Introduction to Real World Statistics

Introduction to Real World Statistics provides students with the basic concepts and practices of applied statistics, including data management and preparation; an introduction to the concept of probability; data screening and descriptive statistics; various inferential analysis techniques; and a series of exercises that are designed to integrate core statistical concepts. The author's systematic approach, which assumes no prior knowledge of the subject, equips student practitioners with a fundamental understanding of applied statistics that can be deployed across a wide variety of disciplines and professions.

Notable features include:

- short, digestible chapters that build and integrate statistical skills with real world applications, demonstrating the flexible usage of statistics for evidence-based decision-making
- statistical procedures presented in a practical context with less emphasis on technical jargon
- early chapters that build a foundation before presenting statistical procedures
- SPSS step-by-step detailed instructions designed to reinforce student understanding
- real world exercises complete with answers
- chapter PowerPoints and test banks for instructors.

Edward T. Vieira, Jr. is an Associate Professor, Research Director, and member of the Institutional Review Board at Simmons College, Boston, Massachusetts, USA. He earned his M.B.A. from Bryant University and Ph.D. from the University of Connecticut. Currently, Dr. Vieira serves on the editorial boards of seven peer-reviewed journals providing statistical and methodological expertise. He has over 30 years of management, research, and consulting experience in areas such as marketing research, community outreach focus groups, organizational research, and education evaluation research.

Introduction to Real World Statistics

With Step-by-Step SPSS Instructions

Edward T. Vieira, Jr.

Routledge
Taylor & Francis Group
NEW YORK AND LONDON

Reprint 2019

First published 2017
by Routledge
711 Third Avenue, New York, NY 10017

and by Routledge
2 Park Square, Milton Park, Abingdon, Oxon, OX14 4RN

Routledge is an imprint of the Taylor & Francis Group, an informa business

Library of Congress Cataloging in Publication Data
Names: Vieira, Edward T., Jr.
Title: Introduction to real world statistics : with SPSS step-by-step instructions / by Edward T. Vieira, Jr.
Description: New York : Routledge, 2017. | Includes bibliographical references and index.
Identifiers: LCCN 2016040764| ISBN 9781138292314 (hardback) | ISBN 9781138292307 (pbk.)
Subjects: LCSH: Mathematical statistics—Data processing. | SPSS (Computer file)
Classification: LCC QA276.45.S77 V54 2017 | DDC 519.50285/53—dc23
LC record available at https://lccn.loc.gov/2016040764

ISBN: 978-0-367-24085-1 (hbk)
ISBN: 978-1-315-23302-4 (ebk)

Typeset in Bembo
by Florence Production Ltd, Stoodleigh, Devon, UK

Visit the companion website: www.routledge.com/cw/vieira

Digitally Printed at Replika Press Pvt. Ltd.

For sale in India, Pakistan, Nepal, Bhutan, Bangladesh and Sri Lanka only.

I dedicate this work to my dearest wife, Rebecca, who gave me the space required to write this textbook.

Contents

PART III: DATA SCREENING, DESCRIBING, AND PROBABILITIES

APPENDICES

Preface

Why Read This Book?

My many years of teaching applied statistics, quantitative analysis, research methods, marketing research, and educational research led me to write this student practitioner-friendly introductory statistics book in an understandable voice. The statistician's perspective dominates many statistics textbooks. Arguably, these books expend space covering statistical formulas and topics that are relatively not easily usable by introductory students. The level of detail often becomes overwhelming and the student experiences a loss of interest in studying statistics. *Introduction to Real World Statistics* focuses on constructing a foundation of understanding where the student can simply use the covered statistical tools without learning formulas or unnecessary details. This "toolkit" approach is designed and presented in a manner that clearly demonstrates how statistics aids in data-driven decision-making. In other words, this book is for the student or practitioner who wishes to learn many important applied statistical techniques required to produce knowledge that will aid informed decision-making.

A topic such as applied statistics must strike a balance between being overly simplistic and not much use to the practitioner student *and* being overly abstract and complex so that the student stays engaged and does not become lost in minutia. *Introduction to Real World Statistics* is written in a nontechnical, clear, and concise writing style. I use significance testing examples to demonstrate whether results are meaningful. This process makes use of a variety of learning tools such as applied exercises, case studies from different fields, datasets, and SPSS output. The topics and exercises are designed to build student confidence one concept at a time in manageable blocks. Like many professional-oriented disciplines, applied statistics often uses more than a single procedure or tool to address a challenge. An understanding of how these tools operate together to produce a targeted outcome is essential. Consequently, the chapters build and take the reader to more integrative blocks of statistics.

Relatedly, it can be sometimes difficult to interpret and apply statistical findings unless we have a broader context. Although applied statistics is the primary focus of this book, statistics does not operate in a vacuum. The veracity of statistics is linked and dependent upon various aspects of research such as sampling, research objectives, and study design. Part II addresses sampling and related issues. The appendix contains information about research objectives and research design.

In *Introduction to Real World Statistics*, terminology is consistent and represents the subject covered in plain "English." Chapter titles are as self-explanatory as possible. For example, instead of a chapter title such as "A One-Way Analysis of Variance Significance Test," it is labeled "ANOVA: Comparing More Than Two Independent Groups' Means to Test for Differences among Them by One Type of Classification." Additionally, glossary terms are in bold print throughout the book.

How are real world applications incorporated? First, a real world situation or snapshot is incorporated in each chapter, which places the chapter's main topic in a real world context so that readers can relate to the content in a concrete and very real way. Second, students understand and learn various statistical procedures and the purposes for these techniques. Third, they learn how to determine which procedures to use under different or unique circumstances. Fourth, they properly implement the technique using SPSS, which is a popular statistical software package. Fifth, students interpret their SPSS produced statistical results. Last, they report their results in a reader-friendly, "plain English" manner. In sum, *Introduction to Real World Statistics* serves as a usable and useful applied statistics toolkit for the student practitioner who wants to understand, do, interpret, and report statistics.

Notable Features

Assumes No Prior Knowledge of Statistics

As the title suggests, *Introduction to Real World Statistics* assumes no prior statistical or SPSS knowledge. We start from the beginning learning fundamental statistical terms, concepts, and statistical techniques and apply them using SPSS step-by-step instructions.

Introduction to Real World Statistics does not cover detailed statistical formulas. Let me explain why through an analogy. Assume that you are a person in the market for a new vehicle for your airport taxi service. You are not required to understand at an engineering level all of the mechanical, electronic, safety, and electrical systems of the vehicle that you may purchase. Being a well-informed consumer, however, you will have *some* understanding of key features. Your focus is on the desired *benefits* derived from a well-engineered, reliable vehicle. In other words, you wish to purchase a vehicle that will provide safety, a margin of comfort, luggage space, and dependability for your airport taxi service customers. This book approaches statistics in the same manner. We focus on practical considerations that provide data-driven knowledge for informed decision-making which minimizes risk based on accurate, precise, valid, and reliable information from sample data. We can answer such questions as: Is there a meaningful difference between consumer preferences for Brand Y over Brand Z? Is Curriculum A more effective than Curriculum B? Is there a meaningful difference among percentage of defective products on the first work shift compared to the second and third shifts across production facilities? Our questions or what we study are only limited by our imagination.

Short Digestible Chapters That Build and Integrate Real World Statistical Skills

Chapters are in smaller comprehensible blocks of content. Statistical procedures and concepts are presented in different contexts, thus demonstrating the flexible usage of statistics for evidence-based decision-making.

The problem sets in this book consist of end-of-chapter real world exercises. The appendix includes a wide array of case studies across disciplines integrating a number of statistical procedures. *Answer* keys are included for exercises and case studies.

An Alternative to the Traditional Hypothesis Testing Approach

Statistics and quantitative analysis textbooks typically devote large amounts of content to describing and explaining the null and alternative hypotheses. I found that students often become so immersed in the details and nuances of hypothesis testing that the main point of the analysis becomes lost to abstract considerations and the reconciliation of those abstractions rather than focusing on the practical aspects of statistics, including the understanding, interpretation, and reporting of findings. *Introduction to Real World Statistics* concentrates on answering questions and testing the truth or falsity of statements in a clear and comprehensible manner.

Interdisciplinary Applications

Introduction to Real World Statistics is a toolkit for data analysis that can be used in numerous disciplines, such as psychology, sociology, gender studies, nursing, health sciences, criminal justice, education and educational leadership, human services, social work, counseling, many aspects of business, including marketing, management, organizational behavior, operations management, and economics, as well as communication. Every effort is made to demonstrate the usage of statistics across a wide range of disciplines.

SPSS Step-by-Step Detailed Instructions with Screenshots

There are many student practitioner-friendly illustrations and examples of systematic statistical procedures covered using SPSS software in the companion website (www.routledge.com/cw/vieira), including datasets, output files, and screenshots. These examples are designed to: (1) reinforce student understanding of the topic; (2) apply the procedure to real world applications; (3) clearly illustrate how to conduct the procedure in SPSS using step-by-step instructions; and (4) link the concept to other related SPSS procedures.

Chapter PowerPoints and Test Bank

Introduction to Real World Statistics includes PowerPoint presentations for each chapter in the companion website (www.routledge.com/cw/vieira). These presentations are designed to summarize key chapter statistical concepts using a number of visuals whenever possible, making them easier to understand. For instructors, the test bank offers closed-ended questions with answers easily adaptable for online applications.

A Systematic Approach to Teaching Statistics

In this book, statistical topics are systematically addressed along the following lines. (1) A topic is introduced. (2) A practical problem is presented. (3) The statistical procedures that speak to the problem are described and explained. (4) The procedures are applied to the practical problem. (5) Steps for conducting the analysis using SPSS are provided, including screenshots. (6) SPSS output screenshots are explained and interpreted. (7) Each chapter ends with applied problem exercises. (8) There are PowerPoint presentations for each chapter. (9) The appendix includes comprehensive case studies and solutions. (10) Additional useful information is located in the appendix.

Book Organization

It is important to note that learning statistics for the first time using *Introduction to Real World Statistics* is best approached by starting from Chapter 1 and then proceeding through each chapter in progression, since subsequent topics build on previous topics. The book is organized into four main parts.

Part I, "Getting Started," introduces the student to statistics and presents examples of why a systematic and scientific approach to real world problems is beneficial. This part also explains kinds of data, types of variables, and addresses key data management issues using SPSS.

Part II, "Sampling Considerations," covers sampling strategies and sample size in the context of missing data and sampling error.

Part III, "Data Screening, Describing, and Probabilities," reviews describing categorical and numeric data, basic probabilities, and screening data distributions for probability statistical analysis.

Part IV, "Statistical Analysis," provides methods for analyzing categorical and numeric variables, including fundamental data analysis techniques for single samples, two sample comparisons, more than two sample analysis, correlation analysis, and two basic types of regression analysis.

The appendices contain a glossary of key terms, solutions to the end-of-chapter exercises, case studies covering different disciplines, including solutions, and information about research objectives, types of studies, a test for more than two related categorical samples, and an additional discussion about regression.

Organized in this manner, *Introduction to Real World Statistics* provides students with the basic concepts and practices of applied statistics, including data management and preparation, an introduction to the concept of probability, which is fundamental to inferential statistics, data screening and descriptive statistics, various inferential statistical analysis techniques, and a series of exercises and cases that are designed to integrate core statistical concepts. This approach provides student practitioners with the fundamentals of applied statistics which can be effectively deployed across various disciplines and professions.

Acknowledgments

I wish to acknowledge and thank my mentors at the University of Connecticut, Sjef van den Berg, Professor C. Arthur VanLear, and especially Professor Emeritus James Watt, who has answered an untold number of my statistics-related emails throughout the years.

PART I

Getting Started

Chapter 1

Introduction to Real World Statistics

LEARNING OBJECTIVES

To be able to:

- define statistics and know its purpose;
- explain the difference between descriptive statistics and inferential statistics;
- know the difference between sample data and census data;
- understand the concept of reification;
- explain why statistics is important in light of naïve science and current developments; and
- know that there are options for addressing violations of statistical assumptions.

1.1 What Is Statistics?

What is statistics? **Statistics** is a branch of applied mathematics that focuses on studying sample data that are representative of a specific population. The sample data are collected and analyzed. What we discover from the data analysis can provide useful decision-making information. Moreover, statistics involves a scientific and systematic process that follows procedures which assure reliability and validity—in other words, the process assures the precision and accuracy of our results.

Statistics is a major part of the research process, a process with interdependent components. The questions to be answered or statements to be tested inform or influence the study design, the sampling strategy, selection of variables, how those variables will be measured, and how those measures will be analyzed. This systematic approach effectively moves in a manner that answers research questions or tests the truth of research statements. These considerations affect the quality and level of our statistical analyses, as well as the results, interpretation of those results, and quality of knowledge that we garner from our results. This process will become more apparent as we explore this book.

Statistics has two general purposes, perhaps best thought of as types of statistics. First, **descriptive statistics** summarizes and describes sample data representative of the population under study. Second, **inferential statistics** examines the relationships between and among variables and helps us draw conclusions that can be generalized to the population, thus allowing us to reduce uncertainty in decision-making.

Having sample data that represent the broader targeted population is critical to our ability to use our findings to make informed decisions. A **sample** is a relatively small representative number of a larger population selected for statistical analysis. If our sample does not represent the population under study, then the conclusions derived from the sample data would be inaccurate and of limited value because the data would not be representative of the population under study. One well-known example of poor sampling techniques was the *Literary Digest* poll for the 1936 U.S. presidential race between Alf Landon and Franklin D. Roosevelt. Landon was incorrectly predicted to defeat Roosevelt with 57% of the vote. Among many of the poll's problems, the selection process was fatally flawed. Lists such as telephone directories and club memberships provided the sample data. In 1936, only upper-middle- and upper-income households could afford telephones and club memberships. These individuals tended to vote for Republican candidates, as was Landon. As we know, President Roosevelt, a Democrat and advocate for the poor and middle-class America, easily won re-election with 62% of the vote. As this example illustrates, poor sampling procedures can result in drawing inaccurate conclusions.

Sample Data vs. Census Data

Again, statistics is a type of applied mathematics used to describe and infer (draw) conclusions about a population under study based on an analysis of a "representative" sample of that population. Alternatively, **census** research polls the entire population under study. The population can consist of every person of a population or all of the output of a manufacturing process during three work shifts. The key point is that a census study includes all population data and not a sample of the population, as is the case for a statistical study.

Why not study the entire population? There are a number of reasons why statistical sampling would be more appropriate. First, the costs of collecting data from a population might be prohibitive. For example, the U.S. Constitution mandates that a census be conducted every 10 years. According to the Congressional Research Service, the decennial census of 2010 cost an estimated $15 billion. If statistical analyses in lieu of a census were possible, the cost of the U.S. census would be substantially less. Second, there is the issue of timeliness. Surveying an entire population can be time-consuming. In addition to years of preparation, in 2010, the U.S. Census Bureau collected data for the entire 12 months of that year. Representative sample data could be collected in a fraction of the time. Third, collecting census data may be impractical. For example, in an experimental design study of millennials, it would be highly unlikely that a team of researchers could recruit all or most millennials to participate in a study requiring their thoughts about aspects of criminal justice or other social issues after being exposed to editorial articles on such topics. Yet these types of experiments could easily be conducted with samples. Last, sampling makes it easier to include individuals who are not easily accessible whether they are undocumented workers or people living "off the grid." We can see that statistical studies offer a viable alternative to census data collection.

1.2 Reification

How do we go from an idea inside someone's mind to measurable statistics? We do so through reification. **Reification** is the process of taking something abstract, such as ideas, thoughts, and feelings, and making them concrete or measurable so that we can tell a story using numbers. For example, what is "work satisfaction"? We can define it abstractly by giving it a conceptual definition or framework. Through reification, however, we can define it concretely so that we can measure it using numbers, which can then be subject to statistical analysis. In our example, the measurable description is the operational definition of work satisfaction.

Let us delve more into these concepts. A conceptual definition for work satisfaction may be "how content an individual is with his or her job." A measurable definition of work satisfaction may measure: happiness, reward, learning new things, helping others . . . These "parts" can be framed as questions and collectively measure work satisfaction in a comprehensive way. For instance, in responding to the question, "How happy am I at work?" respondents would answer by selecting one of five possible answers ranging from 1 = "not at all" through 5 = "intensely happy." The same would apply to rewarding work, learning new things, helping others at work, and so forth. In our example, such questions together measure work satisfaction because they cover all the major aspects of what constitutes a satisfying work experience. In this case, an average of the responses represent the level of work satisfaction. Together, they are the operational definition of work satisfaction.

As we can see, examining and understanding something requires a way of defining it so that we can measure it and statistically analyze it, often in relation to other things. For example, how do women or men behave in certain social shopping contexts? How do women or men in different age groups behave in specific social shopping contexts? Does participation in social services vary by gender and other personal attributes? Once we define these variables, we can then define ways to measure them. Operational variables serve as the basis by which we analyze and understand what we are studying. In our example, we may find that women in different age groups use different types of social services compared to men in the same age group. We may also find that these differences become less pronounced as people age. In this example, we seek to discover patterns of behavior based on different sample characteristics such as gender and age. Knowing these patterns can inform agencies to design needed programs geared to specific populations.

1.3 Naïve Science: The Deception of Common Sense

Talking to people or viewing the occasional news report about researchers studying something that is generally perceived as "common sense" and unworthy of study and resources is sometimes appropriately referred to as **naïve science** or the deception of common sense. It is the popular perspective that anything that appears to be true is true and undeserving of scientific verification. The scientific method and statistics help us uncover the truth, even when the truth seems counterintuitive. For examples, the origin of the word "Malaria" and Copernicus' claim that the sun is the center of the "universe" illustrate this point.

Let us start with Malaria, which is a Latin term meaning "bad air" and refers to a mosquito-transmitted illness. The ancient Roman soldiers would march through odiferous swamps populated by mosquitoes. Some soldiers would become ill. The Romans "reasoned" that the terrible-smelling swamp water air caused the soldiers to become sick. To them, it was cause and effect reasoning. However, the swamp air did not cause illness. The disease-carrying swamp mosquitoes that bit the soldiers caused them to become sick. Common sense failed the Romans.

Copernicus conceived (or conceptualized) that the sun, and not the earth, was the center of the "universe." Most people disagreed with Copernicus, for if one stood in the middle of a field, one would see the sun at dawn in the east, at midday the sun would be overhead, and at dusk it would be in the west. The sun slowly moved across the sky. The moon and stars moved as well. The terra firma earth did not move. To most people, it was apparent that the earth was the center of everything. These beliefs prevailed until Galileo Galilei improved upon the telescope and was able to prove that the earth orbited around the sun as Copernicus theorized, and not the inverse. Therefore, the earth was not the center of the universe.

Along the lines of our Malaria and Copernicus examples, Lilienfeld and his colleagues (2009), in their work on "common sense," discuss 50 myths of psychology, including "Working while in high school will help students build character and value money," "Children who read a lot are not very social or physically fit," and "We know what will make us happy." Scientific research disproved these among other assertions or deceptions of common sense.

What do these examples have in common and how do they relate to statistical research? They reveal that the truth is sometimes counterintuitive. For this reason, research is needed to verify what we think is reality. As part of discovering the truth, statistics is a systematic and mathematical tool used to help us assure sound research.

REAL WORLD SNAPSHOT

In the 2012 article "The Importance of Attitudes in Statistics Education" by Ramirez, Schau, and Emmioglu published in *Statistics Education Research Journal*, these statistics professors emphasized the importance of students' attitudes toward statistics. They stress the importance for instructors to measure their students' attitudes toward statistics because "People forget what they do not use. But attitudes 'stick'" (p. 57). They hold that attitudes about math abilities and expectations for success are the key drivers for success in statistics and math in general. The article examines why it is important for students to:

- believe that they can understand and use statistics,
- think that statistics is useful both in their professional and personal lives,
- recognize that statistics can be interesting,
- be willing to invest the effort needed to learn statistical thinking and skills, and,
- realize that statistics is not easy but it also is not too difficult to learn.

(p. 57)

Ask yourself: How might you use statistics in your personal or professional life? Can you think of fun applications of statistics?

1.4 Importance of Statistics

The previous section illustrates the importance of statistical research. Statistics allows us to make data-driven decisions in an ever-increasingly complex world where experience alone is not sufficient to manage risk and make optimal choices. New and rapidly evolving technologies can easily influence how people think, feel, behave, and learn in different, new, and innovative ways—in some cases, making previous knowledge obsolete and ineffective. Statistics allows us to quickly respond to changes and develop solutions to new and fluid challenges.

In the past, our data analyses were limited to after the fact studies, intentionality research, and some limited behavioral studies slicing away at bridging psychological and behavioral human activities. Collecting data was arduous and conducting accurate statistical analysis was time-consuming and laborious. Today, all of this has changed and continues to change. Statistics and the broader quantitative methodologies are now especially practical because of cost-effective advances in computer hardware and software, as well as the easy capture of online behaviors. We now have massive amounts of online psychological and behavioral data for analysis and the volume continues to grow at an accelerated rate. With big data and predictive analytics, we can integrate computer systems and statistics to analyze massive databases, which will allow us to develop predictive models for online and offline behaviors, sometimes in real time. There are many other types of applications for statistics reaching out to medicine and health sciences, to business and consumer sciences, to the full spectrum of the social sciences. This is certainly an exciting time for the statistics practitioner!

Statistical Assumptions

Most of statistics and the usage of the most effective statistical tools are based on a number of assumptions usually pertaining to the characteristics of the data. Reality often provides us with less than ideal circumstances where some assumptions are not met. Violating some of these assumptions can produce inaccurate results. This book presents suggestions to address some of the more common challenges. Some of these solutions are more practical than others and the details of others are beyond the scope of an introductory statistics textbook. What is important to know is that options are nearly always available to explore.

SUMMARY OF KEY CONCEPTS

- Statistics is a branch of applied mathematics that focuses on studying sample data that are representative of a specific population, as opposed to census data, which are collected from the entire population under study.
- Statistics comes in two general varieties. Descriptive statistics summarizes and describes sample data, which can be generalized to the population. Inferential statistics examines the relationships between and among variables and helps us draw generalizable conclusions as well.
- All sorts of variables can be made measurable through a process of reification or making that which is abstract measurable.
- There are options available to address most violations of statistical assumptions.

INTRODUCTORY APPLIED EXERCISES

1.1 Define statistics and be sure to cite general examples.

1.2 What is a sample? Cite examples.

1.3 Define descriptive statistics. Cite an example.

1.4 Define inferential statistics. Cite an example.

1.5 Are there cases where descriptive variables (or data) can be applied to inferential statistics? Explain your answer.

1.6 Define census data and provide examples. Under what study conditions would census data be appropriate (and easily available)?

1.7 Explain what is naïve science.

1.8 Is it possible to reify everything? Explain your reasoning.

1.9 What is the relationship between a sample and a population?

1.10 Why does the U.S. Census Bureau collect census data rather than using sample data?

1.11 What is different today from data analysis in the past?

1.12 Why can sampling be more accurate than census data collection?

Chapter 2

Statistics: Descriptive, Correlation, and Inferential

LEARNING OBJECTIVES

To be able to:

- define, understand, and learn the purpose of descriptive, correlation, and inferential statistics;
- understand the associative nature of a relationship between two variables;
- understand how the three types of statistics relate to each other; and
- define and understand external validity.

2.1 Introduction to Descriptive, Correlation, and Inferential Statistics

There are three types of statistics that, although they vary, can each take on the role of the others depending on the context. These are descriptive, correlation, and inferential statistics. These types of statistics involve the analysis of a representative sample data drawn from a population under study. At a basic and more involved level, these types of statistics describe data, variables, and relationships between and among variables that can be generalized to the population under study. If the sample truly represents the target population, then the results provide what is known as **external validity**. In other words, sample findings can be applied to the population of interest because the data are a small representation of the larger population and thus contain the same attributes as the population.

2.2 Descriptive Statistics

Descriptive statistics is used to discover the characteristics of data. It involves the summary description of sample data by variable. Variables are described or defined by their attributes from two related perspectives.

First, data from a given variable are described by their distribution as part of the data screening process quite often using significance testing (see Chapter 11). For categorical variable data, the data are described in terms of counts and percentages of those counts in relation to the total count or sample space where there are required minimum frequencies per grouping. We can create various charts and tables that depict the data's characteristics, as discussed in Chapter 9. Numeric variable data are described in terms of the normal distribution. There are a number of graphical and numeric tools that can help assess the distribution of numeric data, as discussed in Chapter 12. These fundamental descriptive statistics provide information that assesses the data's appropriateness for probability statistical analysis or other statistical procedures that accommodate unique data attributes.

Second, after the data screening process is complete, descriptive statistics is used to define variables in summary. This process does not use significance testing. These variables represent attributes of the sample that may be generalized to the population from which it was drawn. The analysis is basic; however, descriptive statistics is important to summarily describe and define the sample by variables that comprise important sample characteristics. For example, we may describe a sample as follows:

> An online questionnaire was completed by 2,823 participants representing a 25% response rate. The average age of a respondent was 45.5 years old. Men comprised 1,223 (43.3%) of the sample and there were 1,600 (56.7%) women. There were 1,200 (42.5%) White participants, 800 (28.3%) Hispanics, 400 (14.2%) Black, 232 (8.2%) Asian, and 191 (6.8%) comprised all other ethnic groups. The average level of education was two years of college. Average household income was $55,000 and average respondent income was $37,000.

Measures of Variation

Think of a world in which everyone or everything was the same. Every person's survey responses would be identical. Every manufactured item would be exactly the same. Every participant would have the same response in a new drug trial. In such a world, there would be little need for research. There would be certainty and no variation. However, the world is not certain. Things vary. Things change. There are differences among the sources of data, as well as within those sources. This is why measures of variation are so important to statistical analysis.

Measures of variation are used to describe the distribution of data, which is critical to many statistical procedures. Variation is a broad statistical term that can be mathematically expressed in a number of ways. In general terms, it refers to differences between observations or differences between what is expected and what is observed in some comparative way.

Variance is an important type of variation measure. It is a statistic used to reveal on average how widely data values vary from the average within the group. If a sample's variance varies greatly from the group average, its variance is large. If it does not, its variance is small. Variance helps us to know something about the spread of a data distribution. A statistic associated with variance is the standard deviation, which is derived from the variance. The standard deviation is more commonly used because it is easily relatable to the data and because it provides the actual average difference a value is from the average observation in a sample. Chapters 11 and 12 cover standard deviation and variance, respectively, in detail.

2.3 Correlation Statistics

Correlation statistics is used to determine whether a relationship exists between two sample variables. It is generally used in inferential statistics and normally refers to a linear relationship. The two variables *may* be those used in descriptive statistics such as educational level and income, where we may wish to determine if there is a relationship between them, for example. These relationships may also be called **associations** or **correlations**. Correlations can be positive or negative, which is the directionality of the linear relationship. Put differently, their presence may increase or decrease together, which is a positive association or relationship. For example, as education and experience increase, generally so does income. Inversely, they may move in the opposite direction, which is called a negative relationship. For instance, in middle-aged individuals, as healthy eating and exercise practices increase, generally physical illness decreases. Correlations reveal the strength and directionality of associations between and among variables (see Chapter 21).

However, we must be careful not to assume that correlations can be used to make "common sense" jumps to cause and effect (A causes B) relationships between two variables. Surely, in children, as age increases, normally so does height (an increase in age *causes* an increase in height). Yet there are many situations where cause and effect are not so clear. For instance, during the winter in New England, there is a positive correlation between pizza delivery and depression. Does this mean that pizza consumption causes depression or perhaps depressed people tend to self-medicate by eating pizza? Alternatively, if we were to introduce cold temperatures and inclement weather, where individuals tend to stay indoors and perhaps become depressed, then perhaps these persons order pizza to be delivered because they do not wish to brave the weather. We can see that relationships (and any potential causality) among these variables can become complicated. Appendix E, "Types of Research Design," and Appendix G, "More on Linear Regression," touch upon causality and their related complexities.

In short, a correlation analysis determines whether a linear relationship exists between two variables, as well as the strength and directionality of that relationship. It is not assumed to be a cause and effect relationship.

2.4 Inferential Statistics

Inferential statistics is used to make conclusions and potential predictions about a population based on the analysis and evidence of data provided from a representative sample of that population. Inferential statistics focuses on the nature of the relationship between and among variables. Often this process involves answering questions and/or testing statements about the population. Some examples are: "Are 18–24 consumers more interested in purchasing remanufactured tablets compared to other age groups?"; "Do women or men patients read online reviews more before selecting a primary care physician?"; and "Older production equipment will be less energy efficient." In the first case, the analysis examines for a relationship between age groups and interest in tablets, and whether younger people are expected have a greater interest in

REAL WORLD SNAPSHOT

A 2016 Pew Research Center study by Lee Rainie titled "Libraries and Learning" found that the majority of Americans think that their local libraries serve the needs of local schools (76%) and families (71%). However, many respondents were unaware of the key educational services offered by their local libraries. Forty-seven percent were unaware of GED services, 47% did not know that their local libraries offered new business start-up programs, and 49% were unaware of library-offered online programs that certify people who have acquired new competencies. Women, young adults, higher-educated adults, and parents were among those most likely to visit local libraries and library websites. Moreover, people who identify themselves as lifelong learners were more likely to use bricks-and-mortar libraries and their websites.

Ask yourself: How might this information be used to increase awareness and library usage of the full array of services offered?

remanufactured tablets. The second example considers gender differences in those patients who research possible primary care physicians; thus, the relationship variables are gender and physician search. In the last instance, the variables are old vs. new equipment and energy efficiency.

The responses to these questions or statements can be generalized to the population under study and serve as the basis for predicting future "events" in the population, whether it involves consumer thoughts, feelings, and/or behaviors; machinery production output under different conditions; drug effectiveness; type of nursing care; and so forth.

2.5 Descriptive, Correlation, and Inferential Statistics

Descriptive, correlation, and inferential statistics can be generalized to the population under study. The difference among these types of statistics rests in the nature of their generalization to the population. Descriptive statistics describes one or more of the population's general attributes. Correlation analysis determines whether a relationship exists between two variables. Inferential statistics examines the nature of the relationships between and among variables. Table 2.1 summarizes the key functions of the three types of statistics.

Table 2.1

Statistics Types Function

Type of Statistics	Screening	Descriptions	Number of Variables	Relationship Among Variables	Nature of Relationship	Generalize to Population
Descriptive	Yes	Yes	≥ 1			Yes
Correlation			2	Yes	Some	Yes
Inferential			≥ 2	Yes	Yes	Yes

Note: Same variables might be used for more than one type of statistics.

These types of statistics provide insights, external validity, and predictability from the sample to the population. The following are examples.

Quality Control/Assurance: A company has 30 production facilities throughout the world and wishes to determine if the percentage of defective parts it produces varies by country of production. The operations management team takes a random sample of 5% of the production machinery's records for analysis. In this case, after the initial data screening, the average number of defective parts produced by 5% of the production machinery is provided and these data are separated by country, which is descriptive. However, we can use inferential statistical procedures to determine whether there are meaningful differences among the countries, which can then be generalized to the entire production of the company by country. In this instance, we do more than simply describe. We examine the relationship between country and production output for meaningful differences.

Motivated to Exercise: A hospital wishes to discover what motivates patients to exercise upon their discharge from the hospital. A sample of patients agreed to complete a survey that included asking demographic information as well as a number of exercise motivation questions. After the initial data screening, the demographic questions provided general descriptive characteristics about a typical patient. The motivation questions described information about typical levels of exercise motivation. These two groups of data serve as describing or defining a typical patient by summarizing data: averaging the numeric variables and counting (taking percentages) various categorical variables, which are discussed in Chapter 3. These variables, along with any other data collected, are examined to reveal whether motivation varies in relation to other variables.

For instance, does level of exercise motivation vary by education, income, or primary care physician? Inferential statistics involves discovering any statistically meaningful differences. The descriptive definition of a typical patient, along with differences among patients by groupings within other variables, can be generalized from the sample to all charged patients who qualify for an exercise program.

SUMMARY OF KEY CONCEPTS

- Statistics consists of three general types: descriptive, correlation, and inferential.
- Descriptive statistics summarizes and describes sample data.
- Correlation statistics explores whether a linear association exists between two variables. It does not examine for a cause and effect relationship.
- Inferential statistics studies the nature of relationships between and among variables.
- All three types of statistics help us draw conclusions that can be generalized to the entire population, thus providing external validity.

DESCRIPTIVE, CORRELATION, AND INFERENTIAL STATISTICS APPLIED EXERCISES

2.1 Define descriptive, correlation, and inferential statistics.

2.2 Additionally, differentiate the three types of statistics by their key functions and provides examples of each.

2.3 What is a correlation? What is an association?

2.4 Define and provide an example of external validity.

2.5 Which type of statistics is used to screen data? Explain your answer.

2.6 Is a correlation typically a linear relationship between two variables? Explain your response.

2.7 What is the focus of inferential statistics?

2.8 In the Pew study Real World Snapshot, what type of data are described? Explain your answer.

2.9 How do descriptive, correlation, and inferential statistics provide more and more information, respectively?

2.10 A new drug is being tested that can reverse the effects of Alzheimer's disease in certain patients. Researchers have sample data for 300 patients who have taken the drug over the minimum six-month period. The data include age, health condition, family history, blood type, sex, and a drug effectiveness score. From these data, provide types of descriptive, correlation, and inferential statistical analyses that can be conducted.

Chapter 3

Data and Types of Variables

LEARNING OBJECTIVES

To be able to:

- understand what is a variable;
- define a conceptual variable and how it becomes measurable;
- define and identify the different kinds of variables;
- know and explain categorical and numeric levels of data and their various subtypes; and
- know that statistical analyses are guided by the level of data comprising a variable.

3.1 Introduction to Variables

A **variable** is a directly or indirectly observable characteristic or property of something that is measurable. It varies or changes particularly in relation to one or more other variables or in comparison to other observations or measurements of the same variable. People vary by age, income, motivation, attitude toward criminal justice, love toward an object or person, and so forth. Their age and income may relate to or affect their attitudes toward various topics. Their attitudes toward a brand, for instance, may affect their motivation to purchase that brand. In education, student learning can vary by teaching style, subject taught, and student demographics, which are all measurable variables.

3.2 Kinds of Variables

Variables vary or change by data points or under certain conditions such as in relation to other variables. Variables can be conceptual and measurable, whether measurement is direct or indirect. The **conceptual definition** is an "idea" definition of a variable. The **measurable definition** is how we measure the conceptual definition.

Understanding and distinguishing different kinds of data or variables is important because it informs the types of statistical analyses that are possible. Some variables are easier to grasp. For instance, age is understandable and can be measured easily. Its conceptual definition is how long a person has lived. Its measurable definition may be the length of existence as reported and analyzed in completed years of life. Thus, age and its measurement are straightforward. However, what about the idea of "attitude?" Attitude is an abstract concept that can be measured indirectly. It may be conceptually defined in different ways. It may be defined as "a psychological tendency that is expressed by evaluating a particular entity with some degree of favor or disfavor" (Eagly & Chaiken, 1993, p. 1). Additionally, there are different aspects of attitude that can be applied to different contexts.

For example, in consumer science, attitude can be measured in terms of specific brands, service level, corporate image, corporate social responsibility, in relation to purchase intention, and so forth. Some brand attitude measures include "like" or "dislike" questions about quality, pricing, accessibility through offline/online retailers, choice of options, sales discounts, and other attitude measures associated with a brand or product, which are indirect ways to measure what constitutes brand attitude.

As we can see, once we have a conceptual framework or know what we wish to measure, what follows is determining how we measure it. We measure variables through collected data on those variables. **Data** are (datum is singular) the recorded individual measurements of variables. Data are the different values associated with a variable such as age in years reported by a sample of people, reported women, men, or LGBTQ gender identification, attitudes such as accepting or rejecting a political message, production output as in units, and so forth. The tools and formats that are used to collect and measure data are collectively called the **measurable framework**. The measurable framework is how we quantify variables. Therefore, a variable has a conceptual definition, which can be abstract, as well as a measurable definition, which is concrete. There are different ways to define variables. What follows are other practical ways of doing so.

3.3 Variables by Type of Data

A variable can be defined by the kind of data collected to measure it. The type of data collected to measure it affects the type of statistical analysis that can be conducted on the variable. Therefore, it is important to know the various types of data, how they can be analyzed, and the limitations of analysis. There are two basic types of variables based on level of data: categorical and numeric. They serve most quantitative analyses.

Categorical Data

Categorical variables consist of a set number of mutually exclusive characteristics or categories, which can be the simple presence or absence of a single variable attribute or a number of attributes within a variable. They are measured by counting instances of the categories within the variable. Thus, categorical variables are the result of a **counting process**. The **counts or frequencies** often include their proportions or percentages in order to provide information about their relationship to other categories within a variable. In SPSS, binary or nominal categorical choices can be recorded as words (**string data**) or numbers. For instance, answering "yes" or "no" to a question can be represented by string data, "yes" or "no," or numeric data, 2 = "yes" and 1 = "no." The categorical choices within a variable consist of all possible outcomes. It is called the **sample space** and can be represented in a table. For example, in a poll of 2,000 eligible voters, 50% (1,000 eligible voters) of respondents reported that they will vote for Candidate Brown, while 40% (800 eligible voters) intend to vote for Candidate White, and 7% (140 eligible voters) plan to vote for Candidate Green. Three percent (60 eligible voters) were undecided. These choices, their counts, and their percentages represent the sample space for this political poll. Again, the actual numbers are the counts (or frequencies) and their percentages provide a proportion in relation to other category counts. In tables, the total sample size is denoted as "N" and subsamples are reported as "n." Percentages are also called **relative frequencies** because they are the percentages or proportions of counts in relation to a larger count, which is often the total sample size. The statistical tools that can be used for categorical data analysis are limited to those incorporating counts and percentages. They are discussed in Chapters 13–15.

Statistically, we attempt to discover a number of relationships within or between categorical variables. We can examine whether there is a meaningful difference between or among categories within a single variable compared to the overall counts. We can also analyze whether there is a relationship between two categorical variables, as well as the properties of that relationship. The following sections describe and explain different kinds of categorical variables.

Binary-Level Data (Variable)

Binary data, also called dichotomous or nominal-level data, only have two possible outcomes. They can also be viewed as the presence or absence of a condition. For examples, "Do you like chocolate ice cream? Yes or No" or "The study was accurate: True or False." A binary formatted question provides the least amount of information. The complementary rule applies to binary variables. That is, if there are only two choices, then both of them must equal 100%. Therefore, in our first example, assuming a sample of 200 (N = 200), if 60% or 120 people selected "yes," then 40% or 80 people must have selected "no." The 200 responses comprise the (total) sample space.

Table 3.1

Summary Count for Chocolate Ice Cream Preference

Response	Count	Percentage
Yes	120	60%
No	80	40%
Totals	200	100%

Note: N = 200

A summary table tallies all of the counts and their respective percentages for all possible categories. In this case, they are "yes" and "no." In summary Table 3.1, every category and data point are included. A summary table is said to be a **one- or single-dimensional table** because it comprises only one variable.

Nominal-Level Data (Variable)

Categorical data with more than two categories are called **nominal-level data.** Let us extend our example to ice cream preference among five different flavors. Sample participants select one out of five flavors. Because we cannot have more than the total amount or 100%, all of the flavor counts equal the total sample size and the percentages add up to 100%. In this case, our sample consists of 200 respondents (N = 200) who answered as follows: chocolate 75 (37.5%); vanilla 50 (25%); cookie dough 32 (16%); strawberry 25 (12.5%); and coffee 18 (9%).

Table 3.2 depicts all of the counts and percentages for one nominal variable with five categories (five flavors of ice cream). Thus, it is a single variable analysis represented by a one-dimensional table of the sample space.

Table 3.2

Summary Count Ice Cream Flavor Preference

Flavor	Count	Percentage
Chocolate	75	37.5%
Vanilla	50	25.0%
Cookie Dough	32	16.0%
Strawberry	25	12.5%
Coffee	18	9.0%
Totals	200	100%

Note: N = 200

Ordinal-Level Data (Variable)

There is one difference between nominal categorical and ordinal categorical variables. **Ordinal categorical-level data** or variables imply an order of magnitude to categories within the variable. There is an increase or decrease in the intensity of categories within the variable. An example would be class standing: freshman, sophomore, junior, and senior, where there is an inherent order to class standing implying greater school credits and being closer to graduating college. Other examples are income range: low, medium, and high; level of education: high school diploma, associates, bachelors, masters, doctorate, and postdoctorate; and rank ordering product attributes by order of personal importance.

In the income example, let us incorporate gender, as described earlier. Both the income variable, which is ordinal categorical, and the gender variable, which is nominal categorical, each have three categories. They are represented in a **contingency table**, which depicts the relationship between two categorical variables each with two or more categories.

It is called a contingency table because the counts are based on or contingent upon another variable's categories. The table consists of counts and percentages. In the example below, we have income range by gender. Since there is no evidence suggesting that income level causes gender identification, the relationship between income categories and gender is apparent. We assume that a person's gender identity may have an effect on a person's income category. The "by" designation indicates that respondent gender may affect reported income range, suggesting that income varies by gender.

Table 3.3 represents reported income level ranges by respondent gender. Since there are two variables, the table is a **two-dimensional table**.

Table 3.3

Income Range by Gender Identification Frequencies

Income Range	Women	Men	LGBTQ	Total
Low Income	90 (51%)	65 (37%)	20 (12%)	175 (35%)
Middle Income	80 (39%)	100 (49%)	24 (12%)	204 (41%)
High Income	45 (37%)	37 (31%)	39 (32%)	121 (24%)
Total	215 (43%)	202 (40%)	83 (17%)	500 (100%)

Note: *N* = 500. Percentages are rounded.

Numeric Data

A **numeric variable** comprises a level of some attribute measured in a sample. The measurements vary among data records and are part of a **measuring process**. This process involves the systematic assignment of numbers to objects and their properties in order to facilitate the use statistics to study and describe concepts or objects and their relationships. There are no predetermined selections or counts, unlike categorical variables. Responses, measures, or observations are measured values. Age in number of years, income in dollars, height in inches, SAT scores, and the number of defective widgets produced in an eight-hour shift are examples of numeric data. There are two basic types of numeric variables: ratio and interval.

For numeric data, we can discover more information about a sample compared to categorical variable counts. Unlike categorical variables, we can calculate means (averages), medians, and standard deviations, examine associations between variables, and create models that predict change in variables. These differences and procedures will become more evident as we explore statistical procedures.

Ratio-Level Data (Variable)

Ratio variables are the most comprehensive and informative level of data. All types of statistical analysis can be applied to ratio variables. Zero is a meaningful value; when the value of a variable equals zero, then there is nothing of that variable; it is absent. For example, zero income includes no income. Moreover, differences are clearly meaningful because we know the exact relationships between the values of the characteristic measured, including their relationship with zero. For instance, one can say that a person who is 40 years old is twice the age of someone who is 20 years old. Likewise, the difference between 10 and 20 years old is the same as the difference between 60 and 70 years old, and the difference between 0 and 1 is as meaningful as the difference between 1 and 2. Examples of ratio variables are age, income, and state funding for nonprofit social services' programs in each of the 50 states. In these cases, a value of zero is possible and meaningful. If nothing exists, then it does not exist!

Interval-Level Data (Variable)

In an **interval variable**, there are equal distances between the values of the characteristic measured. Put differently, the difference between 1 and 2 is the same as the difference between 3 and 4, the difference between 5 and 6, and so forth. However, zero has no meaning and it does not equal nothing or the absence of the variable attribute; thus, relative to "zero," differences are not meaningful. For instance, SAT scores can range from 300 to 800 on a given test. A participant's score can be 300, 301, 302, . . . 798, 799, or 800. There are equal intervals among the 300–800 scores, but there is no zero score; 300 is the lowest value. Therefore, the difference between 0 and 300 is not equal to the difference between 300 and 600. In the first instance, there is no difference. In the second case, the difference equals 300. Similarly, one cannot say that someone who scores 620 on the math portion of the SAT is twice the performance level of a 310 scorer because the minimum score is 300, regardless of answers. In essence, a 300 score is a zero score.

This is also the case when measuring a person's IQ. Since all people have a level of intelligence, IQ does not start at zero. An IQ of 100, which is average, provides a meaning comparison with individual scores. IQ scores below 100 are below average and those above 100 are above average. The SAT 300–800 scores and the IQ 100 average are arbitrary figures used to measure college "aptitude" and "intelligence," respectively.

Scale Response Formatted Variables: A Special Case

Scale data are treated as interval-level data. This is a special case usually involving survey-derived data. Strictly speaking, scale data formats such as 1 = "strongly disagree" through 5 = "strongly agree," 1 = "less important" to 7 = "more important," or 1 = "the least" to 5 = "the most" are ordinal categorical-level data. However, research has shown that treating this type of data as interval data is valid and reliable under many conditions (Carifio & Perla, 2007; Norman, 2010). Considering the supportive research, we will analyze scale-formatted variables as numeric data subject to the rules of normal distribution, which are discussed in Chapter 11.

As we can see, the types of analysis that can be conducted on sample data depends on the level of the data. There are two basic data types. One is categorical and the other is numeric. Table 3.4 summarizes them, including subtypes within each of the two kinds.

Table 3.4

Attributes by Data Type

Data Types/Attributes	Groups[1]	Process	Attributes
Categorical			
Binary Data	2	Counts	Complementary rule
Nominal Data	>2	Counts	No order
Ordinal Data	>2	Counts	Ordered
Numeric			
Ratio Data	n/a	Measurement	Meaningful zero; meaningful differences b/w values
Interval Data	n/a	Measurement	No meaningful zero; equal differences between values
Scale	n/a	Measurement	Treated as interval data

Note: [1]Number of attributes (groups) within a categorical variable including the presence or absence of an attribute or group.

Appropriate Analysis for Variable (Data) Type

We can transform higher levels of data to lower levels of data, but we cannot transform lower levels of data to higher levels of data. In other words, all categorical variable analyses can be done with numeric variables. However, numeric variable analyses cannot be conducted on categorical variables. There is less information available in categorical variable calculations because analyses are limited to counts. With numeric variables, there are more enriching statistical techniques available resulting in much more information. This is why careful attention must be made when constructing or deploying items (questions). Such items should be formatted in a manner suitable to the study at hand. For instance, age data in years can be collected as ratio or categorical data. If one were simply to ask survey participants to record age, the data would be ratio-level and subject to *all* statistical analyses. However, if the age question were formatted in categories, such as "younger than 18," "18–24," "25–34," "35–54," "55–64," and "older than 64," statistical analyses would be limited to counts and percentages.

It is important to note that there may be circumstances where using categorical data formatting is more appropriate. The sensitivity of the variable being measured may be a consideration. For example, participants may be hesitant to report a specific income figure, but they may be willing to select a category such as $50,001–75,000. This may also be the case when reporting age. Additionally, past reporting requirements may be a concern. An organization may have a reason for requesting categorical responses rather than specific ratio-level answers, which may be based on the organization's "philosophy," past practices, or ability to accurately compare new data with existing data.

REAL WORLD SNAPSHOT

C. Caple wrote a 2016 Quick Lesson published by Cinahl Information Systems, which addressed Complex Regional Pain Syndrome, Type 2 (CRPS2), a condition whereby a person experiences severe and chronic pain. The prognosis for patients with CRPS2 varies; however, treatment is more effective when implemented immediately upon diagnosis.

Signs and symptom vary across a spectrum from unyielding pain, to body temperature changes, to excessive hair growth. A variety of statistical assessment tools are used in an attempt to diagnose the condition early. These variables collect different types of data from:

- patient history;
- physical findings of particular interest, such as excessive sweating of the affected area;
- laboratory tests that may be ordered; and
- other diagnostic tests/studies.

Ask yourself: How might the data be formatted? When considering this question, think about the different types of variables discussed in this chapter.

3.4 Variables by Influence

Variables are also defined by the influence they exert (or suggest to exert) on other variables. Thus, there are "independent" variables (or predictors) that influence "dependent" variables. Independent variables can be analyzed based on their single effect on another variable or in combination with other variables known as interaction terms or variables. Dependent variables, which are also called outcome variables, are influenced by independent variables. There are also control variables, which may be included in the analysis in order to determine whether they influence the dependent variable. Control variables are often called **exogenous** ("outside") variables because they are not "created" by the researcher. Examples are age, educational level, and ethnic background.

Independent Variables (Predictors)

An **independent variable** predicts or causes change in another variable. Its effects are measured so that a change or different condition in an independent variable affects or changes a dependent variable in some way. In linear regression, these variables are called the **predictor** and **outcome**, respectively. For example, educational level and number of hours of work per week are two independent variables that might predict game hunting behaviors, which is the dependent variable. The question to be answered is: "Do one's amount of education and how much one works influence whether one becomes a game hunter?" or "Will game hunting behavior vary by educational level and number of hours worked per week?"

An independent variable or predictor can also be an experimental condition such as having participants provide an opinion of a topic, followed by showing participants a news story video about the topic, and then asking them again their opinion of the topic in order to measure any opinion change owing to news story exposure (predictor). The first opinion measure is called the pre-test and the second measure is the post-test. They are the dependent measures. The amount of difference between the two tests is the degree of change in opinion. This difference suggests whether the news story affects (predicts) opinions on the topic covered.

Dependent Variables (Outcomes)

The **dependent variable** changes because of change in the independent variable. That is, the independent variable affects the dependent variable. In the example above, differences in amount of work per week and in educational level are thought to predict hunting behavior. In short, based on information about the predictor variable, we can discover information about the dependent variable.

Control Variables

A variable that the researcher wants to account for so that it does not influence the relationship between the independent variable(s) and the dependent variable is called a **control variable**. Control variables allow us to account for other effects between the independent and dependent variables, which can provide misleading results. For instance, if we were trying to measure customer service satisfaction in bricks-and-mortar women's clothing retail chain stores, we may wish to account for price points, retail space square footage, age of the store, store location, and so forth. These factors may influence general customer service satisfaction in unexpected ways.

Imagine that we want to run trials on a new Alzheimer's disease drug. The independent variable would consist of two conditions: those actually receiving the drug and those receiving the placebo (sugar pill). The dependent variable would be a series of cognitive ability tests completed by the patients over the duration of the study. This type of trial might control for patient diet, stage of Alzheimer's disease, patient weight, level of family support, and other patient illnesses—all factors that could influence the drug's effectiveness. The controls might suggest that the medicine may be less effective for patients on certain diets and with co-occurring illnesses. Accounting for these variables would allow researchers to discover whether the new drug shows promise in treating at least some types of Alzheimer's patients.

Interaction Variables

An **interaction term** is a variable that comprises a combination of usually two but sometimes more than two independent variables. They have a combined effect on a dependent variable. The collective effects can be more or less than the sum of the predictors' effects operating separately on the dependent variable. Think of it this way: the relationship between or among the independent variables somehow affects their relationship together on the dependent variable in a manner different from their individual effects.

For example, consider the effects of advertising and sales discounts on actual sales. If the product price is too high, then advertising may not generate sales increases. Similarly, sales discounts alone are not effective if customers are unaware of them. However, advertising that communicates sales discounts might very well generate additional sales. It is the combination of advertising and sales promotion discounts that have the most meaningful effect on sales, which is the dependent variable.

Let us consider job performance. Assume that we control for all possible variables and also assume that relevant professional experience and education are the two major predictors of job performance. Yet experience alone or education alone will not account for how well someone does at work. Professional experience without education may allow for limited professional success. Education alone without relevant experience might initially impede performance. However, relevant experience and relevant education will optimize someone's chances for doing well at work. As we can see, it is the combination or interaction of these two variables that provide the greatest opportunity for enhanced job performance.

SUMMARY OF KEY CONCEPTS

- The levels of data and variables are closely related.
- A variable is an observable and recordable characteristic of something that is counted or measured.
- What is measured is recorded as data.
- The properties of categorical and numeric levels of data determine the appropriate type of analysis. Within these two kinds of data are subtypes each with unique properties.
- Categorical data result from a counting process.
- Numeric data result from a measuring process.
- Compared to categorical data, numeric data contain more information.

VARIABLES APPLIED EXERCISES

3.1 What is a variable? Provide three examples.

3.2 What is the conceptual definition of a variable? Provide examples.

3.3 What is a measurable definition of a variable? Illustrate with examples.

3.4 When measuring the same phenomenon, can measurable definitions of variables (and conceptual definitions, for that matter) vary? If so, explain why.

3.5 Define data and explain data in relation to variables. Illustrate your understanding with examples.

3.6 What components comprise a measurable framework?

3.7 What are categorical variables? Provide some examples. Be sure to discuss the various types of categorical variables or levels of data.

3.8 What are numeric variables? Provide some examples. Be sure to discuss the various types of numeric variables or levels of data.

3.9 Explain whether the following variables are categorical and/or numeric: mortgage amounts of randomly selected homeowners on the West Coast; political party affiliation; star mass in the Milky Way galaxy; temperatures along the equator; and the top three desirable product features by order of importance.

3.10 How might we conceptualize and measure attitudes of Brand Z sportswear?

3.11 What are string data? Provide an example.

3.12 What are counts or frequencies? Provide an example.

3.13 What are relative frequencies? Provide an example.

3.14 Define a contingency table and provide an example.

3.15 What is a sample space?

3.16 What is a one-dimensional table? Provide a brief example.

3.17 What is a two-dimensional table? Provide a brief example.

3.18 What is the role of a meaningful zero in ratio-level data? Clearly explain your answer and provide an example.

3.19 What is scale-level data? Provide an example.

3.20 Define a control variable.

3.21 If we wish to observe, measure, and analyze the relationship between consumer perceived Brand Z sportswear quality and consumer repeat purchases at retail bricks-and-mortar stores, what might we control for in this study? Identify at least three potential control variables.

3.22 What are independent and dependent variables? Explain their relationship. Be sure to provide an example.

3.23 Define an interaction variable.

3.24 Pair the following six variables into three interaction variables that make sense: lead time for responding to email; education; product Model X recall; relevant professional experience; advertising Model X; and effective interpersonal email communication. Explain their potential effects within the interaction.

Chapter 4

SPSS Statistics Data Management Basics: Preparing Data for Analysis

LEARNING OBJECTIVES

To be able to:

- explain the key functions of data, output, and syntax SPSS files;
- access data in SPSS and from other formats;
- create and format categorical and numeric variables for viewing, analysis, and reporting;
- use the Data and Variable Views' functionality in SPSS;
- cut and paste data using SPSS;
- save data in SPSS and other formats; and
- understand and describe the basic usage of a codebook.

4.1 Introduction to SPSS and Data, Output, and Syntax Files

The SPSS "data management" function is a powerful tool. This chapter introduces some of the basics for getting started using SPSS. SPSS has three main file types: data, output, and syntax. Although our focus will be the data file, we will briefly discuss the output and syntax files. It is important to know that in SPSS (like other software applications), there are numerous ways to conduct the same task. Some require less or more steps and some depend on what you seek to accomplish.

The **data file** holds the data. It is composed of two windows or tabs. These are the **Data View** and **Variable View** tabs. The Data View contains the raw data, which can be manually entered, cut and pasted from another source, opened from an existing SPSS data file, accessed from another data file format, or imported from an external source. Data can also be saved in various spreadsheet formats. The Variable View allows the SPSS user to define the variable's characteristics.

The **output file** contains data analysis output such as tables, graphs, and statistical information, which can be copied and saved to SPSS and other formats. The output file also serves as a record of all activities conducted during the SPSS session.

Although there are numerous ways to access, save, and store SPSS data, we will focus on opening and saving data files in various spreadsheet formats. We will also cover saving output files in SPSS and other formats such as PDF, Word, and PowerPoint.

Last, although SPSS has an extensive, user-friendly pull-down menu of statistical tools, there is a **syntax file** option, where users can customize and specify statistical instructions to be executed in SPSS. Output can be customized as well. Syntax files can be saved for future use.

An asterisk appearing before a named or unnamed data, output, or syntax file indicates that there have been changes to the file that have not been saved. It is important to save files regularly because they may be inadvertently closed or lost during a power outage.

In addition to the SPSS Help Menu, there are three available IBM SPSS resources, which can be downloaded for free from the IBM website. They are the *IBM SPSS Statistics 23 Brief Guide*, which is approximately 100 pages, the *IBM SPSS Statistics Base 23*, and the *IBM SPSS Statistics 23 Command Syntax Reference*, which contains a comprehensive list of commands and instructions for syntax users.

4.2 Setting up the Data File

A data file contains the sample data that will be analyzed. It is formatted as a spreadsheet. The individual records or **cases** of data are located in the rows and the columns organize the data by variables so that the case data (row) are organized by (column) variable. For example, each row may contain data for individual social services clients. Each client's data are located in a case. The columns are the variables each representing information about every client in the data file, such as age, educational level, employment status, ethnic background, number of dependents, residence address, and so forth. These data allow the researcher to discover aggregate information about the clients.

4.3 Key SPSS Data Management Tools

This chapter starts by discussing how to create and format variables in an SPSS data file. Next, the chapter covers manually entering variable data. The discussion also addresses how to access data using different methods, including cutting and pasting into an SPSS data file as well as saving data in SPSS and in other formats. Output and syntax files are discussed. The chapter ends with a description of a codebook. These topics are important in order to prepare data for analysis and storage.

4.4 Opening SPSS

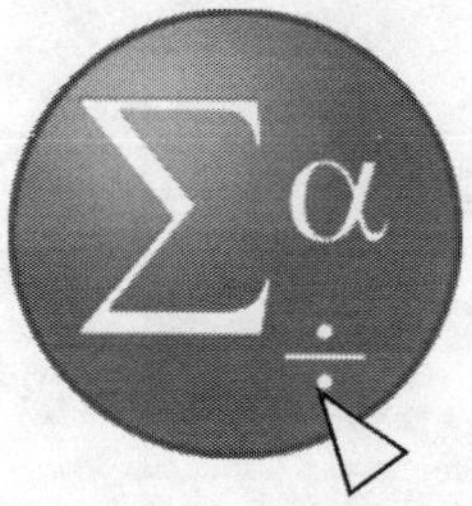

Figure 4.1

Step 1: To launch SPSS, locate the above icon on your desktop and click it.

Step 2: Depending on the default setting, the following "Welcome Dialog" window will open. This is a useful tool to explore the potential of SPSS. Next:

- Click "Cancel."

- If you do not wish to see this window in future SPSS starts, then click the "Don't show this dialog in the future" box located in the bottom-left-hand corner.
- This option can be re-enabled by doing the following:
  - Click onto the "File" tab.
  - Next, select the "Welcome Dialog" option.
  - Make sure the "Don't show this dialog in the future" box is not checked off, which will become the new default setting.

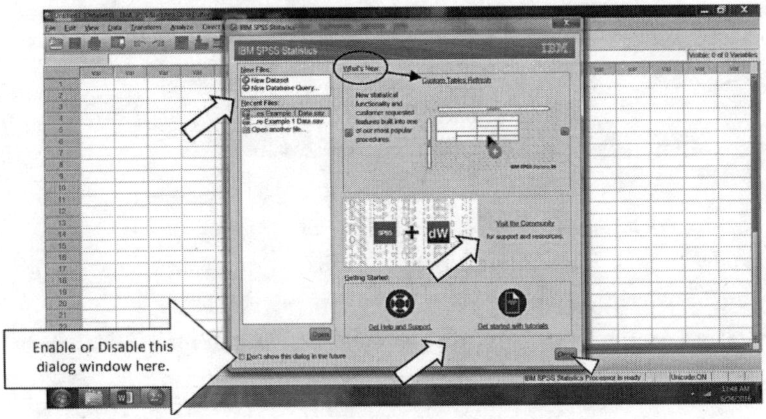

Figure 4.2

For your information: on the upper-left side, there are "New Files" and "Recent Files" options. First, "New Dataset" allows you to open a new SPSS data file for data entry. The "New Database Query" selection allows you to open a non-SPSS dataset such as Excel in SPSS. The "Recent Files" is available for your convenience.

Clicking the "Cancel" button will provide a clean, new spreadsheet. In the center of the window are support resource links, such as information on what's new in SPSS, a community forum, help access, and a number of tutorials.

Alternatively, once SPSS is open, you can open one or more new data files by:

- First, clicking on "File".
- Then click "New" followed by the "Data" option.

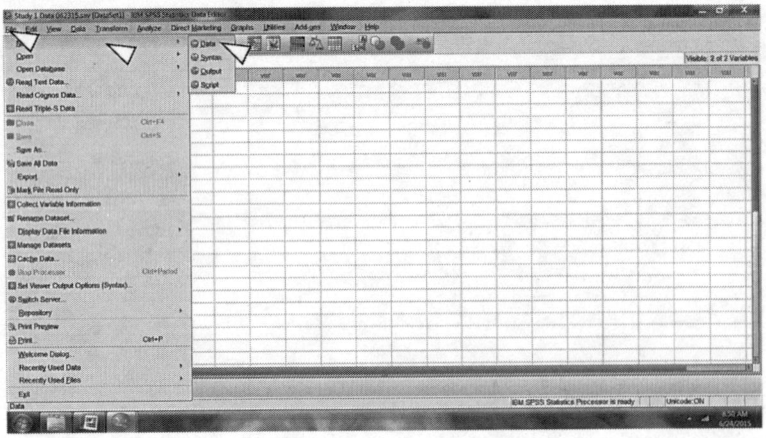

Figure 4.3

4.5 Formatting the Variables' Data

After closing (cancelling) the "Welcome Dialog" window, you will see the following window. The data file has two components or view tabs: "Data View" tab and "Variable View" tab. The "Data View" tab, which is the default view, provides the data by **case rows** organized by **column variables**. The selected tab has a gold background. The case numbers are to the far left. Like Excel, data values can simply be typed in. Each row represents a data record. Each column represents a variable, which is a measured property of something for each case. The cases are specific measurements of a variable. For example, a respondent's data (a case) may contain the person's age (a variable) and intervention effectiveness (another variable) based on a rating system applied to all clients (the cases). Each case row comprises data for a specific client.

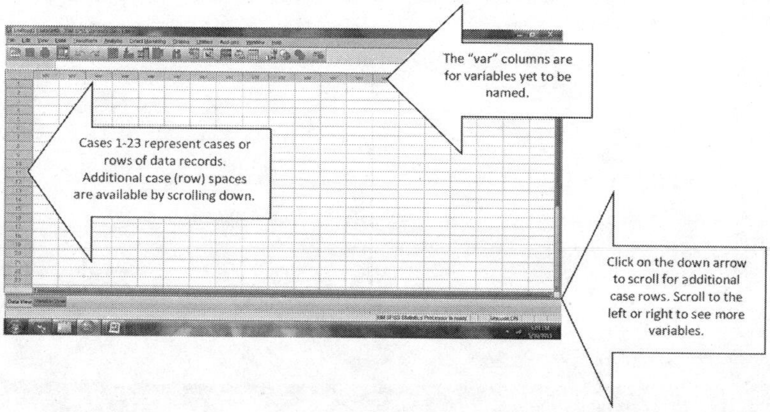

Figure 4.4

Before we enter data, we must format the variable's display as well as enter each variable's properties. This is important because these settings can affect our ability to present and analyze the data. The Variable View will allow us to prepare variables for data entry.

Step 1: Click on the "Variable View" tab. The "Variable View" tab allows us to:

- Define variables (which are located as columns of data);
- Label variables;
- Provide information about variables; and
- Define a number of column variable display attributes, which establish the appearance of the data and variables in the Data View.

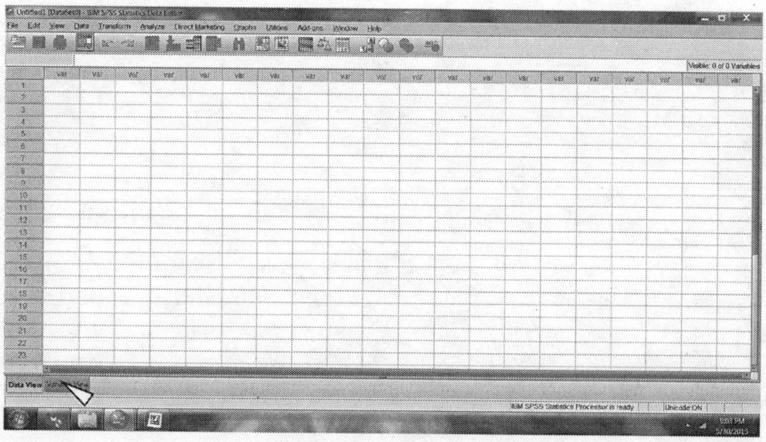

Figure 4.5

We can create new variables or modify existing variables' properties in order to meet our analysis requirements. In the Variable View only, each row represents a variable, which is a column in the Data View. The selected tab has a gold background. Let us address each column item, starting with "Name."

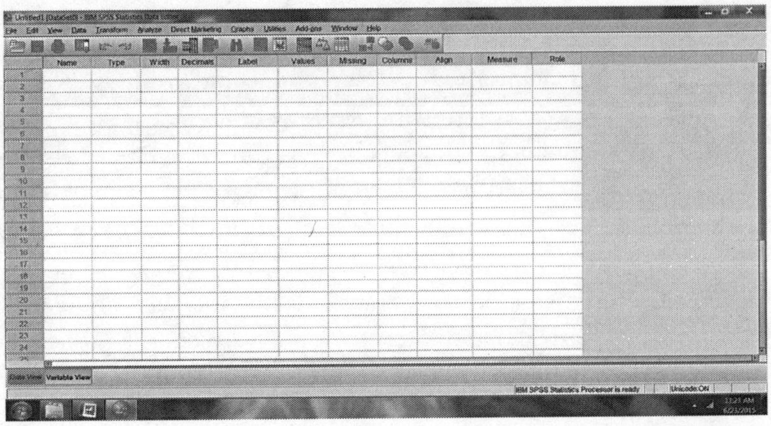

Figure 4.6

Name

Name is the variable name. There are three variable naming rules:

- Names must be one "word" and cannot contain any blank spaces. However, feel free to use the underscore line in place of blank space (e.g. Name_1, Name_2, and so forth). For instance, "HH_Income" might denote Household Income.
- Names must start with a letter.
- Names cannot contain any unusual characters.

Step 2: The first column is "Name." In the first row, which is reserved for the first variable, type in a variable name. The second row is for the second variable, and so forth.

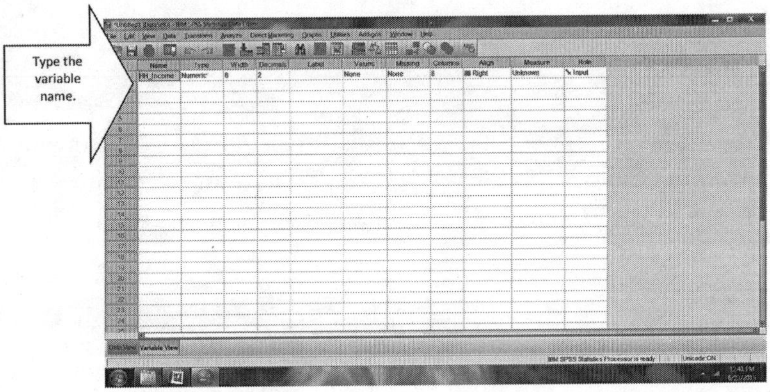

Figure 4.7

Type

Click on the **Type** cell representing the variable row that you wish to work on. A window will open providing a number of variable type formats. Types include Numeric, Comma, Dollar, and String (labels composed of symbols, letters, and/or numbers and suitable for categorical data). Clicking on the "Help" button in the window will provide detailed descriptions of the variable type options. In addition, for numeric values, you can set the number of places to the right of the decimal point.

Step 3: Under the "Type" column, click on the cell in the variable row. Next, do the following:

- Select variable type. In this example, it is numeric.
- Leave the default setting of two places to the right of the decimal point (.XX).
- Last, click the "OK" button.

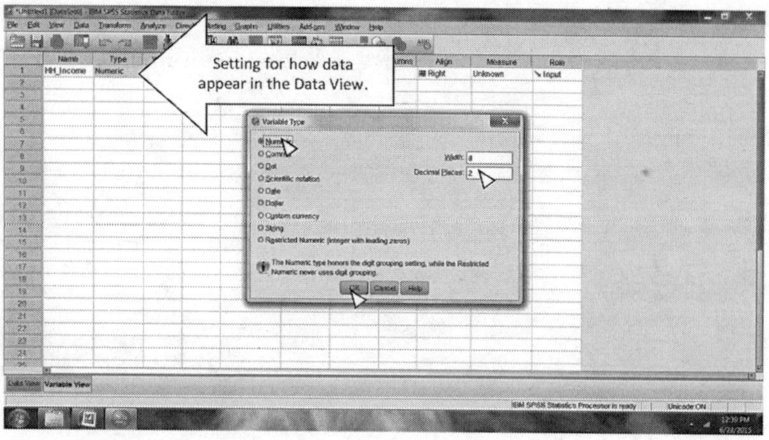

Figure 4.8

Width

The **Width** setting pertains to the length of places to the right of the decimal point, which appears in the Data View. This setting must be at least 1 greater than the decimal place setting. It is common practice to keep the default setting, which is 8.

Step 4: Under the "Width" column, click on a cell in the variable row. Again, do not change the "8" default setting. It can be decreased or increased using the spin control (arrows up or down).

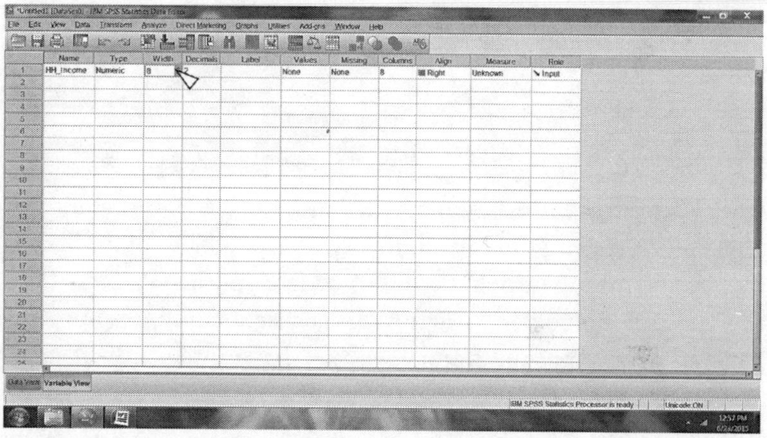

Figure 4.9

Decimals

The number of **Decimal** places can be set here as well as in the "Type" window. Place the cursor in the appropriate variable row "Decimal" cell and either type in or use the spin control to set the number of places to the right of the decimal point. It can be set from no decimal places up to any amount, which will be displayed in the Data View.

Step 5: Set the number of decimal places.

- Under the "Decimal" column, click on a cell in the variable row.
- Set the number of places to the right of the decimal point.

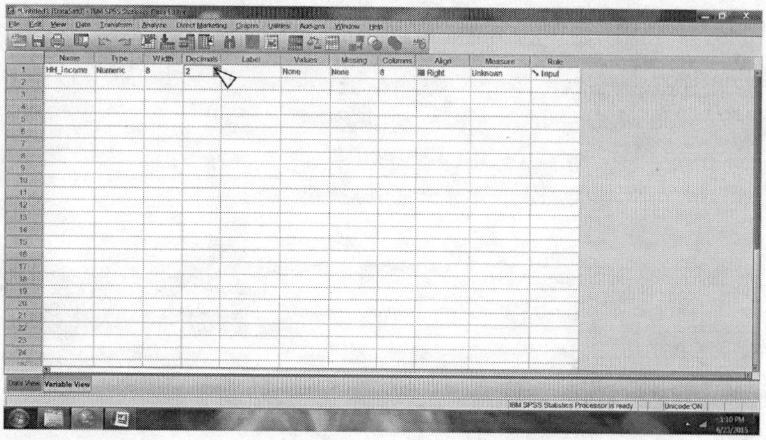

Figure 4.10

Label

Labels represent the variable names and provide more naming flexibility than the "Name" option. Labels can include spaces and any character. Simply type in the label. In the Data View, if a label is provided, running the cursor over the variable name will display the variable label. For example, the variable name "HH_Income" is easier to understand using the label "Household Income." This setting becomes valuable when there are many variables, and especially when these variables have similar names. Additionally, the variable label appears in the SPSS output, which is convenient.

Step 6: Create variable labels.

- Under the "label" column, click on a cell in the variable row.
- Type in the variable label using more descriptive language.

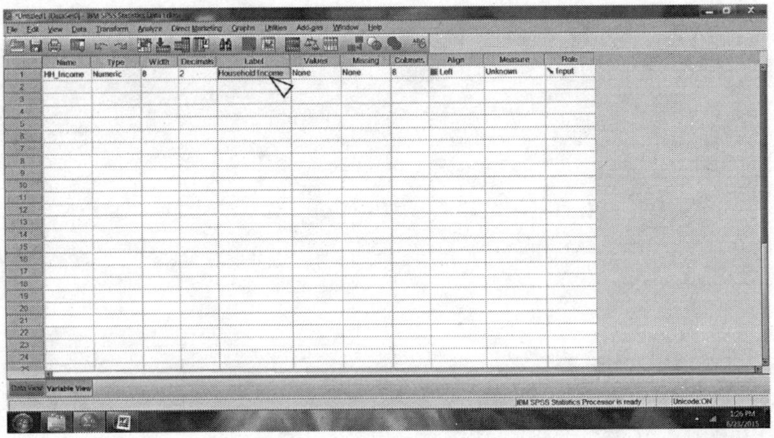

Figure 4.11

Values

The **Values** setting is important if numeric values represent groups or categories in a variable. This information would be contained in the codebook, which is a legend of what the numbers represent, and which will be discussed later in this chapter. Let us take an example. Because of the sensitivity involved in reporting specific income, respondents may be asked to indicate their general income group. Assume that we have three ordinal income categories—Low, Medium, and High—that are coded (recorded) as 1, 2, and 3 in the dataset. Although 1–3 represents the variable values, we can have them *appear* as Low Income, Medium Income, and High Income in any output and in the Data View by clicking the "Value Labels" button (icon with the "A1" double arrow), which replaces 1–3 with the assigned labels.

Step 7: Under the "Values" column:

- Click on a cell in the variable row.
- Click on the blue button with the three dots in the right-hand side of the cell. The "Values" window will open.

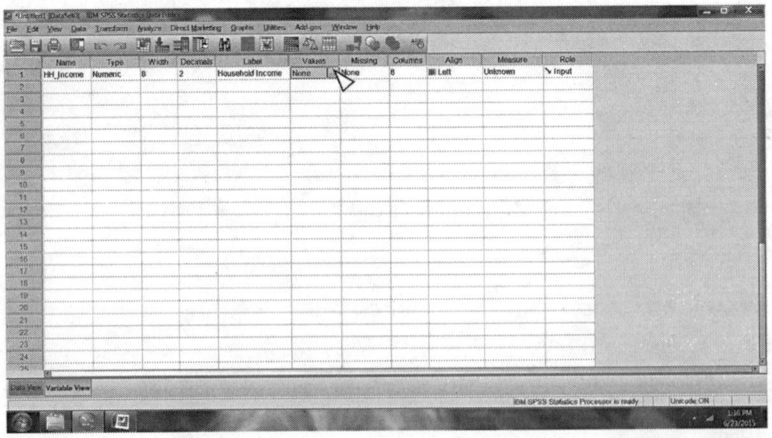

Figure 4.12

Step 8: Create "Values" labels.

- Enter a value and corresponding label.
- Then, click the "Add" button. In this example, they are 1 = "Low Income," 2 = "Medium Income," and 3 = "High Income." There are options to change or remove value labels as well.
- Once completed, click the "OK" button.

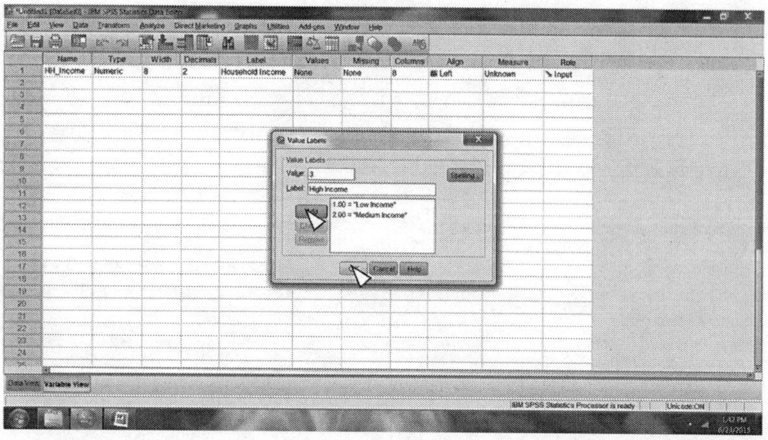

Figure 4.13

Step 9: Alternatively:

- Click the "Data View" tab.
- Then, click the "Value Labels" button.

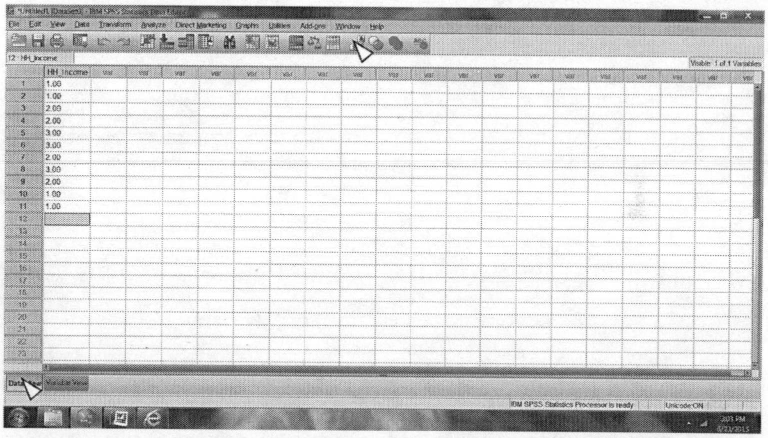

Figure 4.14

Step 10: Now, the Data View contains the variable labels in place of the numeric values. Disabling the "Value Labels" button will return the cells to their original 1–3 values.

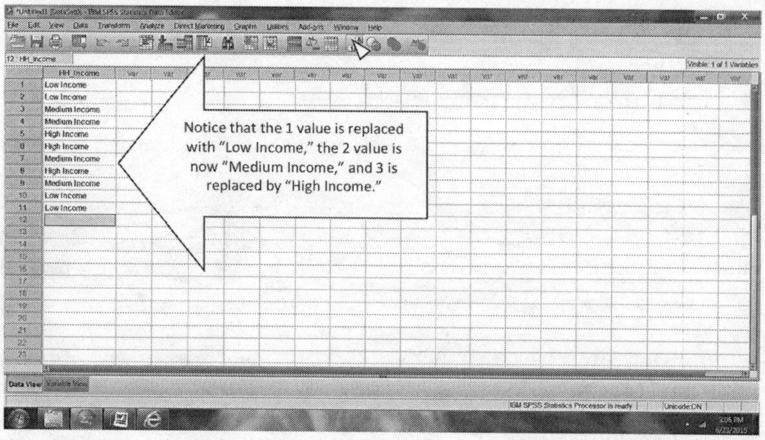

Figure 4.15

Missing

The **Missing** function can be used to code missing data with specific values. The coding should be guided by the reasons why the data are missing. We will skip further discussion of this topic.

Column

Column (Width) can be adjusted by typing in a width value or setting using the spin control. It sets the column width in the Data View, which can also be set by clicking and dragging the column borders in the blue background variable name area, thus expanding or narrowing a column width.

Step 11: Column width.

- Start by clicking the "Variable View" tab.
- Under the "Columns" column, click on the cell in the variable row. It can be decreased or increased using the spin control. It is common practice to keep the default setting, which is 8.

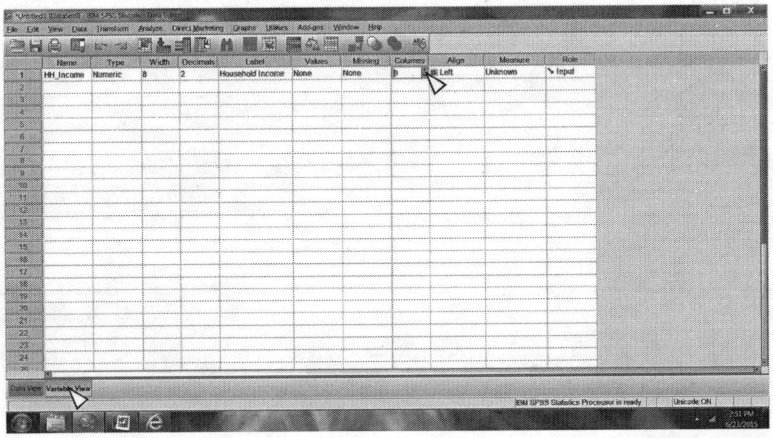

Figure 4.16

Align

The data in the cells can be left, right, or center **aligned**. This affects the Data View.

Step 12: Align the content in the cells.

- Under the "Align" column, click on the cell in the variable row. For illustrative purposes, select the left alignment.
- Click the "Data View" tab.

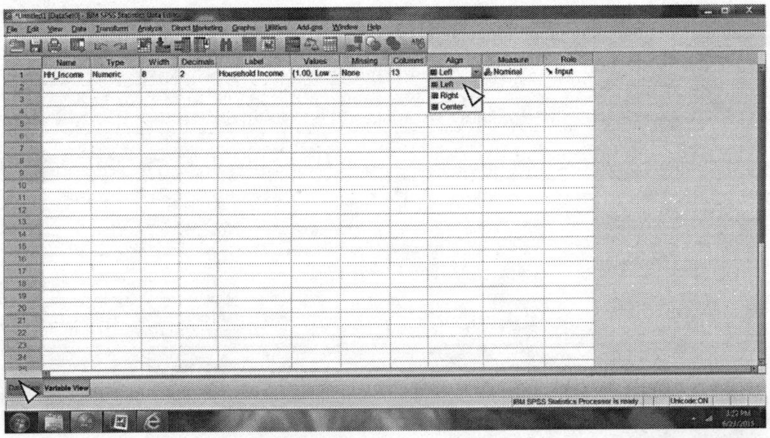

Figure 4.17

Notice that the cell content is aligned to the left. This setting can easily be changed to the right or center.

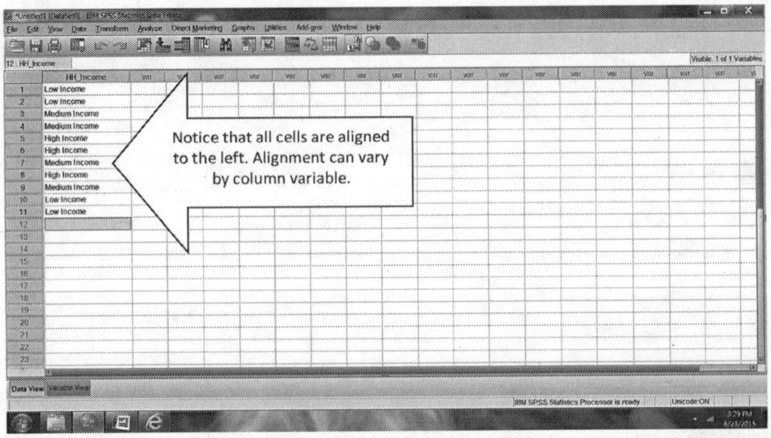

Figure 4.18

Measure

The **Measure** variable property indicates whether the level of data is numeric or categorical. There are three options in the pull-down menu. "Scale" is for numeric data. "Ordinal" is for ordinal categorical data. "Nominal" is for nominal categorical data, including binary.

Step 13: Measures (level of data).

- Click on the "Variable View" tab.
- Under the "Measure" column, click on a cell in the variable row.
- Highlight the "Ordinal" option because our choices suggest an order to our selections, from low, to medium, to high income.

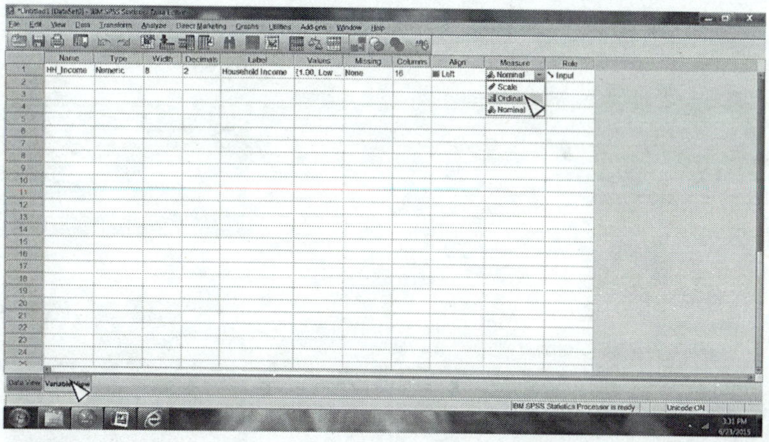

Figure 4.19

Role

This variable property is beyond the scope of our discussion. Suffice to say that this function allows variables to be assigned specific roles.

To exit the data file, simply click on the "X" in the red box located in the top-right-hand corner of the screen or click the "File" tab and then the last option, which is "Exit." If related output or syntax files are open and have not been saved, you will be prompted to save them.

4.6 The SPSS Data File

Data Access

We can populate our data file in three ways. First, we can manually enter data. Second, we can open an existing SPSS file or open another software application's data file in SPSS. Last, we can cut and paste data into the SPSS spreadsheet.

Manual Entry

These days, most data collection is electronic and automated, so manual entry is rare. However, there are situations where some type of manual entry is required. Examples would be paper and pencil surveys or human observational studies where researchers record participant behaviors on paper or audiovisually.

Let us return to the Data View. Now that we have formatted our variable, we can enter (type in the cell) data for Household Income by category (1 through 3), as in our example. Recall that the Variable View contains variables in the rows. The Data View provides the data by case rows organized by column variables.

Following the steps described above and using the Variable View, the numeric variable "Age" was added. Note, in the Data View, variable columns can be created by simply right-clicking your mouse in a column area on the "var" label, which will highlight the column, and then selecting the "Insert Variable" option. This is a useful function when you wish to insert a new variable among existing variables that might already have data.

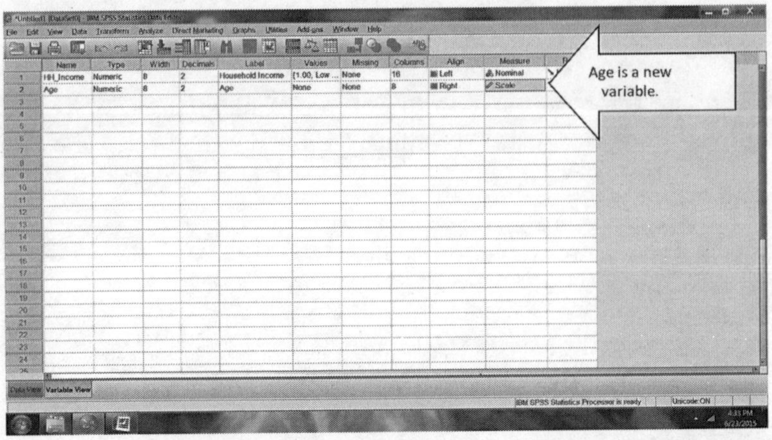

Figure 4.20

Next, click on the "Data View" tab. The Data View contains the manually entered age values. Notice that the alignment is to the right, unlike the "HH_Income" variable. The age values are simply typed in, as were the "HH_Income" values of 1–3.

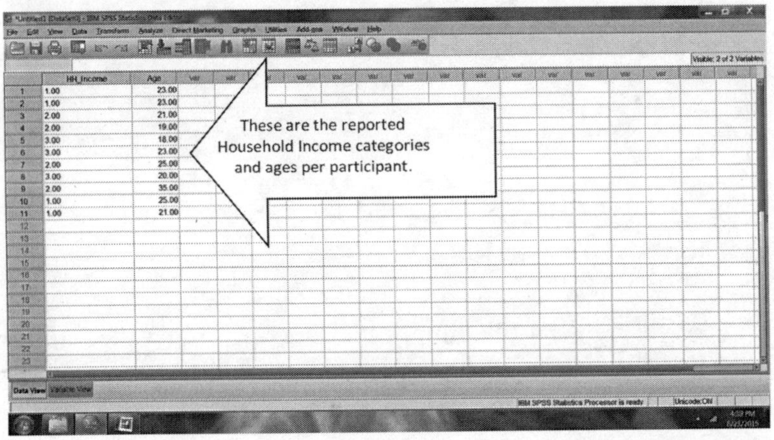

Figure 4.21

Again, to exit the data file, simply click on the "X" in the red box located in the top-right-hand corner of the screen or click the "File" tab and then the last option, which is "Exit." If related output or syntax files are open and have not been saved, you will be prompted to save them.

Opening an Existing SPSS Data File

Step 1: Click on the "Folder" image button.

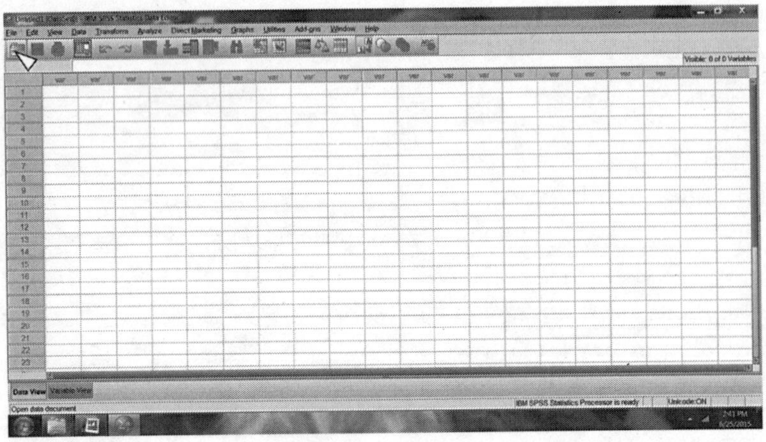

Figure 4.22

The following window will open.

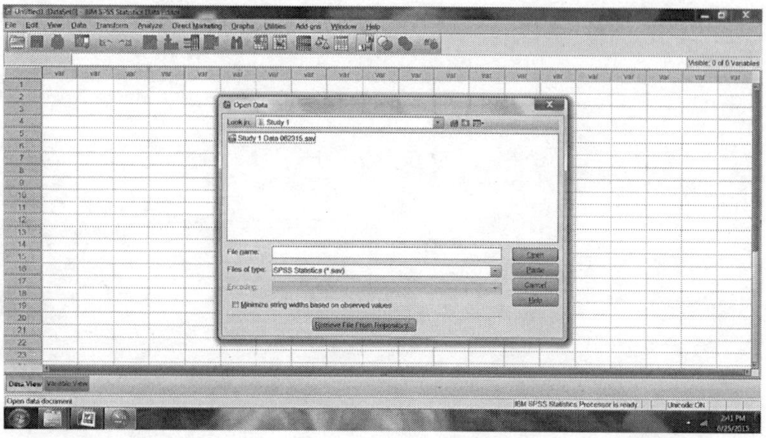

Figure 4.23

Step 2: Open the file.

- Highlight the data file that will be opened.
- Click the "Open" button.

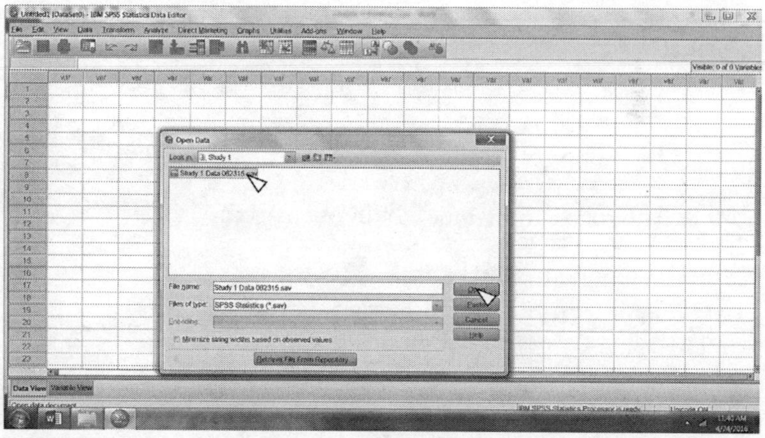

Figure 4.24

The SPSS data file will open. The data are now ready for analysis.

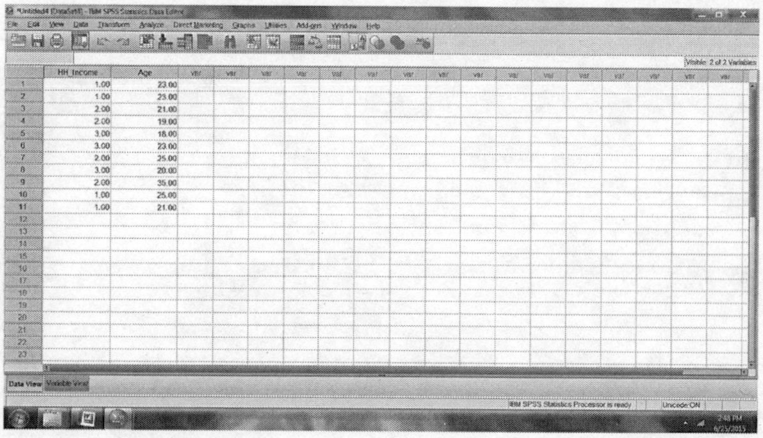

Figure 4.25

Opening Other Formatted Spreadsheet Data Files

The procedure to open an SPSS or other data format file is intuitive. Since data stored in Excel is common, we will illustrate opening an Excel file. Let us start with Step 2 from the above example.

Step 2: Save in another format.

- Click the "Files of type" pull-down menu.
- Select "Excel."

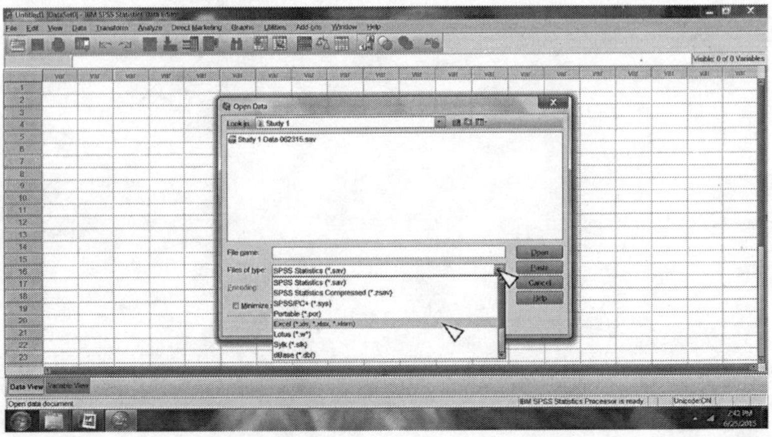

Figure 4.26

Step 3: The following window will open.

- Select (highlight) the Excel file, which will appear in the "Open" window.
- Then, click the "Open" button.

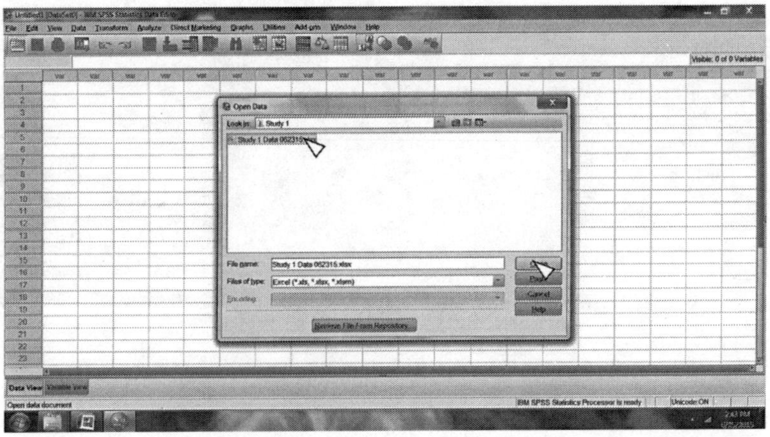

Figure 4.27

Step 4: The following window will appear. Since we know in advance that the variable names are in the first row, leave the box checked. Click the "OK" button.

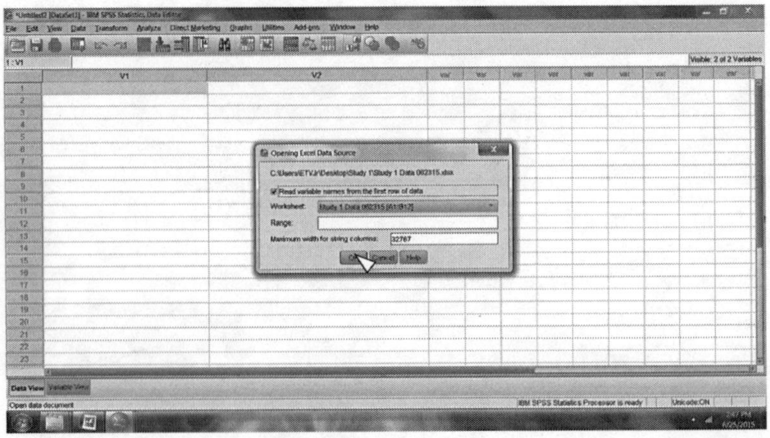

Figure 4.28

The Excel data will open in SPSS as depicted to the right. SPSS sets the variable properties based on an automatic assessment of the values. It is good practice, though, to check the variable properties in the Variable View.

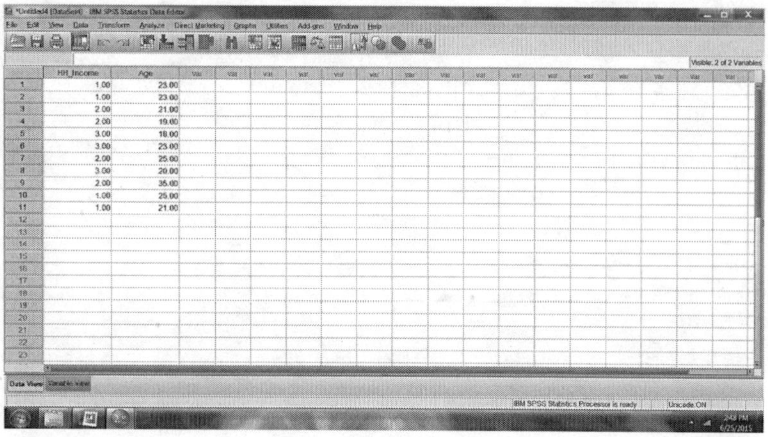

Figure 4.29

Text Files

Data in text files can be opened in SPSS. It is important to know how the data are arranged in the text file, whether there are fixed column widths or organized by delimiters. Delimiters are tabs, spaces, commas, or some other type of symbol separation of the data fields.

Cut and Paste

Sometimes simply copying (or cutting) and pasting data from a file into another data file is convenient. The steps are as follows.

Step 1: Cut and paste.

- Highlight the data that you wish to copy.
- Right-click on the data and then select "Cut" or "Copy."

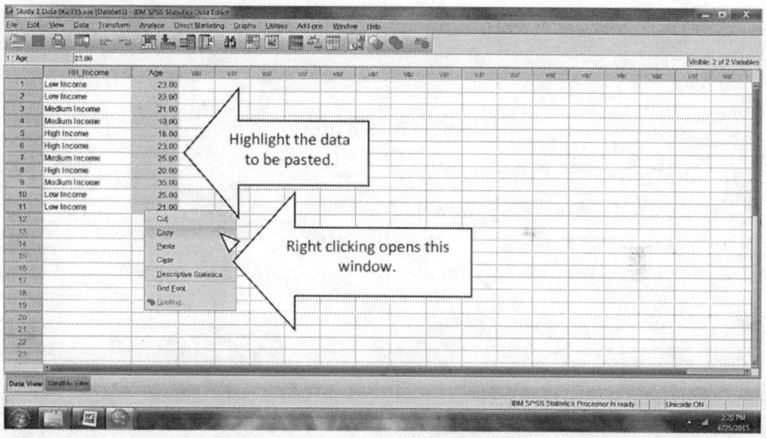

Figure 4.30

Step 2: Go to the file or spreadsheet where you wish to place (paste) the data.

- Select the cell where the first value will be located.
- Right-click and then select the "Paste" option.

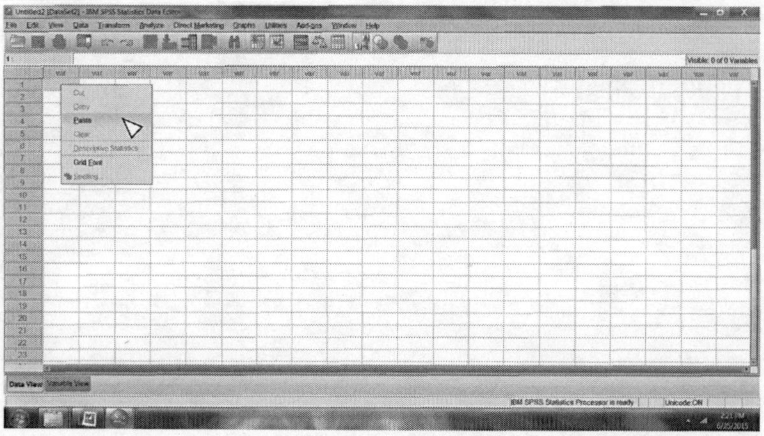

Figure 4.31

Step 3: The data will paste starting from the selected cell. The variable attributes will need to be defined in the Variable View.

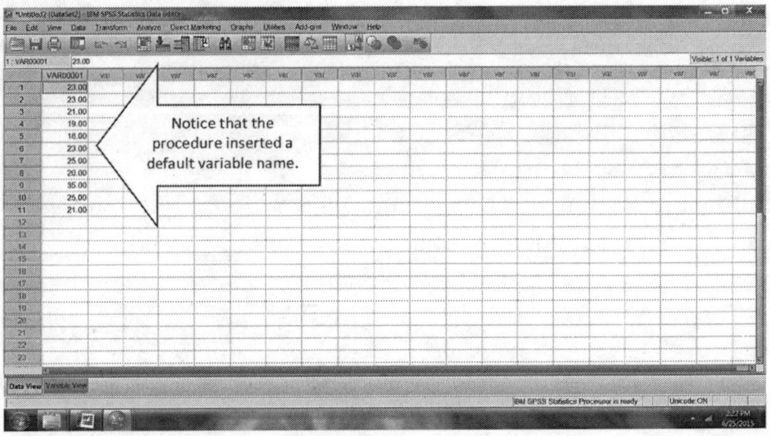

Figure 4.32

Saving the Data File

When finished with data entry or after making a change to the data file, save the file.

Saving Data in SPSS

The steps to save an SPSS data file are as follows.

Step 1: Saving data.

- Click on the "Save" button located on the top-left-hand side.
- Alternatively, the file can be saved by clicking the "File" tab and using the "Save As . . ." option, as shown below.

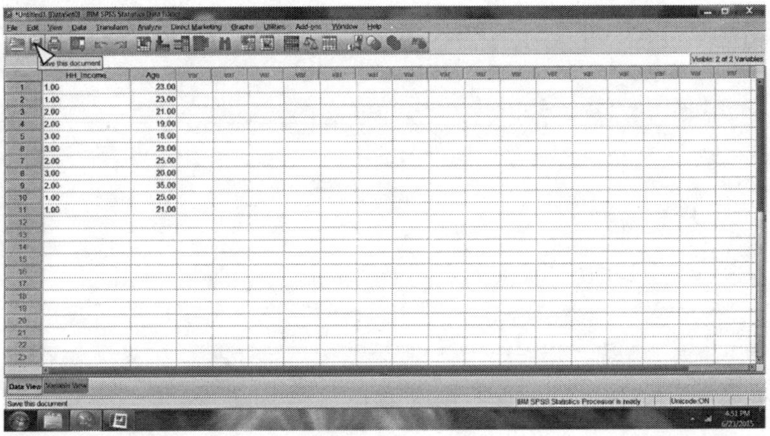

Figure 4.33

The following "Save Data As . . ." window will open.

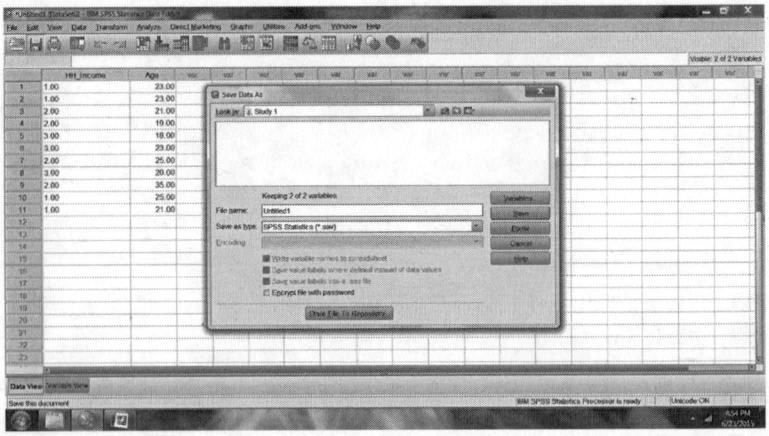

Figure 4.34

Step 2: Place the cursor in the file name area and type a name over the default name. In our example, notice that the file to be saved will be named "Study 1 Data 062315."

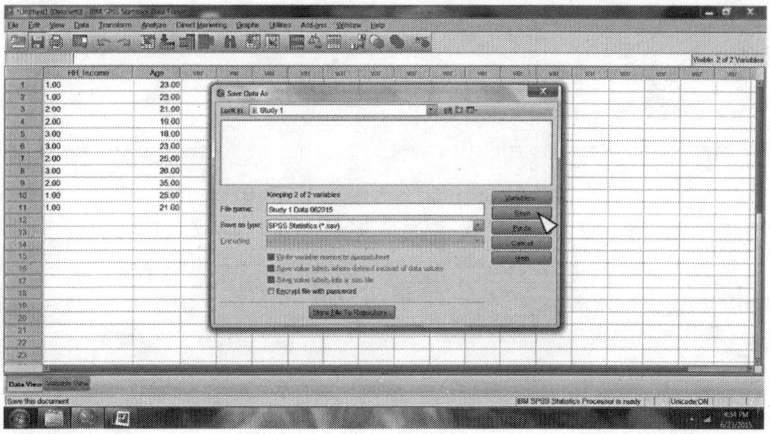

Figure 4.35

- It is good practice to create a name that relates to the analysis as well as indicates the date. This minimizes the confusion associated with having multiple datasets.
- Leave the "Save as type" (*.sav), which is the SPSS data file default format. The ".sav" is the file extension. The "*"is a placeholder for the file name, which will be typed in by the person saving the file.
- Save the SPSS data file in the desired location. In this example, it will be saved in a folder labeled "Study 1."

The save file procedure will create a record of the action in the output file.

Saving Data in Other Spreadsheet Formats

SPSS data files can be saved in other spreadsheet applications such as Excel, SAS, and Strata, among others, as well as generic formats such as tab or comma delimited text files. The procedure below saves the SPSS data in Excel.

After a file name is typed in the "File name" box, do the following:

- Scroll down to "Save as type."
- Select "Excel 2007 through 2010" (*.xlxs). Other formats are available.
- Save the Excel formatted data file in the desired location.

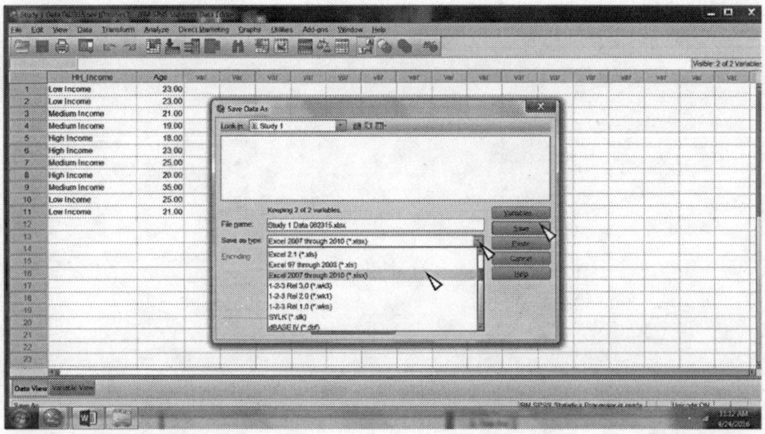

Figure 4.36

4.7 The SPSS Output File

The SPSS output file contains data analysis output, such as tables, graphs, and other statistical information, which can be copied and pasted, saved in SPSS, or exported (saved in another format). The output file also serves as a record of all activities conducted during an SPSS session. It is automatically generated when SPSS is launched. A new output file or existing one can be opened. These files can be saved in numerous common formats for usage later.

Many activities in SPSS, such as saving a file or various analyses and results, are recorded in the output file, including a log of the analyses generated. This convenient record serves as a reminder of the specific analyses conducted should a user wish to run similar analyses at a future time. The specific analysis instructions can be cut and pasted into a syntax file (and also modified) for future usage.

Creating a New SPSS Output File

The SPSS output file can be created in two ways. First, an output file generates once a data file is opened. Second, a new output file can be created from the data spreadsheet or output viewer window. The procedure below describes the latter option.

Step 1: Create a new output file.

- Click on the "File" tab.
- Next, select the "New" option.
- Then, click the "Output" option.

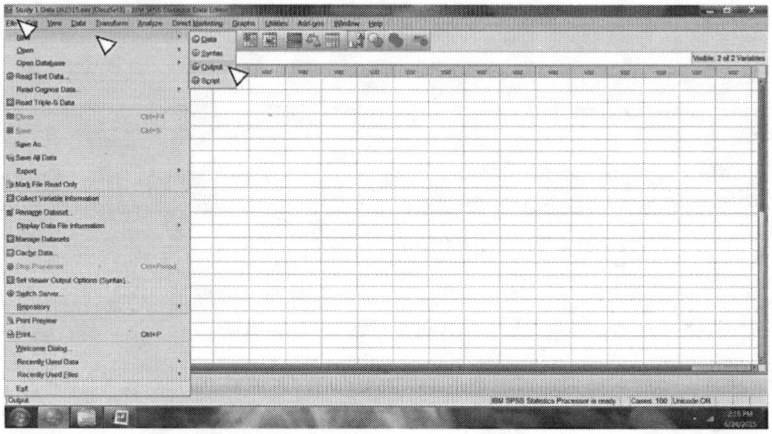

Figure 4.37

The following new output file window will appear.

Figure 4.38

Opening an Existing SPSS Output File

Step 1: Opening an SPSS output file.

- Click on the "File" tab.
- Next, select the "Open" option.
- Then, click the "Output" option.

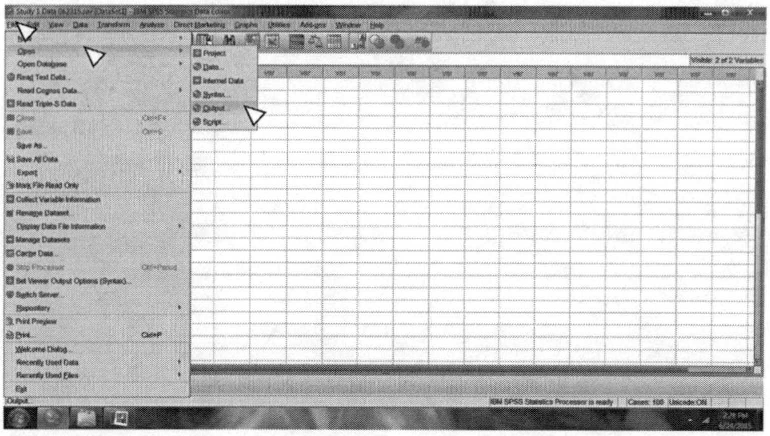

Figure 4.39

Step 2: From the "Open Output" window:

- Locate the desired output file.
- Highlight it until it appears in the "File Name" space.
- Click "Open."

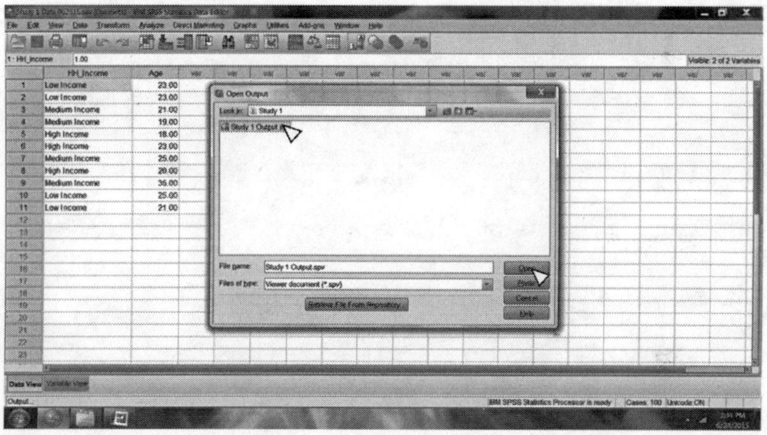

Figure 4.40

The following existing output file window will appear.

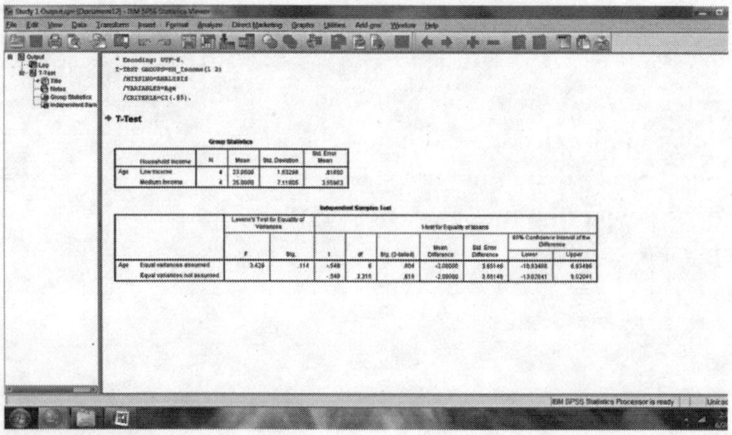

Figure 4.41

Displaying the Full *P*-Value in the Output File

Values in the output file can be fully displayed to the right of the decimal point. This option is useful when examining *p*-values, which is an important concept addressed in Chapter 11. We will cover two related methods.

Here is a sample output file.

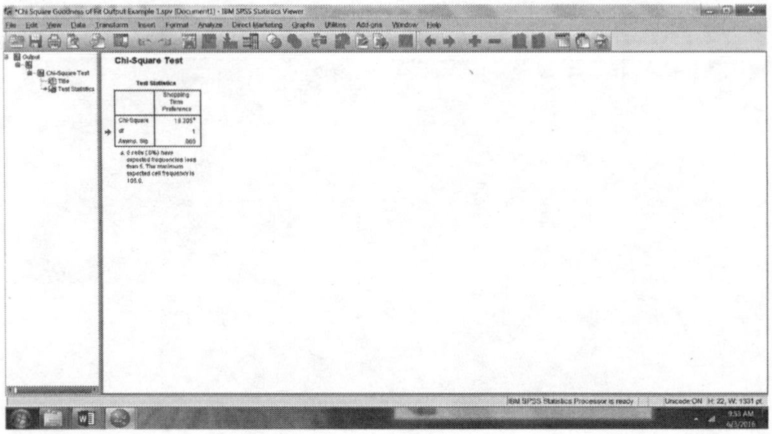

Figure 4.42

In the output file:

- Double-click on the table. Notice that the table title cell now has a black background.
- Place the cursor over the *p*-value, which is .000. A yellow box opens, which now displays the full *p*-value. It is .000019.

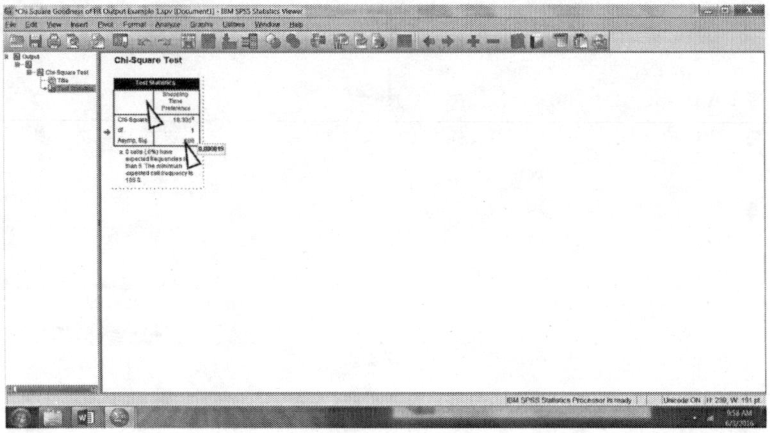

Figure 4.43

Alternatively, after double-clicking the table, simply clicking on the *p*-value cell will reveal the full number. The cell background becomes blue and the *p*-value is in white font.

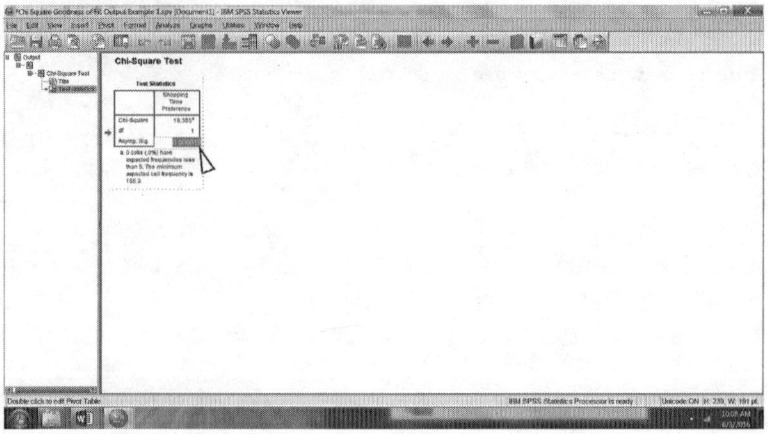

When the *p*-value is very small, it will be displayed in scientific notation as in the example below. **Scientific notation** is a way of reporting very large numbers or very small numbers in a shorthand form. The 1.9E–9 notation indicates that there is a decimal point followed by 8 zeroes, then 1 and 9. The negative value following the "E" represents the number of places before the value that is immediately to the right of the decimal point. Thus, it includes 1 and any values to the left of the decimal point. If less than the number after "E–" are available, then zeroes are used as places. In this example, it is 9. In other words, the *p*-value is .0000000019. This will occur using either of the two methods. Although we will not cover it here, SPSS has options to change the number of decimal places displayed in the output file, which can be saved as such.

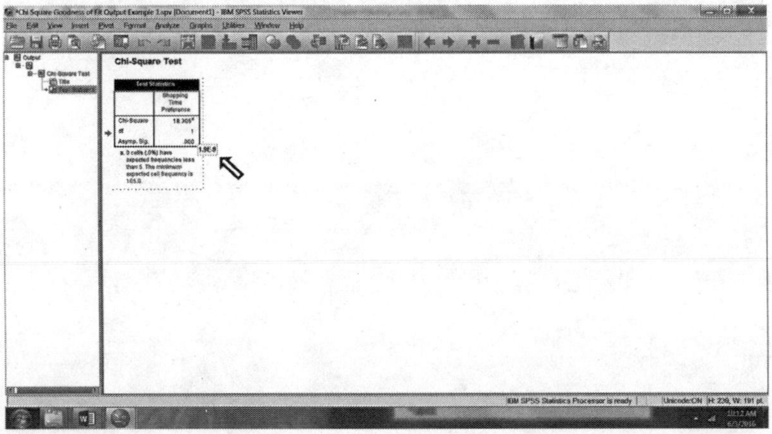

Figure 4.44

Saving an SPSS Output File

The procedure for saving an output file is similar to saving other types of SPSS files. The export function is valuable because it allows the file be saved as a Word, PDF, PowerPoint, and a number of other formats that make it easier for someone to read output who does not have access to SPSS. Let us review the steps for saving and exporting an SPSS output file.

Saving Output for the SPSS Output Viewer

The SPSS output file extension is *.spv, which allows output to be read in the **SPSS Output Viewer** (the output file). The procedure is straightforward and as follows.

Step 1: Saving the SPSS output file.

- Click on the "Save" button located on the top-left-hand side.
- Alternatively, the file can be saved by clicking the "File" tab and using the "Save as" option.

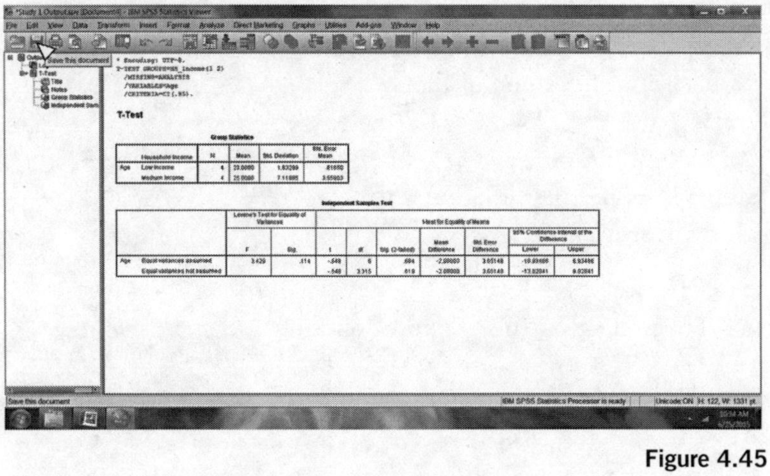

Figure 4.45

The following "Save Output As" window will open.

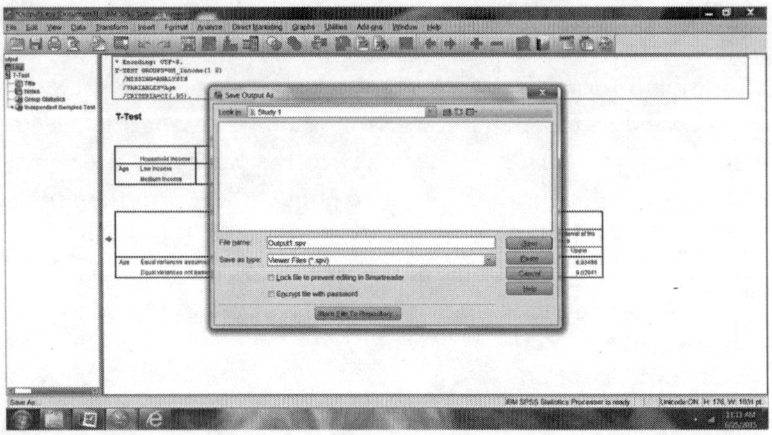

Figure 4.46

Step 2: Place the cursor in the file name space and type a file name. Notice that the file to be saved will be named "Study 1 Output 062315."

- Leave the "Save as type" (*.spv), which is the SPSS output file default format.
- Save the SPSS output file in the desired location. In this example, it will be saved in a folder labeled "Study 1."

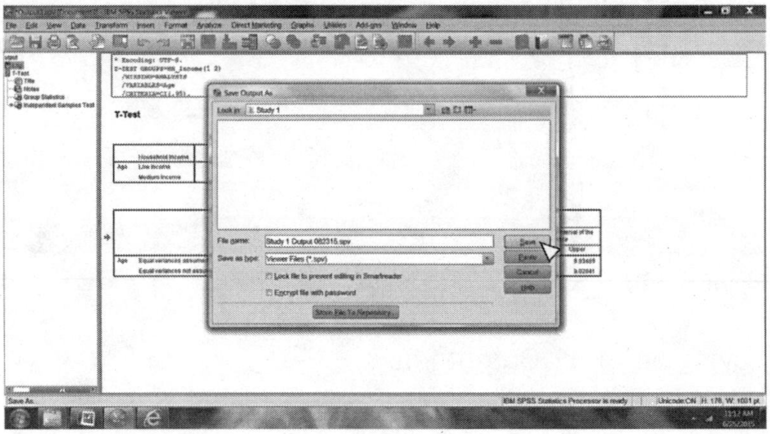

Figure 4.47

Saving SPSS Output in Another Format

The following example illustrates how to "save" an SPSS output file as a PDF file.

Step 1: Saving the SPSS output file to another format.

- Select the "File" tab.
- Then, click on the "Export" option.

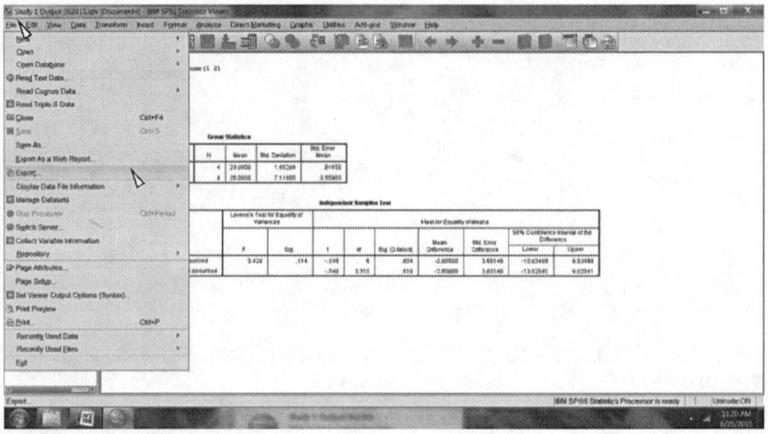

Figure 4.48

The following "Export Output" window will open.

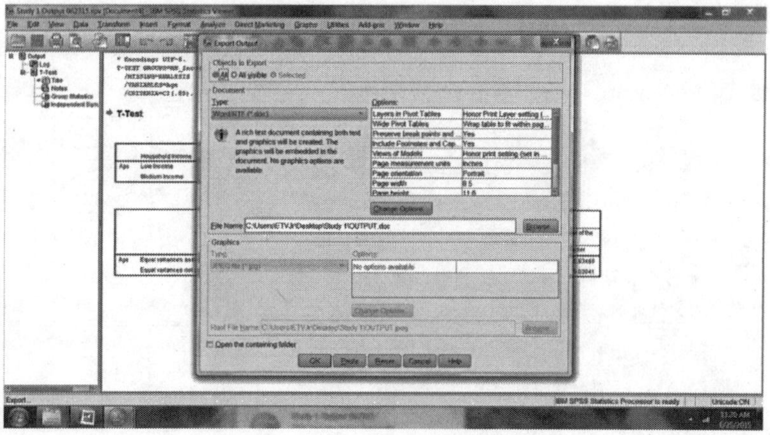

Figure 4.49

Step 2: In the "Export Output" window:

- On the right-hand side where "Document" and "Type" headings are located, click on the blue pull-down menu area.
- Select "Portable Document Format (*.pdf)." Other formats are available.

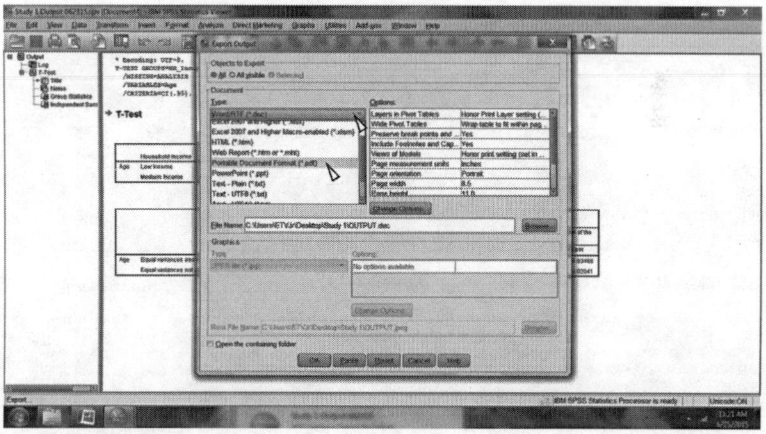

Figure 4.50

Step 3: Now, the exported file will be "Portable Document Format (*.pdf)," as noted in the blue pull-down area. Notice in the "File Name" window to the left of the "Browse" button is an address and default name for the exported PDF file.

- Click on the "Browse" button to select the location where the PDF output file will be saved.

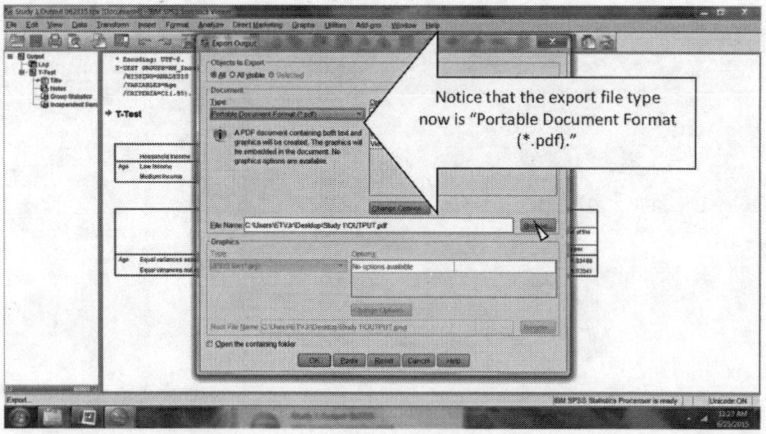

Figure 4.51

Step 4: The "Save File" window will open.

- Once you locate where the exported file will be stored, you can type over the blue highlighted default file name. In this example, the exported output PDF file will be named "Study 1 Output 062315." As a best practice, it is advisable to link the output file to the data file by indicating the study name in both files, including the date signals the version saved. Any systematic naming scheme can be used.
- Last, click the "Save" button.

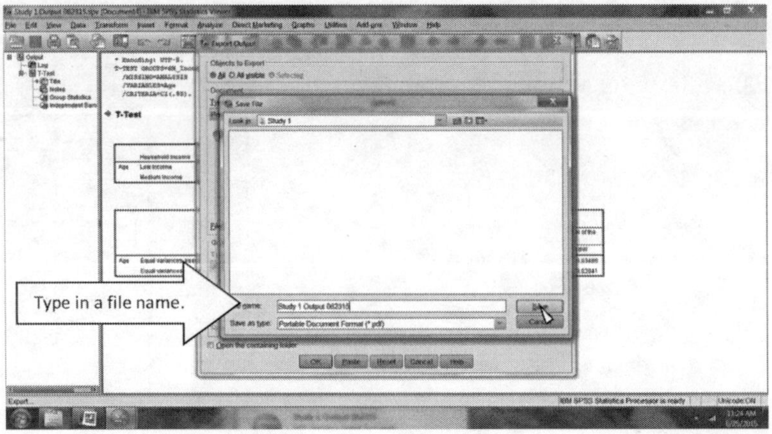

Figure 4.52

Step 5: The following window will open, which verifies the export file type, name, and location. If this information is correct, then click "OK."

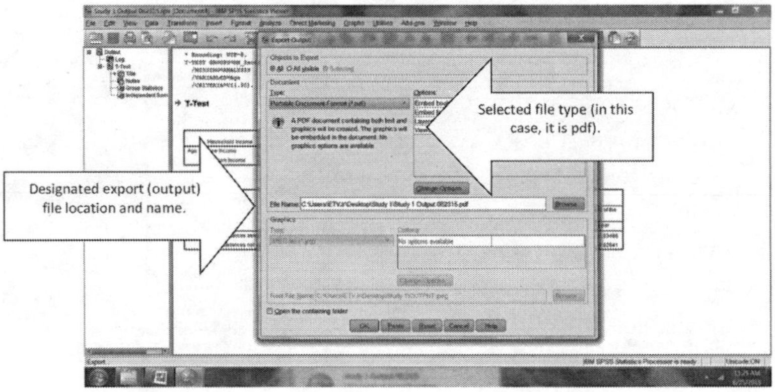

Figure 4.53

As the output file exports, you will see the following "Exporting Progress" window. Once the export is complete, the window will close. The exported output file will be located in the selected area and in the designated format.

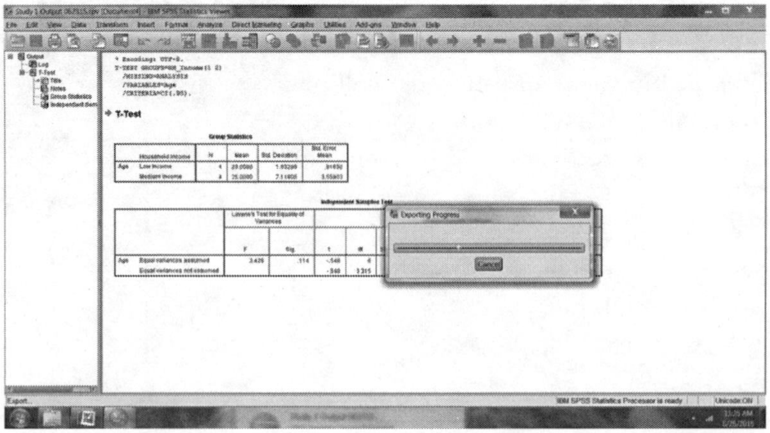

Figure 4.54

4.8 A Brief Review of the Syntax File

Rather than use the SPSS pull-down menu, using a text syntax file allows one to customize the analysis and output to meet specific needs. By typing in commands, the file can automate many SPSS functions, such as running descriptive statistics, graphs, *t*-tests, and regression analysis in a single easy run. The syntax file can be saved for future use. Multiple versions can be saved for different analysis situations. The entire syntax file or parts of it can be run by highlighting a section or selecting all. Once a data file is open, either open an existing syntax file or open a new, empty one. Run the existing syntax or enter commands and run a new one. Existing syntax files can be modified. The syntax file utilizes the data in the most recently accessed data file. Additionally, it can conduct analyses beyond the pull-down menu options. The SPSS syntax guide contains detailed instructions.

Below are examples of a new syntax file with no commands followed by an existing one, which is run.

Step 1: Create a new syntax file.

- Open the data file to be used with the syntax file.
- Click on the "File" tab.
- Select the "New" option.
- Then, click the "Syntax" option.

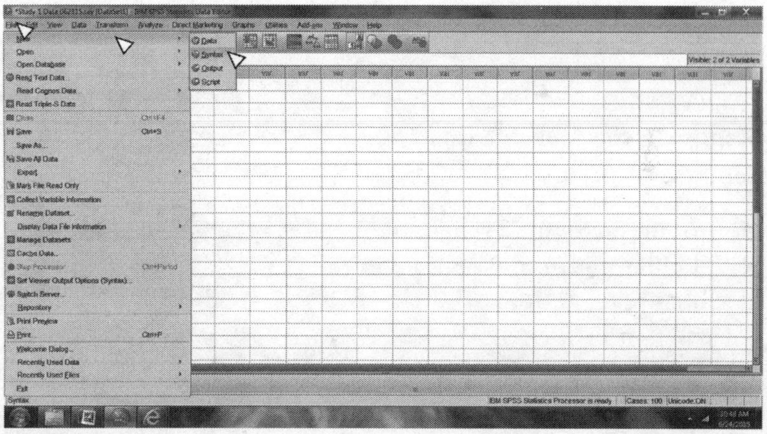

Figure 4.55

The following new syntax file window will open. Simply enter the commands in accordance with the *IBM SPSS Statistics Command Syntax Reference* book.

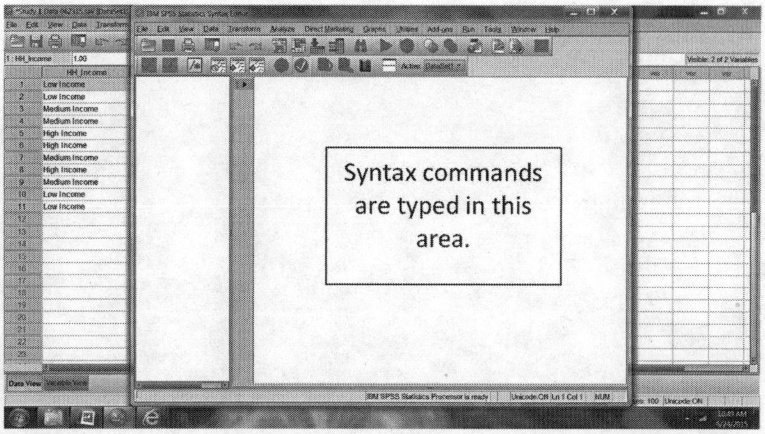

Figure 4.56

To open an existing syntax file, follow the steps below.

Step 1: Open an existing syntax file.

- Open the data file to be used with the syntax file.
- Next, click on the "File" tab.
- Select the "Open" option.
- Last, click the "Syntax" open.

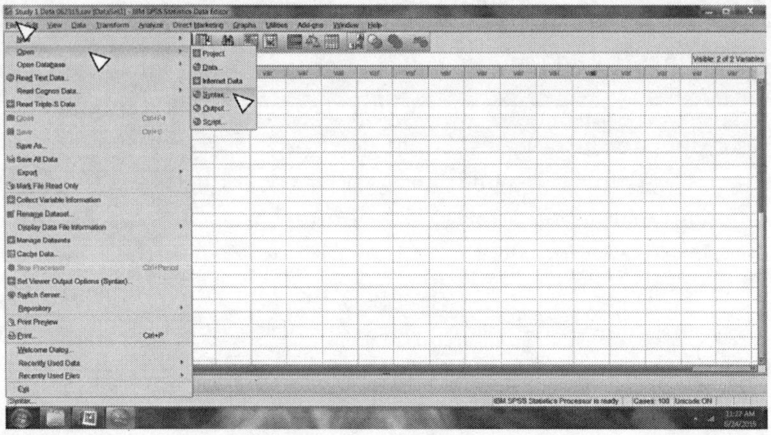

Figure 4.57

Step 2: In the "Open Syntax" window:

- Locate the desired syntax file.
- Highlight it until it appears in the "File Name" space.
- Click "Open."

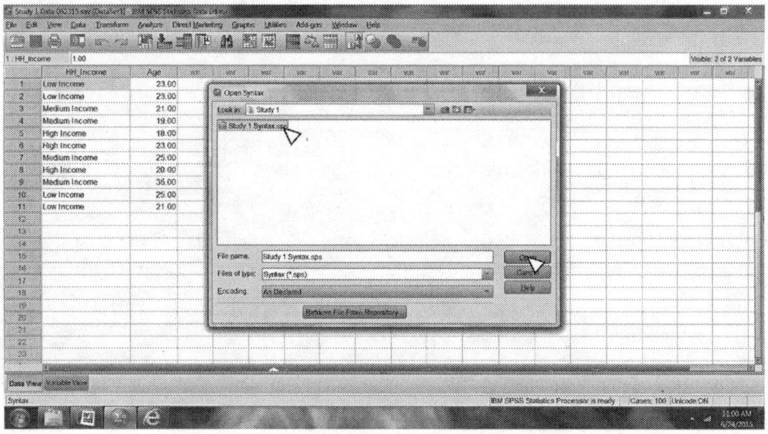

Figure 4.58

The following existing syntax file window will appear.

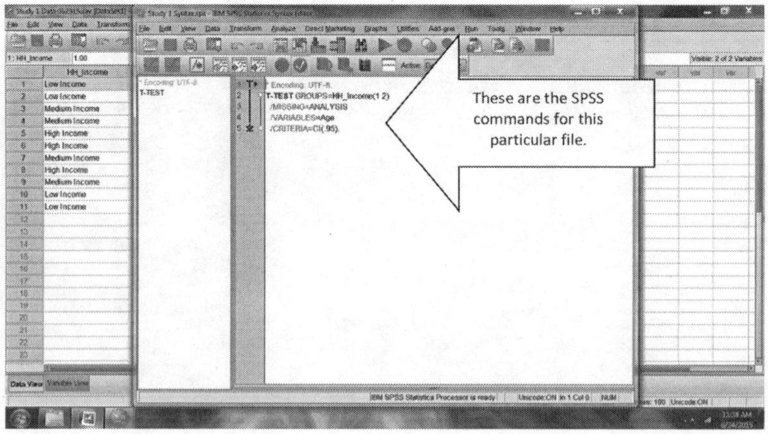

Figure 4.59

Step 4: Continue with the following:

- Click the "Run" tab.
- Then select "All," which will execute the entire syntax file.

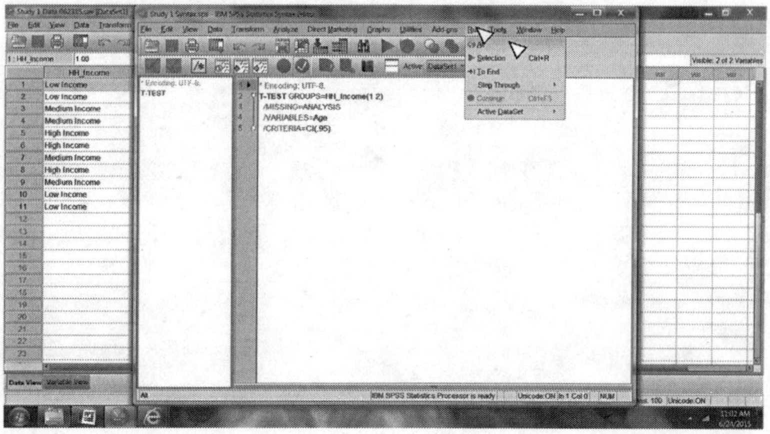

Figure 4.60

The following output will be generated based on the syntax file run.

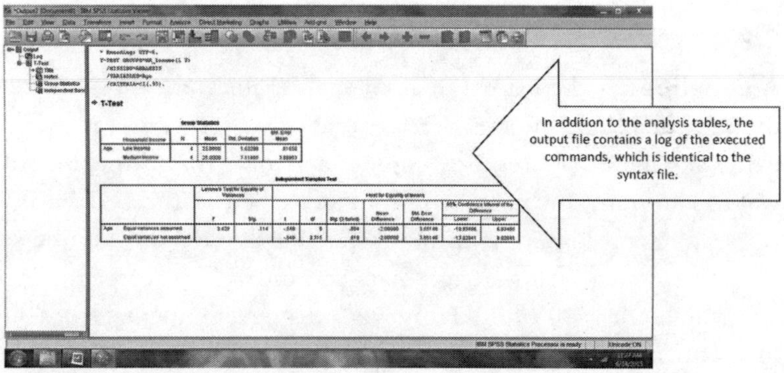

Figure 4.61

Step 5: Select the "File" tab and "Save as" option.

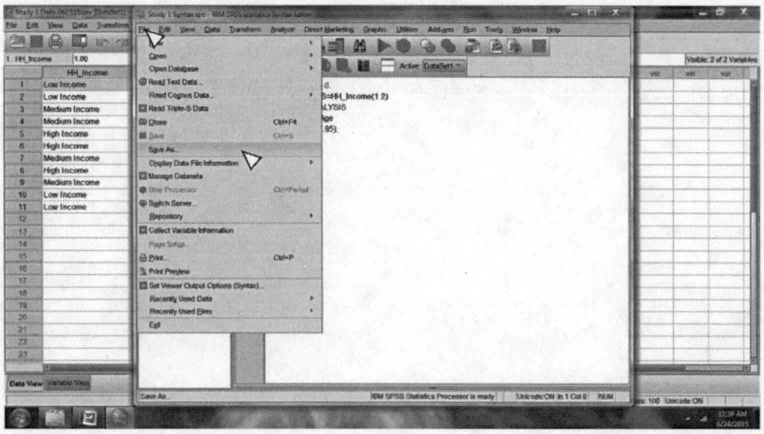

Figure 4.62

Step 6: Either keep the same name or change the syntax file name. The syntax file extension is "*.sps." Do not change the "Encoding" default setting.

- Click the "Save" button.

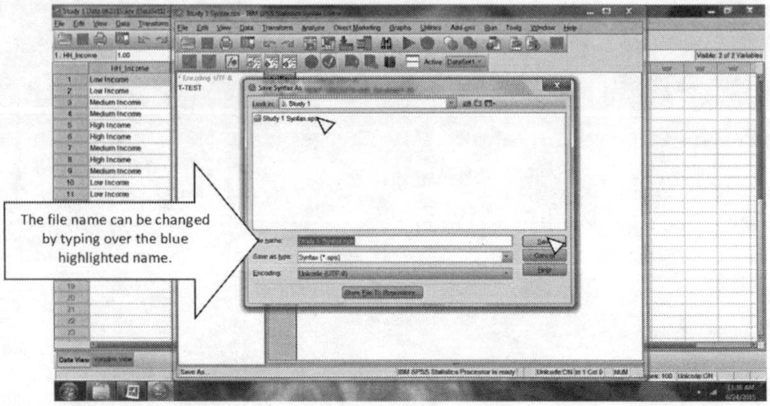

Figure 4.63

4.9 Creating a Codebook

Creating a Codebook from Scratch

A **codebook** is the legend of all of the variables' descriptions and values' formatting. It provides the measurable definitions of the variables. It serves as a reference that is handy when there are many variables that are not easily defined and when variables are transformed (changed in some way). The transformation should be described in the codebook. In short, the codebook makes a daunting spreadsheet with many variables, cases, and numbers manageable.

For instance, data on age that are numeric in years are straightforward; we simply see the age whether it is 10 or 80. However, in a developmental study of children, age may be recorded in months so that we may have values such as 1, 5, 24, 36, 48, and so forth. At the same time, we may have the ages of the primary caregivers in years. These two variables can be confusing unless we have a codebook, which indicates an age variable name and definition for children and an age variable name and definition for primary caregivers. In the case of categorical variables, the codebook provides the definitions of categories, which usually is arbitrarily set. Therefore, the codebook assures accurate interpretation and reporting.

The codebook serves another purpose. Often numbers are used to identify categories within variables in order to reduce data storage requirements. In very large studies, data storage can become an issue. Using numeric values in variables rather than string data consumes less storage and processing time, and is thus cost-effective. Table 4.1 shows an example of a simple codebook.

Table 4.1

Survey Study 1 Codebook

1. *Gender:*
   1 = female; 2 = male; 3 = lesbian; 4 = gay; 5 = bisexual; 6 = transgender; 7 = queer
2. *Age: Age in years*
   Blank space
3. *Your Student Status:*
   1 = full-time student; 2 = part-time student
4. *Highest level of education:*
   1 = bachelors; 2 = some graduate school; 3 = masters; 4 = doctorate
5. *Anticipated year of MBA graduation:*
   Blank space
6. *MBA concentration:*
   1 = Business Analytics; 2 = Financial Analytics; 3 = E-ship; Marketing;
   4 = Sustainability/CSR;
   5 = Nonprofit Management; 6 = Healthcare Management
7. *Most useful undergraduate course taken:*
   Blank space (requires coding)
8. *Commute in minutes: Minutes*
   Blank space
9. *Mode of transportation to/from the University?*
   1 = own vehicle; 2 = mass transits; 3 = combination of own vehicle and mass transit

REAL WORLD SNAPSHOT

According to IMALTD.com, in an effort to reduce costs and improve efficiencies, IMA, a data management consulting firm, was charged with reorganizing Pepsi Bottling for North America (PepsiCo)'s massive database. During the project, IMA scrubbed PepsiCo's entire database, including data from PepsiCo's 63 North American beverage facilities. Additionally, the firm created a master codebook, identified all duplicated and obsolete variables, and singled out variables that were not sufficiently described in the codebook.

The cleaned and more efficient database allowed PepsiCo to develop financial objectives with confidence. In fact, the new corporate master codebook contained 36% fewer variables, and yet consisted of more data. The cleaned and updated database allowed PepsiCo to:

- consolidate vendors;
- consolidate parts numbering;
- implement an aftermarket supplier program;
- create a virtual warehouse for bottling locations to share big-ticket items; and
- develop a supplier buy-back program.

Ask yourself: Can you think of other organizations that might benefit from data scrubbing and database reorganization? What might be some hypothetical situations and benefits?

The SPSS Codebook

Although it is a sound practice to prepare a codebook in advance of data entry and analysis, there are occasions where a dataset does not have an accompanying codebook. SPSS has a codebook feature that may be used to create a codebook or may be used in place of a formal codebook. The steps below illustrate this feature.

Step 1: Assuming that we have an open data file:

- Click the "Analyze" tab.
- Next, select the "Reports" option.
- Then, click "Codebook."

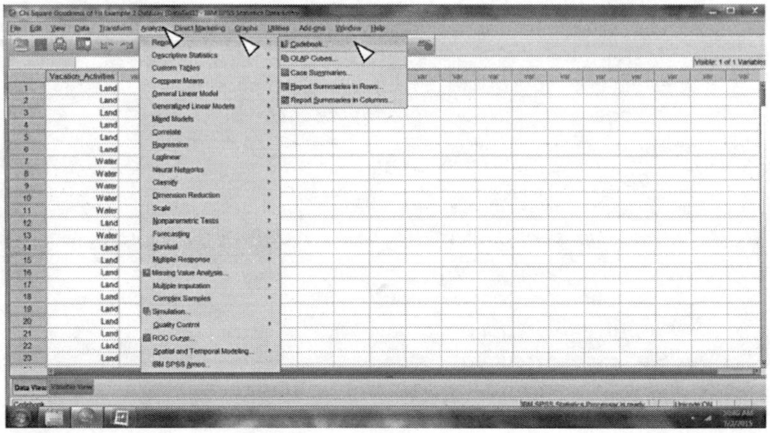

Figure 4.64

The following "Codebook" window will open. Notice that the "Variable" tab is highlighted. Feel free to explore the "Output" and "Statistics" tabs. The "Help" button within each tab provides descriptions of the various codebook options.

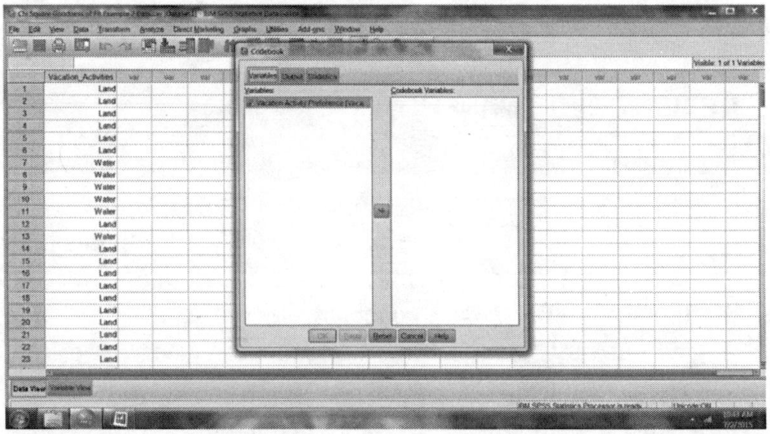

Figure 4.65

Step 2: In the "Codebook" window, do the following:

- In the "Variable" box to the left, highlight the variables that you wish to view.
- Then, click the "Arrow" button so that they are moved to the "Codebook Variable" box on the right.
- Last, click the "OK" button.

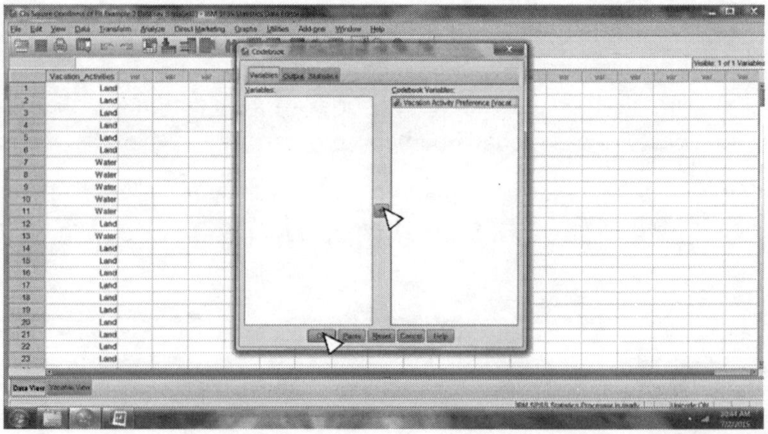

Figure 4.66

The selected variable information output will appear in an output file. This information is contained in a codebook.

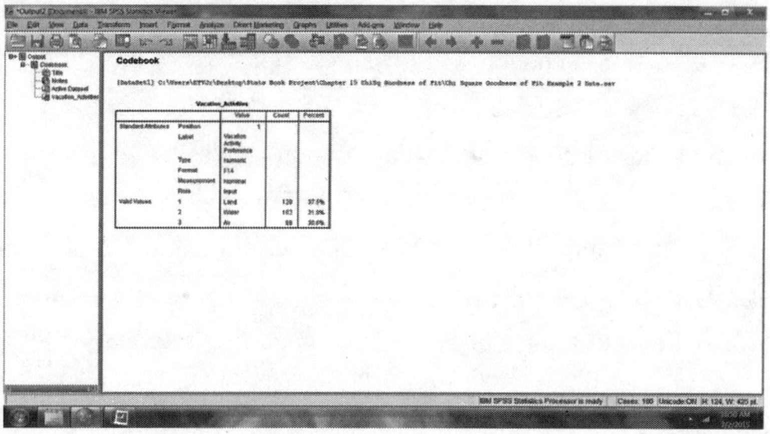

Figure 4.67

SUMMARY OF KEY CONCEPTS

- There are three basic files in SPSS.
- The data and output files are mostly used.
- The data file contains data and is managed through two windows: the Data and Variable Views. In the Data View, the individual records are in the case rows and the variables are in the columns. The variable properties and format, as well as the appearance in the Data and Output Views, are set in the Variable View.
- Sometimes there are multiple ways to conduct a procedure in SPSS.
- Data can be accessed from different spreadsheet applications.
- Data and output files can be saved in multiple formats.
- It is a best practice to maintain a codebook, which defines variables and data in the file.

DATA MANAGEMENT APPLIED EXERCISES

4.1 What is a data file?

4.2 In the SPSS data, define the "Data View" and the "Variable View" tabs.

4.3 What is the output file?

4.4 What is a syntax file?

4.5 What is a case of data and where is it located?

4.6 What is located in a data column?

4.7 Can variable names contain spaces?

4.8 Can variable labels contain spaces?

4.9 In the Variable View, what are the choices in the "Measure" option? Explain each option.

4.10 When opening or saving data files, what are the various formats available?

4.11 When saving (or exporting) output files, what are some of the available formats?

4.12 Can SPSS data be cut and pasted to or from an SPSS data file?

4.13 Can text files be opened in SPSS?

4.14 What is a codebook? Provide examples.

4.15 Does SPSS have a codebook feature? If so, where is it located?

4.16 How does one exit the data or output files?

4.17 What are the three basic SPSS file formats?

4.18 What view allows for more variable information to be inputted?

4.19 In the "Variable View" tab, what types of data measures (levels are data) are available?

4.20 Refer to the codebook in this chapter. Create an SPSS data file based on the codebook. Where the codebook does not have coding, create your own coding scheme. Prepare the data file in the Variable View; however, do not enter any data in the Data View. Save the data file as a .sav file. Save your output file as a Word file. Name the files "Exercise 3.1 Data File Assignment" and "Exercise 3.1 Output File Assignment."

PART II

Sampling Considerations

Chapter 5

Sampling Strategies

LEARNING OBJECTIVES

To be able to:

- understand and explain what is a sample and the sampling process;
- describe the importance of the relationship between a representative sample and target population;
- understand and define what is a sampling element and what is a sampling unit;
- describe the role of a sampling frame in the sample selection process;
- understand and describe what is a probability sample and the role of randomness in the sample selection process;
- describe the relationship of central tendency and dispersion in shaping data distribution;
- describe various types of probability samples;
- understand and describe what is a nonprobability sample;
- describe various types of nonprobability sampling techniques; and
- describe the advantages and disadvantages of the key sampling methods.

5.1 Introduction to the Sampling Process

A sample is a representative small group of a target population. The **target population** is the entire population of interest. The group is subject to statistical analysis with the intention of generalizing results to the population from which it was drawn. **Sampling** is the process by which a representative small group or sample of a population of interest is selected for data collection followed by a statistical analysis of the data. The representative sample must match key characteristics of the population under study because the statistical findings of the analyses will be applied to the population from which the sample was drawn. For example, if we are studying 18–24-year-old men, then our sample must consist of 18–24-year-old men. Therefore, sampling starts with knowing the target population.

The target population must be clearly defined so that it informs the sampling strategy. It is defined by its characteristics. Usually, its approximate size is known. For instance, a population may be defined as all 18–24-year-old persons who identify as male, including all ethnicities, religious traditions, and incomes, and who are enrolled in community colleges on the West Coast. The population may consist of 2 million students. The male student is the basis of analysis. Another example might be all privately held quick service restaurant chains in the United States with at least 50 company-owned locations. The restaurant chain is the basis of analysis.

The targeted population consists of **elements** or individual units. The element serves as the basis of analysis. It is the data source such as male student or restaurant chain. Knowing the approximate size or number of elements in the population is important for sampling because it provides context, indicates magnitude of the results, and can influence sample size strategy especially when the population is small.

Sometimes data are collected from a **sampling unit**, which is also an element or contains a set of (unique) elements so that there may be more than one basis of analysis. For instance, data may be collected from children within households. The household is the sampling unit and each child is an element so that the children are studied in the context of household characteristics. Each row or case consists of information about a household or child that was collected and stored as column variables of data. A variable is a specific piece of information or characteristic about an element or sampling unit.

For sampling purposes, it is also important to know how data will be collected. Will the data come from survey respondents, client records, credit records, machinery output, drug trials, and so forth? The data collection method must be true to the definition of the target population. For instance, credit records of undocumented workers may not yield the extent of their economic impact on the economy since many of these workers may not use credit cards.

The actual data process begins by identifying a **sampling frame**, which is a data source or list of elements composed of the target population. Examples are telephone lists, email lists, Facebook friends, voter registration lists, other types of registration lists, property ownership lists, all the machinery output records from a manufacturing facility, lists of companies, and so forth.

A clearly defined target population and data collection method will inform the sampling frame choices. For example, few retirees in their mid-70s or older may text message; thus, drawing from opt-in texting lists may not provide a representative sample of this retired population, whereas a landline or cell telephone list might be representative of this group.

Last, sometimes researchers use the same sampling frame to draw additional samples. **Sampling without replacement** means that once you select a particular element, you cannot select it again. This approach affects the probability of selecting a specific element. **Sampling with replacement** means that after you select an element, you return it to the frame where it might be selected again, which maintains the same probability of selection. Either approach may not make a substantive difference when the sampling frame is large. However, when the frame or population is relatively small, sampling with or without replacement can make an impact. This is especially so with some organizational research where the sampling frame and organizational population is relatively small. For example, assume that the element is an employee and the sampling frame is the email list of all 1,000 employees. If we draw a sample of 200, each person has a 1 out of 5 chance of being selected. If we draw a second sample of 200 using sampling with replacement, each person still has a 1 in 5 chance (20%) of being selected. However, if we sample without replacement, the second sample probability of being selected is 1 out of 4 (25%) and not 1 out of 5 (20%). On the other hand, the situation changes for a second draw when the frame comprises 30,000 email addresses. If we selected 200 out of 30,000 employees using sampling with replacement, the selection probability is .66 of 1% (200/30,000 or 2/300). If we sample without replacement, the probability is .67 of 1% (200/28,000 or 2/228). As we can see, sampling frame size makes a difference.

The following discussion of sampling strategies examines the key sampling techniques. It is by no means comprehensive.

5.2 Probability Sampling

There is a variety of probability sampling methods. **Probability sampling** is an approach that assures that each element or sampling unit has an equal chance of being chosen. This method uses some form of random selection. Random selection provides normally distributed data, which is an assumption of parametric statistics. **Random** denotes something that is not systematic nor has a pattern, and **normal distribution** is a data distribution that is symmetrical like a bell-shaped curve. Today, we can use all sorts of computer random number generators, assign a number to elements, and then develop a procedure for selecting elements based on random numbers.

The aim of using a random sampling technique is to assure that a sample is representative of the target population. Some techniques more than others draw from a wider spread of the population, which makes the application of probability statistics appropriate. Each random method has its advantages and disadvantages.

Random vs. Representative Sampling

A random sample is not necessarily a representative sample of the target population. If the sampling frame does not represent the target population, then a random sample from the frame would not represent the population. For instance, if the population is 18–24-year-old individuals and we draw a random sample from a sampling frame of 18–34-year-old persons, the sample will not represent the target population of 18–24-year-old individuals only.

Random Sampling and the Shape of Data Distribution

The combination of two attributes determines the shape of data distribution. Thus, the assessment of these two characteristics is necessary in order to determine whether the data are approximately normally distributed. These characteristics are central tendency and dispersion. **Central tendency** is the extent to which data points concentrate around the mean (average) or center of the distribution. It is a measure of symmetry. **Dispersion** is the spread of the data from the mean or degree to which values deviate from the mean. It is a measure of peakedness or flatness. Together, these attributes represent the shape of a variable's data distribution. Randomly selected data provide normal distribution and this allows for accurate probability statistical results. Details of these measures are covered in Chapter 12.

Below is a description of the four major random sampling methods. Each varies in its randomness precision.

Simple Random Sampling

When utilizing **simple random sampling**, every element has a known and equal chance of being selected. Every sample of a fixed size has the same chance of being selected as another sample of the same size. For instance, to draw a simple random sample of 350 customers from an email list of 10,000 customers encompasses generating a random list of 10,000 numbers. From the list, the first 350 numbers or some arbitrary starting point before the last 350 numbers is selected for the sample. As depicted in Table 5.1, the numbers are matched with the corresponding customer on the ordered customer email list of 1 through 10,000 such that 120 is the 120th customer, 543 is the 543rd customer, and 2,536 is the 2,536th customer, and so forth until we reach 350 customers. The result is a simple random sample of 350 customers.

This approach is simple, easy to implement, and provides a level of random selection. The primary disadvantage of simple random sampling is that hidden data patterns or ordered conditions in the list or sampling frame may create a bias in the data and can reduce randomness. For instance,

Table 5.1

Simple Random Sampling *Random Numbers Generated* *(1 – 10,000)*	*Customer Email List (N = 10,000)* *ID Number*	 *Customer Name*
00120	1	Nick B.
00543	2	Rachel C.
02536	3	Alex W.
-	-	
-	120	Mary D.
-	-	
-	543	Susan S.
-	-	
10000	2536	Mike V.

The corresponding random numbers are matched with the email list until the sample reaches 350 names.

if the list consists of ordered levels of consumer creditworthiness (most credit-attractive to least), then a data pattern may be present, and thus the sample may not represent the entire population (the full "range" of creditworthy consumers). Additionally, if the target population size is large or unknown, then identifying a sampling frame that includes the full distribution of elements may be challenging, which makes the selection of a representative sample difficult.

Systematic Random Sampling

In the case of **systematic random sampling**, every element has a known and equal chance of being selected like simple random sampling. However, for systematic random sampling, the methodology varies and is more complex than simple random sampling, but manageable. This method attempts to overcome some of the pitfalls of simple random sampling by selecting elements from the full range of the population or sampling frame.

Referring to the simple random sample example above, first, all of the 10,000 elements on the email list are assigned a consecutive number. Second, the sampling fraction is calculated, which is based on the population (*N*) and desired sample (*n*) sizes. The **sampling fraction** is the desired sample size divided by the population size or (n/N). Let us assume that our entire customer population is 10,000. In this case, it is also the sampling frame. The sampling fraction is: 350/10,000 or 1 in 28.57, rounded down to 28, which provides a slightly higher sample size. This means that we must select one customer from every consecutive group of 28 customers' names from the list of 10,000.

Which customers do we select? First, we generate a random number list of 1 to 28. Let us say that the first number is 15. As shown in Table 5.2, we then select every 15th name from each group of 28 customers for a total close to, if not equal to, 350. For example, the first three selections from the list of 10,000 would be 15th (0 + 15 = 15 from the first group of 28), 43rd (28 + 15 = 43 from the second group of 28), 71st (28 + 28 + 15 = 71 from the third group of 28), and so forth until we reach 350 customers at the end of the customer email list.

Systematic random sampling is a more precise technique that reduces the chance of the sample data not being normally distributed because elements are chosen throughout the list, unlike simple random sampling. However, there is still the potential for data patterns depending on how the sampling frame was developed. If elements were organized by categories that correspond with the sample fraction calculation, then a pattern may emerge. For instance, the groups of 28 could have coincidentally been organized by an opinion leader influence on every 28 or so elements. This pattern could weaken sample randomness and result in a sample not representative

Table 5.2

Systematic Random Sampling *Random Numbers Generated (1 – 28)*	*Customer Email List (N = 10,000)* *ID Number*	*Customer Name*
15 (1st)	1	Nick B.
02 (2nd)	2	Rachel C.
28 (3rd)	3	Alex W.
-	-	
21 (28th)	**15**	**Mary D. (1st element)**
	-	
	43	**Cathy S. (2nd element)**
	-	
	71	**Jerry T. (3rd element)**
	-	
	-	
	-	
	9787[1]	**Jim C. (350th element)**

The first random number, which is 15, serves as the basis for the position selected in each group of 28.

Note: [1] Since the calculations involved non-whole numbers, some rounding of number occurs. The calculation for the last element is as follows: 28.57 rounded down to 28.00; 28 X 350 = 9,800; 9,800 – 28 = 9772; 9772 + 15 = 9787.

of the population. Like simple random sampling, if the target population size is large or unknown, then identifying a sampling frame that includes the full distribution of elements may be challenging.

Cluster and stratified types of sampling attempt to address data pattern challenges and often contain components of random selection.

Cluster (Random) Sampling

Cluster (random) sampling often draws data from natural clusters such as geopolitical locations, company departments, neighborhood blocks, people who shop on certain days, and so forth. The clusters are mutually exclusive and collectively exhaustive subpopulations. The clusters are assumed to be normally distributed data, which are explained in Chapters 11 and 12. Random sampling and clustering methods are combined.

There are two types of cluster sampling. All of the sampling frame clusters are identified, from which a random number of clusters are chosen. Of those clusters, all of the elements are included in the sample. This is called **one-stage cluster sampling**. The process can repeat itself, in which case the randomly selected clusters are broken down further into smaller groups that are also randomly selected. Once the smallest-level clusters are chosen, all of the elements in these smaller groups become part of the sample. This is called **multistage cluster sampling**. For example, a researcher would random sample companies, then departments within those companies or random sample state voting districts, followed by county districts, and then municipal areas. Sampling can also account for population sizes known as **proportionate cluster sampling**, where the cluster sizes in the sample are based on the respective population size. On the other hand, a sample can have an equal number of elements per sample cluster despite different subpopulation sizes, which is called **disproportionate cluster sampling**.

Let us illustrate a multistage cluster example. A circuit board manufacturer wishes to determine the number of low-quality circuit boards produced by specific factories based on customer complaints and dealer in-warranty returns. The sampling strategy is single-stage clustering incorporating simple random sampling. Of the 30 countries representing 120 facilities, eight countries were randomly selected, which are: the United States (10 plants), Canada (3), Mexico (7), Brazil (6), Germany (5), Italy (4), Hungary (3), and Ireland (3). These 41 facilities (sampling units) in eight randomly selected countries (clusters) will participate in the study.

The major benefit of this sampling approach is that researchers can avoid including the entire population, thus reducing study time and costs. There are two key drawbacks of cluster sampling. First, and related to its key advantage, the cluster definitions and criteria for inclusion must be consistent with the study goal and match the target population. If the definitions do not fit, then findings may not address the goal and the results may not be applicable to the target population. Second, arriving at normally distributed clusters can be challenging because some clusters are naturally homogeneous. For instance, it can be difficult to statistically analyze social services' usage patterns within clusters for the full array of individuals' socioeconomic status backgrounds when some geographical clusters are essentially low- or high-income areas.

Stratified Random Sampling

Stratified random sampling involves segmenting the target population into subpopulations or strata based on homogenous characteristics relevant to the study. These characteristics are called stratification variables and have different levels. Once the stratum (or level) combinations are determined for each subpopulation, then a random representative sample is drawn from each. The process has the following requirements:

1. The population is divided into homogenous strata.
2. The strata must be mutually exclusive and exhaustive.
3. Elements are assigned to only one stratum.
4. Random samples are drawn from each stratum.
5. The samples from each stratum are combined into a single sample that is representative of the target population.

This approach is akin to multiple layered clustering where we may have multiple combinations of sample data that possess homogeneous characteristics. For example, the stratification variables may be age and income in which there are four age groups and five income levels, thus providing 20 strata.

Assume that a study goal is to survey intention to purchase a smartphone that is designed as a wristwatch. The wrist phone has different price points. The aim is to collect 35 (n) elements per stratum (each cell), as depicted in Table 5.3. The required sample size is 700 (35 × 20 = 700).

Each stratum or subpopulation element would be drawn based on a simple or systematic

Table 5.3

Stratified Random Sampling Income/Age in Years	18–34	**35–44**	45–65	Over 65	Totals
0–$25,000	35	35	35	35	140
$25,001–$50,000	35	35	35	35	140
$50,001–$75,000	35	35	35	35	140
$75,001–$125,000	35	35	35	35	140
Over $125,000	35	35	35	35	140
Total	175	175	175	175	700

random sampling technique. If the population size of each stratum were known, then the strata sample sizes (n) could be adjusted to correspond with that of the population, which is called **proportionate stratified sampling**. For instance, if 35–44-year-old persons whose incomes are $50,001–75,000 consist of 10% of the target population, then the required sample size would be 70, assuming that the entire sample size is expected to be 700. However, for illustrative purposes, Table 5.3 depicts a **disproportionate stratified sampling** approach where each stratum is not equal to its proportion in the target population.

The stratified random sampling method is the most precise random sampling technique. Its accuracy permits smaller representative samples, which is cost-effective and requires less time to conduct. There are two key drawbacks. First, there is the potential for inaccurate development of stratification variables. Second, since the strata must be mutually exclusive and exhaustive, with more discrete strata come more levels, resulting in a larger required sample size. For example, if the sampling strategy requires a breakdown by binary gender, four levels of income, and three regions of the country, then there would be 2 × 4 × 3 = 24 groups. Each would require a minimum number of cases depending on the type of analysis to be conducted. On the other hand, if the variables were binary gender and four levels of income, there would be 2 × 4 = 8 groups.

REAL WORLD SNAPSHOT

In the United States, prior to a volunteer military force, individuals were required to serve in the armed forces. They were selected via the "Draft Lottery." Dates were drawn and those individuals whose birthdays fell on the drawn dates would be inducted into the military.

In 1969, the lottery procedure consisted of placing 366 small pieces of paper each representing a day of the year, including February 29, in a separate capsule the size of a pecan. One at a time, starting with January, each month was placed in a container and then mixed followed by being emptied into a larger canister, which easily filled. The first 100 draft dates of birth were then drawn from the canister.

According to an article by D. E. Rosenbaum in 1970, the selected birth dates demonstrated a pattern. The months near the end of the year, especially December, were overrepresented. Officials realized that the months at the end of the year filled the top of the canister. Since the canister was tightly filled, it was difficult to draw capsules from deep inside. Thus, there was sampling bias toward the second half of the year for the first 100 draws.

Ask yourself: In order to assure random selection, how might the draft lottery been modified?

5.3 Nonprobability Sampling

Nonprobability sampling is a subjective sampling strategy that does not involve random selection, but is based on some other criterion. There are no assurances that each element has an equal chance of selection, the probability of selection is unknown, and the representativeness of the sample is left to the researcher rather than to an objective measure. There is no formal sampling frame. Consequently, nonprobability sample findings can only be applied to a population representative of the sample. There are four major types of nonprobability sampling methods: convenience, expert, quota, and snowball.

Convenience Sampling

Convenience sampling involves selecting elements based on convenience. Convenience sampling examples include students, coworkers, family members, and other social group members such as Facebook friends and Twitter followers. These elements are easy to access. There is no random component to selection and the sample often does not fully represent the population of interest.

The main advantages of a convenience sample is that it is easy to develop, quickly accessible, and cost-effective. The main disadvantage is that applicability to the target population is limited to the attributes of the sample.

Expert Sampling

Expert sampling involves selecting elements that are available experts on the topic under study. For example, if a study goal is to predict when a likely cure for cancer will occur, the researcher may ask the leading oncologists and oncological researchers. A company may interview its top clients to discover their opinions about a new product or service. Expert sampling has the benefit of being quick and cost-effective. At the same time, it can only be generalized to a narrow population.

Quota Sampling

Quota sampling is based on the judgment of the researcher to set groups and quotas. It consists of two basic steps. First, categories of characteristics (like strata) are created to serve as the basis for groups, including quotas for those groups. These categories attempt to assure that the target population is represented in the sample. Last, quotas (subsample sizes) are assigned to characteristics that are consistent with the target subpopulation sizes. For example, a sample consists of 60% women and 40% men because this represents the breakdown in the target population. Keep in mind that the target population may not represent the general population. The quotas may be guided by other criteria. Unlike stratified random sampling, quota sampling elements are not randomly selected. Table 5.4 is an example of a quota sampling table. The population attributes and quotas are compared with what is required in the sample's composition.

Table 5.4

Quota Sampling

Control Attribute	Population Composition Percentage	Targeted Sample Composition Percentage	Count
Sex			
Women	40	40	400
Men	50	50	500
Other	10	10	100
Total	100	100	1,000
Age Group			
18 - 34	25	25	250
35 - 44	40	40	400
45 - 65	20	20	200
66 & Over	15	15	150
Total	100	100	1,000
Region of Residence			
East Coast	35	35	350
Midwest	20	20	200
West Coast	40	40	400
International	5	5	50
Total	100	100	1,000

Note: The sample size is 1000.

Quota sampling is the nonprobability technique that comes closest to a representative sample because of the inclusion of groups selected by the researcher. Additionally, it is quick and easy to deploy. There is a major disadvantage. The quota-based sample is not random. Thus, generalizing to the target population is limited to the sample and how the groups are defined.

Snowball Sampling

Snowball sampling is appropriate when it is difficult to reach the target population. The sensitive nature of the data and the target population make data collection challenging. For instance, if the U.S. Census Bureau wanted to collect economic data on undocumented workers, it might use snowball sampling. The researchers would initially locate workers receptive to providing data and ask those workers to identify others who might be willing to provide information. The snowball sampling method is effective to recruit victims of unreported domestic violence, workers who operate in some aspect of the underground economy, or people who live off the grid in general.

Snowball sampling involves selecting an initial group of participants using simple random or random systematic sampling techniques. These participants, in turn, identify other target population members for potential recruitment. The process continues until a sufficient number of participants are recruited and enough data are collected. Snowball sampling is often utilized when the target population is small and unique, and creating a sampling frame is extremely difficult.

Keep in mind that although the initial group is selected using random sampling, subsequent participants likely possess characteristics similar to those who referred them, which reduces random chance. Thus, although snowball sampling can recruit those individuals normally out of reach, it comes at a cost. The nature of the referral can provide results not altogether representative of the target population, thus limiting generalizability.

Figure 5.1 is a flow chart depicting the various sampling methods. Tables 5.6 and 5.7 highlight the advantages and disadvantages of probability and nonprobability sampling strategies. As discussed, often methods consist of combinations of the basic sampling methods.

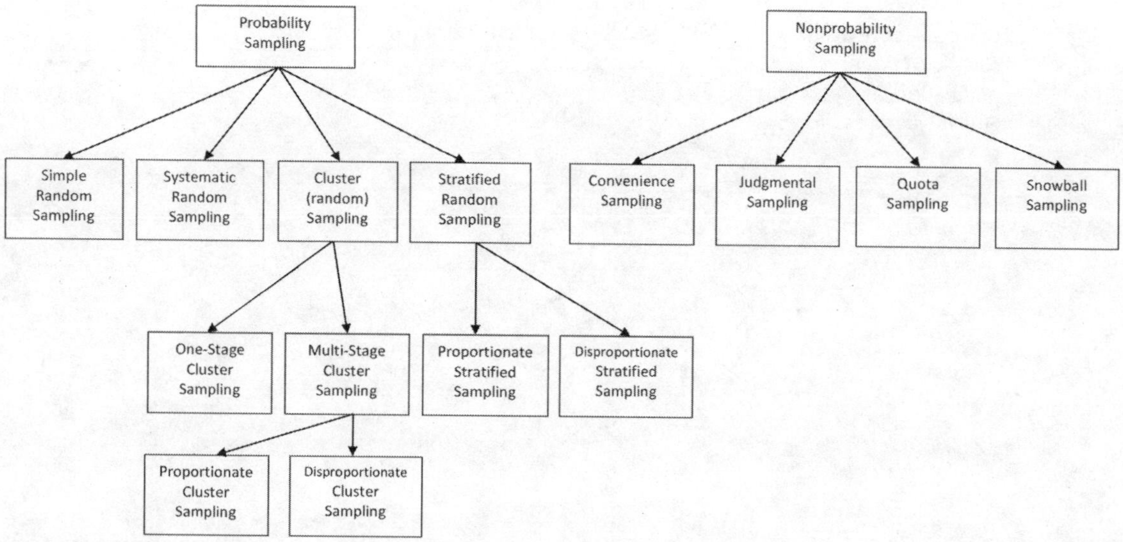

Figure 5.1 Sampling Strategies

Table 5.5 Probability Sampling Strategies Advantages and Disadvantages

Sampling Strategy	Advantages	Disadvantages
Simple Random	▪ Simple and easy to use ▪ Provides a level of random selection ▪ Can generalize from sample to target population	▪ Data patterns can create bias ▪ Elements may not contain full range of values ▪ Probability statistical analysis can be compromised
Systematic Random	▪ Relatively simple and easy to use ▪ Provides a level of random selection ▪ Less likely to have data pattern bias ▪ Can generalize to the target population	▪ Data patterns can create bias ▪ Elements may not contain full range of values ▪ Probability statistical analysis still can be compromised
Cluster (random)	▪ Can provide a level of random selection ▪ Can be time saving and cost effective ▪ Specific populations can be targeted ▪ Can generalize from sample to target population	▪ Defining clusters can be challenging especially as they relate to the target population ▪ Sometimes clusters are homogeneous thus compromising statistical analysis
Stratified Random	▪ Provide the most precise random selection ▪ Can be time saving and cost effective ▪ Specific populations can be targeted ▪ Can generalize from sample to target population ▪ Smaller samples are possible	▪ Defining strata can be challenging especially as they relate to the target population ▪ Number of strata can become challenging resulting in a larger sample size

Table 5.6 Nonprobability Sampling Strategies Advantages and Disadvantages

Sampling Strategy	Advantages	Disadvantages
Convenience	▪ Quick and cost-effective	▪ No random selection ▪ Usually sample does not represent the population ▪ Generalization is limited often to the sample
Judgmental	▪ Quick and cost-effective	▪ Can only generalize to a narrow population
Quota	▪ Quick and cost effective ▪ Of the nonprobability methods, it comes closest to being a representative sample	▪ No random selection ▪ Defining quota groups can be challenging especially as they relate to the target population ▪ Generalization is limited to defined groups and often to the sample
Snowball	▪ Can access hard to reach populations	▪ No random selection ▪ Elements may not represent the target population ▪ Generalization limited to the sample

SUMMARY OF KEY CONCEPTS

- Ideally, a sample is a small representative group of a population under study.
- The population under study is known as the target population.
- A random sample helps assure that the sample represents the target population, and thus allows for probability statistical analysis.
- Probability sampling methods vary in the amount of random selection that they provide.
- Data distribution is determined by the degree of central tendency and dispersion in a dataset.
- A nonprobability sampling strategy, of which there are numerous, is sometimes necessary when an easy, quick, and cost-effective method is required.
- Sometimes strategies are combined.
- Sampling strategies each have advantages and disadvantages.

SAMPLING APPLIED EXERCISES

5.1 Define the term sample and provide two examples.

5.2 Define the process of sampling.

5.3 Define the term target population and provide an example.

5.4 Define the term element and provide three examples.

5.5 Define a sampling unit.

5.6 What is a sampling frame? Provide two examples.

5.7 What is sampling without replacement?

5.8 What is sampling with replacement?

5.9 What is probability sampling? Provide two examples.

5.10 What does random denote in statistics?

5.11 Define central tendency. Explain your answer.

5.12 Define dispersion. Explain your answer.

5.13 What is the relationship between central tendency and dispersion, and how do they relate to the shape of data's distribution?

5.14 Describe simple random sampling.

5.15 Describe systematic random sampling.

5.16 What is a sampling fraction?

5.17 Describe cluster random sampling.

5.18 Define one-stage cluster sampling.

5.19 Describe multistage cluster sampling.

5.20 Describe proportionate cluster sampling.

5.21 Define disproportionate cluster sampling.

5.22 What is a stratified random sample?

5.23 What is a proportionate stratified sample?

5.24 What is a disproportionate stratified sample?

5.25 What is a nonprobability sample?

5.26 Describe convenience sampling and provide two examples.

5.27 Describe expert sampling and provide an example.

5.28 Define quota sampling and provide an example.

5.29 What is snowball sampling? Provide two examples.

5.30 What is the optimal sampling method to collect numeric data from a population where subpopulation areas tend to be homogenous and have different sizes? We want to accurately generalize our findings to the entire population of interest. Explain your answer using appropriate terminology.

5.31 We wish to sample homeless people who suffer from substance abuse in order to collect data about their perspective on what type of social support might help them on the road to recovery. What sampling approach would you suggest and why?

5.32 Cite and explain three examples where expert sampling would be appropriate.

5.33 Describe and explain a hypothetical cases deploying cluster sampling within an organization. Be sure to include the basis for clustering. Justify your hypothetical case.

Chapter 6

Sample Size

LEARNING OBJECTIVES

To be able to:

- understand why proper sample size is important;
- describe the Central Limit Theorem;
- describe power analysis;
- understand and describe statistical power;
- understand the relationship between statistical power and level of confidence;
- understand and describe how to determine sample size in SPSS based on a combination of effect size, level of confidence, and level of acceptable risk; and
- understand how to determine the required sample size in SPSS for specific types of statistical analysis.

6.1 Introduction to Sample Size

This chapter addresses sample size determination for numeric data and categorical data. It is important to note that although the optimal sample size is the ideal situation, it must be acknowledged that often reality dictates something less perfect. When possible, each chapter covers options that account for undersized data samples.

Numeric Data

The sample size is the number of cases or elements in the sample. There are numerous cloud and downloadable free and for-fee applications that can help one calculate appropriate sample sizes. As a rule, in the case of numeric data, a sample size over 30 is required to achieve normal distribution, which yields accurate results. The more the sample distribution is normally distributed, the smaller the required sample size necessary to conduct parametric statistical analysis. By the same token, a larger sample size ensures normal distribution. The importance of the normal distribution in parametric statistical analysis is discussed in Chapter 2. For now, we focus on the relationship between sample size and its distribution.

Central Limit Theorem

The normal distribution relates to the **Central Limit Theorem (CLT)**, which is an important statistical concept. The CLT states that a sample of means from randomly drawn samples will approach normal distribution as the (overall) sample size increases whether or not the population from which the samples are drawn is normally distributed. To illustrate this point, if we were to plot the means of 1,000 samples, all of which were randomly selected, and each contained 500 observations, then the means would be normally distributed. Some means would be less than the mean of all 1,000 means and some means would be greater than the overall mean. The more extreme the value, the fewer the number of observed values.

The normal distribution is assumed for individual observations within a single sample as well. The greater the number of randomly selected observations, the more normally distributed the data. Moreover, a smaller sample is necessary to achieve normality when the target population is assumed to be normally distributed. A larger sample size is required if the population is not assumed to be normally distributed. The general rule of thumb is that the normal distribution is possible when the sample size is over 30, assuming that the sample mean approximates the population mean (see Figure 6.1).

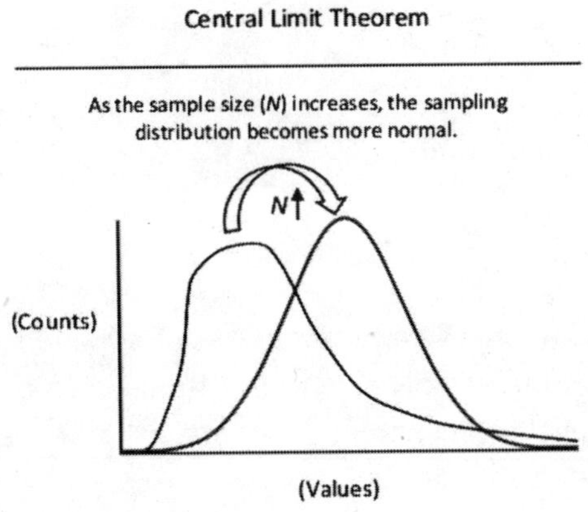

Figure 6.1

Representative samples of normally distributed populations should themselves approximate the normal distribution if they are randomly selected and truly represent the target population. In fact, a random sample's attributes should approximate that of the target population. It is an approximate representation because no sample perfectly represents a population because of sample selection flaws, normally occurring random error, and other natural fluctuations in the data. Statistical procedures account for these factors, which we shall explore in the forthcoming chapters.

Categorical Data

For categorical data, the situation is much simpler. Cell counts should be at least five each.

Quantitative researcher methodologists subscribe to various approaches for determining sample size and many of these methods vary according to anticipated statistical analyses and the kind of data.

Other Considerations

This chapter provides an overview for determining appropriate sample size for specific types of statistical analysis. It does not cover sample size determination for every statistical procedure reviewed in this textbook. The selected procedures include examples that describe as well as cover all of the necessary steps required to establish sample size.

Generally, determining a representative sample size is *not* contingent on the estimated size of the target population. All else being equal for a given statistical procedure, a sample size of

500 to 950 may be appropriate, whether the population consists of 1 million to many millions of potential elements. National survey samples typically comprise as little as 300–400 respondents. However, a very small sample size may not detect significant results or effects when they in fact exist. **Effect** is a general term that refers to meaningful results of some kind that vary by statistical procedure. For instance, an analysis that examines for a difference between two or more sample averages or a study that tests for a correlation between two variables are examples of testing for effects. They are estimates of population **parameters**. In other words, effects are assumed to apply to the target population. Effects from a small sample size may not represent the true nature of the sample when it includes a few extreme values, whose presence can easily influence statistical results. These values can pull the average in the direction of the extreme values, thus not reflecting an average representative of the majority of values. A very large sample size will detect a small "difference" that may serve no practical purpose because it is actually error that increases with sample size and thus becomes noticeable. Based on the three pieces of information discussed below, power analysis can help us determine the appropriate sample size.

6.2 Power Analysis and Sample Size

Power analysis is a statistical tool that calculates statistical power. **Statistical power** is the level of confidence that we have for detecting a potential effect in sample data so that if an effect exists, it will be detected. Statistical power and the following three considerations are interdependent: (1) What potential effects do we hope to detect at a minimum? (2) What is our acceptable level of risk known as alpha level? (3) What is our sample size? Knowing three out of four determines the fourth consideration.

Statistical power is the level of probability of an anticipated effect being statistically meaningful. It is the chance of results being meaningful assuming that they exist. It is expressed as the percentage of confidence that the potential results will be detected. Power provides an assessment based on a combination of: (1) minimum anticipated effect size; (2) alpha level; and (3) sample size. Statistical power is set based on general practices and specific circumstances, which both can influence the combination of the three items.

As a rule of thumb, statistical power is set at 80% or greater. In social science, some researchers set it at 60% or greater. Specific circumstances can inform the level of statistical power. The manual for "IBM SPSS SamplePower3" provides excellent examples of when statistical power would vary. A new drug trial in which researchers wish to determine whether a medication shows promise and warrants further research and development might set power at 95% and alpha at .20 in order to easily detect any possible effect. On the other hand, if a pharmaceutical company wishes to assess a drug's risk of side effects and then submit the results for FDA approval, power might be set at 95% and alpha at .01, which sets a higher threshold for detection by accepting less risk. These concepts will become clearer in our SPSS step-by-step examples.

Expected effect sizes are what we minimally expect to find, whether it involves means testing, categorical variable comparisons, correlations, or regression results. For instance, a study strategy may target correlations of .30 or greater. Expected effects' sizes are often informed by previous research, expert advice, or target goals.

Level of alpha is the level of acceptable risk. This is usually .05 or less, which means that the chance of findings not being statistically meaningful must be <.05 in order to detect effects. Depending on the study aim, alpha might increase or decrease. For example, at a nuclear power plant, a study that examines for serious reactor breaches would set alpha higher and perhaps at .20, which is a lower threshold of significance that increases the likelihood that the study will detect possible breaches. In this case, it is better to be safe than sorry considering the consequences of such a breach. In less risky situations, setting alpha at the standard .05 is acceptable, as would be the case in marketing and educational research. In sum, the circumstances and standard conventions of the subject matter or industry under study guide the alpha level.

Given the required statistical power, anticipated minimum effect sizes, and alpha, we can determine the **sample size**. Generally, the sample size must be sufficiently large enough in order to provide the desired statistical power necessary to generalize to the target population.

Finite Population Correction

In some cases, populations may be small, as in the case of organizational research where the organizational population of interest may be 1,000 or less. As a rule, a sample size should consist of less than 10% of the target population. Violating this rule may yield results that appear real, but actually are not statistically meaningful. In such cases, the finite population correction would be used, which is beyond the scope of our discussion.

Informed Power Analysis

Values for power analysis factors are informed by previous research, expert advice, target goals, a pilot study designed to inform the full study, rules of thumb, or expectations.

REAL WORLD SNAPSHOT

Reid Klion, in his 2013 article "Know Your N: The Importance of Sample Size," discusses a controversy from a number of years ago involving the Gates Foundation. The Gates Foundation funded a study that found that smaller schools usually outperformed larger schools. Upon further examination, statisticians discovered that the smaller schools had smaller sample sizes, and thus they tended to have more variability in the data compared to the larger schools, which had larger sample sizes.

What does this mean? In a small sample size, a few extremely high-performing students can drive the average assessment higher, which may not represent the majority of student performance assessments. This was the case in the Gates Foundation's study. Statisticians actually found that the smaller schools underperformed. Likewise, a few extremely low-performing students can provide results that understate student performance.

Ask yourself: Can you think of other examples where a small sample size might misrepresent the target population?

Comparison of Unequal Sample Sizes

The influence of variable unequal sample sizes on statistical analysis varies. There are a number of factors that come into play. First, the approaches vary based on whether categorical or numeric data are analyzed. Second, measuring the same sample more than once for comparison would require equal sizes for each measurement. Third, the size of the samples to be compared can affect the analysis. Fourth, the degree of difference in the sizes is also a factor. Greater differences would be a cause for alarm.

Additionally, the decision to adjust for unequal sizes requires an assessment of the research situation. The study design, nature of the research, and number of variables are considerations. In light of these factors, some statisticians recommend deleting the extra cases using various strategies, and still others suggest doing nothing. An in-depth exploration of this topic is best left for another discussion.

Data Assumptions

The data are numeric or categorical and representative of the target population are key asumptions. Numeric data should approximate the normal distribution. Sample size or more broadly statistical power is based on other assumptions specific to the intended statistical procedures. The examples below cover a number of common scenarios.

6.3 Examples Using SPSS: Step-by-Step Instructions

SPSS has an add-on called "IBM SPSS SamplePower3" used for determining sample size. The following examples include step-by-step instruction utilizing SamplePower, which cover the major statistical procedures discussed in this textbook, as well as multilevel "clustering" sampling techniques for cluster and stratified sampling.

Example 6.1: Means: One-sample *t*-test that mean = specific value

A hospital administrator wants to determine whether her hospital's emergency room patients wait time for non-life-threatening conditions is different from the local average of 120 minutes. She estimates her patients' average wait time is 90 minutes, ranging from no waiting to a wait of 360 minutes. The alpha is .05 and she wants to be 95% confident in the results. The data will be numeric. What sample size is necessary to run this study?

An anticipated standard deviation (spread of the data, see Chapter 11) is often known through pilot testing, previous research, or expert advice. However, sometimes it is unavailable. If we assume that the data are normally distributed, there is a rule of thumb for estimating the standard deviation, which is dividing the range of the data by four:

Standard deviation = (maximum value – minimum value) / 4

The range is the difference between expected minimum and maximum values of the data. With normally distributed data, four standard deviations encompass 95% of the data, which accounts for a 95% level of confidence.

Let us apply the formula to our known information: Standard deviation = (360 – 0) / 4 = 90. The steps in SPSS SamplePower3 are below.

Step 1: Launch SPSS.

- Run the cursor on "Add-ons."
- Select "Applications."
- Then, select "IBM SPSS SamplePower."

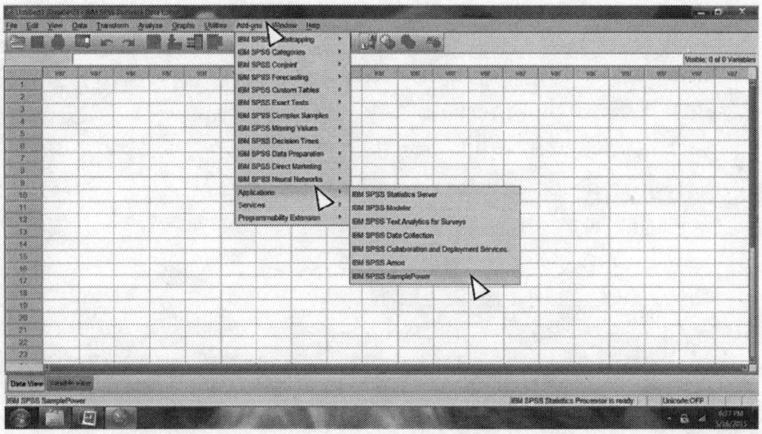

Figure 6.2

Step 2: The "Select an interface" window will open.

- Click the button to the left labeled "Click here to use the classic interface."

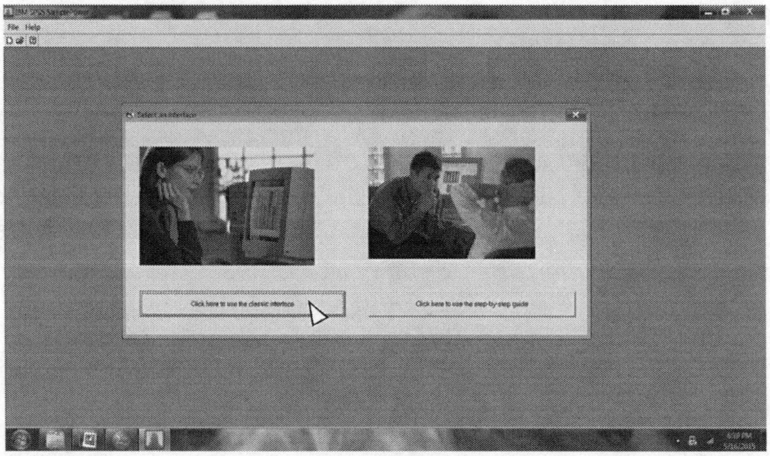

Figure 6.3

Step 3: The following "Procedures" window will open.

- Click the "Means" tab.
- Next, select the radio button for "One-sample *t*-test that mean = specific value."
- Last, click the "OK" button.

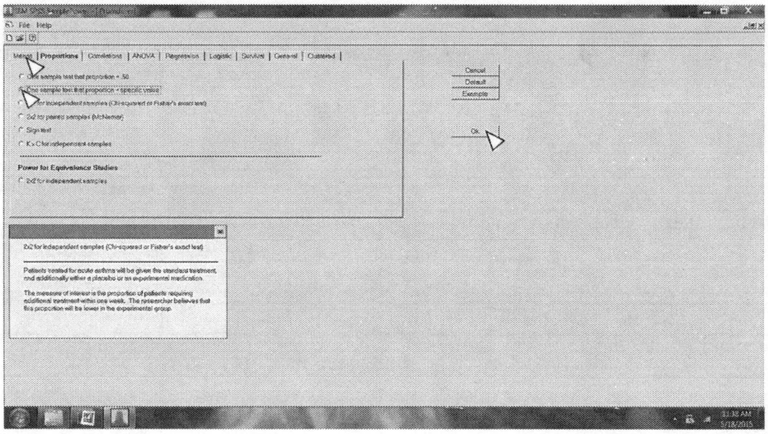

Figure 6.4

Step 4: The "One-sample *t*-test" window will appear.

- Since the administrator thinks that the hospital's average wait time is 90 minutes, then enter 90 minutes in the "Population Mean—Expected mean" area.
- Using the spin control, enter 120 minutes in the "Population Mean—Test against the constant" area because we are comparing the anticipated 90 minutes against the reported local average wait time of 120 minutes.
- Since we calculated a standard deviation of 90 minutes assuming that the data are normally distributed, enter 90 in the "Standard Deviation" area.

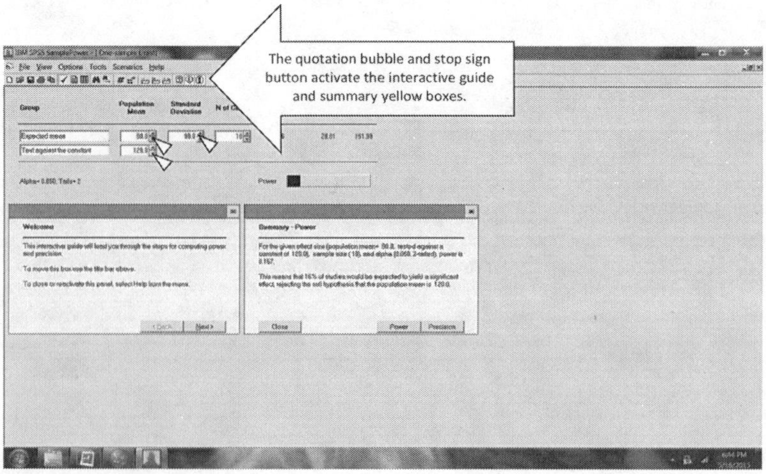

Figure 6.5

Step 5: Next, move the cursor to the "N of Cases" spin control.

- Vary the "N of Cases" (sample size) until the "Power" bar reaches 95% confidence. We can see that a sample size of 120 will provide us with 95% confidence (statistical power) given the anticipated effects (90 minutes and 120 minutes), standard deviation of 90 minutes, and alpha = .05, which is not visible but is the default (automatic) setting.

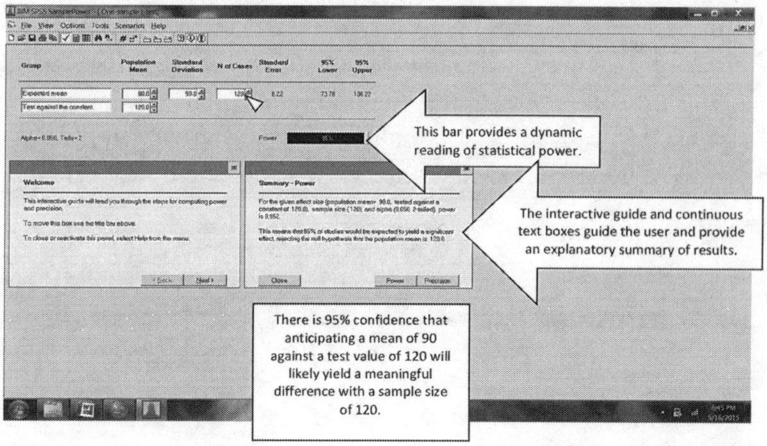

Figure 6.6

Step 6: Generate a text report of your power analysis.

- Click the "View" button.
- Next, select the "Text report" option.
- Last, click the "Next" button.

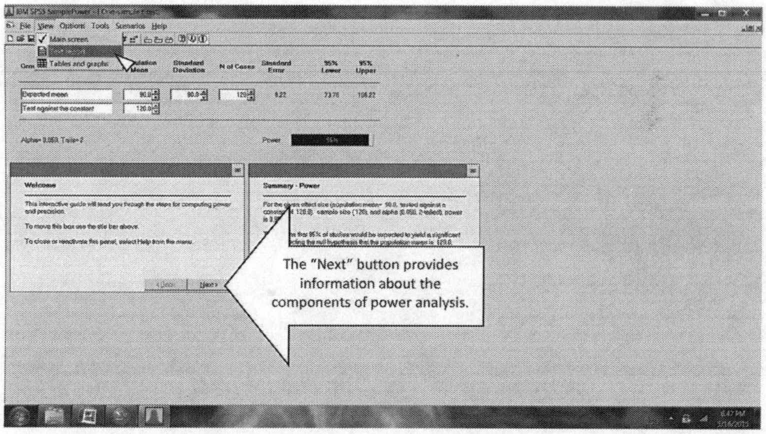

Figure 6.7

This is the text report, which summarizes the power analysis. For our purposes, it contains more information than we will need.

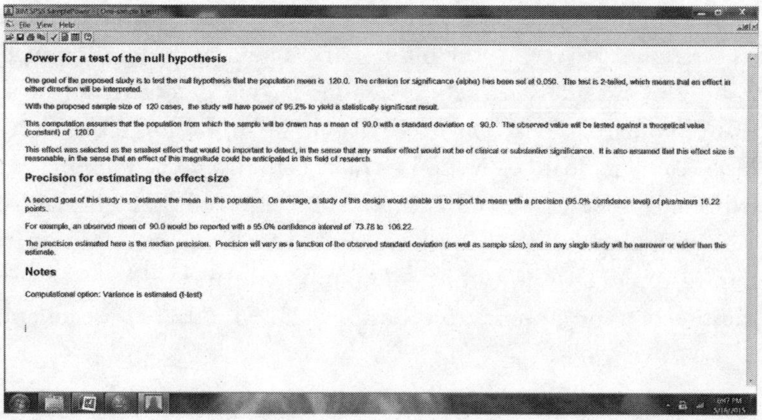

Figure 6.8

Interpretation

Anticipating a sample average patient wait time of 90 minutes for non-life-threatening conditions ranging from no wait to 120 minutes, and a reported average wait time of 120 at other local hospitals, we can be 95% confident that a random sample of 120 wait times will detect any potential differences between the hospital and other local hospitals. The risk of finding inaccurate results will be 5% or less.

Step 7: Exit SamplePower.

- Click on the "X" located in the top-right side. A window offering the option to quit the program will appear.
- Click the "OK" button.

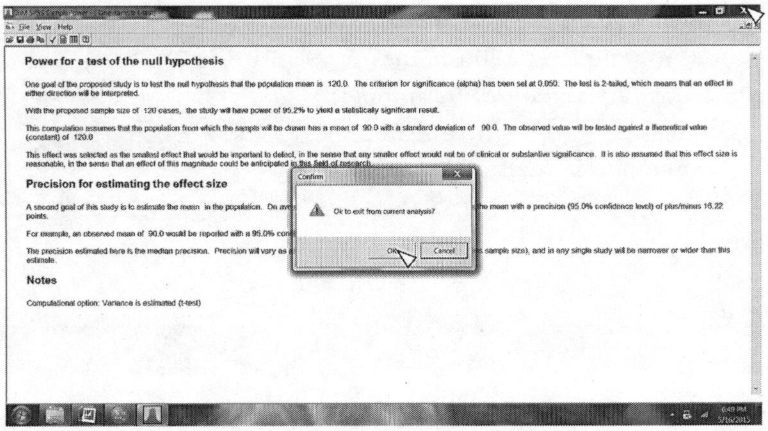

Figure 6.9

For the remaining examples, the first and last steps are skipped. Below are the steps followed by an interpretation.

Example 6.2: Means: Paired *t*-test that mean = 0

This example entails determining whether an email campaign increases interest in a new healthcare insurance program. Participants were asked whether they would consider changing their existing healthcare insurance carrier. After receiving a number of promotional emails and telephone sales calls from a new insurer, they were asked again whether they would consider changing their healthcare insurance carrier. The responses were formatted in a scale ranging from 1 = "not at all interested" to 7 = "very interested." The minimum difference between the before-marketing responses and after-marketing response to be detected is 1.00 based on the seven-point scale. Both standard deviations were based on previous research findings. The pre-test (before-marketing) standard deviation, which is the typical difference in responses from the average, is expected to be 1.70, and the post-test (after-marketing) standard deviation is expected to be 1.40. Results after such campaigns tend to have less variation from the average. The required statistical power is 80%. The minimum correlation that the researcher wishes to detect between the pre-test and post-test responses is .25. The data are scale and treated as numeric.

Step 1: First, open SamplePower.

- Select the "Means" tab.
- Next, click the radio button corresponding to "Paired *t*-test that mean difference = 0."
  Last, click the "OK" button.

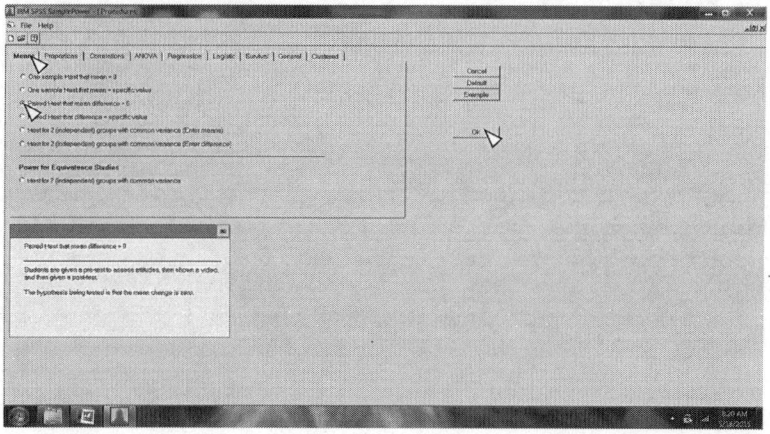

Figure 6.10

Step 2: The window right will appear.

- Select the minimum mean difference that is anticipated, which is 1.0.
- In the box located at the lower right-hand corner, enter the standard deviations for each group in the "SD for each rating" area, which are 1.70 and 1.40.
- Next, enter the expected minimum correlation between both ratings (groups), which is .25. The "SD of the difference" will automatically appear in the top-left-hand corner box.
- Last, adjust the sample size so that 80% power or confidence is achieved, which is a sample size of 31.

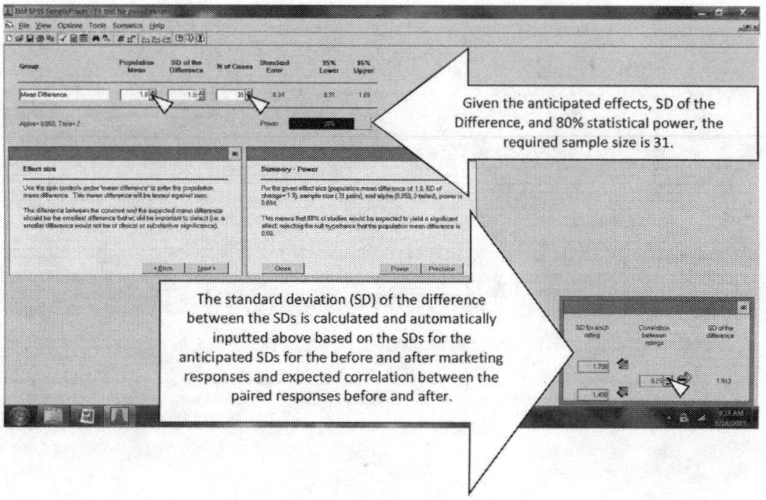

Figure 6.11

Interpretation

Anticipating with 80% confidence whether an email campaign will increase interest by at least one point based on a seven-point scale requires a random sample size of 31. It is assumed that the before-marketing standard deviation is 1.70 and the after-marketing standard deviation is 1.40. The paired groups' anticipated correlation is at least .25. Acceptable risk of making a mistake (level of alpha) is 5% or less.

Example 6.3: Proportions: One-sample test that proportion = ".50"

In this example, respondents will be asked if they will be able to maintain their current standard of living over the long term and into old age. The response options are "yes" or "no." Statistical power is set at 80% and alpha is .05. The minimum proportion for yes or no is set at .60. That is to say, the minimum difference desired to be detected in comparison to a 50/50 split (50% = yes and 50% = no) is expected to be a proportion of .10 (.60 – .50 = .10). The data are categorical. Determine the appropriate sample size.

Step 1: Open the SamplePower window.

- Select the "Proportion" tab.
- Then, click the radio button corresponding to "One-sample test that proportion = .50."
- Last, click the "OK" button.

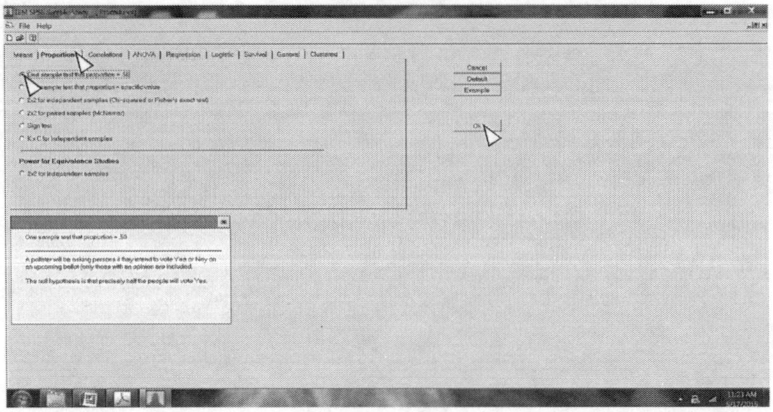

Figure 6.12

Step 2: The window right will appear.

- Set the anticipated minimum proportion ("Proportion Positive") to .60.
- Adjust the sample size until "Power" is 80%. The appropriate sample size is 192.

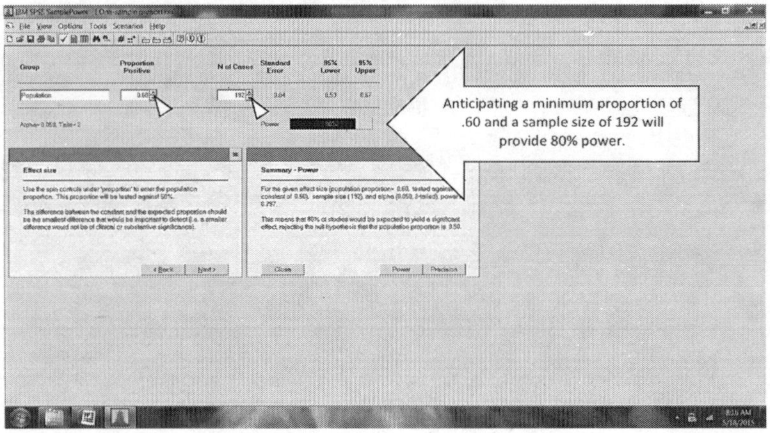

Figure 6.13

Interpretation

The sample size needed to determine whether respondents perceive that they will be able to maintain their current standard of living over the long term and into old age is based on detecting differences of .10 or greater in their "yes" or "no" responses. Therefore, maintaining or not maintaining their lifestyle is anticipated to be 60% or more of the sample. A random representative sample of 192 is required to detect such a difference. The level of alpha is 5% or less.

Note: The "Proportion Positive" is the proportion that is anticipated. It is compared against a proportion of .50 or 50/50 even split of responses: yes or no. The difference (.10) between the Proportion Positive and .50 is the smallest that is anticipated.

Example 6.4: Proportions: 2 × 2 for independent samples (chi-square or Fisher's exact test)

This example adds an additional aspect to the one covered above. All else is similar other than examining for a difference in standard of living outlook based on respondent sexuality: female or male. Thus, there is another category layer. Again, respondents will be asked if they will be able to maintain their current standard of living over the long term and into old age. The response options will be "yes" or "no." Statistical power is set at 80% and alpha is .05. The minimum proportion for yes or no by sexuality is set at .55 vs. .45. Put differently, the minimum difference to be detected in comparison to a 50/50 even split (50% = yes and 50% = no by sexuality) is .55 – .45 = .10 in the expected population as represented by the sample. The data are categorical. Determine the appropriate sample size.

Step 1: Open the SamplePower window.

- Select the "Proportion" tab.
- Then, click the radio button corresponding to "2 × 2 for independent samples (chi-square or Fisher's exact test)."
- Last, click the "OK" button.

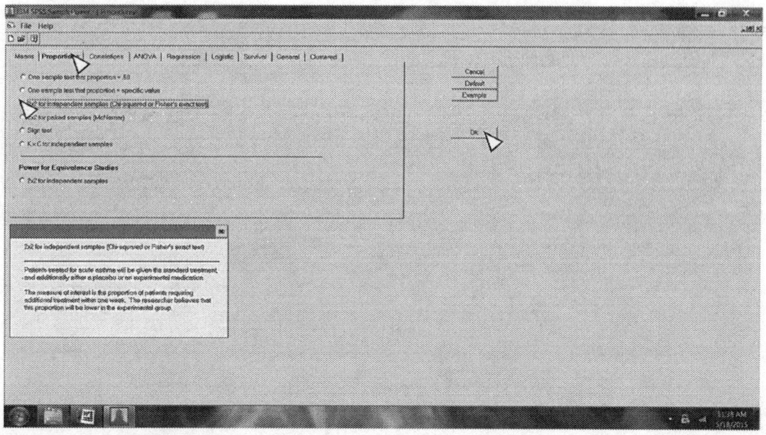

Figure 6.14

Step 2: The window to the right will appear.

- Since we wish to determine if there is a difference of at least .10 by sexuality, then set Populations 1 and 2 to .55 and .45, respectively. The order does not matter.
- Adjust "*N* Per Group," the sample size(s), until "Power" is 80%. As you can see, men and women each require 390 respondents for a total of 780 participants.

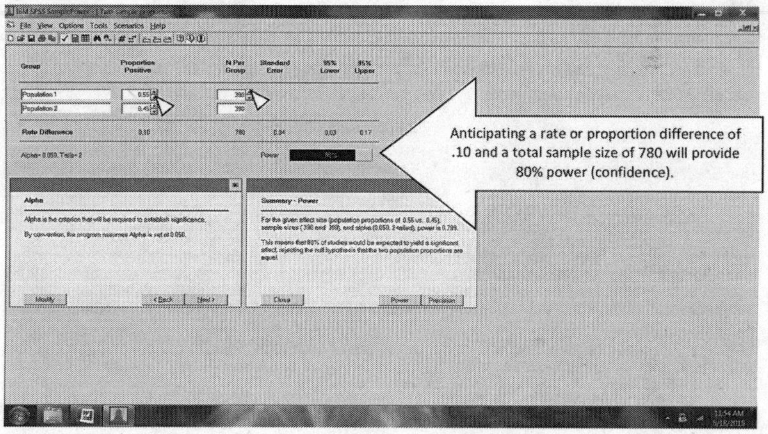

Figure 6.15

Interpretation

In order to be 80% confident to determine whether there is an expected difference of at least 10% between women's and men's responses about their future standard of living, a total sample of 780 is required or 390 participants per women and men each. Alpha is 5% or less.

Example 6.5: Correlations: One-sample test that correlation = 0

A career consulting firm intends to examine the relationship between education and career advancement. Previous research found correlations from .30 to .78 depending on the position. A correlation is an association between to variables. Education is measured as number of completed years of college. Career advancement will be a subjective measure captured using a scale (1 = "little advancement" to 7 = "much advancement") and treated as numeric data. What sample size is appropriate to detect at least a .30 correlation with 90% confidence?

Step 1: Open the SamplePower window.

- Select the "Correlation" tab.
- Then, click the radio button corresponding to "One-sample test that correlation = 0."
- Last, click the "OK" button.

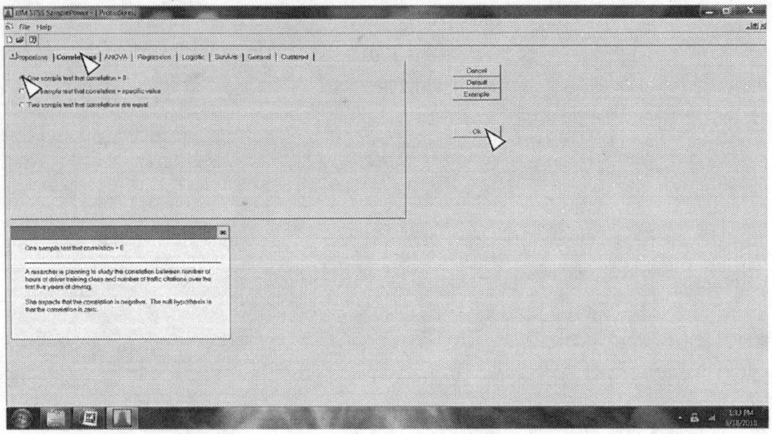

Figure 6.16

Step 2: The window to the right will appear.

- Set the "Population Correlation" to .30, the minimum anticipated correlation.
- Adjust the sample size in "*N* of Cases" until power is set at 90%. The appropriate sample size is 108.

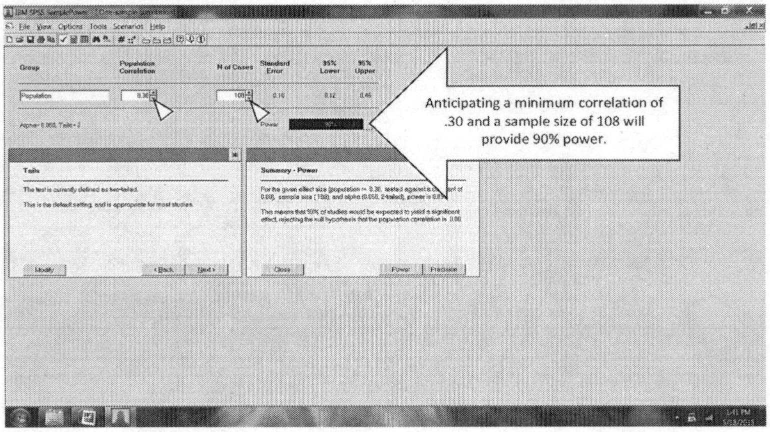

Figure 6.17

Interpretation

A sample size of 108 is required in order to be 90% confident that, if it exists, a correlation of .30 or greater will be detected between education and career advancement. Alpha is 5%.

Example 6.6: ANOVA: One-way analysis of variance

In this example, purchase intention for a wristwatch smartphone will be researched based on four income groups. Purchase will be self-reported by consumers using a seven-point scale ranging from "no intention to purchase" to "will definitely purchase." Alpha is .05, level of confidence is 80%, and the researchers wish to detect any potential effect sizes as low as .10. Two (2) is the anticipated standard deviation based on the scale. What sample size is necessary to meet these requirements?

Following ordered steps will assure accurate results.

Step 1: Open the SamplePower window.

- Select the "ANOVA" tab.
- Then, click the radio button corresponding to "One-way analysis of variance."
- Last, click the "OK" button.

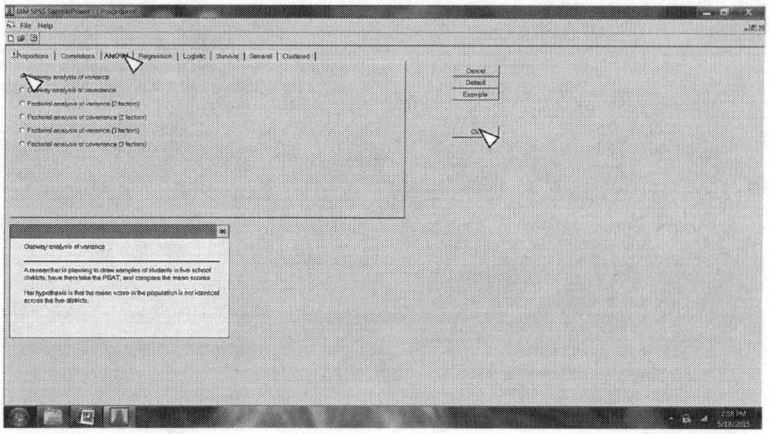

Figure 6.18

Step 2: The window to the right will appear.

- In the "Factor Name" area, change "Factor A" to "Income Level."
- Enter "2" in the "SD within cell" box, after which the blue "Compute" button will appear. "Variance within cell" will be automatically computed.
- Click the "Compute" button.

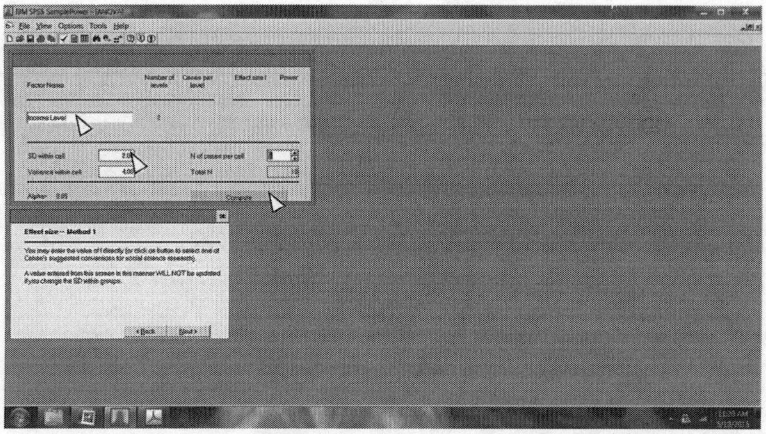

Figure 6.19

Step 3: The window to the right will appear.

- Click in the "Effect size *f*" box.

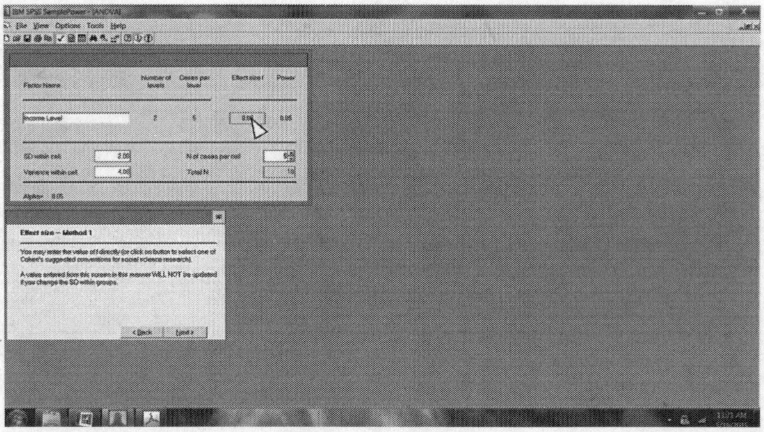

Figure 6.20

Step 4: The following window will open.

- First, and importantly, enter "4" as the number of income groups.
- There are four methods for selecting effect size. Since we have a desired *f* effect size, we select the first option (tab): "Enter *f*."
- Select the "Small *f* = .10," which is selected in this example, "Medium *f* = .25," "Large *f* = .40," or type a different "*f*."
- Last, click the yellow "Compute" button.

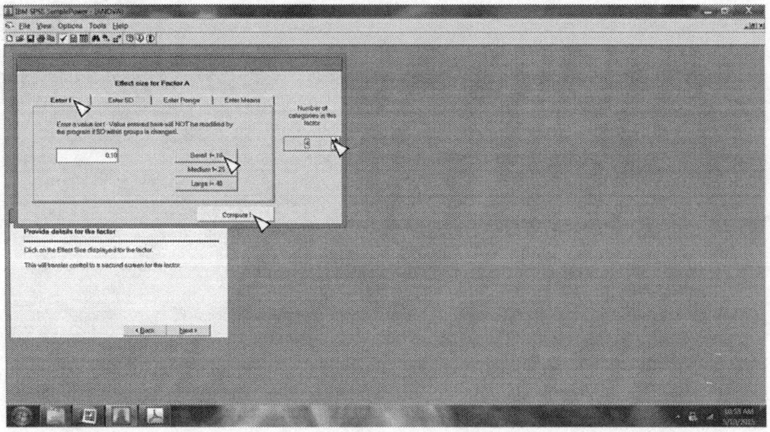

Figure 6.21

Step 5: The yellow "Compute" button changes to a blue "Register *f*" button.

- Click the "Register *f*" button.

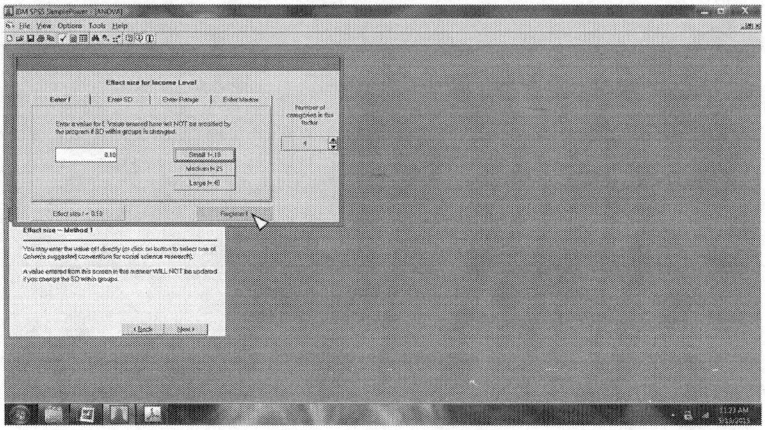

Figure 6.22

Step 6: The following window will appear.

- Adjust the "*N* of cases per cell" sample size so that power equals 80%. Note that the total is automatically calculated as the cell size is set. As we can see, in order to meet this study's requirements, a sample of 275 for each of the four income groups is needed for a total of 1,100 (275 × 4).

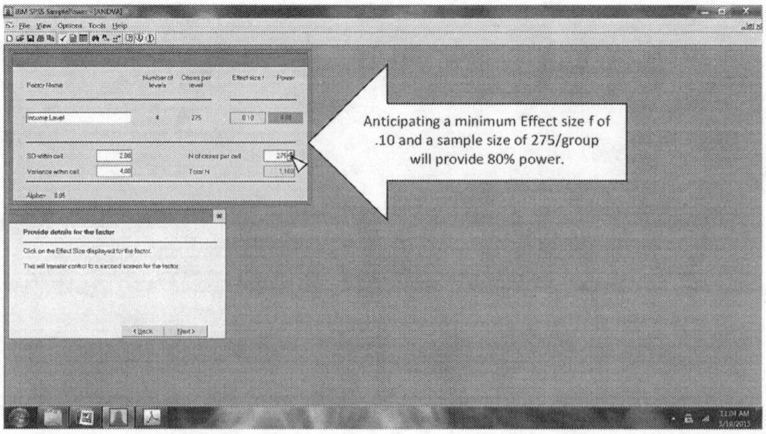

Figure 6.23

Interpretation

In order to detect a minimum potential effect size of .10 with 80% confidence requires a total sample size of 1,100 or 275 participants per each of the four income groups. The anticipated standard deviation is 2.00 based on the seven-point scale.

Note: "Effect size *f*" is the pooled (shared) standard deviation between income levels divided by the standard deviation of each income group. This will make sense after a review of Chapter 18.

Example 6.7: Regression: One set of predictors

A human resources researcher intends to determine the extent of the effects of individual education and relevant professional experience on one's income. The data are numeric. The researcher wants to determine if at least 15% of income is predicted by level of education and if professional experience contributes to 10% of income level for a total of 25%. The level of confidence is 80% per independent variable and alpha is 5%. What sample size is necessary to meet these requirements?

Note: Independent variables predict the dependent variable (see Chapter 3).

Step 1: Open the SamplePower window.

- Select the "Regression" tab.
- Then, click the radio button corresponding to "One set of covariates followed by set of predictors."
- Last, click the "OK" button.

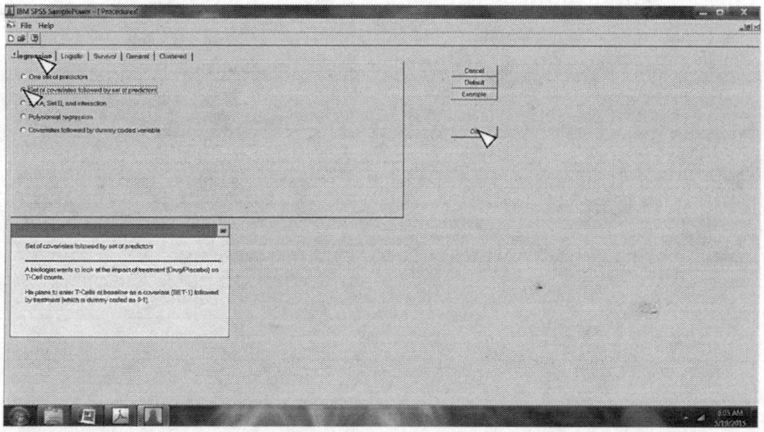

Figure 6.24

Step 2: The window to the right will appear.

- In the yellow areas, type in the predictor variable names. It is good practice to list them in order of *R*-square contribution (see Chapter 23) from most to least, but it is not necessary, especially if they are expected to make equal contributions.
- Under the area titled "Incremental to *R*-Squared" and "Number Variables in Set," select 1 for both variables.

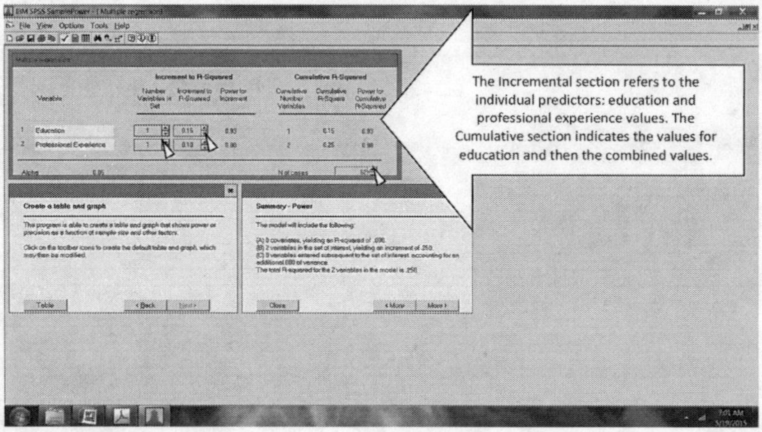

Figure 6.25

- For the "Incremental *R*-Squared," select .15 for education and .10 for professional experience.
- Set the sample size in "*N* of cases" to a number where at least 80% "Power of Increment" appears for each predictor variable. In this case, education is 93% and professional experience is 80%, the minimum acceptable confidence level. These values are achieved when the sample size is 62. The combined variable power for the total analysis is 98% accounting for 25% of the change in income.

Interpretation

A random and representative sample of 62 is required in order to examine with 93% confidence whether education and, with 80% confidence, whether professional experience explain at least 15% and 10%, respectively, of income level. This sample size provides 98% confidence that if the combined effects of 25% exist, they will be detected.

Example 6.8: Clustering

This tool can be used to determine sample sizes for cluster and stratified (multilevel) sampling techniques using numeric data.

In this example, a researcher intends to determine with 80% confidence if there is a difference in favorable responses to eight tablet brands based on whether a consumer is right- or left-handed. The minimum anticipated effect size is .20 (*d*). What sample size per cell (tablet brand by handedness) is required?

Step 1: Open the Samplepower window.

- Select the "clustered" tab.
- Then, click the "ok" button.

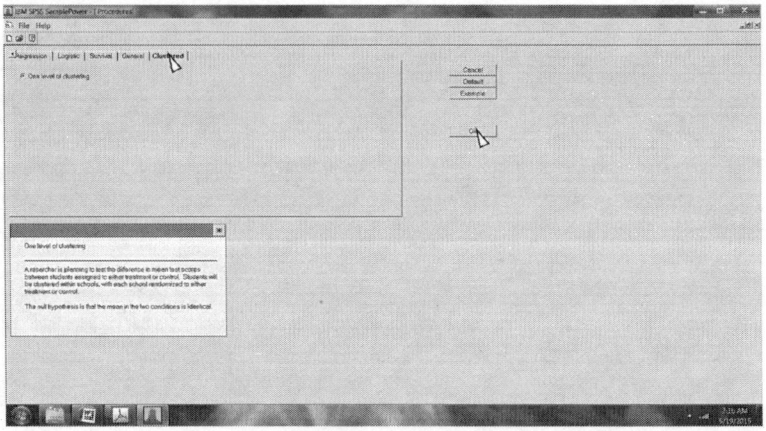

Figure 6.26

Step 2: The window to the right will appear.

- In the "interactive guide—welcome" window, click the "next" button.

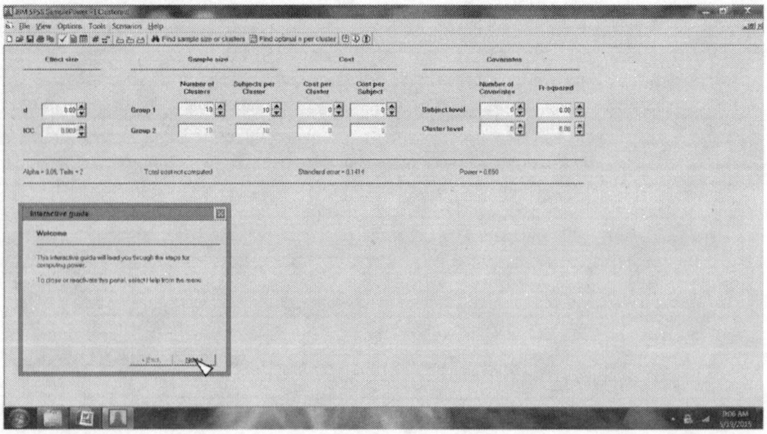

Figure 6.27

Step 3: The window then changes to "interactive guide—labels for groups."

- Select the "modify" button.

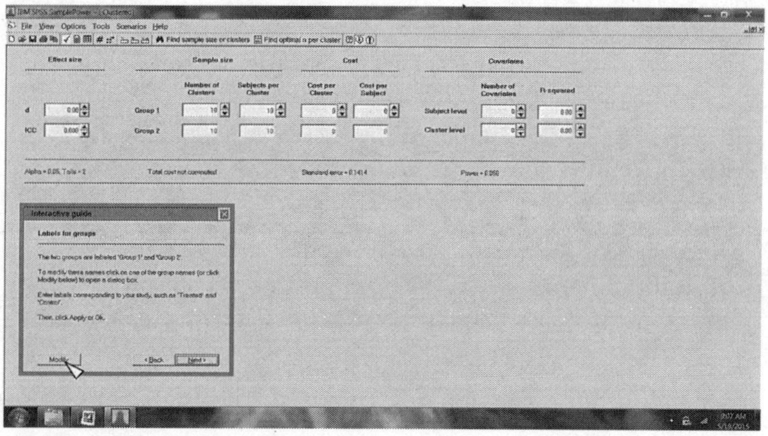

Figure 6.28

Step 4: The "assign labels" window will open.

- For "Name for subject," enter "consumer."
- For "Name for cluster," enter "tablet brand."
- For "Name for first group," enter "right-handed."
- For "Name of second group," enter "left-handed."
- Last, click the "Apply" button.

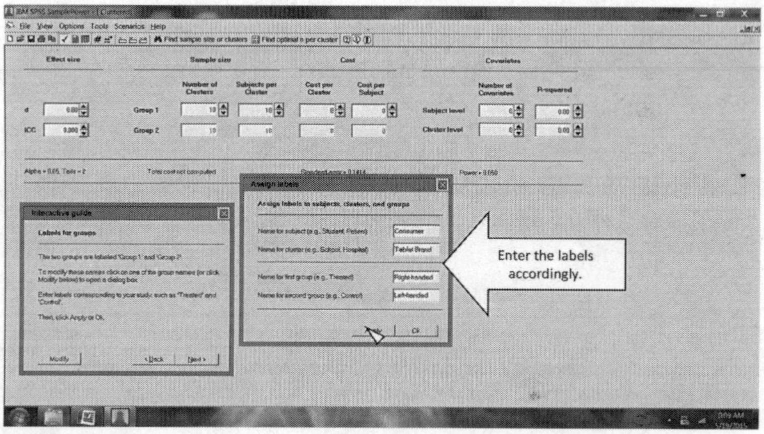

Figure 6.29

Step 5: The "assign labels" window will close.

- Although there is an option to vary cell sizes, we will assume that all cells are equal.
- Enter "8" for number of tablet brands per handedness.
- Set "*d*" at .20.
- Adjust the sample size until power is 80%. The required sample size per cell is 57.

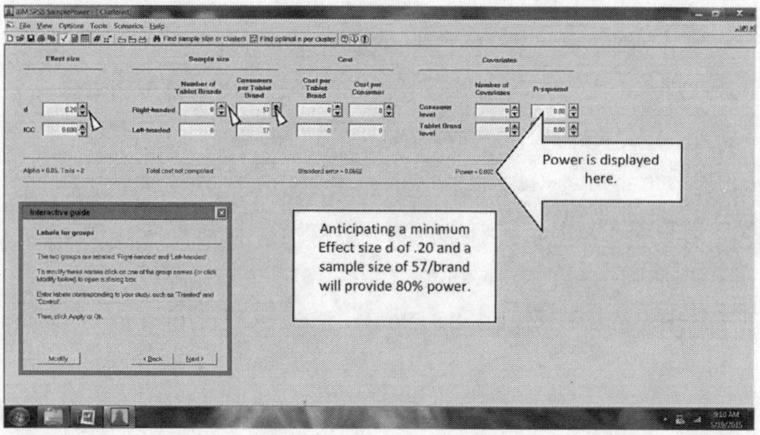

Figure 6.30

Interpretation

Given a level of 80% confidence, an anticipated minimum $d = .20$ effect, and 16 cell combinations (8 tablet brands by [2] right- *and* left-handedness), we will require 57 participants per condition, which will be a total sample of 8 tablets × 2 handedness × 57 number per possible combination = 912.

Note: "*d*" refers to the difference between two group means as a percentage of their pooled (shared) standard deviation. It is a standardized measure of effect size. For example, $d = .20$ tells us that the difference between the two group means is .20 or 1/5 of the standard deviation between them (see Chapters 11 and 12). This indicates that if the means do not differ by .20 standard deviations or more, then the difference is trivial. Usually, $d = .20$ is considered a small effect size, .50 is a medium effect size, and .80 is a large effect size.

SUMMARY OF KEY CONCEPTS

- The sample size is the number of cases or elements in the sample.
- The Central Limit Theorem is a unique property of the normal distribution.
- Statistical power is the level of certainty in results expressed as a percentage.
- Statistical power is the degree of certainty in arriving at minimum statistical results based on sample size and level of acceptable risk.
- The effect size is the strength of the results and applies to a specific statistical procedure.
- The probability that results are not a mistake is the level of risk or alpha, which is usually 5% or less.
- SamplePower is an SPSS add-on used to determine sample size based on power analysis and the type of statistical analysis used.

SAMPLE SIZE APPLIED EXERCISES

6.1 What is the Central Limit Theorem?

6.2 What is a sample size? Provide one example.

6.3 For categorical data, is there a minimum expected cell count? If so, what is it?

6.4 Generally, is sample size based on the total target population size? Explain your answer.

6.5 What is an effect? Provide an example.

6.6 What is an expected effect size? Provide an example.

6.7 Is it possible to have a sample that is too large?

6.8 What is statistical power?

6.9 Describe the components of statistical power.

6.10 What is alpha? Explain your answer.

6.11 Generally and briefly explain the concept of finite population correction.

6.12 What are some factors that inform how unequal sample sizes are addressed?

6.13 What is the name of the SPSS application provided to determine an appropriate sample size?

6.14 What is the rule of thumb for estimating a standard deviation in normally distributed data?

6.15 For what types of variables can an appropriate sample size be determined?

6.16 In reporting the required sample size, what statistics are included?

6.17 What is a useful feature of SamplePower 3?

6.18 A manufacturer wishes to know whether the diameter of its machined parts varies from 10 mm by sample testing output. The anticipated mean is 7.30 mm. In the past, the standard deviation was 6.50 mm. What sample size is necessary in order to be 90% confident in the sample results?

6.19 You wish to determine if tuna is preferred more on the West Coast or East Coast in fine dining restaurants. Restaurant patrons will provide their preference by answering a question formatted in a five-point scale with responses ranging from 1 = "not preferred at all" to 5 = "preferred most or all of the time." The standard deviation will be 1 and the confidence level is 80%. What sample size is required? The minimum expected difference (effect) based on the five-point scale is .5 (for example, 4.5 and 4.0).

6.20 Education researchers wish to determine whether household income, owning one or more dogs, and having educated parents will predict whether children will attend college. The anticipated minimum effect sizes are .10 for income, .10 for education, and .05 for dog ownership. The overall confidence level is 95%. What is the required sample size?

Chapter 7

Sources and Types of Statistical Error

LEARNING OBJECTIVES

To be able to:

- understand and describe statistical error;
- differentiate between sampling and nonsampling error;
- describe random and systematic sampling error;
- Describe random and systematic nonsampling error.
- Understand that error can influence the normal distribution and statistical results.

7.1 Introduction to Sources of Statistical Error

In statistics and especially numeric data, **statistical error** is any deviation in sample data from the population of interest based on: (1) data collection methods; and (2) sources of data. Less error in sample data increases our ability to accurately measure, describe, and predict population attributes and behavior. Some error is due to natural (random) fluctuations and other inaccuracies are systematic (follow a pattern). For example, someone in a positive mood may respond differently compared to when that person is in a negative mood; this is a natural fluctuation. Having children complete a cognitive capacity exercise in a number of classes, some of which were unintentionally exposed to distractions that are not part of the study, might yield different response patterns by classroom, which thus causes systematic error. Both of these sources of error can move data away from the normal distribution, in which case statistical probability can become unstable and inaccurate.

There are a number of sampling considerations as they relate to error. First, the population from which the data are drawn is the intended population under study. The population could be the economy, a market, new drug trials, manufacturing quality control measures, social services clients, students, and so forth. Second, for parametric statistics (numeric data), the data are assumed to be normally distributed (bell-shaped). If the sample data represent the population, then they too will be normally distributed, which allows results to be applied to the target population. However, if the sample data contain high levels of error, then the distribution will stray from normal and probability statistics can become meaningless. Thus, our ability to make inferences from the sample to the population is diminished. This suggests that if numeric data are not normally distributed, it is due to increased error caused by poor sample selection (sampling error) and/or poor data collection methods (nonsampling error). We now delve further into these concepts.

REAL WORLD SNAPSHOT

Since the beginning of the twenty-first century, the rate of global warming has slowed down. Opponents of global warming indicate that the "new" trend supports their position and that previous research findings were plagued with systematic statistical errors that overestimated global warming claims.

Two scientists, Marotzke and Forster, decided to investigate the new temperature pattern by running a number of statistical analyses on the available data. In a 2015 article, they reported their findings. After their thorough step-by-step review of over 100 climate change models, they could not find an explanation for the change in the temperature trend other than random fluctuations in the earth's climate. They held that climate is subject to change, and thus it can be unpredictable in the short term.

They reported that the earlier increasing temperature trends have been much longer than the current pattern and that the current trend still demonstrates a consistent rise in the temperature as predicted by the vast majority of statistical models. The study concluded that the downward change in rate of global warming is based on random error and global warming is quite real.

Ask yourself: What other variables might contribute to change in weather patterns?

7.2 Sampling Error

Error related to sample selection is a source of inaccuracy, some of which can be part of the normal, random fluctuation of sample variance or it can be systematic demonstrating a pattern.

Random Sampling Error

Random sampling error occurs when the sample selected is an imperfect representation of the target population. The differences between the sample and population do not demonstrate a pattern, but are inherently random. Natural differences commonly occur between and among samples drawn from the same population. However, a more representative sample will have less random sampling error. For example, political polls that deploy similar scientific or systematic sampling techniques often yield somewhat different results. Pollsters endeavor to minimize random sampling error so that they can produce accurate results.

Systematic Sampling Error

Sampling error that demonstrates a pattern in the data is called **systematic sampling error**. For instance, **coverage error** occurs when the sample does not represent a cross section of the target population, resulting in selection bias. This can create skewed data distribution commonly known as **systematic response error**. For instance, university researchers often use college/university students in their studies. Drawing from students to collect data about their shopping habits cannot be generalized to the population as a whole, but only to college/university students, who may very well possess consumer shopping habits, at least in part, unique to people at that stage in life. Systematic response error is addressed below in the nonsampling error section.

A particular type of coverage error is **sampling frame error**, which is the difference between the actual target population and population as defined by the sampling frame. A **sampling frame** is the source of data from which a sample is drawn. Examples are children enrolled in an elementary school, a list of people participating in social services programs, a list of ex-offenders taking part in a support program, and so forth. More specifically, if a researcher wishes to run an opinion poll of all adults about a number of local social issues, drawing a sample solely from property ownership lists would result in sampling frame error because such lists would not include non-propriety-owning adults in the community.

The source of data can skew data. For example, if researchers test for adherence to quality control specifications at a factory and keep drawing from the same shift, responses may be skewed in comparison to an average of all three shifts or in comparison to one of the other shifts. The same could apply to work days. If data are drawn only from Monday, there may be more data fluctuation or skew compared to other days. It might be because the first day back from the weekend requires a mental adjustment. In any case, drawing only from Monday does not present an accurate picture of quality assurance adherence. **Ceiling effect** data are skewed to the left, illustrating many high values. **Flooring effect** data are skewed to the right, denoting many low values. Figures 7.1 and 7.2 illustrate these effects.

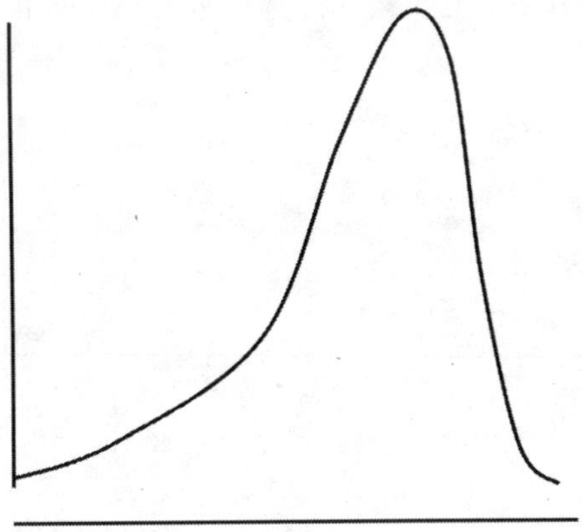

Figure 7.1 Ceiling Effect

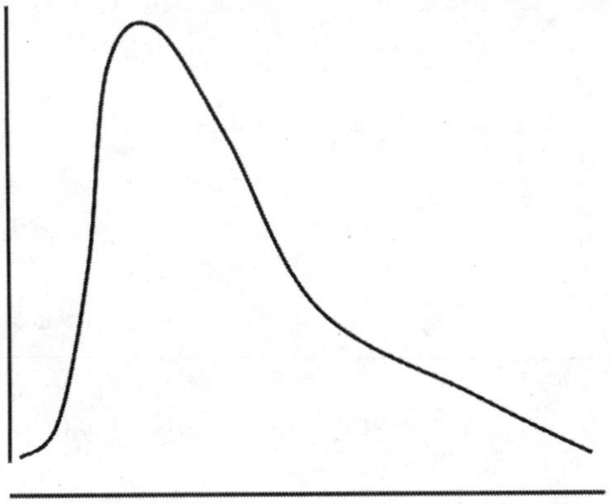

Figure 7.2 Flooring Effect

7.3 Nonsampling Error

Sampling practices, data format, or the nature of the data collection environment can be sources of inaccurate results. Nonsampling error can be random as well as systematic.

Nonsampling Random Error

Nonsampling random error results from sources other than those ascribed to sampling. Some error may be caused by the intrinsic fluctuation of data and other error may be caused by the unit of measurement such as people, a chemical process, financial trends, weather conditions, or some other aspect of the measurement environment. For instance, some survey questions may not have been clearly understood by some respondents, resulting in a wider range of responses. Alternatively, responses from survey participants may not be accurate because individuals might be compelled to provide socially acceptable responses to sensitive issues rather than deviate from what is perceived as acceptable answers, which then become a source of nonsampling random error.

Nonsampling Systematic Error

Nonsampling systematic error demonstrates a pattern in the data not attributed to sampling. It is caused by the study design, some aspect of the study environment, and/or measurement error. The error follows a discernible pattern and is controllable. For example, a production manager monitors productivity of machine operators but is unaware that some machines were overhauled. The increased production is in part owing to the overhaul. The researcher may very well see a pattern emerge and adjust the analysis accordingly in order to gain an accurate picture of operator productivity.

There are different types of nonsampling systematic error. First, there is **measurement error**, which is error due to a flaw in data collection or measurement. In the case of surveys, questions must be clearly worded and understood. Response categories should contain all possible groupings (exhaustive) and they must not overlap (mutually exclusive). Therefore, if a researcher includes an education question, then he/she must incorporate all categories of education from those with no education, those with doctorate degrees, and those groups between these two categories. To the second point, two adjacent annual income categories should not be as follows: $25,000–$45,000 and $45,000–$65,000. This format allows those respondents earning $45,000 to select either option, which can produce inaccurate results. Therefore, $25,001–$45,000 and $45,001–$65,000 are appropriate.

Questions that do not account for the full range of responses can result in ceiling or flooring effects that skew the data distribution, producing non-normal distributions, which produce inaccurate probabilities and unstable results. These effects were discussed above. However, the reason for them is different in this case. For example, if children were asked several comprehension questions about their understanding of a story that they read by selecting 1 = "I understood nothing" to 5 = "I understood everything," assuming that the story was very simple and easily understood by virtually all of the children, then the responses would not be bell-shaped, but skewed to the left, indicating a ceiling effect. In this case, either a more challenging story should be used or younger children should have been selected to participate in the study. In any case, the solution should be informed by the research goal.

Another type of response error is caused by **social desirability effects**. Study respondents provide answers that are socially desirable even if they actually do not subscribe to those responses. This is especially the case when the issue is socially sensitive, such as reporting attitudes about lifestyles or behaviors, as well as personal values and religious beliefs.

A related process is the **Hawthorne effect**. Responses are guided by participant perceptions of what they think the researcher wants them to answer or do. They do this in appreciation for the attention given them by the researcher.

All of these sources of error are threats to the normal distribution assumption and the accuracy of statistical results.

SUMMARY OF KEY CONCEPTS

- Statistical error can misrepresent the nature of data because of a sample selection flaw, data source dynamic, or measurement error.
- Sampling error results from weaknesses in the sampling process.
- Nonsampling error is a consequence of shortcomings in the measurement instrument or data source characteristics.
- Sampling and nonsampling error can be random or systematic.

- Random error comprises normal fluctuations in the data and is usually beyond the researcher's control.
- Systematic error demonstrates a pattern involving some aspect of the study design.
- Statistical error can threaten normal distribution and the accuracy of statistical results.

STATISTICAL ERROR APPLIED EXERCISES

7.1 Define statistical error.

7.2 Define random sampling error and provide one example.

7.3 Define systematic sampling error and provide one example.

7.4 What is coverage error?

7.5 What is a systematic response error? Provide an example.

7.6 What is a sampling frame error? Provide an example.

7.7 What is a ceiling effect?

7.8 What is a flooring effect?

7.9 What is nonsampling random error? Provide an example.

7.10 Define nonsampling systematic error and provide an example.

7.11 Define measurement error and offer an example.

7.12 What is a social desirability effect? Provide an example.

7.13 What is the Hawthorne effect?

7.14 What is problematic about the following question? "What is your party affiliation: Democrat, Republican, or Independent?"

7.15 What is problematic about the following question? "What is your age range: 18–25, 25–45, 45–65, 65 and older?"

7.16 What is problematic about the following scenario? Asking only progressive Democrats if they will vote for a conservative Republican.

7.17 What is the difference between sampling and nonsampling error?

7.18 What is the difference between random and systematic error?

7.19 Explain how random fluctuations in data can appear to influence data trends. Cite the Real World Snapshot example.

7.20 Think of situations where people complete a survey. Such self-reported data can be subjective and not accurately represent a situation. Can you think of circumstances where this might be the case? How might you reduce these effects?

Chapter 8

Missing Data

LEARNING OBJECTIVES

To be able to:

- explain why missing data can threaten the accuracy of statistical results;
- describe the concept of imputation;
- describe the three different types of missing data analysis;
- know and describe the various methods for addressing and replacing missing data; and
- address missing data using expectation maximization.

8.1 Introduction to Missing Data

Data are measurement values or individual observations represented in cases and based on or structured according to a variable's data format. This chapter uses the terms data and values interchangeably.

Often datasets may have missing values for certain variables or cells so that cases (rows of individual responses) are incomplete. For example, sample data from production output over 30 days on 50 pieces of machinery may have missing data for some days on certain machinery. It might be that certain units of machinery malfunctioned or were not operating owing to scheduled maintenance, and thus no production output was recorded.

Individuals surveyed about their eating habits may not answer certain questions because the topic is sensitive. People may be hesitant for various reasons to report specific income, gender, or ethnic background.

There are three key reasons for addressing missing data. First, less data can reduce statistical power or the level of confidence to detect potential effects (see Chapter 6 for a review of sample size and statistical power). Second, missing data can threaten the normal distribution assumption, which can diminish the soundness of statistical results.

Third, it is important to understand the nature of missing sample data. Missing data that are random with no particular pattern are normal. However, missing data that are not random may reveal valuable information. For instance, the lack of data for certain production days may suggest that for those equipment units, there is a pattern of operation that requires identification and addressing in order to maximize productivity. It could be the machinery model, operator characteristics, training requirements, pattern of some aspect of maintenance, or even the practices of the supervisor, among other factors, that influence production. Thus, the missing data can reveal a dynamic that is important for analysis even though it may not have been considered beforehand.

Using various methods in SPSS, we can replace missing values with values that are consistent with patterns in the existing data. This is known as **imputation**. Imputation allows us to replace missing values with predicted values, thus adding to statistical power (confidence in our results).

As a rule, we can impute missing data as long as the number of missing values represents less than 2% of all data values and the total of complete cases is greater than 30. With smaller datasets, this percentage may be less, depending on the circumstances. With very large datasets, some researchers allow for a 5% maximum of missing values. Statistical power analysis can inform the researcher about what constitutes a sufficient sample size.

Why is adherence to the 5% rule important? It is first important to acknowledge that the impact of missing data on statistics can be serious, leading to biased estimates of parameters, loss of information, decreased statistical power, increased standard errors, and weakened generalizability of findings. Most statistical procedures automatically eliminate cases with missing data, which can decrease statistical power. Consequently, results may not be meaningful because of the reduction. A larger sample size with adequate power might yield statistically significant effects not detected by a smaller size. Moreover, if the remaining "complete" sample is not random, results may not be accurate. Assuming a sufficiently large sample, removing no more than 5% of the missing data cases assures that the data are random and that there is satisfactory statistical power.

Before we "impute" missing values, we must determine whether the data are missing randomly. If the data are systematically (not randomly) missing, then any replacements may not accurately represent what the values would have been had they not been missing. In other words, the pattern in the missing data must also be considered before replacement. It is important to note that patterns may not be captured in the various approaches to replace missing data. Therefore, in cases where there is a pattern in missing data, there are alternatives to imputation, which are discussed later. Let us start with missing value analysis.

8.2 Missing Value (Data) Analysis

There are three missing data conditions. First, there is **missing completely at random (MCAR)**. This is a condition in which there is no pattern between any missing values and any values in the dataset. For example, there is no pattern among respondents who did not report their income and other variables in the dataset, such as educational level, age, or ethnicity.

Second, there is the **missing at random (MAR)** condition. Missing values are not random. However, within subsets, missing values are indeed random. For example, in a hypothetical study of income level and ethnicity, certain ethnic groups did not report income as frequently as other groups. However, within ethnic groups, there is no pattern between missing income values and amount of income. In MAR situations, missing value analysis should be conducted on the clearly defined subsets of a variable.

Third, there is the **missing not at random (MNAR)** condition. The missing values are not random, but demonstrate a pattern between the missing value and at least one other value in the dataset. For instance, respondents with greater education (e.g. reported completed years of post-secondary education) tend to report income more so compared to persons with less education and income. This same pattern emerges even when considering other variables, such as gender, ethnicity, location of residence, and so forth.

We can determine whether there is a pattern in missing data using an SPSS add-on called **Missing Value Analysis** and **Little's MCAR Test**. This test determines whether missing data are MCAR and requires at least two variables to detect a pattern. Determining MAR would require formatting the data into subsets before running the test.

If the data are MCAR, there are a number of imputation methods available, which are discussed below. For MAR conditions, these same methods are appropriate for defined subsets. For instance, age, which is numeric data, can be analyzed by gender, which is categorical.

If there is a pattern in the data, the following options are viable: (1) collect more data to increase the number of complete cases; (2) limit statistical analysis to MAR subsets and report results accordingly; (3) analyze the data listwise or pairwise; or (4) provide a caveat in the write-up.

REAL WORLD SNAPSHOT

A 2009 SPSS white paper reported a case study about a consumer goods company usage of data from a few questions on a warranty card as the basis to inform its marketing decision-making. The initial analysis ignored missing data from the sample. After an analysis of the missing data, the expectation-maximization method was used to replace missing values. The results varied, especially in terms of occupation, which moved from any to nonprofessional occupations as depicted below.

Demographic Characteristics	**Incomplete Data**	**Expectation-Management Replacement Data**
Marital Status	Married Women	Married Women
Income	\$18,000–\$42,000	\$17,000–\$39,000
Occupation	Any	Nonprofessional

Based on forecasted promotional spending, simulation research generated the following results for the before and after imputation dataset. Imputation provided a more accurate picture of the typical customer, which allowed for more precise targeting, resulting in a higher response rate to promotions, more sales, and profits.

Incomplete Data	**Expectation-Maximization Replacement Data**
100,000 names purchased	100,000 names purchased
Total cost for mailing: \$100,000	Total cost for mailing: \$100,000
Response rate: 2%	Response rate: 4%
Total number of responses: 2,000	Total number of responses: 4,000
Closed sales: 1,000	Closed sales: 2,000
Average revenue per sale: \$100	Average revenue per sale: \$100
Total revenue: \$100,000	Total revenue: \$200,000
Profit: \$0	Profit: \$100,000

Ask yourself: Can you think of areas of research plagued by high missing data rates that might benefit from replacing missing data techniques?

8.3 Methods for Replacing Missing Values

It is important to note that the selection of an imputation method should be informed by the aim of your study and the analyses that will be conducted. Some methods require that the data be reformatted or split before imputation. An in-depth discussion of these considerations is beyond our discussion but worth mentioning.

Estimation methods for replacing or imputing missing values broadly fall into two categories: "traditional" and "new." The traditional approaches include listwise (casewise), pairwise, series mean, mean of nearby points, median of nearby points, linear interpolation, and linear trend at point. They are available in the standard version of SPSS located at the "Transform" tab. Other than the listwise and pairwise approaches, traditional imputation are based on the relationships of the *single* (column) variable's values. Mean of nearby points, median of nearby points, linear interpolation, and linear trend at point are used for time series analysis. Series means is also used to replace missing values by simply replacing missing values with the average for the variable.

Newer methods are expectation maximization (EM) and multiple imputation (MI), which are available as add-ons labeled "Missing Value Analysis" and "Multiple Imputation—Analyze Patterns and Impute Missing Data Values," respectively. EM and MI consider the relationships among all of the sample data in the calculation and prediction of imputed values.

There are a number of imputation assumptions. First, with the exception of listwise, pairwise, and MI, the data must be numeric. Second, after the imputation, the complete sample size must be sufficiently large enough to achieve the desired statistical power. Third, the missing values do not constitute more than 5% of the complete dataset values. Last, the missing values are MCAR or MAR (well-defined subsets).

Note that references to values used to impute refer to valid values. Blank cells do not constitute a valid value, but are missing values, whether or not they occur next to each other.

Listwise (Casewise)

The **listwise** or casewise procedure is an option in many statistical procedures. Selecting this option simply removes all incomplete cases from the analysis, whether composed of numeric or categorical data. This reduces sample size and can weaken statistical power.

Pairwise

The **pairwise** approach simply removes all incomplete cases on an analysis-by-analysis basis, whether the data are numeric or categorical. If two variables are compared, each with a different number of complete cases, the analysis will be conducted based on the variable with the smaller number of complete cases. Therefore, if there are missing values, then the sample sizes for each analysis may not be equal.

For example, if there are 50 responses to an income question and 75 responses to an education question, then the income analysis would be based on the 50 income-reported cases and the education analysis would be based on the 75 responses. If the 75 education responses were compared to 150 individuals who reported ZIP codes, a correlation analysis would be based on the 75 education response cases. As we can see, the major drawback is that the sample size will likely have different distributions because the data analyzed will vary based on missing values.

Series Mean

The **series mean imputation** involves substituting the variable mean for missing values. For example, if the values in the variable are 3, 4, 3, –, 5, 4, 5, –, 5, then the imputed value would be (3 + 4 + 3 + 5 + 4 + 5 + 5 =) / 7 = 4.14. Therefore, the variable values would be 3, 4, 3, 4.14, 5, 4, 5, 4.14, 5. Series mean imputation can be conducted in SPSS by clicking the "Transform" tab followed by selecting "Replace Missing Values." Although the simple mean procedure is straightforward, it is problematic for two major reasons.

First, the mean underestimates how far the sample mean is likely to be from the population mean. This might make the data appear more normally distributed than in actuality. Second, the series mean is an average of all the values for a given variable (cases for a variable) and it does not account for patterns among the variables' values within the case. For instance, simply taking an average of income from all respondents with varying income levels fails to detect the relationships among educational level and other measures of economic status with income level. In reality, income is likely understated or overstated by taking an average and not considering other factors.

Mean of Nearby Points

The **mean of nearby points imputation** imputes missing values with the mean of surrounding valid values. The researcher sets the span of nearby value points above and below the missing value in the variable. The nearby points are used to compute the mean. The span is based on valid values so that any missing values will be skipped and the next valid value will be selected. If, as might be the case in the beginning or end of the variable values, there is not a valid value, then no imputation will occur. This procedure requires numeric data.

For example, as noted in Table 8.1, the case values are arranged as 1, **2**, **1**, –, **4**, **2**, 3. If the mean calculation span consists of 2 or the 2 closest valid values above and below the missing value, then the imputation would result in "2.25" replacing the missing value. The calculation is: (2 + 1 + 4 + 2 = 9) / 4 = 2.25.

Again, this method assumes that nearby variables represent similar values, and thus would be representative of the missing value. Like the series mean imputation, mean of nearby points does not account for relationships or the pattern among all of the case variables.

Table 8.1

Mean of Nearby Points

Missing Value	Imputed Missing Value
1	1
2	**2**
1	**1**
?	**2.25**
4	**4**
2	**2**
3	3

Median of Nearby Points

The **median of nearby points imputation** replaces missing values with the median of the surrounding values. The span of nearby points is the number of values above and below the missing value used to calculate the median. The number of values is determined by the researcher. Again, the span is based on valid values so that any missing values will be skipped and the next valid value will be selected in the variable. If there is no valid value, then no imputation will occur for the missing data.

Like the mean of nearby points, the median of nearby points does not account for patterns among all of the case variables.

Linear Interpolation

Linear interpolation imputation replaces missing values using a linear interpolation formula, which is based on patterns detected in two data points. The last valid value above (before) the missing value and the first valid value below (after) the missing value are used. If the first or last case in the variable has no data, then the missing value is not replaced.

For example, in the following missing values array: **6, –, 2 . . . 2, –, –, 5**, linear interpolation would impute to: 6, 4, 2 . . . 2, 3, 4, 5; thus, the missing values are replaced with 4, 3, and 4, as depicted in Table 8.2.

Table 8.2

Linear Interpolation

Missing Value	Imputed Missing Value
6	1
-	**4**
2	1
.	.
.	.
.	.
2	2
-	**3**
-	**4**
5	5

Linear Trend at Point

Linear trend at point imputation replaces missing values with the linear trend for that point based on all values in the variable. Put differently, missing values are replaced with their predicted values. Unlike linear interpolation, where only the valid values immediately above (before) and below (after) are considered, all of the data in the variable are included.

8.4 New Data Replacement Methods

Expectation Maximization

Arguably, **Expectation-Maximization (EM) imputation** is recommended for most missing values analyses and imputation using numeric data. It employs a single imputation process and predicts missing values based among the variables' data patterns within each case. For example, assume that respondents who have little training or education earn less than those who are highly educated. A record missing an income value that accompanies a low education value for the same respondent would likely be replaced with an income value similar to complete responses containing reported low education levels.

EM imputation is easily executed in SPSS. Once an expected value is imputed, it goes through a repeated process of testing and replacing that value until a maximum solution is reached. Thus, in a single procedure, it can test for missing value pattern analysis, as well as impute and replace missing data.

EM tends to underestimate standard error, which overestimate statistical power. Since EM is easy to use and interpret, many researchers find it a reasonable trade-off.

Multiple Imputation

Like EM, **multiple imputation (MI)** accounts for all case values. It employs multiple imputations, which are set by the researcher. Generally no more than five imputations provide sufficient randomness. The average of the results is the replacement value. Generally, MI is more complex and provides more accurate results compared to EM. It can be used with nominal categorical, ordinal categorical, and numeric data.

Remember that with the exception of MI, all imputation methods require numeric data. Imputation used on nonrandom missing data can yield dubious results. Lastly, the percentage of missing values must not exceed 5%, depending on the sample size.

8.5 Examples Using SPSS: Step-by-Step Instructions

The following examples demonstrate MCAR and NMAR missing values. MAR is beyond the scope of our discussion. We will first assure that the data are numeric. Second, we will analyze for missing value patterns and determine the percentages of missing values. If the missing values are MCAR and the missing rate is sufficiently low, we will conduct EM imputation. EM is the preferred method considering its precision and ease of use.

Example 8.1: The MCAR Case

A dataset consists of three variables: GDP, lobster consumption in pounds, and enrollments in college courses. The sample consists of 120 cases, some of which have missing values. First, we will determine if the missing values are numeric and MCAR. Second, we will examine whether the percentages of missing data are acceptable. Third, we will impute missing values using EM. Last, the procedure will be reported in standard format. For those interested in running the imputation, the dataset is named "Missing Data MCAR Exercise 1."

Step 1: Open SPSS.

- Locate the appropriate folder and data file, then highlight it.
- Next, click the "Open" button.

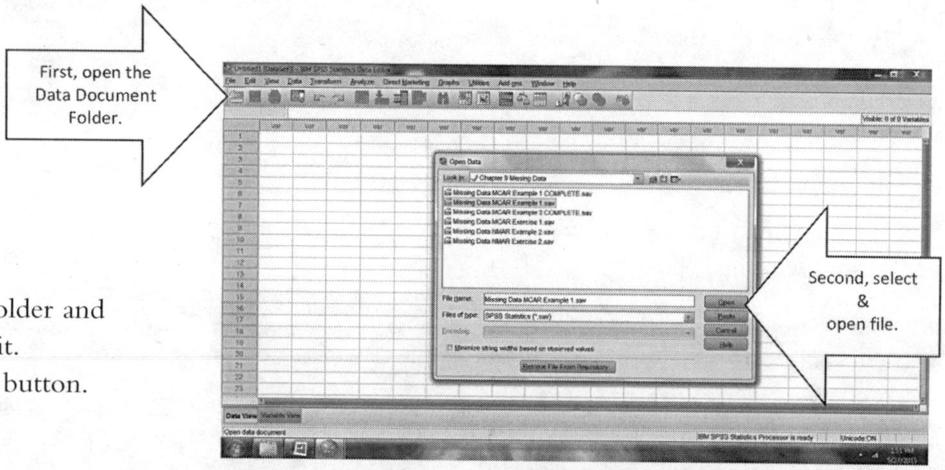

Figure 8.1

Step 2: Scroll down the data file to discover any missing data values.

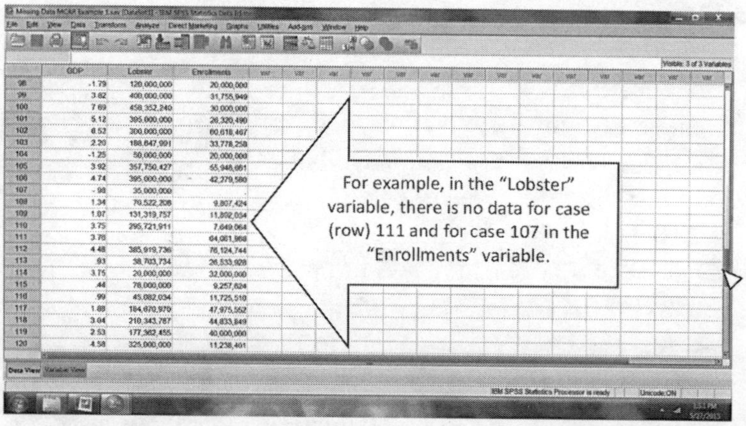

Figure 8.2

Step 3: Assuming that missing values are found, take the following steps:

- Select the "Analyze" tab.
- Then, select "Missing Value Analysis."

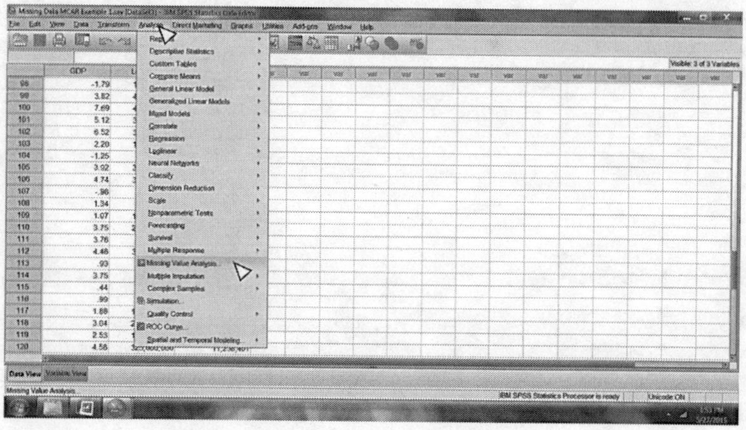

Figure 8.3

Step 4: The "Missing Value Analysis" window will open.

- Highlight all study variables located in the box to the left.
- Then, click the "Arrow" button so that the variable moves to the "Quantitative Variables" box, which will be used for all numeric data, including scale. Ignore the "Categorical Variable" box.
- Check off "EM."
- Last, click the "EM" button.

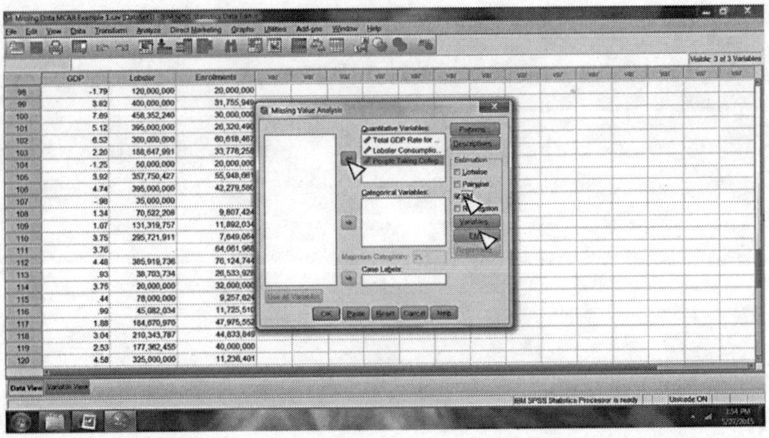

Figure 8.4

Step 5: The "Missing Value Analysis: EM" window will open.

- Check off "Save completed data."
- Click "Create a new dataset." This will allow us to keep the original dataset with missing values as well as create a new complete dataset with the imputed missing data.
- In the "Dataset name" window, type a brief name that identifies the new dataset with the original dataset. It must be one word with no space between letters or symbols. In our case, the name is "Example1."
- Last, click the "Continue" button.

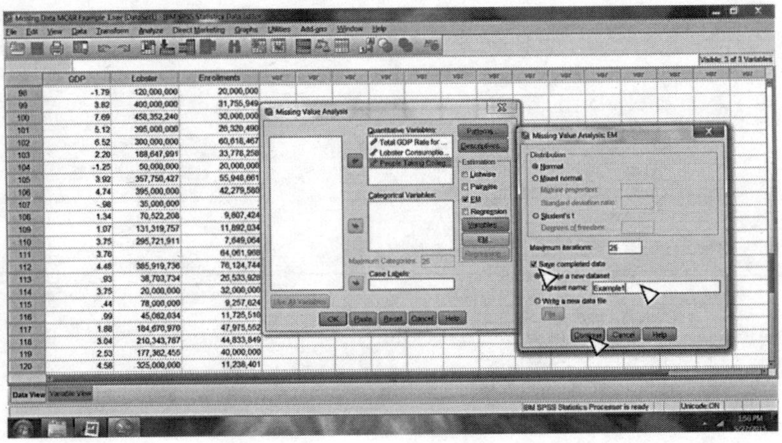

Figure 8.5

Step 6: In the "Missing Value Analysis" window, click the "OK" button.

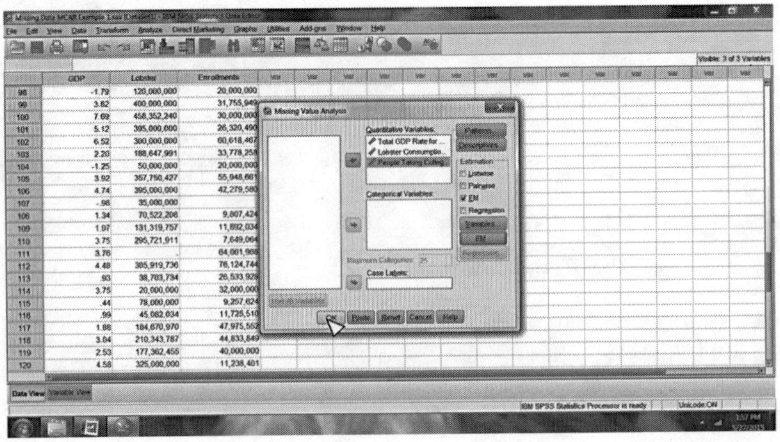

Figure 8.6

Step 7: The "Save completed data" selection created an unnamed and unsaved complete dataset with imputed missing values. The name that was typed in the box is in brackets.

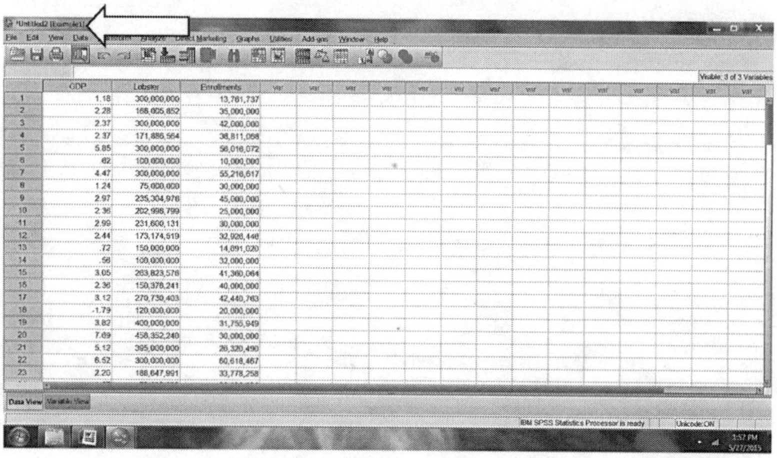

Figure 8.7

Step 8: The complete dataset must be saved.

- Click the "Save" button on the top-left-hand side.
- When the "Save Data As" window appears, type a name that links the dataset file to the study and original dataset and then click on the "Save" button located in the "Save Data As" window.

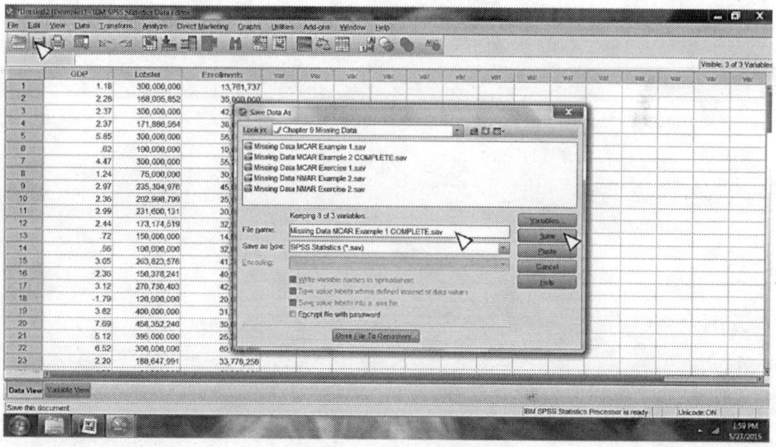

Figure 8.8

Step 9: Scroll down the dataset to review the data. There are no missing values in the new, complete dataset. Since the two datasets are saved, you can exit SPSS anytime.

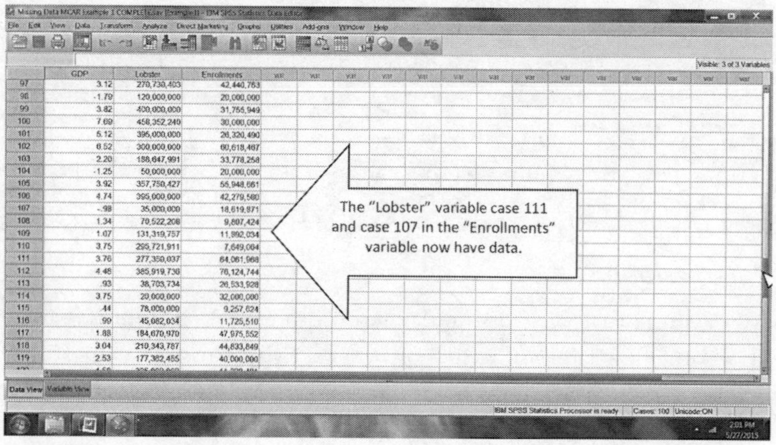

Figure 8.9

Interpretation

We will only utilize two output tables: "Univariate Statistics" and "EM Means." We assume that the missing data are numeric. Since Little's MCAR is $p = .71$, the missing values are assessed as MCAR (see Table 8.3). A p-value of .05 or less would indicate that the missing data are likely not MCAR, and thus are NMAR. As depicted in Table 8.4, the percentages of missing data per variable are well below 2% and the complete sample size is greater than 30.

The imputed missing variables are available in the complete dataset named "Missing Data MCAR Example 1 COMPLETE."

Table 8.3

EM Means[a]

GDP	Lobster	Enrollments
2.5306	211877700.0	3212167.99

a. Little's MCAR test: Ch... DF = 6, Sig. = .712

"Sig." represents the p-value (level of risk), which is .712.

Table 8.4

Univariate Statistics

	N	Mean	Std. Deviation	Missing		No. ...emes[a]
				Count	Percent	L...
GDP	119	2.5290	2.02486	1	.8	
Lobster	118	211846443.9	118081640.7	2	1.7	
Enrollments	118	33342393.36	16926287.67	2	1.7	

a. Number of cases outside the range (Q1 - 1.5*IQR, Q3 + 1.5*IQR).

Missing values are represented in counts and in percentages. For instance, the GDP variable has one missing value representing .8% of the total sample size of 120.

Write-Up

The sample size is 120. Little's MCAR was not meaningful ($p = .71$), indicating that the missing data do not follow a pattern. The percentage of missing values ranges from .8% to 1.7% (1–2 missing values/variable), which is well within the acceptable 5%. Expectation-maximization imputation was conducted, which provided a complete dataset.

Example 8.2: The NMAR Case

The dataset consists of two variables: years of college and income. The sample consists of 575 cases, some of which have missing values. First, we will determine if the missing values are numeric and MCAR. Second, we will examine whether the percentages of missing data are acceptable. Third, we will impute missing values using EM. Last, the procedure will be reported in proper format.

Interpretation

We assume that the missing data are numeric. As noted in Table 8.5, since Little's MCAR is $p < .001$, the missing values are assessed as NMAR or not missing at random, which precludes imputation. The percentages of missing data per variable are approximately 2% (see Table 8.6). Since the missing value percentage is low and the sample size is 575 (and greater than 30), we have the following options: (1) collect more data to

Table 8.5

EM Means[a]

Collegeyears	Income
5.03	$56,057.28

a. Little's MCAR test: Chi-Square = 28.340, DF = 2, Sig. = .000

P-value is less than .001.

Table 8.6

Univariate Statistics

	N	Mean	Std. Deviation	Missing		No. of Extremes[a]	
				Count	Percent	Low	High
Collegeyears	568	5.03	.986	7	1.2	0	0
Income	562	$56,376.67	$20,663.614	13	2.3	0	5

a. Number of cases outside the range (Q1 - 1.5*IQR, Q3 + 1.5*IQR).

increase the number of complete cases; (2) limit statistical analysis to MAR subsets and report results accordingly; (3) analyze the data listwise or pairwise; or (4) provide a caveat in the write-up.

How to proceed will be informed by the required sample size, which will be determined using power analysis (see Chapter 6). However, it appears that the listwise procedure may be effective since the percentages of missing values are low.

Write-Up

Assuming that the data approximate the normal distribution, the listwise procedure is recommended because there is the likelihood of missing value patterns (Little's MCAR, $p < .001$). The missing value rates are approximately 2% or less and the sample size will be 562, representing a small loss of data.

SUMMARY OF KEY CONCEPTS

- Imputation is a statistical procedure used to replace missing data.
- Missing data can be replaced if the sample size is sufficient and imputation accounts for no more than 5% of the cases.
- Missing completely at random is a condition in which there is no pattern between any missing values and any values in the dataset.
- Missing at random indicates that values are not random, except within subsets, where missing values are random.
- The missing not at random condition represents missing values that are not random, but demonstrate a pattern between the missing value and another value in the dataset.
- For randomly missing data, there are alternatives for replacing data.
- In the case of patterns in missing data, there are a number of options available.
- Expectation maximization offers an attractive approach to replacing data.

MISSING DATA APPLIED EXERCISES

8.1 What is the value to having nonrandom missing data?

8.2 What is imputation?

8.3 What is missing at random (MAR)?

8.4 What is missing completely at random (MCAR)?

8.5 What is missing not at random (MNAR)?

8.6 What is listwise?

8.7 What is pairwise?

8.8 Define series mean imputation.

8.9 Define mean of nearby points imputation.

8.10 What is the median of nearby points imputation?

8.11 Define linear interpolation imputation.

8.12 Define linear trend at point imputation.

8.13 What is expectation-maximization (EM) imputation?

8.14 Define multiple imputation (MI).

8.15 What options are available when a dataset has nonrandom missing data?

8.16 Why is adherence to the 5% rule important?

8.17 How might missing data have a negative impact on one's statistical analysis?

8.18 A dataset consists of three variables: social status of restaurant, service level, and average check (bill). The sample consists of 400 cases, some of which have missing values. First, determine if the missing values are numeric and MCAR. Second, determine whether the percentages of missing data are acceptable. Third, impute any missing values using EM. Last, report findings in the examples' format. The data file name is: Missing Data MCAR Exercise 1.

8.19 This dataset consists of eight variables where PR professionals reported their preference for eight types of PR tasks. The sample consists of 255 cases, some of which have missing values. First, determine if the missing values are numeric and MCAR. Second, determine whether the percentages of missing data are acceptable. Third, impute any missing values using EM. Last, report findings in the examples' format. The data file name is: Missing Data NMAR Exercise 2.

8.20 What is Little's MCAR Test?

PART III

Data Screening, Describing, and Probabilities

Chapter 9

Describing Categorical Variables

LEARNING OBJECTIVES

To be able to:

- understand and explain the purpose for using categorical data;
- understand and explain that categorical data involve counts and percentages;
- understand and learn how to construct pie and bar charts;
- understand and know the components of frequency tables;
- describe the concept of joint counts;
- differentiate between summary and contingency tables;
- in SPSS, learn how to tabulate categorical data and create charts and tables; and
- learn how to report categorical descriptive results.

9.1 Introduction to Describing Categorical Variables

Categorical variables result from a counting process. Each variable is composed of groups or categories, each with **frequencies** or tallies that represent the number of occurrences of the category within the variable. Thus, categorical values must be whole numbers or integers. For example, we may have a sample of 200 participants who completed a preference survey about their interest in communication media. The choices of cell phone, tablet, laptop, desktop, and smart TV are the categories within the variable "communication medium preference." For example, the 200 participants' preference might be rendered as follows: cell phone = 50, tablet = 40, laptop = 42, smart TV = 38, and desktop = 30 for a total of 200 preferences. These values represent the **counts** or frequencies (choices) of the participants for a preferred specific communication medium.

In our example, from the frequencies, we can calculate the **proportions** or relative frequencies, which are the percentages of the counts per category based on the total sample size of 200, such as: cell phone = 25% (n = 50), tablet = 20% (n = 40), laptop = 21% (n = 42), smart TV = 19% (n = 38), and desktop = 15% (n = 30) for a total of 100%. It is a best practice to present both proportions and frequencies because they provide the relative counts and the magnitude of those counts, respectively.

Categorical variables can be dichotomous (binary), nominal, or ordinal, as discussed in Chapter 3. We can organize and present categorical data using various charts and tables. Specifically, we will cover pie charts and column (row) charts, as well as a number of tables incorporating one or more variables.

Finally, it is important to note that categorical data descriptive statistics involves describing or defining the sample data based on variables designed to represent the data's characteristics.

REAL WORLD SNAPSHOT

In a 2016 Pew Research Center article, Cohn and Caumont discuss 10 demographic trends that are shaping the United States and the world. Demographic trends impact nations, change cultures, and affect how people feel and think about themselves and their society.

The 10 trends are as follows:

- Americans are more diverse than in the past and this pattern will increase.
- Asia has replaced Latin America and Mexico as the largest source of immigrants.
- As a result of immigration shifts, American politics is changing.
- Young adults born after 1980 are becoming the most influential population segment.
- Women's role in the labor force and society has substantially grown.
- The American family continues to change.
- The middle class now represents 50% of America, and continues its downward spiral.
- The number of adults who do not identify with a religious tradition has increased.
- The world's religions are shifting.
- The world's population is aging.

These demographic trends will influence governmental policies both domestically and internationally. The economic shifts and political trends will inform how nations address economic recessions and use resources—all in light of political and other stakeholder interests. Demographic trends are clearly a window to the future.

Ask yourself: Can you think of areas that will be influenced by demographic trends and why so?

9.2 Charting Categorical Variables

Categorical data are described using various charts. Two popular types are pie charts and bar charts. Charts can be constructed in SPSS using tools available in the "Analysis" tab and in the "Graphs" tab. Both approaches will be covered in this chapter.

Pie Chart

Typically, a **pie chart** is an image shaped as a circle, in which parts or slices are different colors representing the counts and percentages of those counts within each category of the variable. The pie chart represents the sample space of all of the counts. The following are instructions for constructing a pie chart with two or more categories.

Dichotomous (Two-Category) Pie Chart

A **dichotomous or binary pie chart** contains the counts and percentages of a categorical varaiable that has only two groups, such as "Yes," "Low," or "Women," and the absence of that same attribute, such as "No," "High," or "Men," respectively, so that the sample space consists of "Yes" and "No," "Low" and "High," or "Women" and "Men." When there are only two categories or groupings, then the Complement Rule applies. The **Complement Rule** involves a variable with only two categories. It states that the sum of the probabilities of an event (one category) and its complement (the other category) must equal 1.00 or 100% of all possible outcomes. For instance, if .65 or 65% of respondents answered "Yes," then 35% must have answered "No." If 41% or .41 reported "Low," then 59% reported "High." If 55% of participants are women, then 45% comprise men, assuming binary gender reporting.

Example 9.1: A Pie Chart with Two Categories

In this example, we have loan default data from 700 small business owners. The variable is formatted as "Yes" (coded 1) for those small business owners who defaulted on their loans and "No" (coded 0) for those who did not default. We will create a pie chart that depicts the counts and percentages of small business defaults. The SPSS file named "Categorical Data Descriptives Example 1" contains the data for this illustration.

Step 1: Open SPSS.

- Locate the appropriate folder and data file.
- Click the "Open" button.

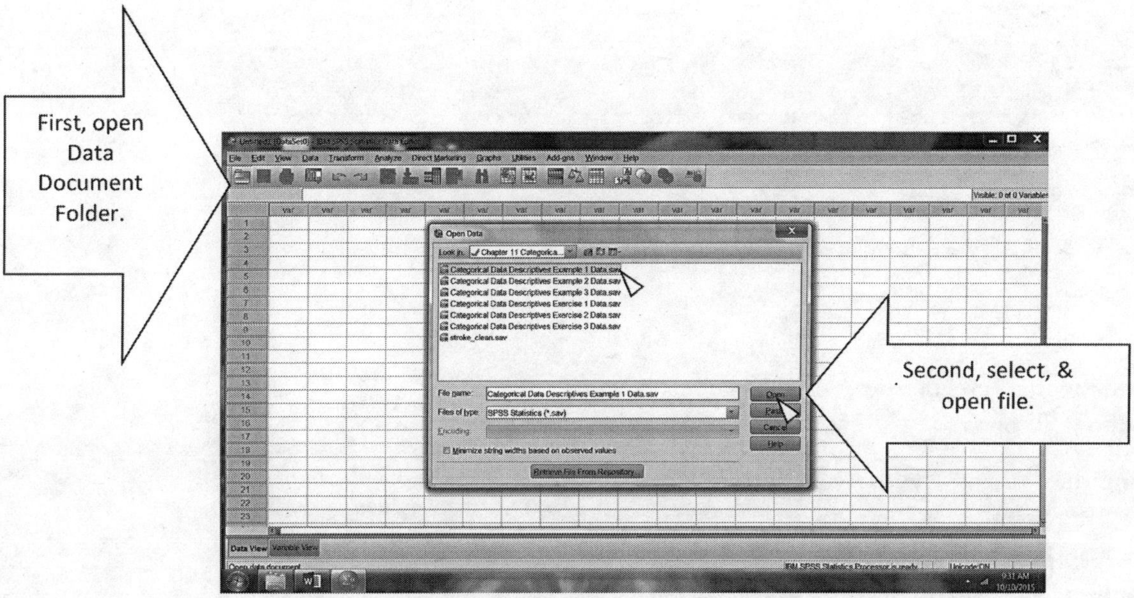

Figure 9.1

There are three options for constructing pie charts in SPSS, which are demonstrated below.

Of the chart tools covered below, Option 1 is limited to a pie chart, but also includes a frequency table option, which can make interpretation a bit easier. Options 2–3 do not include frequency tables, but offer many other charts, options, and graphical tools.

Option 1

Step 2: First, we must run the frequency descriptives.

- Click the "Analyze" tab.
- Select "Descriptive Statistics."
- Last, click "Frequencies."

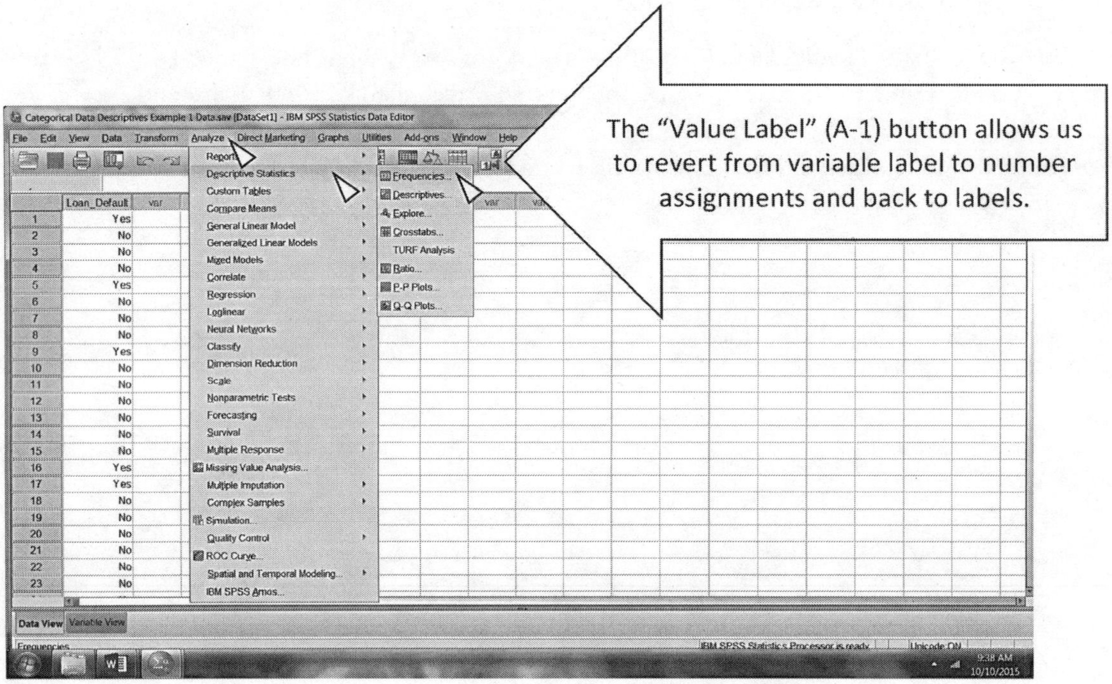

Figure 9.2

Step 3: The following "Frequencies" (counts) window will open.

- By clicking the "Arrow" button, move the "Previous defaulted_loans" variable from the left window to the "Variables" window on the right by highlighting the variable.
- Leave the "Display frequency table" box checked.
- Last, click the "Charts" button on the right.

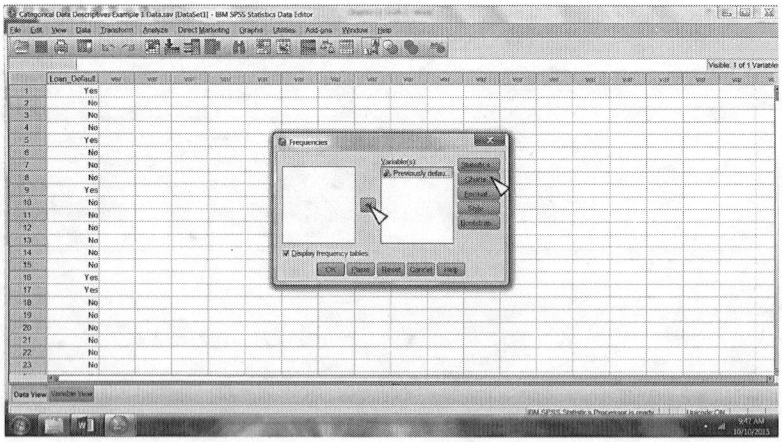

Figure 9.3

Step 4: The "Frequencies: Charts" window will open.

- Click the "Pie charts" radio button.
- Leave all other default values as is. Click the "Continue" button in the bottom-left-hand corner.

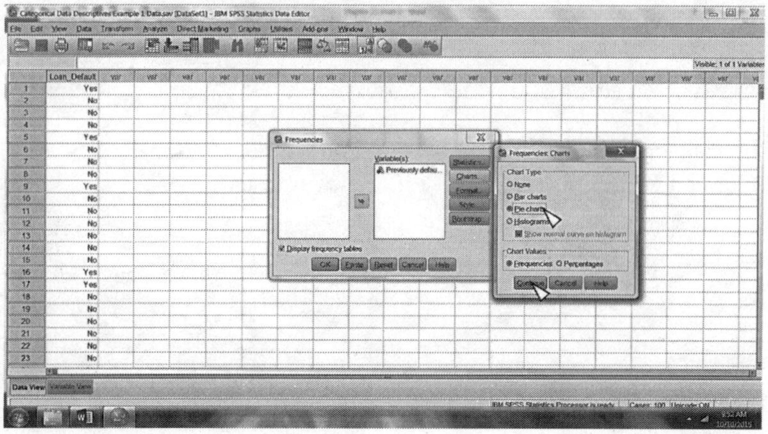

Figure 9.4

Step 5: Click the "OK" button, which will generate the frequencies table and pie chart output.

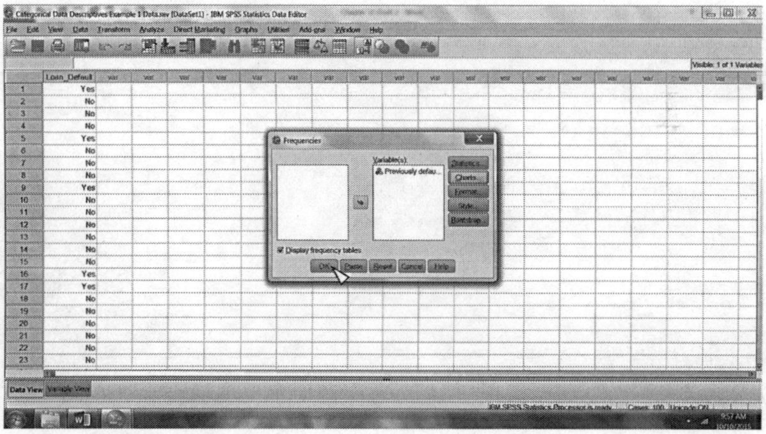

Figure 9.5

The following is the output. The pie chart requires editing.

Table 9.1

Previously defaulted loans

		Frequency	Percent	Valid Percent	Cumulative Percent
Valid	No	517	73.9	73.9	73.9
	Yes	183	26.1	26.1	100.0
	Total	700	100.0	100.0	

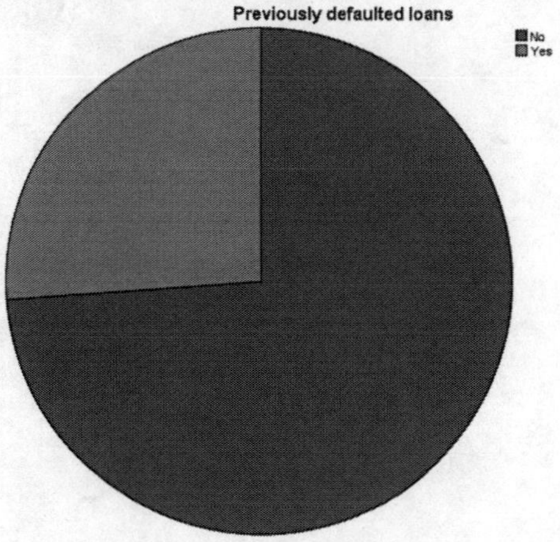

Figure 9.6

Step 6: For editing, do the following:

- Right-click on the pie chart.
- Select the last option, "Edit Content."
- Last, click the "In Separate Window" option.

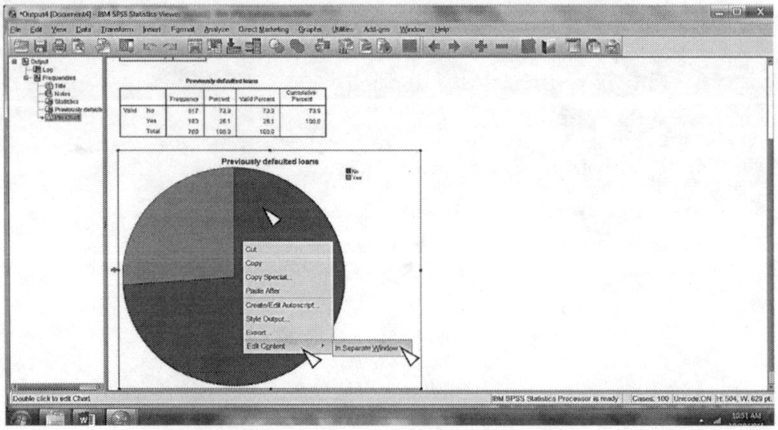

Figure 9.7

Step 7: The following "Chart Editor" window will open.

- Right-click on the new window.
- Select "Show Data Labels."

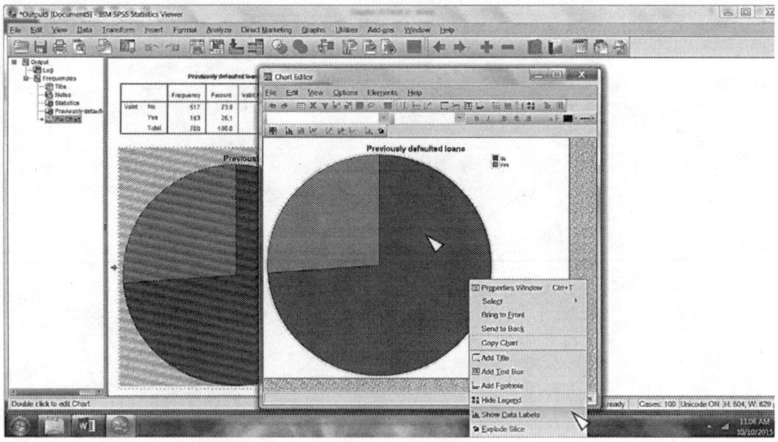

Figure 9.8

Step 8: The following "Properties" window will open. This window can be used to adjust the chart size, edit text and numbers, as well as customize the colors and add borders.

- Click onto the "Data Value Labels" tab.
- In the "Not displayed" box, highlight "Percent."

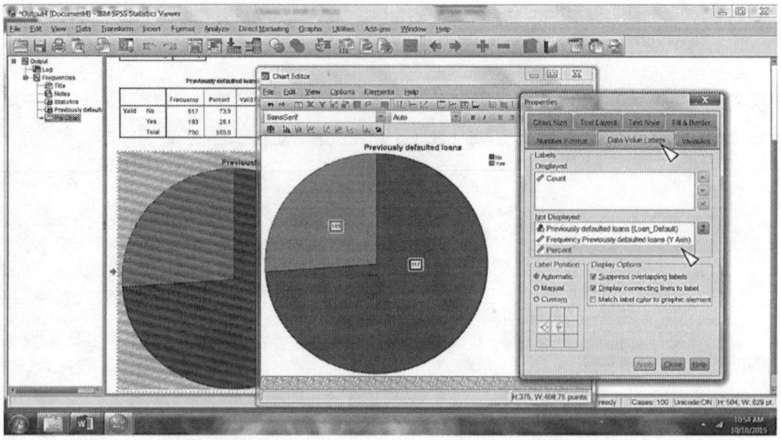

Figure 9.9

Step 9: Once "Percent" is highlighted, do the following:

- Click the "Arrow" button so that "Percent" is now in the "Displayed" box with "Count."
- Next, click the "Apply" button.

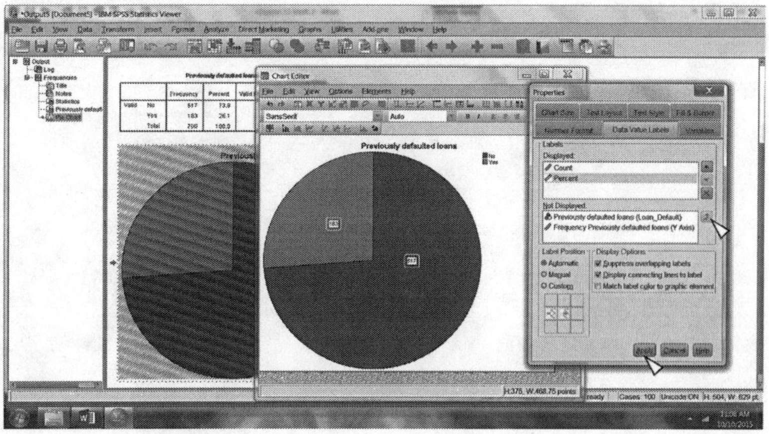

Figure 9.10

Step 10: Notice that both counts and percentages are now displayed, which is a best practice for depicting categorical data.

- Click the "Close" button located in the bottom-right side of the "Properties" window.

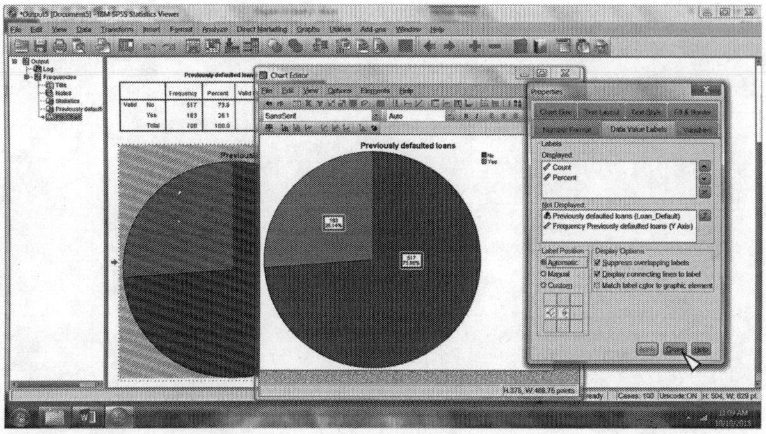

Figure 9.11

Step 11: In the "Chart Editor" window:

- Click on "File."
- Then, select "Close."

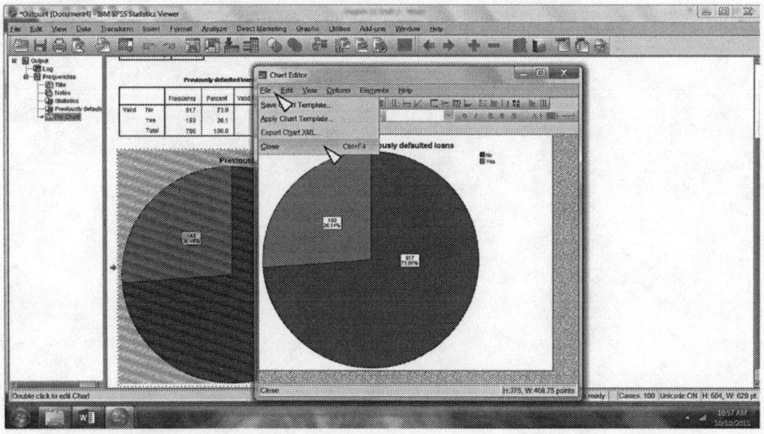

Figure 9.12

The output file will now contain the edited version of the pie chart and can be saved (see Chapter 4).

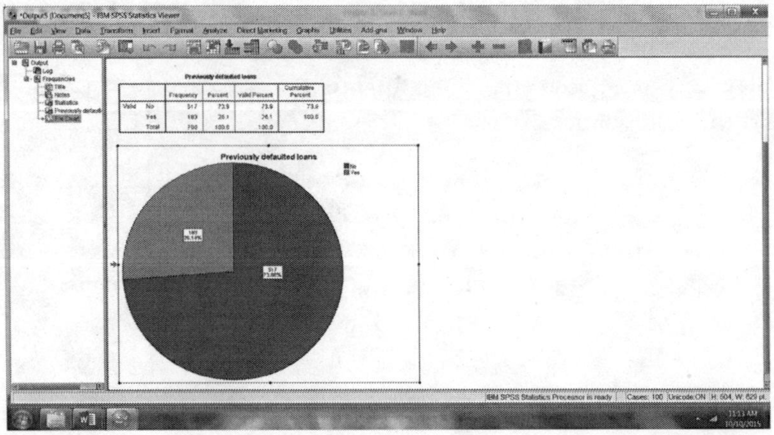

Figure 9.13

Step 12: Additionally, the pie chart can be copied and pasted to a number of file formats, including Word, by doing the following:

- Right-click on the pie chart.
- Then, select the "Copy" option. Now it can be pasted into an open file.

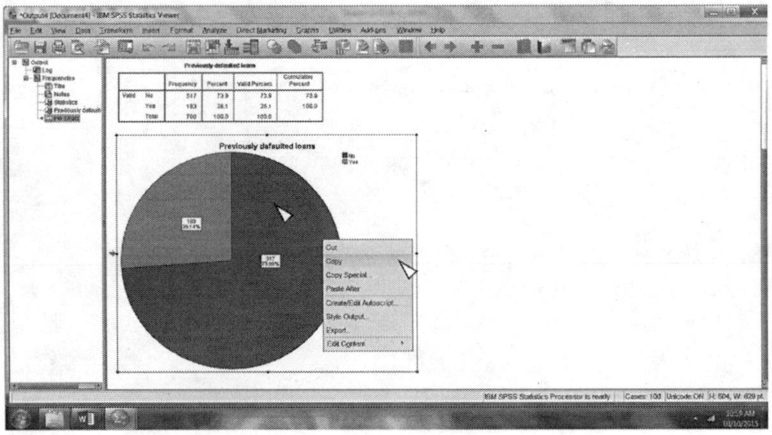

Figure 9.14

Step 13: Place the cursor in an open Word file, for example, and right-click, then select "Paste."

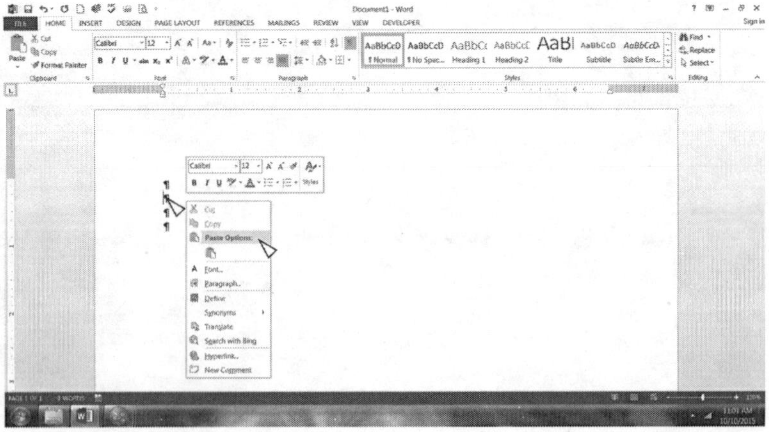

Figure 9.15

The following will be pasted into the Word document.

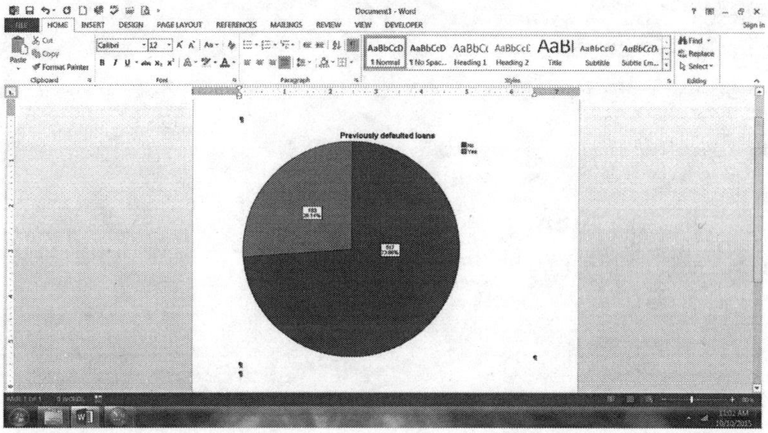

Figure 9.16

Option 2

The "Graphs Legacy" option offers a selection of graphics, including pie charts, bar charts, scatter plots, and box plots, among others.

Step 1: In the open SPSS file, do the following:

- Select "Graphs."
- Next, click onto "Legacy Dialogs."
- Last, select "Pie . . ."

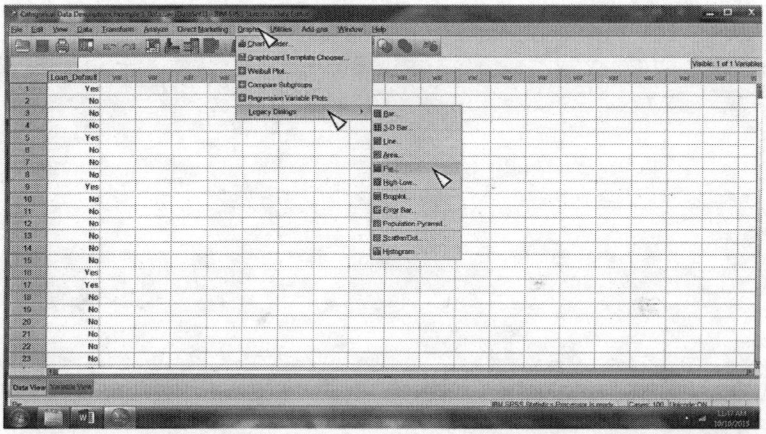

Figure 9.17

Step 2: The "Pie Charts" window will open.

- Leave the default setting "Summaries for groups of cases."
- Click the "Define" button.

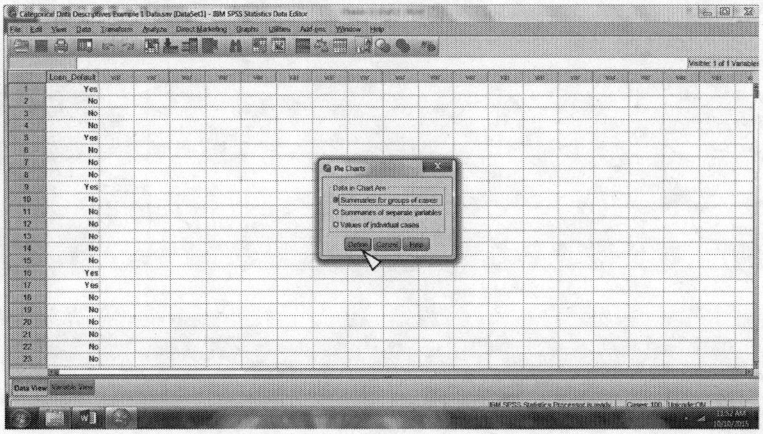

Figure 9.18

Step 3: The following "Define Pie Summaries for Groups of Cases" window will open.

- Highlight the "Previous defaulted_loans" variable.
- Click the Arrow button that corresponds to "Define Slices by."

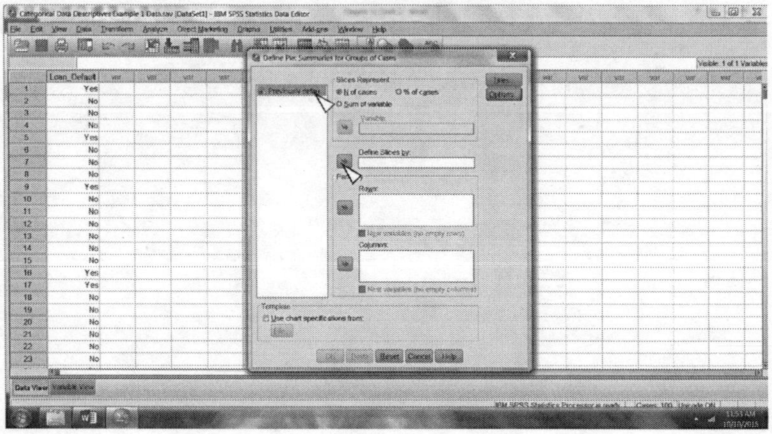

Figure 9.19

Step 4: Next, click the "OK" button located on the bottom-left-hand corner.

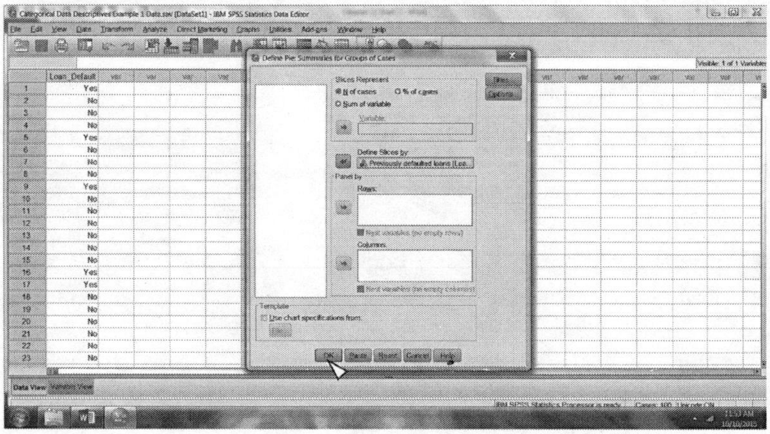

Figure 9.20

The following output will be produced.

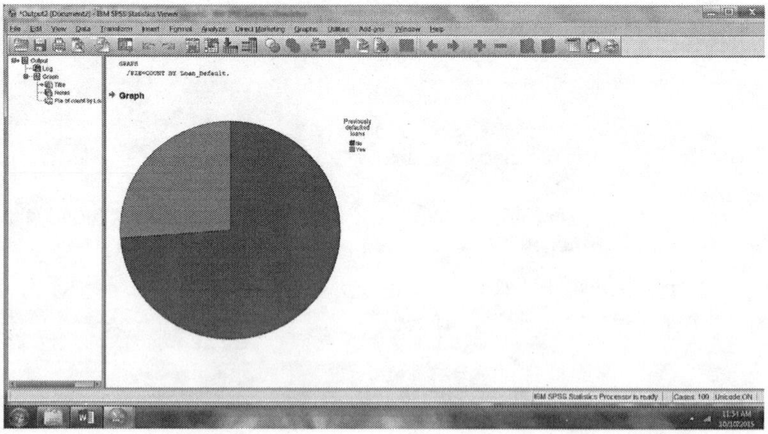

Figure 9.21

Next, follow Steps 6–11 in Option 1 for customizing the pie chart before saving the file.

Option 3

"Chart Builder" provides more options for building graphics and allows for specific types of customization.

Step 1: In the open SPSS file window, do the following:

- Select the "Graphs" tab.
- Click onto the "Chart Builder" option.

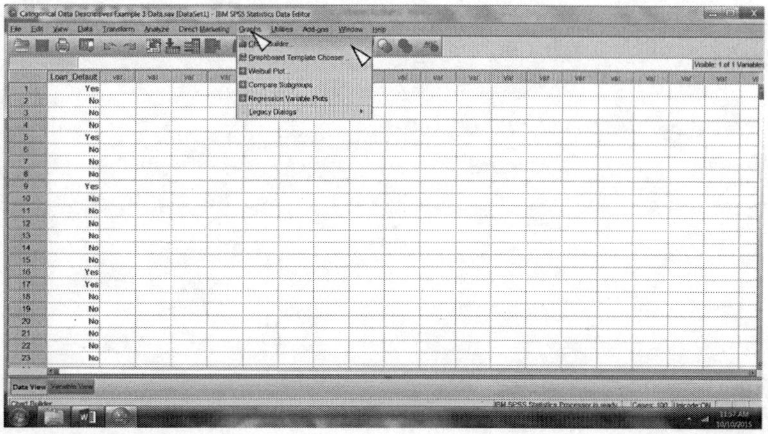

Figure 9.22

Step 2: The following "Graph Builder" window will open.

- First, click onto the "Gallery" Tab.
- Then, in the "Choose from" window, select "Pie/Polar."

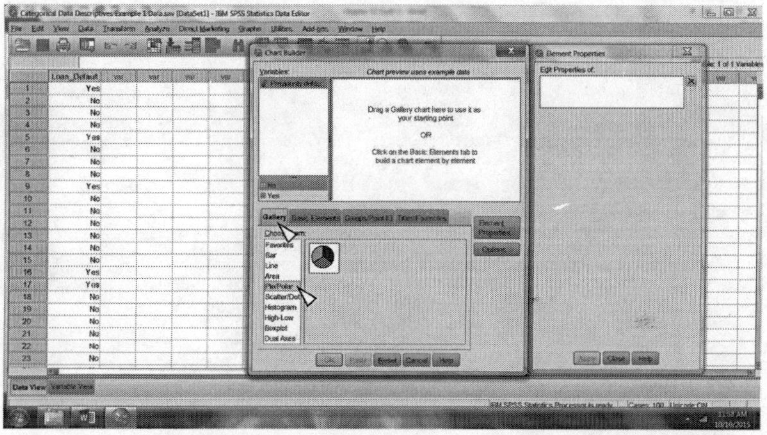

Figure 9.23

Step 3: Double-click on the pie chart image and the pie chart will then appear in the chart preview window.

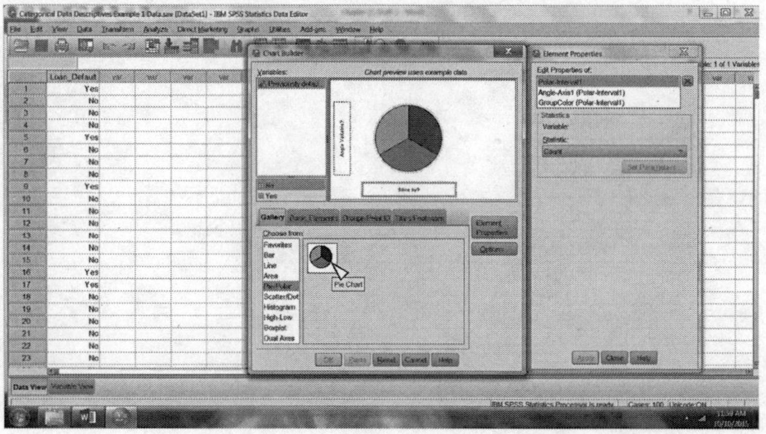

Figure 9.24

Step 4: Working from the "Variables" window, do the following:

- Drag the "Previously defaulted_loans" variable from the variable box on the left side to the "Slice by?" box located within the pie chart image on the right.

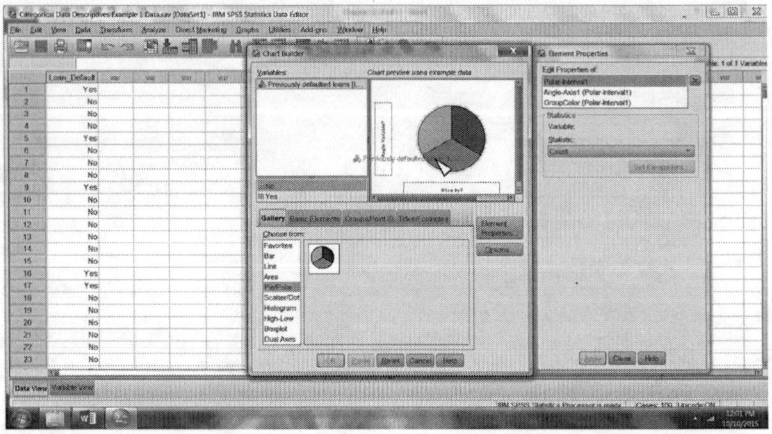

Figure 9.25

Step 5: Click onto the "OK" button located on the bottom-left of the "Chart Builder" window.

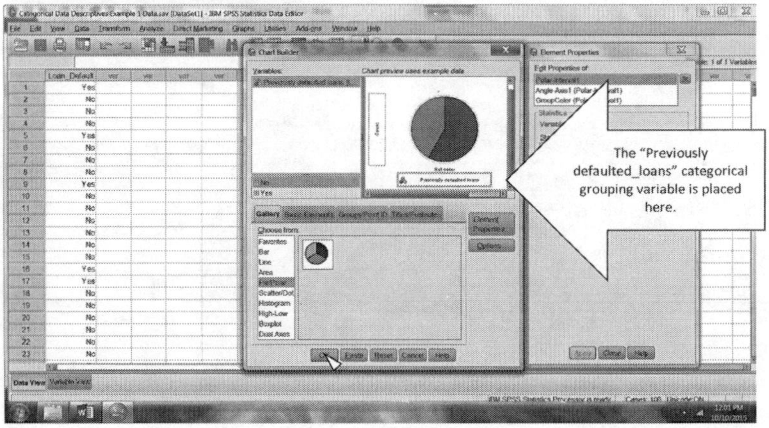

Figure 9.26

The following output will be created.

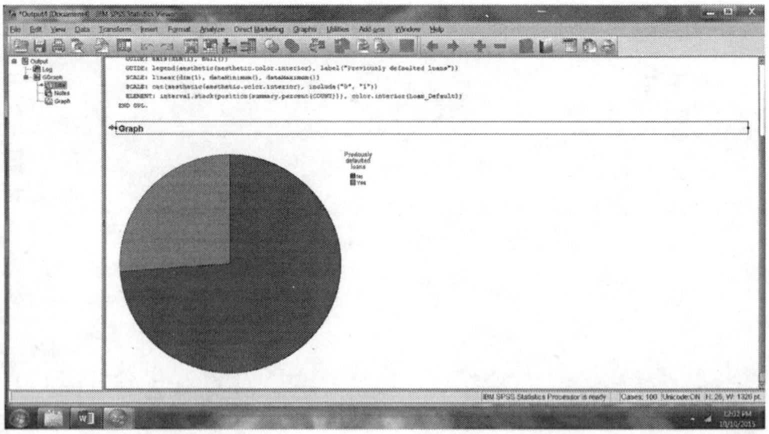

Figure 9.27

Next, follow Steps 6–11 in Option 1 to customize the pie chart. Last, save the data and output files for your records.

Describing and Reporting

The categorical variables comprise two groups about whether small businesses previously defaulted on loans: "Yes" and "No." The sample data consisted of 700 representative small businesses throughout the United States provided by the Business Agency.

Write-up

A study was conducted that analyzed the default loan rate of a representative sample of 700 small businesses throughout the United States. Five hundred and seventeen (73.9%) did not default on their small business loans. One hundred and eighty-three (26.1%) reported loan defaults. Figure 9.28 represents the breakdown.

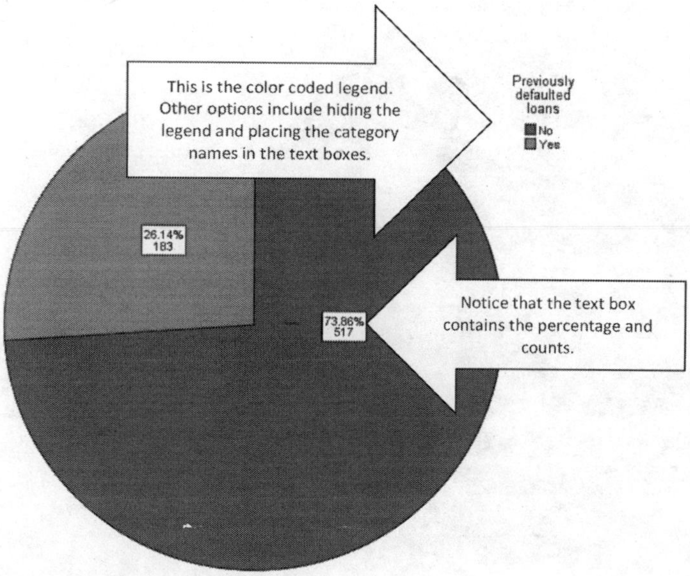

Figure 9.28 Breakdown of Small Business Default Loans

Multiple Category Pie Chart

A **multiple category pie chart** is used to depict a categorical variable with more than two categories. It should not contain more than seven categories, at which point interpreting the chart becomes challenging. Both the counts and percentages are reported. At least the **mode** or most frequently appearing category should be cited in the descriptive narrative. In the case of more than one mode (bimodal or multimodal), report all of the highest count ties.

Example 9.2: A Pie Chart with More Than Two Categories

A sample of 850 survey participants were asked their level of education based on the following possible responses: "Did not complete high school" (coded 1); "High school degree" (coded 2); "Some college" (coded 3); "College degree" (coded 4); and "Post-undergraduate degree" (coded 5). In this example, we follow all of the SPSS steps in Example 9.1 Option 1. Additionally, the legend was removed and replaced by category names. The image editing mode offers many more options. The SPSS file named "Categorical Data Descriptives Example 2" contains the data for this illustration.

Describing and Reporting

The categorical variable comprises five categories encompassing various educational levels from no high school degree to graduate degree. The sample data consists of 850 participants.

Write-up:

A survey study was conducted asking 850 participants about their level of education. The breakdown was as follows: "Did not complete high school" (54.1%, n = 460); "High school degree" (27.6%, n = 235); "Some college" (11.9%, n = 101); "College degree" (5.58%, n = 49); and "Post-undergraduate degree" (.6%, n = 5). "Did not complete high school" is the mode. Figure 9.29 depicts the results.

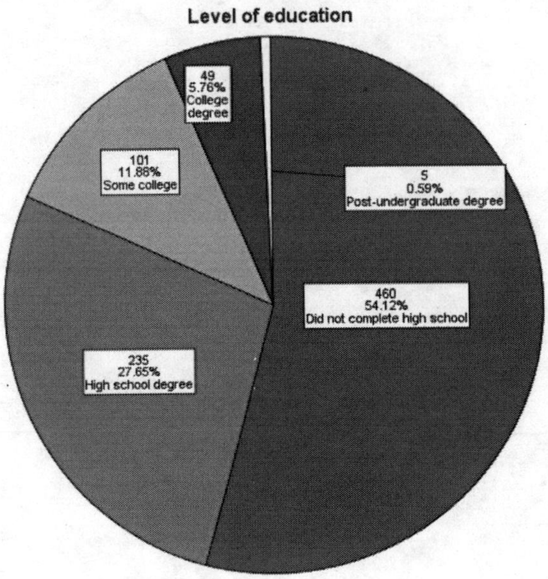

Figure 9.29 Breakdown of Respondent Level of Education

When reporting the number of a subset of the sample, use "*n*." The upper-case "*N*" is used to report the entire sample size.

Bar Chart

A **bar chart** represents the counts and percentages of those counts for each category of a (categorical) variable. The counts are depicted in vertical or horizontal bars, which can be colored. Both counts and percentages are reported. Bar charts make it easy to label, read, and understand categorical data, especially when there are more categories to compare.

Example 9.3: A Bar Chart with More Than Two Categories

Let us take the example immediately above and depict the data in a bar chart. We will skip the SPSS steps because they are identical to the procedure in Example 9.1 Option 1, with the exception of Step 4, where we would select the "Bar Chart" option. The SPSS file named "Categorical Data Descriptives Example 3" contains the data for this example.

Describing and Reporting

Write-up

A survey study was conducted asking 850 participants about their level of education. The breakdown was as follows: "Did not complete high school" (54.1%, n = 460); "High school degree" (27.6%, n = 235); "Some college" (11.9%, n = 101); "College degree" (5.58%, n = 49); and "Post-undergraduate degree" (.6%, n = 5). "Did not complete high school" is the mode. Figure 9.30 depicts the results.

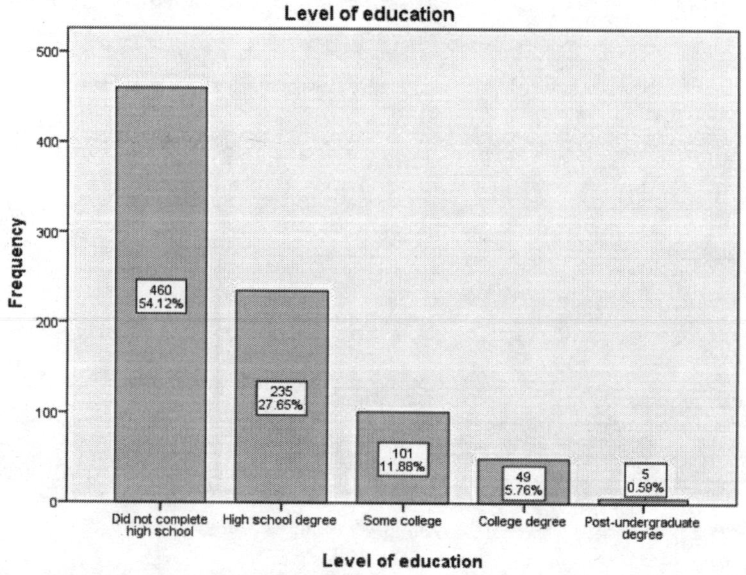

Figure 9.30 Breakdown of Respondent Level of Education

9.3 Categorical Variable Tables

Unlike typical charts, tables can represent one or more categorical variables, including overlapping or joint counts. A table composed of counts and percentages is collectively called a frequency table. A **frequency table** represents the counts of one or more categorical variables as well as the counts of the groups within the variables and between the variables. Frequency tables can make understanding categorical data easier.

In SPSS, a frequency table typically provides more information than simply counts and percentages. First, it includes **cumulative percentages**, which are the increasing or cumulating percentage as each additional group's count is added to the subtotal. Second, they are based on **valid cases**, which are the counts adjusted for missing sample data (cases with no cell data), as well as **valid percentages**, which are the percentages adjusted for missing sample data. For example, using valid values, in a sample of 100, if an analysis of two variables involves 10 missing cases, then the percentages would be based on a count of 90 rather than the total incomplete case sample size of 100. In a sample consisting of 50 females, women would comprise 55.55% (50 / 90), which is the "valid percentage." However, if the total case number were used in the calculation, the "percentage" would be 50.00% (50 / 100). If no data are missing, then the two percentages are equal. Unless there are specific reasons for using the "Percent" column values, it is best practice to use the "Valid Percent" figures. Last, these tables can provide counts and percentages for groups within groups, which is discussed in the next chapter.

Single Variable Tables

A frequency table comparing a single categorical variable with two or more categories is called a one- or single-dimensional table. It is also called a **summary table**. Let us return to the data in Examples 9.1 (previous defaulted loans) and 9.2 (level of education) and create frequency tables for each.

Example 9.4: A Single Categorical Variable with Two Categories Table

To simply create a frequency table for the data in Example 9.1, follow Steps 1–3 in Example 9.1 Option 1. Skip the chart instructions. Instead, be sure to select the "Display frequencies table" box.

Describing and Reporting

The following output is generated. Forty-two cases contain missing data. This accounts for the difference between the "Percent" column, which is based on 700 cases, and the "Valid Percent" column, which is based on the 658 cases with data. Six percent of the data was missing. Chapter 8 addresses assessing and remedying missing data.

Table 9.2 Previously defaulted loans

Previously defaulted loans

		Frequency	Percent	Valid Percent	Cumulative Percent
Valid	No	481	68.7	73.1	
	Yes	177	25.3	26.9	
	Total	658	94.0	100.0	
Missing	System	42	6.0		
Total		700	100.0		

Valid percentages adjust for missing data.

Write-up

A study was conducted that analyzed the default loan rate of a representative sample of 700 small businesses throughout the United States. The analysis was based on 658 valid cases. Four hundred and eighty-one (73.1%) did not default on their small business loans. One hundred and seventy-seven (26.9%) reported loan defaults. Table 9.3 represents the breakdown.

Table 9.3 Previously defaulted loans

Previously Defaulted Loans

Loan Status	Frequencies	Percentages
Yes	481	73.1%
No	177	26.9%
Total	658	100.0%

Note: "Yes" = defaulted and "No" = no default. Missing data = 42.

Only report valid percentages.

Only the valid cases are indicated and information about missing data is reported in the "Note" area.

Example 9.5: A Single Categorical Variable with More Than Two Categories Table

To create a frequency table for the data in Example 9.2, we follow Steps 1–3 in Example 9.1 Option 1. Again, be sure to select the "Display frequencies table" box.

Describing and Reporting

The following table output is generated. Since there are no missing data, the "Percent" equals the "Valid Percent" values. The "Cumulative Percent" totals 100%.

Table 9.4 Level of Education

Level of education

		Frequency	Percent	Valid Percent	Cumulative Percent
Valid	Did not complete high school	460	54.1	54.1	54.1
	High school degree	235	27.6	27.6	81.8
	Some college	101	11.9	11.9	93.6
	College degree	49	5.8	5.8	99.4
	Post-undergraduate degree	5	.6	.6	100.0
	Total	850	100.0	100.0	

Cumulative percentages are tallied from the previously listed ones.

Percentages or proportions can be reported as whole numbers or to one or two decimal places (xx%, xx.x%, or xx.xx%) so long as the reporting is consistent. Keep in mind that the formatting chosen can influence whether rounded percentages equal 100%.

Write-up

A survey study was conducted asking 850 participants about their level of education. The breakdown was as follows: "Did not complete high school" (54.1%, n = 460); "High school degree" (27.6%, n = 235); "Some college" (11.9%, n = 101); "College degree" (5.6%, n = 49); and "Post-undergraduate degree" (.6%, n = 5). "Did not complete high school" is the mode. Table 9.5 depicts the results.

Table 9.5 Level of Education

Education	Frequencies	Percentages
Did not complete high school	460	54.1%
High school degree	235	27.6%
Some college	101	11.9%
College degree	49	5.8%
Post-undergraduate degree	5	0.6%
Total	850	100.0%

Note: N = 850.

Multiple Variable Tables

Multidimensional tables contain two or more variables each with two or more categories so that there are joint counts. These distributions are depicted in a contingency table. A distribution involving two categorical variables is represented by a two-dimensional table. Distributions for three variables are three-dimensional. Beyond three dimensions makes interpretation challenging.

Contingency tables are generated using one of two SPSS tools. These techniques involve crosstabs or the Analysis (Custom Tables) functions. The former approach is recommended. The **crosstabs** function creates a contingency table and allows for various types of categorical variables' analyses involving joint counts. In fact, contingency table and crosstabs are terms often used interchangeably.

Two Variables

We can examine two categorical variables based on the relationship between them. Each variable must have two or more categories. For example, we can examine car color preference among seven colors by gender or occupation. We can examine the presence of high blood pressure by ethnicity.

Example 9.6: Two Categorical Variables Each with Two or More Categories Table

In this example, we construct a contingency table examining age categories by gender, assuming women (1) and men (2). The categorical variable for age group is as follows: younger than 25 years old (1), 25–49 (2), 50–74 (3), and 75 and older (4). The sample size is 995. The SPSS file named "Categorical Data Descriptives Example 6" contains the data for this analysis. The following are the SPSS steps.

Step 1: Open SPSS.

Locate the appropriate folder and data file, then click open.

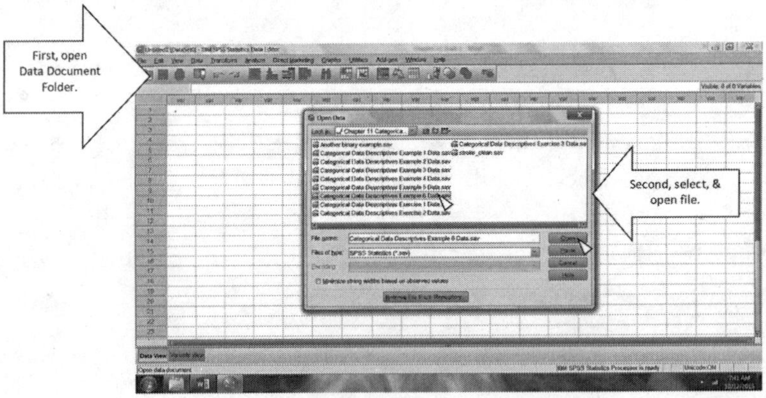

Figure 9.31

The following data file will appear.

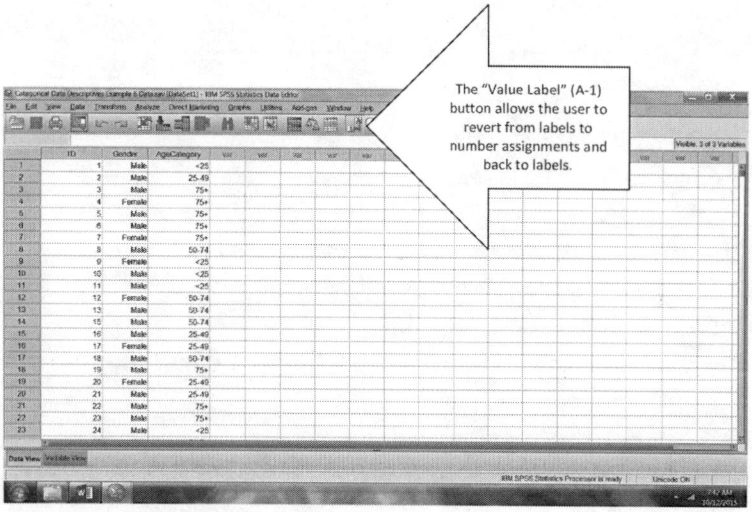

Figure 9.32

Step 2: After the SPSS file opens, do the following:

- Click the "Analyze" tab.
- Select "Descriptive Statistics."
- Last, click onto "Crosstabs."

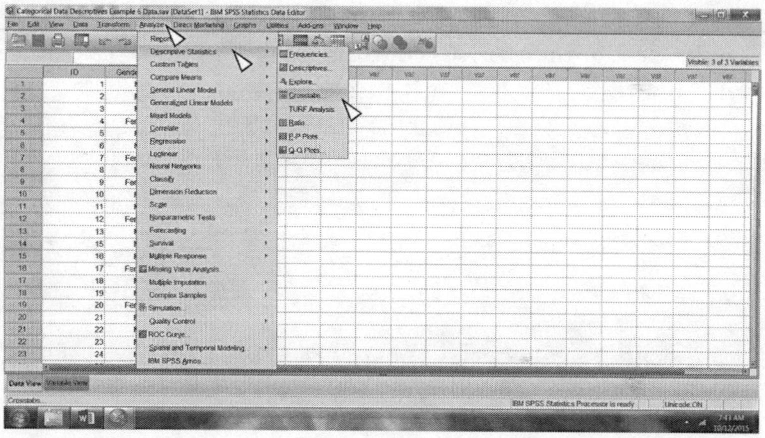

Figure 9.33

Step 3: The following "Crosstabs" window will appear.

- Highlight the "Gender" variable.
- Next, click the arrow button in the "Row(s)" window.
- Place the "Age Category" variable in the "Column(s)" window.
- The placement of variables as such should make interpretation easier.
- Last, click the "Cells" button on the right side.

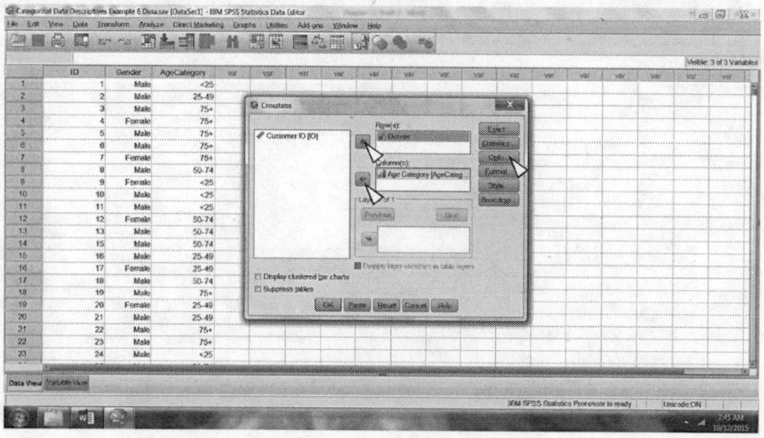

Figure 9.34

Step 4: The following "Crosstab Cell Display" window will open.

- Leave only the "Observed" box checked in the "Counts" area and "Round Cell Count" radio button in the "Noninteger weights" area.
- In the "Percentage" area, only select the "Total" box. This will provide sufficient information in order to construct a contingency table.
- Last, click the "Continue" button located in the bottom-left side of the window.

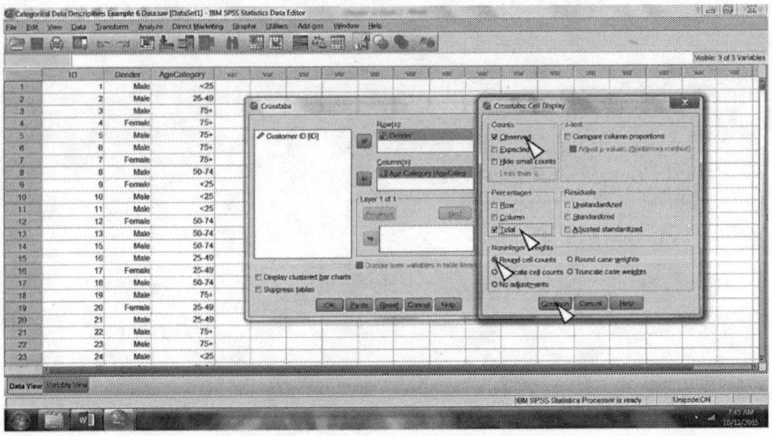

Figure 9.35

Step 5: To run the analysis, click the "OK" button on the bottom-left side.

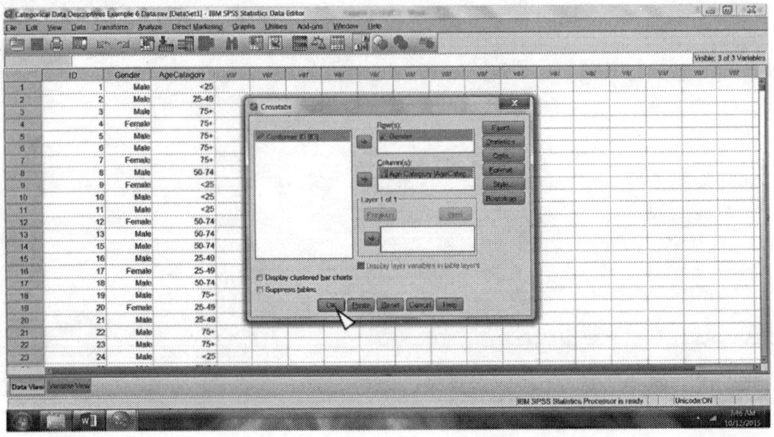

Figure 9.36

The "Case Processing" and "Crosstabulation" tables are generated in an output file. Our focus is the latter table.

Last, save the data and output files for your records.

Describing and Reporting

As represented in Table 9.6, these counts and percentage are for single and joint gender/age categories. For instance, the sample consists of 477 (47.9%) women and there are 113 (11.4%) women who are under 25 years old. Chapter 14 discusses contingency tables in detail.

Table 9.6 Gender/Age Category Crosstabulation

The age categories comprise the columns and gender composes the rows. The total age category counts equal 100% as well as the total gender counts. Chapter 14 discusses these counts in detail.

Gender * Age Category Crosstabulation

			Age Category				
			<25	25-49	50-74	75+	Total
Gender	Female	Count	113	113	125	126	477
		% of Total	11.4%	11.4%	12.6%	12.7%	47.9%
	Male	Count	129	135	116	138	518
		% of Total	13.0%	13.6%	11.7%	13.9%	52.1%
al		Count	242	248	241	264	995
		% of Total	24.3%	24.9%	24.2%	26.5%	100.0%

Write-up

A survey study of 995 participants was conducted to determine age group by gender (women and men). The age category breakdown was: younger than 25 years old (24.3%, $n = 242$); 25–49 (24.9%, $n = 248$); 50–74 (24.2%, $n = 241$); and 75 and older (26.5%, $n = 264$). Women comprised 477 (47.9%) and there were 518 (52.1%) men. Table 9.7 depicts the breakdown by gender.

Table 9.7 Age Category by Gender

Age Category by Gender

Gender	Younger than 25	25–49	50–74	75 and Older	Totals
Women	113 (11.4%)	113 (11.4%)	125 (12.6%)	126 (12.7%)	477 (47.9%)
Men	129 (13.0%)	135 (13.6%)	116 (11.7%)	138 (13.9%)	518 (52.1%)
Total	242 (24.3%)	248 (24.9%)	241 (24.2%)	264 (26.5%)	995 (100.0%)

Note: $N = 995$.

Three Variables

We can also examine the relationship among three categorical variables each with two or more categories.

Example 9.7: Three Categorical Variables Each with Two or More Categories Table

The SPSS steps are similar to Example 9.6, except for Step 3, which is where we start.

Step 3: The following "Crosstabs" window will appear.

- Highlight the "Gender" (woman or man) variable, then click the arrow button in the "Row(s)" window.
- Place the "Age Category" (18–24, 25–34, 35–49, 50–64, and 65+) variable in the "Column(s)" window.
- Next, place "Union Member" (yes or no) in the "Layer 1 of 1" box. Additional layers or breakdowns can be added. The more layers, the more difficult it becomes to interpret the data distribution. The placement of variables should optimize readability.
- Last, click the "Cells" button on the right side.

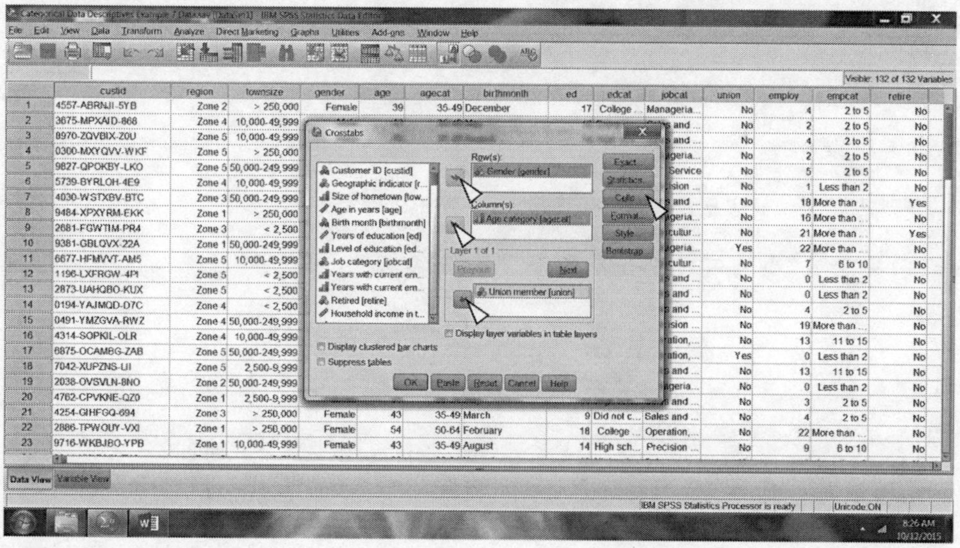

Figure 9.37

Step 4: The "Crosstab Cell Display" window will open.

- Leave only the "Observed" box checked in the "Counts" area.
- In the "Percentage" area, only select the "Total" box. This will provide sufficient information in order to construct a contingency table.
- Last, click the "Continue" button located in the bottom-left side of the window.

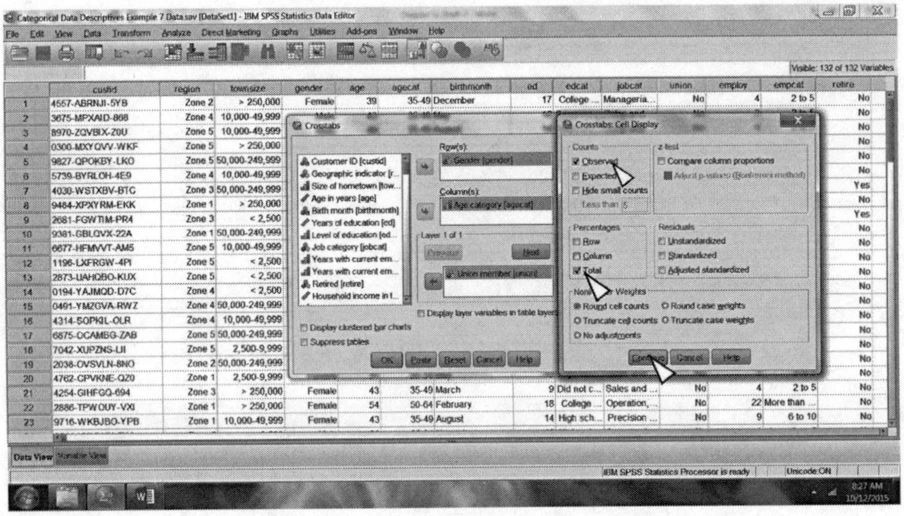

Figure 9.38

Step 5: Click the "OK" button in the bottom-left side.

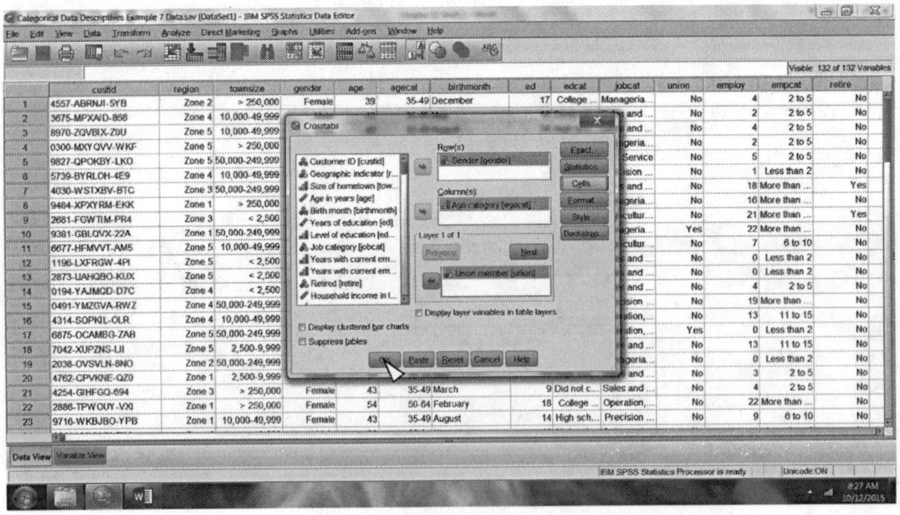

Figure 9.39

Again, an output file is generated, which can be saved.

Describing and Reporting

The contingency Table 9.8 consists of three categorical variables. Age categories are broken down to union membership status and then further categorized by gender. The total sample size is 80. Non-union members comprise 69 (69 / 80 = .8625 or 86.25%) participants and union members consist of 11 (11 / 80 = 13.75%) people. These counts are further tallied by gender. In the case of union membership, there are 6 men and 5 women. Notice that the percentages are in relation to the specific categorical variable and add up to 100%. SPSS offers options for row and column percentages, as shown in Step 4. All joint counts are depicted in the table.

Table 9.8 Gender/Age Category/Union Member Crosstabulation

The age categories comprise the columns followed by union member status in the rows, which is further broken down by gender.

Gender * Age category * Union member Crosstabulation

Union member				Age category 18-24	25-34	35-49	50-64	>65	Total
No	Gender	Male	Count	5	3	6	10	6	30
			% of Total	7.2%	4.3%	8.7%	14.5%	8.7%	43.5%
		Female	Count	4	9	11	7	8	39
			% of Total	5.8%	13.0%	15.9%	10.1%	11.6%	56.5%
	Total		Count	9	12	17	17	14	69
			% of Total	13.0%	17.4%	24.6%	24.6%	20.3%	100.0%
Yes	Gender	Male	Count	0	0	0	5	1	6
			% of Total	0.0%	0.0%	0.0%	45.5%	9.1%	54.5%
		Female	Count	1	1	1	1	1	5
			% of Total	9.1%	9.1%	9.1%	9.1%	9.1%	45.5%
	Total		Count	1	1	1	6	2	11
			% of Total	9.1%	9.1%	9.1%	54.5%	18.2%	100.0%
Total	Gender	Male	Count	5	3	6	15	7	36
			% of Total	6.3%	3.8%	7.5%	18.8%	8.8%	45.0%
		Female	Count	5	10	12	8	9	44
			% of Total	6.3%	12.5%	15.0%	10.0%	11.3%	55.0%
	Total		Count	10	13	18	23	16	80
			% of Total	12.5%	16.3%	22.5%	28.7%	20.0%	100.0%

Of the 11 reported union members, 6 are men and 5 are women.

In reporting the descriptives, the reporting table is constructed so that it is easier to understand.

Write-up

A sample of 80 women and men were asked their age group and their union status. There were 44 (55.00%) women and 36 (45.00%) men. Sixty-nine (86.25%) were non-union members and 11 (13.75%) were union members. The age group distribution was as follows: 18–24 (12.50%, n = 10); 25–34 (16.25%, n = 13); 35–49 (22.50%, n = 18); 50–64 (28.75%, n = 23); and 65+ (20.00%, n = 16). Table 9.9 represents the counts by combinations of the various categories.

Table 9.9 Age Category by Union Status and Gender

Age Category by Union Status and Gender

	Union Member (13.75%, n = 11)		Non-Union Member (86.25%, n = 69)		
Age Category	Women	Men	Women	Men	Total
18-24	1 (1.25%)	0	4 (5.0%)	5 (6.25%)	10 (12.50%)
25-34	1 (1.25%)	0	9 (11.25%)	3 (3.75%)	13 (16.25%)
35-49	1 (1.25%)	0	11 (13.75%)	6 (7.50%)	18 (22.50%)
50-64	1 (1.25%)	5 (6.25%)	7 (8.75%)	10 (12.50%)	23 (28.75%)
65+	1 (1.25%)	1 (1.25%)	8 (10.00%)	6 (7.50%)	16 (20.00%)
Total	5 (6.25%)	6 (7.50%)	39 (48.75%)	30 (37.50%)	80 (100.00%)

SUMMARY OF KEY CONCEPTS

- Categorical data is depicted using counts of occurrences and the percentages of those counts.
- Pie charts are effective representations of categorical data when there are no more than seven categories at most.
- Bar charts are appropriate when there are more than a few categories.
- Tables are broadly called frequency tables.
- Frequency tables are summary, dimensional, and contingency.
- Tables can represent complex categorical variable combinations.
- Tables can depict one or more variables each with multiple groups.
- In SPSS, charts and tables can be customized to suit reporting requirements.
- Charts and tables can be copied and pasted into applications such as Word or PowerPoint.

DESCRIBING CATEGORICAL VARIABLES APPLIED EXERCISES

9.1 What is a sample frequency?

9.2 What is a sample count?

9.3 What is a sample proportion?

9.4 What is a sample percentage?

9.5 What is a relative frequency?

9.6 What is a contingency table? Provide a brief narrative example.

9.7 What is a joint count?

9.8 Describe a pie chart using an example.

9.9 Describe a dichotomous pie chart using an example.

9.10 Define the Complement Rule.

9.11 Define a multiple category pie chart.

9.12 What is a mode?

9.13 What is a bar chart?

9.14 What is a frequency table?

9.15 What is a cumulative percentage?

9.16 What is a valid case?

9.17 What is a valid percentage?

9.18 Describe a summary table.

9.19 What is a one- or single-dimensional table?

9.20 What is a multidimensional table?

9.21 Describe a two-dimensional table.

9.22 Define crosstabs.

9.23 A pharma company ran a trial on a new cholesterol medication that lowers overall cholesterol within eight hours. One thousand and forty-eight patients with high cholesterol agreed to participate in the trial. Run descriptive statistics on the trial results based on the data available in the file. Provide a brief narrative and pie chart, including counts and percentages. The data file name is "Categorical Data Descriptives Exercise 1 Data."

9.24 A hospital wished to determine how many patients were prescribed nitroglycerin over a given period. A sample of patient records was reviewed to discover whether they were prescribed nitroglycerin. Run descriptive statistics on the record results based on the data available in the file. Provide a brief narrative and table, including counts and percentages. The data file name is "Categorical Data Descriptive Exercise 2 Data."

9.25 A healthcare research firm conducted a study with 217 people diagnosed with various eating disorders. Run descriptive statistics on the distribution of the disorders based on the data available in the file. Provide a brief narrative and bar chart, including counts and percentages. The data file name is "Categorical Data Descriptive Exercise 3 Data."

Chapter 10

Basic Probabilities for Categorical Variables

LEARNING OBJECTIVES

To be able to:

- understand the purpose of basic probabilities;
- understand and describe categorical variable basic probability;
- describe sampling with and without replacement;
- understand and explain simple, joint, and conditional probabilities; and
- learn how to calculate probabilities using the Multiplication Rule and Addition Rule.

10.1 Introduction to Basic Probability

An understanding of basic probability will make categorical variable significance testing, as covered in Chapters 13–15, easier to understand. A **probability** is the chance of something occurring by random chance. Occurrences are the counts of something taking place and its probability is in relation to other possible outcomes. We will discuss simple (marginal), joint, and conditional probabilities, as well as the Addition Rule and Multiplication Rule, as they apply to probabilities.

Usually, categorical data analysis involves counting the frequencies of groups within one or two variables. In the case of two variables, the joint frequencies overlap. These frequencies serve as the basis for the probabilities of single or joint categories occurring. For example, if we have 3 red balls, 5 green balls, and 2 brown balls in a hat, the probability of randomly drawing a brown ball is 2 out of 10 (2 / 10) or .20 or 20%, assuming that each of the 10 balls has an equal chance of being selected.

10.2 Assumptions

For our purposes, there are a number of assumptions required for random probability to occur. **Events** are outcomes (or potential categories within a categorical variable) based on counts and probabilities. First, events (e.g. colored balls being randomly drawn) must be **independent events** so that the chance of an event occurring is independent of any other event taking place. In the case of the ball example, the draw of a ball is not dependent on some other condition, nor does

REAL WORLD SNAPSHOT

The digital divide is alive and kicking, according to John Horrigan. In a 2016 Pew Research Center study titled "Lifelong Learning and Technology," he reported that individuals with access to online devices are more likely to be lifelong learners. Persons with smartphones and home high-speed connections reported the highest percentage amount of personal learning. Those who reported having only a smartphone or high-speed internet represented the middle percentage of lifelong learners. At the bottom were respondents who lacked either of these items. Figure 10.1 depicts the percentages by learning venue.

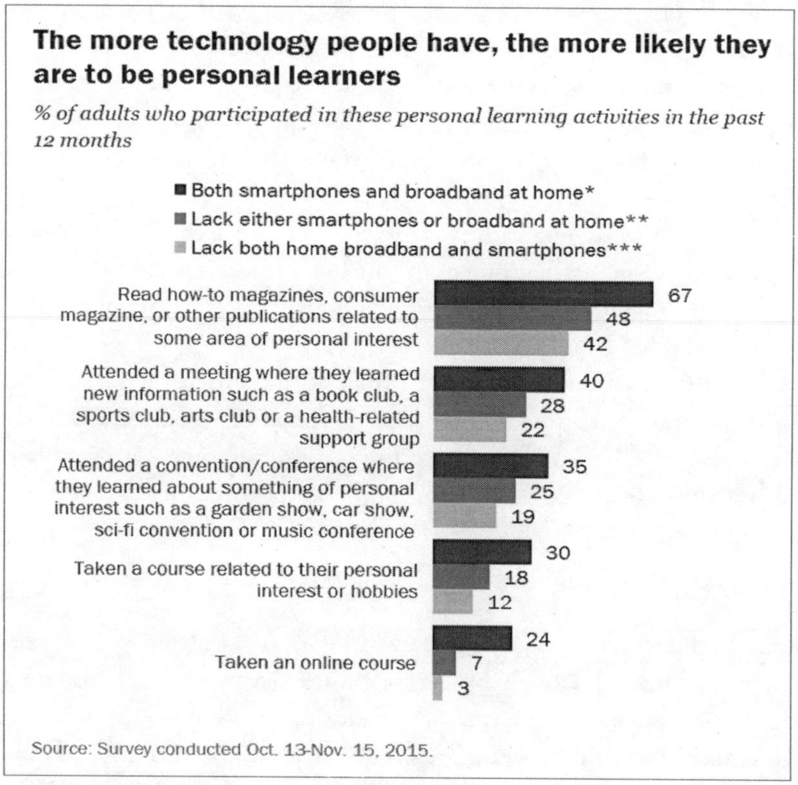

Figure 10.1 Depicting Categorical Data

Note: * 56% of all adults have both smartphones and broadband at home. ** 44% of all adults lack either smartphones or broadband at home. *** 19% of all adults have neither home broadband nor a smartphone.

Ask yourself: Can you think of any other variables that might shed light on what contributes to lifelong learning?

it affect the random drawing of another ball. In other words, the chances of selection are equal. Therefore, if we were to draw a brown ball in the example above, we will then replace that brown ball before drawing again. When an element drawn for sampling is returned to the sampling frame (source) before another element is drawn so that the chances of elements being selected always remain the same, it is said to be **sampling with replacement**. However, if we draw a ball and it is not returned to the sampling frame, the remaining elements' chances of selection change and will continue to change with each subsequent draw. This is called **sampling without replacement**.

Going back to our example, when sampling with replacement, the chance of drawing a brown ball always remains at 20%. Let us assume that we do not replace the ball. The probability of drawing a brown ball now changes from 20% to 1 out of 9 (1 / 9) or .1111 or 11.11%. In this case, the second event's probability is affected by the first event because there is one less brown ball, so that the probability of selecting the same color ball decreases.

Second, in the case of categorical variables, values or observations are counts or the number of occurrences of a specific event. For example, there are 90 out of 100 right-handed people, 8 out of 100 left-handed people, and 2 out of 100 ambidextrous people.

Third, categories or groups within the categorical variable must be **mutually exclusive**. That is to say, counts cannot be assigned to two or more categories. For example, we cannot have the following age group counts: birth–17, 18–24, 24–35, 35–44, 44–54, 54–64, and 65+. As we can see, there is overlap in the age categories. For instance, 18–24 and 24–35 both contain age 24. Some 24-year-olds may be counted in the 18–24 group while others may be counted in the 24–35 group. The following is appropriate and presents an accurate picture: birth–17, 18–24, 25–34, 35–44, 45–54, 55–64, and 65+.

Fourth, contingent upon the study goals, the categories must be **exhaustive**. All categories must be represented so that no counts are left out of the analysis. In the example above, assuming that all ages are examined, every age group must be represented. All counts in all categories must be included in order to determine accurate probabilities.

Last, the categories must be depicted in their most basic form, and at the same time capture the various joint or overlapping category counts. The proportions or probabilities are then calculated from this information. The simple, joint, and grand total counts are represented in a table. The conditional probabilities are derived from simple and joint counts.

10.3 Simple (Marginal) Probability

A **simple probability** is the chance of a single event occurring. It involves one or two categorical variables. It is an event described by a single category and in relation to the total sample size. The total sample size is the denominator (bottom number of the fraction). Table 10.1 depicts results of a study by gender about preference for one of three ice cream flavors. Two hundred individuals participated in the study. A simple event pertains to a specific gender or specific preferred ice cream flavor. For instance, 100 out of 200 or 50% (**100** / 200 = .50) of all participants are men and women comprise the other 50%, assuming binary gender. In the case of ice cream flavors, 90 out of 200 or 45% (**90** / 200 = .45) of all respondents prefer chocolate ice cream. Therefore, a simple event is calculated as:

Count for specific event / Count of total sample

Simple probabilities are also called marginal probabilities because they occur in the margins of the matrix, as shaded in Table 10.1.

Additionally, when only two categories or events are possible, then the Complement Rule applies. This means that the total probability for both events must equal 100% so that if the probability for one event is 60%, the other event's probability is 40%.

10.4 Joint Probability

A **joint probability** is the chance of two events occurring at the same time each from one of two categorical variables. Thus, it is the total count of two categories based on the total sample

Table 10.1

Preference for Ice Cream Flavor

Gender/Flavor	Chocolate	Vanilla	Coffee	Total
Men	50	30	20	100
Women	40	30	30	100
Total	90	60	50	200

Note: *N* = 200

Men comprise 100/200 = .50 or 50% of the sample.

Women comprise 100/200 = .50 or 50% of the sample.

Chocolate ice cream is the preference for 90/200 = .45 or 45% of the sample.

Table 10.2

Of all of the respondents, 25% (50/200 = .25) consist of men who prefer chocolate ice cream.

The combination of women and preference for coffee ice cream comprises 30/200 = .15 or 15% of the sample.

Preference for Ice Cream Flavor

Gender/Flavor	Chocolate	Vanilla	Coffee	Total
Men	50	30	20	100
Women	40	30	30	100
Total	90	60	50	200

Note: *N* = 200

size. These events and their probabilities are depicted in the counts or values "inside" of the table, as shaded in Table 10.2.

Like simple probability, a joint probability is always based on the total sample size count. In Table 10.2, 200 is in the denominator and the numerator consists of the count of the two events. A joint probability is the intersection of the two events. For instance, the probability of women and coffee ice cream is 30 out of 200 or 15% (**30** / 200 = .15). Of all respondents, 15% consist of women who prefer coffee ice cream. Of all respondents, 25% (**50** / 200 = .25) consist of men who prefer chocolate ice cream. When interpreting and reporting joint probability, it is important to include that the proportion is in relation to the total sample size. Therefore, a joint event is calculated as:

Count for Event 1 + Count for Event 2 / Count of total sample

10.5 Conditional Probability

Conditional probability is the chance of an event occurring within a subgroup of the total sample. It is the total count of a category (or event occurring) within a subset of the sample. A conditional probability is the chance of occurring given a category in the sample. Think of it as the chance of an event occurring within a category.

Table 10.3

Among men, 30% (30/100 = .30), prefer vanilla ice cream.

Preference for Ice Cream Flavor

Gender/Flavor	Chocolate	Vanilla	Coffee	Total
Men	50	30	20	100
Women	40	30	30	100
Total	90	60	50	200

Note: N = 200

Among those who prefer chocolate ice cream, 44.44% (40/90 = .4444) are women.

The subtotal category count within the sample is the denominator and the numerator is the count for the specific event. In Table 10.3, given men (or within the category of men), how many prefer vanilla ice cream? The answer is **30** / 100 or .30. Therefore, of all of the men, 30% prefer vanilla ice cream. Of those respondents who prefer chocolate ice cream (within the chocolate preference category), how many are women? Given the chocolate selection, 44.44% (**40** / 90 = .4444) are women. As we can see, conditional probabilities are not clearly evident in the contingency table. They must be calculated from the available information.

10.6 Tables

Basically, tables are one-dimensional or two-dimensional. The former is also called a summary table and the latter is commonly known as a contingency table. A single-dimensional table consists of one categorical variable with two or more categories. Only simple probabilities can be calculated for a single variable table, as shown in Table 10.4. For instance, the probability of a person preferring water activities is 102 / 320 = .319 or nearly 32%. Here, there are three categories that must total 100% or 1.00.

Some tables are more complex or contingent upon other events. They involve combinations of two (and sometimes more) categorical variables, each of which has two or more categories. In Table 10.5, the age variable is defined as "younger" and "older."

Table 10.4

Observed Preferred Type of Vacation Activity

Activity	Frequencies	Percentages
Land	120	37.5%
Water	102	31.9%
Air	98	30.6%
Total	320	100.0%

Note: N = 320

Preferred type of vacation activity is not broken down by another categorical variable.

Table 10.5

Below preferred type of vacation activity categorical variable is broken down by the age group categorical variable.

Vacation Activity Preference by Age Category

Activity/Age Category	Younger Category	Older Category	Total
Land	10 (3.1%)	110 (34.4%)	120 (37.5%)
Water	62 (19.4%)	40 (12.5%)	102 (31.9%)
Air	80 (25.0%)	18 (5.6%)	98 (30.6%)
Total	152 (47.5%)	168 (52.5%)	320 (100%)

Note: $N = 320$.

As we can see, the entire sample is necessary for a full range of probability computations.

10.7 Multiplication Rule in Probability

The **Multiplication Rule** in statistics is used to determine the probability of two or more events occurring such as events A and B. Since the events are assumed to be independent, the probability is calculated by taking the cross-product of each probability (in other words, the probabilities are multiplied by each other). For instance, if we wish to know the probability of flipping a coin twice resulting in two heads, we would calculate the following: .50 × .50 = .25, which indicates that the chances of flipping a coin twice resulting in two heads is 25%. The chances of flipping a coin three times resulting in three heads would be: .50 × .50 × .50 = .125 or 12.5%. The formula is as follows:

$$\text{probability of event}_1 \times \text{probability of event}_2 \times \ldots \text{probability of event}_k$$
$$= \text{probability of events occurring}$$

where

k = number of events occurring

10.8 Addition Rule in Probability

The **Addition Rule** in statistics is used to determine the probability of one or another event occurring such as event A or event B. Since the events are assumed to be independent, the probability of one of the events taking place is calculated by simply adding together the probabilities of each occurring. For example, the probability of flipping a coin resulting in a heads or tails is: .50 + .50 = 1.00 or 100%. The formula is as follows:

$$\text{probability of event}_1 + \text{probability of event}_2 + \ldots \text{probability of event}_k$$
$$= \text{probability of events occurring}$$

where

k = number of events occurring

SUMMARY OF KEY CONCEPTS

- There are three types of basic probabilities involving categorical variables: simple, joint, and conditional.
- Sampling can be with or without the replacement of drawn elements.
- Events are outcomes based on probabilities.
- Events are based on categories within a variable and may involve simple or joint counts.
- The categories that potentially comprise events are mutually exclusive and exhaustive
- The Multiplication Rule and the Addition Rule are used to calculate the probabilities involving two or more events, or one or another event, occurring.

CATEGORICAL DATA PROBABILITY APPLIED EXERCISES

10.1 Define probability.

10.2 Define event and provide an example.

10.3 What is an independent event?

10.4 What is sampling with replacement?

10.5 What is sampling without replacement?

10.6 Concerning categorical variables, what does mutually exclusive mean?

10.7 In the case of categorical variables, define exhaustive.

10.8 Define simple probability.

10.9 Define joint probability.

10.10 Define conditional probability.

10.11 What is the Multiplication Rule?

10.12 What is the Addition Rule?

10.13 The following are counts for home design preferences for potential homeowners:

Saltbox: 30
Raised Ranch: 105
Colonial: 100
Garrison: 25
Tutor: 50
Contemporary: 40

$N = 350$

What are the probabilities that potential homeowners will prefer each home design?

10.14 Based on their undergraduate majors, students were asked about their intention to attend graduate school. There were two categorical variables. The first variable was about graduate school intention where respondents selected one of three possible answers: “No Intention,” “Undecided,” and “Intends to Go.” The responses were categorized by major: “Healthcare,” “Math/Science,” “Engineering,” “Business,” and “Education.” The following is the contingency table representing only frequency (count) data. Note that such a table would normally include relative frequencies (percentage proportions).

Interest in Graduate School by Major Category

Intent to Go to Graduate School	Health-care	Math/ Science	Engin-eering	Busi-ness	Edu-cation	Total
No Intention	8	13	23	29	7	80
Undecided	11	7	9	7	6	40
Intends to Go	12	10	10	8	40	80
Total	31	30	42	44	53	200

Note: $N = 200$.

Prepare a table that includes proportions. In narrative, indicate all of the simply, joint, and conditional probabilities. Be sure to interpret your results in plain English.

10.15 Why must categorical choices be mutually exclusive and exhaustive?

10.16 What is the Complement Rule?

10.17 What is a marginal probability and why is it called so?

10.18 Do conditional probabilities require information about marginal probabilities?

10.19 When applying the Multiplication Rule to probability analysis, what is an important assumption?

10.20 What is the difference between the Multiplication Rule and the Addition Rule?

Chapter 11

The Concepts of Data Distribution, Probability Values, and Significance Testing

LEARNING OBJECTIVES

To be able to:

- understand and describe the role of normal distribution in probability statistics when analyzing numeric data;
- understand and explain what is a standard deviation and its place in the normal distribution;
- understand *z*- and *t*-distributions;
- calculate and understand *z*-scores;
- understand and interpret the *p*-value;
- define what is acceptable risk in terms of alpha;
- understand what is statistical significance;
- understand and describe what is a confidence interval;
- know how to assess whether results are statistically significant; and
- describe what is a chi-square test for categorical data.

11.1 Introduction to Data Distribution and Probability

This chapter explains concepts that are both abstract and concrete at the same time. The normal distribution, chi-square distribution, probabilities (statistical chance of something occurring), and how they relate to each other are abstract to many individuals, especially since they are constructs that we do not think about in our everyday lives. Yet these concepts have concrete applications to real world situations.

Let us start by defining some key terms. **Observations**, **data**, **data points**, and **values** are the information that we collect and are used interchangeably. An effect is a result, finding, or outcome derived from statistical analysis. An **effect** is statistically significant. A statistically significant effect is meaningful because it is not likely to occur by random chance. *It is important to know and report that the findings are "likely" results because the probability of their occurring by chance is low, but still possible.* **Distribution** is where data values or measured observations fall when examined together as a variable. **Normality** or **normally distributed** data is symmetrical like a bell-shaped curve. Last, when we refer to sample data, we assume that the data were randomly collected and are representative of the target population. In principle, **random sampling** is defined as the condition where every element or data source has an equal chance of being selected. Sampling techniques are deployed to approximate this condition as closely as possible.

The normal distribution is an important concept in statistics. Depending on what is measured, most phenomena are normally distributed. For example, a demographic study of Canadians might yield an average age of 41 years old. Some Canadians would be very young, others would be very old, but most would be closer to 41, whether younger or older.

In the case of numeric data, the normal distribution serves as the basis for probabilities, which we will discuss later in this chapter. Most sample observations are somewhat less than or somewhat greater than the **mean** (average value or observation). As illustrated in Figure 11.1, the number of values decrease as they deviate more from the mean.

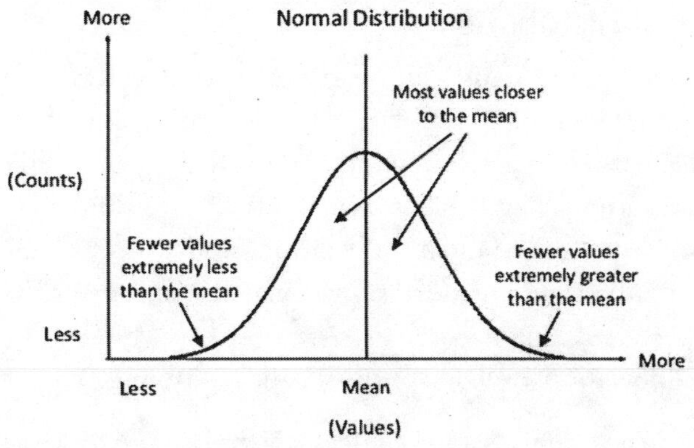

Figure 11.1 Normal Distribution

Chi-square probability distribution is based on a series of distributions that pertain to categorical data. It is dependent on the number of categories or groups within the categorical variable. With categorical variables, which consist of counts, data can only be whole numbers where the probability is about the group count in relation to the total sample. Because of this attribute, tests involving the chi-square distribution are part of **nonparametric statistics**, which is a type of probability statistics based on the degrees of freedom (number of groups within the variable), and oftentimes the data are rank ordered. Nonparametric statistics does not require normally distributed data.

A probability is the chance of something occurring by random chance. At some level, we often consider probabilities in our decision-making, whether at work or in our personal lives. Recall high school and the senior prom? I recall one friend who would not ask a fellow student to the prom unless he "assessed" that the chances of the person accepting his invitation were "high." This assessment practice does not change in adulthood. For instance, before one decides to voluntarily assume new tasks at work, at some level one assesses whether she or he can successfully and effectively complete the work. In both of these examples, a rudimentary probability is calculated and serves as the basis for decision-making.

Probability statistics is a scientific and systematic approach for determining the chances of events occurring and being meaningful based on the attributes of a sample. For instance, we can uncover whether actual seating wait times in a restaurant are different from a presumed time. We can also determine if there is a relationship between wait time and day of the week or time of the day. These approaches can be applied to categorical data as well as numeric data. As you will see, statistical methods are formal, systematic, and usually more accurate than our everyday informal assessments.

11.2 Numerical Data Distribution

We assume that **numeric data** can be Likert scale, interval, or ratio-level. Numeric variables arise from a measuring process. In statistics, a bell-shaped distribution of random observations (collected data) is said to be normally distributed, as depicted in Figure 11.1.

Many phenomena in nature, especially in the social sciences and physical world, follow the normal distribution so that populations of things, whether they are measured people's attitudes collected using a survey, machinery output from production records, or new drug trial effectiveness rates, are normally distributed.

Standard Deviation and the Normal Distribution

The sample **standard deviation** is a calculated statistical measure that applies to the sample and can be inferred to the target population. The sample standard deviation represents the typical (or standardized) difference in a variable between each observation and the mean. It allows us to determine the spread of the data distribution. The smaller the standard deviation, the closer the observations are to the mean. The larger the standard deviation, the more spread out the observations are away from the mean. The standard deviation affects the amount of peakedness of the data distribution.

To calculate the sample standard deviation by hand requires the following steps:

- Compute the differences between each value and the mean of the values.
- Square each of the differences.
- Sum the squared differences.
- Divide the total squared differences by the sample size minus 1 ($N - 1$).
- Take the square root of what was divided, which is the sample standard deviation.

The formula is as follows:

$$S = \frac{\sqrt{\sum_{i=1}^{n}\left(X_i - \bar{X}\right)^2}}{n-1}$$

where

S = standard deviation
n = sample size
X_i = individual (i) value of the variable X
$\bar{X}$ = sample mean

The differences are squared because in a normal distribution, half the values are below the mean and half of them are above the mean. The calculation results in negative and positive differences that, when added together, cancel each other, resulting in zero, which is not possible since there are differences between the individual observations and their mean. For example, in the data 2, 3, 4, 5, and 6, the mean is 4. When the differences are added, the sum equals:

$2 - 4 = -2$

$3 - 4 = -1$

$4 - 4 = 0$

$5 - 4 = 1$

$6 - 4 = 2$

$-2 + (-1) + 0 + 1 + 2 = 0$

$\sqrt{0} / (5 - 1) = 0$

$\sqrt{0} / 4 = 0$

In our example, when we square the differences, the results are:

$2 - 4 = -2 \times -2 = 4$

$3 - 4 = -1 \times -1 = 1$

$4 - 4 = 0 \times 0 = 0$

$5 - 4 = 1 \times 1 = 1$

$6 - 4 = 2 \times 2 = 4$

$4 + 1 + 0 + 1 + 4 = 10$

$= \sqrt{10} / (5 - 1)$

$= \sqrt{10} / (4)$

$= \sqrt{2.5}$

$S = 1.58$

Since we square the differences, we now take the square root of the total difference to return the variation to its original value in absolute terms. Moreover, one is subtracted from the sample size because samples tend to understate the standard deviation. This adjustment compensates for the smaller standard deviation and is thus more representative of the true population standard deviation.

In a normal distribution, one standard deviation above the mean represents 34.13% of all observations and one standard deviation below the mean represents 34.13% so that both one standard deviation above and below the mean comprise 68.26% of all observations in the sample distribution. Two standard deviations above the mean and two standard deviations below the mean represent 95.44% of all values. Three standard deviations comprise 99.74%. The curve never touches the *x*-axis (horizontal line) because we can never reach 100% probability, which is called an asymptotic function.

In sum, the standard deviation captures how far the individual observations are on average from the mean of the data. Thus, we can describe normally distributed data based on the average difference of the observations from the mean using the standard deviation. Most values, or more precisely 99.74% of the observations, fall within three standard deviations or within three times the average standardized difference from the mean. As we move away from the mean, the number of observations declines. In other words, 68.26% of observations rest within one standard deviation to the left and right of the mean. Two standard deviations add another 27.18%, totaling 95.44%. Three standard deviations add another 4.30%, totaling 99.74%, which is depicted in Figure 11.2. Any values beyond three standard deviations are considered **outliers** or extreme values. The 68–95–99.7 standard deviation distribution breakdown is called the **Empirical Rule**.

Referring to Figure 11.2, the sample mean age is 25 years old. The standard deviation for age is 6 years. As we can see, ages 19 (25 – 6) to 31 (25 + 6) years old comprise about 68% of the sample and fall within one standard deviation of the mean. Approximately 95% of the sample's ages fall between 13 (25 – [6 × 2]) and 37 (25 + [6 × 2]) years old, which is within two standard deviations of the mean. Generally, data points beyond two standard deviations are considered to have a low probability of occurring by chance. Any data points beyond three standard deviations

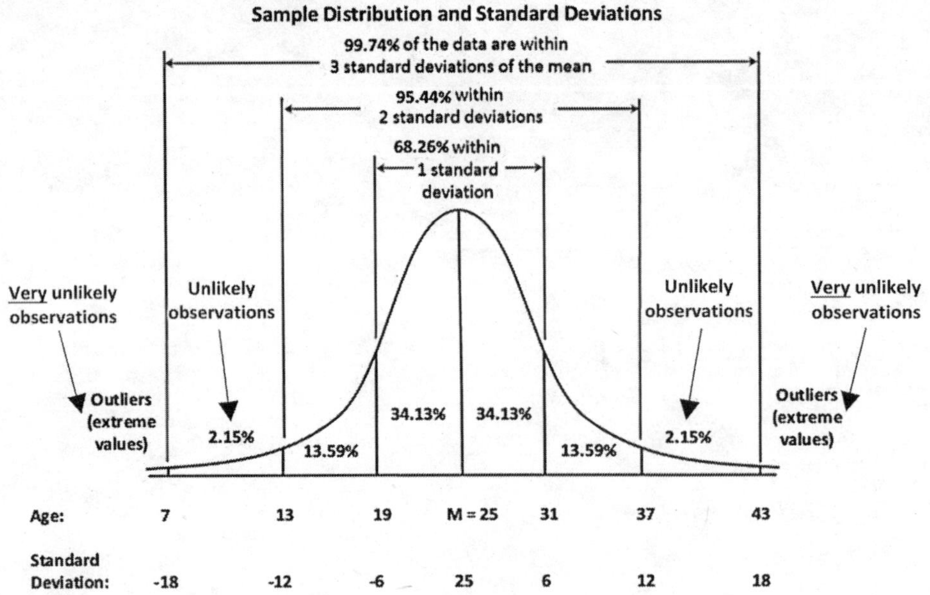

Figure 11.2 Sample Distribution and Standard Deviations

Note: Although the figures are precise, in practice, we round one standard deviation on either side of the mean to 68%. We round two standard deviations on either side of the mean to 95% so that there is 2.5% on each end of the curve remaining (tails).

are extreme values and considered to be outliers, which indicates that they are highly unlikely to occur by chance. Depending on the aim of the study, outliers may be removed from the analysis.

Assuming normal distribution, we can discover the probability of a value occurring. More specifically, the normal distribution makes it easy to identify extreme values with a low probability of occurring, as well as those that are common. Low probability results are considered to be statistically significant findings representing a meaningful effect.

REAL WORLD SNAPSHOT

Six Sigma is a data-driven approach for reducing mistakes in product manufacturing or services provided by reducing variation in their quality. It was developed by Motorola in 1986 and applied to many companies, including General Electric (www.isixsigma.com/new-to-six-sigma/getting-started/what-six-sigma/).

Six Sigma is based on decreasing the number of errors to levels that exceed six standard deviations below and six standard deviations above the average required quality of produced goods or services. Therefore, errors cannot exceed 3.4 defective parts per 1 million produced. Said differently, Six Sigma requires that 99.9999998027% of produced goods or services meet quality standards.

Is Six Sigma effective? At Motorola, sales increased fivefold, profit increased by 20%, and, over 11 years, $14 billion were saved as a result of implementing Six Sigma. At General Electric, three years after deploying it, the company saved $2 billion. After a $30 million investment in the program, Bechtel Corporation saved $200 million (www.qualitygurus.com/).

Ask yourself: Can you think of companies or organizations that might benefit from Six Sigma?

Therefore, when we refer to statistics using numeric data, we think of a representative normally distributed sample of a target population. We assume that the data follow one of two types of normal distribution.

Z-Distribution and *Z*-Scores

The normal distribution follows the Empirical Rule. A perfectly normal distribution is called the ***z*-distribution** (also called the **standard normal distribution**). It approximates a 68–95–99.7 distribution and is used to determine the probability of individual values occurring when the standard deviation of the target population is known.

In a *z*-distribution, the mean is represented as zero and the observations are expressed in relation to the standard deviation and are known as *z*-scores. A ***z*-score** is a standardized observation based on the original value. It is calculated and determined independent of the normal distribution so that the distribution remains the same whether it represents the *z*-scores or the original values.

Z-scores between –1 and 1 (standard deviation) approximately consist of 68% of the scores. *Z*-scores between –2 and 2 comprise 95% of the scores. Those *z*-scores between –3 and 3 encompass 99.7% of the scores. The smaller or larger the *z*-score value, the farther it is from the mean. Additionally, data values are considered outliers if their *z*-scores are less than –3 or greater than 3. The distribution of observations follow the pattern displayed in Figure 11.2.

Again, converting sample data to *z*-scores does not change the shape of the distribution. It simply provides information about the location of an observation in the sample distribution using the standard deviation as a reference point. Thus, observations can be pinpointed where they are located in terms of the Empirical Rule. Moreover, a number of statistics measures use some form of the *z*-score in their calculations, especially those that assess normal distribution.

A *z*-score is computed by subtracting the mean from the data point value and then dividing the result by the sample standard deviation. The following formula converts an original value to its *z*-score:

$$Z = \frac{X - B}{S}$$

where

Z = *z*-score
X = original observation
$\overline{X}$ = sample mean
S = sample standard deviation

For instance, if a math mean SAT score is 490 with a standard deviation of 100, what is the *z*-score for someone who scores 620 or 130 above the mean? Subtract the mean from the individual score over the standard deviation. This results in a *z*-score of 1.30, revealing that an SAT score of 620 is 1.30 standard deviations above the mean of 490. Put differently, if the standard deviation is 100 and 620 is 1.3 standard deviations above 490, then 1.3 × 100 = 130 and 490 + 130 = 620.

$$Z = \frac{X - B}{S} = \frac{620 - 490}{100} = \frac{130}{100}$$

$$Z = 1.30$$

A score of 620 is 1.3 standard deviations above the mean and is not considered an outlier.

The z-score applies to a given test group, where the mean is 490 and the standard deviation is 100. Thus, 1.30 is relative to the studied sample.

A z-score can be converted to its original value by doing the following:

$$X = (Z \times S) + \bar{X}$$

where

X = original observation
$\bar{X}$ = sample mean
Z = z-score
S = sample standard deviation

For example, the SAT z-score can easily be converted back to its original metric by multiplying the z-score and standard deviation, and then adding the result to the mean.

$$X = (Z \times S)\ \bar{X}$$

$$= (1.3 \times 100) + 490$$

$$= 130 + 490$$

$$\mathbf{X = 620}$$

In both formulas, sample data and statistics were used because in practice population parameters are often unavailable.

In short, z-scores help us determine where original values fall in the distribution compared to what we would expect in a perfectly normal distribution. Since in most cases the standard deviation is unknown, we turn to the t-distribution.

T-Distribution

Again, in most cases, the population standard deviation is unknown. When this happens, the sample distribution, called the ***t*-distribution**, is used. It is the distribution from which we infer to the target population. It approximates the z-distribution and is symmetrical, but varies slightly to account for sample fluctuations not present in the perfect distribution. As we can see in Figure 11.3, the t-distribution is flatter and has thicker tails, representing more extreme observations in the tails, which indicate greater fluctuations in sample data as opposed to the target population's z-distribution.

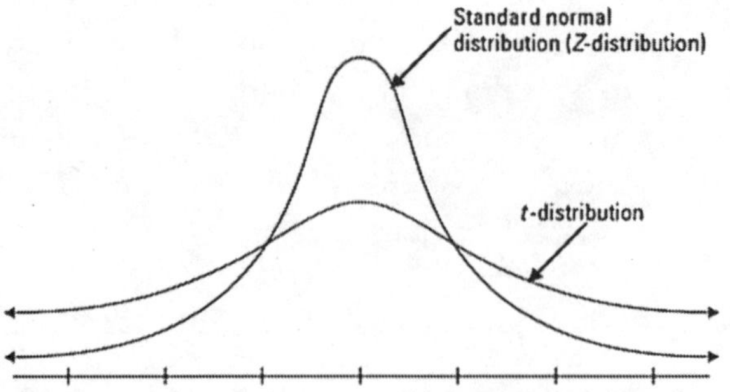

Figure 11.3 The *Z* and *T* Normal Distributions

Note: *T*-distributions can closely resemble *z*-distributions. This example clearly contrasts the difference between them.

Probability Based on the Normal Distribution

Distribution is the spread of a variable's data points as represented by the number of times a data value appears in the distribution. The distribution's attributes are discovered by data screened using graphs, plots, and statistical tests.

In short, if we expect a population to be normally distributed, then we can expect that same pattern in a representative sample of the population. For the most part, a representative and sufficiently large enough sample of a population should be approximately normally distributed.

The distribution of the data points represents the chances of specific values being selected based on their location in the distribution. Similar chances or probabilities apply to the sample and its population. For instance, assume that a population of balls consists of the following color distribution:

1 blue ball (10% of all balls)

2 red balls (20% of all balls)

4 brown balls (40% of all balls)

2 green balls (20% of all balls)

1 purple ball (10% of all balls)

The probability of selecting a green ball is 2 out of 10 or 20%. The probability of selecting a brown ball is 4 out of 10 or 40%. We assume that each ball has an equal chance of being drawn.

As seen in Figure 11.3, the instances of values diminish as they deviate further from the mean. Thus, the probability of those values occurring becomes less likely. For instance, an observation that is two or more standard deviations from the mean has a probability of less than 5% of occurring. Less than 5% indicates a low probability of random selection, thus suggesting that if it is present, it is likely meaningful. In the age example in Figure 11.3, less than 5% of sample participants are either less than 13 years old or greater than 37 years old. Therefore, if each participant's age were randomly drawn from a hat, there would be less than a 5% chance of drawing someone whose age was less than 13 or greater than 37 years old.

These same principles apply to statistical analysis. If the result has a low probability of occurring (say less than 5%), then it is likely that the effect is meaningful because it is not likely to occur by chance alone.

Thus, the condition of normal distribution is critical for probability statistics based on the number of standard deviations whether one, two, or three, accounting for 68%, 95%, and 99% of observations, respectively. Probabilities or the chances of events being meaningful are based on standard deviations. It stands to reasons that the farther an observed value is from what would be expected in a normal distribution, the greater the likelihood that the observed result or value is statistically significant (meaningful). It thus represents a real difference.

Probability Value (*P*-Values)

Since statistics involves the probability of an effect occurring, understanding the *p*-value ("*p*" for probability) is important. It is the basis of **significance testing**, which is a statistical procedure that determines whether there is no difference or meaningful result based on the probability of the value occurring. The ***p*-value** is the probability of an effect occurring, assuming that the data are normally distributed. It is expressed as a probability percentage or random chance of occurrence. The higher the *p*-value, the higher the probability that the effect in the sample data is due to chance alone. A *p*-value of .75 or $p = .75$ indicates that the chances of having this result by chance is 75% or 75 out of 100; it is a common result, and thus not meaningful. If $p = .003$, then the likelihood that the result is by chance is .3% or 3 out of 1000, which clearly demonstrates a small likelihood of such an effect taking place. It is therefore an unusual occurrence, suggesting a meaningful effect. Standards that constitute a meaningful result are discussed in the next section.

Level of Significance (Alpha) and Significance Testing

At what level does a *p*-value demonstrate a statistically meaningful result? Again, the *p*-value represents the expected probability of an effect happening, assuming normally distributed sample data. In a sense, we might say that the *p*-value is the **level of risk** that we are willing to accept when concluding that a statistical finding is meaningful and not by chance alone. Therefore, the expected normal distribution probabilities can be used to set an acceptable level of risk.

The level of risk or threshold for assessing whether an effect is statistically significant or meaningful is called the **level of significance** or **alpha**. It is set arbitrarily, but guided by standard conventions. Alpha is the maximum probability that we are willing to accept that an effect is likely caused by chance, and is thus not statistically meaningful. Remember that the alpha refers to effects that transpire within a specific number of standard deviations. Even those that are beyond three standard deviations can still randomly occur. However, the probability of their happening is very low.

Referring back to the Empirical Rule, if the effect were *within* one standard deviation, the probability of occurring would be 68%. An observed effect that is beyond two standard deviations has an expected chance of occurring of less than 5%. Therefore, there is 2.5% at each end of the two tails because we do not know whether the difference is less than or greater than in the comparison. We would expect this effect less than 5% (2.5% × 2) of the time, which is an unlikely event.

In social work, health studies, education, social sciences, and consumer sciences, the typical alpha is set at .05 or 5%. An alpha of .05 indicates that we are willing to accept a probability of less than 5% that our results are by chance alone. We can say that any results associated with *p*-values less than .05 are considered statistically significant or meaningful. Back to our age example, there is less than a .05 probability of drawing ages less than 13 or greater than 37 by chance, suggesting that drawing such an "extreme" age is meaningful. On the other hand, if $p \geqslant .05$, the result would not be statistically meaningful because the chance of random occurrence is 5% or greater and thus unacceptable risk.

We can think of this another way. Consider the curve and the values representing the differences between what is being compared. In the case of two means, equal averages would have no differences. However, the greater the difference, the more extreme it becomes so that it eventually falls in the 5% shaded area of meaningful differences (2.5% at each tail). It would be likely that the two means are statistically significantly different from each other.

For instance, Figure 11.4 depicts a bolded hypothesized true population mean of 5 and a bolded random representative sample mean of 4. The goal is to determine if the population mean differs from 5. The sample mean is "less" by one unit, which is the difference. There is a high probability of having 4 as a mean. Under these conditions, the difference of 1 is not sufficiently large enough for it to stand out and represent a meaningful difference. Therefore, we conclude that it is likely that the population mean is not different from 5. On the other hand, if the mean were 1, which represents a difference of 4 or if the mean were greater than 8, which also represents a difference of greater than 4, then there would be a statistically significant difference between the hypothesized mean and the sample mean. It would be unlikely that the population mean was 5.

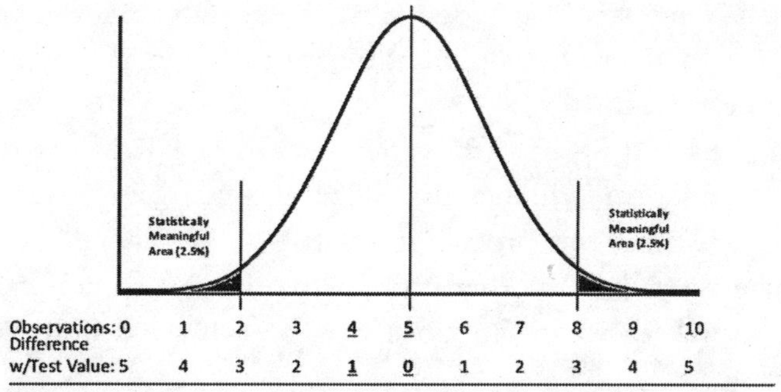

Figure 11.4 Sampling Distribution

Note: The test mean is 5 and the sample mean is 4. This figure illustrates the differences between the test mean and various sample means

Significance testing is based on the probability that there is no difference or meaningful result. The probability is that of random chance. It is important to note that we cannot calculate the probability of a specific number occurring such as 54 or 60. Numeric data is continuous and can be broken down to infinity (e.g. how many points exist that are less than 1?). Thus, *p*-values and other statistical results can only be approximated for numeric data. This is why results are reported in intervals or other ways that involve the open-ended less than (<) or greater than (>) reporting.

As we can see, where a value is located in the normal distribution of a given dataset reveals the probability of it occurring. The data points that are farther away from the mean are less likely to occur, but when they do take place they suggest a meaningful finding. *A result that has a probability of less than 5% of occurring by chance signals a meaningful result because it is rare. On the other hand, a finding that has 5% or more of a probability of occurring does not indicate a meaningful result and is considered too risky to be considered meaningful. The* p-*value is that probability based on a representative sample of the target population, and thus the results can be generalized (inferred) to that population.*

11.3 Categorical Data Distribution

A categorical variable has dichotomous, nominal, or ordinal data. The observations are the result of a counting process. Therefore, categorical data consist of counts or frequencies and the proportions or percentages of those counts in relation to the total sample size or to subgroups within the variable.

Any analysis of categorical data can only involve counting and calculating proportions of those counts for comparative purposes. Therefore, we cannot calculate a mean or standard deviation as we can for numeric data. We cannot have a count of 1.5 or 1.7. Counts are whole numbers. A categorical variable's probabilities of specific outcomes can be determined using the **chi-square probability set of distributions**, which are based on the number of groups within the variable. "χ^2" is the chi-square symbol.

The Chi-Square Significance Test

The chi-square distribution is related to the normal distribution. It involves a number of calculations, including squaring observations, and hence the χ^2. The chi-square distribution allows us to discover the distribution of count differences between and among two or more groups within a categorical variable or between two categorical variables such as the presence or absence of some attribute. Some examples are: a response of "yes" or "no" to some question such as,

"Do you support Candidate B?"; "right" and "left" handedness by gender; and worker certification rating of production equipment where there are five different types of machinery—single press, double press, triple press, laser, and heat press.

The calculations involve determining and squaring the differences in each category or group and then summing them in order to discover whether the differences between expected and observed are statistically significant. Because the probability is based on difference and not whether a difference is less than or greater than another group's frequencies or counts, the χ^2 distribution squares the differences so that there are no negative values. It starts from zero (for no difference) to extreme differences.

Degrees of Freedom

Degrees of freedom (*df*) is the number of data points that are free to vary. In some cases, all of the data can vary. In other cases, change is limited and based on a specific formula. For example, let us assume that we have a sample of six values from six cases that total 24. If five of the values are: 5, 3, 2, 4, and 6, then the sixth value must be 4 in order to total 24. In this case, $df = n - 1 = 6 - 1 = 5$.

For the chi-square test, the *df* is the number of groups minus one (1). *Df* is the number of categories where counts can vary based on the total sample count. Assume there is a binary variable where the categories are "left-handed" or "right-handed." The formula is $df = n - 1$, n = number of groups within a categorical variable. If 90 people are right-handed, then 10 must be left-handed. Only one of the two groups is allowed to vary because there is one degree of freedom ($n - 1 = 1$). If we have a sample of 210, where there were three groups, the $df = 3 - 1 = 2$. For example, 210 people select from among three flavors of ice cream: chocolate, coffee, and vanilla. If 150 selected chocolate and 50 selected vanilla, then 10 people must have selected coffee for a total of 210. In this instance, two groups are allowed to vary. When two categorical variables are considered, the formula for *df* is:

(Categorical variable$_1$ number of groups – 1) × (Categorical variable$_2$ number of groups – 1)

For example, an analysis that aimed to determine if class standing (freshman, sophomore, junior, and senior) influences whether students preferred one of three groups of course electives would require the following *df*:

df = (Four class standings: 4 –1) × (Three elective groups: 3 – 1)

$df = 3 \times 2$

$df = 6$

Figure 11.5 represents different χ^2 distributions based on the groups within the categorical variable minus one. Instead of categories, we say that the chi-square distribution is based on the degrees of freedom (*df*).

The shape of the curve is influenced by the *df* or number of groups within the categorical variable. When $df = 1$, the presence of a group is compared with the absence of that one group. When there are fewer groups, the opportunity for a difference is limited. This is represented in the curve that spikes near zero, which indicates a high probability of little difference. However, as the number of groups or *df* increases, so do the probabilities for differences increase, because there are more comparisons among groups within the variable, and thus more opportunities for variation. The change is clearly evident in the $df = 3$ curve and higher *df*. In fact, $df = 10$ is symmetrical and approaches the normal distribution.

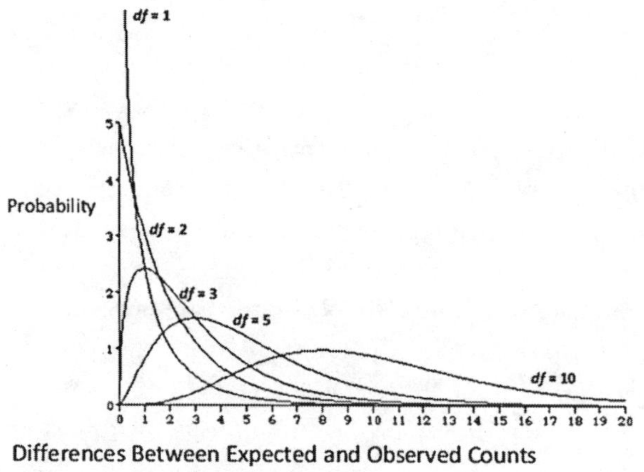

Figure 11.5 Chi-Square Distributions by Degrees of Freedom

Note: *df* = degrees of freedom (number of groups – 1)

Two Types of Expected Observations

There are two types of expectations. An **expectation** is an outcome that is anticipated based on the counts and their respective percentages in the sample space. The first is what we would expect from random and equal chance. For example, if we flip a coin, the probability of a head or tail facing us is 50%. In other words, there is an even probability that either heads or tails will emerge. Imagine we have four balls in a hat. One ball is red, another is blue, another is white, and the fourth ball is green. There is a 25% probability or chance that the ball will be blue, for example. Each colored ball has an equal chance of being selected. These probability distributions are called **uniform probability distributions** because each group within the categorical variable has a uniform random chance of selection.

On the other hand, expectations may not be uniform as in the following case:

1 blue ball (10% of all balls)

2 red balls (20% of all balls)

4 brown balls (40% of all balls)

2 green balls (20% of all balls)

1 purple ball (10% of all balls)

The random chance of selecting a green ball is .20. The probability of selecting a brown ball is .40. Therefore, not all probabilities are equal, which is called a **non-uniform probability distribution**. By default, SPSS calculates probabilities based on uniform probability. However, SPSS allows for unequal probability analysis as well, which is covered in Chapter 13. SPSS provides *p*-values for chi-square tests and includes *df* and other statistics.

Probability (*P*-Values) Based on the Chi-Square Distribution

Although the categorical chi-square distribution is different from the numeric normal distribution, many of the same probability principles apply. The statistical significance test and the level of significance (alpha) follow the same principles and interpretation.

11.4 Confidence Intervals

Another parametric estimate used more often with estimates such as the single sample *t*-test is the confidence interval. Keep in mind that a parameter is a true measure of a target population based on a randomly drawn representative sample of that population. Parameters can include point estimates such as means, medians, proportions, correlations, differences between values, and so forth. A **point estimate** is the value of a single *sample* statistic. A **confidence interval (CI) estimate** is a range of numbers constructed around a point estimate. Thus, we can develop CIs for a host of point estimates. A CI indicates the boundaries where a true population parameter lies based on a certain level of confidence expressed as a percentage.

Typically, the level of confidence for intervals is 95% or 99%, and sometimes 90%. The level of confidence indicates that, in principle, if we drew all possible samples of the sample size in question, the mean would fall within the interval at the stated level of confidence. For example, if an analysis revealed a 95% CI for a true mean between 20 and 35, then we could be confident that 95 out of 100 representative samples would have a mean between 20 and 35 inclusive. The remaining 5% would likely be less than or greater than the interval. The reason for calculating an interval stems from the natural fluctuations in samples, and thus in their means. Chapter 7 discusses types and sources of error. CIs provide further insight and information in addition to significance testing.

Let us take an example starting with the following 10 data points:

2, 3, 4, 5, 6, 7, 8, 9, 10, 11

Mean	=	6.50
Standard deviation	=	3.03
Sample size	=	10

Table 11.1 illustrates the key points about CIs. The mean is the center point of the confidence interval. The end points are included in the interval. For example, 6.50 falls in the middle of 4.74–8.26 and the other CIs. In other words, 6.50 – 1.76 = *4.74* and 6.50 + 1.76 = *8.26*. The wider the CI, the larger the difference each end will be from the sample mean. For instance, the difference increases from 1.76 to 2.17 as we move from 90% to 95%. We can see that the larger the percentage of confidence, the wider the interval in order to assure the level of confidence. Assuring more confidence comes at the expense of precision, as we can see in the wider interval and larger potential difference from the sample mean.

Table 11.1

Confidence Interval Statistics

Level of Confidence	Confidence Interval	Difference From Sample Mean
90%	4.74 – 8.26	$\pm$ 1.76
95%	4.33 – 8.67	$\pm$ 2.17
99%	3.39 – 9.61	$\pm$ 3.11

Note: Assume the same sample size for all levels of confidence and for inferring the interval of the true population means within each expressed level of confidence.

The Central Limit Theorem, which is covered in Chapter 6, plays a role in interval width. It states that as a sample size increases, it becomes more normally distributed. More normally distributed data contain less error, and thus narrow the interval. Therefore, assuming no change in level of confidence, a larger representative sample offers greater precision.

11.5 Conclusion

The probability principles and concepts discussed above can be applied to many statistical analyses involving numeric variables as well as categorical variables. The calculations for the various procedures can be summed up in the *p*-value, which provides the probability of sample results occurring by chance alone. The lower the *p*-value, the greater the chance that results are statistical significant or meaningful. Additionally, CIs offer more information that helps us understand the data better. Part IV, "Statistical Analysis," covers the various statistical procedures using SPSS.

SUMMARY OF KEY CONCEPTS

- In order to have accurate numeric data-based statistical results, the assumption of normally distributed data is important.
- Normally distributed data are assumed for numeric variables in order to determine probabilities.
- Standard deviation is a valuable statistical measure that helps determine the spread of data and can be used to compare a dataset to the normal distribution.
- The *z*-distribution is the ideal normal distribution, whereas the *t*-distribution, derived from the sample, represents a more practical picture of data.
- *Z*-scores are a way to understand the location of an observation in the distribution.
- Whether a *p*-value indicates a significance finding is based on an acceptable level of risk or alpha, which is arbitrarily set but follows standard conventions.
- Significance testing applies to categorical data as well.
- The chi-square test is used to determine statistical significance.
- Categorical data are tested in terms of what is expected compared to what is observed.
- Confidence intervals provide more information about point estimates.

DISTRIBUTION AND SIGNIFICANCE TESTING APPLIED EXERCISES

11.1 Define observations, data, and data points in statistical terms.

11.2 Define a statistical effect and provide an example.

11.3 What is a distribution?

11.4 What is a normal distribution?

11.5 What is a chi-square probability distribution?

11.6 What is nonparametric statistics?

11.7 Define probability.

11.8 What is probability statistics?

11.9 What is the Central Limit Theorem?

11.10 What is a standard deviation?

11.11 What is the Empirical Rule?

11.12 What is the *z*-distribution?

11.13 What is the standard normal distribution?

11.14 What is a *z*-score?

11.15 What is the *t*-distribution?

11.16 What is significance testing?

11.17 Define what is a *p*-value?

11.18 Relative to statistical analysis and *p*-values, what is the level of risk?

11.19 What is the level of significance?

11.20 In statistics, what is alpha?

11.21 What are uniform probability distributions?

11.22 What are non-uniform probability distributions?

11.23 Define degrees of freedom (*df*).

11.24 When alpha or level of significance is .05, explain what *p*-values of .001 and .340 represent.

11.25 What do observations more than three standard deviations out in the distribution constitute and why?

11.26 What is the basis for categorical data analysis?

11.27 What is a parameter?

11.28 What is a point estimate? Indicate examples.

11.29 What is a confidence interval estimate? Indicate examples.

11.30 What is a confidence interval?

11.31 What is (are) the relationship(s) between (among) confidence interval precision, level of confidence, and sample size?

Chapter 12

Numeric Variables: Data Screening and Removing Outliers

LEARNING OBJECTIVES

To be able to:

- understand the purpose for data screening and removing outliers;
- understand and describe the shape of a data distribution based on central tendency and dispersion;
- know how to manually calculate a mean, median, and mode;
- describe skewness and kurtosis distribution shapes;
- describe and know how to calculate the Coefficient of Variation and range;
- know how to assess normal distribution using various statistical measures;
- understand and explain how outliers can influence statistical results;
- describe the major ways to identify outliers; and
- know how to identify and remove outliers in SPSS using the simple outlier removal and outlier labeling rule techniques.

12.1 Introduction to Numeric Data Screening and Removing Outliers

As covered in Chapter 3, numeric data and statistics involve a measuring process composed of Likert-type scale, interval, and ratio levels of data. The basis of probability statistics and numeric data is the normal distribution. The sample distribution's shape is based on its central tendency and dispersion, which are discussed in the next sections. There are different types of normality, of which some are univariate (examining a single variable), others are bivariate (examining the relationship between two variables), and some are multivariate (examining the relationship among three or more variables). Measures used to examine numeric data distribution are called descriptive statistics. Descriptive statistics is used to discover the characteristics of data. It provides a summary description of sample data by variable.

This chapter concentrates on the **univariate normal distribution**, which focuses on a single variable and whether the data in that variable are normally distributed. The assumption is that a randomly selected representative sample of the target population will approximate that population and will be normally distributed. It is approximated because there is no sample that perfectly represents a population because of sampling error and natural fluctuations in the data.

Normally distributed numeric data lends itself to probability statistical analysis. Chapter 11 covers the important relationship between normal distribution and probability statistics.

Violations of normal distribution can simply involve the inclusion of a number of outliers, which can be systematically removed. Although there are various data transformation or normalization techniques available when the overall distribution is not normal, this chapter focuses on data that are largely normally distributed, with the exception of a number of outliers, which can be removed using various techniques. Therefore, the outliers are removed as part of the data screening process in a distribution that would otherwise be normal.

The following is in introduction to key concepts associated with describing and assessing numeric data distribution in a single variable. In situations where the relationships analyzed are between (bivariate) or among (multivariate) variables, the screening process is addressed in the relevant chapters in this book.

REAL WORLD SNAPSHOT

Although electronic health records (EHR) information systems can yield tremendous benefits such as better healthcare and cost savings, there has been a growing trend in undesirable practices with negative consequences. Hasan and Padman (2006) reported that 37% of patient medical records may be inaccurate and almost 70% are incomplete.

Poor EHR designs and untrained staff have caused serious EHR-related errors that lead to mistakes that threaten patient safety or, at the very least, decrease the quality of care. According to Bowman (2013), the trend in unintended consequences also may lead to fraud and abuse as well. One area of misuse is the cutting and pasting of data records without carefully reviewing the content for accuracy. Another problem is the erroneous input of data, such as transposing data, leaving out important information, and entering the incorrect gender or age. Last, EHR are not up to date, resulting in mistreatment. Healthcare practitioners are guided by patient EHR and make healthcare decisions based on the assumptions that records are accurate and up to date. The accuracy of records cannot be taken for granted, and until a uniform system is implemented across healthcare providers, EHR deficiencies will continue to plague the record system.

Ask yourself: From a general perspective, what might be the first steps to address the challenges associated with EHR?

12.2 Measuring Central Tendency

Central tendency is the extent to which data points concentrate around the mean (average) or center of the distribution. It is a measure of symmetry. The symmetry of a variable's data distribution can vary. Distributions can be asymmetric, skewed to the left or to the right, and have two or more peaks (multimodal) caused by different values influencing the data distribution.

There are a number of central tendency measures. We will focus on the mean, median, mode, and skewness statistics.

Mean

The mean is the average value of the data points comprising a variable. It is the variable's sum of its case values divided by the number of values in the sample. Outliers can influence the mean, which we will discuss shortly. The mean equation is:

$$\bar{X} = \text{sum of values / number of values}$$

where

$\bar{X}$ = the variable mean

For example, if the data are 5, 2, 4, 4, 5, 6, 8, the mean ($\bar{X}$) is:

$\bar{X} = (5 + 2 + 4 + 4 + 5 + 6 + 8) / 7$

$\bar{X} = 34 / 7$

$\bar{X} = 4.8571$

Median

The **median** is the middle value of the cases ordered from smallest to largest. Half the values are lower than the median and half the values are greater than the median. Outliers do not influence the median. The median equation is:

Median = $(n + 1) / 2$ ranked value

where

If there is an odd number of values, the median is the middle ranked value
If there is an even number of values, the median is the average of the two middle ranked values.

For example, if the data are:

Ranked values: 2, 4, 4, **5**, 5, 6, 8

↑

Ranks: 1st, 2nd, 3rd, **4th**, 5th, 6th, 7th

Median = $(n + 1) / 2$ ranked value

Median = $(7 + 1) / 2$

= 4th ranked value

Median = 5

If the data are:

Ranked values: 10, 12, 15, **18**, **20**, 22, 25, 30

↑ ↑

Ranks: 1st, 2nd, 3rd, **4th**, **5th**, 6th, 7th, 8th

Median = $(8 + 1) / 2$

= 4.5th ranked value

Median = 4.5th ranked value

Median = $(18 + 20) / 2$

Median = 19

Mode

The mode is the value that appears most frequently in the variable. If there is no one value that appears most, then there is no mode. The data can have more than one mode such as a bimodal or trimodal distribution. Outliers do not influence the mode. The following are examples:

For 1, 3, 4, 5, 4, 5, 6, 4, 7, 8, 9, 8, mode = 4

For 20, 40, 50, 60, 50, 80, 90, 100, 80, bimodal = 20 and 80

For 0, 0, 0, 3, 5, 6, 7, 8, 9, 3, 9, 3, 4, 9, trimodal = 0, 3, and 9.

Coefficient of Skewness

The median and mode statistics define the shape of the data in relation to the mean. Together, these three measures relate to the skewness of the data. **Skewness** indicates that there is an imbalance of the data values below or above the mean, which affects the symmetry in the distribution. It helps us discover the relationship of the data values to the mean. Skewness is thus a way to determine how and to what extent values relate to the mean.

A skewed data distribution is not bell-shaped. There are two basic types of skewed distributions. They are right or positive skew and left or negative skew. Figure 12.1 depicts both types compared to the normal distribution. In the first case, the data have a right skew because the mean is greater than the median and median is greater than the mode. A few outliers drive the mean higher then what would be expected based on the majority of values (mode and median). The inverse holds in the third case, where the distribution has a left skew. The mean is less than the median and mode because it is driven by a few low-value outliers. On the other hand, when the distribution is perfectly symmetrical, the mean, median, and mode are equal. These distributions illustrate why it is important to assess and address asymmetrical or non-normal distributions before analyzing the data. If the distribution is not normal, then the results will likely be misleading, producing inflated or deflated means as well as skewed probabilities.

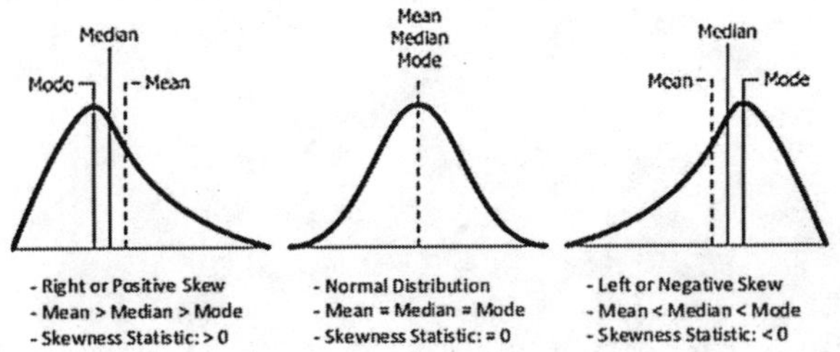

Figure 12.1 Basic Central Tendency Distributions

SPSS and other software packages provide the **Coefficient of Skewness** statistic, which measures the degree of symmetry in a variable's distribution based on the mean. The statistic can also be based on the median or mode. As a general rule of thumb, a skewness statistic from –1 to 1 demonstrates relative symmetry, with 0 being perfectly symmetrical. A positive skewness statistic indicates right skew and a negative value indicates left skew. For example, a –.20 or .20 is more symmetrical than a –.85 or .85. Less than –1.00 or greater than 1.00 represent violations of symmetry.

Let's apply central tendency distributions to data and review their descriptive statistics in Table 12.1. As we can see, the presence of an outlier skews the distribution. In the right skew case, the value 15 is an outlier. Compared to normally distributed data, the mean and median are higher. Skewness is nearly double the acceptable maximum score.

Table 12.1

Measures of Central Tendency

Descriptive Statistic	*Right Skew Distribution*	*Normal Distribution*	*Left Skew Distribution*
Data Values:	2, 3, 4, 5, 6, & **15**	2, 3, 4, 5, & 6	2, 3, 4, 5, 6, & **-15**
Mean:	5.83	4.00	0.83
Median:	4.50	4.00	3.50
Skewness:	1.96	0.00	-2.27

Note: The bold value is an outlier.

There are other types of non-normally distributed data. Figure 12.2 represents multimodal distributions. There are numerous reasons why distributions are not symmetrical. The nature of the study, the data collection mechanism, and sampling techniques can all contribute to non-normality.

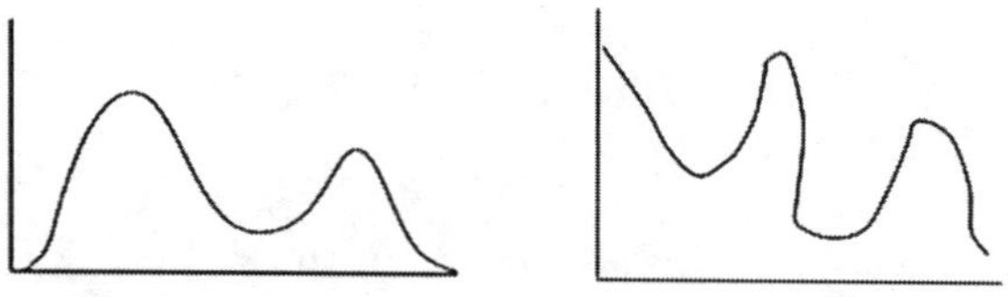

Figure 12.2 Other Distributions

12.3 Measuring Dispersion

Dispersion is the spread of the data from the mean. It is the degree to which values deviate from the mean and can be observed as the peakedness or flatness in the distribution. In other words, are the data spread out over a flat-like distribution, are the data tightly packed so that there are two short tails and a high peak, or are they somewhere in the middle of these two conditions?

There are a number of dispersion measures. We will focus on range, which involves minimum and maximum values; standard deviation; Coefficient of Variation; and the Coefficient of Kurtosis statistic.

Range

The **range** is the difference between the largest value and the smallest value. Technically, it is called the **exclusive range** because it does not include the endpoints. The equation is:

$$\text{Range} = X_{\text{largest}} - X_{\text{smallest}}$$

For example, in the following data, 2, 3, 4, 5, 6, 4, 5, 6, 3, the range is:

$$\text{Range} = 6 - 2$$

$$\text{Range} = 4$$

The smallest and largest values are also the minimum and maximum values. In this instance, they are 2 to 6. This is the simplest descriptive measure for dispersion.

The **inclusive range** includes the endpoints. The equation is:

$$\text{Inclusive range} = (X_{\text{largest}} - X_{\text{smallest}}) + 1$$

For example, in the following data, 2, 3, 4, 5, 6, 4, 5, 6, 3, the range is:

$$\text{Inclusive range} = (6 - 2) + 1$$

$$\text{Inclusive range} = 4 + 1$$

$$\text{Inclusive range} = 5$$

Most of the time, the (exclusive) range is reported.

Variance

Variance is a measure of variation in which the difference between each value and the mean are squared and then summed. The summed total is then divided by the sample size minus 1. This provides a measure of the average variation from the mean. The formula is:

$$\text{Variance} = \frac{\sum_{i=1}^{n}(X_i - \bar{X})^2}{n-1}$$

where

n = sample size
X_i = individual (i) value of the variable X
$\bar{X}$ = sample mean

From the data 2, 3, 4, 5, and 6, the variance is:

2 – 4	=	–2 × –2	=	4
3 – 4	=	–1 × –1	=	1
4 – 4	=	0 × 0	=	0
5 – 4	=	1 × 1	=	1
6 – 4	=	2 × 2	=	4
4 + 1 + 0 + 1 + 4			=	10
Variance			=	10 / (5 – 1)
Variance			=	2.5

Standard Deviation

The sample standard deviation represents the typical (standardized) difference in a sample dataset between each value and its mean. The smaller the standard deviation, the closer the observations are to the mean. The larger the standard deviation, the more spread and further away the observations are from the mean. The standard deviation determines the flatness or peakedness of the data distribution curve.

Coefficient of Variation

The **Coefficient of Variation (CV)** is a statistic that represents the standard deviation as a percentage of the mean. For instance, if the standard deviation is 50 and the mean is 200, then the CV is 25%. Likewise, if the CV is 150% and the mean is 200, then the standard deviation is 150% of the mean, and thus it is 300. Larger CVs are associated with flatter and spread out distributions. Smaller CVs are associated with a greater peak and concentrated distributions. The formula is:

CV = (Sample Standard Deviation / Sample Mean) × 100

What if there are similar standard deviations but different means? A larger mean would result in a smaller CV, whereas a smaller mean would result in a larger CV. In the latter case, the standard deviation represents a larger percentage of a smaller mean. For example, if the standard deviation is 1.5 and mean is 6, then the CV is 25%. On the other hand, if the standard deviation is 1.5 and mean is 5, then the CV is 30%.

Coefficient of Kurtosis

The **Coefficient of Kurtosis** statistic measures the degree of peakedness or flatness in the distribution based on the standard deviation. As a general rule of thumb, kurtosis from −1 to 1 demonstrates a relatively normal peak in the distribution, with 0 being perfect. A positive kurtosis statistic indicates more peak and a negative value indicates more flatness.

There are three basic types of kurtosis, as depicted in Figure 12.3.

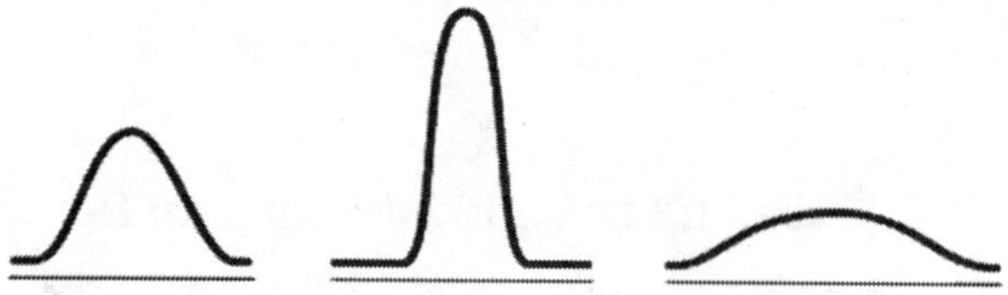

Figure 12.3 Kurtosis

- A **mesokurtic distribution** is the normal distribution. The peak of this distribution is neither high nor low. It is considered to be a baseline for the other two classifications. A mesokurtic distribution that is perfectly distributed has a kurtosis statistic equal to 0. Its CV and standard deviation are between those of the leptokurtic and platykurtic distributions.
- The **leptokurtic distribution** has a high peak that is thin and tall. The tails of the distribution are relatively short and heavy. The data values are concentrated in the center more so than a normal distribution. The leptokurtic distribution has a kurtosis statistic greater than 0 because of its high peak. The CV and standard deviation are smaller than those of the mesokurtic or platykurtic distributions.
- A **platykurtic distribution** is flat (low peak) and the data are spread out more than the normal distribution. Both tails are long. The platykurtic distribution has a kurtosis statistic less than 0, which represents flat distributions. The CV and standard deviation are larger than those of the mesokurtic or leptokurtic distributions.

Table 12.2 depicts the effect of outliers on dispersion. As we can see below, removing them reduces the spread of the data and influences the overall shape of the distribution. Outliers increase the minimum and maximum values, thus they increase the range. Outliers also increase the standard deviation, CV, and can change the kurtosis statistic. In the case of the leptokurtic distribution, the higher statistical measures are consistent with data that contains outliers. The platykurtic data represents a flat distribution.

Like what skewness is to central tendency and distribution symmetry, **kurtosis** is a general measure of peakedness or flatness in the distribution. Together, they constitute the total shape of the data distribution.

Table 12.2

Measures of Dispersion

Descriptive Statistics	*Leptokurtic Distribution*	*Mesokurtic (Normal) Distribution*	*Platykurtic Distribution*
Data Values:	**−8**, 2, 4, 5, 5, 6, 6, 6, 7, 8, & **16**	2, 4, 5, 5, 6, 6, 6, 7, & 8	2, 4, 5, 6, 7, 8, 9, 10, & 11
Min./Max.:	−8.00–16.00	2.00–8.00	2.00–11.00
Range:	24.00	6.00	9.00
Mean	5.18	5.44	6.89
Stand. Deviation:	5.61	1.74	2.93
CV	1.08%	32%	42%
Kurtosis:	3.94	0.99	−.76

Note: The bold values are outliers. The mean is included because it is required to calculate the CV.

The discussion above is meant to provide a sufficient introduction to the important factors for determining and assessing data distribution. Below is a discussion of the key tools for evaluating distributions followed by approaches that assess and remedy outlier violations of normality.

12.4 Screening Data: Identifying and Removing Outliers

Our focus is to determine the overall normality in the distribution followed by identifying and removing outliers in a distribution that would otherwise be fairly normal. There are numerous descriptive visual and statistic tools available for describing and assessing distributions. A visual inspection of the distribution is a good start because it provides an overview of the distribution as well as context for where and how outliers impact the distribution. Next, the skewness, kurtosis, and Shapiro-Wilk statistics, which directly or indirectly incorporate the statistics covered above, offer precise measures of distribution, especially valuable when screening very large datasets. We will conduct these analyses for identifying and removing outliers using SPSS. First, let us start by understanding a bit more about outliers.

Outliers

According to Tabachnick and Fidell (2013), there are a number of basic causes for outliers. First, data may have been incorrectly entered. Second, coding that indicates missing data could be mistakenly read as actual data. Third, some of the sources of data are not from the targeted population resulting in outliers. Last, a flaw in the measurement metric can cause outliers such as a range restriction in values so that some observations become skewed indicating a ceiling or floor effect. In other cases, the research or sampling design failed to account for extreme values in underrepresented but targeted subgroups. For instance, in a study aimed at determining the level of social service usage for clients, including those people "off the grid," survey questions may not accommodate their unique needs or provide a full range of potential responses.

Keep in mind that the removal or retention of outliers depends also on the study aim. Some research may examine for new trends, which alert decision-makers to potential areas of concern. For example, the emergence of foreclosures in a stable real estate market or the appearance of an exotic disease may signal changes in the status quo. Therefore, it is important for outlier policy to be informed by the study goal and objectives.

The identification of outliers and whether any or all of them are removed depends on the shape of the data distribution. Arguably, some experts note no more than 10% of the data should be removed because there is the potential for altering the nature of the variable's data and its relationship to other variables. Based on the distribution, identifying and selecting which outliers to remove can yield significantly different results. In more extreme violations of normal distribution, data transformations in conjunction with outlier removal may be more appropriate, especially when achieving normality would require removing more than 10% of the data. Unless there is a sound reason to include outliers, every effort should be made to remove them.

Visual Assessment

There are numerous visual tools available to assess for outliers. The Normal Q-Q Plot and simple dot plot are excellent graphical tools. The **Normal Q-Q Plot** places observations along a straight line that represents a perfect normal distribution. Any values off the line are potential outliers depending on their location off the line. The **simple dot plot** depicts the observations as dots in a distribution, which, in turn, can be visually evaluated. Both methods allow for the identification and removal of outliers. They are demonstrated in the examples section.

Statistical Measures

Along with visual representations of the data, statistical measures describe the data and its distribution by reporting the mean, median, standard deviation, minimum/maximum values, range, skewness and kurtosis statistics, and other statistics, including the important Shapiro-Wilk statistic.

The **Shapiro-Wilk test** is one among a number of significance tests used to evaluate whether a data distribution approximates a normal distribution. If the *p*-value is significant (less than the alpha), then it is likely that the distribution does not approximate normality. Generally, significant results have a *p*-value of less than .05.

Methods for Identifying and Removing Outliers

Some of the basic methods for identifying and removing outliers are: (1) the simple outlier removal approach; (2) standardizing scores and then removing outliers guided by their *z*-scores and the standard deviation; (3) trimming or truncating; (4) winsorizing; and (5) the outlier labeling rule technique.

Below is a brief discussion of these approaches. Again, these techniques work best when data are approximately normally distributed.

Simple Outlier Removal

The **simple outlier rule** involves identifying outliers by examining data graphs and statistical measures such as the kurtosis and the skewness statistics as well as the Shapiro-Wilk test of normality. The outliers are then removed followed by running the same analyses once more to assess for normality. Illustrations are provided in the examples section.

Standard Deviation Rule

The **standard deviation rule** involves standardizing or converting the observations to their *z*-scores, rank-ordering the *z*-scores, and then removing outliers using the three standard deviation baseline. Recall that each *z*-score unit represents the data's standard deviation. Some researchers propose that with sample sizes up to 80, all *z*-scores > 2.50 should be identified as outliers and removed. For sample sizes over 80, all *z*-scores > 3.00 should be removed.

Trimming or Truncating

Trimming is the removal of a percentage of outliers at each tail of the distribution. Usually, trimming is symmetrical so that a specific percentage of outliers below the mean and the same specific percentage of outliers above the mean are removed. The percentage removed below or above can vary based on the distribution. In the case of skewed data, trimming can be asymmetrical. A 10% trim involves the removal of the bottom 5% most extreme or lowest values and the top 5% most extreme values.

Winsorizing

Winsorizing is similar to trimming with one major difference. In lieu of removing the lower and upper-end outliers, the values are replaced with the first observation in the data that is not an outlier but next to the removed outlier. Therefore, in a 2% trim, if 2 and 3 are identified as the lowest 1%, however 4 is not in the 1%, then 2 and 3 are each replaced with a 4. This procedure is appropriate when there are no more than two or three outliers.

Outlier Labeling Rule

The **outlier labeling rule** is a multistep approach for identifying and removing outliers utilizing the 25th and 75th percentiles and a simple formula. It is an attempt to precisely identify outliers. In order to accommodate for small as opposed to large sample sizes, there is a slight variation in the formula. This method is best explained through illustration, as provided in the examples section.

Data Removal and Analysis

The removal of observations can be listwise or pairwise. In a listwise removal, the cases containing the outliers are deleted from the dataset. A pairwise removal consists of removing outliers on a variable-by-variable basis so that the analyzed sample size might vary by the variables in the analysis. If the sample size is sufficiently large, then the listwise approach is preferred because pairwise could potentially affect analyses between and among variables. Pairwise is preferred when as many cases as possible are needed because of a relatively small sample size.

Data Screening and the Removal of Outliers Assumptions

There are a number of data screening and removal of outliers assumptions. First, the data must be numeric. Second, for the removal of outliers to be beneficial, the overall data must be fairly normally distribution. Third, the sample size must be sufficiently large after removing outliers. Fourth, data removal should not exceed 10% of the original data. Finally, as best as can be known, removing outliers will not alter the nature of the data.

12.5 Examples Using SPSS: Step-by-Step Instructions

This section focuses on the simple outlier removal approach and the outlier labeling rule. The first approach is appropriate when outliers are straightforward and fairly easily identifiable. The latter method systematically identifies and removes outliers that are not readily apparent.

Example 12.1: Simple Outlier Removal

This study consists of data from 58 economists who were asked whether they think that the overall economy is stable. Responses were received via text message based on an 11-point scale ranging from 1 = "not at all" to 11 = "thoroughly stable." The data must be screened for normal distribution and, if necessary, prepared prior to analysis. Alpha = .05. The SPSS file named "Outlier Example 1 Data" contains the data. The SPSS steps are as follows.

Step 1: Open SPSS.

- Locate the appropriate folder and data file.
- Next, highlight it.
- Last, click the "Open" button.

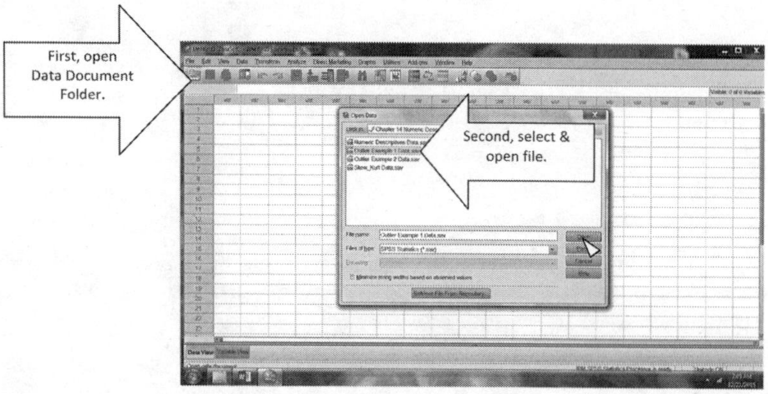

Figure 12.4

Step 2: First, we must screen the data for normal distribution.

- Select the "Analyze" tab.
- Next, choose "Descriptive Statistics."
- Last, click "Explore."

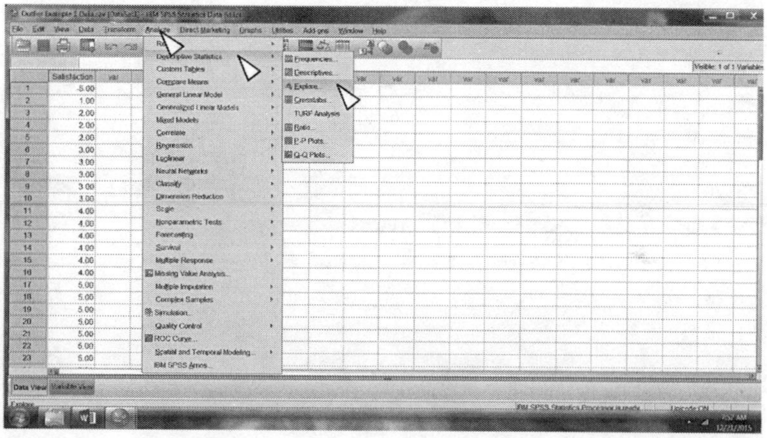

Figure 12.5

Step 3: The "Explore" window will open.

- Highlight the "*Satisfied* . . ." variable and place it in the "Dependent List" box by clicking the "Arrow" button.
- Click the "Plots" button.
- In the "Explore Plots" window:
  - Check "None" in the box plot area.
  - Below that, check "Normality plots with tests."
  - Click the "Histogram" radio button in the "Descriptives" box.
  - Select the "Continue" button located in the bottom-left. The "Explore Plots" window will close.
- Last, click the "OK" button. Output is generated.

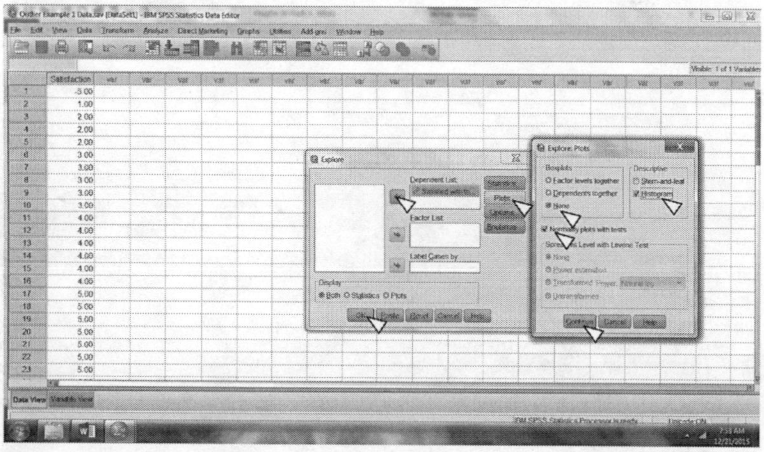

Figure 12.6

Graphs can be edited by right-clicking onto the graph and then selecting the "Edit Content" option. In the accompanying output, the graphs have been edited to depict whole numbers.

Step 4: In addition to a histogram, a univariate scatter plot can be generated.

- First, select the "Graphs" tab.
- Next, click "Legacy."
- Last, click "Scatter/Dot."

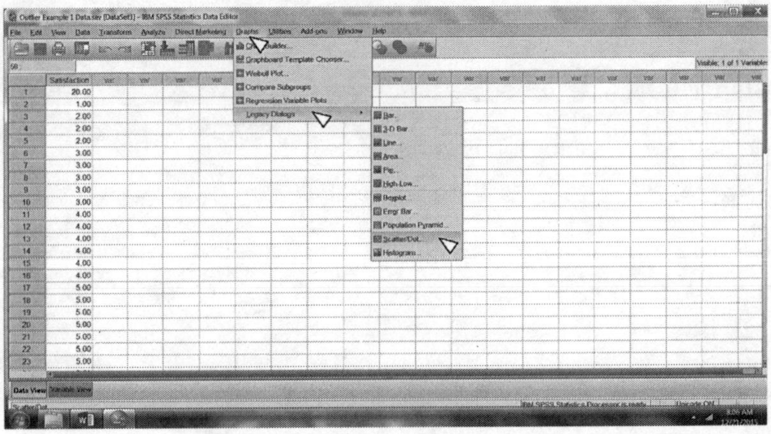

Figure 12.7

Step 5: In the "Scatter/Dot" window, select the "Simple Dot" button on the right side.

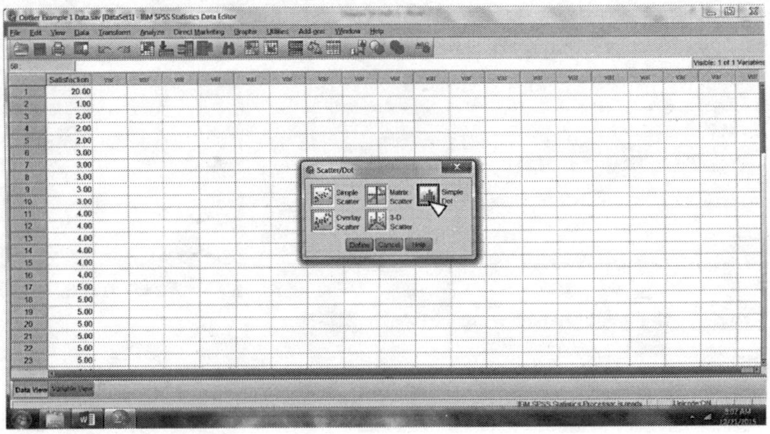

Figure 12.8

Step 6: The "Define Simple Dot Plot" window will open.

- Highlight the "Satisfied . . ." variable located in the box on the left.
- Then, click the "Arrow" button placing it in the "X-Axis Variable" box located on the top-right side.

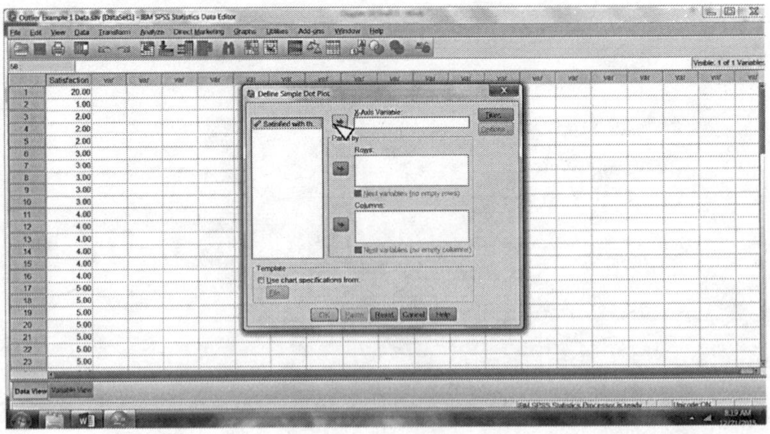

Figure 12.9

Step 7: Still in the "Define Simple Dot Plot" window:

- Click the "Titles" button on the far right. The "Titles" window will open.
- In the "Line 1" box located in the "Title" area, type a title for the dot plot.
- Last, click the "Continue" button on the bottom-left side.

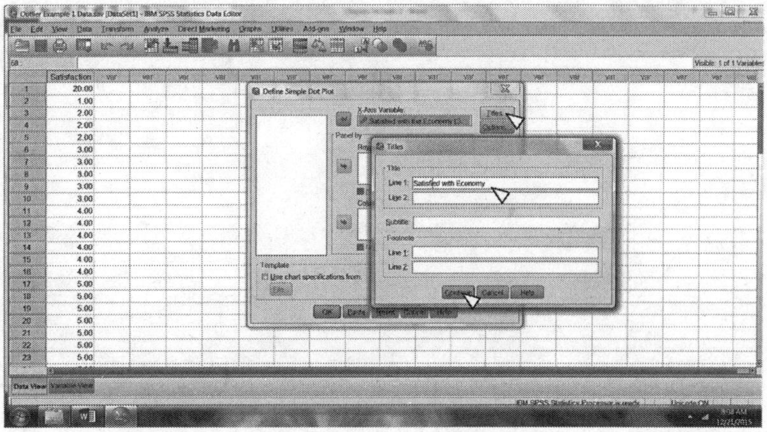

Figure 12.10

Step 8: In the "Define Simple Dot Plot" window, click the "OK" button located in the bottom-left side. Output is generated. Again, output can be edited by right-clicking onto the image and then selecting the "Edit Content" option.

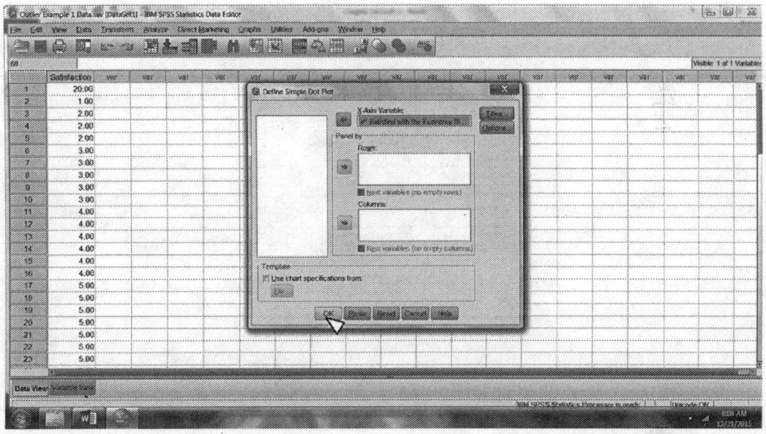

Figure 12.11

Be sure to save the data and output files for your records.

SPSS Output Interpretation

We ran a number of statistical and visual descriptive analyses. Below, we examined the descriptives and tests of normality tables, as well as the histogram, Normal Q-Q Plot, and XGraph (dot plot). After the removal of any outliers, we rerun the analyses to examine for improvement.

The data are numeric. The sample size is larger than 30. The histogram below suggests that although the data are close to being normally distributed, they appear peaked, especially in relation to two outliers, one at each tail. Further examination is needed.

The "Descriptives" table supports the histogram distribution. First, there are minimum values of –5.00 and 20.00 and the range is 25.00 where the measurement scale is 1 to 11, indicating the presence of outliers. Although skewness is within the acceptable bounds of –1.00 to 1.00, kurtosis is high at 6.252. This indicates a high peak. The skewness statistic and the near equality of the mean and median (and mode for that matter) indicate symmetry in the distribution. Thus, although the data are symmetrical, the distribution is peaked more than the normal distribution.

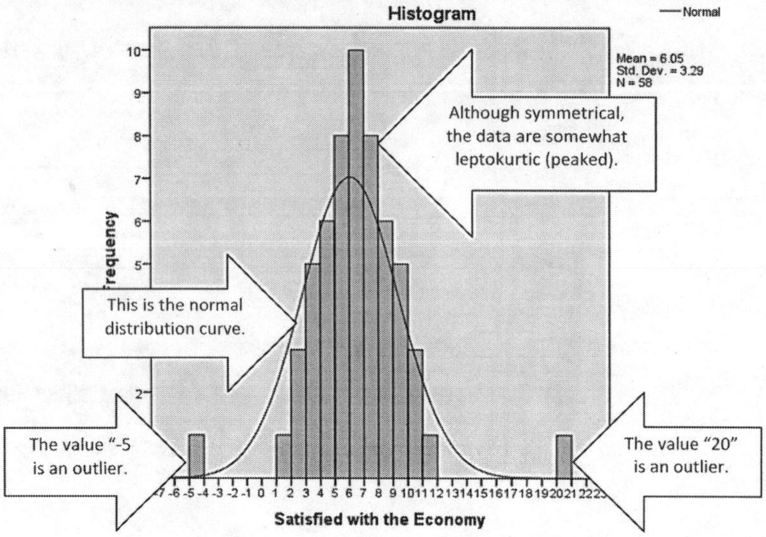

Figure 12.12

Table 12.3

Descriptives

			Statistic	Std. Error
Satisfied with the Economy	Mean		6.0517	.43195
	95% Confidence Interval for Mean	Lower Bound	5.1868	
		Upper Bound	6.9167	
	5% Trimmed Mean		6.0000	
	Median		6.0000	
	Variance		10.822	
	Std. Deviation		3.28966	
	Minimum		-5.00	
	Maximum		20.00	
	Range		25.00	
	Interquartile Range		4.00	
	Skewness		.672	.314
	Kurtosis		6.252	.618

The "Mean" is the average score including the outliers. The median is slightly less than the mean.

The "Std. Deviation" is the spread of the data and is a measure of dispersion.

The "Minimum and "Maximum" values are outside of 1-11. This suggests the presence of outliers at the lower and upper ends of the distribution.

The "Skewness" Statistic is within the -1.00 to 1.00 value. "Kurtosis" is higher indicating a high peak in the data.

Table 12.4

Tests of Normality

	Kolmogorov-Smirnov[a]			Shapiro-Wilk		
	Statistic	df	Sig.	Statistic	df	Sig.
Satisfied with the Economy	.111	58	.074	.894	58	.000

a. Lilliefors Significance Correction

The "Shapiro-Wilk" Statistic is significant at $p < .001$ indicating that the distribution is not likely normal.

Table 12.4 indicates the Shapiro-Wilk statistic. The alpha or acceptable level of risk is .05. Since the Shapiro-Wilk test is statistically significant at $p < .001$, the chance that the distribution does not vary from normality is very low or less than 1 out of 1,000, which is not acceptable risk. Therefore, it is likely that the data deviate from the normal distribution.

Next, we attempt to identify the outliers by examining the Normal Q-Q Plot. The two outliers identified in the histogram are clearly evident in the Q-Q Plot. The line represents where normally distributed data is located, which is the intersection between the "Expected Normal" distribution and the actual "Observed Value" data.

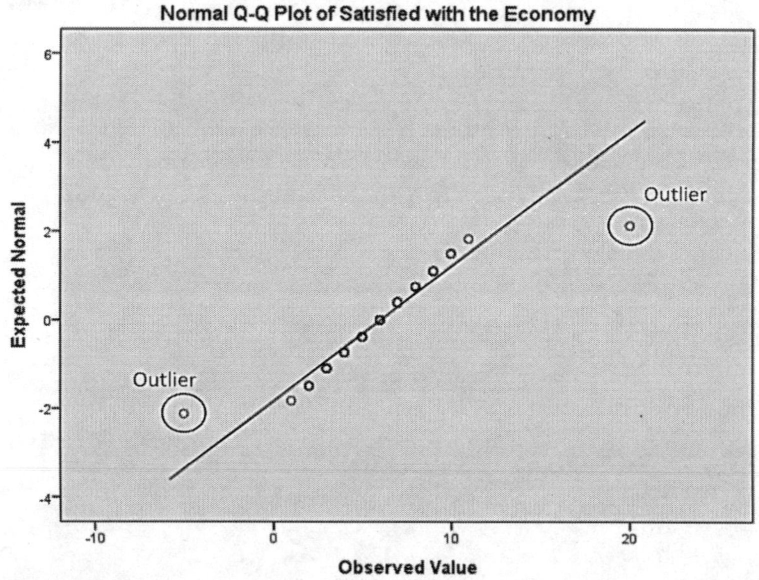

Figure 12.13

For comparative purposes, the simple scatter plot below also depicts the two outliers in the original metric, which are –5.00 and 20.00.

Figure 12.14

We can now identify the specific cases containing the two outliers using the Normal Q-Q Plot in the output.

Step 9: In the output "Normal Q-Q Plot of Satisfied with the Economy" image window, do the following:

- First, make sure that the dataset from which the output was generated is open.
- Next, right-click on the plot image, which will open a window that contains options.
- Select "Edit Content" followed by "In Separate Window."

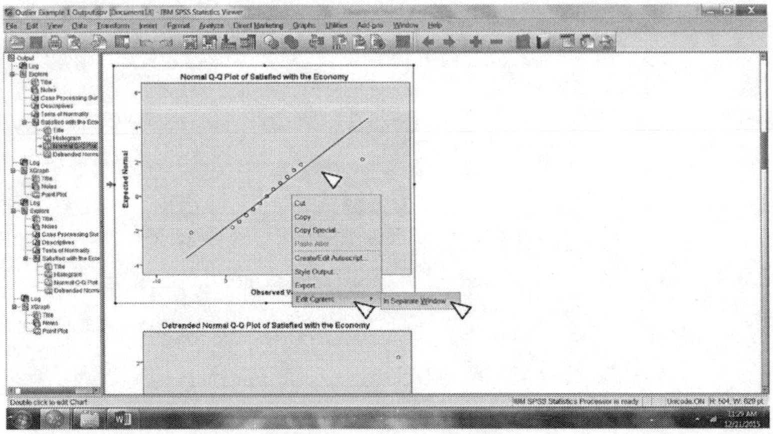

Figure 12.15

Step 10: The "Chart Editor" window will open.

- Right-click onto an outlier. All the data points will be highlighted and a window containing options will open.
- Choose "Select."
- Then, click "This Marker." Now, only the selected outlier data point will be highlighted and the "Properties" window will open.

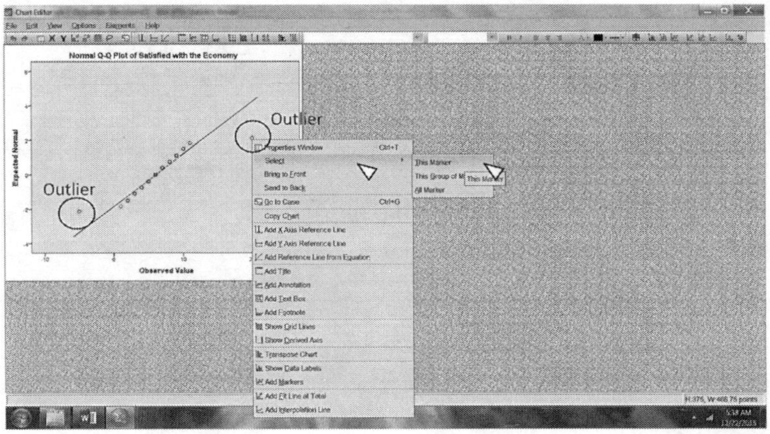

Figure 12.16

Step 11: Ignore the "Properties" window.

- Right-click on the highlighted outlier.
- The same window containing options will open. Click "Go to Case."

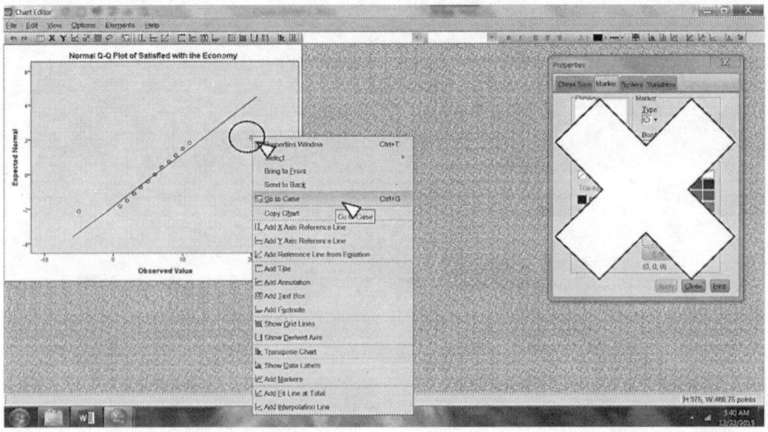

Figure 12.17

The following data window will open highlighting the selected outlier.

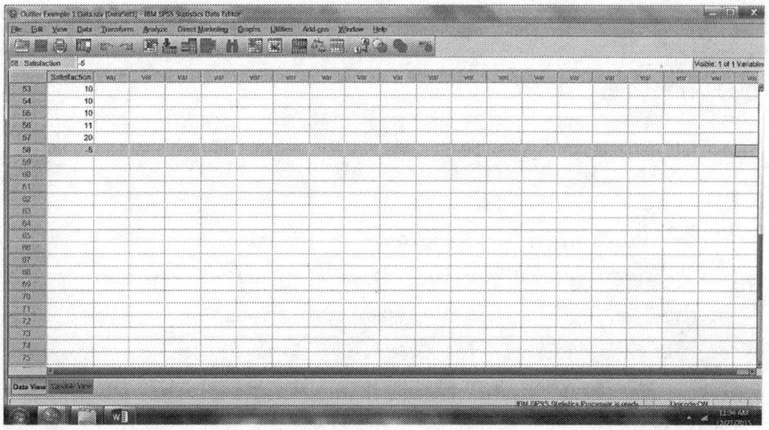

Figure 12.18

Step 12: From the data window, do the following:

- Click onto the cell containing the outlier.
- Right-click inside of the cell and a window will open.
- Select the "Clear" option by left-clicking it. The value will be removed. This removal approach will highlight the entire case across multiple column variables. Be sure to only remove the outlier in question.
- It is best to save a version of the dataset containing all of the outliers as well as the "clean" dataset.

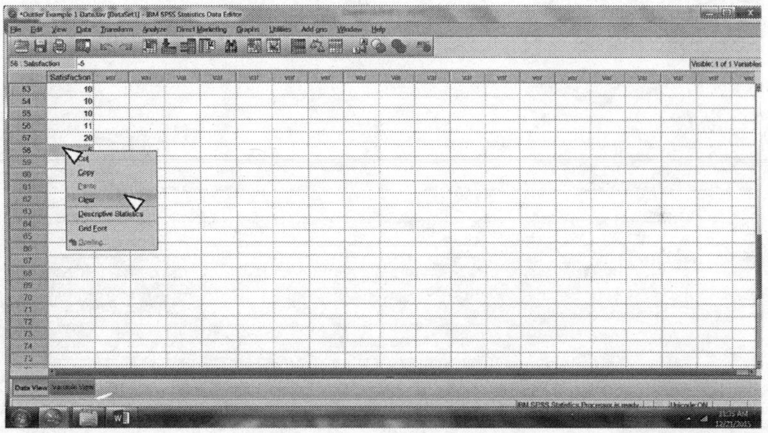

Figure 12.19

Follow the same procedure for all outliers. Since there are only two, representing 3.4% (2 out of 58) of the total data, we have not violated the 10% maximum number of removals rule.

We now rerun the descriptive statistics to examine for improvement.

Notice that the histogram now resembles a normal distribution much better without the two outliers. In the first histogram, in order for all of the data points to fit on one graph, the columns were thinner and appeared to form a different distribution compared to the one to the right in Figure 12.20. However, other than the outliers, the distributions of the data points in both histograms are similar.

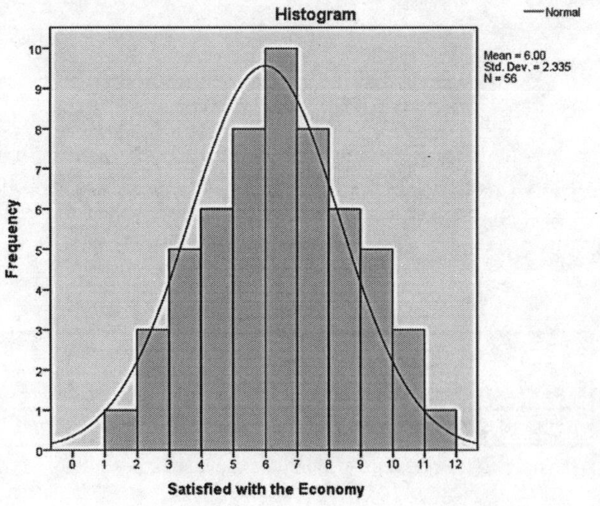

Figure 12.20

In Figure 12.21, the simple dot scatter graph tails are now shorter and more in line with normally distributed data.

After removing the outliers, the mean has changed from 6.0517 to 6.0000. The mean and median are now equal. The standard deviation is decreased from 3.28966 to 2.33550, indicating less spread in the data, which demonstrates that the average distance of a data point from the mean decreased. Consistent with the change in standard deviation, the minimum and maximum values are now 1.00 and 11.00 along with a range of 10.00. Both skewness and kurtosis statistics are within the values of –1.00 and 1.00. Skewness is .000, which demonstrates perfect symmetry. Kurtosis is much improved going from 6.252 to –.578.

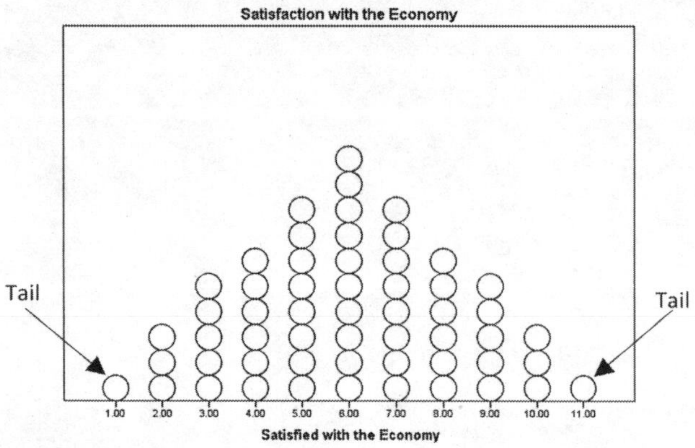

Figure 12.21

Table 12.5

Descriptives

			Statistic	Std. Error
Satisfied with the Economy	Mean		6.0000	.31209
	95% Confidence Interval for Mean	Lower Bound	5.3745	
		Upper Bound	6.6255	
	5% Trimmed Mean		6.0000	
	Median		6.0000	
	Variance		5.455	
	Std. Deviation		2.33550	
	Minimum		1.00	
	Maximum		11.00	
	Range		10.00	
	Interquartile Range		4.00	
	Skewness		.000	.319
	Kurtosis		-.578	.628

As shown in Table 12.6, the Shapiro–Wilk test for normality is now not meaningful at p = .387, indicating that the distribution does not deviate from normal. However, it is possible to have a nonsignificant p-value in a distribution containing outliers, especially in larger sample sizes where the outliers have less of an impact on the overall distribution.

Table 12.6

Tests of Normality

	Kolmogorov-Smirnov[a]			Shapiro-Wilk		
	Statistic	df	Sig.	Statistic	df	Sig.
Satisfied with the Economy	.089	56	.200*	.978	56	.387

*. This is a lower bound of the true significance.

a. Lilliefors Significance Correction

The Normal Q-Q Plot clearly approximates a normal distribution. All of the data points touch or nearly touch the expected normal line.

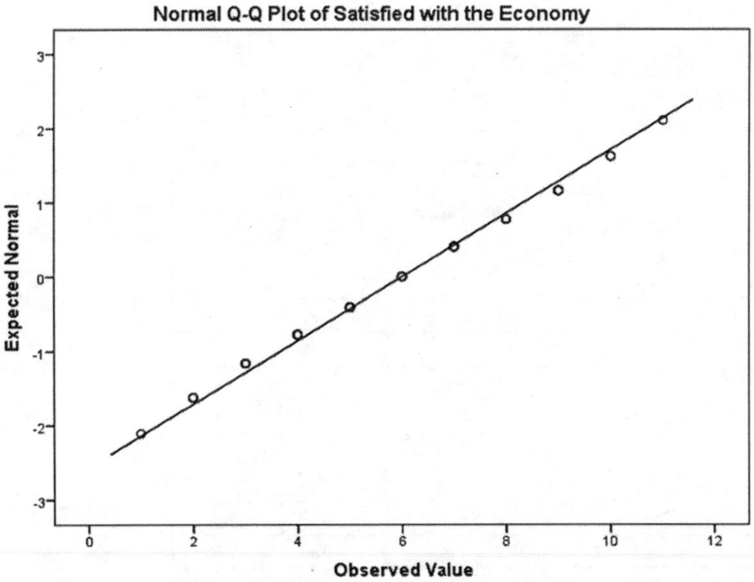

Figure 12.22

In sum, upon the removal of the two outliers and subsequent data screening, the data approximate normal distribution and are thus appropriate for parametric statistical analysis.

Example 12.2: Outlier Labeling Rule Removal

This example applies the outlier labeling rule method to the data in the example above. All of the output is similar, with the exception of the additional "Percentile" and "Extreme Values" output tables, as well as the use of a formula. Alpha is .05. The SPSS file named "Outlier Example 2 Data" contains the data. The SPSS steps are similar to those covered above, except for the following.

Once the "Explore" window is open:

- Click the "Statistics" button located on the top-right side.
- The "Explore Statistics" window will open. Select "Descriptives," "Outliers," and "Percentiles."
- Last, click the "Continue" button located on the bottom-left side. All the other steps are identical to the first example.

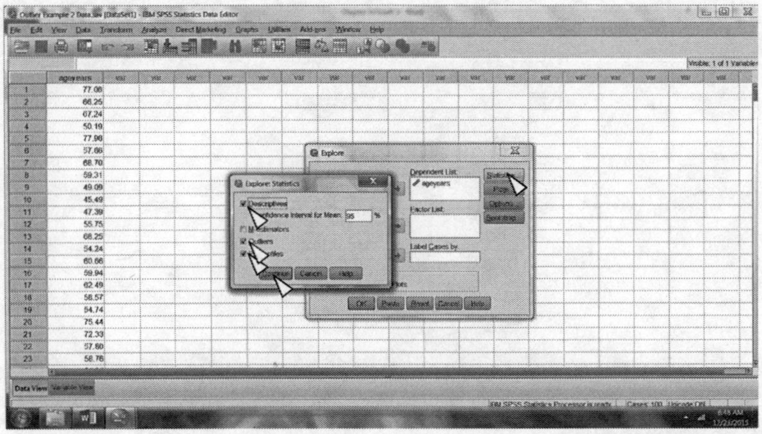

Figure 12.23

SPSS Output Interpretation

As expected in Table 12.7, the descriptive statistics are identical to the first example.

Table 12.7

Descriptives

			Statistic	Std. Error
Satisfied with the Economy	Mean		6.05	.432
	95% Confidence Interval for Mean	Lower Bound	5.19	
		Upper Bound	6.92	
	5% Trimmed Mean		6.00	
	Median		6.00	
	Variance		10.822	
	Std. Deviation		3.290	
	Minimum		-5	
	Maximum		20	
	Range		25	
	Interquartile Range		4	
	Skewness		.672	.314
	Kurtosis		6.252	.618

The outlier labeling rule requires information from the "Percentile" and "Extreme Values" tables as well as three calculations. In order to calculate the lower and upper bounds values for outliers, we must first determine the reference values based on the 25th and 75th percentiles located on the "Weighted Average Definition 1" row of the "Percentile" table. In our example, they are 4.00 and 8.00, respectively. The reference formula is as follows:

(75th percentile – 25th percentile) × k = Reference Value

where

k (constant) = 1.50

Note that some statisticians prefer $k = 2.20$ when the data are fairly normally distributed and the same size is < 300.

Next, the lower and upper values are calculated as follows:

(75th percentile + Reference Value) = upper value

(25th percentile – Reference Value) = lower value

where

Upper value: > outliers

Lower value: < outliers

Table 12.8

These are the 25th & 75th percentiles

Percentiles

		Percentiles						
		5	10	25	50	75	90	95
Weighted Average(Definition 1)	Satisfied with the Economy	1.95	2.90	4.00	6.00	8.00	9.10	10.05
Tukey's Hinges	Satisfied with the Economy			4.00	6.00	8.00		

In this example, the calculations are as follows:

$$(8.00 - 4.00) \times 1.50 = 6.00$$

where

$$k \text{ (constant)} = 1.50$$

Next, the lower and upper values are determined as follows:

$$(8.00 + 6.00) = 14.00$$

$$(4.00 - 6.00 = -2.00.$$

Therefore, outliers are values that are –2.00 or less and 14.00 and greater.

The "Extreme Values" table depicts the five highest and five lowest values. This table is useful when sample sizes are no more than 200–300. In large datasets, the 10 most extreme observations may not represent all outliers. Moreover, if the distribution is not close to normal, it is possible that there will be outliers not listed in the table. In this example, we locate all values $\leqslant -2.00$ and $\geqslant 14.00$. These observations are the outliers in this sample data, which will be removed before running analysis.

Table 12.9

Extreme Values

			Case Number	Value
Satisfied with the Economy	Highest	1	57	20
		2	56	11
		3	53	10
		4	54	10
		5	55	10
	Lowest	1	58	-5
		2	1	1
		3	4	2
		4	3	2
		5	2	2

These two outliers should be removed. Their case (row) number locations are indicated to help find them.

Before removing any outliers, be sure to save the original data file as well as the file that does not contain outliers.

Table 12.10 summarizes the simple outlier removal and outlier labeling rule methods. The bold steps are is the major difference between these two approaches.

Table 12.10

Comparing the Simple Outlier Removal & Outlier Labeling Rule Methods

Simple Outlier Removal	Outlier Labeling Rule
1) Run the descriptive statistics	1) Run the descriptive statistics
2) Observe the histogram & assess	2) Observe the histogram & assess
3) Review the descriptive statistics & assess	**3) Review the percentile and extreme values output**
4) Identify the outliers in the Normal Q-Q Plot	**4) Calculate the lower/upper outlier values**
5) Remove the outliers using the Q-Q Plot output file	**5) Remove the identified outliers based on Step 4 results**
6) Rerun the descriptive statistics & verify normality	6) Rerun the descriptive statistics and verify normality
7) Conduct statistical analyses	7) Conduct statistical analyses

Note: The bolded steps are the differences between both approaches.

12.6 Other Remedies for Non-Normal Data Distribution

Measures of central tendency and dispersion help us discover and understand the shape of a variable's data distribution. If removing the outliers does not produce normality, there are a number of options. (1) If possible, correct inaccurately recorded data. (2) Additional data can be collected, which may bring the distribution closer to normal. (3) Data can be transformed so that they become normalized for analysis. The type of transformation depends on the shape of the distribution. For reporting purposes, transformed data results can be back-transformed (reversed) so that interpretation becomes easier. (4) Nonparametric tests can be used in lieu of parametric tests. These tests rank-order the data. (5) If all else fails, a caveat could be included in the write-up indicating that the results may not be stable.

SUMMARY OF KEY CONCEPTS

- The shape of a data distribution is based on its central tendency and dispersion attributes.
- Central tendency can be assessed using the mean, median, mode, and Coefficient of Skewness statistics.
- Dispersion can be evaluated using the range, standard deviation, Coefficient of Variation, and Coefficient of Kurtosis statistics.
- Skewness and kurtosis distributions come in various shapes.
- The Shapiro-Wilk significance test is a measure of overall normal distribution.
- Providing that the distribution is fairly normal, the removal of outliers contributes to the accuracy of results.
- There are a number of methods for identifying and removing outliers.
- SPSS offers a variety of techniques for identifying and removing outliers such as the simple outlier removal approach and the outlier labeling rule technique.

NUMERIC DATA SCREENING AND REMOVING OUTLIERS APPLIED EXERCISES

12.1 What is a univariate normal distribution? Provide an example.

12.2 What is central tendency?

12.3 What is a mean?

12.4 What is the mean of the following data array: 21, 22, 2, 3, 6, 8, 12, 12, 12, 16, 18?

12.5 What is a median?

12.6 What is the median from the following data array: 21, 22, 2, 3, 6, 8, 12, 12, 12, 16, 18, 20, 25, 22, 20?

12.7 Define the term mode.

12.8 Using the data in Question 12.6, what is the mode?

12.9 Define the term skew.

12.10 Using the data in Question 12.6, what are the mean and median? What do they suggest about skew?

12.11 What is the Coefficient of Skewness?

12.12 What is dispersion?

12.13 Define range in statistical terms.

12.14 What is an exclusive range?

12.15 What is an inclusive range?

12.16 What is a sample standard deviation?

12.17 What is the Coefficient of Variation (CV)?

12.18 What is the Coefficient of Kurtosis?

12.19 What is kurtosis?

12.20 What is a mesokurtic distribution?

12.21 What is a leptokurtic distribution?

12.22 What is a platykurtic distribution?

12.23 What is a Normal Q-Q Plot?

12.24 What is a simple dot plot?

12.25 What is the Shapiro-Wilk test?

12.26 What is the simple outlier rule?

12.27 What is the standard deviation rule?

12.28 Define trimming.

12.29 What is winsorizing?

12.30 Define the outlier labeling rule.

12.31 From the following dataset, determine the mean, median, mode, standard deviation, Coefficient of Variation, skewness, kurtosis, and the Shapiro-Wilk statistic: 10, 8, 2, 3, 9, 4, 5, 6, 5, 12, 1. Are the sample data normally distributed? Explain your response.

12.32 From the following dataset, determine the mean, median, mode, standard deviation, Coefficient of Variation, skewness, kurtosis, and the Shapiro-Wilk statistic: 42, 36, 25, 30, 25, 50, 52, 55, 60, 20, 18, 20. Are the sample data normally distributed? Explain your response.

12.33 What is the maximum percentage of outlier data that can be removed from a data array?

12.34 The dataset consists of production in units for 500 machines worldwide. The data must be screened for normal distribution, and, if necessary, remove any outliers. Use the outlier labeling rule method. Alpha = .05. The SPSS file named "Outlier Exercise 1 Data" contains the data.

12.35 The dataset comprises 200 records of minutes to complete a task. The data must be screened for normal distribution, and, if necessary, remove any outliers. Use the simple outlier removal method. Alpha = .05. The SPSS file named "Outlier Exercise 2 Data" contains the data.

12.36 What is variance?

PART IV

Statistical Analysis

Categorical Variables

Chapter 13

Chi-Square Goodness of Fit Test: Comparing Counts in a Single Variable with Two or More Categories

LEARNING OBJECTIVES

To be able to:

- learn the purpose of a chi-square goodness of fit test;
- learn the steps involved to detect meaningful differences between and among counts in categories within a single variable using the chi-square statistic;
- learn how to use SPSS to run a chi-square goodness of fit test;
- know the data assumptions in order to conduct a chi-square test;
- learn how to interpret chi-square results; and
- learn how to report significant and nonsignificant chi-square results.

13.1 Introduction to the Chi-Square Goodness of Fit Test

The **chi-square goodness of fit significance test** compares the observed (from a sample) frequencies or counts and expected counts in each category within a single categorical variable. Proportions are the percentages of the counts. Thus, when we compare counts, we also are comparing proportions (percentages). This type of procedure is a **between-subjects analysis** because it compares counts among the sample cases. We look for the presence or absence of something. The SPSS chi-square procedure tests that all categories within the variable contain an equal number of counts as would occur by chance. It is called an R × 1 chi-square goodness of fit test design. The "R" denotes the number of categories, which must be two or more, and the "1" indicates one sample. "χ^2" is the chi-square symbol. There are two chi-square test options for comparing category counts within a variable. They vary based on the assumption of expected counts and are best explained through illustrations.

First, assume that we wish to ask a sample of 200 consumers to each report one favorite brand of ice cream from among four brands. The 200 preference ratings are the observed counts. We would test to determine whether the brands have equal favorability ratings based on the sample ratings, which happens to be the SPSS default setting. In other words, we would expect the selections to be as follows: Brand A = 50 (25%); Brand B = 50 (25%); Brand C = 50 (25%); and Brand D = 50 (25%). Therefore, the test compares the sample data counts against equal counts for each category within the variable. The goodness of fit test compares what is expected by chance to what is actually observed. A good fit would have equal or near equal counts across categories. In our example, a good fit would have ice cream preference equal to or near 50 preferences per brand.

In the second case, the sample can be tested against specified counts. We might change our example above to the following expectations: Brand A = 20 (10%); Brand B = 100 (50%); Brand C = 35 (17.5%); and Brand D = 45 (22.5%). Thus, the test compares the observed counts against expected specified counts for each category within the variable. In this instance, a good fit would have ice cream preferences equal to or near Brand A = 20, Brand B = 100, Brand C = 35, and Brand D = 45.

13.2 Calculating and Understanding the Chi-Square Statistic

A one-sample chi-square test is single-dimensional because there is only one variable. Let us take a hypothetical leadership example and calculate if there is a statistically significant difference in perceived management style assuming an equal chance of selection. One hundred and twenty mid-level managers were asked to select from one of three categories which best represents their management style. We assume that alpha is .05. Twenty-five reported a delegate management style, 80 played more a supportive role, and 15 indicated that they more directly involved in managing their staff. We assume that all of the data requirements are met. Table 13.1 depicts the observed counts per category.

Table 13.1

Self-reported Management Style

Delegate	Support	Direct	Total
25	80	15	120

Note: Only one management style was selected per respondent. *N* = 120.

Once we determine the expected counts, the chi-square test involves a number of calculations from which we derive the chi-square test statistic. The test statistic is then tested for significance. The steps are as follows.

(1) What would we expect if the categories were evenly distributed? To answer this question requires that the total count be divided by the number of categories. The formula is:

Total Count / The number of categories within the variable

In this case, it is: 120 / 3 = 40. Therefore, we would expect to find by chance 40 selections per management style.

(2) The chi-square test compares what is expected by chance and what is observed. Each observed count is subtracted from the expected count, then squared, and then divided by the expected observation. This calculation for each category is added together. The final result is a measure of difference between the observed and the expected counts. If the chi-square statistic equals zero, then there is no difference between the observed and what we expect. In other words, zero indicates that there is likely no difference among the category counts. The larger the chi-square statistic, then the larger the difference between what is observed and what is expected, likely signaling at least two differences between observed and expected counts. When the comparison pertains to one sample, the formula is:

$$\chi^2 = \sum_{\text{alt cells}} \frac{(O-E)^2}{E}$$

where

χ^2 = the chi-square statistic
Σ = summation sign
O = observed count
E = expected count

Going back to the counts in Table 13.1, Table 13.2 represents the chi-square statistic calculations. Again, the expected count is subtracted from the observed count. The difference is called the **residual**. The residual is squared and then divided by the expected count. This procedure is conducted for each category and then they are summed. In this case, the chi-square value is 61.24.

Table 13.2

Chi-square Calculation for Management Style Survey

Category	O (observed counts)	E (expected counts)	(O – E) Residual	$(O - E)^2$	$(O - E)^2/E$
Delegate	25	40	15	225	5.62
Support	80	40	40	1,600	40.00
Direct	15	40	25	625	15.62
Totals	120	120	-	-	χ^2 **= 61.24**

Note: Only one management style was selected per respondent. *N* = 120.

(3) To determine whether 61.24 is statistically significant requires a number of additional steps. However, SPSS calculates the intermediate steps and provides the chi-square statistic and *p*-value in the output. In this case, $\chi^2 = 61.24$ is statistically meaningful, indicating the likelihood that the three reported management styles are not equally distributed. The *p*-value is very low at <.001. Therefore, we can say that the reported management styles likely vary.

REAL WORLD SNAPSHOT

In an article entitled "Recommendations for the Development of a New Operational Classification System for the Foodservice Industry" published in the *Journal of Hospitality & Tourism Research*, Barrows and Vieira (2012), used chi-square good of fit tests to help classify the top 400 national restaurant chains by sales.

There are many different classification systems in use by industry and researchers. Although many of the systems offer certain benefits, arguably they do not provide realistic groupings for purposes of industry benchmarking. The new system proposed by the authors incorporates operational factors such as service level and menu type, which were analyzed using quantitative methods.

Chi-square tests aided in the discovery of six restaurant segments, which were:

- Upscale steakhouses such as Texas Roadhouse, Bugaboo Creek, and Sagebrush Steakhouse.
- Quick service (fast food) such as McDonald's, Burger King, and Wendy's.
- Fast casual such as Panera Bread, Chipotle's, and Tijuana Flats.
- Casual/upscale such as Legal Seafood, Olive Garden, and Joe's American Bar & Grill.
- Cafeteria/buffet such as Souper Salad, Ponderosa, and Golden Corral Buffet & Grill.
- Delivery such Papa John's, Godfather's Pizza, and Little Caesar's.

Ask yourself: What other variables might be introduced in this classification system that can be analyzed using the chi-square goodness of fit procedure?

13.3 Data Assumptions

Since we are analyzing sample data, we need to use probability statistics in order to discover whether there is a difference between observed category counts and what we expect those counts to be. We must start with the following data assumptions.

- The sample is representative of the target population. For example, if 45–54-year-old middle-income men from the West Coast is the target population, then the sample must represent this targeted population or the findings will not be applicable to this group.
- The sample is randomly drawn, as we covered in Chapter 5.
- The categories being compared are independent of each other. In our examples, the categorical counts represent different respondents or data elements.
- There is a minimum of two categories so that comparison is possible.
- The categories contain all necessary groupings and they do not overlap (mutually exclusive). Therefore, if a study includes *all* levels of education, then a category for no education, one for doctorate degrees, as well as those categories between these two categories, must be included. Doing this will provide the complete sample space. To the second point, two adjacent annual income-level categories must not overlap, such as \$25,000–\$45,000 and \$45,000–\$65,000. This format allows those respondents earning \$45,000 to select either option, which can produce inaccurate results. Therefore, \$25,000–45,000 and \$45,001–\$65,000 are appropriate. Following this approach contributes to accurate results.
- Each case or count is present in only one category. For instance, in a three-shift work day, machine operators can only be counted in one of the three work day shifts.
- The expected counts for each category are at least 1 and no more than 20% of the categories have expected counts that are less than 5.

13.4 Examples Using SPSS: Step-by-Step Instructions

This section contains three step-by-step chi-square (goodness of fit) test examples: one 2 × 1 indicating significant findings, another 3 × 1 yielding nonsignificant results, and a third 3 × 1 with specified expected percentages with significant and nonsignificant findings.

Example 13.1: Equal Expected Counts: The Significant Case

A sample of 210 retail shoppers were asked if they prefer shopping mornings or evenings. They simply responded "morning" *or* "evening." The two possible responses were coded 1 = "Morning" and 2 = "Evening." It is assumed that each time of the day has an equal chance of being selected. Is there a difference in shopping time preference? Alpha = .05. The SPSS file named "Chi-Square Goodness of Fit Example 1 Data" contains the data. The SPSS steps are as follows.

Step 1: Open SPSS. Locate the appropriate folder and data file, then click open.

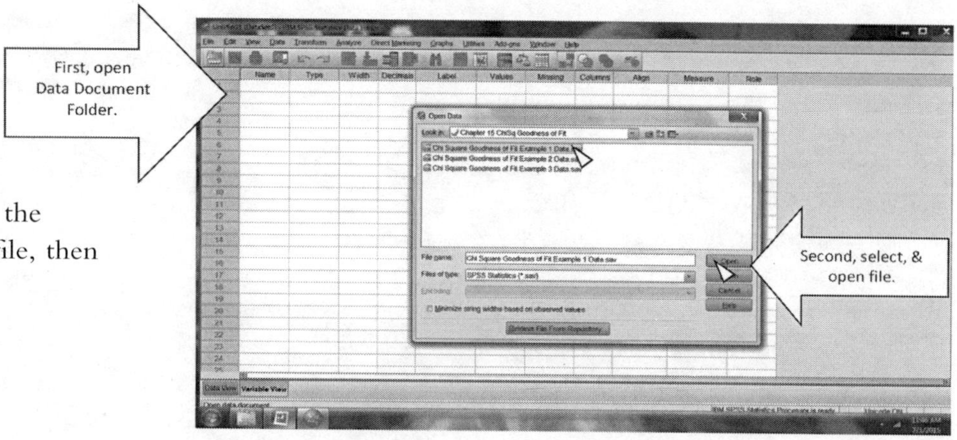

Figure 13.1

Step 2: First, run the frequency descriptives.

- Click the "Analyze" tab.
- Select "Descriptive Statistics."
- Last, choose "Frequencies."

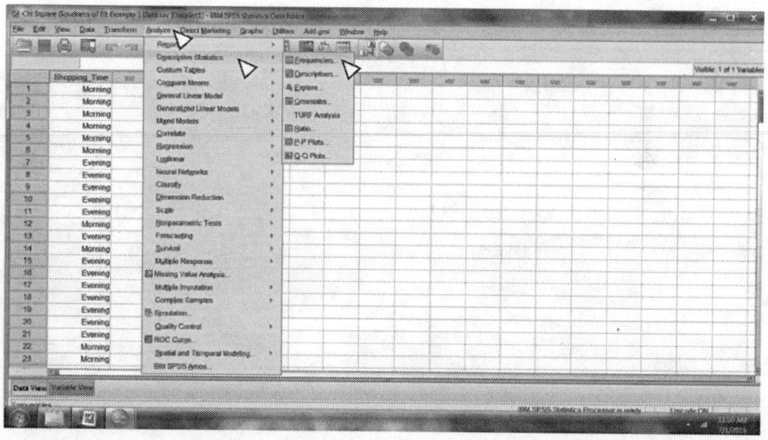

Figure 13.2

Step 3: The "Frequencies" window will open.

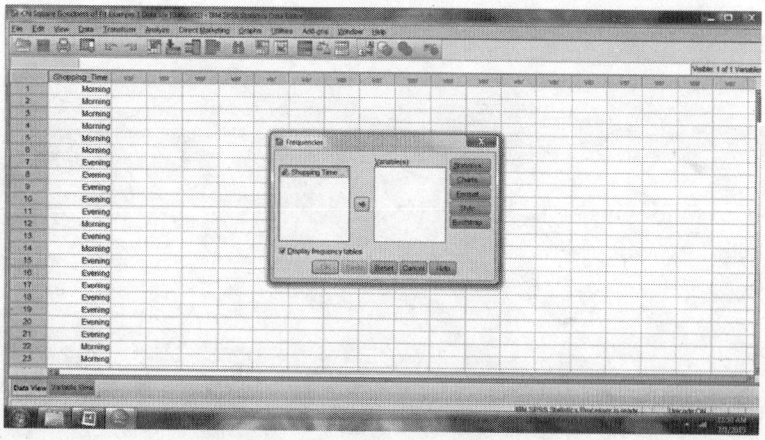

Figure 13.3

Step 4: In the "Frequencies" window, do the following:

- Highlight the "Shopping Time" variable in the left box.
- Next, leave the "Display Frequency table" box checked and click on the "Arrow" button, moving the variable to the "Variables" box.
- Last, click onto the "OK," which will generate the frequencies table.

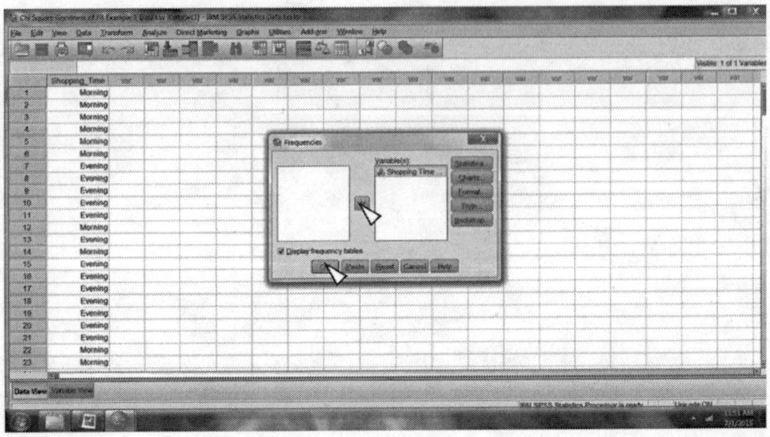

Figure 13.4

Step 5: Next, do the following:

- Click the "Analyze" tab.
- Select "Nonparametric Tests."
- Choose "Legacy Dialogs."
- Last, pick the "Chi-square" option.

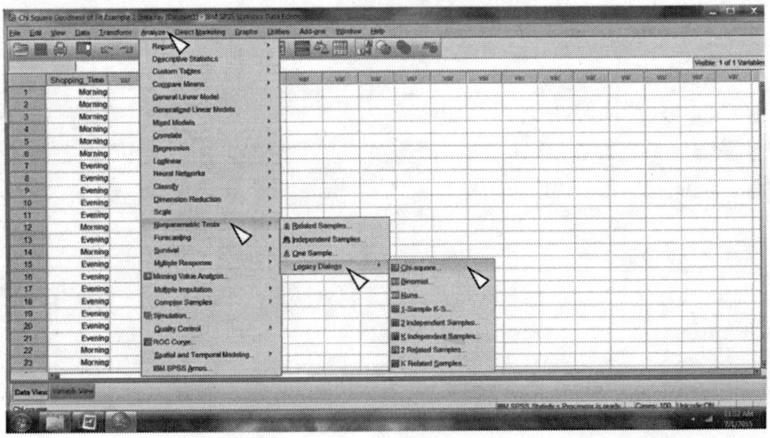

Figure 13.5

The following "Chi-square Test" window will open.

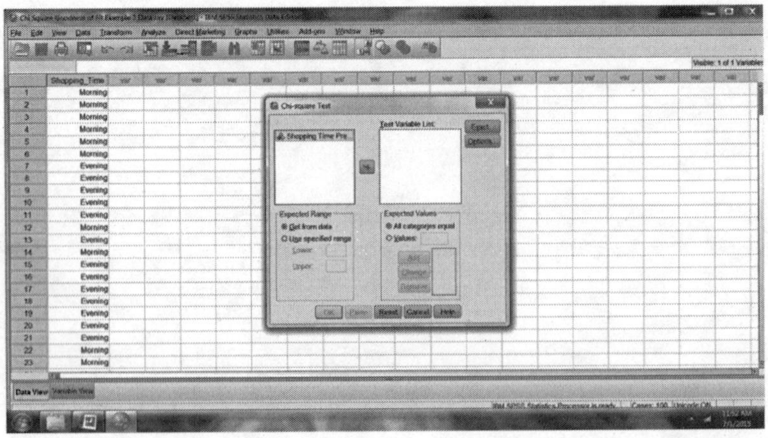

Figure 13.6

Step 6: In the "Chi-square Test: window:

- Move the "Shopping Time" from the left box to the "Test Variable List" box on the right by highlighting the variable and then clicking on the "Arrow" button.
- Last, click onto the "OK," which will generate the chi-square goodness of fit test output.

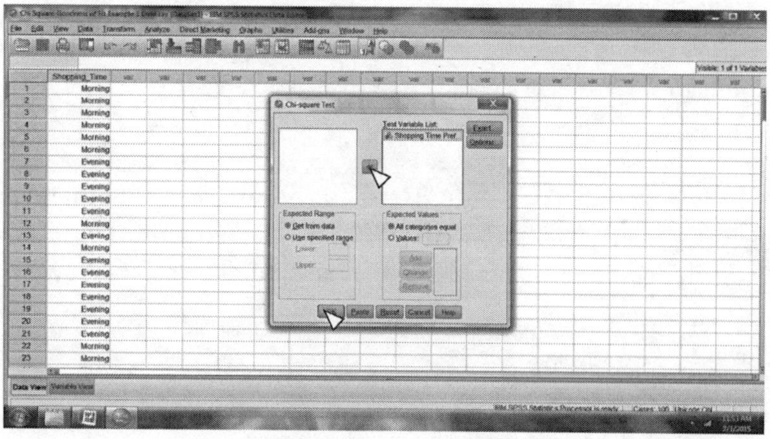

Figure 13.7

Last, save the data and output files for your records. Chapter 4 covers the save procedures.

SPSS Output Interpretation

The descriptive frequencies, observed and expected frequencies, and test statistics tables are necessary in order to interpret the results.

Data Screening

In this example, the following assumptions are met.

- We assume that the sample is random and representative of the target population.
- The observations are independent.
- There is a minimum of two categories.
- As depicted in Table 13.2, the expected observations each have at least counts of 5.

In cases where the minimum cell count is not met or small cell counts exceed 20%, we have two options. First, more data can be collected to increase the low cell counts. Second, contiguous (adjacent) categories can be combined so that the new grouping meets the minimum count requirements, providing that the combined categories make sense being placed in one category.

The tables tell the story. They provide us with a descriptive picture of the data distribution and suggest whether there are meaningful differences between or among category counts. Because there is one variable, Table 13.3 is called a one-way or single-dimensional table. It reveals that 35.2% (74) shoppers prefer to shop during the morning, while 64.8% (136) prefer to shop during evenings. The total sample size is 210.

Table 13.3

We will use the values in the "Frequency" and "Valid Percent" columns.

Shopping Time Preference

		Frequency	Percent	Valid Percent	Cumulative Percent
Valid	Morning	74	35.2	35.2	35.2
	Evening	136	64.8	64.8	100.0
	Total	210	100.0	100.0	

The "Valid Percent" column accounts for missing observations. In a sample of 100, if an analysis of two variables involved 10 missing cases, then the percentages would be based on a count of 90 rather than the total incomplete case count of 100. More specifically, if a sample consists of 50 females, then women would comprise 55.55% (50 / 90) of the sample, which is the "valid percentage" value. However, the "percentage" value is based on the total sample size, which is 50.00% (50 / 100). If no data are missing, then the two percentages are equal. Unless there are specific reasons to use the "Percent" column values, it is best practice to use the "Valid Percent" column figures. The "Cumulative Percent" pertains to the valid cases or percentages.

Table 13.4

Shopping Time Preference

	Observed N	Expected N	Residual
Morning	74	105.0	-31.0
Evening	136	105.0	31.0
Total	210		

The "Residual" column represents the difference between observed and expected counts where the observed counts are the reference point.

Chi-Square Goodness of Fit Test Analysis

Table 13.4 contrasts the observed and expected counts. As per Step 1, the expected equal counts are 105 for morning shopping preference and 105 for evening shopping preference, which total 210 of the observations. As per Step 2, the "Test Statistics" table to the right indicates the chi-square statistic and *p*-value.

Table 13.5

Test Statistics

	Shopping Time Preference
Chi-Square	18.305[a]
df	1
Asymp. Sig.	.000

a. 0 cells (.0%) have expected frequencies less than 5. The minimum expected cell frequency is 105.0.

Asymp. Sig. is the *p*-value for the chi-square test, which is $p < .001$. All expected frequencies are ≥ 5.

As per Step 3 using Table 13.5, the differences between observed and expected counts are assessed for statistical significance. The chi-square goodness of fit test has a *p*-value < .001. Therefore, in all likelihood, we can conclude that there is a meaningful difference between preferences for morning and preferences for evening shopping because there is a very low probability that there is an equal split in preference. Thus, the results suggest that consumers generally prefer to shop during the evening (64.8%, $n = 136$) more than during the morning (35.2%, $n = 74$).

As discussed in Chapter 11, a *p*-value of <.000 indicates that the probability that these results are not meaningful (or are by chance) is less than 1/1000; thus, these results are statistically meaningful. This is so because it is certainly less than our <.05 (5 / 100) alpha, which is the level of risk that we are willing to accept. We usually report *p*-values that are .000 or less (for example, .0000004) as $p < .001$. *P*-values that are equal to or higher than .001 are reported to three places to the right of the decimal point (for example, .130 or .006). As covered in Chapter 4, clicking on the *p*-value in the SPSS output file will indicate the exact value.

Reporting Results

This example would be reported as follows.

Write-Up

Based on a representative sample of 210 shoppers, a chi-square goodness of fit test was calculated comparing the counts of preference for shopping during the morning and during the evening. It was assumed that an equal number of shoppers would prefer morning and evening shopping times. A meaningful difference from the expected counts was found ($\chi^2(1) = 18.305$, $p < .001$). More retail consumers preferred evening shopping (64.8%, $n = 136$) compared to morning shopping (35.2%, $n = 74$).

As depicted in Table 13.6, the percentages are the **standardized counts** so that we can easily compare the counts' percentages in the two categories. Only the valid cases are indicated and information of missing data would be reported in the "Note" area.

The "χ^2" is the chi-square symbol for the chi-square test statistic, which is 18.305. In this case, the degrees of freedom (*df*) is the number of categories that can vary. The "(1)" represents *df*, which is calculated as n − 1 or 2 − 1 = 1. For instance, with a sample of 210, once one count for a category is set such to 74, then the other category must have a count of 136 because they both total 210. All of these statistics are typically reported.

Table 13.6

Observed Preferred Shopping Time

Time	Frequencies	Percentages
Morning Shopping	74	35.2%
Evening Shopping	136	64.8%
Total	210	100.0%

Note: ($\chi^2(1) = 18.305$, $p < .001$). $N = 210$.

Example 13.2: Equal Expected Counts: The Nonsignificant Case

A sample of 320 consumers were asked if they prefer land- (e.g. biking), water- (e.g. boating), or air- (e.g. air-gliding) based vacation activities. It is assumed that each type of activity has an equal chance of being selected. Is there a difference in preferred type of vacation activity? Alpha = .05. The SPSS file named "Chi-Square Goodness of Fit Example 2 Data" contains the data for this study.

We will skip the SPSS steps because they are identical to the first example.

SPSS Output Interpretation

Data Screening

We make the following assumptions:

- The sample is random and representative of the target population.
- The observations are independent.
- There is a minimum of two categories.
- As shown in Table 13.8, all of the expected observations each have at least counts of 5.

The following one-way table provides us with a descriptive picture of the data distribution. It reveals that 37.5% (120) of vacationers prefer land-based activities, 31.9% (102) prefer water-based activities, and 30.6% (98) are drawn to air-based fun things. The total sample size is 320.

Table 13.7

Vacation Activity Preference

		Frequency	Percent	Valid Percent	Cumulative Percent
Valid	Land	120	37.5	37.5	37.5
	Water	102	31.9	31.9	69.4
	Air	98	30.6	30.6	100.0
	Total	320	100.0	100.0	

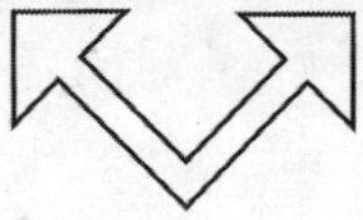

Chi-Square Goodness of Fit Test Analysis

Table 13.8 contrasts the observed and expected counts, as well as providing residuals (differences between them). Equal counts were expected, as indicated by an expected count of 106.7 for each activity category, which is a 1/3 per each of the three categories totaling 100% of the observations. The "Test Statistics" table below indicates whether the differences between the observed and expected counts are meaningful.

The chi-square goodness of fit test has a *p*-value = .276, which indicates that the probability of these findings being by chance alone is 27.6%. This is an unacceptable level of risk, especially since our alpha or the acceptable level is < 5%. Therefore, there is no statistically meaningful difference among preferences for type of vacation activities.

Table 13.8

Vacation Activity Preference

	Observed N	Expected N	Residual
Land	120	106.7	13.3
Water	102	106.7	-4.7
Air	98	106.7	-8.7
Total	320		

Table 13.9

Test Statistics

	Vacation Activity Preference
Chi-Square	2.575[a]
df	2
Asymp. Sig.	.276

a. 0 cells (.0%) have expected frequencies less than 5. The minimum expected cell frequency is 106.7.

Reporting Results

When a variable has only two categories, a significant finding clearly indicates that the difference rests between the two categories. However, when there are more than two categories, the differences between and/or among categories may not be clear. In these situations, you will note the usage of the phrases "There is likely no *overall* difference . . ." or "There is likely a difference between the expected counts and observed counts *in at least two categories* . . ."

This example would be reported as follows. Note that depending on the reporting requirements, it may not be necessary to include a table if the results are not significant.

Write-Up

Based on a representative sample of 320 vacationers, a chi-square goodness of fit test was calculated comparing the counts of preference for type of vacation activity: land-, water-, or air-based. It was assumed that an equal number of shoppers would prefer each type of activity. No overall meaningful difference from the expected counts was found ($\chi^2(2) = 2.575$, $p = .276$). It is likely that vacationers do not prefer one type of vacation activity more than the other two types of vacation activities.

The chi-square statistic is 2.575. The *df* is 2 because n − 1 or 3 − 1 = 2. For instance, with a sample of 320, once one count is set, such as 120 and another at 102, then the other must be 98.

Example 13.3: Specified Expected Counts: Both Cases

A sample of 320 consumers were asked if they prefer land- (e.g. biking), water- (e.g. boating), or air- (e.g. air-gliding) based vacation activities. This time, however, the researchers expect that 192 (60%) of vacationers will prefer land-based activities, 96 (30%) will prefer water-based activities, and 32 (10%) will engage in air-based activities. Test these percentages. Alpha = .05. The SPSS file named "Chi-Square Goodness of Fit Example 3 Data" contains the data for this study.

All of the steps are similar to the previous examples, except for the following.

Step 1: In the "Expected Values" area, click the "Values" radio button.

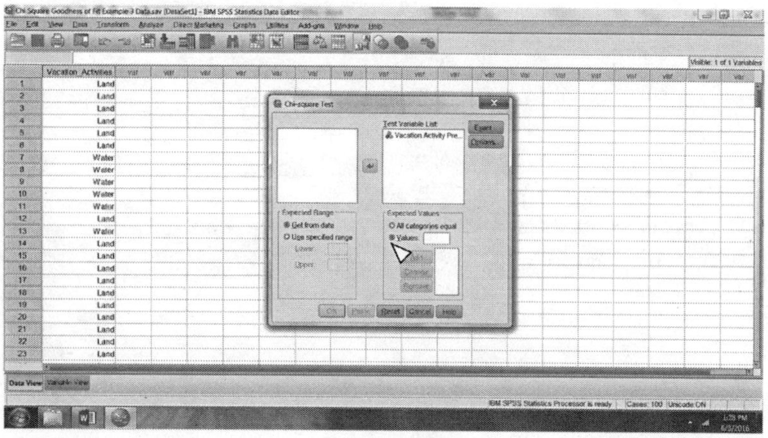

Figure 13.8

Step 2: The order of each entry is important because it corresponds to the ascending order of the category values such that Land = 1, Water = 2, and Air = 3. The first expected count of the list corresponds to the lowest group value of the variable and the last entered count corresponds to the highest value. In the "Values" box:

- Enter the expected counts for each category of preferred vacation activity starting with "Land," which was coded first, followed by "Water," which was coded second, and then "Air."
- After each count is typed in, click the "Add" button.

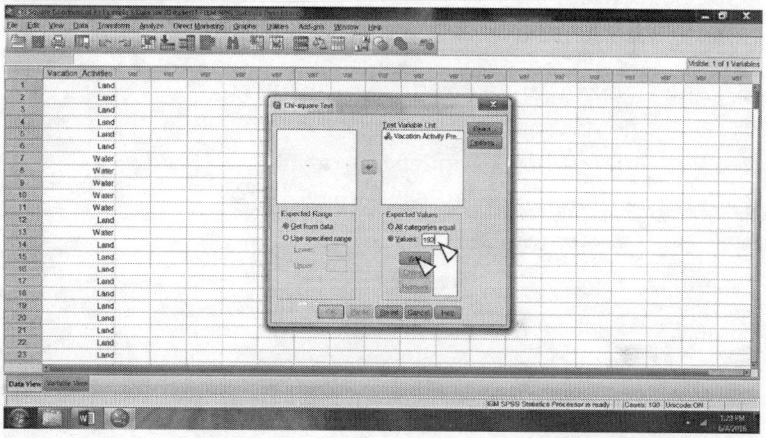

Figure 13.9

The category counts will appear in the box next to the "Add" button.

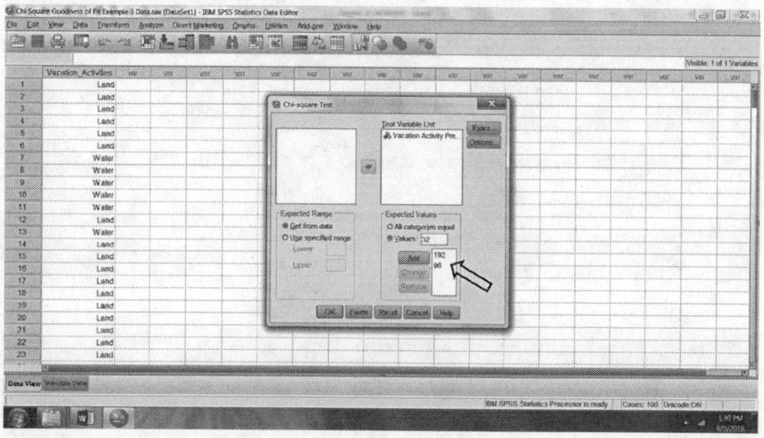

Figure 13.10

Step 4: These counts relate to the total number of data points so that they represent 192 / 320, 96 / 320, and 32 / 320.

- When finished adding category counts, click the "OK" button. The output is generated.

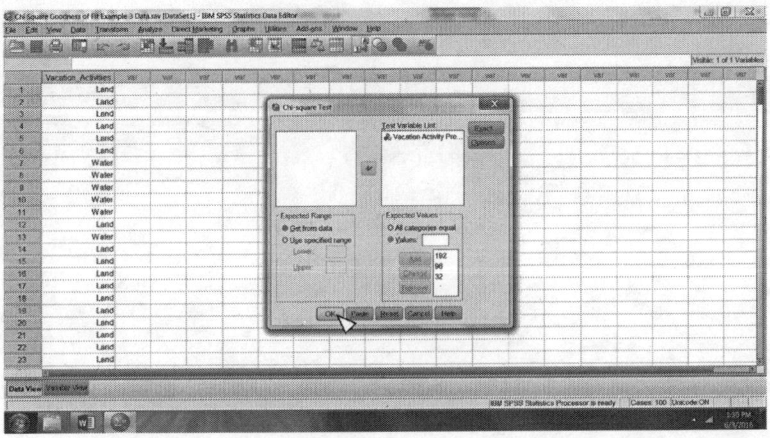

Figure 13.11

SPSS Output Interpretation

We first screen the data.

Data Screening

Again, all of the data assumptions have been met.

- The sample is random and representative of the target population.
- The observations are independent.
- There is a minimum of two categories.
- The expected counts are at least five per category.

Table 13.10

Vacation Activity Preference

		Frequency	Percent	Valid Percent	Cumulative Percent
Valid	Land	120	37.5	37.5	37.5
	Water	102	31.9	31.9	69.4
	Air	98	30.6	30.6	100.0
	Total	320	100.0	100.0	

Table 13.10 reveals that 37.5% (120) of vacationers prefer land-based activities, 31.9% (102) prefer water-based activities, and 30.6% (98) are drawn to air-based fun things. The total sample size is 320.

Chi-Square Goodness of Fit Test Analysis

As we can see in Table 13.11, the expected counts vary from the sample observed values. The "Test Statistics" table below indicates whether the differences between the observed and specified expected counts are statistically meaningful.

The chi-square goodness of fit test has a *p*-value < .001, which indicates that the probability of these findings being by chance alone is very low. This risk is acceptable since our alpha is < .05. Therefore, we conclude that results suggest that vacationers' observed preferences differ from the specified expected category count in at least two types of vacation activity.

Table 13.11

Vacation Activity Preference

	Observed N	Expected N	Residual
Land	120	192.0	-72.0
Water	102	96.0	6.0
Air	98	32.0	66.0
Total	320		

Table 13.12

Test Statistics

	Vacation Activity Preference
Chi-Square	163.500[a]
df	2
Asymp. Sig.	.000

a. 0 cells (.0%) have expected frequencies less than 5. The minimum expected cell frequency is 32.0.

Reporting Significant Results

As noted in Example 13.2, when a variable has two categories, a significant finding clearly indicates that the difference is between the two categories. When there are three or more categories, the differences between and/or among categories may not be clear. In these situations, you will note the usage of the phrases "There is likely no *overall* difference . . ." or "There is likely a difference between the expected counts and observed counts *in at least two categories* . . ." This example would be reported as follows.

Write-Up

Based on a representative sample of 320 vacationers, a chi-square goodness of fit test was calculated comparing specified expected preferences for type of vacation activity: land (60%, n = 192), water (30%, n = 96), and air (10%, n = 32) and observed preferences. A meaningful difference was found between the expected counts and observed counts in at least two categories ($\chi^2(2)$ = 163.500, p < .001). As depicted in Table 13.13, although the water activity preference appears similar (31.9%, n = 102), this is not likely the case for land- and air-related vacation activities (37.5%, n = 120 and 30.6%, n = 98, respectively).

Table 13.13

Observed Preferred Type of Vacation Activity

Activity	Frequencies	Percentages
Land	120	37.5%
Water	102	31.9%
Air	98	30.6%
Total	320	100.0%

Note: ($\chi^2(2)$ = 165.500, p < .001). N = 320.

Reporting Nonsignificant Results

Nonsignificant results would be reported as follows.

Write-Up

Based on a representative sample of 320 vacationers, a chi-square goodness of fit test was calculated comparing specified expected preferences for type of vacation activity: land (60%, n = 192), water (30%, n = 96), and air (10%, n = 32) and observed preferences. No overall meaningful difference between the expected counts and observed counts was found ($\chi^2(2)$ = .583, p = .747). Therefore, it is likely that the observed counts are similar to what was expected. Table 13.14 depicts the observed counts and percentages.

Table 13.14

Observed Preferred Type of Vacation Activity

Activity	Frequencies	Percentages
Land	188	58.8%
Water	102	31.9%
Air	30	9.4%
Total	320	100.0%

Note: ($\chi^2(2)$ = .583, p = .747). N = 320.

In the case of nonsignificant specified expected counts, it is optional whether to include a table.

SUMMARY OF KEY CONCEPTS

- The steps for conducting a single sample chi-square goodness of fit significance test involve determining the expected counts and discovering the differences between the expected and observed counts by following a number of calculations resulting in a chi-square statistic. Essentially, the larger the value of the statistic, the greater the probability of finding a significant difference in the category counts.
- The chi-square goodness of fit test can easily be conducted in SPSS.
- SPSS output provides a *p*-value for the chi-square statistic.
- The data assumptions for running a chi-square test are: the sample is random and representative of the target population; the counts are independent; there is a minimum of two categories; and the expected counts are at least 1 and do not comprise more than 20% of the categories.
- Reporting is straightforward for significant and nonsignificant results.

CHI-SQUARE GOODNESS OF FIT TEST APPLIED EXERCISES

13.1 What is a chi-square goodness of fit test? Provide two examples.

13.2 What is a between-subjects analysis? Offer one example.

13.3 In the context of a chi-square goodness of fit test, define residual.

13.4 When conducting a chi-square goodness of fit analysis, what are the data assumptions?

13.5 Although SPSS runs the chi-square, conceptually what are the required steps in the process?

13.6 How many samples and categories are involved when conducting a chi-square goodness of fit analysis?

13.7 In terms of the expected counts, how are they determined?

13.8 A manufacturing facility is considering reorganizing work hours and aims to survey employees on their preferred work shift: 1st, 2nd, or 3rd shift. There is a sample of 106 employees and it is assumed that each shift has an equal chance of being selected. Determine if there is a difference in desired work shift. Alpha is .05. The data file name is "Chi-Square Goodness of Fit Exercise 1 Data."

13.9 Referring back to Exercise 13.8, assume that work shift preference varies such that specified expectations are that 53 (50%) prefer the first shift, 37 (35%) prefer the second shift, and 16 (15%) prefer the third shift. Do the data support these expectations? Alpha is .05. The data file name is "Chi-Square Goodness of Fit Exercise 2 Data."

13.10 There are four political parties under study: Democrat, Republican, Independent, and Libertarian. A sample of 50 likely voters indicated which political party offers a presidential candidate who they are likely to support. Determine if there is a difference among the parties. There is an equal chance of selection. The data file name is "Chi-Square Goodness of Fit Exercise 3 Data."

13.11 Taking the same data in Exercise 13.10, run the analysis again expecting the breakdown to be as follows: Democrat (16), Republican (15), Independent 13), and Libertarian (6). Is there a statistically significant difference among party affiliations? The data file name is "Chi-Square Goodness of Fit Exercise 4 Data."

13.12 Betterment Services offers group mental wellness counseling. Clients were required to attend sessions rotated during morning, afternoon, and evening times for a given day once per week. This format was for six months so that clients attended 26 sessions. A representative sample of 120 participants who experienced "positive affects" were asked to self-report which time of the day was most beneficial to their "feeling better." In order to force a choice, the specific answer format was morning, afternoon, or evening. Although not covered in this exercise, other factors were accounted for in the study. Determine if there is a difference in feelings of wellness based on time of the day assuming an equal distribution of answers. The data file name is "Chi-Square Goodness of Fit Exercise 5 Data."

13.13 Using the data from Exercise 13.12, the researchers expect that of the 120 study participants, 50% (60) will feel better during the afternoon session, 30% (36) during the evening session, and 20% (24) during the morning session. Test this idea. The data file name is "Chi-Square Goodness of Fit Exercise 6 Data."

Chapter 14

Chi-Square Test of Independence: Comparing Counts between Two Variables Each with Two or More Categories

LEARNING OBJECTIVES

To be able to:

- understand and explain the purpose of a chi-square test of independence;
- know how to manually calculate a chi-square statistic;
- understand and describe the various chi-square designs;
- know and describe how to conduct the chi-square test of independence in SPSS;
- describe under what conditions specific statistical tests are appropriate for assessing results;
- accurately interpret chi-square test of independence results; and
- learn how to report significant and nonsignificant chi-square test results.

14.1 Introduction to the Chi-Square Test of Independence

Crosstabs (cross-tabulations table) chi-square test of independence is a significance test that assesses whether there is a relationship between two categorical variables each with two or more categories. The counts (and percentages of those counts) between two variables each with counts in two or more categories is the basis of the comparison. The data are set up in a contingency table and the marginal counts provide the expected counts that are compared with the combinations of categories, one each from the two variables, which are called **joint counts (or joint frequencies)**. **Marginal counts (or totals)** are the row and column totals. They are called so because they are located in the margins of the table.

The chi-square design is based on the number of categories per variable. The anticipated independent variable is usually located in the columns (C). The dependent variable is placed in the rows (R). The crosstabs is said to have an R × C or row by column design. "χ^2" is the chi-square symbol.

We can use chi-square tests to answer such questions as: Are people who live in rural or urban areas likely to be pet owners? We assume that the residency area is independent of pet ownership and that pet owner may in part be influenced by his or her residence. This is said to be a 2 × 2 chi-square test of independence test design because there are two categories within each variable. Since it comprises two variables, it is a two-dimensional analysis.

Chi-square tests can have more than two categories per one or both variables. For example, we might seek to answer the research question: Is there a relationship between undergraduate college major and intention to attend graduate school? Let us assume that the categories of majors are

Healthcare, Math/Science, Engineering, Business, and Education. The dependent variable can be framed as intention to attend graduate school, no intention to attend graduate school, and undecided. This would be a 3 × 5 chi-square test of independence design. It is a best practice to keep the number of categories within each variable to an amount that can be reasonably well interpreted.

As we can see, the crosstabs procedure counts the observed counts (frequencies) of the joint categories and compares them against the total sample expected counts for each category in order to determine if there is a difference. The chi-square statistical significance test of independence within the SPSS Cross Tab procedure is used to determine if the overall differences between the observed and expected counts is statistically meaningful thus representing a likely relationship between the two variables.

14.2 Calculating and Understanding the Chi-Square Test of Independence

Let us go back to our pet ownership example. Two hundred people were surveyed. They were asked if they owned one or more pets and if they lived in a rural or non-rural area. We assume that alpha is .05. Table 14.1 represents the breakdown.

Table 14.1

Pet Ownership by Type of Residence

Pet Ownership	Type of Residence		
	Rural	Nonrural	Total
Owns Pets	45	120	165
Does not own Pets	5	30	35
Total	50	150	200

Note: We will assume a sample of 200.

Once we determine the expected counts, the chi-square test involves a number of calculations from which we derive the chi-square test statistic. The test statistic is then tested for significance. The steps are as follows.

(1) For each count, the expected frequency or count is tabulated by multiplying the row total of that cell by the column total of that same cell and then dividing the result by the total sample size. This tabulation determines the row and column joint category expected counts. Table 14.2 provides the expected counts for our example. The formula is:

$$\text{Expected frequency} = \frac{(\text{Row total}) \times (\text{Column total})}{\text{Total sample size}}$$

where

Expected frequency	=	what count is expected based on the anticipated distribution
Row total	=	sum of the counts in the row
Column total	=	sum of the counts in the column
Total sample size	=	overall sample size

For instance, the expected frequency for pet owners who reside in a rural area is:

Expected frequency = (165 × 50) /200

Expected frequency = (8,250) / 200

Expected frequency = 41.25

Table 14.2

Pet Ownership by Type of Residence

Pet Ownership	Type of Residence		
	Rural	Nonrural	Total
Owns Pets	Observed: 45	Observed: 120	165
	Expected: 41.25	Expected: 123.75	
Does not own Pets	Observed: 5	Observed: 30	35
	Expected: 8.75	Expected: 26.25	
Total	50	150	200

Note: We will assume a sample of 200.

Knowing the row, column, and grand total sizes allows us to tabulate the expected counts. Recall from Chapter 10 the Multiplication Rule? This is the probability of two events or conditions co-occurring. The same reasoning applies to this procedure. That is to say, they are derived from subsets of the sample frame. Along these lines, we can also calculate the expected frequencies using proportions. In our example, of the *total* sample, 165 / 200 = 87% own pets and 34 / 200 = 17.5% do not own pets. Therefore, of the rural people, of which there are 50, we would expect 87.5% to own pets. We can say that 87.5% × 50 = 41.25 are expected to own pets. The same logic applies to all of the expected frequencies. As we can see, the marginal totals and grand total are required in order to calculate the expected counts.

(2) The chi-square test of independence compares the observed counts in each combination of categories and what is expected based on the category total in relation to the total sample size. If there is no difference between the observed and what we expect, then the chi-square statistic equals zero. In other words, zero indicates that there is likely no difference among the joint category counts with what would be expected as a whole in the sample. However, a large chi-square statistic suggests that there is at least one meaningful difference between the observed counts and expected counts. The two variable formula is:

$$\chi^2_{\text{STAT}} = \sum_{\text{all cells}} \frac{(O - E)^2}{E}$$

where

χ^2_{STAT} = the chi-square statistic
Σ = summation sign
O = observed count
E = expected count

Going back to the counts in Table 14.2, Table 14.3 represents the chi-square statistic calculations. Again, the expected count is subtracted from the observed count. The difference is called the **residual**. The residual is squared and then divided by the expected count. This procedure is conducted for each category and then they are summed. In this instance, the chi-square test value is 2.58.

Note that the 2 × 2 design is a special case. The residuals will have the same absolute value although they will be positive and negative. This is not the case in other two sample designs, whether or not they are symmetrical. However, as we shall see in the examples section, most of the same principles apply.

Table 14.3

Chi-square Calculation for Pet Owner and Residency Area

Intersection	O (observed counts)	E (expected counts)	(O – E) Residual	$(O-E)^2$	$(O-E)^2/E$
Owns Pet/Rural	45	41.25	3.75	14.06	0.34
Owns Pet/Nonrural	120	123.75	-3.75	14.06	0.11
No Pet/Rural	5	8.75	-3.75	14.06	1.60
No Pet/Nonrural	30	26.25	3.75	14.06	0.53
					$\chi^2 = 2.58$

Note: There is only one pet ownership status and residency status per respondent. $N = 200$.

(3) To determine whether $\chi^2 = 2.58$ is statistically significant requires a number of additional steps. SPSS calculates the intermediate steps and provides the chi-square statistic and *p*-value in the output. Here, 2.58 is not statistically meaningful ($p = .107$), indicating that there is likely no relationship between where one resides and pet ownership.

14.3 Data Assumptions

Since we are analyzing sample data, we need to use probability statistics in order to discover whether there is a relationship between two categorical variables. To tell an accurate story of these two variables requires that we meet the following assumptions.

- The sample is representative of the target population.
- The sample is randomly drawn, as we covered in Chapter 5.
- The categories being compared are independent of each other. In our examples, the categorical counts represent different respondents or data elements.
- There is a minimum of two categories per variable.
- Based on the study goal, the variables contain all relevant categories and are mutually exclusive.
- Each case or count is present in only one category.
- Equal category sizes are preferred for the independent variable categories.
- Each expected joint category count is at least 5.

> **REAL WORLD SNAPSHOT**
>
> In a 2015 study entitled "More Than Just Writing: Handedness and Substance Use," Bradley Martin, MSW, explored the possible relationship between handedness and substance use disorders. Ninety-six individuals ages 18–62 completed a survey. Eighty-seven (90.6%) identified as right-handed and 9 (9.4%) identified as left-handed. A significant result was found ($\chi^2(1) = 4.077$, $p = .043$). Five (55.6%) left-handed respondents reported participating in a treatment plan compared to 21 (24.1%) for right-handed respondents. Although this study did not incorporate any of the participants' psychological and physical attributes, these results suggest that handedness orientation may influence alcohol and/or drug use.
>
> **Ask yourself**: What other factors might influence the relationship between handedness and substance abuse? Does this finding suggest something else?

14.4 Examples Using SPSS: Step-by-Step Instructions

The following three chi-square tests of independence examples are a 2 × 2 design indicating significant results, another 2 × 2 design yielding nonsignificant results, and a 3 × 5 design with significant and nonsignificant results.

Example 14.1: A 2 × 2 Chi-Square Test of Independence: The Significant Case

We have a total sample of 182 people consisting of 91 "18–34-year-olds" and 91 "35-over-year-olds," who were asked whether they were interested in learning about a private pension fund. They simply selected one of the two age categories and answered "Yes" or "No" to interest in the pension fund. The objective is to determine whether there is a relationship between age category *and* interest in private pension funds. Alpha = .05. The SPSS file named "Chi-Square Independence Example 1 Data" contains the data for this study.

The analysis requires two variables: "Age Group" (18–34-year-olds or 35-over-year-olds) and "Interest in Learning about Pensions" (Yes or No).

Step 1: Open SPSS.

- Locate the appropriate folder and data file.
- Then, click open.

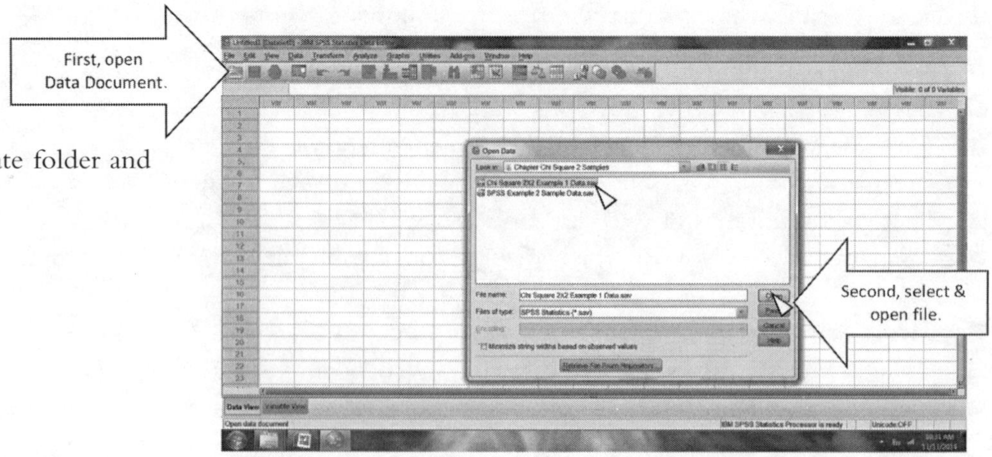

Figure 14.1

Step 2: Once the data file is open:

- Select the "Analyze" tab.
- Next, go to "Descriptive Statistics."
- Last, click "Crosstabs."

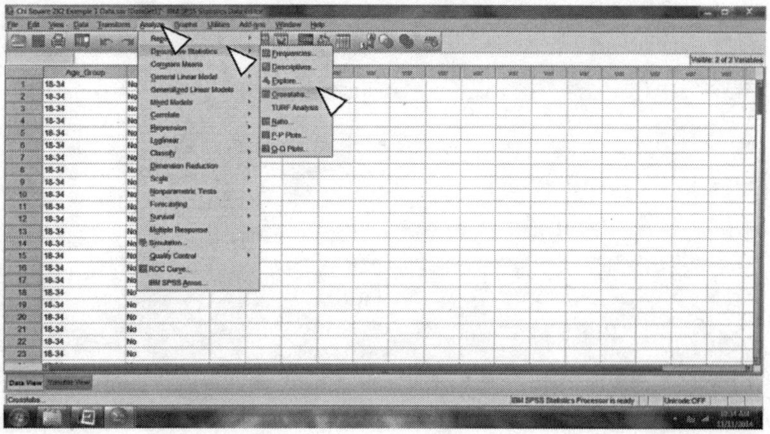

Figure 14.2

You will see the "Crosstabs" window.

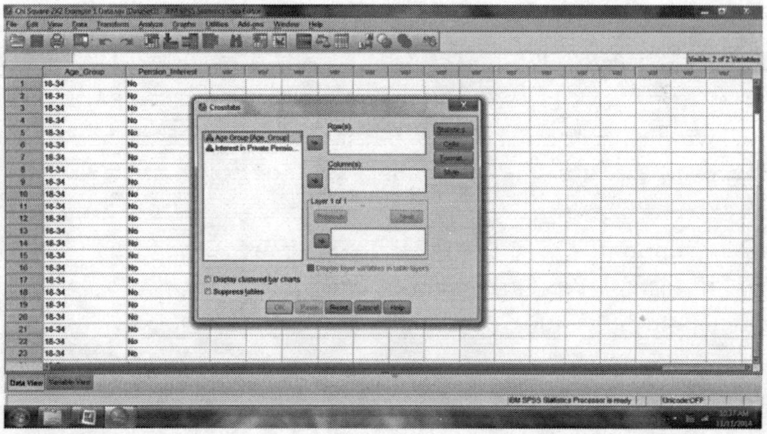

Figure 14.3

Step 3: In the "Crosstabs" window:

- Assign "Age Group" to the column(s) box. Usually, assigning what you think is the "predictor" (influencing) variable to the column(s) box makes interpreting the tables easier.
- Assign "Pension Interest" to the row(s) box.

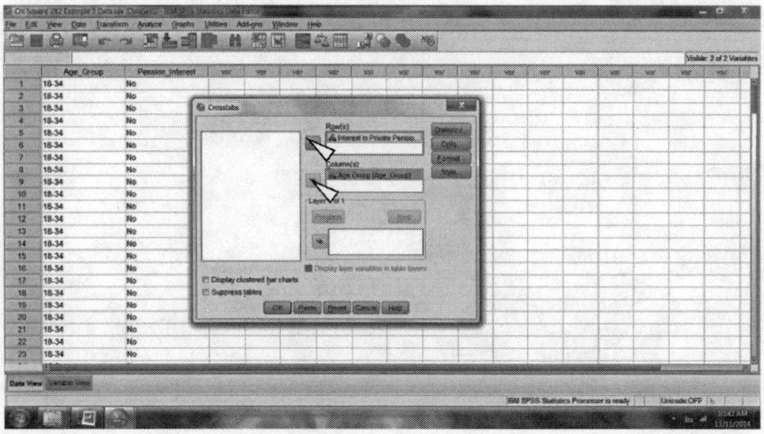

Figure 14.4

Step 4: After the variables are assigned to rows or columns:

- Click onto the "Statistics" button.
- The "Crosstabs Statistics" window will open.
  - Next, select the "Chi-Square" and "Phi and Cramer's V" radio buttons.
  - Last, click "Continue."

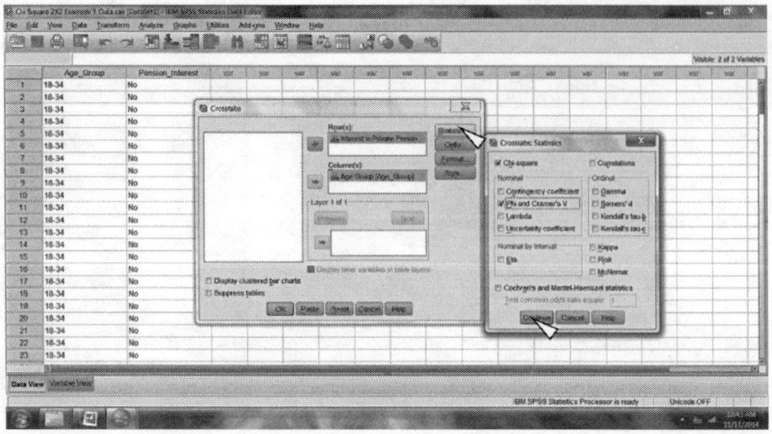

Figure 14.5

Step 5: Back in the "Crosstabs" window:

- Click the "Cells" button.
- The "Crosstabs: Cell Display" window will open.
  - In the "Counts" area, check off the "Observed" and "Expected" options.
  - In the "Percentages" area, check off the "Column" and "Total" options, which will make interpreting the table easier.
  - Last, click the "Continue" button.
- Finally, click "OK" to run the chi-square analysis.

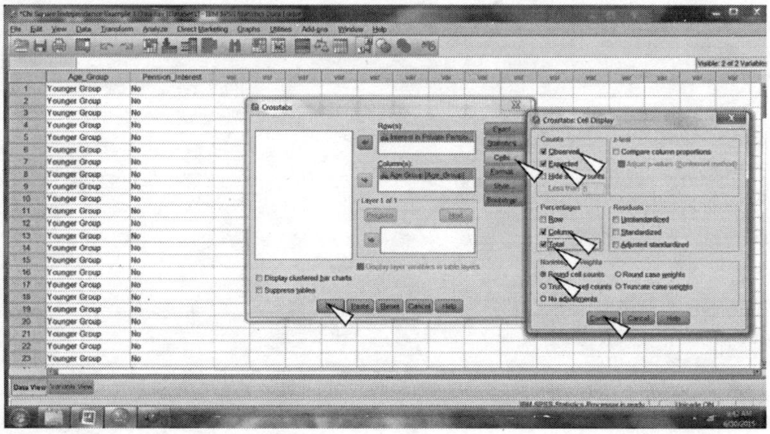

Figure 14.6

Last, save the data and output files for your records. Chapter 4 covers the save procedures.

SPSS Output Interpretation

The case processing summary, Crosstabs (with percentages), chi-square significance test, and symmetric tables are generated. The latter three are discussed below.

Data Screening

As per Table 14.4, all combinations of categories have a minimum of five observations. In cases where this condition is not met, there are three options. First, more data can be collected using a stratified sampling technique focusing on the low cell count conditions (see Chapter 5 for a review of sampling strategies). Second, in crosstabs with more than two categories in a variable, and depending on the counts, we can combine two contiguous (adjacent) categories in order for the new category to reach a minimum expected count of 5, providing that the categories make sense together. Last, we can evaluate the data based on the Fisher Exact Test, which accounts for low cell counts. This test is covered below.

These tables tell the story about the data. Table 14.4 provides descriptive crosstabs of the data. A crosstabs is a contingency table. Because there are two variables, it is called a two-way table.

Table 14.4

Interest in Private Pension * Age Group Crosstabulation

			Age Group		
			Younger Group	Older Group	Total
Interest in Private Pension	No	Count	71	8	79
		Expected Count	39.5	39.5	79.0
		% within Age Group	78.0%	8.8%	43.4%
		% of Total	39.0%	4.4%	43.4%
	Yes	Count	20	83	103
		Expected Count	51.5	51.5	103.0
		% within Age Group	22.0%	91.2%	56.6%
		% of Total	11.0%	45.6%	56.6%
Total		Count	91	91	182
		Expected Count	91.0	91.0	182.0
		% within Age Group	100.0%	100.0%	100.0%
		% of Total	50.0%	50.0%	100.0%

Based on the entire sample, we would expect to find 43.4% (79) persons not interested in a private pension and 56.6% (103) of the sample interested in the pension, as well as 50.0% (91) from the younger group and 50.0% (91) from the older group, as highlighted in Table 14.5. When the total counts are not equal, count assessments can be misleading. For this reason, including percentages is useful. The **percentages** are the standardized (or relative) counts so that we can easily compare the counts' percentages of the different joint categories, of which there are 2 × 2 = 4 in this example.

Table 14.5

Interest in Private Pension * Age Group Crosstabulation

			Age Group		
			Younger Group	Older Group	Total
Interest in Private Pension	No	Count	[illegible]	[illegible]	79
		Expected Count	[illegible]	[illegible]	79.0
		% within Age Group	[illegible]	[illegible]	43.4%
		% of Total	[illegible]	[illegible]	43.4%
	Yes	Count	[illegible]	[illegible]	103
		Expected Count	[illegible]	[illegible]	103.0
		% within Age Group	[illegible]	[illegible]	56.6%
		% of Total	[illegible]	[illegible]	56.6%
Total		Count	91	91	182
		Expected Count	91.0	91.0	182.0
		% within Age Group	100.0%	100.0%	100.0%
		% of Total	50.0%	50.0%	100.0%

Basis of Expected counts.

Basis of Expected counts.

What interests us is whether there is a significant relationship between private pension interest and age category. Put differently, does one's age category influence whether one is interested in a private pension? The differences between the expected counts (which are based on the marginal totals and overall total) and the observed counts determine whether the chi-square test reveals a meaningful relationship.

Table 14.6

Interest in Private Pension * Age Group Crosstabulation

			Age Group		
			Younger Group	Older Group	Total
Interest in Priva nsion	No	Count	71	8	[illegible]
		Expected Count	39.5	39.5	[illegible]
		% within Age Group	78.0%	8.8%	[illegible]
		% of Total	39.0%	4.4%	[illegible]
	Yes	Count	20	83	[illegible]
		Expected Count	51.5	51.5	[illegible]
		% within Age Group	22.0%	91.2%	[illegible]
		% of Total	11.0%	45.6%	[illegible]
Total		Count	[illegible]	[illegible]	[illegible]
		Expected Count	[illegible]	[illegible]	[illegible]
		% within Age Group	[illegible]	[illegible]	[illegible]
		% of Total	[illegible]	[illegible]	[illegible]

Observed ("Count") from sample and the "Expected Count" based on the marginal and sample totals.

As depicted in Table 14.6, of the observed counts, we can see that 71 or 78% of the younger category are not interested in a private pension compared to 8 or 8.8% of the older group. In both cases, we would have expected 39.5 each (or one 39 and the other 40). For instance, the expected count calculation for the younger group (or older group for that matter when using a 2 × 2 design) who are not interested in a pension is: (79 × 91) / 182 = 7,189 / 182 = 39.5.

Thus, there appears to be a difference in lack of interest by age group. In the case of those who are interested in a private pension plan, 20 or 22% of the younger respondents express interest, whereas 83 or 91.2% of the older category of respondents are interested. Overall, we would have expected 51.5% for each group (one 51 and the other 52). Clearly, the older group is more interested in private pension plans.

Chi-Square Test of Independence Analysis

The "Chi-Square Tests" table indicates whether differences are statistically significant. The "Asymp. Sig. (2-sided)" column comprises the p-values for the various statistical measures. Since we have at least five expected counts in each cell, we use the Pearson chi-square statistic, which has a p-value of <.000. The **Pearson chi-square statistic** is the chi-square statistic used when there is a sufficient sample size (see Chapter 6 on sample size determination) in addition to meeting all of the data assumptions. Assuming that our alpha is .05, we are willing to accept a probability of less than 5% that these results are by chance and not meaningfully different from the expected counts. Since $p < .000$ (.050 > .000), these findings are statistically significantly different from what we would expect. Therefore, based on the sample data, it is likely that there is a meaningful relationship between age groups and interest in private pensions. That is to say, interest in private pensions varies by age group.

The **Continuity Correction statistic** is a conservative measure that adjusts for an undersized sample in a 2 × 2 chi-square analysis *only*. If the Pearson Chi-square and Continuity Correct are both significant or both nonsignificant, then report the Pearson chi-square statistic. If they are inconsistent, where they are not both significant or not both nonsignificant, then the Continuity Correct statistic becomes the basis of assessment and is reported.

The **Fisher Exact Test (two-sided)** statistic automatically generates for 2 × 2 chi-square analysis *only*. It may be reported if at least one expected joint category has a count less than 5. If both the Pearson Chi-square statistic and Fisher Exact Test statistic are significant or both are nonsignificant, then report the Pearson chi-square statistic. If they are inconsistent where one is significant and the other is not significant *and* there is one category that has an expected count <5, then the Fisher Exact Test statistic is used for assessing and is reported. Alternatively, the beginning of this chapter covers options that address combining expected counts that are less than 5.

Table 14.7

Chi-Square Tests

	Value	df	Asymp. Sig. (2-sided)	Exact Sig. (2-sided)	Exact Sig. (1-sided)
Pearson Chi-Square	88.774[a]	1	.000		
Continuity Correction[b]	85.979	1	.000		
Likelihood Ratio	99.107	1	.000		
Fisher's Exact Test				.000	.000
N of Valid Cases	182				

a. 0 cells (0.0%) have expected count less than 5. The minimum expected count is 39.50.

b. Computed only for a 2x2 table

Table 14.8, the **Symmetric Measures table**, provides additional information about the relationship between age category and interest in private pension responses. It is akin to a "correlation." Of the two statistics reported, Cramer's *V* accounts for all categories and is thus preferred over the limited Phi statistic. In this example, the Cramer's *V* statistic is .698 and meaningful ($p < .000$).

Table 14.8

Symmetric Measures

		Value	Approx. Sig.
Nominal by Nominal	Phi	.698	.000
	Cramer's V	.698	.000
N of Valid Cases		182	

Since **Cramer's *V*** is the "correlation" between the two categorical variables, squaring it will provide the variance explained. The **variance explained** is the percentage of the relationship between the two variables that can be explained by the sample data. Squaring .698, .698 × .698, yields an explained variance of .487. That is to say, the sample data explain 48.7% of the relationship between age category and interest in private pension categories. Therefore, in this case, the data *suggest* that 48.7% of whether one is interested in pensions may be explained by one's age.

In summary, since the Pearson chi-square test has a *p*-value <.001, indicating a meaningful relationship between age group and interest in private pensions, we can conclude that based on a representative sample, there is evidence that indicates one's age group and interest in private pensions are related. The results suggest that age influences whether one is interested in pensions. The opposite would not make sense.

Reporting Results

The following is a suggested write-up of the results.

Write-Up

Based on a representative sample of 182 participants consisting of 91 respondents 18–34 years and 91 respondents 35 years and older, a chi-square of independence was calculated comparing the counts of those interested in a private pension based on younger and older age groups. A significant relationship was found ($\chi^2(1) = 88.774$, $p < .001$). The data explain nearly 49% ($p < .001$) of the relationship between private pension interest and age group, suggesting that age affects whether someone is interested in pensions. As depicted in Table 14.9, those individuals who were 35 and older (91.2%) were more likely to be interested in private pensions than persons who were 18–34 years old (22.0%).

Table 14.9

Interest in Private Pension Participation by Age Group

Income Range	Younger Group	Older Group	Total
Interested in Private Pension	20 (11.0%)	83 (45.6%)	103 (56.6%)
Not Interested in Private Pension	71 (39.0%)	8 (4.4%)	79 (43.4%)
Total	91 (50.0%)	91 (50.0%)	182 (100%)

Note: ($\chi^2(1) = 88.774$, $p < .001$). Cramer's $V = .698$ ($p < .001$). $N = 182$.

As shown in Table 14.9, the age groupings are in the columns because they likely predict pension interest. The percentages are the standardized counts so that we can easily compare the counts as percentages in the different categories (four joint combinations of age and pension interest). The expected percentage of those interested in private pensions is 56.6%. For older respondents, 91.2% were interested in the private pension and, by contrast, only 20.0% of the younger participants expressed a similar interest. This table makes an observed and expected count (and percentage) visual comparison easily understandable.

In this case, the degrees of freedom (*df*) is the number of joint categories that can change within the total sample size before the remaining number(s) become fixed. The "(1)" represents *df*, which is calculated as follows: $(r - 1) \times (c - 1) = (2 - 1) \times (2 - 1) = 1 \times 1 = 1 = df$. Let us illustrate the idea behind *df* for this type of analysis. Because the *df* refer to joint category counts, the rows and columns are multiplied. There are 103 persons interested in private pensions. Let us take the younger group interested in private pensions' count. Because 20 of the 103 are younger, then 83 must be older, and the other two joint counts thus become predetermined as well. Therefore, only 20 or any other single joint count can vary, which represents one degree of freedom. For our purposes, it is important to know how to determine the *df* for reporting (see Table 14.10).

Table 14.10

Degrees of Freedom Calculation in A Chi-square Test of Independence

(20)	? = 83	*20 + 83* = 103
? = 71	? = 8	*71 + 8* = 76
20 + 71 = 91	*83 + 8* = 91	*91 + 91* = 182

The 88.774 is the chi-square statistic for this dataset and a reporting requirement. A *p*-value of <.000 indicates that the probability of the results occurring by chance alone is less than 1 out of 1,000. This is very low and certainly less than the .05 (5 / 100) alpha. *P*-values that are .000 or less are presented as $p < .001$. *P*-values that are equal to or higher than .001 are exactly reported to three places to the right of the decimal point (for example, .130 or .006). Clicking on the *p*-value in the SPSS output file will indicate the exact value. Last, *N* represents the sample size.

Example 14.2: A 2 × 2 Chi-Square Test of Independence: The Nonsignificant Case

For this example, we will skip the SPSS steps because they are identical to the procedure above. We wish to examine whether there is a relationship between individuals who are conservative or liberal and their smoking habits. Participants selected conservative or liberal and "Yes" or "No" to whether they smoke. Alpha = .05. The sample data file name is "Chi-Square Independence Example 2 Data."

SPSS Output Interpretation

The case processing summary, Crosstabs (with percentages), chi-square significance test, and symmetric tables are generated. We focus on the latter three tables.

Data Screening

Table 14.11 gives us a descriptive picture of the variables' data. We assume that all of the data requirements have been met.

Table 14.11

Smoker Status * Political Perspective Crosstabulation

			Political Perspective		
			Conservative	Liberal	Total
Smoker Status	Nonsmoker	Count	48	54	102
		Expected Count	49.8	52.2	102.0
		% within Political Perspective	80.0%	85.7%	82.9%
		% of Total	39.0%	43.9%	82.9%
	Smoker	Count	12	9	21
		Expected Count	10.2	10.8	21.0
		% within Political Perspective	20.0%	14.3%	17.1%
		% of Total	9.8%	7.3%	17.1%
Total		Count	60	63	123
		Expected Count	60.0	63.0	123.0
		% within Political Perspective	100.0%	100.0%	100.0%
		% of Total	48.8%	51.2%	100.0%

Based on the entire sample, we would expect to find 82.9% (102) nonsmokers and 17.1% (21) smokers, as well as 48.8% (60) conservative and 51.2% (63) liberal. In this example, all of the marginal totals vary.

Table 14.12

Smoker Status * Political Perspective Crosstabulation

			Political Perspective		
			Conservative	Liberal	Total
Smoker Status	Nonsmoker	Count	[illegible]	[illegible]	102
		Expected Count	[illegible]	[illegible]	102.0
		% within Political Perspective	[illegible]	[illegible]	82.9%
		% of Total	[illegible]	[illegible]	82.9%
	Smoker	Count	[illegible]	[illegible]	21
		Expected Count	[illegible]	[illegible]	21.0
		% within Political Perspective	[illegible]	[illegible]	17.1%
		% of Total	[illegible]	[illegible]	17.1%
Total		Count	60	63	123
		Expected Count	60.0	63.0	123.0
		% within Political Perspective	100.0%	100.0%	100.0%
		% of Total	48.8%	51.2%	100.0%

The size of the differences between the expected and observed counts determine whether the chi-square test indicates a meaningful relationship between political perspective and smoker status. Table 14.13 presents the joint category counts.

Table 14.13

Smoker Status * Political Perspective Crosstabulation

			Political Perspective		
			Conservative	Liberal	Total
Smoker Status	Nonsmoker	Count	48	54	[illegible]
		Expected Count	49.8	52.2	[illegible]
		% within Political Perspective	80.0%	85.7%	[illegible]
		% of Total	39.0%	43.9%	[illegible]
	Smoker	Count	12	9	[illegible]
		Expected Count	10.2	10.8	[illegible]
		% within Political Perspective	20.0%	14.3%	[illegible]
		% of Total	9.8%	7.3%	[illegible]
Total		Count	[illegible]	[illegible]	[illegible]
		Expected Count	[illegible]	[illegible]	[illegible]
		% within Political Perspective	[illegible]	[illegible]	[illegible]
		% of Total	[illegible]	[illegible]	[illegible]

Chi-Square Test of Independence Analysis

Table 14.14 indicates whether the difference is statistically meaningful. "Asymp. Sig. (2-sided)" comprises the *p*-values for the various statistical measures. Since we have at least five expected counts in each cell, with 10.2 being the lowest, and the Continuity Correction statistic is consistently not significant as are the other tests, we use the Pearson chi-square statistic, which has a *p*-value of .400. Since $p = .400$ ($.050 < .400$), these findings are not significantly different from what we would expect. Based on the sample data, there is likely no meaningful relationship between smoking and political perspective.

Table 14.14

Chi-Square Tests

	Value	df	Asymp. Sig. (2-sided)	Exact Sig. (2-sided)	Exact Sig. (1-sided)
Pearson Chi-Square	.709[a]	1	.400		
Continuity Correction[b]	.363	1	.547		
Likelihood Ratio	.710	1	.399		
Fisher's Exact Test				.476	.274
N of Valid Cases	123				

a. 0 cells (.0%) have expected count less than 5. The minimum expected count is 10.24.

b. Computed only for a 2x2 table

As shown in Table 14.15, because the Pearson chi-square is not significant (less than .05), Cramer's V is not significant as well, (V = .076, p = .400).

Table 14.15

Symmetric Measures

		Value	Approx. Sig.
Nominal by Nominal	Phi	-.076	.400
	Cramer's V	.076	.400
N of Valid Cases		123	

In summary, since the Pearson chi-square test has a p-value of .400, there is no significant relationship between political perspective and smoker status. Thus, we can conclude that based on a representative sample, there likely is no evidence indicating that one's political perspectives and whether one smokes are related.

Reporting Results

The following is an example of reporting a chi-square test of independence. Note that depending on the reporting requirements, it may not be necessary to include a table if the results are not significant.

Write-Up

Based on a representative sample of 123 participants consisting of 102 nonsmokers and 21 smokers, a chi-square of independence was calculated comparing counts of these two groups by their reported conservative or liberal political perspective. No significant relationship was found ($\chi^2(1)$ = .709, p = .400). It is likely that there is no relationship between one's self-reported political perspective and whether one smokes.

Example 14.3: A 3 × 5 Chi-Square Test of Independence: Both Cases

Again, we will skip the SPSS steps because they are nearly identical to the procedure above, with the exception of the Continuity Correction and Fisher Exact Test statistics, which are only generated for a 2 × 2 chi-square design. In this analysis, we will determine if there a relationship between undergraduate college major and the intention to attend graduate school after graduation. The anticipated independent variable consists of the following categories of majors: Healthcare, Math/Science, Engineering, Business, and Education. The dependent variable is composed of intention to attend graduate school, no intention to attend graduate school, and undecided.

This is thus a 3 × 5 design. Alpha = .05. The sample data file name is "Chi-Square Independence Example 3 Data."

SPSS Output Interpretation

We focus on the Crosstabs (with percentages), chi-square significance test, and symmetric tables.

Data Screening

Table 14.16 offers us a descriptive picture of the variables' data. We assume that all of the data requirements have been met.

Table 14.16

Intention to Attend Grad School * Major Grouping Crosstabulation

			Major Grouping					
			Healthcare	Math/Science	Engineering	Business	Education	Total
Intention to Attend Grad School	No	Count	8	13	23	29	7	80
		Expected Count	12.4	12.0	16.8	17.6	21.2	80.0
		% within Major Grouping	25.8%	43.3%	54.8%	65.9%	13.2%	40.0%
		% of Total	4.0%	6.5%	11.5%	14.5%	3.5%	40.0%
	Undecided	Count	11	7	9	7	6	40
		Expected Count	6.2	6.0	8.4	8.8	10.6	40.0
		% within Major Grouping	35.5%	23.3%	21.4%	15.9%	11.3%	20.0%
		% of Total	5.5%	3.5%	4.5%	3.5%	3.0%	20.0%
	Yes	Count	12	10	10	8	40	80
		Expected Count	12.4	12.0	16.8	17.6	21.2	80.0
		% within Major Grouping	38.7%	33.3%	23.8%	18.2%	75.5%	40.0%
		% of Total	6.0%	5.0%	5.0%	4.0%	20.0%	40.0%
Total		Count	31	30	42	44	53	200
		Expected Count	31.0	30.0	42.0	44.0	53.0	200.0
		% within Major Grouping	100.0%	100.0%	100.0%	100.0%	100.0%	100.0%
		% of Total	15.5%	15.0%	21.0%	22.0%	26.5%	100.0%

Based on the entire sample, and as depicted in Table 14.17, we would expect to find 40.0% (80) who do not intend to attend graduate school, 20.0% (40) who are undecided about attending graduate school, and 40.0% (80) who intend to go to graduate school. Likewise, we expect to find 15.5% (31) Healthcare, 15.0% (30) Math/Science, 21.0% (42) Engineering, 22.0% (44) Business, and 26.5% (53) Education majors.

Table 14.17

Intention to Attend Grad School * Major Grouping Crosstabulation

			Major Grouping					
			Healthcare	Math/Science	Engineering	Business	Education	Total
Intention to Attend Grad School	No	Count	[illegible]	[illegible]	[illegible]	[illegible]	[illegible]	80
		Expected Count	[illegible]	[illegible]	[illegible]	[illegible]	[illegible]	80.0
		% within Major Grouping	[illegible]	[illegible]	[illegible]	[illegible]	[illegible]	40.0%
		% of Total	[illegible]	[illegible]	[illegible]	[illegible]	[illegible]	40.0%
	Undecided	Count	[illegible]	[illegible]	[illegible]	[illegible]	[illegible]	40
		Expected Count	[illegible]	[illegible]	[illegible]	[illegible]	[illegible]	40.0
		% within Major Grouping	[illegible]	[illegible]	[illegible]	[illegible]	[illegible]	20.0%
		% of Total	[illegible]	[illegible]	[illegible]	[illegible]	[illegible]	20.0%
	Yes	Count	[illegible]	[illegible]	[illegible]	[illegible]	[illegible]	80
		Expected Count	[illegible]	[illegible]	[illegible]	[illegible]	[illegible]	80.0
		% within Major Grouping	[illegible]	[illegible]	[illegible]	[illegible]	[illegible]	40.0%
		% of Total	[illegible]	[illegible]	[illegible]	[illegible]	[illegible]	40.0%
Total		Count	31	30	42	44	53	200
		Expected Count	31.0	30.0	42.0	44.0	53.0	200.0
		% within Major Grouping	100.0%	100.0%	100.0%	100.0%	100.0%	100.0%
		% of Total	15.5%	15.0%	21.0%	22.0%	26.5%	100.0%

Chi-Square Test of Independence Analysis

Of the observed counts, 23 Engineering graduates did not intend to attend graduate school while the expected count was nearly 17. A similar pattern emerged for Business graduates, where 29 indicated no interest in graduate school compared to an expected count of nearly 18. The opposite was true for Education graduates, in which 21 were expected to not be interested in graduate school when the actual sample count was 7. The undecided counts were unremarkable. It appears that Education graduates intend to go to graduate school more than the other college major students, and Business and Engineering students tend to have less interest in graduate school compared to the other majors. Table 14.18 presents the major categories and intention category counts.

Table 14.18

Intention to Attend Grad School * Major Grouping Crosstabulation

Observed ("Count") from sample and "Expected Count" based on sample "Total."

			Major Grouping					
			Healthcare	Math/Science	Engineering	Business	Education	Total
Intention to Attend Grad School	No	Count	8	13	23	29	7	[illegible]
		Expected Count	12.4	12.0	16.8	17.6	21.2	[illegible]
		% within Major Grouping	25.8%	43.3%	54.8%	65.9%	13.2%	[illegible]
		% of Total	4.0%	6.5%	11.5%	14.5%	3.5%	[illegible]
	Undecided	Count	11	7	9	7	6	[illegible]
		Expected Count	6.2	6.0	8.4	8.8	10.6	[illegible]
		% within Major Grouping	35.5%	23.3%	21.4%	15.9%	11.3%	[illegible]
		% of Total	5.5%	3.5%	4.5%	3.5%	3.0%	[illegible]
	Yes	Count	12	10	10	8	40	[illegible]
		Expected Count	12.4	12.0	16.8	17.6	21.2	[illegible]
		% within Major Grouping	38.7%	33.3%	23.8%	18.2%	75.5%	[illegible]
		% of Total	6.0%	5.0%	5.0%	4.0%	20.0%	[illegible]
Total		Count	[illegible]	[illegible]	[illegible]	[illegible]	[illegible]	[illegible]
		Expected Count	[illegible]	[illegible]	[illegible]	[illegible]	[illegible]	[illegible]
		% within Major Grouping	[illegible]	[illegible]	[illegible]	[illegible]	[illegible]	[illegible]
		% of Total	[illegible]	[illegible]	[illegible]	[illegible]	[illegible]	[illegible]

Table 14.19 indicates whether the differences are statistically meaningful. Since the Pearson chi-square statistic's $p < .000$ ($.05 > .000$), these findings are significantly different from what we would expect. Based on the sample data, there is a meaningful relationship between undergraduate college major and intention to attend graduate school after graduation. In a 2 × 2 analysis, if the results were statistically meaningful, it would be clear that the difference rests between the two categories. This is not always obvious when there are more than two categories. A meaningful result indicates that there is a difference between at least one joint category's observed and expected counts. Post hoc tests, such as the Marascuilo procedure, column comparison proportions z-tests, and residual analysis, can precisely reveal where differences exist. The details of these procedures are beyond our discussion.

Chi-Square Tests

	Value	df	Asymptotic Significance (2-sided)
Pearson Chi-Square	52.125[a]	8	.000
Likelihood Ratio	52.316	8	.000
Linear-by-Linear Association	5.061	1	.024
N of Valid Cases	200		

a. 0 cells (0.0%) have expected count less than 5. The minimum expected count is 6.00.

Table 4.19

As shown in Table 14.20, since the Pearson chi-square is significant, we would expect the Cramer's V to be significant, which it is ($V = .361$, $p < .000$).

Table 14.20

Symmetric Measures

		Value	Approximate Significance
Nominal by Nominal	Phi	.511	.000
	Cramer's V	.361	.000
N of Valid Cases		200	

In summary, since the Pearson chi-square test has a p-value of .000, we can conclude that based on a representative sample, there is evidence to suggest that one's college major and intention to attend graduate school are related.

Reporting Significant Results

The following is the write-up for this example.

Write-Up

A representative sample of 200 recent graduates organized by college major were asked about their intention to attend graduate school after graduation. A chi-square test of independence was calculated comparing the counts of graduate school intentionality by college major. A significant relationship was found ($\chi^2(8) = 52.125$, $p < .001$). The data explain 13% ($p < .001$) of the relationship between major and graduate school intentionality, suggesting that major has an influence on whether someone is interested in graduate school. Those who majored in Education were more likely to be interested in attending graduate school (75.5%) compared to the other majors. Those who majored in Engineering (23.8%) and Business (18.2%) were less likely to be interested in graduate school compared to the other major categories (see Table 14.21).

Table 14.21

Interest in Graduate School by College Major Category

Intent to Go to Graduate School	Healthcare	Math/Science	Engineering	Business	Education	Total
No Intention	8 (4.0%)	13 (6.5%)	23 (11.5%)	29 (14.5%)	7 (3.5%)	80 (40.0%)
Undecided	11 (5.5%)	7 (3.5%)	9 (4.5%)	7 (3.5%)	6 (3.0%)	40 (20.0%)
Intends to Go	12 (6.0%)	10 (5.0%)	10 (5.0%)	8 (4.0%)	40 (20.0%)	80 (40.0%)
Total	31 (15.5%)	30 (15.0%)	42 (21.0%)	44 (22.0%)	53 (26.5%)	200 (100%)

Note: ($\chi^2(8) = 52.125$, $p < .001$). Cramer's $V = .361$ ($p < .001$). $N = 200$.

Reporting Nonsignificant Results

Nonsignificant results would be reported as follows.

Write-Up

A representative sample of 200 recent graduates organized by college majors were asked about their intention to attend graduate school. A chi-square test of independence was calculated comparing the counts of graduate school intentionality by major. No significant relationship was found ($\chi^2(8) = 5.718$, $p = .679$). Therefore, it is likely that there is no relationship between college major and intention to attend graduate school.

SUMMARY OF KEY CONCEPTS

- The chi-square test of independence is a significance test that involves counts within categorical data.
- Chi-square tests of independence require two variables each with two or more categories.
- The chi-square measures the size of the difference between the observed and expected joint counts.
- There must be a minimum of a count of 5 in all expected joint categories.
- Expected counts are based on the marginal total counts and the sample size.
- The "Crosstabs" tool in SPSS can be used to generate chi-square test of independence results.
- The 2 × 2 chi-square design includes a number of statistics applicable to unique data attributes.
- Assessing and interpreting the chi-square results involves the chi-square statistic and *p*-value in order to determine statistical significance.

CHI-SQUARE TEST OF INDEPENDENCE APPLIED EXERCISES

14.1 What is the chi-square test of independence?

14.2 What is a crosstabs?

14.3 What is a joint count?

14.4 Define marginal totals.

14.5 What are standardized counts?

14.6 What is the Pearson chi-square statistic?

14.7 Define the Continuity Correction statistic.

14.8 What is the Fisher Exact test (two-sided)?

14.9 What are Symmetric Measures?

14.10 Define Cramer's *V*.

14.11 What is variance explained?

14.12 By hand, calculate the expected counts for the following contingency table.

Perceptions of Global Warming by Political Affiliation

Global Warming Is Real	**Political Party**		
	Democrat	**Republican**	**Total**
Yes	160	75	235
No	15	100	115
Total	175	175	350

Note: We will assume a sample of 350.

14.13 By hand, calculate the chi-square statistic and what is the *df* for the data in Exercise 14.12.

14.14 In narrative, explain why the differences between the observed and expected counts determine whether the two variables are related. Include the reasoning for the expected counts.

14.15 Based on the following information in the table, determine the *df* and three missing counts.

Perceptions of Global Warming by Political Affiliation

Global Warming Is Real	**Political Party**		
	Democrat	**Republican**	**Total**
Yes	?	150	470
No	?	?	230
Total	350	350	700

Note: We will assume a sample of 350.

14.16 What is the Pearson chi-square statistic for the data in Exercise 14.15?

14.17 Conduct a crosstabs chi-square analysis to determine if there is a relationship between type of protein diet selection (soy or meat) and gender (woman or man). Do women or men prefer soy or meat as a protein source of food? Alpha = .05. Explain your answer. Report your results in the format covered in this chapter and, if necessary, include a table. Should it be necessary, include the Continuity Correction and/or Fisher Exact Test statistics, as well as providing any necessary solutions to problematic data. The data file name is "Chi-Square Independence Exercise 1 Data."

14.18 Conduct a crosstabs chi-square analysis to determine if there is a relationship between working first or second shift and mood (positive or negative). Alpha = .05. Explain your answer. Report your results in the format covered in this chapter and, if necessary, include a table. Should it be necessary, include the Continuity Correction and/or Fisher Exact Test statistics, as well as providing any necessary solutions to problematic data. The data file name is "Chi-Square Independence Exercise 2 Data."

14.19 Conduct a crosstabs chi-square analysis to determine if there is a relationship between college status (full-time or part-time) and preference for a statistics e-book or a statistics hard-copy book in a statistics course. Alpha = .05. Explain your answer. Report your results in the format covered in this chapter and, if necessary, include a table. Should it be necessary, include the Continuity Correction and/or Fisher Exact Test statistics, as well as providing any necessary solutions to problematic data. The data file name is "Chi-Square Independence Exercise 3 Data."

14.20 Conduct a crosstabs chi-square analysis to determine if there is a relationship between pet ownership and college attendance. Alpha = .05. Explain your answer. Report your results in the format covered in this chapter and, if necessary, include a table. Should it be necessary, include the Continuity Correction and/or Fisher Exact Test statistics, as well as providing any necessary solutions to problematic data. The data file name is "Chi-Square Independence Exercise 4 Data."

Chapter 15

Chi-Square Test of the Same Sample: Comparing Counts of the Same Sample Measured Twice Using a Categorical Variable

LEARNING OBJECTIVES

To be able to:

- understand and explain the purpose of a repeated measures McNemar chi-square test;
- understand that repeated counts involve data from the same sample;
- know when to use a McNemar-Bowes chi-square test;
- know and describe how to conduct the repeated measures chi-square test in SPSS;
- accurately interpret the repeated measures chi-square test results; and
- learn how to report significant and nonsignificant repeated measures chi-square test results.

15.1 Introduction to the Same Sample Measured Twice Using a Categorical Variable

The **McNemar** and the **McNemar-Bowker Chi-Square Significance Test** examine counts (and percentages of those counts) between the same cases or sample measured twice, usually using a Time 1 variable and a Time 2 variable with two or more identical categories of the variable being measured. The test is a paired version of a chi-square test known as a repeated measures design. It calculates whether there is a meaningful difference between the same sample counted twice on the same dependent categorical variable, which is called a **within-subjects analysis**. In order to statistically *compare* time points, there must be a minimum of two categories of what will be counted. The first time period categorical variable is usually placed in the columns (C) and serves as the baseline count. The **baseline count** establishes the counts from which the subsequent counts are compared for differences. The second time period categorical variable is usually placed in the rows (R) so that we have a crosstabs design or R × C (row by column) design.

Any differences between count points is related to time or to time in conjunction with a treatment. In the first instance, it is simply the effect of time on the two counts. In the second case, a **treatment**, which is an experimental condition or some type of intervention, is introduced and the frequencies are examined for differences between the baseline and post-treatment counts. The time-related component is the independent "variable" and the counted condition of potential change is the dependent "variable." The crosstabs or contingency table-like analysis organizes the data into joint categories.

For instance, we can use crosstabs, and the **McNemar test** in particular, to answer binary formatted questions such as: Do people change in their support for a program over time ("Yes" or "No" responses)? Do people change their views on pet ownership *after* watching ads that encourage pet ownership? The first time (before exposure to the ad) would contain binary formatted data as "Yes" or "No" responses to interest in pet ownership. The second time would record responses to the same question after participants are exposed to the "pet ownership" ads. These examples are called a 2 × 2 crosstabs McNemar chi-square test of repeated measures because there are only two response choices: "Yes" or "No," and the same sample is measured twice. The design is 2 categories × 2 times.

Although the crosstabs test examines for difference between only two independent time points, the categorical dependent variable can have more than two categories, which would require an R × 2 crosstabs **McNemar-Bowker test** of repeated measures design. The "R" indicates that there are more than two categories and the "2" indicates two time points. For example, we can extend our illustration above to a variable with three groups by adding an "Undecided" category, thus having a 3 × 2 design. In this case, responses for the before and after pet ads repeated measures would be "Yes," "No," or "Undecided." The joint combinations of the two variables consist of "Time 1" or "Time 2" and "Yes," "No," or "Undecided." The count of "Undecided" responses "before" exposure to the pet ad is one joint category. The before and after "No" counts are compared, the before and after "Yes" counts are compared, and the before and after "Undecided" counts are compared for statistically meaningful differences among them. A statistically significant result indicates there is a time effect owing to ad exposure.

In short, the analysis involves a paired comparison of counted responses within each case to examine whether the counts change between the first time and second time points

15.2 Data Assumptions

Since we are analyzing a sample, we have the following data assumptions:

- The sample is representative of the target population. For example, if 45–54-year-old middle-income men from the West Coast is the target population, then the sample must represent this targeted population or the findings will not be applicable to this group.
- The sample is randomly drawn, as we covered in Chapter 5.
- The groups being compared are dependent in some way, which is usually indicated by the same cases or origin of the data points being measured twice and then analyzed by paired or matched comparison. In our examples, the categorical counts represent the same respondents examined at two different times.
- The independent "time" variable comprises only two time or count points.
- There is a minimum of two categories in the dependent variable.
- Based on the study goal, the dependent variable contains all relevant categories and they are mutually exclusive.
- Each count is assigned to only one category.
- Since this is a repeated measures procedure, each time point has an equal number of cases. For example, if we are studying whether a sample of people are more likely to smoke over two time periods, we require the same people to be measured over the two time points, thus each time point has the same sample size.
- Last, each joint category contains at least five counts.

REAL WORLD SNAPSHOT

In a 2004 published study entitled "Knowledge of Sleep in Italian High School Students: Pilot-Test of a School-Based Sleep Educational Program," Cortesi and colleagues evaluated the effects of a sleep educational program on high school student knowledge about sleep and its importance to quality of life. The study examined changes from baseline knowledge compared to knowledge after completing a 2-hour interactive sleep educational course, as well as after 3 months.

Five hundred and forty students, ages 17–19 years, who were attending three secondary public schools, participated. They were randomly assigned to the educational condition or to the control condition. Changes in their sleep knowledge were examined by the differences in the counts of correct answers of the two post-course surveys compared to baseline responses. The McNemar statistic was one of the tests used in the analysis.

A series of paired tests compared joint counts at the three time points. The counts were based on a number of sleep-related questions. Virtually all of the repeated counts McNemar chi-square tests were statistically significant at $p < .001$, indicating that the number of correct answers to questions about sleep increased after exposure to the course. In many cases, the increased correct answers were maintained 3 months later. These findings suggest that a 2-hour course describing sleep, sleepiness, and the risk of poor sleep on daytime functioning can improve participants' level of knowledge on the importance of sleep.

Ask yourself: Can you think of a follow-up study that might contribute to assuring that students actually receive a sufficient amount of sleep?

15.3 Examples Using SPSS: Step-by-Step Instructions

The following crosstabs McNemar and McNemar-Bowker tests of repeated counts examples are covered using SPSS: one 2 × 2 indicating significant results, one 2 × 2 yielding nonsignificant results, and a 4 × 2 with significant and nonsignificant results.

Example 15.1: A Crosstabs 2 × 2 Repeated Measures McNemar Test: The Significant Case

We have a sample of 200 voters who were surveyed about their support for Candidate A before and after the candidate participated in three debates. This study was to determine if the debates influenced support for the candidate. Alpha = .05. The SPSS file named "2X Repeated Chi-Square Example 1 Data" contains the data for the analysis. The SPSS steps are as follows.

The analysis requires two variables: "Pre-Debate" support (1 = "No" and 2 = "Yes") and "Post-Debate" support (1 = "No" and 2 = "Yes").

Step 1: Open SPSS.

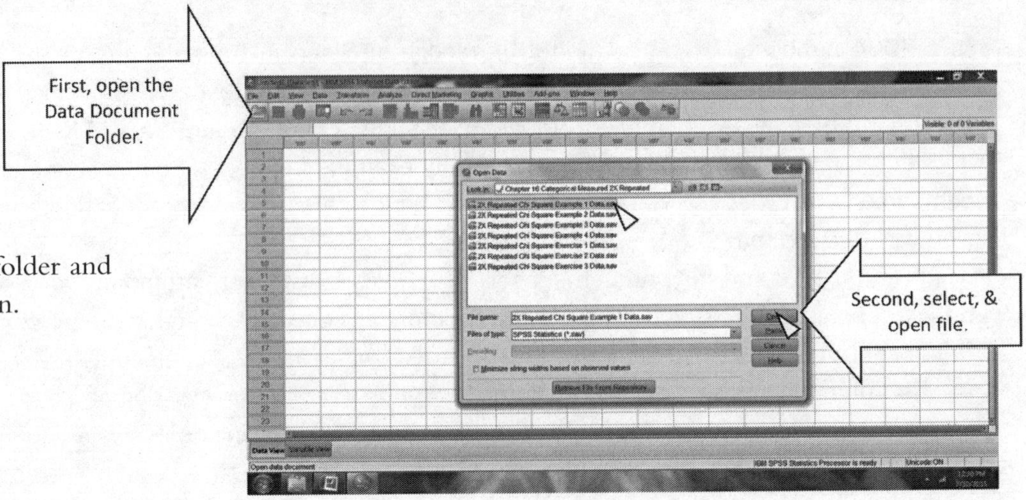

Locate the appropriate folder and data file, then click open.

Figure 15.1

Step 2: After the data file opens:

- Select the "Analyze" tab.
- Then, highlight "Descriptive Statistics."
- Last, click onto "Frequencies."

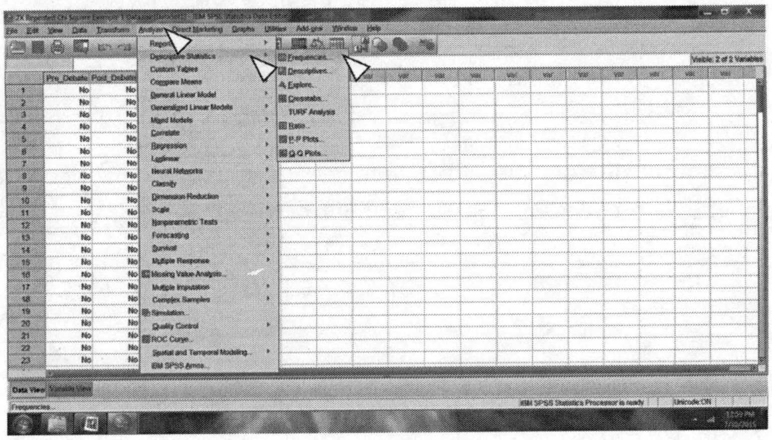

Figure 15.2

Next, you will see the following window.

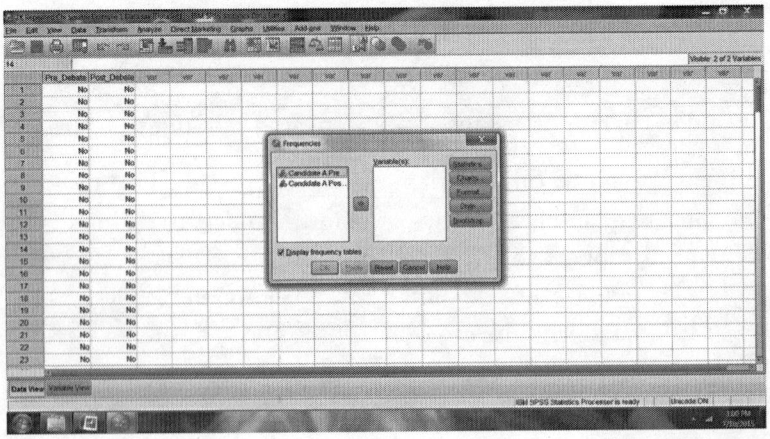

Figure 15.3

Step 3: In the "Frequencies" window, do the following:

- Highlight both variables in the left-hand side box and then click the "Arrow" button so that both the "Candidate A Pre-debate" and the "Candidate A Post-debate" variables are located in the "Variable(s)" box on the right-hand side. Leave everything else as is.
- Click the "OK" button located in the bottom-left-hand corner of the window. This procedure will generate frequency tables for later use.

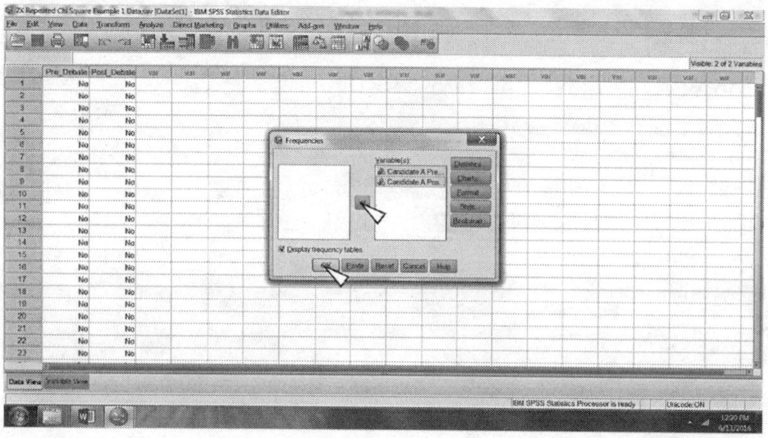

Figure 15.4

Step 4: Next, do the following:

- Click on the "Analyze" tab.
- Select "Descriptive Statistics."
- Last, click "Crosstabs."

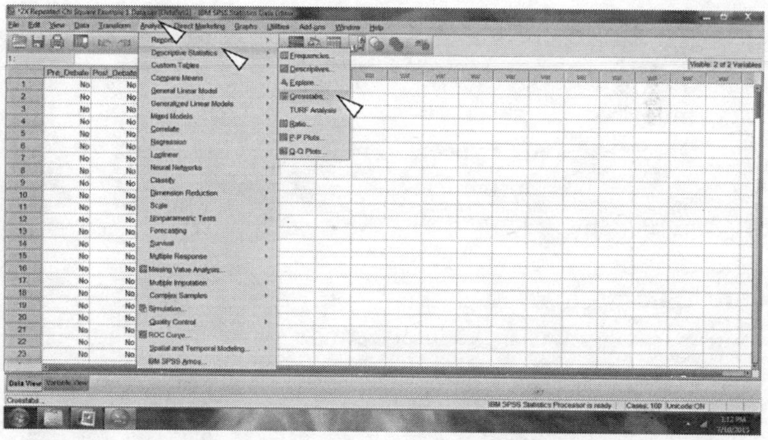

Figure 15.5

Step 5: The "Crosstabs" window will open.

- Since the "Candidate A Pre-debate" may influence the "Candidate A Post-debate," place the "pre-debate" variable in the column(s) box on the right by highlighting the variable.
- Then, click the "Arrow" button.
- Place the "post-debate" in the row(s) on the right using the same procedure.
- Last, click the "Statistics" button on the top-right-hand side of the window.

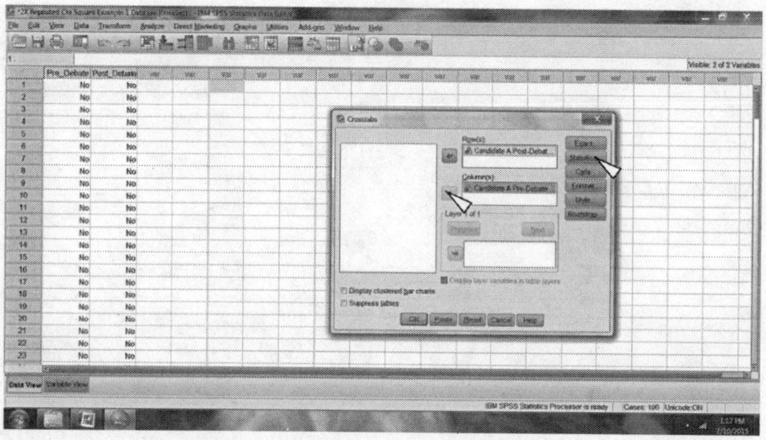

Figure 15.6

Step 6: The following "Crosstabs Statistics" window will open.

- Check off the "McNemar" box located in the bottom-right-hand corner.
- Then, click "Continue."

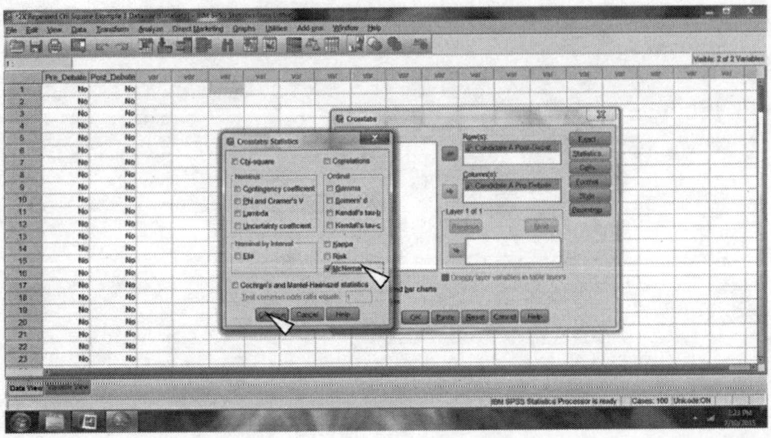

Figure 15.7

Step 7: Next, in the "Crosstabs" window, do the following:

- Click the "Cells" button.
- When the "Crosstabs Cell Display" window opens, check off "Observed" and "Expected" in the "Counts" box on the left-hand side.
- On the same side, in the "Percentages" area, check off "Total." Selecting only the "Total" percentages will make interpreting the table easier.
- Finally, click the "Continue" button in the bottom-left-hand side of the window.

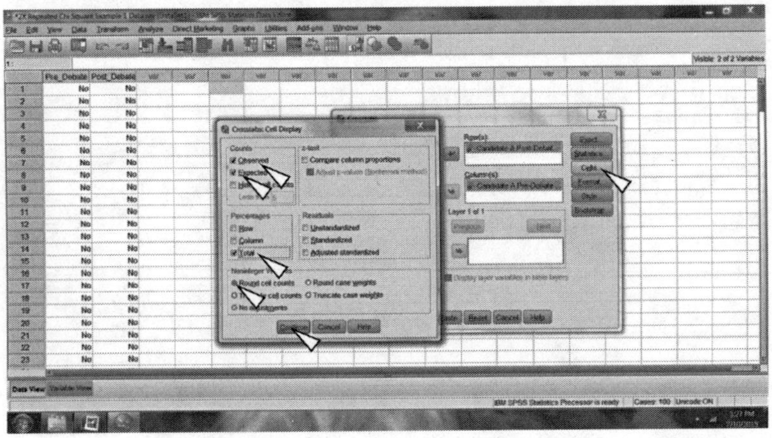

Figure 15.8

Step 8: Select "OK," located in the bottom-left-hand side of the "Crosstabs" window, to run the analysis. More output will be generated.

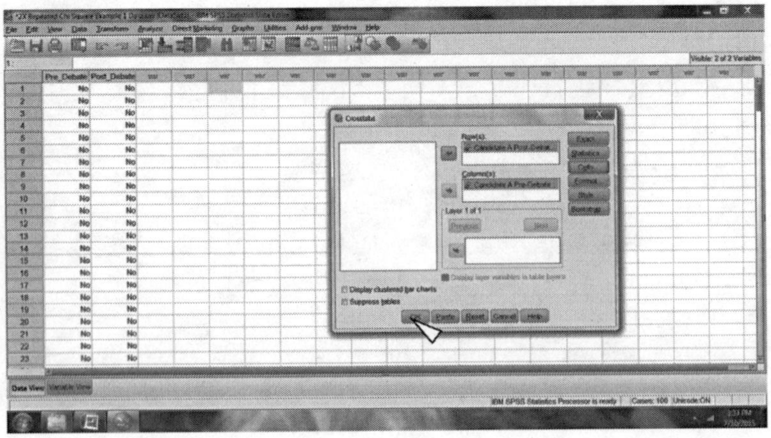

Figure 15.9

Last, save the data and output files for your records. Chapter 4 covers the save procedures.

SPSS Output Interpretation

Frequency tables, Crosstabs (with percentages), McNemar chi-square significance test, and a number of other tables were generated. We will focus on the frequency, Crosstabs, and McNemar chi-square test tables.

Data Screening

Table 15.1 is two-way because the dependent categorical variable is compared at two time points. We examine the "Yes" counts because the analysis focuses on candidate support. As depicted in Table 15.1, all joint categories have at least a count of 5. Had some joint counts been less than 5, there are two options. First, more data can be collected using a stratified sampling technique focusing on the low joint counts. Second, if additional data cannot be collected, a caveat would be included in the write-up indicating that the results may not be stable.

Table 15.1

Candidate A Post-Debate Poll * Candidate A Pre-Debate Poll Crosstabulation

			Candidate A Pre-Debate Poll		
			No	Yes	Total
Candidate A Post-Debate Poll	No	Count	71	36	[illegible]
		% of Total	35.5%	18.0%	[illegible]
	Yes	Count	76	17	[illegible]
		% of Total	38.0%	8.5%	[illegible]
Total		Count	147	53	200
		% of Total	73.5%	26.5%	100.0%

The joint counts are 71, 36, 76, and 17.

Table 15.2

Candidate A Pre-Debate Poll

		Frequency	Percent	Valid Percent	Cumulative Perc[illegible]
Valid	No	147	73.5	73.5	[illegible]
	Yes	53	26.5	26.5	[illegible]
	Total	200	100.0	100.0	

Pre-debate support for Candidate A was 26.5% (n=53).

Table 15.3

Candidate A Post-Debate Poll

		Frequency	Percent	Valid Percent	Cumulative Perc[illegible]
Valid	No	107	53.5	53.5	[illegible]
	Yes	93	46.5	46.5	[illegible]
	Total	200	100.0	100.0	

Post-debate support for Candidate A was 46.5% (n=93).

Tables 15.2 and 15.3 provide us with the marginal count descriptive picture of the sample data. We use the "Valid Percent" column, which adjusts for missing observations. On the other hand, the "Percent" column is based on the total case count, regardless of incomplete data in cases. Unless there are specific reasons to use the "Percent" column values, it is best practice to use the "Valid Percent" column figures. The "Cumulative Percent" is based on the valid cases or percentages.

Chi-Square Test for Repeated Counts Analysis

Based on a representative sample of the same voters, before the three debates, Candidate A's support was 26.5% (n = 53). After the debates, Candidate A's support was 46.5% (n = 93). We now need to determine whether the difference is statistically meaningful by analyzing the paired responses utilizing the McNemar chi-square test.

The McNemar Chi-Square Test result in Table 15.4 indicates that the difference in support between before and after the debates is statistically significant. Since our alpha is .05, we are willing to accept a probability of less than 5% that these results are by chance alone, and thus not meaningfully different. The p-value of .000 indicates a risk much less than 5%. Therefore, there is likely a difference in support between the two time points. Support for Candidate A changed after the debates.

Table 15.4

Chi-Square Tests

	Value	Exact Sig. (2-sided)
McNemar Test		.000[a]
N of Valid Cases	200	

a. Binomial distribution used.

The p-value is less than .000. Since alpha is .05, there is a difference in candidate support. "N of Valid Cases" is the sample size.

Reporting Results

The following is an example of reporting the McNemar chi-square test results. Only the valid cases are indicated and information of missing data would be reported in the "Note" area. The write-up focuses on support for the candidate.

Write-Up

Based on a representative sample of 200 voters, who were asked if they supported Candidate A before and after the three debates, a McNemar Chi-Square test was conducted. A significant difference in support was found ($p < .001$). As depicted in Table 15.5, prior to the debates, 26.5% (n = 53) voters supported Candidate A. After the debates, 46.5% (n = 93) of the same voters supported the candidate, representing a change in support.

Table 15.5

Comparison of Support for Candidate A Before and After the Three Debates

Support	Before Debates	After Debates
Yes	53 (26.5%)	93 (46.5%)
No	147 (73.5%)	107 (53.5%)
Total	200 (100.0%)	200 (100.0%)

Note: McNemar Chi-Square Test ($p < .001$). N = 200.

Likewise, looking at it differently, before the debates, 73.5% (n = 147) indicated that they would not support Candidate A. After the debates, non-supporters comprised 53.5% (n = 107) of the polled voters (p <.001), demonstrating a decrease in lack of support.

A p-value of <.000 indicates that the probability that these results are not meaningful is less than 1/1,000. This is very low and certainly less than our .05 (5 / 100) alpha, which is the level of risk that we are willing to accept. We usually report p-values that are .000 or less (for example, .0000004) as p < .001. P-values that are equal to or higher than .001 are reported exactly to three places to the right of the decimal point (for example, .130 or .006).

Example 15.2: A Crosstabs 2 × 2 Repeated Measures McNemar Test: The Nonsignificant Case

For this example, we will skip the SPSS steps because they are identical to the procedure above. This study tests ad campaign effectiveness for a new wrist cell phone. Four hundred consumers were asked if they would consider purchasing a wrist cell phone before and after viewing ads about the product. The response data consisted of a simple "yes" or "no" answer. Determine if the ad campaign changed interest in the wrist cell phone. Alpha = .05. The SPSS file named "2X Repeated Chi-Square Example 2 Data" contains the data for the analysis.

SPSS Output Interpretation

Again, we will focus on the Frequency, Crosstabs, and McNemar chi-square test tables.

Data Screening

All of the data assumptions have been met. Importantly, all joint categories have at least a count of 5. The joint counts are 218, 89, 76, and 17.

Table 15.6

Post Ad Campaign Interest * Pre Ad Campaign Interest Crosstabulation

			Pre Ad Campaign Interest		
			No	Yes	Total
Post Ad Campaign Interest	No	Count	218	89	307
		% of Total	54.5%	22.3%	76.8%
	Yes	Count	76	17	93
		% of Total	19.0%	4.3%	23.[illegible]
Total		Count	294	106	400
		% of Total	73.5%	26.5%	100.0%

Table 15.7

Pre Ad Campaign Interest

		Frequency	Percent	Valid Percent	Cumulative Percent
Valid	No	294	73.5	73.5	73.5
	Yes	106	26.5	26.5	100.0
	Total	400	100.0	100.0	

Table 15.8

Post Ad Campaign Interest

		Frequency	Percent	Valid Percent	Cumulative Percent
Valid	No	307	76.8	76.8	76.8
	Yes	93	23.3	23.3	100.0
	Total	400	100.0	100.0	

Tables 15.7 and 15.8 provide us with marginal count information. Actually, interest in the wrist cell phone appears to have decreased from 26.5% to 23.3%. Now we must examine whether this difference is statistically significant.

Chi-Square Test for Repeated Counts Analysis

In Table 15.9, the McNemar chi-square test result indicates that the difference in interest before and after the ad campaign is not statistically meaningful ($p = .350$). Thus, it is likely that the ad campaign did not change interest in purchasing the wrist cell phone.

Table 15.9

Chi-Square Tests

	Value	Exact Sig. (2-sided)
McNemar Test		.350[a]
N of Valid Cases	400	

a. Binomial distribution used.

Reporting Results

Since the results are not significantly meaningful, there is no accompanying table.

Write-Up

Based on a representative sample of 400 consumers, who were asked if they were interested in a wrist cell phone before and after being exposed to an ad campaign, a McNemar Chi-Square test was conducted. A nonsignificant difference in interest was found ($p = .350$). It is likely that the ad campaign made no different in changing interest in the wrist cell phone.

Note that the write-up focuses on interest in the wrist cell phone.

Example 15.3: A Crosstabs 4 × 2 Repeated Measures McNemar-Bowker Test: Both Cases

Although this illustration comprises two time points like the previous examples, there are four categories in the dependent variable, of which only one was selected per participant. The McNemar-Bowker test is used to determine if an overall difference exists among the categories or candidates in this case. It does not address where the specific differences lie.

Four candidates are running for governor of California: Brown, Moniz, Feinstein, and Pileggi. A pollster wishes to determine whether there is a shift in voter support among the four candidates after a major debate. Sample data from eligible voters consisted of the same voters polled before and after the debate. Alpha = .05. The SPSS file named "2X Repeated Chi-Square Example 3 Data" contains the data for the analysis.

The analysis requires two variables: "Pre-Debate" selection (1 = "Brown," 2 = "Moniz," 3 = "Feinstein," and 4 = "Pileggi") and "Post-Debate" selection (1 = "Brown," 2 = "Moniz," 3 = "Feinstein," and 4 = "Pileggi").

Again, we will skip the SPSS steps. Although there are more than two categories in the variable we wish to measure, we still checked off the McNemar box. The McNemar-Bowker Chi-Square test output will automatically be generated.

SPSS Output Interpretation

We will focus on the frequency, Crosstabs, and McNemar-Bowker chi-square test tables.

Data Screening

Table 15.10 provides the counts. All of the data assumptions have been met. We examine the "Yes" counts because our aim is to examine candidate support.

Table 15.10

Support for Each Candidate Time 2 * Support for Each Candidate Time 1 Crosstabulation

			Support for Each Candidate Time 1				Total
			Brown	Moniz	Feinstein	Pileggi	
Support for Each Candidate Time 2	Brown	Count	5	5	11	5	26
		% of Total	3.7%	3.7%	8.1%	3.7%	19.3%
	Moniz	Count	6	10	5	21	42
		% of Total	4.4%	7.4%	3.7%	15.6%	31.1%
	Feinstein	Count	5	9	8	14	36
		% of Total	3.7%	6.7%	5.9%	10.4%	26.7%
	Pileggi	Count	9	7	8	7	31
		% of Total	6.7%	5.2%	5.9%	5.2%	23.0%
Total		Count	25	31	32	47	135
		% of Total	18.5%	23.0%	23.7%	34.8%	100.0%

Table 15.11

Support for Each Candidate Time 1

		Frequency	Percent	Valid Percent	Cumulative Percent
Valid	Brown	25	18.5	18.5	18.5
	Moniz	31	23.0	23.0	41.5
	Feinstein	32	23.7	23.7	65.2
	Pileggi	47	34.8	34.8	100.0
	Total	135	100.0	100.0	

Table 15.12

Support for Each Candidate Time 2

		Frequency	Percent	Valid Percent	Cumulative Percent
Valid	Brown	26	19.3	19.3	19.3
	Moniz	42	31.1	31.1	50.4
	Feinstein	36	26.7	26.7	77.0
	Pileggi	31	23.0	23.0	100.0
	Total	135	100.0	100.0	

According to Tables 15.11 and 15.12, and based on a representative sample of targeted voters, before the debate, the candidates' percentages of support were as follows: Brown = 18.5% (n = 25), Moniz = 23.0% (n = 31), Feinstein = 23.7% (n = 32), and Pileggi = 34.8% (n = 47). After the debate, the breakdown was as follows: Brown = 19.3% (n = 26), Moniz = 31.1% (n = 42), Feinstein = 26.7% (n = 36), and Pileggi = 23.0% (n = 31). We need to determine whether the overall difference is statistically meaningful using the McNemar-Bowker Chi-Square Test.

Chi-Square Test for Repeated Counts Analysis

Table 15.13 illustrates that the McNemar-Bowker Chi-square test indicates that for at least one candidate, there is a difference in support between before and after the debate (p = .039). Although the difference appears apparent for Moniz (from 23.0% to 31.1%) and Pileggi (34.8% to 23.0%), it is not always straightforward. There are other statistical procedures that can determine where the specific differences exist, which are beyond the scope of our discussion. In any case, these results suggest that after the debates, Candidate Moniz gained support at the expense of Candidate Pileggi while the other candidates essentially remained unchanged.

Table 15.13

Chi-Square Tests

	Value	df	Asymptotic Significance (2-sided)
McNemar-Bowker Test	13.263	6	.039
N of Valid Cases	135		

Reporting Significant Results

The following is the McNemar-Bowker chi-square test write-up.

Write-Up

Based on a representative sample of 135 voters, who were asked which candidate they supported for governor of California before and after a major debate, a McNemar-Bowker Chi-Square test was conducted. A significant difference among candidates was found ($\chi^2(6) = 13.263$, $p = .039$), indicating that there was a meaningful difference between at least one candidate. Before a major debate, the candidates' support was as follows: Brown = 18.5% (n = 25), Moniz = 23.0% (n = 31), Feinstein = 23.7% (n = 32), and Pileggi = 34.8% (n = 47). After the debate, the breakdown was: Brown = 19.3% (n = 26), Moniz = 31.1% (n = 42), Feinstein = 26.7% (n = 36), and Pileggi = 23.0% (n = 31). It is likely that after the debate, Moniz's support increased at the expense of Pileggi while the other candidates essentially remained unchanged. Table 15.14 represents the levels of support.

Table 5.14

Comparison of Support for Candidates Before and After the Debate

Support	Before Debate	After Debate
Brown	25 (18.5%)	26 (19.3%)
Moniz	31 (23.0%)	42 (31.1%)
Feinstein	32 (23.7%)	36 (26.7%)
Pileggi	47 (34.8%)	31 (23.0%)
Total	135 (100.0%)	135 (100.0%)

Note: McNemar-Bowker Chi-Square Test ($\chi^2(6) = 13.263$, $p = .039$). $N = 135$.

Because the p-value is .039, the analysis revealed at least one before and after meaningful difference among the candidates.

Reporting Nonsignificant Results

The following is a nonsignificant write-up of the same example above. The SPSS file named "2X Repeated Chi-Square Example 4 Data" contains the data for the analysis.

Write-Up

Based on a representative sample of 135 voters, who were asked which candidate they supported for governor of California before and after the three major debates, a McNemar-Bowker Chi-Square test was conducted. A nonsignificant difference among candidates was found ($\chi^2(6) = 2.273$, $p = .893$), indicating that there were no meaningful differences among candidates' support before and after the debate. It is likely that the debate had no effect on the candidates' support.

SUMMARY OF KEY CONCEPTS

- The repeated measures McNemar chi-square test is a significance test that counts categorical data at two time points from the same sample in order to examine for within-subject differences.
- The time variable is independent and the category variable is dependent. The test determines if time or some specific exposure between the two time points affects category selection.
- In a chi-square test of the same sample, there are only two data collection time points, but there can be more than two dependent variable categories.
- If there are more than two categories in the dependent variable, the McNemar-Bowker chi-square test is used.
- The chi-square test is used to calculate whether there are statistically significant differences in the categorical variable by time point.
- There must be a minimum of five counts in all joint categories (category by time).
- Conducting the analysis in SPSS and reporting results are straightforward.

CHI-SQUARE TEST OF TWO RELATED SAMPLES MEASURED TWICE APPLIED EXERCISES

15.1 What is the McNemar chi-square significance test? Cite an example.

15.2 What is the McNemar-Bowker chi-square significance test? Cite an example.

15.3 What is a within-subjects analysis? Cite an example.

15.4 In the McNemar chi-square test, what are the independent and dependent variables?

15.5 In the McNemar-Bowker chi-square test, what are the independent and dependent variables?

15.6 Does a repeated counts analysis involve a dependent or independent sample? Explain your answer.

15.7 Why is it necessary to have an equal number of data cases per time point?

15.8 In the sleep education program Real World Snapshot, assuming alpha is .05, would an overall *p*-value of .02 still produce statistically significant results? Explain your response.

15.9 Protection Home Security (PHS) wants to test the effectiveness of its sales force. Six hundred potential customers were asked whether they were interested in home security before and then after receiving a sales call from a PHS representative. Responses were "Yes" or "No." From the sample data, determine whether the sales call had a likely effect on consumers' interest in home security. Alpha is .05. The SPSS file named "2X Repeated Chi-Square Exercise 1 Data" contains the data for the analysis.

15.10 Venus Tablets wants to test whether trial usage of its new tablet will increase interest in the device. One hundred and seventy consumers were surveyed about their interest in the tablet prior to using the product for 2 weeks. After the trial, they were again asked whether they were interested in the Venus tablet. Responses were framed as "Yes" or "No." Did the trial usage make a difference? Alpha is .05. The SPSS file named "2X Repeated Chi-Square Exercise 2 Data" contains the data for the analysis.

15.11 Cornucopia Medical wants to test the feasibility of offering customized health insurance plans. The company asked 120 individuals about whether they were interested, not interested, or undecided (about their interest) in the product. They were then given information about Cornucopia's customized health insurance program. Then, they were asked again whether the plan interests them. Does providing information about customized health insurance plans likely increase interest in such products? Alpha is .05. The SPSS file named "2X Repeated Chi-Square Exercise 3 Data" contains the data for the analysis.

Numeric Variables

Chapter 16

T-Test: Comparing a Single Sample Mean to a Specific Value

LEARNING OBJECTIVES

To be able to:

- understand and explain what is a single sample *t*-test;
- know and explain the purpose of confidence intervals;
- understand the data assumptions for conducting a single sample *t*-test;
- conduct a single sample *t*-test in SPSS;
- interpret and explain single sample *t*-test and confidence interval output; and
- know how to report significant and nonsignificant *t*-test and confidence interval results.

16.1 Introduction to the Single Sample *T*-Test

The **single sample *t*-test** compares the mean (average) of a single sample and some specific (test) value in order to determine if there is the likelihood of a statistically significant difference between them. The test value is often suspected to represent the true population mean. For example, a researcher may wish to discover if the current typical customer who visits Store ABC is indeed 35 years old. A quality assurance officer may want to test whether the number of substandard parts produced varies from 25 parts per production shift, which is thought to be the true shift mean.

There are two types of single sample *t*-tests for numeric data. If the population standard deviation (it is called the sigma) is known, then we use a *z*-statistic. However, in most cases, the sigma is unknown, in which case the *t*-statistic is used. In fact, the SPSS pull-down menu offers the *t*-test approach for a single sample *t*-test. The *t*-test is based on the sample standard deviation. All *t*-tests are based on sample data.

Let us return to the Store ABC example. We assume an alpha of 5%, which means that results with less than a 5% chance of occurring will be our acceptable level of risk. In the normal distribution curve, the .05 is divided by two because statistically significant values can be less than or greater than the mean. Thus, there are 2.5% observations at each tail. Figure 16.1 illustrates the normal distribution for two samples each with a different sample mean. In Sample 1, the mean is 34 and the test value is 35. The sample mean is clearly not in the Statistically Meaningful Area where significant values would be located. This is supported by $p = .78$, which is greater than .05. There is likely no difference between the Sample 1 mean and the test value. We conclude that 35 years old is likely the true population mean age.

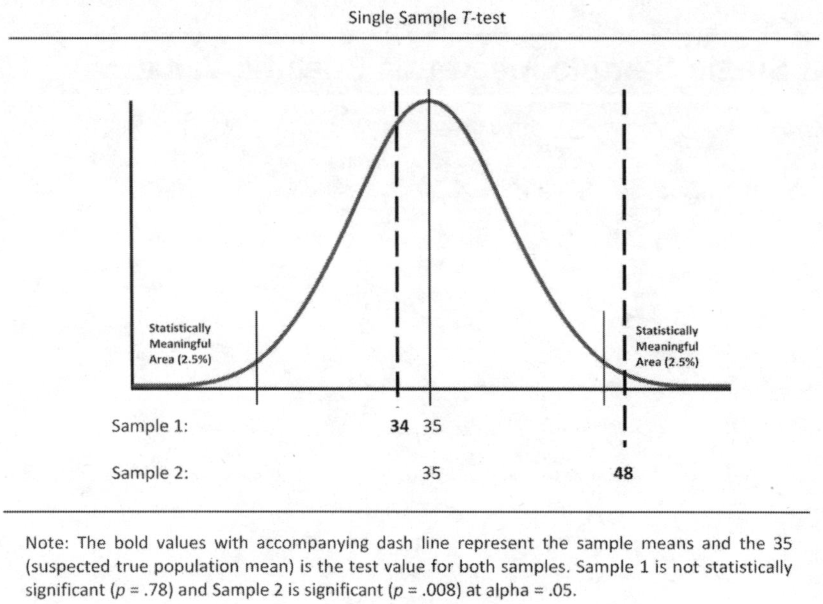

Figure 16.1

However, Sample 2 tells another story. Although the test value is still 35, the sample mean is now 48. In this sample, the sample mean is much more different than the test value. The sample mean falls in the Statistically Meaningful Area. This is consistent with the *p*-value of .008, which is clearly greater than .05, and thus is statistically significant. Therefore, based on Sample 2, 35 years old is not likely the true population mean.

Additionally, single sample *t*-tests that examine greater than or less then relationships between sample means and test values are available; however, they are beyond the score of this textbook. The next section covers confidence intervals, which are often reported along with *t*-test results.

16.2 Confidence Interval for a Single Sample *T*-Test

In SPSS, another statistical tool available with the single sample *t*-test is the **confidence interval (CI)**. The CI comprises the boundaries within which the true population mean falls. It is an interval because of the natural fluctuations associated with drawing multiple samples (see Chapter 7). If we were to draw all possible random samples of the same size from the same target population, the confidence interval would provide us with a statistical interval with a certain level of confidence ("certainty").

The CI is about where the sample mean stands in relation to the test value (often the assumed population mean). That is, it is based on the sample. For this reason, the sample mean is in the middle of the CI. SPSS produces a "difference" interval that applies to the sample mean from which we produce a confidence interval for the true population mean, which is covered in the Examples section. The difference interval inclusively encompasses the inclusive lower and upper limits of the sample mean difference from the test value.

If the initial difference interval includes zero, then the *p*-value for the single sample *t*-test will not be statistically significant because zero indicates possibly no difference between the test value and sample mean within the level of confidence. Likewise, if the calculated true mean interval includes the test value, then again there will not be a statistically significant difference between the test value and sample mean because both likely rest within the interval.

A 95% level of confidence is standard. However, guided by the situation, 99% or 90% are also relatively common confidence intervals. Taking 95% as an example indicates that if we take 100 random representative samples of the same size, then 95 out of 100 times, it is likely that the difference between the test value and mean would fall within the calculated interval based on the sample data. Five out of 100 times, it is likely that the difference falls outside of the interval.

The confidence interval is included in this analysis because it offers more information about the true assumed population mean. In fact, there are other related procedures, such as bootstrapping, that can increase the precision of CIs, and means testing for that matter. Chapter 11 discusses confidence intervals in general.

REAL WORLD SNAPSHOT

A 2003 study by Parmesan and Yohe entitled "A Globally Coherent Fingerprint of Climate Change Impacts Across Natural Systems" studied possible relationships between animal behavioral trends and climate change. Part of the study examined the range boundaries of 99 bird species. Using a test value of zero change, single sample *t*-tests were conducted over seven decades to examine changes in bird boundary patterns in areas that experienced climate change. Significant findings were found ($t(98) = 2.52$, $p = .013$). The bird species' range limit likely moved northward on average 6.1 kilometers in the direction of climate change. The study was 95% confident that the average range boundary move northward was between 3.70 and 8.50 kilometers.

Ask yourself: What other single sample *t*-tests and variables might provide information on the relationship between animals and climate change?

16.3 Data Assumptions

The *t*-test has a number of data assumptions:

- The data are numeric.
- The sample data are in the same format as the test value.
- Data are randomly selected and representative of the target population.
- The sample data are fairly normally distributed.
- The sample size is greater than 30.

16.4 Examples Using SPSS: Step-by-Step Instructions

Using the single sample *t*-test SPSS procedure, the following two examples compare a test value and sample mean to examine whether there is a difference between them.

Example 16.1: Single Sample *T*-Tests: The Significant Case

According to previous Store ABC marketing research, the typical customer is 35 years old. We want to determine if the shopper mean age has changed since that previous research. In the current sample, we have 171 Store ABC retail patrons. The variable is age in years, thus we have numeric data, which make them conducive to means testing. Alpha = .05. The SPSS file named "*T*-Test Single Sample Example 1 Data" contains the data for this analysis. For the purposes of an SPSS introduction, we will focus on the basic steps.

Step 1: Open SPSS.

Locate the appropriate folder and highlight the data file. Next, click the "Open" button.

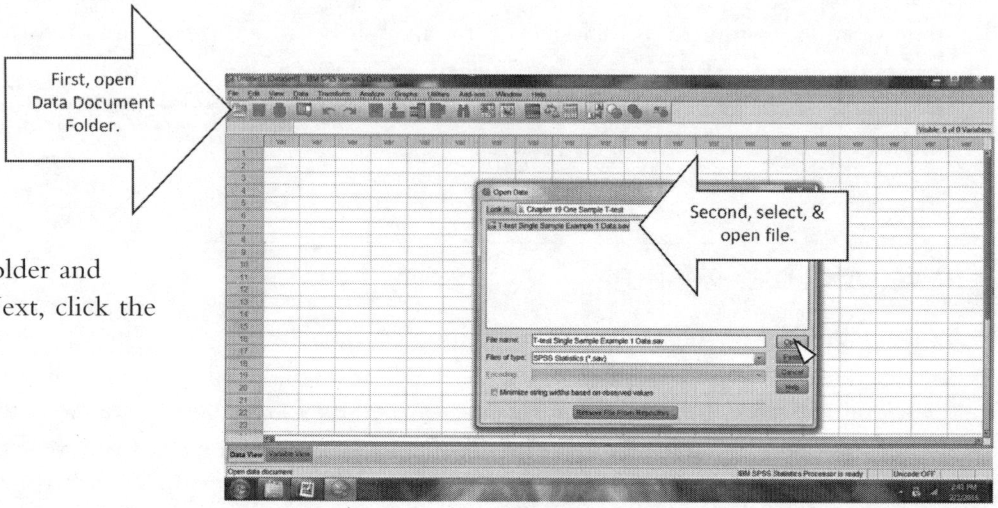

Figure 16.2

Step 2: In the data file, do the following:

- Select the "Analyze" tab.
- Then, choose "Descriptive Statistics."
- Last, click "Explore."

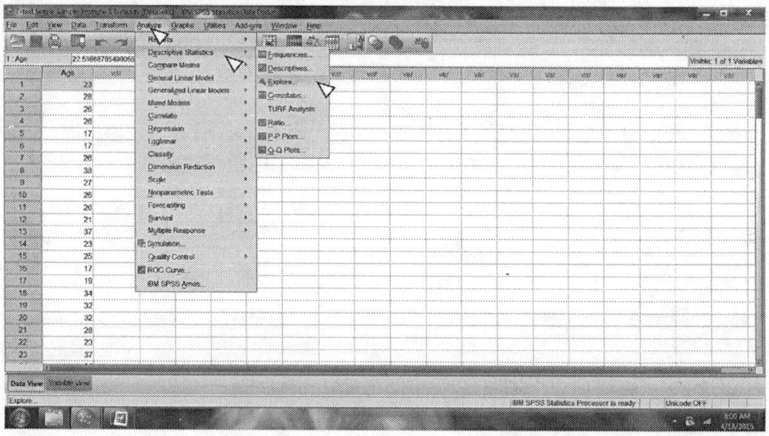

Figure 16.3

Step 3: The "Explore" window will open.

- Highlight the "Age" variable and place it in the "Dependent List" box by clicking the "Arrow" button.
- Click the "Plots" button.
  - In the "Explore Plots" window, only check "None" in the box plot area.
  - Below that, check "Normality plots with tests."
  - Click the "Continue" button.
- Last, click the "OK" button. Output is generated.

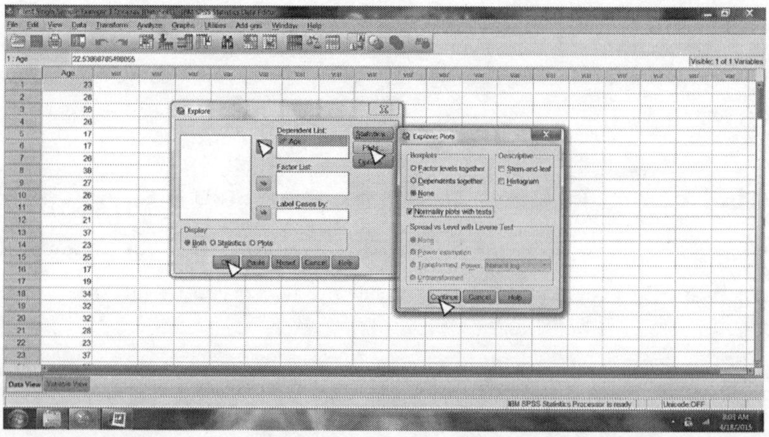

Step 4: Do the following:

- Select the "Analyze" tab.
- Pick "Compare Means."
- Last, click "One-Sample *T*-Test."

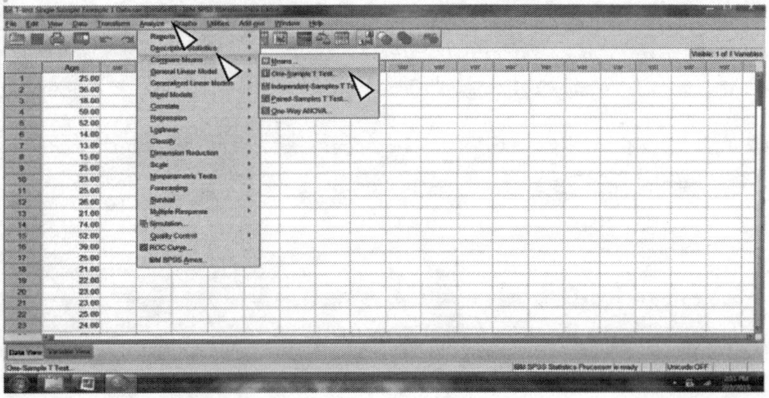

Figure 16.5

Step 5: The "One-Sample *T*-Test" window will open:

- Assign the "Age" variable to the "Test Variable(s)" box by highlighting and then clicking the "Arrow" button.

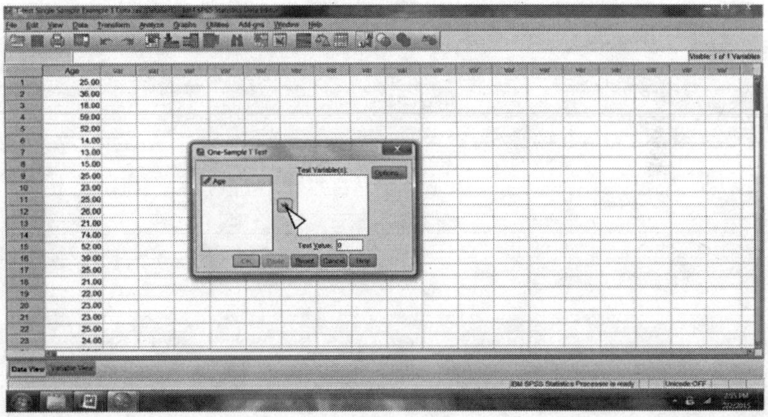

Figure 16.6

Step 6: Because we want to know whether the current typical customer is 35 years old, enter 35 as the test value. After that, click on the "Options" button located on the top-right of the "One-Sample *T*-Test" window.

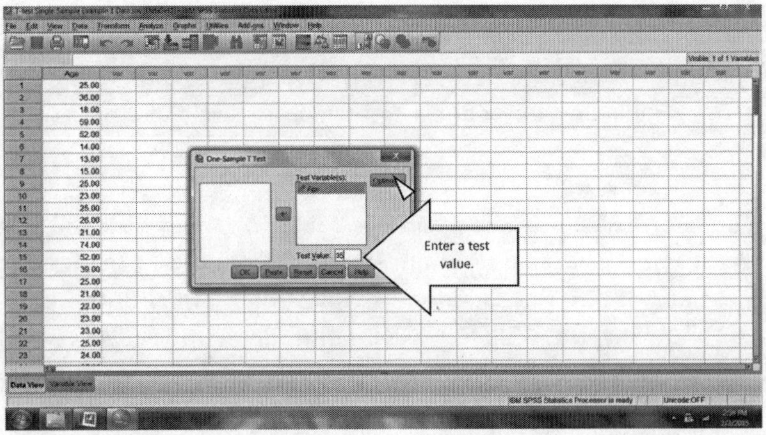

Figure 16.7

Step 7: Once you click the "Options" button, the "One-Sample *T*-Test Options" window will open:

- The default "Confidence Interval Percentage" is 95%. Do not change this percentage. Leave the default "Missing Data" setting as is. If you wish to learn more about missing data, then click the "Help" button at the bottom-right-hand side of the window.
- Click the "Continue" button located in the bottom-left of the window.

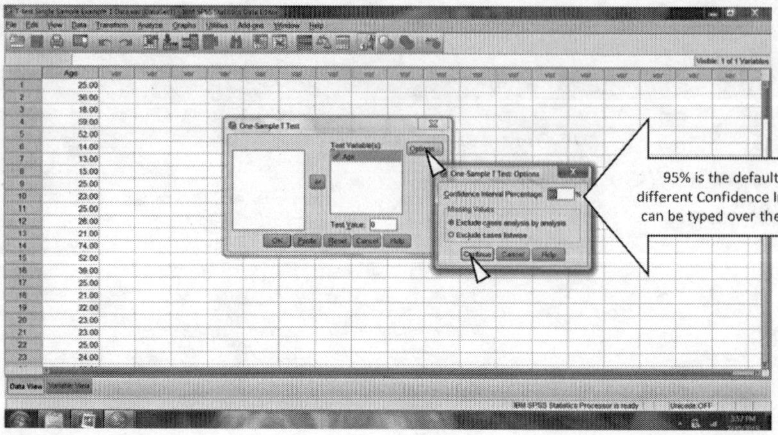

Figure 16.8

Step 8: Click the "OK" button to run the analysis. The analysis generates an output file.

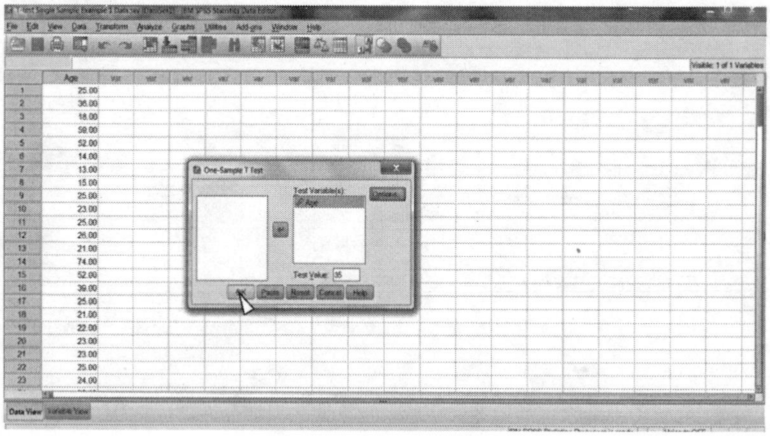

Figure 16.9

Last, save the data and output files for your records.

SPSS Output Interpretation

In addition to the descriptive statistics tables and graphs, the one-sample *t*-test output, one-sample statistics table and one-sample test tables are available.

Data Screening

The sample size is greater than 30. Table 16.1 comprises the tests for normality. As we can see, the Shapiro-Wilk statistic is not statistically significant (p = .76). Because p = .76 is greater than our alpha of .05, the data do not violate the normal distribution assumption.

If the Shapiro-Wilk test were statistically significant, we would consider other options. First, providing that the sample size is sufficiently large, we can examine the Normal Q-Q Plot derived from the Descriptive/Explore analysis output to identify and remove any outliers (extreme observations), which might then give us a fairly normal distribution (see Chapter 12). Next, we could collect more data with the hope that the distribution becomes normal, which is in line with the Central Limit Theorem. Third, depending on the data distribution, a transformation could be conducted to normalize the data. Last, a popular nonparametric alternative to the parametric single sample *t*-test is the "Wilcoxon one-sample signed ranks test," which accounts for non-normal data distribution. The last two approaches are beyond the scope of our discussion. If we cannot normalize the data, then we must be cautious in drawing conclusions. When the data are not normal, it is appropriate to provide a caveat in the reporting noting that the results may not be stable.

Table 16.1

Tests of Normality

	Kolmogorov-Smirnov[a]			Shapiro-Wilk		
	Statistic	df	Sig.	Statistic	df	Sig.
Age	.043	171	.200*	.994	171	.769

*. This is a lower bound of the true significance.

a. Lilliefors Significance Correction

"Sig" denotes a p-value of .769.

As we can see in Table 16.2, the sample consists of 171 customers. The store patron sample mean age is 27.17 years. The standard deviation or patrons' age varies on average 6.01 years from the mean. The "Standard Error Mean" statistic is an estimate of the average difference among means that are drawn from multiple representative same size samples of the target population. Since we do not require the standard error of the mean for our analysis, please ignore it.

Table 16.2

One-Sample Statistics

	N	Mean	Std. Deviation	Std. Error Mean
Age	171	27.17	6.010	.460

Single Sample *T*-Test Analysis

Using a single sample *t*-test, we ran our analysis to determine if there is a meaningful difference in the sample average age of a Store ABC customer compared to a previous study that indicated the mean age to be 35 years old.

As Table 16.3 reveals, because the *p*-value is <.001, there is a meaningful difference between 27.17 years and 35.00 years when alpha is .05. Therefore, it is likely that the current Store ABC patrons' average age of 27.17 years is different from 35 years old.

Table 16.3

P-value is less than .001.

One-Sample Test

	Test Value = 35					
					95% Confidence Interval of the Difference	
	t	df	Sig. (2-tailed)	Mean Difference	Lower	Upper
Age	-17.035	170	.000	-7.829	-8.74	-6.92

As depicted in Table 16.3, the "Mean Difference" of –7.829 refers to the difference between the sample mean of 27.17 and the test value of 35.00. The "Lower" and "Upper" 95% confidence intervals represent where the sample mean stands in relation to the test value. The average age of a Store ABC patron is anywhere from 6.92 to 8.74 years younger than the 35 years old mean reported in a previous study.

Put differently, the negative lower and upper interval values denote that the sample mean of 27.17 is anywhere between 6.92 and 8.74 less than the test value of 35. From here, we can calculate a 95% CI of the mean. Since the difference interval pertains to the sample mean in relation to the test value, we need to add the lower and upper limits of the interval to the test value in order to arrive at a mean CI. After all, the test value is what we are examining.

$$LL = (TV + LD) \text{ and}$$

$$UL = (TV + UD)$$

where

LL = lower limit
TV = test value
LD = lower limit
UD = upper limit

In the example, it is calculated below:

$$LL = 35.00 + (-8.74)$$

$$= 26.26 \text{ and } UL$$

$$= 35.00 + (-6.92)$$

$$= 28.08$$

$$LL = 26.26 \text{ and}$$

$$UL = 28.08.$$

Therefore, we are 95% confident that the true average customer's age is between 26.26 and 28.08.

Reporting Results

When reporting the confidence interval for the single sample *t*-test, report the mean lower and upper values and not the differences.

Write-Up

A single sample *t*-test was conducted that compared the previously reported typical Store ABC patron mean age of 35 years old to a current representative sample of 171 customers. A significant difference was found ($t(170) = -17.03$, $p < .001$). It is likely that the mean age of 27.17 (SD = 6.01) years old is different from the previous study mean of 35 years old. Thus, the average age of the store patron has changed. Furthermore, we are 95% confident that the true mean age of a Store ABC customer is between 26.26 and 28.08 years old.

(OR we can apply directionality)

A single sample *t*-test was conducted that compared the previously reported Store ABC patron mean age of 35 years old to a current representative sample of 171 customers. A significant difference was found ($t(170) = -17.03$, $p < .001$). It is likely that the mean age of 27.17 (SD = 6.01) years old is less than the previous study mean of 35 years old. Thus, the average age of the store patron has decreased. Furthermore, we are 95% confident that the true mean age of a Store ABC customer is between 26.26 and 28.08 years old.

The "*t*" is the *t*-test statistic. The "(170)" represents the degrees of freedom (*df*), which is the number of data points that can vary (see Chapter 11). Its formula is $n - 1$ because there is one sample. In our case, it is $171 - 1 = 170 = df$. The details of this concept are beyond the scope of this textbook. It is only important to know how to determine the *df* for reporting purposes.

Consistent with the *t*-test statistic, $p < .001$ is a statistically significant result. It indicates that the likelihood of these findings occurring by chance is very low or less than 1/1,000. We usually report *p*-values that are .000 or less, such as $p < .001$. "*SD*" denotes standard deviation.

Example 16.2: Single Sample *T*-Tests: The Nonsignificant Case

In this example, we wish to examine whether the mean Mercy Hospital patient wait time varies from 15 minutes. Survey sample wait time data were collected from a representative sample of 236 patients. Respondents indicated the number of minutes that they waited before being called into an examination room. Alpha = .05. The sample data file name is "*T*-Test Single Sample Example 2 Data."

We will skip the SPSS steps because they are identical to the first example.

SPSS Output Interpretation

Data Screening

The sample size is greater than 30. The Shapiro-Wilk statistic is $p = .85$, indicating that the sample meets the normal distribution assumption.

Table 16.4

Tests of Normality

	Kolmogorov-Smirnov[a]			Shapiro-Wilk		
	Statistic	df	Sig.	Statistic	df	Sig.
Wait Time in Minutes	.031	236	.200*	.996	236	.856

*. This is a lower bound of the true significance.

a. Lilliefors Significance Correction

As we can see in Table 16.5, based on the sample, the mean wait time of the 236 patients is 14.90 minutes. The standard deviation or typical wait time varies on average 3.00 minutes from the sample mean.

Table 16.5

One-Sample Statistics

	N	Mean	Std. Deviation	Std. Error Mean
Wait Time in Minutes	236	14.9041	3.00850	.19584

Single Sample *T*-Test Analysis

As Table 16.6 reveals, because the *p*-value is .625, it is likely there is no meaningful difference between 14.90 and 15.00 minutes when alpha is .05. Therefore, there is no evidence to suggest that the average patient wait time varies from 15 minutes.

Table 16.6

One-Sample Test

	Test Value = 15					
					95% Confidence Interval of the Difference	
	t	df	Sig. (2-tailed)	Mean Difference	Lower	Upper
Wait Time in Minutes	-.490	235	.625	-.09595	-.4818	.2899

As depicted in Table 16.6, the "Mean Difference" of −.09595 refers to the difference between the 14.90 and 15.00. Again, the "Lower" and "Upper" 95% confidence intervals represent where the sample mean stands in relation to the test value. The average wait time is anywhere from .4818 minutes less to .2899 minutes more than the test value of 15 minutes. Therefore, we are 95% confidence that the average patient wait time is between 14.52 (15.00 + (−.4818)) and 15.28 (15.00 + .2889) minutes.

Notice that the lower difference value is negative and the upper difference value is positive so that the interval goes from less than to greater than the test value, thus including zero (no difference between the test value and sample mean). The mean interval also includes the test value of 15.00. The inclusion of zero and the test value in the intervals are consistent with $p = .625$, a result that does not represent a statistically significant difference. Both statistics indicate that it is highly likely that there is no difference between the sample mean and the test value. Therefore, it is likely that the true mean wait time at Mercy Hospital does not differ from 15.00 minutes.

Reporting Results

Again, when reporting the confidence interval for the single sample *t*-test, report the lower and upper means and not the differences. Usually, nonsignificant findings do not include a table.

Write-Up

A single sample *t*-test was conducted that examined whether Mercy Hospital patient wait times vary from 15 minutes. Sample wait time data were collected from a representative sample of 236 patients. A nonsignificant difference was found ($t(235) = -.490$, $p = .625$). In all likelihood, there is no evidence to indicate that the average patient wait time of 14.90 ($SD = 3.00$) is different from 15 minutes. Thus, current wait times do not vary from 15 minutes. Furthermore, we are 95% confident that the true average patient wait time falls between 14.52 and 15.28 minutes.

SUMMARY OF KEY CONCEPTS

- The single sample *t*-test is a significance test that compares a test value (often suspected as the true population mean) and a representative sample mean.
- The SPSS difference confidence interval provides a difference interval between the test value and sample mean.

- The difference interval pertains to the sample mean in relation to the test value.
- The single sample *t*-test and confidence have a number of data assumptions.
- Conducting the *t*-test and CI procedures in SPSS is easy.
- Both the *t*-test and confidence interval statistics are reported, thus providing a wealth of information about the data.
- Interpreting SPSS output and reporting significant and nonsignificant findings are straightforward.

SINGLE SAMPLE *T*-TEST APPLIED EXERCISES

16.1 In general terms, define a single sample *t*-test.

16.2 What is a confidence interval?

16.3 If a confidence interval of the difference between the sample mean and test value contains a zero, will the *p*-value of the single sample *t*-test be significant or nonsignificant? Explain your answer.

16.4 In a single sample *t*-test, if a confidence interval of the true mean contains the test value, will the single sample *t*-test results be significant or nonsignificant? Explain your answer.

16.5 Pharma 1st wishes to test the efficacy of a new Alzheimer's disease drug on a group of Alzheimer's patients. The instrument was formatted using a response scale where 1 = "no apparent cognitive ability" to 12 = "no apparent cognitive impairment." These treatment-free patients were never administered this test by a licensed practitioner until now. However, previous research findings indicate that individuals in this age group who did not receive any type of treatment typically scored 9.13. Is there a difference between the sample intervention group average score and the typical no intervention 9.13 score (test value)? Alpha = .01. Explain your answer. Report results in the format provided in this chapter. Be sure to include the confidence interval. The data file name is "*T*-Test Single Sample Exercise 1 Data."

16.6 A professor has been recording student motivation in her highly popular yet demanding classes over a number of years using the same survey. Recently, she collected representative data from her current classes using the same survey. Responses were formatted as: 1 = "not motivated at all" to 7 = "highly motivated." She has an average of all previously collected data. To date, the mean motivation score is 6.12. Is there a difference between the collective previous samples of student motivation and the motivation of her current students? Alpha = .05. Explain your answer. Report results in the format provided in this chapter. Be sure to include the confidence interval. The data file name is "*T*-Test Single Sample Exercise 2 Data."

16.7 In a production facility, the general manager suspects that the shoe production output of newer replacement machinery is different from the older replaced equipment average output. This may be the case because the new machinery requires additional adjustments and the operators require additional training and experience operating the new equipment. By the same token, the new equipment should produce more output than the older outdated machinery. The general manager directed her operations management research team to compare a sample of the current production output with the overall average of the older equipment's output. The overall average 24-hour production run on the old machinery was 1,200 pairs. Determine if there is a difference in output. Alpha = .05. Explain your answer. Report results in the format provided in this chapter. Be sure to include the confidence interval. The data file name is "*T*-Test Single Sample Exercise 3 Data."

16.8 Using a sample of those persons who completed its course, GOFORIT! wishes to determine whether students in general perform differently on the SAT for the first time after completing its SAT preparation course compared to first-time test takers who have no preparation. Based on past data, where students took the same format SAT for the first time and did not prepare for the test, test takers averaged 998 on their total Math/English scores. Determine whether those test takers who completed the SAT preparation class scored differently than the 998 previously reported average score. Alpha = .05. Explain your answer. Report results in the format provided in this chapter. Be sure to include the confidence interval. The data file name is "*T*-Test Single Sample Exercise 4 Data."

Chapter 17

T-Test: Comparing Two Independent Samples' Variable Means

LEARNING OBJECTIVES

To be able to:

- understand the purpose and explain the basic principles of a two independent samples *t*-test;
- describe the data assumptions for two independent samples *t*-tests;
- understand the role of normal distribution and equality of variance in a two independent samples *t*-test;
- know that there are two types of two independent samples *t*-test involving pooled and separate variances;
- screen the data in order to select the appropriate two independent samples *t*-test;
- conduct two independent samples *t*-tests in SPSS;
- learn and explain how to calculate and report confidence intervals; and
- interpret and report two independent samples significant and nonsignificant results.

17.1 Introduction to the Two Independent Samples *T*-Test

The **two independent samples *t*-test** is a significance test that compares the means between two independent samples (groups) in order to determine if there is the likelihood of a statistically meaningful difference between them. The representative sample means serve as estimates of their true population means.

Typically, data elements (participants) are assigned to an experimental condition or control group, which serve as the two samples. The exposure to the condition, or lack thereof, is the independent variable and the subsequent measurement of both groups is the dependent variable. Comparing the two groups for amount of differences between their mean scores indicates whether the independent variable has an effect on the dependent variable. For the comparison to be valid, the same information in the same format must be collected from both samples. For instance, an analysis may compare height in which both samples are measured in inches or a study may examine infants' amount of food consumption to one of two baby food brands where each sample eats one of the two brands of food measured in ounces.

Sometimes the independent variable is not quite an "experiment." For instance, in the case of comparing urban and rural views about education, the urban or rural residency designation is the independent condition and the views on education is the dependent variable. The goal is to determine whether residency designation affects views about education.

Other examples are: a researcher may wish to discover if the level of hospital patient satisfaction varies if patients visit the emergency room on Wednesday as opposed to Friday; or a restaurant chain human resources director may wish to learn whether his company offers higher starting salaries compared to his largest competitor. As we can see, the two independent samples *t*-test examines whether samples representing independent populations are different in some way from each other.

Let us consider whether urban and rural dwellers support farm subsidies. We assume an alpha of 5%. Our focus is on the difference between the mean scores about farm subsidy support based on whether the people live in an urban or rural setting. Thus, we have an urban sample and a rural sample. Responses may be formatted as 0 = "no support for farm subsidies" to 5 = "total support for farm subsidies." Figures 17.1 and 17.2 illustrate the normal distribution for nonsignificant and significant scenarios. In both situations, the means vary, thus the differences vary. The question is: Is the difference between the two sample means (Urban sample – Rural sample) sufficiently large enough to represent a statistically significant result?

In Figure 17.1, which is the nonsignificant *t*-test, the difference of –2 (or 2 for that matter) does not fall in the area of a statistically meaningful differences between the two means. The *p*-value for such a nonsignificant difference would be $\geq .05$, where each tail accounts for 2.5% of the largest differences whether greater than or less than in terms of the first sample in the comparison. A difference of "2" is not sufficiently large enough for there to be a statistically significant difference between the urban and rural sample means.

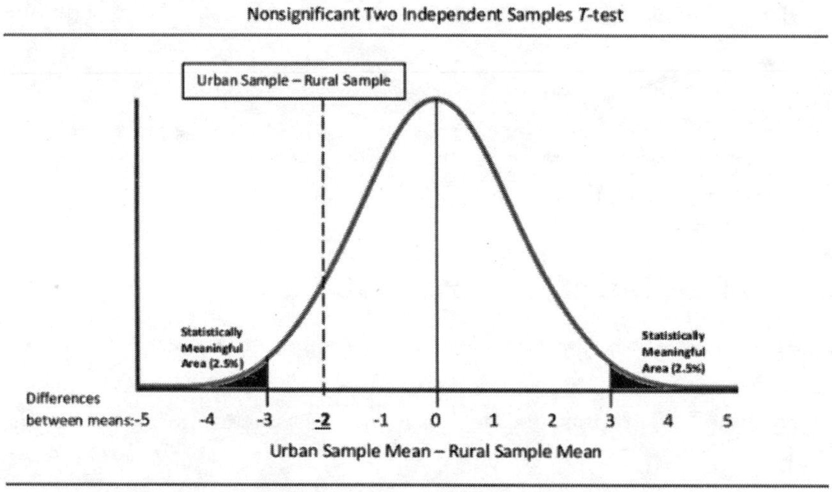

Note: Responses were based on a scale from 0 to 5. The urban sample mean is 3 and the rural sample mean is 5 indicating a difference of -2 between them. It is negative because the urban sample was assigned the first sample. If it had been the rural sample, then the difference would be 2. In either case, a difference of 2 does not fall in the Statistically Meaningful Area.

Figure 17.1

On the other hand, in the significant *t*-test case (Figure 17.2), the difference of 4 is sufficiently large enough to represent a statistically meaningful finding. The *p*-value would be $< .05$. In this illustration, it is likely that urban residents are more supportive than rural residents. Perhaps in the interim the urbanites realized the importance of a reliable food source for which they have become dependent and, at the same time, the ruralites developed a fiercely independent perspective.

In any case, the characteristics of each sample's distribution affects how the means' comparison is calculated. The pooled *t*-test or the separate *t*-tests are used based on whether the two distributions have similar variances. The next section covers the concept of equality of variance and what is the appropriate *t*-test to apply based on variance.

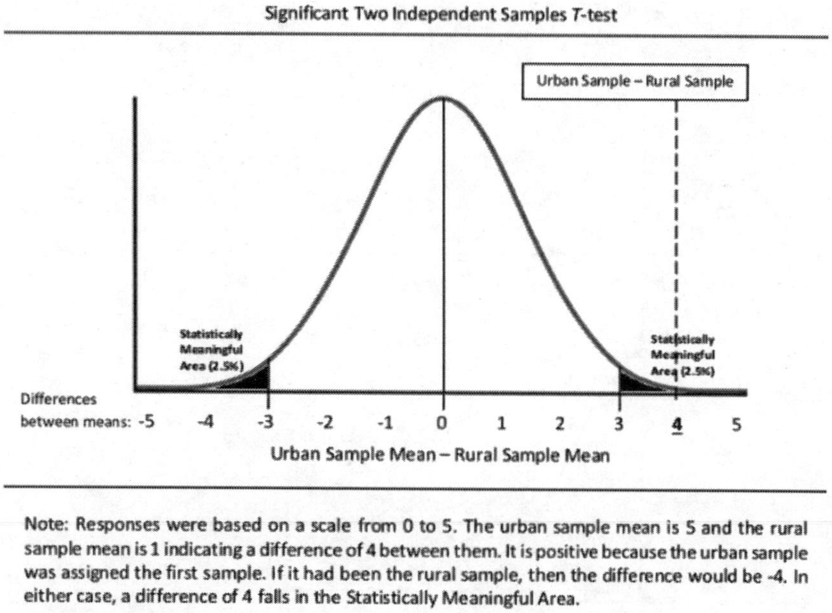

Figure 17.2

17.2 Equality of Variance

As covered in Chapter 11, variance is the spread or dispersion of the data. It is how far the data are from the mean. Variance is the data's standard deviation squared. In order to determine which two independent samples *t*-test to use requires knowing whether the two samples share similar variances. This is known as **equality of variance**. Keep in mind that if both samples are fairly normally distributed and share similar variances, then their distributions will look alike. We assume that the two samples meet the normal distribution assumption—that is, they are both symmetrical although their variances may be different. We first assess whether there is equality of variance and then select the appropriate *t*-test based on the assessment. Let us start by reviewing equal and unequal variances.

In Figure 17.3, distributions A and B share similar variances. This is evident in the similar shapes of the two distributions. Although their means likely differ, their variances and standard deviations are alike. As a general rule of thumb, if one variance is no more than double the other, usually there will be equality of variance.

On the other hand, distributions C and D appear to violate the equality of variance assumption. Notice that, although symmetrical, the distributions are clearly different, which is consistent with the differences in the variances and standard deviations. Distribution D's variance is more than double that of distribution C.

Even though the 2X rule of thumb provides a rough idea of what to expect, the **Levene Test for Equality of Variance** is a significance test that should be used to more precisely assess variance in distributions. It is discussed in the Examples section.

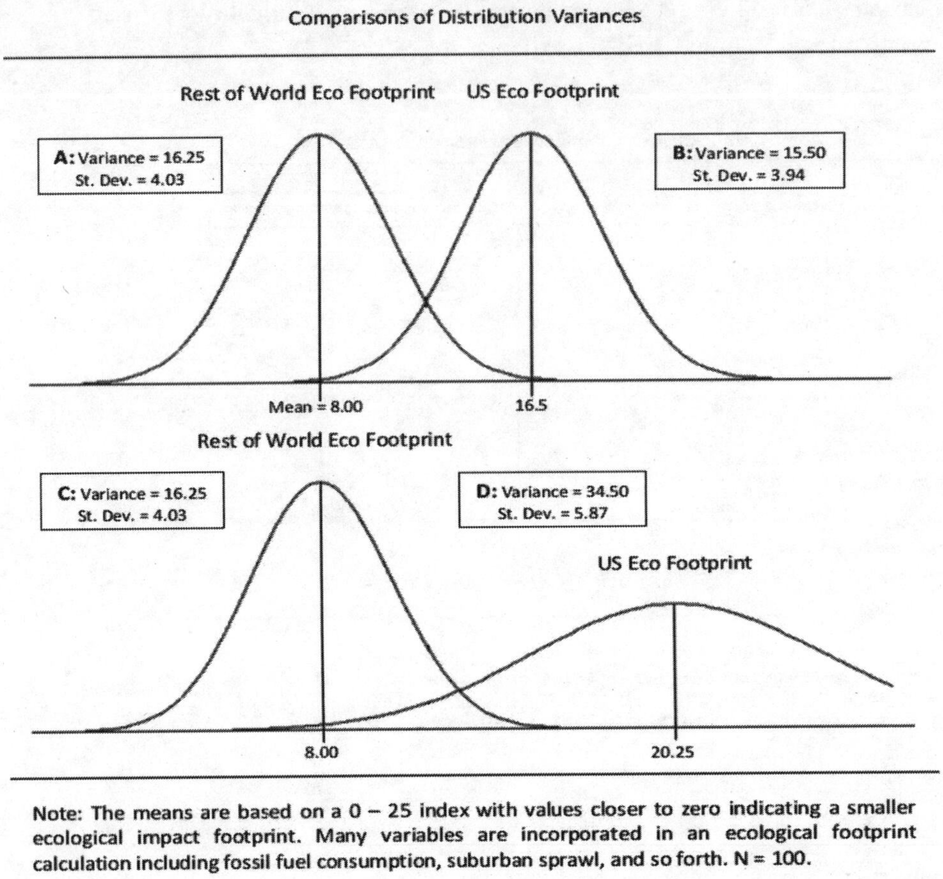

Figure 17.3

REAL WORLD SNAPSHOT

Animal-assisted therapy (AAT) involves mostly dogs, but also cats, birds, guinea pigs, fish, horses, dolphins, and other animals serving as therapists to help persons who are in need of some type of healing. The parties involved are the patient, a trained animal as therapist, and the animal handler, who all act to help the patient achieve target therapeutic goals.

In 2009, Braum and colleagues published an article entitled "Animal-Assisted Therapy as a Pain Relief Intervention for Children," which examined possible effects of AAT on reducing pain in children. A sample of 57 children, ages 3–17, agreed along with their parents to participate in the study. Two independent samples *t*-tests, among other tests, were used to assess the effectiveness of the AAT intervention.

The article reported that those children who received AAT in essence experienced statistically significant less pain than children not exposed to the therapy. The pain reduction was four times more for the AAT children. According to the researchers, the study provides evidence that AAT can be used as an effective method for pain reduction in children. They posit that exposure to a friendly animal releases endorphins and lymphocytes, which facilitate feelings of well-being and boost the immune response, respectively.

Ask yourself: What other variables might affect the relationship between a therapy animal and a patient?

Pooled or Separate Two Independent Samples *T*-Test

Once equality of variance is assessed using the Levene test, then one of two *t*-tests is selected based on the test results. If the Levene test is not significant indicating equality of variance, then the **pooled two independent samples *t*-test** is used. The data are combined into a single variance for the test. If the test is significant, revealing a violation of equality of variance, the **separate two independent samples *t*-test** is appropriate, in which the separate variances are incorporated in the analysis.

SPSS calculates the *t*-test deploying both methods. They are labeled **equality of variance assumed** for the pooled *t*-test and **equality of variance not assumed** for the separate *t*-test. Again, which test to use is based on the Levene test result.

17.3 Data Assumptions

This test has a number of assumptions:

- The two samples' data are numeric, in the same format, and in the same variable.
- Each sample size is over 30.
- The samples are randomly drawn and independent of each other. The samples should not contain data from the same source, such as data from the same people.
- The sample is representative of the target population.
- (Ideally), the samples have the same number of cases.
- Both samples are fairly normally distributed.
- There is equality of variance. The samples' data distributions are similar. Usually, one sample's data variance is no more than double that of the other sample.
- There is a grouping (independent) variable to identify each sample's data.

17.4 Examples Using SPSS: Step-by-Step Instructions

Using the two independent samples *t*-test SPSS procedure, the following two examples each compare two independent means to determine if there is a meaningful difference between them.

Example 17.1: Two Independent Samples *T*-Tests: The Significant Case

A hospital wishes to learn if emergency room (ER) patients experience different levels of satisfaction based on whether they visit the ER on Wednesday or Friday. Should there be a difference in satisfaction ratings, the Director of Emergency Services would consider instituting additional ER training requirements. Within one week of discharge, patients were sent a satisfaction survey based on a seven-point scale with responses ranging from 1 = "not satisfied at all" to 7 = "totally satisfied." The hospital collected data from 552 patients over a 30-day period. The study aim is to determine if Wednesday and Friday patient satisfaction varies. Alpha = .05. The SPSS file named "*T*-Test Two Independent Samples Example 1 Data" contains the data for this analysis.

The analysis requires two variables: a grouping (independent) variable (Wednesday = 1 and Friday = 2) and a dependent variable (scores of the satisfaction question formatted in a scale format from 1 to 7). The grouping variable identifies the sample from which the dependent variable data are measured and compared. What follows are the SPSS steps.

Step 1: Open SPSS.

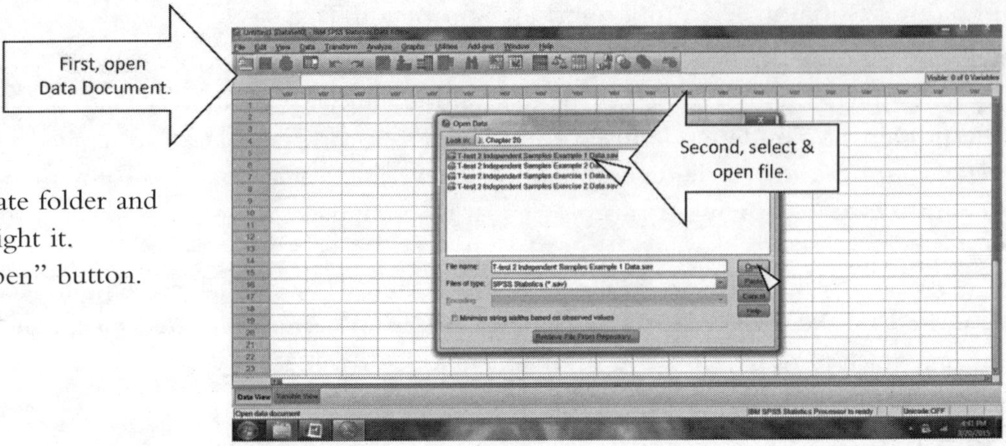

- Locate the appropriate folder and data file, then highlight it.
- Next, click the "Open" button.

Figure 17.4

Step 2: After the data file is open:

- Select the "Analyze" tab.
- Then, highlight "Descriptive Statistics."
- Last, click "Explore."

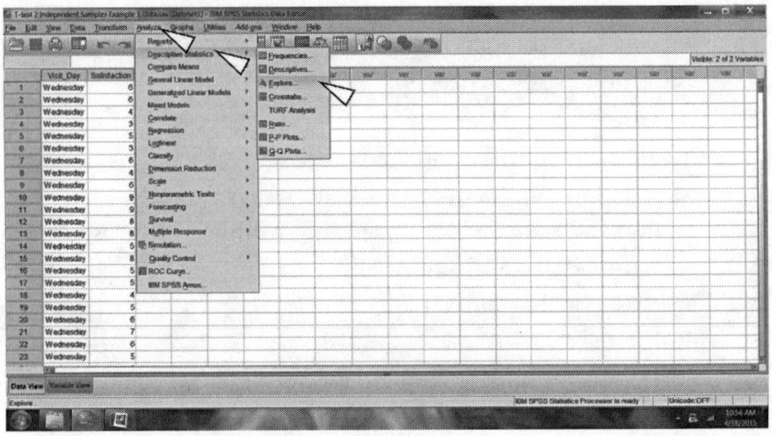

Figure 17.5

Step 3: After the "Explore" window is open:

- Highlight the "Satisfaction" variable and place it in the "Dependent List" box by clicking the "Arrow" button.
- Place the "Visit Day" variable in the Factor List.
- Click the "Plots" button.
- In the "Explore: Plots" window:
  - Only check "None" in the box plot area.
  - Below that, check "Normality plots with tests."
  - In the "Spread vs Level with Levene Test" area, make sure "None" is selected.
  - Next, click the "Continue" button.
- Last, in the "Explore" window, click the "OK" button. Output is generated.

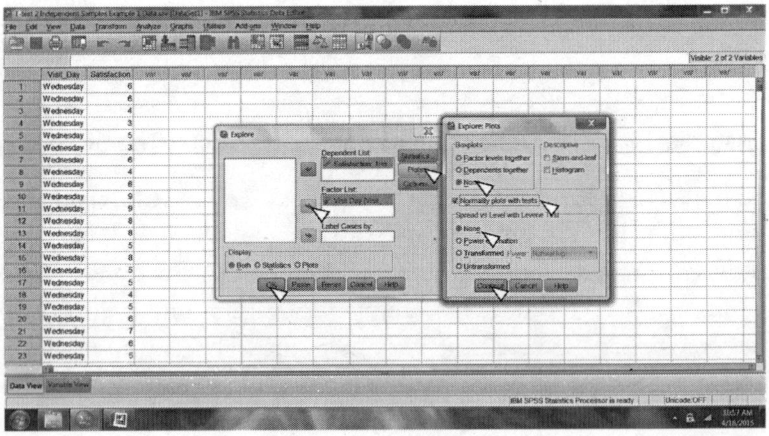

Figure 17.6

Step 4: Back in the data file, do the following:

- Select the "Analyze" tab.
- Highlight "Compare Means."
- Last, click "Independent Samples *T*-Test."

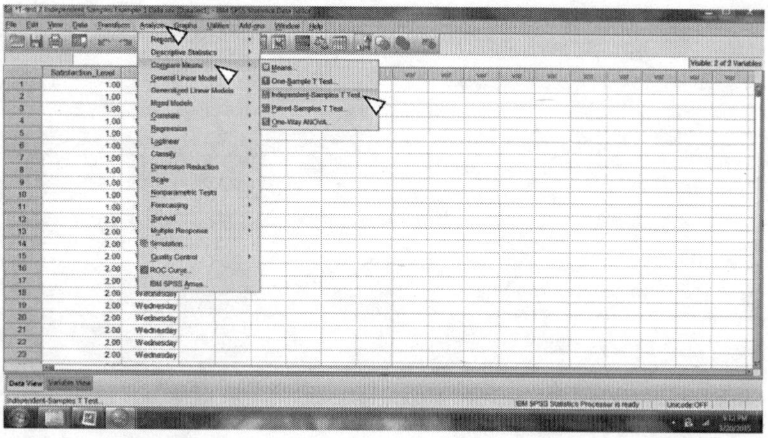

Figure 17.7

Step 5: After the "Independent Sample *T*-Test" window opens, follow these steps:

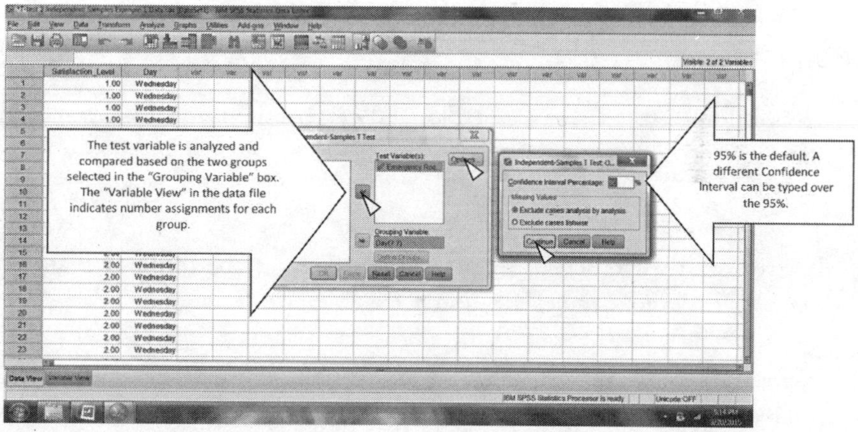

Figure 17.8

- Assign the "Emergency Room Visit Satisfaction Level" variable to the "Test Variable(s)" box by highlighting it and then clicking the "Arrow" button.
- Using the same procedure, assign the "Day of the Week" variable as the Grouping Variable.
- Next, click the "Options" button.
  - Do not change the "95% Confidence Interval."
  - Click "Exclude cases listwise," which will assure equal sample sizes. If you wish to learn more about missing data, then click the "Help" button at the bottom-left-hand side of the window.
  - Last, click the "Continue" button.

Step 6: Back in the "Independent Samples *T*-Test" window:

- Click the "Define Groups" button.
- After the "Define Groups" window opens:
  - Since Wednesday is coded 1 and Friday is coded 2 in the dataset, enter these numbers in the Group 1 and Group 2 boxes, respectively.
  - Last, click the "Define Groups" box's "Continue" button.

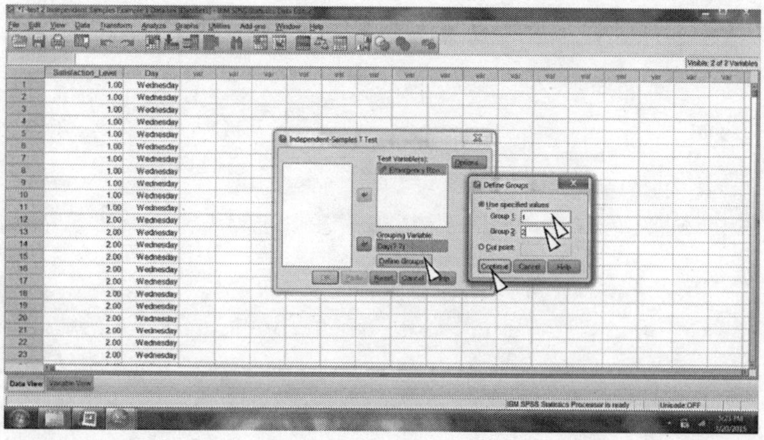

Figure 17.9

Step 7: Click the "OK" button to run the independent samples analysis. An output file will be generated.

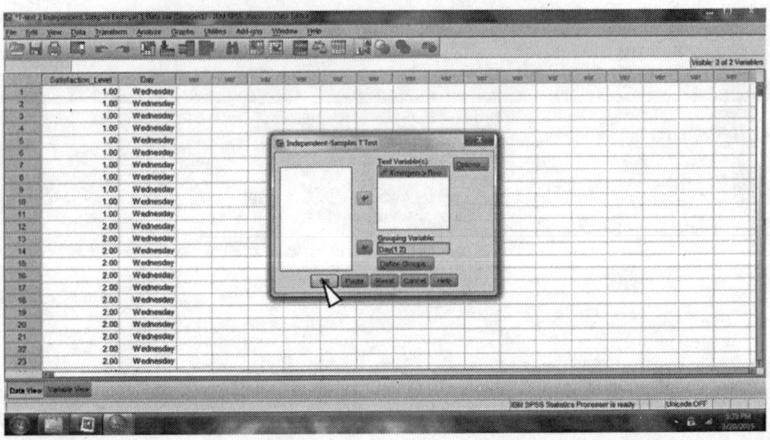

Figure 17.10

Last, save the data and output files for your records.

SPSS Output Interpretation

In addition to the descriptive tables and graphs, the two independent samples *t*-test output group statistics and independent samples test tables are available. Below is a discussion of the output.

Data Screening

There are two data screening procedures. First, each sample is examined for normal distribution. Second, the two samples are tested for equality of variance.

Normal Distribution

Each sample size is over 30. We can determine whether the sample data meet the normal distribution assumption by assessing the Shapiro-Wilk statistic in the tests for normality table. As depicted in Table 17.1, the Shapiro-Wilk statistic is not statistically significant for Wednesday (p = .68) or for Friday (p = .61), indicating that the samples do not violate the assumption.

Table 17.1

Tests of Normality

		Kolmogorov-Smirnov[a]			Shapiro-Wilk		
	Visit Day	Statistic	df	Sig.	Statistic	df	Sig.
Satisfaction: 1=not at all TO 10=totally satisfied	Wednesday	.033	336	.200*	.997	336	.689
	Friday	.027	232	.200*	.995	232	.619
	Sunday	.041	294	.200*	.994	294	.250

*. This is a lower bound of the true significance.

a. Lilliefors Significance Correction

"Sig" denotes a p-value of .689 for Wednesday and .619 for Friday.

Ideally, each sample should have the same number of observations; however, in reality, they often vary. The general rule of thumb is that the bigger sample size should not be 1.5× larger than the smaller sample size. In other words, if the smaller sample size is 232, the larger sample size should be no greater than 232 × 1.5 = 348. As we can see in Table 17.2, the total sample consists of 568 ER patient visits, of which 336 visited on Wednesday and 232 visited on Friday. The sample sizes meet this criterion.

Non-normally distributed data and violation of the 1.5× rule increase the likelihood of producing inaccurate results. There are methods for correcting non-normal data distribution and accommodating the 1.5× rule. We could collect more data with the hope that the distribution becomes normal with close to equal sample sizes. In addition, providing that the sample size is sufficiently large, we can examine the Normal Q-Q Plot derived from the Descriptive/Explore analysis output to identify and possibly remove any outliers. These steps might then give us a fairly normal distribution and close to balanced sample sizes. Chapter 12 covers options to address these conditions.

Another option is a data transformation, which, depending on the non-normal shape, might normalize the distribution. If correcting for data non-normality is impractical, the **Mann-Whitney *U*** nonparametric test is available. This test is less sensitive to violations of normality because it is based on rank-ordering the data. When the test is used to compare two means, equality of variance is not a consideration. In SPSS, it is located in the "Nonparametric Tests" area of the pull-down menu under "Legacy Dialogs." Data transformations and nonparametric means testing are beyond the scope of our discussion. If none of the solutions for addressing non-normal distribution suffice, then include a caveat in the write-up.

The Wednesday mean satisfaction score is 5.58 with a standard deviation of 1.62. The Friday mean satisfaction score is 4.82 with a standard deviation of 1.61. Their standard deviations are nearly equal, which appears to indicate that the typical difference between individual satisfaction scores and its sample mean are close to identical in both samples. The "Standard Error Mean" statistic is an estimate of the average difference of means from multiple representative same size samples of the target population. We do not use this statistic.

Table 17.2

Group Statistics

	Visit Day	N	Mean	Std. Deviation	Std. Error Mean
Satisfaction: 1=not at all TO 10=totally satisfied	Wednesday	336	5.58	1.621	.088
	Friday	232	4.82	1.611	.106

'N' = sample size.size.

Equality of Variance

In our example, there is no meaningful difference between the shape of the two variables' data distribution because $p = .927$. Therefore, as indicated in Table 17.3, we base the assessment on the "Equal variances assumed" statistics.

Two Independent Samples *T*-Test Analysis

Using a two independent samples *t*-test, we ran our analysis to determine if there is a meaningful difference between the Wednesday and Friday ER patient visits' satisfaction scores. Table 17.3 contains information about the Levene Test for Equality of Variance, the significance test for the Wednesday and Friday mean scores, and the 95% confidence interval for the difference between the two true mean scores.

Table 17.3

The Independent Samples *T*-test *p*-value is < .000.

Independent Samples Test

		Levene's Test for Equality of Variances		t-test for Equality of Means					95% Confidence Interval of the Difference	
		F	Sig.	t	df	Sig. (2-tailed)	Mean Difference	Std. Error Difference	Lower	Upper
Satisfaction: 1=not at all TO 10=totally satisfied	Equal variances assumed	.008	.927	5.508	566	.000	.760	.138	.489	1.031
	Equal variances not assumed			5.514	498.697	.000	.760	.138	.489	1.031

The Levene Test *p*-value is .927.

The Wednesday mean score is .489 to 1.031 larger than the Friday mean.

The "Equal variances assumed"—"*T*-Test for Equality of Means"—"Sig. (2-tailed)" statistic indicates that $p < .001$ for the two sample comparison, which is the pooled *t*-test. This is a meaningful finding because .000 < .05. Therefore, it is likely that the satisfaction rates between Wednesday and Friday vary. If equal variances were not assumed, we would select the *p*-value associated with "Equal variances not assumed," which is the separate samples *t*-test. In many cases, the *p*-value will be consistently significant or nonsignificant for both assumptions. However, in cases where it is close to the alpha, the significance may vary depending on the equality of variance assumption.

We have a 95% confidence interval for the difference between the Wednesday patient satisfaction true population mean and the Friday satisfaction true population mean. This interval is the set of possible differences between both populations, as represented in their samples. It pertains to the first sample in relation to the second sample, which makes sense because the Wednesday mean is larger and the interval values are positive; thus, it represents an interval of by how much the Wednesday mean is larger with a 95% level of confidence. The average Wednesday ER patient satisfaction score ($M = 5.58$) is anywhere from .48 to 1.03 larger than the average Friday ER patient satisfaction score ($M = 4.82$). Applying these values, we are 95% confident that the Wednesday true mean score is between 5.30 and 5.85, which includes 5.58 but does not include 4.82, suggesting a meaningful difference.

Based on the *p*-value and confidence interval, there is a low probability that these results are not meaningful. Providing that the sample represents patients who visit the ER on the study days, these findings can be applied to all of the hospital's Wednesday and Friday ER room patients.

Reporting Results

Write-Up

A two independent samples *t*-test was conducted that compared the Wednesday and Friday ER patient satisfaction mean scores of 568 patients (Wednesday [$N = 336$] and Friday [$N = 232$]). Patient responses ranged from 1 = "not satisfied at all" to 7 = "totally satisfied." A significant difference was found ($t(566) = 5.50$, $p < .001$). It is likely that the Wednesday mean patient satisfaction score of 5.58 ($SD = 1.62$) is different from the Friday patient mean score of 4.82 ($SD = 1.61$). Thus, on average, ER patient satisfaction varies between those patients who visit the ER on Wednesday as opposed to Friday. Furthermore, we are 95% confident that the Wednesday ER patient satisfaction true mean score is anywhere from .48 to 1.03 higher than the Friday ER patient satisfaction mean score.

(OR we can apply directionality)

A two independent samples *t*-test was conducted that compared the Wednesday and Friday ER patient satisfaction mean scores of 568 patients (Wednesday [$N = 336$] and Friday [$N = 232$]). Patient responses ranged from 1 = "not satisfied at all" to 7 = "totally satisfied." A significant difference was found ($t(566) = 5.50$, $p < .001$). It is likely that the Wednesday mean patient satisfaction score of 5.58 ($SD = 1.62$) is greater than the Friday patient mean score of 4.82 ($SD = 1.61$). Thus, ER patient satisfaction on average is higher for Wednesday visits compared to Friday patient visits. Furthermore, we are 95% confident that the Wednesday ER patient satisfaction true mean score is anywhere from .48 to 1.03 higher than the Friday ER patient satisfaction mean score.

The "(566)" represents the degrees of freedom (*df*), which is the number of data points that can vary. Its formula is n – number of samples. In our case, it is $568 - 2 = 566 = df$. "*SD*" denotes standard deviation.

Example 17.2: Two Independent Samples *T*-Tests: The Nonsignificant Case

Burger Queen is revising its management training program. In order to attract the best management trainees, it must offer competitive starting salaries. Its major competitor for human capital is McDanno's. Through a trade association affiliation, Burger Queen was able to collect salary data about McDanno's. The goal is to determine if Burger Queen's management trainee starting salary is different from McDanno's. The total sample size is 62; there were 31 respondents each from Burger Queen and McDanno's. Alpha = .05. The data file name is "*T*-Test 2 Independent Samples Exercise 2 Data."

The analysis requires two variables: a grouping variable (Burger Queen = 1 and McDanno's = 2) and a dependent variable (reported gross annual salary).

We will skip the SPSS steps because they are identical to the first example.

SPSS Output Interpretation

Data Screening

Normal Distribution

The sample size is greater than 30 for each restaurant chain. As depicted in Table 17.4, the Shapiro–Wilk statistic for both samples is not meaningful (Burger Queen, $p = .82$ and McDanno's, $p = .31$), indicating that the samples do not violate the normal distribution assumption.

Table 17.4

Tests of Normality

		Kolmogorov-Smirnov[a]			Shapiro-Wilk		
	Quick Service Restaurant	Statistic	df	Sig.	Statistic	df	Sig.
Annual Salary	Burger Queen	.113	31	.200*	.980	31	.826
	McDanno's	.106	31	.200*	.961	31	.316

*. This is a lower bound of the true significance.

a. Lilliefors Significance Correction

As we can see in Table 17.5, the total sample consists of 62 managers. Respondents were evenly split between the two quick service restaurant chains. The Burger Queen mean reported salary is $49,931.88 with a standard deviation of $9,465.79. The McDanno's mean reported salary is $47,928.85 with a standard deviation of $10,001.77.

Table 17.5

Group Statistics

	Quick Service Restaurant	N	Mean	Std. Deviation	Std. Error Mean
Annual Salary	Burger Queen	31	$49,931.88	$9,465.793	$1,700.107
	McDanno's	31	$47,928.85	$10,001.771	$1,796.371

Equality of Variance

The Levene Test for Equality of Variance compared the data distributions between the two samples. It was not meaningful (p = .52). Therefore, we assume that the variances do not differ significantly.

Two Independent Samples *T*-Test Analysis

The output in Table 17.6 contains information about the equality of variances, the comparison of the Burger Queen and McDanno's management trainee mean scores, and the 95% confidence interval for the difference between the two salaries' true population average scores.

The *t*-test for "equal variances assumed" indicates $p = .42$, which is not statistically significant. Therefore, there is likely no meaningful difference between $49,931.88 and $47,928.85. We conclude that there is no evidence to suggest that salaries vary between Burger Queen and McDanno's.

We are 95% confident that the average Burger Queen management trainee starting salary is anywhere from $2,944.34 less than to $6,950.41 more than the average starting salary at McDanno's, which includes a difference of zero. That is to say, we are 95% confident that the Burger Queen mean salary is between $44,984.51 and $54,879.26, which contains the McDanno's mean salary of $47,928.85.

Table 17.6

Independent Samples Test

		Levene's Test for Equality of Variances		t-test for Equality of Means						
									95% Confidence Interval of the Difference	
		F	Sig.	t	df	Sig. (2-tailed)	Mean Difference	Std. Error Difference	Lower	Upper
Annual Salary	Equal variances assumed	.413	.523	.810	60	.421	$2,003.037	$2,473.320	-$2,944.340	$6,950.413
	Equal variances not assumed			.810	59.819	[illegible]	$2,003.037	$2,473.320	-$2,94[illegible]8	[illegible]0.722

Based on the *p*-value and confidence interval, there is a high probability that there is no difference between starting salaries.

Reporting Results

Write-Up

A two independent samples *t*-test was conducted that compared the average management trainee starting salaries between Burger Queen and McDanno's. A total of 62 salaries were collected, which were equally split between the two quick restaurant chains. A nonsignificant difference was found ($t(60) = .81$, $p = .42$). There is no evidence to suggest that the Burger Queen ($M =$ \$49,931.88 [$SD =$ \$9,465.79]) and McDanno's ($M =$ \$47,928.85 [SD = \$10,001.77]) mean salaries vary. Thus, on average, there is likely no difference between starting salaries. Furthermore, we are 95% confident that the true population average Burger Queen salary is anywhere from \$2,944.34 less than to \$6,950.41 greater than the average McDanno's salary.

SUMMARY OF KEY CONCEPTS

- The two independent samples *t*-test is a significance test that compares two representative sample means.
- There are a number of data assumptions when conducting a two independent samples *t*-test.
- In addition to normal distribution, the data must be assessed for equality of variance, which is done automatically when running the analysis.
- The analysis requires a grouping (independent) variable and a data (dependent) variable.
- The grouping variable identifies the sample from which the dependent variable data are measured and compared.
- The pooled and separate two independent samples *t*-tests are associated with "Equal variances assumed" and "Equal variances not assumed."
- Conducting two sample *t*-tests and calculating confidence intervals from differences intervals are straightforward in SPSS.

TWO INDEPENDENT SAMPLES *T*-TEST APPLIED EXERCISES

17.1 Define a two independent samples *t*-test. Provide an example.

17.2 What is equality of variance?

17.3 What is the Levene Test for Equality of Variance?

17.4 Define pooled two independent samples *t*-test.

17.5 What is a separate two independent samples *t*-test?

17.6 To what does the term "equality of variance assumed" refer?

17.7 To what does the term "equality of variance not assumed" refer?

17.8 What is the Mann-Whitney *U* test?

17.9 A local hospital offered two 6-month weight management programs to individuals who were 40–60 pounds overweight. One hundred and forty-six clients enrolled and completed one of these two plans over a 6-month period. Among other information, weight loss data were collected over the 6-month period. There were 62 participants in the *Protein Focus* program and 84 participants in the *Calorie Factor* plan. Based on the data from the two samples, is there any evidence to suggest that one program is more effective than the other by the end of the 6-month program? Explain your answer. Report results in the format provided in this chapter. Be sure to include the confidence interval. Alpha = .05. The data file name is "*T*-Test 2 Independent Samples Exercise 1 Data."

17.10 Primary caregivers (N = 57), who were responsible for one or more minor children, and "empty nesters" (N = 50) were surveyed about their willingness to purchase delivered groceries online. Individuals responded to a scale question: 1 = "not at all willing" to 7 = "willing all of the time." Determine if there is a likely difference in responses between these two groups. Explain your answer. Report results in the format provided in this chapter. Be sure to include the confidence interval. Alpha = .05. The data file name is "*T*-Test 2 Independent Samples Exercise 2 Data."

17.11 "Nursing" staff, including nurses, nursing assistants, and orderlies, sustain over 35,000 reported injuries per year. An occupational research firm seeks to discover the level of reported proper patient lifting and moving techniques employed by nursing staff based on whether they work in short-term hospital care facilities compared to long-term care nursing homes. Is there a difference between these two groups of healthcare workers? Five hundred nursing workers completed a survey, of which 235 worked in hospitals and 265 worked in long-term care nursing homes. The question of interest asked them if they employed proper patient lifting and moving techniques in order to minimize injury to themselves. Responses were anchored in the following format: 0 = "I do not use proper patient lifting and moving techniques" to 5 = "I always use proper patient lifting and moving techniques." Explain your answer. Report results in the format provided in this chapter. Be sure to include the confidence interval. Alpha = .05. The data file name is "*T*-Test 2 Independent Samples Exercise 3 Data."

17.12 The total annual cost in dollars was calculated per individual inmate at federal prisons and at state prisons. The representative sample consisted of 500 federal inmates from various institutions throughout the USA and 500 state inmates from 40 states for a total sample size of 1,000. Determine if there is a difference in costs between federal inmates and the collective data on state inmates. Explain your answer. Report results in the format provided in this chapter. Be sure to include the confidence interval. Alpha = .05. The data file name is "*T*-Test 2 Independent Samples Exercise 4 Data."

17.13 A group of researchers studied whether the amount of open family dialogue related to whether children grew up to be more accepting of "justified" violence, such as war, capital punishment, and other forms of physical violence, for "good" reason. Two hundred and twenty-five adults 18–22 years old completed a survey. One hundred and twenty-five were classified as raised in "more open" dialogue families and 100 were grouped as reared in "less open" dialogue families. The participants were asked whether they thought that some situations warranted a physically violent response. Responses were framed in a seven-point scale: 1 = "violence is never justified" to 7 = "there are situations where violence is totally justified." Does the high or low level of family dialogue relate to support for physical violence under certain situations? Explain your answer. Report results in the format provided in this chapter. Be sure to include the confidence interval. Alpha = .05. The data file name is "*T*-Test 2 Independent Samples Exercise 5 Data."

17.14 Two representative samples of undergraduate students eligible to vote were selected to indicate their likelihood to vote in the forthcoming presidential election. One sample viewed the last presidential debate of the major candidates and the other group did not view the debate. Each sample consisted of 175 students for a total of 350 participants. The question was formatted in a five-point scale as follows: 0 = "I do not intend to vote in the next presidential election" to 5 = "I absolutely intend to vote in the next presidential election." Does exposure to the final presidential debate relate to whether undergraduate students intend to vote in the presidential election? Explain your answer. Report results in the format provided in this chapter. Be sure to include the confidence interval. Alpha = .05. The data file name is "*T*-Test 2 Independent Samples Exercise 6 Data."

Chapter 18

Analysis of Variance (ANOVA): Comparing More Than Two Independent Samples' Means to Test for Differences among Them by One Type of Classification

LEARNING OBJECTIVES

To be able to:

- understand the purpose and explain the basic principles of a one-way ANOVA, including the role of variance;
- describe the data assumptions for one-way ANOVA;
- understand the role of normal distribution and equality of variance in one-way ANOVA;
- know how to address violations of the key assumptions of ANOVA;
- conduct a one-way ANOVA in SPSS;
- understand and describe ANOVA confidence intervals; and
- interpret and report significant and nonsignificant ANOVA results.

18.1 Introduction to One-Way ANOVA

The **one-way analysis of variances (one-way ANOVA) *F*-test** compares the means among more than two independent representative samples (groups) in order to determine the likelihood of a statistically significant difference between at least two of the samples. This ANOVA is called one-way because there is one independent variable categorized in groups. The independent or grouping variable is a categorical variable in which each category identifies one of the samples. The samples represent the target populations. The dependent variable is numeric and compared based on the sample designations indicated in the independent variable. Essentially, ANOVA compares the means of the dependent measure of each group. The overall ANOVA *F*-test is called an **omnibus test**. There are more complex ANOVAs involving more variables, which are beyond our discussion.

ANOVA involves one or two major steps, depending on whether the omnibus test is significant. If it is not significant, then the analysis stops because no differences exist among the means and we conclude that the samples' means likely do not differ. A significant ANOVA indicates that there is a meaningful difference between at least two of the means. At that point, we must determine where the differences among the samples specifically exist. For this, we must conduct **post hoc testing**.

For example, a national sales manager may wish to discover whether there are differences in sales generated by region of the country. A university may wish to assess if there are differences in number of undergraduate applicants among the states of New York, California, and Texas.

As we can see, ANOVA examines whether two or more samples identified as categories within an independent or grouping variable vary in some way from each other.

18.2 Variance

The topic of variance leads to an important question, which does not escape serious students of statistics. Why is comparing more than two means called analysis of variance rather than perhaps "analysis of means?" We know that variance is a measure of the spread of the data or the differences of the data points from the mean. To determine whether more than two means significantly differ requires calculating three types of variances.

The first is the variance within each sample, which is called **within-sample variance**. This measure represents random variance. Second, there is variance between means, which is called **between-samples variance**. The within-sample variance is required in order to calculate the between-samples means' variance. Last, there is the **total variance**. When there is equality of variance, the samples are pooled together in order to determine variance, which is based on the grand mean. The **grand mean** is the mean of all of the data across samples for the variable being analyzed. These three variances are required for us to test for means differences. However, it is the difference in variance between the within-sample and between-samples variances that determines means' differences.

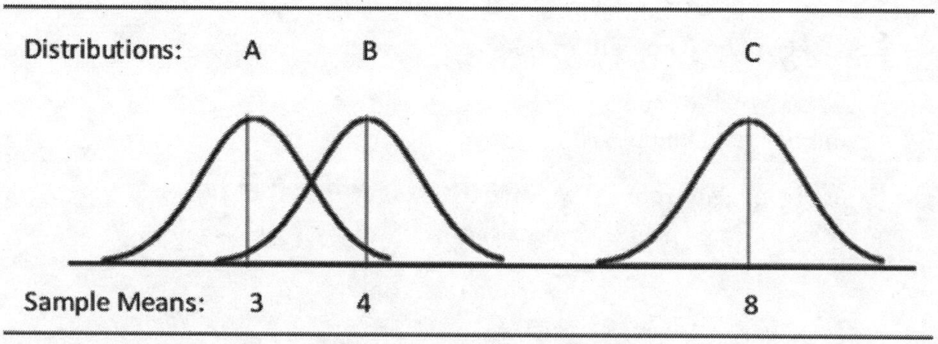

Note: The distributions illustrate equality of variance.

Figure 18.1 Equality of Variance in More Than Two Distributions

In Figure 18.1, the variances are similar yet the means vary. In other words, if the sample distributions were represented on a graph line, they would look similar but potentially vary on their location on the line because of different means. The distributions would look alike and could overlap to a degree or they could not overlap at all, suggesting a meaningful difference of means so that if the distributions are further apart, then their means will be further apart, and thus they are more likely to be statistically significantly different.

Table 18.1 depicts the relationships between variances and means within and among the distributions. If the within variances are similar to the variance among the means, then there is a likelihood that there is no statistically significant difference among them. However, as the difference in variance increases, so does the possibility of finding at least one significant difference among the means. In our example, the within-sample average differences are 1.20 each and the among (between) mean difference is 2.00, signaling a possible significant difference among the means, as suggested by Distribution A's mean of 8 compared to the two other means.

Table 18.1

Variances Within and Among Distributions

Distributions	Data	Absolute Differences (equality of "variance")	Mean
Within A	1, 2, 3, 4, 5	2, 1, 0, 1, 2 Average Difference = 1.2	3
Within B	2, 3, 4, 5, 6	2, 1, 0, 1, 2 Average Difference = 1.2	4
Within C	6, 7, 8, 9, 10	2, 1, 0, 1, 2 Average Difference = 1.2	8
Among Means	3, 4, 8	2, 1, 3 **Average Difference = 2.0**	5

Note: This table attempts to simplify the relationships under discussion. Five (5) is the grand mean. Distributions A - C have equal sample sizes.

As we can see, equality of variance is an important assumption for standard one-way ANOVA. If the samples share similar variances and are equal in size, then they can only differ in means, which is what we want to examine. SPSS provides the *p*-value of the overall ANOVA.

If the overall ANOVA is statistically significant, then we examine the post hoc test to determine where precisely those mean differences lie. SPSS provides output and *p*-values for paired comparison of the sample combinations. For example, three samples would require three comparisons such as:

Sample A and Sample B

Sample B and Sample C

Sample C and Sample A

For sampling planning, it might be useful to determine the number of comparisons ahead of time. The formula for determining the number of paired comparisons is:

$$\frac{G!}{\left(2 \times (G-2)!\right)}$$

where

G = number of samples (groups)
! = factorial (e.g. 4! = 1 × 2 × 3 × 4 = 24)

Let us apply the formula to our three samples illustration:

= $G! / (2 \times (G-2)!)$

= $3! / (2 \times (3-2)!)$

= $1 \times 2 \times 3 / (2 \times 1)!$

= $6 / (1 \times 2)$

= 3 comparisons

REAL WORLD SNAPSHOT

In a 2003 study entitled "Effectiveness of Drug Treatment Courts: Evidence from a Randomized Trial," Gottfredson, Najaka, and Kearley studied 235 offenders over a two-year period who were randomly assigned to one of three conditions: a highly structured drug court treatment program ($n = 67$), drug court with typically less structured treatment options ($n = 72$), and a control group where participants appeared in court but were not required to seek drug treatment ($n = 96$).

The study aim was to learn whether increased treatment structure and monitoring actually decreased recidivism rates over the two-year period. The data comparison involved comparing rearrest percentages among the three groups: more structure, less structure, and no structure (control group).

The percentage of the highly structured treatment participants who were rearrested (56.7%) was statistically significantly less ($p < .05$) than the less structured treatment (75.0%) and no treatment control groups (81.3%). In fact, the highly structured group averaged less than one new arrest compared to over two new arrests for each of the other groups. The findings were 95% confident that the true population average percentage is 44.5–68.9% for the highly structured group, 64.8–85.3% for the less structured participants, and 73.3–89.2% for the control group. Using ANOVA, the study results suggest that highly structured court supervised treatment programs are effective in reducing the rate of drug offender recidivism.

Ask yourself: What follow-up research might be helpful to shed additional light on this topic?

18.3 Data Assumptions

ANOVA has a number of assumptions:

- The dependent variable's data are numeric, in the same format, and in the same variable.
- Each group's sample size is over 30.
- The samples are randomly selected and independent of each other. The samples do not contain data from the same source such as data from the same people.
- The sample is representative of the target population.
- (Ideally), all groups are equal size.
- The groups (samples) each are fairly normally distributed.
- There is equality of variance among the groups.
- The grouping (independent) variable identifies each sample's data.

18.4 Strategies for Addressing Violations of Assumptions

Like the two independent samples *t*-test, the Levene Test for Equality of Variance is used to determine the equality of variance assumption, in which case the samples are pooled for analysis. However, there are a number of situations in which some of the key assumptions are not met. Remedies depending on the nature of the violation are addressed below. Table 18.2 illustrates under what data conditions to use the specified tests. Normality, equality of variances, and equal sample sizes are critical assumptions.

Table 18.2

Testing More than Two Means Options

Overall Test Statistic & Post Hoc Test/ Data Attributes	*Normal Distribution*	*Equality of Variance*	*Equal Sample Sizes*
One-way ANOVA *F*-test/Tukey (HSD)	Yes	Yes	Yes
One-way ANOVA *F*-test/Scheffe	Yes	Yes	No
Welch test/Games-Howell	Yes	No	No
Brown-Forsythe test/Games-Howell	Mostly	No	No

Note: These test options are not exhaustive, but are the more popular approaches for addressing data with such characteristics.

We discussed the classic one-way ANOVA *F*-test. The **Tukey (HSD) post hoc test** is deployed when the data are fairly normally distributed, there is equality of variance, and the sample sizes are equal. When the sample sizes are not equal, we simply use the **Scheffe post hoc test**. The **Welch** and **Brown-Forsythe tests** (located in the robust tests of equality of means table), along with the **Games-Howell post hoc test**, are used when we cannot assume equality of variance and equal sample sizes. The Brown-Forsythe test is preferred when the distributions are close to violating the normality assumption. However, so long as the samples approximate the normal distribution, it is a safe bet to use the Welch test. A nonparametric alternative to the last two omnibus tests is the **Kruskal-Wallis test**, which is not as sensitive to detecting differences as the other statistical tests and thus might miss significant effects.

18.5 Examples Using SPSS: Step-by-Step Instructions

Using the SPSS ANOVA procedure, the following two examples each compare more than two independent means to determine whether there are differences among them.

Example 18.1: ANOVA *F*-Test: The Significant Case

The new accounting manager for Briarcliffe Hospital wants to learn if there is a difference in the typical number of days an insured patient stays in the hospital by insurance carrier. The data cover the last year and there are four major insurance carriers: Medicare/Medicaid, Blue Cross/Blue Shield, Universal Health, and Patriot Insurance. Do hospital stay durations vary by insurance carrier? Alpha = .05. The SPSS file named "One-Way ANOVA Example 1 Data" contains the data for this analysis.

The analysis requires two variables: a grouping variable (Medicare/Medicaid = 1, Blue Cross/Blue Shield = 2, Universal Health = 3, and Patriot Insurance = 4) and a dependent variable (hospital stay in days). The basic SPSS steps are as follows.

Step 1: Open SPSS.

- Locate the appropriate folder and data file, then highlight it.
- Next, click the "Open" button.

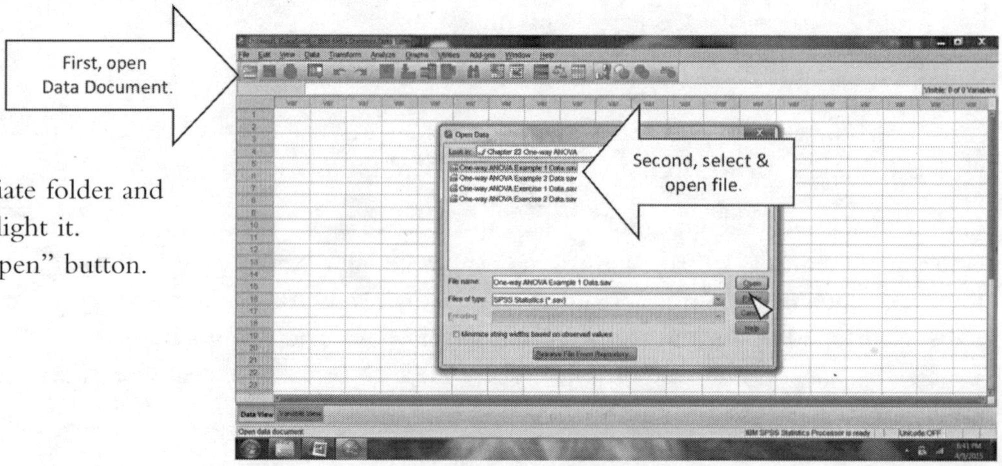

Figure 18.2

Step 2: After the data file opens:

- Select the "Analyze" tab.
- Highlight "Descriptive Statistics."
- Last, click "Explore."

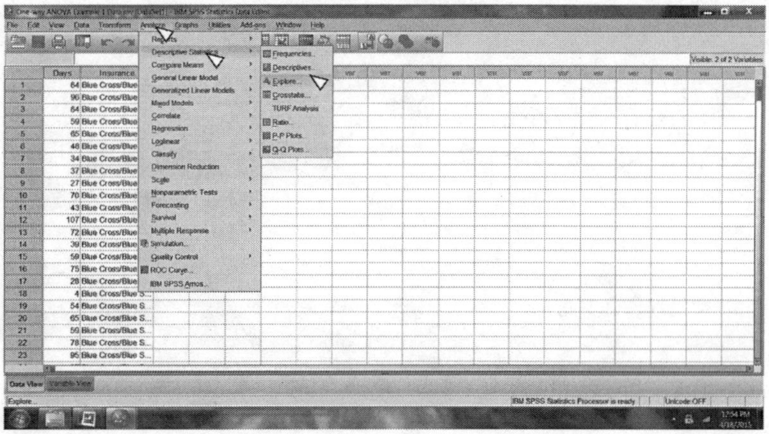

Figure 18.3

Step 3: In the "Explore" window:

- Highlight the "Days" variable and place it in the "Dependent List" box by clicking the "Arrow" button.
- Place the "Insurance" variable in the Factor List.
- Click the "Plots" button.
  - In the "Plots: Explore" window, only check "None" in the box plot area.
  - Below that, check "Normality plots with tests."
  - Next, click the "Continue" button.
- Last, click the "OK" button. Output is generated.

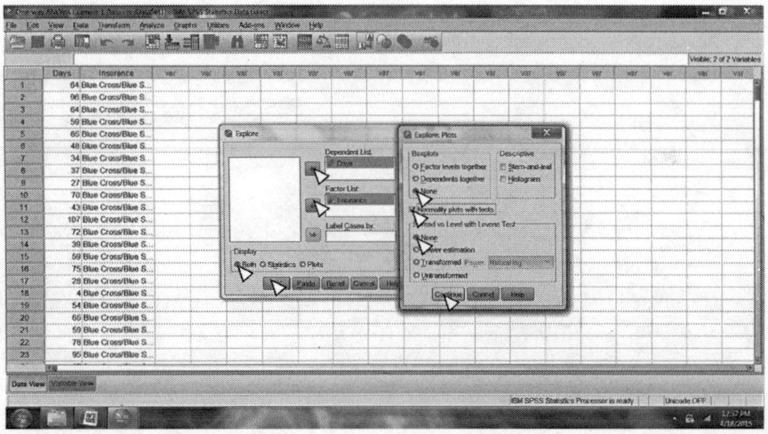

Figure 18.4

Step 4: Back in the data file:

- Select the "Analyze" tab.
- Highlight "Compare Means."
- Click on "One-Way ANOVA."

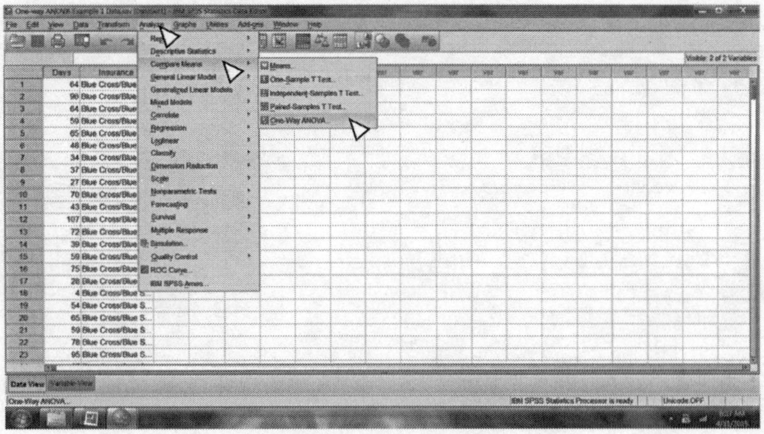

Figure 18.5

Step 5: Next, in the "One-Way ANOVA" window:

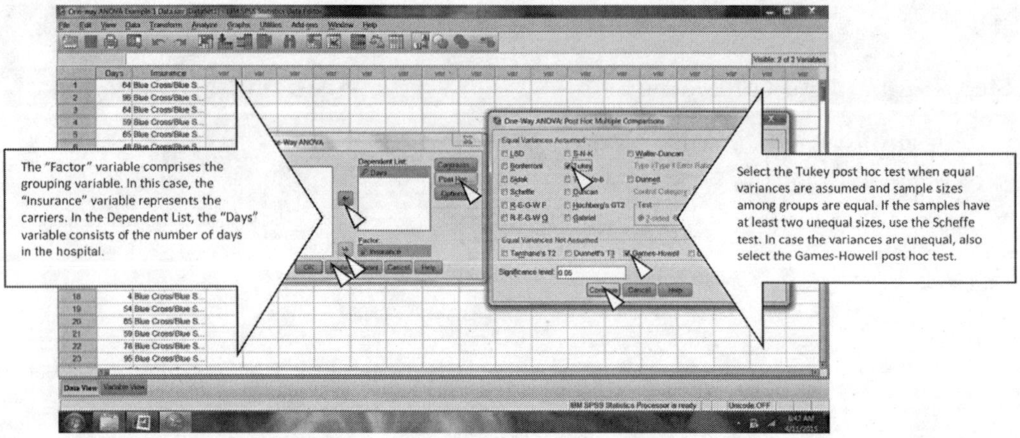

Figure 18.6

- Assign the "Days" variable to the "Dependent List" box by highlighting it and then click the "Arrow" button.
- Using the same procedure, assign the "Insurance" variable to the "Factor" box.
- Next, click the "Post Hoc" button.
  - In the "One-Way ANOVA Post Hoc Multiple Comparisons" window, check off the "Equal Variances Assumed Tukey" and "Equal Variances Not Assumed Games-Howell" settings. If the sample sizes are unequal, select the Scheffe test in place of Tukey's.
- Last, click the "Continue" button.

Step 6: In the "One-Way ANOVA" window:

- Click the "Options" button.
- After the "One-Way ANOVA Options" window opens, in the "Statistics" area, check off "Descriptive," "Homogeneity of variances test," "Brown-Forsythe," and "Welch."
- Under "Missing Values," select the "Exclude cases analysis by analysis" default setting.
- Last, click the "Continue" button.

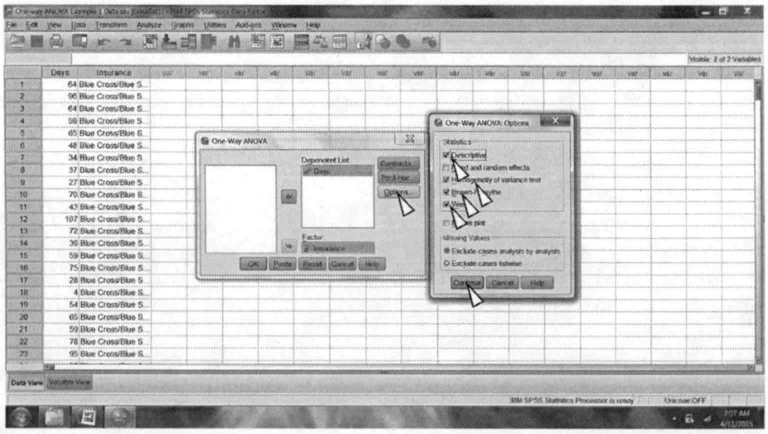

Figure 18.7

Step 7: In the "One-Way ANOVA" window, click the "OK" button to run the ANOVA. An output file will be generated with the analyses tables.

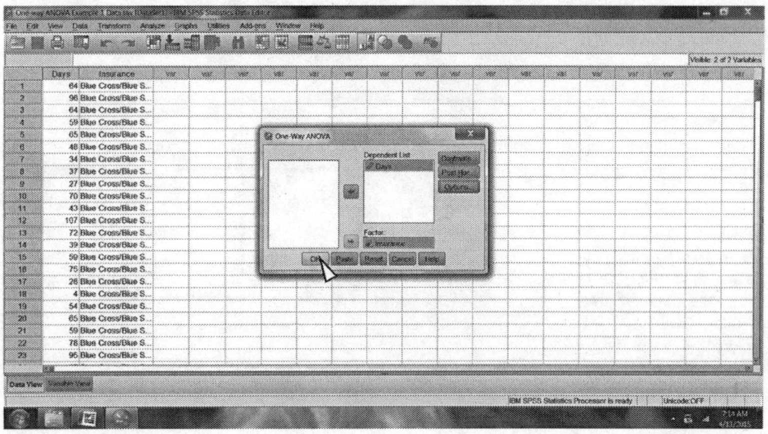

Figure 18.8

Save the data and output files for your records.

SPSS Output Interpretation

In addition to the descriptive tables and graphs, the ANOVA descriptives, test of homogeneity of variances, ANOVA, robust tests of equality of means, post hoc tests, and homogeneous subsets tables are available. Below is a discussion of the output.

Data Screening

The sample sizes are each over 30. We can determine whether the sample data are fairly normally distributed by assessing the Shapiro-Wilk statistic in the tests for normality table. As depicted in Table 18.3, Blue Cross/Blue Shield, $p = .90$, Universal Health, $p = .52$, Patriot Insurance, $p = .39$, and Medicare/Medicaid, $p = .29$. The Shapiro-Wilk statistics p-values for the carriers are all greater than .05, indicating that the samples approximate the normal distribution. If the Shapiro-Wilk p-value were less than .05, we would consider other options, as covered in Chapter 12.

Table 18.3

Tests of Normality

	Insurance	Kolmogorov-Smirnov[a]			Shapiro-Wilk		
		Statistic	df	Sig.	Statistic	df	Sig.
Days	Blue Cross/Blue Shield	.058	100	.200*	.993	100	.907
	Universal Health	.060	100	.200*	.988	100	.528
	Patriot Insurance	.046	100	.200*	.986	100	.399
	Medicare/Medicaid	.075	100	.178	.985	100	.298

*. This is a lower bound of the true significance.

a. Lilliefors Significance Correction

"Sig" denotes the p-values for each insurance carrier's data distribution.

As we can see in Table 18.4, the total sample consists of 400 insured patients. There are 100 patients per insurance carrier. The average stay in days by insurance carrier are Blue Cross/Blue Shield 60.35 days with a standard deviation of 19.93 days; Universal Health 60.60 days with a standard deviation of 20.23 days; Patriot Insurance 59.97 days with a standard deviation of 18.76 days; and Medicare/Medicaid 88.01 days with a standard deviations of 19.20 days. Their standard deviations are similar, indicating that the typical difference between individual hospital stays and its sample mean are not very different.

Table 18.4

Descriptives

Days

	N	Mean	Std. Deviation	Std. Error	95% Confidence Interval for Mean		Mini	Maximum
					Lower Bound	Upper Bound		
Blue Cross/Blue Shield	100	60.35	19.931	1.993	56.40	64.31		
Universal Health	100	60.60	20.235	2.023	56.58	64.61		
Patriot Insurance	100	59.97	18.763	1.876	56.25	63.70		
Medicare/Medicaid	100	88.01	19.207	1.921	84.20	91.82		132
Total	400	67.23	22.877	1.144	64.99	69.48	4	132

Mean 95% Confidence Interval.

Another measure used to complement ANOVA is the confidence interval. Based on the table above, we are 95% confident that the typical average Blue Cross/Blue Shield patient stay in the hospital is anywhere from 56.40 to 64.31 days. We are 95% confident that the true population Medicare/Medicaid average patient stay is anywhere from 84.20 to 91.82 days, and so forth for the other insurance carriers.

Additionally, we must determine whether the data distributions have similar shapes or variances. Table 18.5 provides us with this information. The Levene test assesses equality of variances. Since $p = .785$, the equality of variance assumption is met. The group data distributions are approximately similar to each other.

Table 18.5

Test of Homogeneity of Variances

Days

Levene Statistic	df1	df2	Sig.
.356	3	396	.785

"Sig." represents the p-value.

ANOVA (Analysis)

Since the samples are fairly normally distributed, there is equality of variance and equal sample sizes, we use the general ANOVA *F*-test and, if significant, the Tukey (HSD) post hoc test results. We first assess whether there is at least one different between groups based on the ANOVA *p*-value in Table 18.6. The output in the table contains the overall test for means differences in hospital stay days. Our focus is the "Sig." value, which is the *p*-value. The *p*-value is $< .001$, indicating that there is a meaningful difference between at least two insurance carrier groups.

Table 18.6

ANOVA

Days

	Sum of Squares	df	Mean Square	F	Sig.
Between Groups	57577.569	3	19192.523	50.254	.000
Within Groups	151235.299	396	381.907		
Total	208812.868	399			

"Sig." represents the p-value for the overall ANOVA.

On the other hand, if $p \geqslant .05$, we would stop and conclude that there are no statistically significant differences in hospital stays by insurance carrier.

Should any of the data assumptions be violated, Table 18.2 suggests alternative tests.

Because there is at least one meaningful difference between insurance carriers, we must determine which specific insurance companies differ among them through multiple comparisons, which require post hoc testing.

We use the Tukey (HSD) Multiple Comparisons results. As Table 18.7 reveals, the significant or meaningful differences between group means are indicated by asterisks and *p*-value less than .05. The table also includes a 95% confidence interval for the difference between the reference group mean and its comparison to each of the other groups. It appears that those patients insured by Medicare/Medicaid are more likely to stay longer in the hospital compared to patients insured by other carriers. The sample reveals no differences among the patients insured by other carriers.

This claim is further supported by the 95% confidence intervals of differences. In all multiple comparisons other than those involving Medicare/Medicaid, the interval includes zero or the possibility of no difference between the group mean comparisons. Keep in mind that the descriptives table contains the 95% confidence intervals for each group's mean.

Table 18.7

The asterisk reveals a significant comparison b/w the inference & other group(s).

Multiple Compa

Dependent Variable: Days

	(I) Insurance	(J) Insurance	Mean Difference (I-J)	Std. Error	Sig.	95% Confidence Interval	
						Lower Bound	Upper Bound
Tukey HSD	Blue Cross/Blue Shield	Universal Health	-.248	2.764	1.000	-7.38	6.88
		Patriot Insurance	.377	2.764	.999	-6.75	7.51
		Medicare/Medicaid	-27.660*	2.764	.000	-34.79	-20.53
	Universal Health	Blue Cross/Blue Shield	.248	2.764	1.000	-6.88	7.38
		Patriot Insurance	.625	2.764	.996	-6.50	7.76
		Medicare/Medicaid	-27.411*	2.764	.000	-34.54	-20.28
	Patriot Insurance	Blue Cross/Blue Shield	-.377	2.764	.999	-7.51	6.75
		Universal Health	-.625	2.764	.996	[illegible]	6.50
		Medicare/Medicaid	-28.037*	2.764	.000	[illegible]	-20.91
	Medicare/Medicaid	Blue Cross/Blue Shield	27.660*	2.764	.000		
		Universal Health	27.411*	2.764	.000		
		Patriot Insurance	28.037*	2.764	.000		
Games-Howell	Blue Cross/Blue Shield	Universal Health	-.248	2.840	1.000		
		Patriot Insurance	.377	2.737	.999	[illegible]	7.47
		Medicare/Medicaid	-27.660*	2.768	.000	[illegible]	-20.49
	Universal Health	Blue Cross/Blue Shield	.248	2.840	1.000	-7.11	7.61
		Patriot Insurance	.625	2.759	.996	-6.52	7.78
		Medicare/Medicaid	-27.411*	2.790	.000	-34.64	-20.18
	Patriot Insurance	Blue Cross/Blue Shield	-.377	2.737	.999	-7.47	6.72
		Universal Health	-.625	2.759	.996	-7.78	6.52
		Medicare/Medicaid	-28.037*	2.685	.000	-34.99	-21.08
	Medicare/Medicaid	Blue Cross/Blue Shield	27.660*	2.768	.000	20.49	34.83
		Universal Health	27.411*	2.790	.000	20.18	34.64
		Patriot Insurance	28.037*	2.685	.000	21.08	34.99

*. The mean difference is significant at the 0.05 level.

This is alpha.

The reference group is in the (I) column.

Confidence Interval for the difference between the specific comparison.

"Sig." is the p-value. Note that a p-value of less than .05 will have an asterisk.

In summary, it is likely that Medicare/Medicaid patient hospital stays are longer than those patients covered by other insurance carriers based on $p < .001$ and the confidence intervals. We assume that the sample patients truly represent typical insured hospital patients.

Reporting Results

Write-Up

A one-way ANOVA was conducted that compared 400 hospital admissions by one of four types of insurance coverage. Each insurance carrier had a sample of 100 stays. A significant difference was found, $F(3,396) = 50.24$, $p < .001$. A Tukey (HSD) test was done to determine the specific differences. The Medicare/Medicaid patient stays ($M = 88.01$ days, $SD = 19.20$ days) were likely different than Blue Cross/Blue Shield ($M = 60.5$ days, $SD = 19.93$ days, $p < .001$), Universal Health ($M = 60.60$ days, $SD = 20.23$ days, $p < .001$), and Patriot Insurance ($M = 59.97$ days, $SD = 18.76$ days, $p < .001$). However, no differences were found among the other insurance carriers. Table 18.8 summarizes the results, including confidence intervals for the true population means.

(OR we can apply directionality)

A one-way ANOVA was conducted that compared 400 hospital admissions by one of four types of insurance coverage. Each insurance carrier had a sample of 100 stays. A significant difference was found, $F(3,396) = 50.24$, $p < .001$. A Tukey (HSD) test was done to determine the specific differences. The Medicare/Medicaid patient stays ($M = 88.01$ days, $SD = 19.20$ days) were likely to be longer than Blue Cross/Blue Shield ($M = 60.5$ days, $SD = 19.93$ days, $p < .001$), Universal Health ($M = 60.60$ days, $SD = 20.23$ days, $p < .001$), and Patriot Insurance ($M = 59.97$ days, $SD = 18.76$ days, $p < .001$). However, no differences were found among the other insurance carriers. Table 18.8 summarizes the results, including confidence intervals for the true population means.

Table 18.8

Hospital Stay in Days by Insurance Carrier ANOVA

Insurance Carrier	Days *Mean* (*SD*)	95% Confidence Interval for the True Mean
Blue Cross/Blue Shield	60.35 (19.93)	56.40 – 64.31
Universal Health	60.60 (20.23)	56.58 – 64.61
Patriot Insurance	59.97 (18.76)	56.25 - 63.70
Medicare/Medicaid	88.01 (19.20)	84.20 - 91.82

Note: $F(3,396) = 50.24$, $p < .001$). Tukey (HSD) post hoc test was used. $N = 400$ or $n = 100$/carrier.

The "F" is the F-test statistic and is required in the write-up. "SD" denotes standard deviation. The "3" in "(3,396)" represents the between groups degree of freedom (*df*), which is the number of groups – 1 or 4 – 1 = 3. The "396" represents the sample size. It is the total sample size – number of groups or 400 – 4 = 396 = *df*.

Example 18.2: ANOVA *F*-Test: The Nonsignificant Case

Complex Cable wishes to test consumer interest in a new cable service bundled product called "It's All That." Before deciding whether to market It's All That, Complex Cable will "pre-test" interest in the service. The three targeted regions are the East Coast, Midwest, and West Coast. Participants were asked whether they would seriously consider purchasing the new service bundle by responding to the following question: 1 = "not at all interested in It's All That" to 7 = "Would definitely try It's All That." Determine which region shows the most promise, if any? Alpha = .05. The SPSS file named "One-Way ANOVA Example 2 Data" contains the data for this analysis.

The analysis requires two variables: a grouping variable (East Coast = 1, Midwest = 2, and West Coast = 3) and a dependent variable (1 = "not at all interested in It's All That" to 7 = "Would definitely try It's All That").

We will skip the SPSS steps because they are identical to the first example.

SPSS Output Interpretation

The output tables in this section provide the required analyses and tell the story about the data.

Data Screening

Each sample size is greater than 30. As depicted in Table 18.9 and according to the Shapiro-Wilk statistic, all of the samples approximate the normal distribution: East Coast (p = .50), Midwest (p = .48), and West Coast (p = .74).

Table 18.9

Tests of Normality

		Kolmogorov-Smirnov[a]			Shapiro-Wilk		
	Region	Statistic	df	Sig.	Statistic	df	Sig.
Interest_Level	East Coast	.050	157	.200*	.992	157	.507
	Midwest	.033	173	.200*	.992	173	.486
	West Coast	.036	164	.200*	.994	164	.749

*. This is a lower bound of the true significance.

a. Lilliefors Significance Correction

As we can see in Table 18.10, the total sample consists of 494 respondents. The sample sizes per region vary. The average interest scores for "It's All That" by region are East Coast 5.04 with a standard deviation of 1.41; Midwest 5.08 with a standard deviation of 1.27; and West Coast 5.08 with a standard deviation of 1.39. Their standard deviations are similar, suggesting equality of variances.

We are 95% confident that the typical average Complex Cable customer interest score in "It's All That" for the East Coast is 4.81–5.26, for the Midwest 4.89–5.27, and for the West Coast 4.86–5.29.

Table 18.10

Descriptives

Interest_Level

	N	Mean	Std. Deviation	Std. Error	95% Confidence Interval for Mean		Minimum	Maximum
					Lower Bound	Upper Bound		
East Coast	157	5.04	1.410	.113	4.81	5.26	1	9
Midwest	173	5.08	1.276	.097	4.89	5.27	2	8
West Coast	164	5.08	1.394	.109	4.86	5.29	1	8
Total	494	5.06	1.357	.061	4.94	5.18	1	9

In Table 18.11, the Levene test indicates that in all likelihood, the group variances or data distributions do not violate the equality of variances assumption (p = .43).

Table 18.11

Test of Homogeneity of Variances

Interest_Level

Levene Statistic	df1	df2	Sig.
.840	2	491	.432

ANOVA (Analysis)

Because we have fairly normally distributed data and equality of variances, but have unequal sample sizes, we will assess the data using the ANOVA *F*-test and, if necessary, the Scheffe post hoc test. Table 18.12 indicates the ANOVA results. Since $p = .956$, it is likely that there are no differences in Complex Cable customer interest in "It's All That" service by region of the country. We assume that the sample customers represent the three regions. At this point, we stop further analysis.

Table 18.12

ANOVA

Interest_Level

	Sum of Squares	df	Mean Square	F	Sig.
Between Groups	.167	2	.083	.045	.956
Within Groups	907.1	491	1.848		
Total	907.3	493			

Reporting Results

Write-Up

A one-way ANOVA was conducted that compared 494 Complex Cable customers' interest in "It's All That" service by the East Coast (n = 157), Midwest (n = 173), and West Coast (n = 164). A nonsignificant difference was found, $F(2,323.81) = .04$, $p = .956$. It is likely that customer interest in the new cable service does not vary by region. With 95% confidence, the true population average Complex Cable customer interest score in "It's All That" for the East Coast is 4.81–5.26, for the Midwest 4.89–5.27, and for the West Coast 4.86–5.29.

SUMMARY OF KEY CONCEPTS

- The ANOVA is a significance test that compares more than two representative sample means.
- There are a number of data assumptions when conducting an ANOVA.
- In addition to normal distribution, the data must be assessed for equality of variance and equal sample sizes.
- The analysis requires a grouping (independent) variable and a data (dependent) variable.
- The grouping variable identifies the samples from which the dependent variable data are measured and compared.
- There are a number of statistical tools available to address violations of the data assumptions.
- Conducting ANOVA and calculating confidence intervals are straightforward in SPSS.

ONE-WAY ANOVA *F*-TEST APPLIED EXERCISES

18.1 What is a one-way analysis of variances (one-way ANOVA) *F*-test? Provide an example.

18.2 Generally, what is the ANOVA omnibus test?

18.3 What is a post hoc test?

18.4 Generally, what is within-sample variance?

18.5 Generally, what is between-samples variance?

18.6 Generally, what is total variance?

18.7 What is a grand mean?

18.8 What is the Tukey (HSD) post hoc test?

18.9 What is the Scheffe post hoc test?

18.10 What is the Welch test?

18.11 What is the Brown-Forsythe test?

18.12 When do we use the Games-Howell post hoc test?

18.13 What is the Kruskal-Wallis test?

18.14 What tests should be utilized if equality of variances is not met and the sample sizes are unequal?

18.15 What tests should be deployed if the sample sizes are not equal?

18.16 In ideal conditions, what tests should be used?

18.17 In ANOVA, what do the confidence intervals represent?

18.18 "We Sell," a sales/marketing company, wants to determine whether July monthly sales in dollars per salesperson varies by its three districts (Philadelphia, New York, and Boston). The last July sales figures are available for the analysis. Which district generated the most sales? Explain your answer. Report results in the format provided in this chapter. Be sure to include the confidence intervals. Alpha = .05. The data file name is "One-Way ANOVA Exercise 1 Data."

18.19 A local college wants to learn whether different faculty ranks (assistant, associate, and full professors) perceive that they are provided with the resources necessary to be effective teachers. The dean wishes to learn if the three faculty ranks share the same or vary on views about this topic. The key question answered by faculty was: "Do you think that the college provides you with sufficient resources to be an effective teacher?" Answers were formatted as follows: 1 = "I have no resources to help me be an effective teacher" to 10 = "I have more resources than I will ever need to help me be an effective teacher." Determine if there is a difference in perceptions based on the answers to this question. Explain your answer. Report results in the format provided in this chapter. Alpha = .05. Be sure to include the confidence intervals. The data file name is "One-Way ANOVA Exercise 2 Data."

18.20 Shoe ($n = 525$), Technology ($n = 476$), Food ($n = 525$), and Major Appliance ($n = 453$) retailers were surveyed about their assessment of the economy. They responded to a question that asked: "Are you optimistic about the current economic conditions?" 1 = "not optimistic at all" to 5 = "very optimistic" was the answer format. Determine if there is any difference in level of economic optimism by these four retail sectors. Explain your answer. Report results in the format provided in this chapter. Be sure to include the confidence intervals. Alpha = .05. The data file name is "One-Way ANOVA Exercise 3 Data."

18.21 An Italian automobile manufacturer launched a new line of three fuel-efficient midsized vehicles. Data was collected from 50 cars of each brand, which are the Avanti, Forte, and Pronto. Determine whether there is a difference in gas mileage as measured in miles per gallon of gas. Explain your answer. Report results in the format provided in this chapter. Be sure to include the confidence intervals. Alpha = .05. The data file name is "One-Way ANOVA Exercise 4 Data."

Chapter 19

Paired *T*-Test: Comparing the Means of the Same Sample Measured Twice Using a Numeric Variable

LEARNING OBJECTIVES

To be able to:

- understand the purpose and explain the basic principles of a paired *t*-test;
- describe the data assumptions for the paired *t*-test;
- understand the role of a "difference" variable in assessing the normal distribution;
- know how to address violations of the key assumptions of the paired *t*-test;
- conduct a paired *t*-test in SPSS;
- understand and describe paired *t*-test confidence intervals; and
- interpret and report significant and nonsignificant paired *t*-test results.

19.1 Introduction to the Paired Sample *T*-Test

The **paired sample *t*-test** usually compares the means (averages) between the same sample measured twice in order to determine if there is the likelihood of a statistically significant difference between both measurements. The sources of data are individuals or objects such as individuals asked questions about a brand before and then after viewing commercials or machinery level of production before and after an upgrade. This type of research is called a within-subjects design because the focus is to measure change between each corresponding pair of data points within each case (or single source of data). The basis or data for the analysis are the differences between the two measurements.

The paired *t*-test is also called a **dependent samples *t*-test**, **related samples *t*-test**, **same samples *t*-test**, **repeated measures *t*-test**, **matched samples *t*-test**, or **correlated samples *t*-test**. This test can vary slightly in terms of the nature of the related data, which will be discussed below. To avoid confusion, we will simply call it the paired *t*-test.

First, the paired *t*-test usually involves a pre-test—treatment—post-test design. This is where individuals or objects are measured in order to establish a baseline, followed by exposure to a treatment or some other condition. Last, the same measurements are again taken and compared in order to detect differences in the paired measurement data. The treatment is an independent variable of some type. It can be an intervention, change in condition, or exposure to an experiment—all commonly referred to as the treatment.

The first measurement point is called a pre-test from which differences are measured from the post-test or second measurement point. A statistically significant difference suggests a

treatment effect. In other words, the treatment condition is the independent variable and the difference between the measurements is the dependent variable measurement. If the difference is sufficiently large to produce a statistically significant result, then the difference is likely the result of a treatment effect. For example, measuring for differences in the level of knowledge about fly fishing before and after a fly fishing lecture or measuring for differences in the amount of physical flexibility in patients before they begin physical therapy and six weeks after following a physical therapy regimen require statistical analysis using the paired *t*-test.

Second, the simple passage of time can act as the treatment (independent variable) between two measurements of the same sample. For instance, the fly fishing individuals who attended the lecture are tested on their knowledge about fishing immediately after the lecture and then again three weeks later in order to measure their retention of the material over time.

Third, the same data elements may be exposed to two different conditions and then studied for differences. For instance, consumers asked their opinions about the taste of two new brands of coffee. Here, the cases are related. These same individuals' assessments of the two brands are influenced by their tastes and personal preferences. The two brands are the independent condition and the responses (or differences in them) are the dependent variable.

Fourth, sometimes the same group is not measured twice, but two related groups are measured once and compared, which is called a matched *t*-test. They are related if one data point of the pair tells us something about the other data point (Howell, 2014). Each sample contributes one data point so that together they comprise the paired unit of analysis. For instance, therapy effectiveness can be measured by asking the client and therapist a number of questions. They are likely to share similarities (correlates), such as familiarity with each other. They are also likely to share differences. The issue is whether the differences are significant.

Sometimes the similarities between the paired data cannot be easily removed. **Carry-over effect** is the shared variance that can negate at least some of the treatment effect. For example, let us assume that a number of students who took the SAT and scored poorly wish to improve their scores by taking an online SAT preparation course. These same students take the SAT once more and demonstrate improved scores. There are likely two sources for the improvement. First, the preparation course improved the students' SAT test-taking skills, which is the treatment effect. Second, familiarity with having already taken the course also contributes to an improved score, which is a carry-over effect. If the students were to take the SAT multiple times, their scores, on average, would naturally improve. By analyzing the difference between paired scores, we can mitigate some or much of the carry-over effects.

There are more complex paired *t*-test analyses related to study designs. Suffice to say, they exist, and that paired *t*-tests are dependent, related, matched, and, in most cases, the same sample measured twice.

19.2 Paired *T*-Test Calculations

As we can see, it is reasonable to assume that the same individuals or objects being measured twice would behave alike during both measurements times, thus producing similar results. Therefore, any differences between them likely occur because of the introduction of a treatment. This is why paired *t*-testing focuses on the paired differences, which is represented by the following formula:

$$D_i = X_{1i} - X_{2i}$$

where

i = a specific paired case of data
D_i = the difference between the paired data points
X_{1i} = first data value of the pair of a specific case
X_{2i} = second data value of the pair of a specific case

Let us review an example. A bank has been experiencing an increased number of procedural situations requiring that the branch manager provide guidance. The manager kept monthly records of the number of "assists" per each of the five branch staff persons. The manager decided to institute mandatory training for all branch staff. After the training, she continued to maintain "assistance" records. She now wishes to know if the training reduced the requests for procedural help. Table 19.1 depicts the paired data and the new difference variable for the five employees.

Table 19.1

Calculating the Difference Variable for the Paired *T*-test

Staff Person (i)	Before Training Number of Requests for Assistance (X_{1i})	After Training Number of Requests for Assistance (X_{2i})	Difference Variable ($D_i = X_{1i} - X_{2i}$)
Ed	6	4	-2
Becky	15	7	-8
John	3	1	-2
Rachel	0	0	0
Monica	4	0	-4
			Total = -16

Note: The data represent the most recent monthly totals before and after the completion of the training program. The difference variable mean = -16/5 = -3.2

From this point, the mean, variance, standard deviation, and other statistics are calculated using the new "difference" variable.

Paired *T*-test

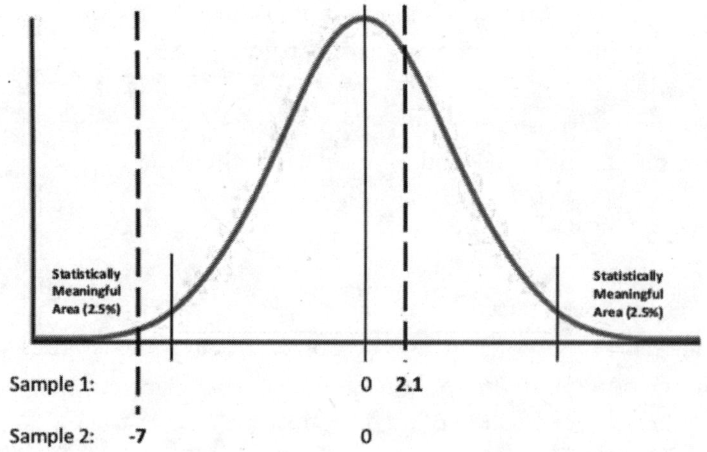

Note: Sample 1 is not statistically significant (p = .780) and Sample 2 is significant (p = .009) at alpha = .05. The bold 2.1 and -7 represent the mean difference in the respective samples. The 0 indicates that there is no difference between the means of each group of the paired comparison.

Figure 19.1

Essentially, the paired *t*-test is a single sample *t*-test in which the test value is zero and the sample consists of the differences between the paired data. If they do not statistically vary from zero, then there is no meaningful difference between the paired data points, as illustrated in Sample 1 of Figure 19.1, where the mean difference is 2.1 and the paired *t*-test *p*-value is .780. On the other hand, a mean difference of –7 is statistically significant ($p = .009$). Interestingly, if we were to run a single sample *t*-test with a zero test value on the difference variable, the results would be identical to the paired *t*-test. The paired *t*-test in SPSS runs the calculations and provides a *p*-value, among other statistics. The question to be answered is whether the mean difference statistically significantly varies from zero. Applying these two samples to our bank training example, the first sample suggests that the training made no difference. The second sample implies that the training was effective.

Additionally, effect size statistics are available and may be explored. Descriptions of these statistics can be accessed by clicking on the "Help" button located in the appropriate SPSS pull-down menu.

REAL WORLD SNAPSHOT

In 2007, Brock and Smith published the article "Using Digital Videos Displayed on Personal Digital Assistance (PDAs) to Enhance Patient Education in Clinical Settings" in the *International Journal of Medical Informatics*. The study aim was to evaluate the effects of using videos to education patients in a clinical setting.

Fifty-one English-speaking patients from various backgrounds, who were being treated for HIV/AIDS, agreed to participate in the study. At visit one, via a survey instrument, baseline measures were taken on patients' knowledge of the disease, knowledge of medications, and knowledge of adherence behaviors. Patients were then given PDAs to watch videos that provided information on the three subject areas. Upon their return to the healthcare facility at visit two, they completed the same survey again. The responses between the two time points were analyzed using paired *t*-tests.

The patients demonstrated statistically significant knowledge increases in the three areas ($p < .005$). The results suggest that digitally based videos are an acceptable approach for teaching patients about their related healthcare. Additionally, the results revealed that this intervention is efficient and effective across an array of ages, educational levels, backgrounds, and locations.

Ask yourself: Can you think of other areas where this approach would be helpful?

19.3 Data Assumptions

The paired *t*-test has a number of assumptions:

- The paired sample represents the target population.
- The paired variables must have matching or paired data, and thus have equal sample sizes.
- The data pairs must come from the same or a related source. In other words, the two samples are dependent in some way.
- The paired data must be numeric and in the same format.
- The sample size should be greater than 30.
- The differences between the paired data approximate the normal distribution.

19.4 Examples Using SPSS: Step-by-Step Instructions

Using the paired-sample *t*-test SPSS procedure, the following significant and nonsignificant examples each compare the paired data to determine whether there is a difference between them.

Example 19.1: Paired-Sample *T*-Tests: The Significant Case

A manufacturer of specialized microcircuits is alarmed about the number of defective parts produced by operators in an eight-hour shift, which is costly. In an effort to minimize the number of defects, the general manager instituted a new quality assurance training program. All operators are required to complete the training. The general manager directed the operations management team to compare the before-training and after-training number of defects per operator in order to discover whether the new training program makes a difference in the number of defects produced. Data were collected from 118 records. Alpha = .05. The data file name is "*T*-Test Paired-Sample Example 1 Data."

The analysis requires three variables: the number of defects prior to training, the matched number of defects after training, and, in order to assess for normal distribution, the differences between the two variables. Note that parts are calculated to two places to the right of the decimal point because some circuit production overlapped shifts. For purposes of an SPSS introduction, we will focus on the basic steps.

Step 1:
Open SPSS 22.0.

Locate the appropriate folder and data file, then highlight it. Next, click the "Open" button.

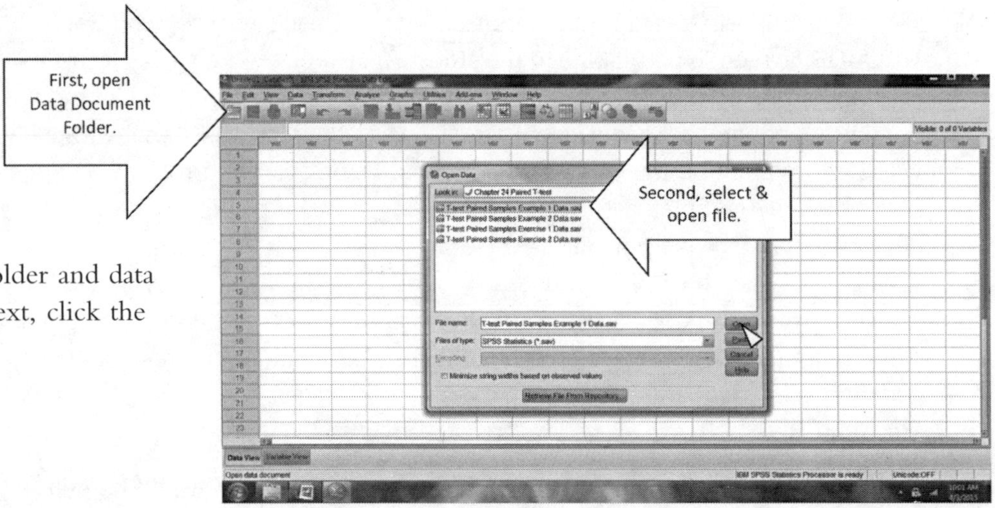

Figure 19.2

Step 2: The data file view will be opened. First, we must create a difference variable to test the normal distribution assumption.

- Select the "Transform" tab.
- Next, click the "Compute Variable" option.

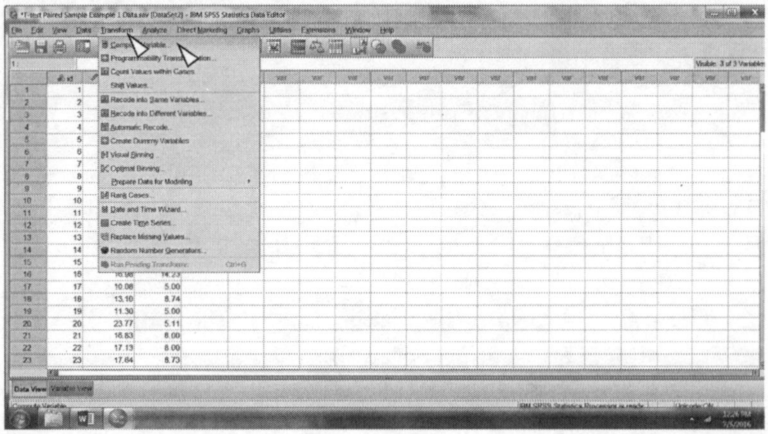

Figure 19.3

Step 3: The "Compute Variable" window will open.

- In the "Target Variable" box located on the top-left side, type in "Difference."
- Highlight the "Pretrain" variable and then click the "Arrow" button, placing it in the "Numeric Expression" box.
- Next, click the "-"sign located on the top-left side of the keypad.
- Highlight the "Aftertrain" variable and click the "Arrow" button.
- Last, click the "OK" button.

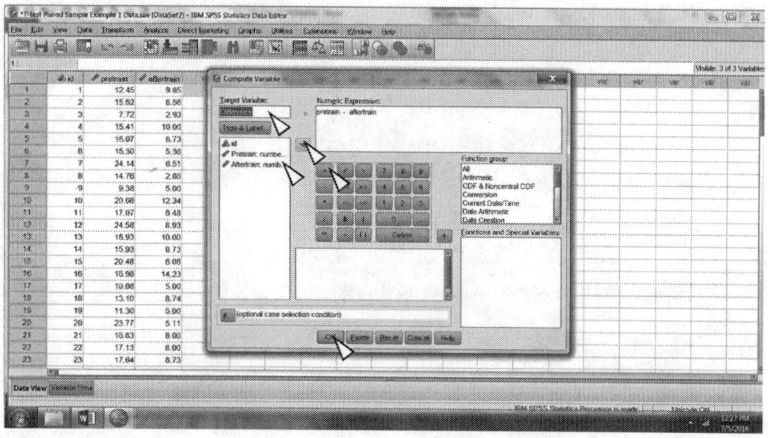

Figure 19.4

Step 4: As we can see, the new "Difference" variable was generated, which is the "Pretrain" minus the "Aftertrain" variables.

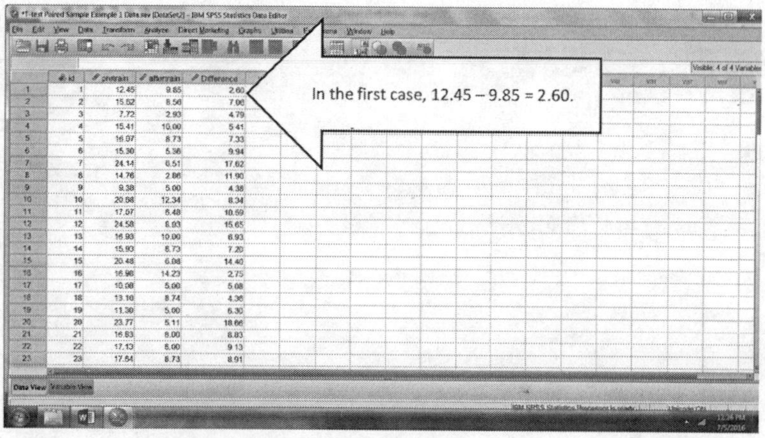

Figure 19.5

Step 5: The "Difference" variable is assessed for normal distribution.

- Select the "Analyze" tab.
- Next, highlight "Descriptive Statistics."
- Last, click "Explore."

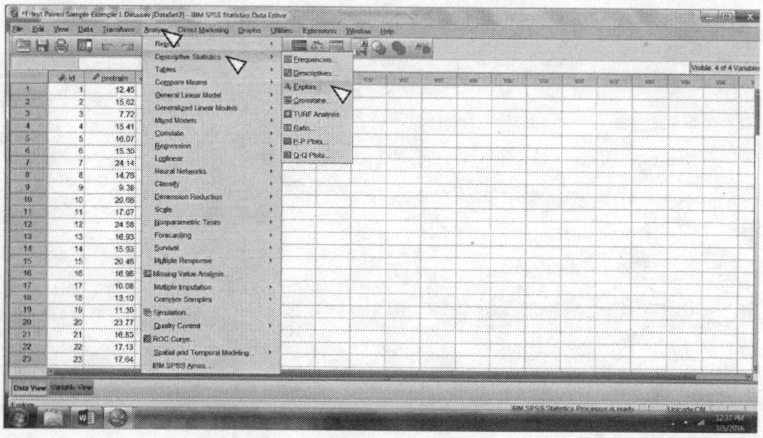

Figure 19.6

Step 6: The "Explore" window will open.

- Highlight "Difference" and then click the "Arrow" button for the "Dependent List" box, placing it in that area.
- Next, click the "Plots" button. The "Explore Plots" window will open.
  - Only check "None" in the box plot area.
  - Check "Normality plots with tests."
  - Click the "Continue" button.
- Last, click the "OK" button. Output is generated.

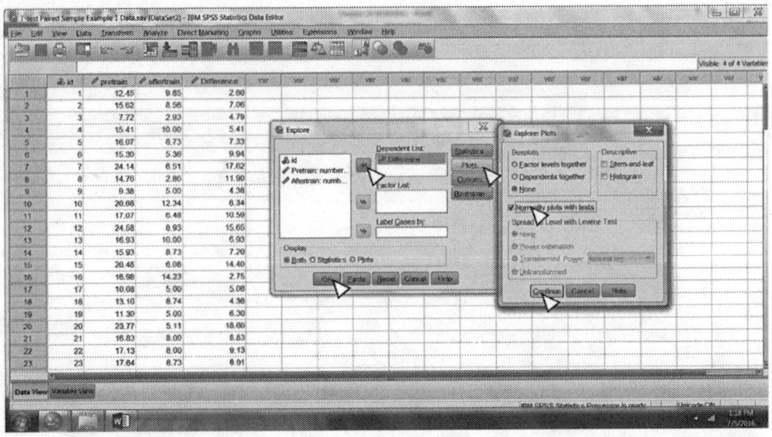

Figure 19.7

Step 7: Run the paired *t*-test.

- Select the "Analyze" tab.
- Next, highlight "Compare Means."
- Last, click "Paired-Samples *T*-Test."

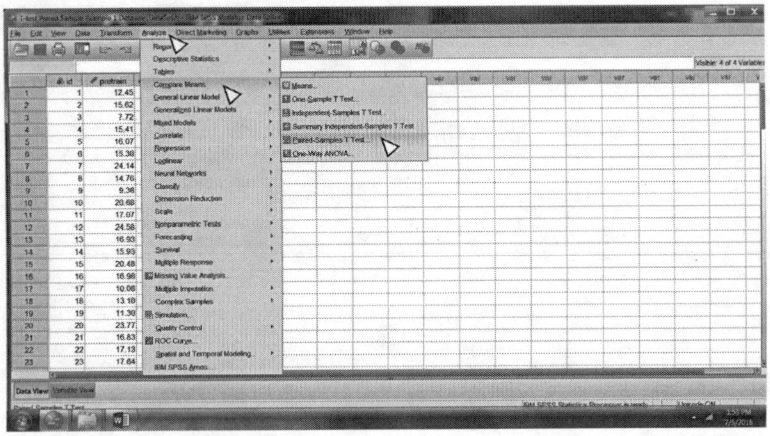

Figure 19.8

Step 8: The "Paired-Samples *T*-Test" window will open.

- In the Paired *T*-Test (Paired Variables area) window, assign the "Pretrain" variable to the "Variable 1" box. Use the "Arrow" button to assign the variable.
- Highlight and assign "Aftertrain" to the "Variable 2" box.
- Next, click the "Options" button.
- The "Paired-Samples *T*-Test Options" window will open.
  - This is where the confidence level can be changed. Do not change the percentage of the "95% Confidence Interval."

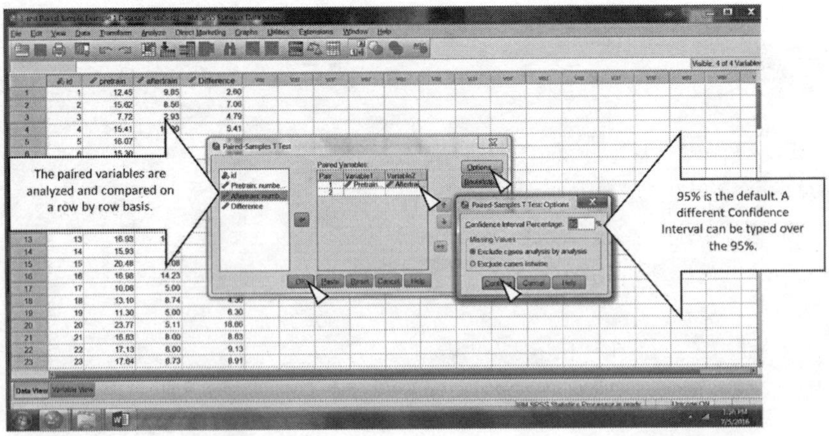

Figure 19.9

- Assuming that the two variables have the same sample size, leave the "Exclude cases analysis by analysis" default setting. If they are not equal, then select "Exclude cases listwise." If you wish to learn more about missing data, then click the "Help" button at the bottom-right-hand side of the window.
- Click the "Continue" button.

- In the "Paired-Samples *T*-Test" window, click the "OK" button. Output is generated.

Last, save the data and output files for your records.

SPSS Output Interpretation

In addition to the descriptive tables and graphs, the paired-sample *t*-test output paired-samples statistics, paired-samples correlations, and paired-samples test tables are available. Below is a discussion of the output.

Data Screening

The tests for normality Table 19.2 indicates a Shapiro-Wilk statistic of $p = .374$ for the difference between the paired data. Since $.374 > .05$, we can assume that the normality assumption is met and that the data approximate the normal distribution.

Table 19.2

Tests of Normality

	Kolmogorov-Smirnov[a]			Shapiro-Wilk		
	Statistic	df	Sig.	Statistic	df	Sig.
Difference	.075	118	.097	.988	118	.374

a. Lilliefors Significance Correction

This is the Shapiro-Wilk *p*-value.

If the data violated the normal distribution assumption, there are a number of options available. First, if possible, more data should be collected, which might bring the data to normality. Second, following the practices covered in Chapter 12, outliers can be removed. Third, nonparametric tools can be used. If the data are symmetrical (not skewed), but not normally distributed, the **Wilcoxon signed ranks test** is appropriate. It is located in the Nonparametric Tests, Legacy Dialogs areas of the SPSS pull-down menu under "Two Related Samples Tests." If the data are not symmetrical, then the **sign rest** option is appropriate. Both of these tests are not as sensitive as the paired *t*-test, and because they offer less statistical power and, thus, may not detect an effect when the pair *t*-test would have done so. Last, the data could be transformed based on its shape using one of the methods available in SPSS. The transformation would normalize the distribution. If none of these solutions for addressing non-normally distributed data suffice, then include a caveat in the results write-up.

As we can see in Table 19.3, the total sample consists of 118 operators' data for before-training and after-training number of defects by operator in an eight-hour shift. The before-training mean number of defects score is 17.17 and the standard deviation is 4.89. The after-training mean number of defects score is 8.31 and the standard deviation is 2.72.

Table 19.3

Paired Samples Statistics

		Mean	N	Std. Deviation	Std. Error Mean
Pair 1	Pretrain: number of defects	17.1692	118	4.89093	.45025
	Aftertrain: number of defects	8.3139	118	2.72654	.25100

The "Paired-Samples Correlations" table indicates the level of relatedness between the two datasets. In other words, if data are correlated, a low-value data measurement in the first variable of the pair would also be low in the second measurement. Both paired data can have relatively high, medium, or low values and be correlated. If they both have similar relative values, then they will be positively correlated. If the paired data move in opposite directions, then they will be negatively correlated. Strong patterns are significant. If there is no pattern, then they will be "uncorrelated" and not significant. The correlation is independent of whether or not there is a meaningful difference between the two sample means. It may reveal that the treatment has different effects on the individual or objects in the sample.

Note that if the paired data are not correlated, then the two samples are not dependent and conducting a two independent samples *t*-test can be used because it provides greater statistical power.

Table 19.4

Paired Samples Correlations

		N	Correlation	Sig.
Pair 1	Pretrain: number of defects & Aftertrain: number of defects	118	.776	.000

P-value.

In this example, the data are related because a correlation (*r*) of .77 ($p < .001$) is strong and statistically significant. Therefore, the data maintain the same pattern across both samples. Therefore, the samples are related.

Paired-Sample *T*-Test Analysis

Using a paired-sample *t*-test, we ran our analysis to determine if there is a meaningful difference between the number of defects per operator before quality assurance training compared to after the training for the same operators. The output in Table 19.5 contains the paired mean difference, the standard deviation of the mean difference, and the 95% confidence interval for the difference between the pre-and after-training number of defects per operator in an eight-hour shift.

As the Table 19.5 "Paired-Sample Test" depicts, there is likely a statistically significant difference between the before-training (M = 17.17 [SD = 4.89]) and after-training (M = 8.31 [SD = 2.72]) number of defects per operator average scores because $p < .001$. The after-training production contains fewer defects compared to the before-training production.

The before-training/after-training sample average difference is 8.855 defects. We also have a 95% confidence interval for the difference between the before-training/after-training mean

Table 19.5

Paired Samples Test

		Paired Differences					t	df	Sig. (2-tailed)
					95% Confidence Interval of the Difference				
		Mean	Std. Deviation	Std. Error Mean	Lower	Upper			
Pair 1	Pretrain: number of defects - Aftertrain: number of defects	8.85530	3.26678	.30073	8.25972	9.45088	29.446	117	.000

P-value.

These values pertain to the difference between the paired data (the two related samples).

scores. This interval is the "range" of possible differences between both datasets and applies to the before-training number of defects parts' (the first sample) average score in relation to the after-training or second sample average number of defective parts. Based on the sample data, we are 95% confident that the true population average before-training number of defects ($M = 17.17$) is anywhere from 8.26 to 9.45 defective parts more than the after-training number of defects average ($M = 8.31$).

As covered in Chapter 16, each true population mean's confidence interval can be derived from the interval of the difference by calculating the following:

Before-training mean interval	=	(8.31 + 8.26) to (8.31 + 9.45)
	=	16.57 to 17.76
After-training mean interval	=	(17.17 – 9.45) to (17.17 – 8.26)
	=	7.72 to 8.91.

In summary, based on the *p*-value and confidence interval, there is a very low probability that these results occurred by chance and thus they are statistically meaningful. These findings can be applied to all before-training and after-training production providing that the sample represents the target population pre- and after-training production per operator in an eight-hour shift.

Reporting Results

The confidence interval can be based on differences or means depending on the study aim. In the write-ups below, they are framed as differences.

Write-Up

A paired-sample *t*-test was conducted that compared the number of defects by operators in an eight-hour shift before and after they received quality assurance training. There were 118 operators. The before-training mean number of defects was 17.17 ($SD = 4.89$) and the after-training mean number of defects was 8.31 ($SD = 2.72$). A significant difference was found ($t(117) = 29.44$, $p < .001$). It is likely that there is a difference between the before-training and after-training number of defects produced by operators in an eight-hour shift. Furthermore, we are 95% confident that the before-training number of defects' true population average is anywhere from 8.26 to 9.45 higher than the true population average number of defects for those same operators after they received training.

(OR we can apply directionality)

A paired-sample *t*-test was conducted that compared the number of defects by operators in an eight-hour shift before and after they received quality assurance training. There were 118 operators. The before-training mean number of defects was 17.17 ($SD = 4.89$) and the after-training mean number of defects was 8.31 ($SD = 2.72$). A significant difference was found ($t(117) = 29.44$, $p < .001$). It is likely that the quality assurance training reduces the number of defects produced by operators in an eight-hour shift. Furthermore, we are 95% confident that the before-training number of defects' true population average is anywhere from 8.26 to 9.45 higher than the true population average number of defects for those same operators after they received the training.

The "(117)" represents the degrees of freedom (*df*), which is the number of data points that can vary. Its formula is $n - 1$ because there is one sample. In our case, it is $118 - 1 = 117 = df$. $P < .001$ is a meaningful probability, which indicates that the likelihood of these findings occurring by chance is less than .1% or less than 1 / 1,000; therefore, the results are meaningful.

Example 19.2: Single Sample *T*-Tests: The Nonsignificant Case

Marketers repositioned the e-Phone so that it will be marketed to the 54 years old and older market. They developed a new email ad campaign directed at this target market and intend to test whether the new campaign will increase brand awareness by the end of a four-week email campaign. The study participants were asked about the brand before the campaign started and then after four weeks. The marketing researchers were charged to determine whether the four-week email campaign increases e-Phone brand awareness. For the pre- and post-tests, 100 participants responded online by using a sliding bar scale from 0 = "I am unaware of the brand" to 5 = "I definitely dream of the brand in my sleep." In order to increase reliability, the bar accommodated responses between each whole number. Alpha = .05. The data file name is "*T*-Test Paired-Sample Example 2 Data."

The analysis requires three variables: the level of brand awareness prior to the email ad campaign, the matched level of brand awareness scores after the email ad campaign, and the difference between both measurements. We will skip the SPSS steps because they are identical to the first example.

SPSS Output Interpretation

Data Screening

As depicted in Table 19.6, the Shapiro-Wilk statistic is $p = .707$, which is nonsignificant, indicating that the difference data approximate the normal distribution.

Table 19.6

Tests of Normality

	Kolmogorov-Smirnov[a]			Shapiro-Wilk		
	Statistic	df	Sig.	Statistic	df	Sig.
Difference	.072	100	.200*	.991	100	.707

*. This is a lower bound of the true significance.

a. Lilliefors Significance Correction

The total sample consists of 100 consumers who were asked twice about e-Brand awareness. The pre-campaign mean awareness score is 2.98 with a standard deviation of .27. The post-campaign mean awareness score is 3.01 with a standard deviation of .44.

Table 19.7

Paired Samples Statistics

		Mean	N	Std. Deviation	Std. Error Mean
Pair 1	Precampaign	2.9872	100	.27006	.02701
	Postcampaign	3.0196	100	.44493	.04449

As depicted in the "Paired-Samples Correlations" table, because $r = .149$, $p = .14$, the data are not correlated. The awareness scores in general do not maintain the same pattern across both data points.

Table 19.8

Paired Samples Correlations

		N	Correlation	Sig.
Pair 1	Precampaign & Postcampaign	100	.149	.140

Paired Sample *T*-Test Analysis

The output in Table 19.9 contains the paired mean difference, the standard deviation of the mean difference, and the 95% confidence interval for the difference between the pre-and post-email campaign consumer awareness mean scores.

The average difference between the pre- and post-ads is −.03249. As Table 19.9, "Paired-Samples Test," reveals, there is no meaningful difference between the pre-campaign ($M = 2.98$) and after-campaign ($M = 3.01$) average awareness scores because $p = .505$. Therefore, the email campaign likely had no effect on consumer e-Brand awareness.

Table 19.9

Paired Samples Test

		Paired Differences					t	df	Sig. (2-tailed)
					95% Confidence Interval of the Difference				
		Mean	Std. Deviation	Std. Error Mean	Lower	Upper			
Pair 1	Precampaign - Postcampaign	-.03249	.48498	.04850	-.12872	.06375	-.670	99	.505

We have a 95% confidence interval for the difference between the two mean awareness scores. This interval is the "range" of possible differences between the paired data. We are 95% confident that the true population average pre-campaign awareness mean is anywhere from .12872 below to .06375 above the true population post-campaign mean awareness score. Notice that the lower interval value is negative and the upper interval value is positive, which includes the possibility of a zero or no difference. This is consistent with $p = .505$, a nonsignificant finding.

In summary, based on the *p*-value and confidence interval, there is a high probability that these results are not meaningful. This conclusion can be applied to all pre-campaign and post-campaign awareness for the target population.

Reporting Results

Write-Up

A paired-sample *t*-test was conducted that compared the *e*Brand awareness scores of those 54 years old and older consumers before being exposed to an email ad campaign to those same consumers after being exposed to a four-week email campaign. Consumers could select 0 = "no brand awareness" through 5 = "total brand awareness." One hundred consumers participated.

A nonsignificant difference was found ($t(99) = 1.34$, $p = .70$). There is no evidence to indicate that the pre-campaign awareness mean score of 2.98 ($SD = .27$) varies from the after-campaign awareness mean score of 3.01 ($SD = .44$). Thus, it is likely that the email campaign had no effect on eBrand awareness. Furthermore, we are 95% confident that the true population average pre-campaign brand awareness is between .04 less than and .24 greater than the true population post-campaign average awareness.

SUMMARY OF KEY CONCEPTS

- The paired *t*-test is a significance test that compares the means between two related samples by focusing on the difference between paired data points.
- Usually, a paired *t*-test compares the values for the same individuals or objects measured twice. Often there is some type of treatment or independent condition between the two measurement points.
- In order to remove any naturally occurring variance between both measurements and determine whether there is a treatment effect, the analysis is based on the difference between the paired data.
- There are a number of data assumptions when conducting a paired *t*-test.
- The normal distribution assumption applies to the difference (variable) between the paired data, which must be created to assess this assumption.
- There are a number of statistical tools available to address violations of the data assumptions.
- Conducting a paired *t*-test and calculating confidence intervals are straightforward in SPSS.

PAIRED-SAMPLES *T*-TEST APPLIED EXERCISES

19.1 What is a paired *t*-test?

19.2 What are other names for the paired *t*-test?

19.3 Define treatment. Cite an example.

19.4 What is a carry-over effect? Cite an example.

19.5 What is the Wilcoxon signed ranks test?

19.6 What is a sign test?

19.7 Free-Air is a new asthma preventative medication in trials. At the onset of an asthmatic attack, an individual takes two puffs, which prevent a full asthmatic episode. Asthmatic attack data were collected for six months from patients who never used any type of medicine. The same patients provided data while using Free-Air for six months. Researchers must determine whether Free-Air is effective at reducing full asthmatic episodes. Explain your answer. Report results in the format provided in this chapter. Alpha = .05. Be sure to include the 95% confidence interval. The data file name is "*T*-Test Paired-Sample Exercise 1 Data."

19.8 A local hospital offered a six-month weight management program to individuals who were 40–60 pounds overweight. Clients enrolled and completed the *Protein Focus* program over a six-month period. Among other information, client weight in pounds was collected before and after the six-month period. Based on the data from the sample, is there any evidence to suggest that *Protein Focus* is effective as a six-month program? Explain your answer. Report results in the format provided in this chapter. Be sure to include the

95% confidence interval. Alpha = .05. The data file name is "*T*-Test Paired-Sample Exercise 2 Data."

19.9 Two hundred drivers were asked to do their normal weekly driving using two different gasoline brands. They were to receive a full tank of gas at the beginning of the week, and at the end of the week the amount of gas consumed would be measured along with the miles traveled. A week later, the gas tank would be drained and replaced with the second brand of gas, where the procedure would be repeated. Determine whether Brand A or Brand B offered greater gas mileage. Explain your answer. Report results in the format provided in this chapter. Be sure to include the 95% confidence interval. Alpha = .05. The data file name is "*T*-Test Paired-Sample Exercise 3 Data."

19.10 Referring back to Exercise 19.9, was there a difference in the miles traveled between the two weeks? Explain your answer. Report results in the format provided in this chapter. Be sure to include the 95% confidence interval. Alpha = .05. The data file name is "*T*-Test Paired-Sample Exercise 4 Data."

19.11 Father and mother dyads were asked whether they believed that communication between them and their children, ages 3–17, was open and easily flowed bidirectionally. Two hundred and fifty parental dyads participated by completing an online survey. The question was framed as follows: "Is there open communication between you and your children so that everyone has the opportunity to easily express him/herself openly in a family setting?" 0 = "Not at all open for everyone" to 5 = "Everyone can say what he/she wants." Based on this question, do parents have similar views about whether they have an open communication family? Explain your answer. Report results in the format provided in this chapter. Be sure to include the 95% confidence interval. Alpha = .05. The data file name is "*T*-Test Paired-Sample Exercise 5 Data."

19.12 A sample of 120 clients from Balanced Health participated in a pilot study designed to increase knowledge about mental health challenges and raise awareness about behavioral wellness options. Clients completed an online baseline survey that measured their knowledge about mental health and behavioral choices. They were then provided with weekly website links over a three-week period followed by their completing another survey that measured their knowledge and awareness levels. Did the website links increase client knowledge about mental health and behavioral choices? Scores for both surveys were based on 100 points. Explain your answer. Report results in the format provided in this chapter. Be sure to include the 95% confidence interval. Alpha = .05. The data file name is "*T*-Test Paired-Sample Exercise 6 Data."

Chapter 20

General Linear Model Repeated Measures: Comparing Means of the Same Sample Measured More Than Twice Using a Numeric Variable

LEARNING OBJECTIVES

To be able to:

- understand the purpose and explain the basic principles of a one-way repeated measures general linear model;
- describe the data assumptions for repeated measures;
- understand what is sphericity in repeated measures;
- know how to address violations of the key assumptions of repeated measures;
- understand and describe repeated measures confidence intervals;
- interpret paired comparisons of the measurement points;
- understand profile plots and contrast analysis;
- conduct a one-way repeated measures general linear model in SPSS; and
- interpret and report significant and nonsignificant repeated measures results.

20.1 Introduction to General Linear Model Repeated Measures

In Chapter 19, we covered the paired *t*-test, where a sample is measured twice in order to determine whether the two measurements significantly vary. Similar comparisons can be made for measurements made more than twice on the same or related samples. Thus, the measurements are related in some way. This analysis is often called **one-way repeated measures ANOVA** or **general linear model (GLM) repeated measures**. It is called one-way because there is only one independent variable. As we covered in Chapter 19, an independent variable can be a treatment or some other condition imposed on the sample. Often the first measurement point establishes a baseline before the introduction of the treatment, which is followed by at least two subsequent measurement points. The independent variable can be an experimental condition, exposure to multiple other conditions, or the passage of time itself. It can also be the related nature among different samples, such as children, mother, and father in a family unit of measurement, which share variances but also possess differences.

We can apply significance testing to one-way repeated measures ANOVA in order to determine whether there are differences between and/or among means in at least one paired comparison. If the overall test is statistically significant, then **post hoc significance testing** is used to identify specifically where the differences lie.

Let us describe some examples of repeated measures analysis. Some tracking studies collect the same data from the same sample or sampling frame over a number of times in order to determine whether changes occur in the data over time. For instance, data may be collected about attitudes toward political candidates during the course of a campaign. Students may be tested during a semester and their test answers can serve as the basis for measuring learning across the term. In order to study progress over time, mental health researchers can survey clients on their mental health well-being a number of times during the course of a therapy and/or drug regimen. Repeated measures designs can also be applied to drug production quality control, in which drug quality can be measured and compared on a regular basis. Similarly, it can be used to compare quality before and two or more times after the introduction of operator training, machinery maintenance, or equipment upgrades.

Like most, if not all, significance testing, the one-way repeated measures general linear model procedure has a number of assumptions.

REAL WORLD SNAPSHOT

In a 2009 article by Faber and Kuo entitled "Children with Attention Deficits Concentrate Better after Walk in the Park," which was published in the *Journal of Attention Disorders*, the researchers found that children with Attention Deficit Hyperactivity Disorder (ADHD) who walked for 20 minutes in a park concentrated better ($M = 4.41$, $SD = 1.18$) than after they walked in a neighborhood ($M = 3.71$, $SD = 1.21$, $p = .007$) or downtown ($M = 3.82$, $SD = 1.07$, $p = .02$) ($F(2,16) = 4.72$, $p = 02$).

A sample of 17 children professionally diagnosed with ADHD, ages 7–12, participated in the study. Each child with a guide present took three walks over three weeks. The walks occurred at the same time and day of the week. Upon completion of each walk, the child would be driven to the healthcare facility and completed a scored concentration exercise (the Digit Span Backwards technique) and a number of other measures. In summary, the park walk was a more positive experience compared to the other two walks, where there was no significant difference between them.

Ask yourself: What other considerations might be accounted for in such a study?

20.2 Data Assumptions

There are a number of assumptions:

- The measurement variables are numeric.
- The sample represents the target population.
- The variables are fairly normally distributed.
- The sample size is over 30.
- There are at least three related (correlated) measurement points.
- There is sphericity or the variances of the differences between all possible pairs of groups are approximately equal.
- There is one independent variable or main effect.

20.3 Strategies for Addressing Violations of Assumptions

We assume that the data are numeric, representative of the target population, and there are at least three measurement points, which are correlated. Non-normally distributed data increases the likelihood of producing inaccurate results. If the normality assumption is not met, we have a number of options. (1) We can collect more data with the hope that the distribution becomes normal. (2) We can examine the Normal Q-Q Plot derived from the Descriptive/Explore analysis output to identify and possibly remove any outliers (extreme observations), which might then give us a fairly normal distribution (see Chapter 12 for a review of this procedure using numerous SPSS tools) (3) A data transformation can be implemented to normalize the data. (4) If none of these solutions suffice, include a caveat in the write-up.

If the data are not correlated, it is optional to conduct an independent samples ANOVA, which is covered in Chapter 18. Most of the time, though, we assume that this assumption is met and conduct the one-way repeated measures ANOVA (aka repeated measures general linear model).

Table 20.1

One-way Repeated Measures ANOVA Overall Test Criteria

Reference	Epsilon	Sphericity Assumed	Within-Subjects Test
Sphericity Assumed	N/A	Yes[1]	Sphericity Assumed
Greenhouse-Geisser	< .75[2]	No[3]	Greenhouse-Geisser
Greenhouse-Geisser	$\geq$ .75[2]	No[3]	Huynh-Feldt

Note: [1]Represents a nonsignificant Mauchly Sphericity Test result. [2]From the Epsilon column in the Within-Subjects Test table. [3]Indicates a significant result.

In repeated measures analysis, **sphericity** is an assumption. It is the condition where the variances of the differences between all possible pairs of groups are similar. Like the paired *t*-test, the focus is on differences between or among the measurement points. Some analysts claim that this assumption is not met approximately 80% of the time. Sphericity is assessed using the **Mauchly's significance test**. The results of this test determine which overall test is appropriate. SPSS provides alternative overall tests when this assumption is violated. Table 20.1 is a guide to test selection based on the Mauchly results. **Epsilon** is a value that applies to Greenhouse-Geisser and Huynh-Feldt corrections for violation of the sphericity assumption. They range from 0 to 1, with 1 indicating perfect sphericity. The correction applies to degrees of freedom and is automatically calculated in SPSS. When the Mauchly test is not significant, use the "**sphericity assumed**" statistics. The **Greenhouse-Geisser**, **Huynh-Feldt**, and **lower-bound** omnibus tests correct for violations of sphericity. The lower-bound is rarely used because it is unstable under a number of conditions. When sphericity is violated and the Greenhouse-Geisser epsilon is less than .75, then use the Greenhouse-Geisser test. If the Greenhouse-Geisser epsilon is equal to or greater than .75, then use the Huynh-Feldt test.

The **Bonferroni post hoc test** is appropriate for all repeated measures analysis. The **partial eta squared** indicates the percentage change in the data explained by the independent variable. It is an effect size related to the independent variable condition. Plotting means and **contrast analysis** can also provide insights about the data, as we shall see in the examples that follow.

20.4 Examples Using SPSS: Step-by-Step Instructions

Using the one-way repeated measures general linear model procedure, the following examples illustrate significant and nonsignificant results.

Example 20.1: GLM Repeated Measures: The Significant Case

A computer chip processor manufacturing wishes to determine whether its new training program for manufacturing staff has resulted in increased chip productivity. A random sample of production records for 475 operators were incorporated in the analysis. There were four measurement points. Production records were included immediately before the training (*Pretraining*), after *Part 1* (of the training), after *Part 2* (of the training), and then after all of the training was completed two weeks later (*Posttraining*). Did the training make a difference in chip production per minute output? If so, describe where the differences were found and the nature of the differences. Alpha = .05. The name of the data file is "GLM Repeated Measures Example 1 Data."

The analysis requires numeric production output variables for the four measurement points. These variables consist of the number of units produced per minute.

Step 1: Open SPSS.

Locate the appropriate folder and data file, then highlight it. Next, click the "Open" button.

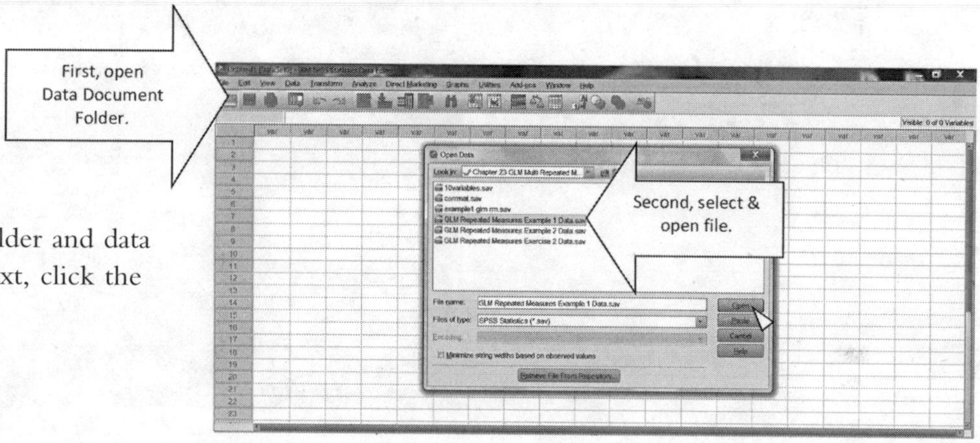

Figure 20.1

Step 2: Once the data file is open, we screen the data for normal distribution.

- Select the "Analyze" tab.
- Highlight "Descriptive Statistics."
- Click "Explore."

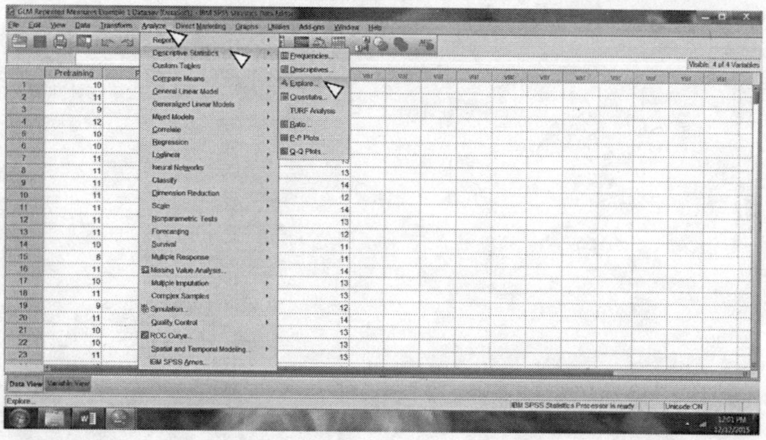

Figure 20.2

Step 3: After the "Explore" window opens:

- Highlight the "*Pretraining*," "*Part1*," "*Part2*," and "*Posttraining*" variables and place them in the "Dependent List" box by clicking the "Arrow" button.
- Click the "Plots" button. The "Explore: Plots" window will open.
  - Check "None" in the box plot area.
  - Check the "Normality plots with tests" option.
  - Click the "Continue" button.
- Last, click the "OK" button. Output is generated.

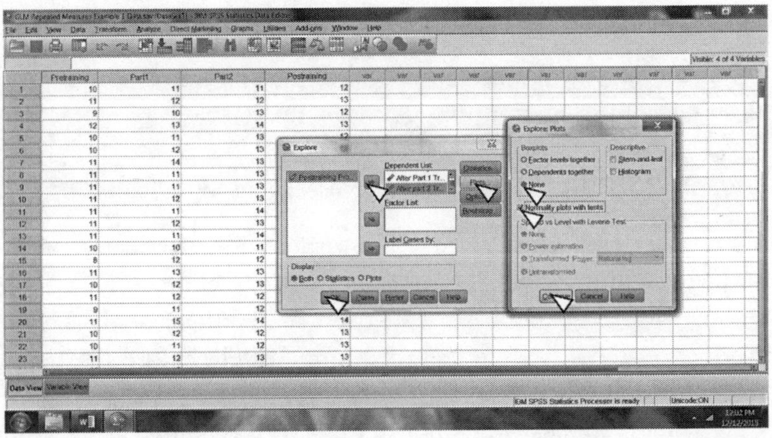

Figure 20.3

Step 4: In the "Data File" window:

- Click the "Analyze" tab.
- Select "General Linear Model."
- Last, click "Repeated Measures."

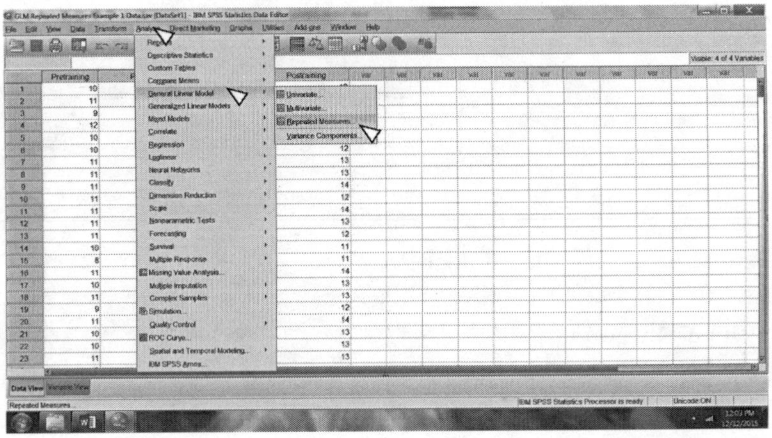

Figure 20.4

Step 5: The "Repeated Measures Define Factor(s)" box will open.

- Since there are four measurement points, enter "4" in the "Number of Levels" box.

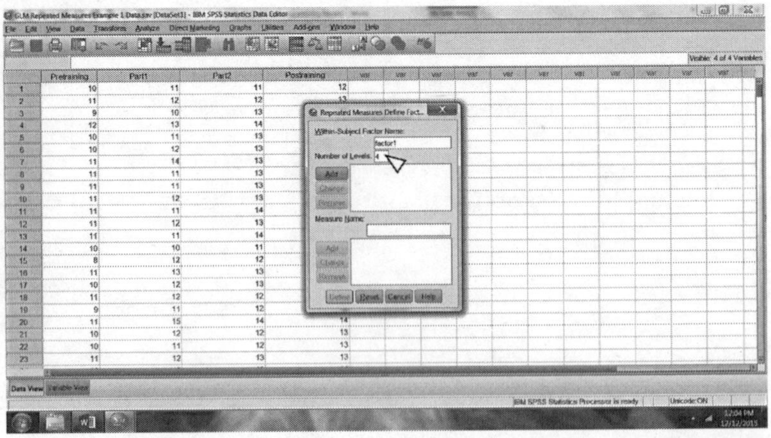

Figure 20.5

Step 6: In the same window:

- Change the "factor1" label to a more appropriate name, such as "Production_Over_Time."
- Click the "Add" button to the left.

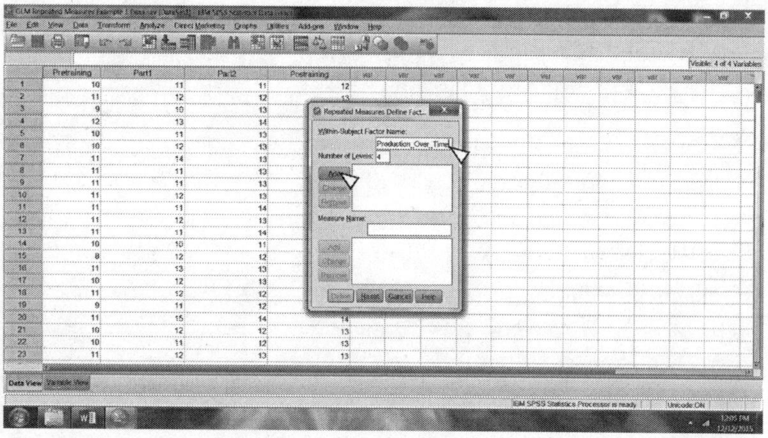

Figure 20.6

Step 7: Once the "Production_Over_Time" is moved to the box below its initial location, click the "Define" button located on the bottom-left side.

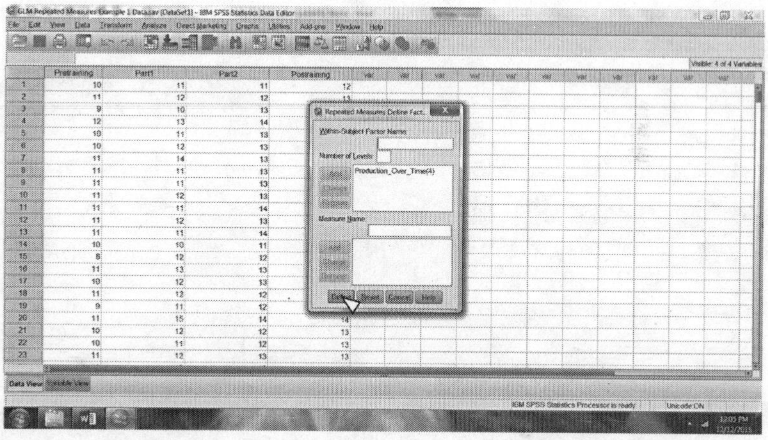

Figure 20.7

Step 8: The "Repeated Measures" window will open.

- Highlight the first "? (1)," then highlight the first variable time point.
- Click the "Arrow" button, thus assigning the variable to the first spot in the "Within-Subjects Variables" box on the right side.
- Repeat the procedure for the other three variables. It is important to maintain the time order from *Pretraining* to *Part1* to *Part2* to *Posttraining*.
- Last, click the "Plots" button on the right side.

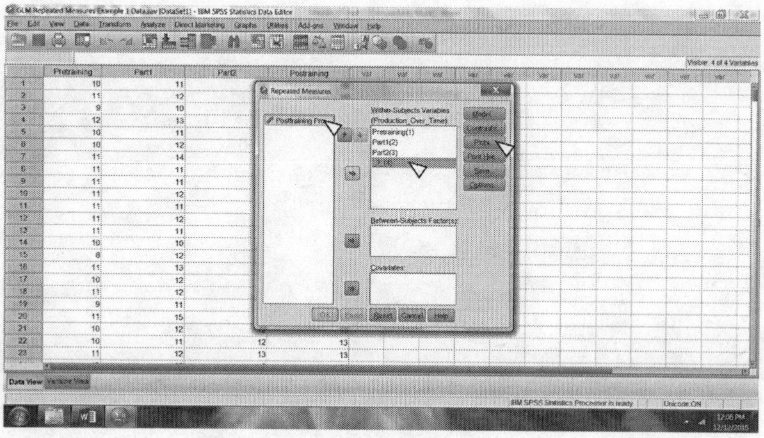

Figure 20.8

Step 9: The "Repeated Measures: Profile Plots" window will open.

- On the left in the "Factors" window, highlight "Production_Over_Time" and then click on the "Arrow" button, placing it in the "Horizontal Axis" box.
- Next, click the "Add" button located above the "Plots" box.

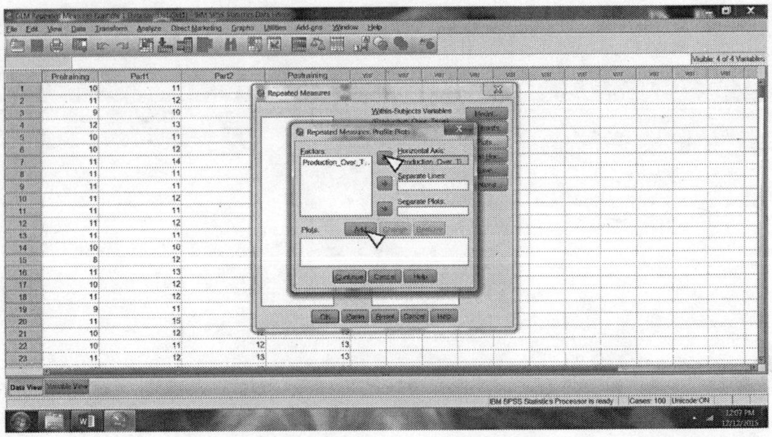

Figure 20.9

Step 10: Notice that the "Production_Over_Time" variable now appears in the "Plots" box. Click the "Continue" button located on the bottom-left side of the window.

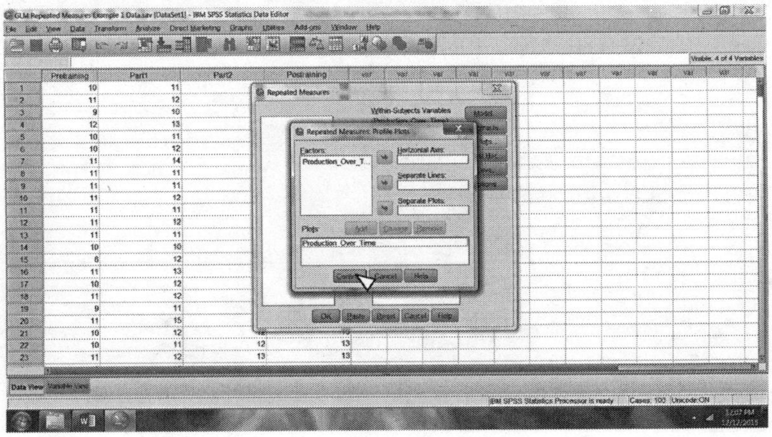

Figure 20.10

Step 11: After the "Repeated Measures: Profile Plots" window closes, click the "Options" button on the bottom-right side.

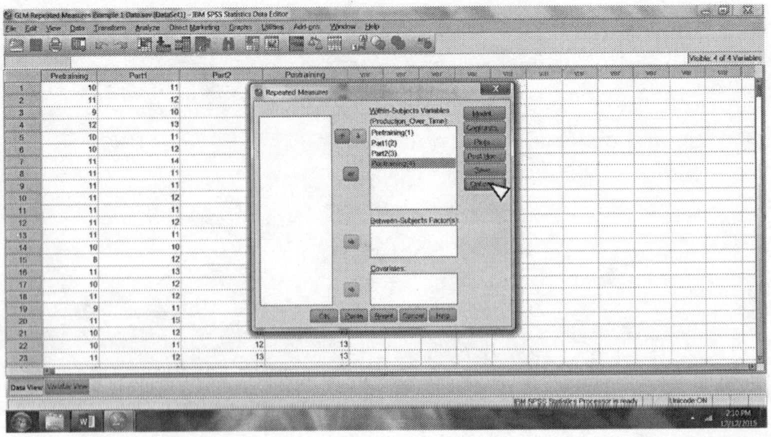

Figure 20.11

Step 12: The "Repeated Measures: Options" window will open.

- Highlight the "Production_Over_Time" variable located in the "Factor(s) and Factor Interactions" box on the left.
- Click on the "Arrow" button, placing it in the "Display Means for:" box on the right.
- Check the "Compare main effects" box on the right.
- Next, pull down the "Confidence interval adjustment" menu and select "Bonferroni."

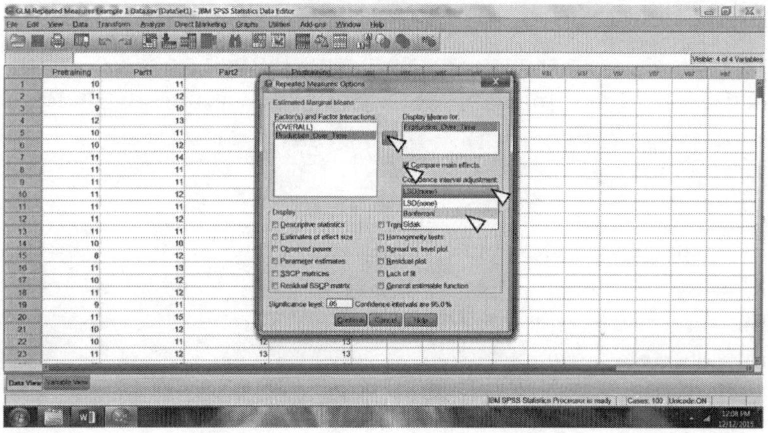

Figure 20.12

Step 13: After "Bonferroni" appears in the "Confidence interval adjustment" area:

- In the "Display" area, check "Descriptive statistics."
- Select "Estimates of effect size."
- Last, click the "Continue" button located on the bottom-left side.

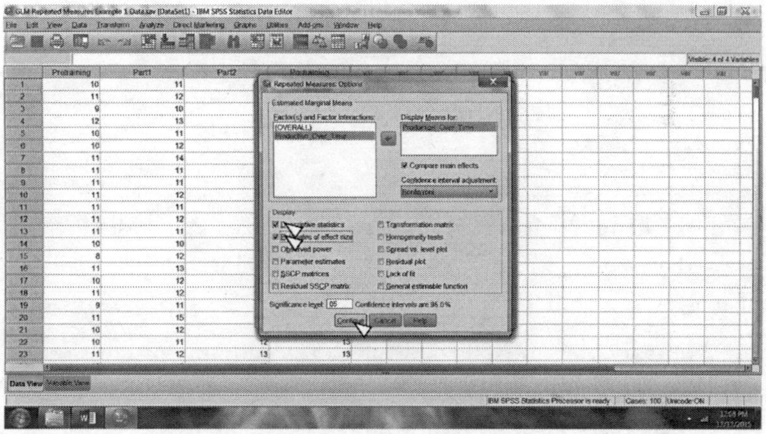

Figure 20.13

Step 14: Finally, click the "OK" button located on the bottom-left side. The analysis will generate output.

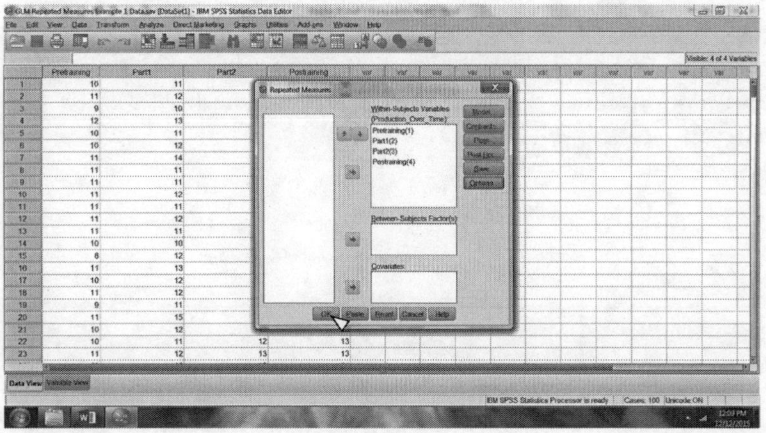

Figure 20.14

Last, save the data and output files for your records.

SPSS Output Interpretation

We will focus on the tests for normality, Mauchly's test of sphericity and tests of within-subjects effects tables and, if necessary, the tests of within-subjects contrasts and pairwise comparisons tables, as well as the **profile plot**. Below is a discussion of the output.

Data Screening

The data are numeric and we assume that they represent the target population. The sample size is greater than 30. There is one main effect, which is training over time. There are four measurement points.

The four time measurement variables meet the normal distribution assumption as indicated in Table 20.2. The Shapiro-Wilk normality test p-values are all >.05.

Table 20.2

Tests of Normality

	Kolmogorov-Smirnov[a]			Shapiro-Wilk		
	Statistic	df	Sig.	Statistic	df	Sig.
Pretraining Production	.025	475	.200*	.998	475	.727
After Part 1 Training Production	.031	475	.200*	.997	475	.564
After Part 2 Training Production	.023	475	.200*	.997	475	.430
Posttraining Production	.030	475	.200*	.997	475	.495

*. This is a lower bound of the true significance.

a. Lilliefors Significance Correction

"Sig" denotes the p-values for the Shapiro-Wilk Test of Normality.

General Linear Model Repeated Measures Analysis

Now that we determined that the four variables are normally distributed, we begin the process of analyzing whether training affects production output over time. The following steps are needed:

- The variables are screened for paired differences equality of variance in order to select the proper overall test.
- If the overall test is significant, post hoc analysis is appropriate.
- Whether or not the overall test is meaningful, examining trends in the means using profile plotting and contrast analysis may be informative.

Mauchly's test of sphericity tests for sphericity (equality of variance in the paired differences). A significant result indicates that the variances of the differences are not likely similar. In this example, $p < .001$ is significant, thus revealing that the variances do not meet the sphericity assumption. Since this is the case and the Greenhouse-Geisser epsilon is ⩾.75, the Huynh-Feldt overall test is appropriate.

Table 20.3

Mauchly's Test of Sphericity[a]

Measure: MEASURE_1

					Epsilon[b]		
Within Subjects Effect	Mauchly's W	Approx. Chi-Square	df	Sig.	Greenhouse-Geisser	Huynh-Feldt	Lower-bound
Training_Influence	.878	61.551	[illegible]	.000	.931	.937	.333

Tests the null hypothesis that the error covari... ...alized transformed dependent va...es is proportional to an identity matrix.

a. Design: Intercept
Within Subjects Desi...

b. May be used to adj... ...averag... ...sts of significance. Correct... ...Tests of Within-Subjects E...

The "Sig." column represents the p-value for the sphericity (homogeneity or equality of variance test), which is significant.

Since Greenhouse-Geisser is ≥ .75, we select the Huynh-Feldt Epsilon.

Table 20.4 is the "Tests of Within-Subjects Effects." It contains the overall tests for repeated measures. Because the Huynh-Feldt test is significant ($p < .001$), there is at least one meaningful paired comparison between the means of the four time points. Further, the "partial eta squared" tells us that 75.9% of the change in the production (average) scores can be explained by the effects of the training over time. The Huynh-Feldt test, along with the partial eta squared, suggest that the training affects productivity over time.

Table 20.4

Training over time accounts for 75.9% of the change in the production output.

The *p*-value.

Tests of Within-Subjects Effects

Measure: MEASURE_1

Source		Type III Sum of Squares	df	Mean Square	F	Sig.	Partial Eta Squared
Training_Influence	Sphericity Assumed	2013.271	3	671.090	1491.312	.000	.759
	Greenhouse-Geisser	2013.271	2.793	720.801	1491.312	.000	.759
	Huynh-Feldt	2013.271	2.811	716.124	1491.312	.000	.759
	Lower-bound	2013.271	1.000	2013.271	1491.312	.000	.759
Error(Training_Influence)	Sphericity Assumed	639.900	1422	.450			
	Greenhouse-Geisser	639.900	1323.931	.483			
	Huynh-Feldt	639.900	1332.577	.480			
	Lower-bound	639.900	474.000	1.350			

Table 20.5 depicts the means and 95% confidence intervals for the four production output variables. For example, the "Pretraining" mean score of chips manufactured per minute is 9.945 or nearly 10 chips. We are 95% confident that the true population mean number of chips made during the pretraining time period was between 9.855 and 10.035. Note that in a one-way repeated measure analysis, the estimated marginal means are equal to the descriptive means.

Table 20.5

Each mean represents the average number of chips produced per minute during each measurement point.

These 95% confidence intervals represent the lower and upper bounds of the means.

Estimates

Measure: MEASURE_1

Training_Influence	Mean	Std. Error	95% Confidence Interval Lower Bound	95% Confidence Interval Upper Bound
1	9.945	.046	9.855	10.035
2	11.688	.046	11.598	11.778
3	12.450	.046	12.360	12.540
4	12.480	.046	12.390	12.570

Table 20.6 depicts where the specific differences were found as noted by the asterisk. The number on the far left represents the measurement time that is compared; its column title is "(I) Training_Influence." The "(J) Training_Influence" is the other time and is matched with in a paired comparison. The "Sig." column depicts the *p*-value for each matched comparison. Notice that in the two comparisons where there is no asterisk, the *p*-values are greater than .05. The "95% Confidence Interval for Difference" is the interval for the difference between the measurement time all the way on the left and its comparison measurement point. For instance, in the case of Pretraining Production Output (1) (M = 9.945) and Part 2 training (3) (M = 12.450), there is

likely a meaningful difference between them because $p < .001$. There is 95% confidence that the Pretraining Production Output true population mean is anywhere between 2.411 and 2.599 less than the Part 2 training true population mean. That is to say, the confidence interval pertains to the measurement time period in the (I) column compared to the (J) column.

Results indicate that the main training over time effect occurred between or by the second and third measurement times, suggesting a cumulative learning effect that improved productivity. There was a positive difference between Part 1 training ($M = 11.688$) and pretraining ($M = 9.945$) output and then again from Part 1 training to after Part 2 training ($M = 12.450$). The only production output time comparison that was not statistically different was between Part 2 training and Posttraining ($M = 12.480$). Thus, most of the benefit from training occurred immediately by the completion of Part 2 training and not at the Posttraining measurement, which occurred two weeks later. Effects were essentially immediate.

Table 20.6

These are the bounds of the Time 1 variable in (I) compared to the Time 3 variable in column (J).

This is the *p*-value.

Here, Time 1: Pretraining is compared to Time 3: Part 2 Training.

Pairwise Comparisons

Measure: MEASURE_1

(I) Training_Influence	(J) Training_Influence	Mean Difference (I-J)	Std. Error	Sig.[b]	95% Confidence Interval for Difference[b] Lower Bound	Upper Bound
1	2	-1.744*	.041	.000	-1.852	-1.635
	3	-2.505*	.036	.000	-2.599	-2.411
	4	-2.536*	.046	.000	-2.657	-2.414
2	1	1.744*	.041	.000	1.635	1.852
	3	-.762*	.046	.000	-.883	-.640
	4	-.792*	.046	.000	-.914	-.670
3	1	2.505*	.036	.000	2.411	2.599
	2	.762*	.046	.000	.640	.883
	4	-.030	.046	1.000	-.152	.091
4	1	2.536*	.046	.000	2.414	2.657
	2	.792*	.046	.000	.670	.914
	3	.030	.046	1.000	-.091	.152

Based on estimated marginal means

*. The mean difference is significant at the .05 level.

b. Adjustment for multiple comparisons: Bonferroni.

We can also examine for a trend in the data by examining the Profile Plots as well as the Contrast tests. As illustrated in Figure 20.15, the means increase from the Pretraining time variable to the Part 2 training variable and then level off from Part 2 to Posttraining. Thus, the trend starts as increasing and is linear, and then becomes a quadratic (curve-like) pattern at the latter two measurement points. This effect is supported by the contrasts tests.

The "Tests of Within-Subjects Contrasts" analyzes for polynomial patterns in the four measurements. There are significance tests for three types of data patterns: Linear (straight line), Quadratic ("U" or inverted "U" shape line), and Cubic (a more complex curved line). The results reveal a linear-quadratic relationship ($p < .001$) consistent with the profile plots.

Eighty-eight percent of the pattern in the data is linear and 67.8% of the data pattern is quadratic. Most of the pattern is linear, which includes some curvature.

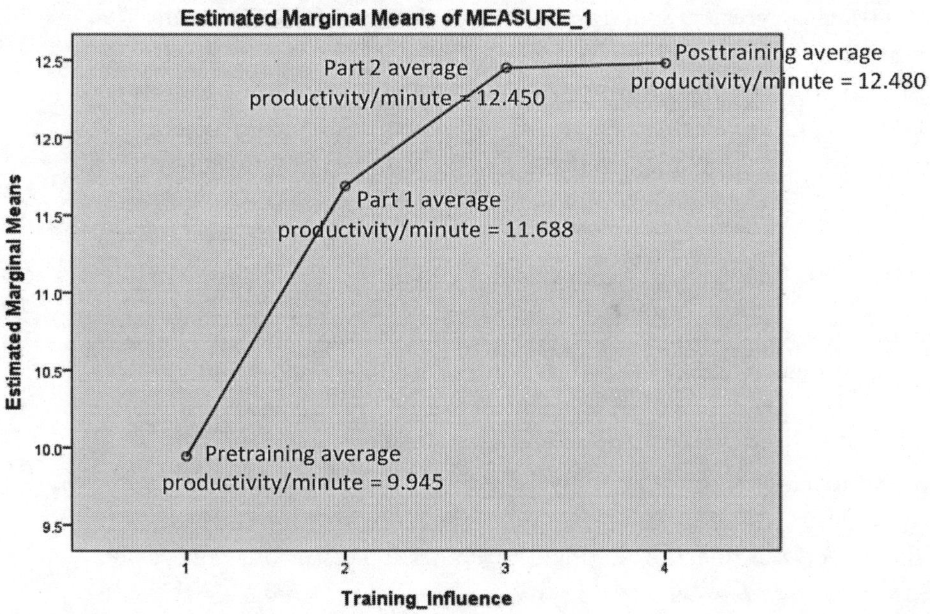

Figure 20.15

Table 20.7

The Partial Eta Squared indicates that 88.2% of the change in the means supports a linear trend and that 67.8% of the change in the means supports a quadratic trend.

Type of trend effect.

The *p*-values.

Tests of Within-Subjects Contrasts

Measure: MEASURE_1

Source	Training_Influence	Type III Sum of Squares	df	Mean Square	F	Sig.	Partial Eta Squared
Training_Influence	Linear	1663.202	1	1663.202	3538.728	.000	.882
	Quadratic	348.579	1	348.579	995.940	.000	.678
	Cubic	1.490	1	1.490	2.811	.094	.006
Error(Training_Influence)	Linear	222.780	474	.470			
	Quadratic	165.900	474	.350			
	Cubic	251.220	474	.530			

Reporting Results

The standard deviations were located in the descriptive statistics output not illustrated in this section. Oddly enough, they are similar to at least two decimal places to the right. Contrasts results usually are not reported unless there is a specific reason to do so. Sometimes they are reported, if significant, along with nonsignificant repeated measures results. They are more useful when there are many measurement points.

Write-Up

A repeated measures ANOVA with a Huynh-Feldt correction determined that the mean Chip output per minute statistically differs over time after training (F(2.793, 1,323.931) = 1,491.312, $p < .001$). Training over time explained 75.9% of the change in production output. Bonferroni comparisons revealed that Part 1 training likely increases chip production (M = 11.68, SD = 1.00, $p < .001$) over pretraining output (M = 9.945, SD = 1.00) and that Part 2 training output

(M = 12.45, SD = 1.00, $p < .001$) was greater than Part 1 training output. There was no improvement from Part 2 training output to posttraining output two weeks later (M = 12.480, SD = 1.00, p = .990). Consistent with these findings, the data indicated a significant linear ($F(1,474)$ = 3538.728, $p < .001$) and quadratic effect ($F(1,474)$ = 995.940, $p < .001$) where output increased and then flattened suggesting that most of the benefit from training occurred by the completion of Part 2 training.

Example 20.2: GLM Repeated Measures: The Nonsignificant Case

The quality assurance manager of a manufacturing facility wishes to test four different quality assurance protocols in order to determine whether any of them produced a reduction in the number of defective plastic molded parts produced during a month. Since no consistent quality assurance system was in place and the aim was to focus on the performance among the five protocols, no pre-protocol measurement was taken. The study occurred over five months where a single protocol was implemented during a full month. Quality assurance reports provided the number of defective parts produced per 475 injection molding machines. The *same* machinery and operator records were used for the five protocols. The protocols were numbered 1–5. Did any of the protocols reduce the number of monthly defective plastic molded parts? If so, describe where the differences were found. Alpha = .05. The name of the data file was this analysis is "GLM Repeated Measures Example 2 Data."

The analysis requires numeric production output variables for the five measurement points. These variables consist of the number of defective units produced in a month.

SPSS Output Interpretation

We will focus on the tests for normality, Mauchly's test of sphericity, and tests of within-subjects effects tables and, if necessary, the tests of within-subjects contrasts and pairwise comparisons tables, as well as the profile plot.

Data Screening

The data are numeric and we assume that they represent the target population. There is one main effect, which is type of training protocol. There are five measurement points, each representing usage of a specific protocol.

The five protocol variables are approximately normally distributed, as indicated in Table 20.8. The Shapiro-Wilk normality test p-values are all >.05.

Table 20.8

Tests of Normality

	Kolmogorov-Smirnov[a]			Shapiro-Wilk		
	Statistic	df	Sig.	Statistic	df	Sig.
QA Protocol 1	.029	475	.200*	.996	475	.354
QA Protocol 2	.032	475	.200*	.997	475	.600
QA Protocol 3	.032	475	.200*	.997	475	.589
QA Protocol 4	.020	475	.200*	.998	475	.849
QA Protocal 5	.025	475	.200*	.996	475	.369

*. This is a lower bound of the true significance.

a. Lilliefors Significance Correction

General Linear Model Repeated Measures Analysis

Mauchly's test of sphericity is not significant because $p = .194$. This indicates that the sphericity assumption is not violated. The variances are similar. The sphericity assumed test is applicable.

Table 20.9

Mauchly's Test of Sphericity[a]

Measure: MEASURE_1

Within Subjects Effect	Mauchly's W	Approx. Chi-Square	df	Sig.	Epsilon[b]
					Gree
Protocol_Effects	.974	12.357	9	.194	

Tests the null hypothesis that the error covariance matrix of the orthonormalized tran to an identity matrix.

a. Design: Intercept
Within Subjects Design: Protocol_Effects

b. May be used to adjust the degrees of freedom for the averaged tests of significance. Corrected tests are displayed in the Tests of Within-Subjects Effects table.

The "Sig." column represents the *p*-value for the sphericity (homogeneity or equality of variance test).

The "Tests of Within-Subjects Effects" reveals that the sphericity assumed statistic is not significant ($p = .949$). It is likely that there is no difference in the five protocols affecting the number of defective plastic molded parts produced by the machinery. The partial eta squared is essentially zero, telling us that there is no connection between type of protocol and number of defective parts. Therefore, there is no need for the Bonferroni post hoc test results.

Table 20.10

Tests of Within-Subjects Effects

Measure: MEASURE_1

Source		Type III Sum of Squares	df	Mean Square	F	Sig.	Partial Eta Squared
Protocol_Effects	Sphericity Assumed	25063.103	4	6265.776	.179	.949	.000
	Greenhouse-Geisser	25063.103	3.947	6349.352	.179	.948	.000
	Huynh-Feldt	25063.103	3.985	6289.929	.179	.949	.000
	Lower-bound	25063.103	1.000	25063.103	.179	.672	.000
Error(Protocol_Effects)	Sphericity Assumed	66215932.37	1896	34924.015			
	Greenhouse-Geisser	66215932.37	1871.043	35389.848			
	Huynh-Feldt	66215932.37	1888.719	35058.642			
	Lower-bound	66215932.37	474.000	139696.060			

Table 20.11 depicts the means and 95% confidence intervals for the five protocol variables. For example, the Protocol 1 mean number of defective parts is 498.043 for the month. We are 95% confident that the true population mean number of defective parts produced during usage of the first protocol was between 480.714 and 515.373.

As illustrated in Figure 20.16, although the means may appear to vary from each other because of the scale, there is no difference or trend in any of the means of the five protocols' outputs. This lack of pattern is supported by the contrasts tests below.

As shown in the "Tests of Within-Subjects Contrasts" table, all of the contrasts are nonsignificant. The partial eta squared statistics are each virtually zero. This is so because there is likely no relationship among the measurement points.

Table 20.11

Each mean represents the average number of chips produced per minute during each measurement point.

These 95% confidence intervals represent the lower and upper bounds of the means.

Estimates

Measure: MEASURE_1

Protocol_Effects	Mean	Std. Error	95% Confidence Interval	
			Lower Bound	Upper Bound
1	498.043	8.819	480.714	515.373
2	489.923	8.320	473.574	506.271
3	496.942	8.580	480.083	513.801
4	493.174	8.487	476.496	509.851
5	490.723	8.469	474.081	507.365

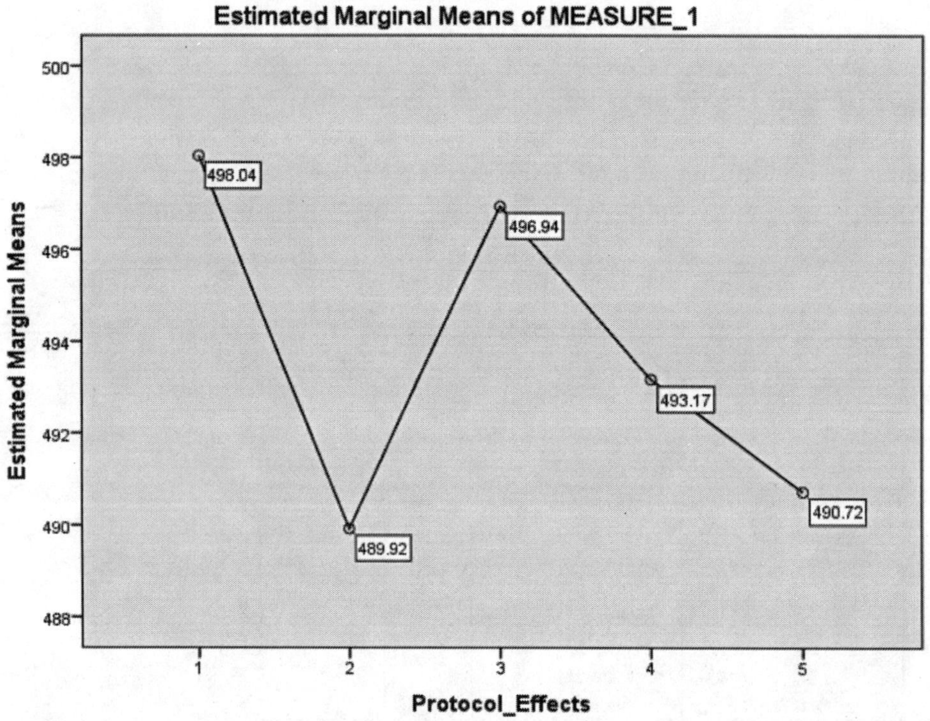

Figure 20.16

Table 20.12

Tests of Within-Subjects Contrasts

Measure: MEASURE_1

Source	Protocol_Effects	Type III Sum of Squares	df	Mean Square	F	Sig.	Partial Eta Squared
Protocol_Effects	Linear	6161.400	1	6161.400	.156	.693	.000
	Quadratic	10.374	1	10.374	.000	.986	.000
	Cubic	9074.732	1	9074.732	.262	.609	.001
	Order 4	9816.597	1	9816.597	.316	.574	.001
Error(Protocol_Effects)	Linear	18775039.89	474	39609.789			
	Quadratic	16277492.72	474	34340.702			
	Cubic	16426069.74	474	34654.156			
	Order 4	14737330.02	474	31091.414			

Reporting Results

Although not reported below, some analysts include the grand mean and its standard deviation when the results are nonsignificant since these statistics represent the total sample.

Write-Up

A repeated measures general linear model determined that the mean number of defective plastic parts per month did not statistically differ by quality assurance protocol ($F(4, 1{,}896) = .179$, $p = .949$). No other effects were found.

SUMMARY OF KEY CONCEPTS

- The one-way repeated measures ANOVA or general linear model is used to discover difference among three or more related measurements.
- Repeated measures has a number of data assumptions.
- Sphericity is a key data assumption that is often not met.
- Sphericity is equality of variance for the differences in the paired comparisons.
- There are a number of remedies to address violations of data assumptions.
- The overall repeated measures tests available are sphericity assumed, Greenhouse-Geisser, and Huynh-Feldt.
- Measurement point and paired difference confidence intervals are provided in the SPSS output.
- The Bonferroni post hoc test is widely used to learn where specific paired mean differences lie.
- Profile plots and contrast analysis offer additional insights about repeated measures data.
- Conducting a one-way repeated measures ANOVA (aka general linear model) in SPSS is straightforward.
- Reporting significant and nonsignificant repeated measures results are clear-cut.

One-Way Repeated Measures ANOVA Applied Exercises

20.1 What is a one-way repeated measures ANOVA?

20.2 What is a general linear model (GLM) repeated measures?

20.3 In repeated measures, what is the overall repeated measures test?

20.4 What is a post hoc significance testing?

20.5 Conceptually, define sphericity.

20.6 What is the purpose of Mauchly's significance test?

20.7 Conceptually, what is the sphericity assumed test?

20.8 What is the Greenhouse-Geisser statistic?

20.9 Define epsilon in the context of repeated measures analysis.

20.10 What is the Huynh-Feldt test in general?

20.11 What is the lower-bound in the context of repeated measures?

20.12 Generally, what is the Bonferroni post hoc test?

20.13 Regarding repeated measures, what is a partial eta squared?

20.14 Pertaining to repeated measures, what is contrast analysis?

20.15 Generally, what is a profile plot?

20.16 Once data have been screened for normality, what are the basic steps required to conduct a one-way repeated measures ANOVA (aka general linear model)?

20.17 A study followed the holiday spending of 380 families over three seasons. The same families, whose average annual household income was reported from $0 to $75,000, were asked how much they spent on holiday gifts for seasons 2013, 2014, and 2015. Were there differences in spending, and, if so, were there any patterns? Explain your answer. Report results in the format provided in this chapter. Alpha = .05. The data file name is "GLM Repeated Measures Exercise 1 Data."

20.18 A new on-demand video stream company wanted to test the brand awareness effectiveness of its new ad format. An advertising customer purchased space over a four-week period to run ads. The video streaming company had a list of opt-in regular subscribers who agreed to answer a short survey about their "viewing habits" over four weeks. The question was formatted in a scale where 1 = "not aware at all of Brand A" to 10 = "totally aware of brand A." The survey was distributed immediately before the campaign and then after each of four weeks so that there were five data collection points from the same participants. Nine hundred and twenty-five subscribers responded to all of the surveys. Did the ad campaign increase brand awareness? If so, what was the nature of the awareness effect? Explain your answer. Report results in the format provided in this chapter. Alpha = .05. The data file name is "GLM Repeated Measures Exercise 2 Data."

20.19 A medical research firm received a grant to determine if the color of nurses' uniforms affected patient moods. A local hospital agreed to ask patients to participant in this study. The patients did not have life-threatening illnesses. Fifty-five of the participants completed the five tablet-based "mood" survey. The responses were formatted in a smiley face pull bar scale from 1 = "I'm in a very sad mood" to 5 = "I'm in a great mood," including increments between 1 and 5 in order to increase reliability. The study transpired over five days. The nurses wore the same style uniform only the color varied as follows: Day 1 = Whatever uniform the nurse typically wore, Day 2 = Green, Day 3 = Navy Blue, Day 4 = White, and Day 5 = Beige. Is uniform color related to patient mood? Explain your answer. Report results in the format provided in this chapter. Alpha = .05. The data file name is "GLM Repeated Measures Exercise 3 Data."

20.20 At an afternoon session, 138 high school juniors were surveyed about their knowledge on the three branches of the U.S. federal government and how they are organized in providing checks and balances. After completing the survey, they immediately attended a two-hour workshop that consisted of a PowerPoint lecture by a teacher on the three branches followed by some related small group activities. At the end of the session, they were administered the same survey. Three weeks later, they completed the same survey once more. Each survey was based on 100 points. Did student knowledge increase over the short term and was it sustained three weeks later? Explain your answer. Report results in the format provided in this chapter. Alpha = .05. The data file name is "GLM Repeated Measures Exercise 4 Data."

Chapter 21

Correlation Analysis: Looking for an Association between Two Variables

LEARNING OBJECTIVES

To be able to:

- understand the purpose and describe what is a correlation;
- describe the basic idea behind a correlation;
- understand the roles of strength and directionality in describing the relationship between two variables;
- describe the data assumptions for correlation analysis;
- describe what is homoscedasticity;
- understand when to use Pearson, Spearman, and partial correlations;
- conduct correlation analysis in SPSS; and
- interpret and report significant and nonsignificant correlations.

21.1 Introduction to Pearson, Spearman, and Partial Bivariate Correlations

Up to this point, we have covered descriptive statistics and compared the means and variances of one or more samples by studying the differences between them. Now, we examine the relationship between two variables. A **bivariate correlation** (*r*) measures the degree to which two variables relate to each other. It is used to determine whether a linear (straight-line) relationship between variables exists, as well as the strength and direction of that relationship. Bivariate indicates two variables and correlation focuses on "co" as in the relationship between two variables. We will simply call it a correlation.

When we talk about a correlation between two variables, we refer to an association between them. An association indicates that when one variable differs, so does the other in a consistent way, whether the difference is in the same or opposite direction. Changes in the variables are reflected in variance within and between the variables. In other words, when matched, on average, they correspond in similar ways in relation to each other. If they are related, they maintain a linear (straight-line) association so that they covary in a pattern.

Covariance involves the degree to which the variables vary together. Correlation analysis is the statistical tool needed to measure the strength and direction of the covariance. For example, we may wish to examine whether there are relationships between people's answers to different survey questions, different economic indicators and GDP, individual production output and machinery operator age, individual waiting in line times and hour of the day, years of post-high school education and income, lifestyle and life expectancy, and so forth.

Often we have an idea which variable "explains" in a very general sense (or for that matter predicts) some or most of the variance in another variable. We may know this because of previous research, experience, expertise, or face validity. **Face validity** is the extent to which a finding or measurement is well founded and accurate based on common sense or face value. In the examples above, it is likely that in a correlation between education and income, most of the variance in income is explained by educational level. An argument can be made for many if not all of the examples above about which variables are the "predictors" in the relationships.

However, although correlation analysis can be used to explain the relationship between two variables, it does not establish cause and effect. Explaining variance in one variable when change occurs in another does not necessarily indicate causality, but it does reveal an association. The actual causes of variance in the dependent variable may rest in other variables. For example, in a study of fire impact, a study found that there was a strong positive relationship between fire damages and number of fire trucks. Might we conclude that perhaps too many fire trucks actually do more harm than good? Upon subsequent analysis, it was revealed that the number of fire trucks and fire damage were both due to the size of the fire. As we can see, correlation analysis is a tool that helps us describe the degree to which two variables relate to each other, but it does not provide evidence for causality. Chapter 22 addresses predictability and the precise nature of the relationship between variables using linear regression.

Explained Variance (r^2)

There is another important feature of the correlation statistic. It can be converted into an **effect size** statistic, which is a statistical measure of the degree to which one or more variables influence one or more other variables. By squaring the correlation, we arrive at the r^2, which is the total variance in the variables that can be explained by their linear relationship. Essentially, it is the variance explained by the line divided by the total variance. Variance explained or the explained variance is also called the **coefficient of determination**. The explained variance is the percentage of the joint data points that fall on the line of best fit, which will be covered soon. The explained variance reveals the percentage of the *shared variance* in the two variables. It is the percentage of the variance between the two variables that can be explained by the sample data. Think of r^2 as the degree or percentage of consistency in the relationship between two variables.

Figure 21.1 represents three scenarios using Venn diagrams. We can think of explained variance as overlapping variance. In the first case, 81% of the variance is shared or overlaps, followed by 36% and then 0% in the second and third cases, respectively.

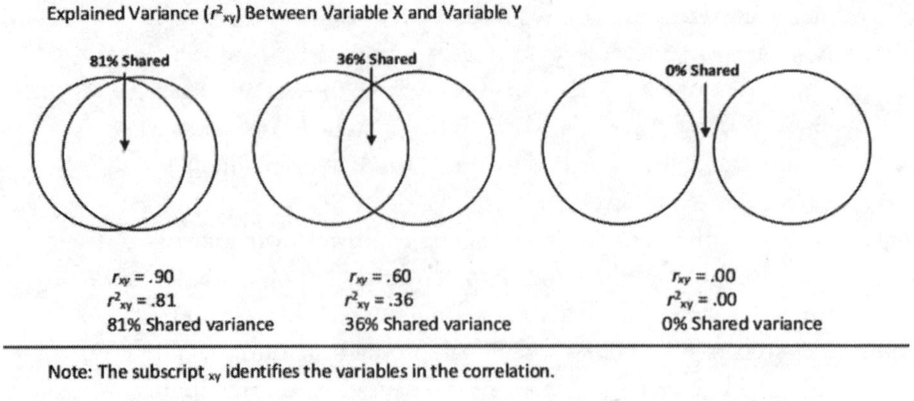

Figure 21.1

Since the explained variance is a percentage, then the unexplained variance (or variance not accounted for by the other variable or the line of best fit) is $1 - r^2$ = **unexplained variance**. Taking our education and income example, assume that $r^2 = .56$. This indicates that 100% – 56% = 44% of the variance in these variables is attributable to other variable(s) and error.

Last, explained variance is a useful statistic to report because it explains the relationship between two variables. It is intuitive and fairly easy to grasp, especially for those individuals who do not have a statistics background.

21.2 Strength and Directionality of Correlations

A correlation is a standardized numeric value that indicates the strength and direction of the relationship between two variables. As we shall discuss below, it can retain a value from –1 to 1. Negative one or positive one indicates a perfect negative or positive correlation, respectively. The correlation is between two variables and does not account for the potential influence of other variables. For this reason, it is called a **zero-order correlation**. In the case of SPSS and other statistical software packages, zero-order correlations can be run concurrently on more than two variables in order to provide a bigger picture of the relationships between pairs of variables. An example is provided in the Examples section.

A correlation analysis is a significance test. Usually, a nonsignificant correlation is very small. A small significant correlation may not have any practical value. However, the particular research aim and context informs the assessment.

Correlation Strength

The **strength of a correlation** is the degree to which the variables have similar variances. If the differences in the variables corresponds perfectly, then the correlation will be –1 or 1. Less than perfect correlations will be between –1 and 1. Correlations close to "0" demonstrate a lack of association, indicating little or no correlation. Table 21.1 identifies ranges of correlations and their strength. Strength is assessed independent of whether the correlation is positive or negative. Typically, correlations are reported to two places to the right of the decimal place. If it is negative, then the value is preceded by a "–"or negative sign. Correlations are subject to significance testing. Small deviations from $r = 0$ are not likely significant. Larger deviations from $r = 0$ are less likely to occur by chance, and thus, when they take place, they are usually significant. In principle, correlations cannot be less than –1 or greater than 1.

Table 21.1

Correlation Range	Strength
.00	No correlational relationship
-.01 to -.30 or .01 to .30	Weak
-.31 to -.50 or .31 to .50	Moderate
-.51 to -.70 or .51 to .70	Strong
-.71 to -.99 or .71 to .99	Very strong
-1.00 or 1.00	Perfect

Note: These values and assessment apply to Pearson, Partial, and Spearman correlations. Typically, correlations must have $p < .05$ to be meaningful.

Correlation Directionality

Directionality of a correlation is about the nature of covariance in terms of whether a variable consistently increases, decreases, or moves in the opposite direction of the other variable where one increases and the other decreases. This is called a **monotonic** relationship, which means that the degree of covariance may change, yet it maintains the same direction. In other words, the slope can vary, but does not change direction. If they vary in the same direction, then it is a positive correlation as in the education and income and healthy lifestyle and life expectancy noted examples—more of one is associated with more of the other or less of one is associated with less of the other. A **positive correlation** is $0 < r \leq 1$. If the variables move in the opposite direction, it is a negative correlation. A **negative correlation** is $0 > r \geq -1$. For example, as income increases, poverty decreases or as education increases, ignorance decreases.

Linear Correlation Strength and Directionality Together

The following graphs represent some of the various correlations. Figure 21.2a represents positive (top curve) and negative (bottom curve), strong, and significant correlations between education and income. Note the *r*'s and *p*-values. The variable thought to be independent is located in the *x*-axis (horizontal line) and the dependent variable is assigned the *y*-axis (vertical line).

Figure 21.2b illustrates a moderate, positive and negative, significant correlations between experience and income. Figure 21.2c demonstrates weak relationships that are not significant.

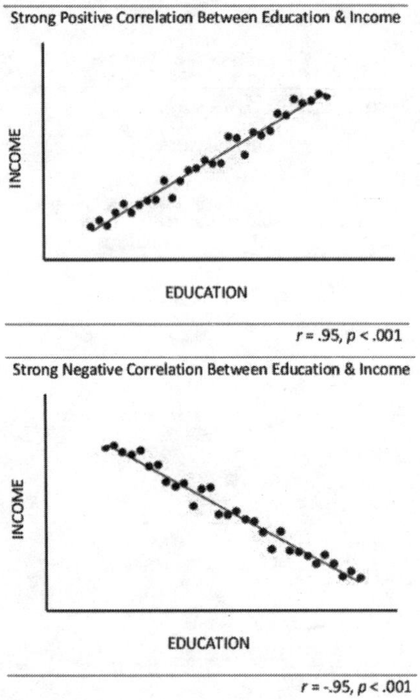

Figure 21.2a

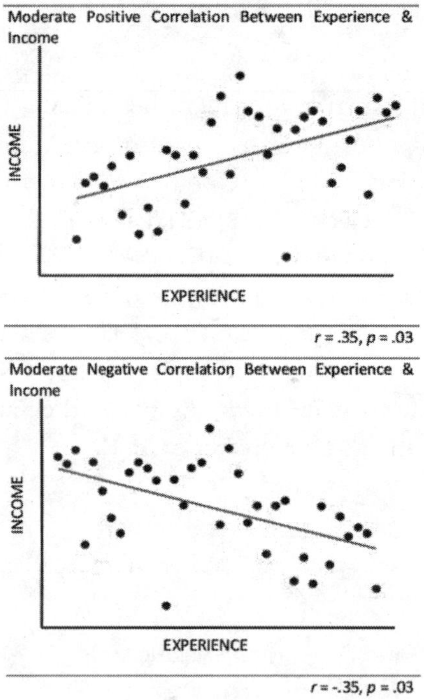

Figure 21.2b

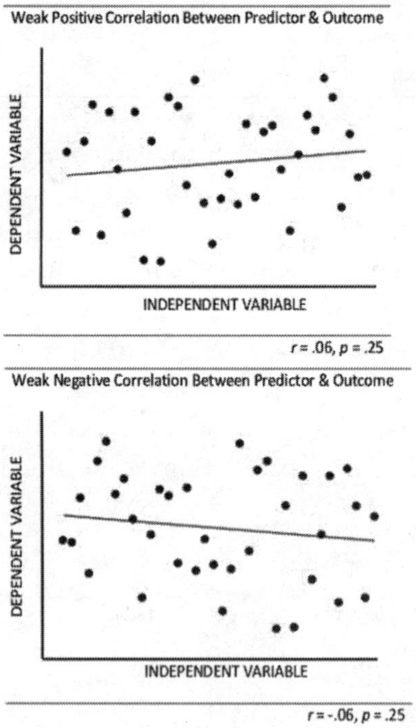

Figure 21.2c

Figure 21.3 is an extreme case of no relationship, which of course is not significant. The line has no slope. Variance in the independent variable has no corresponding variance in the dependent variable. Both the weak and no correlation data distributions are close enough to zero to be nonsignificant.

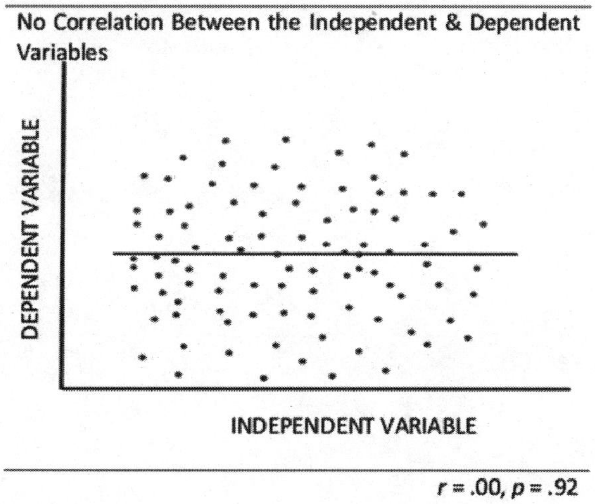

Figure 21.3

21.3 Calculating a Correlation for Numeric Data

Before covering the Pearson correlation example below, let us discuss some important assumptions for this type of correlation analysis.

Linearity is a pattern in a joint distribution that maintains the same slope between two variables in a straight line. It occurs when the variance between two variables is constant in their respective directions. Linearity addresses the validity of the relationship. **Validity** is the extent to which a finding or measurement is well founded and accurate.

Homoscedasticity refers to the degree in which the covariance of the joint values fit along the line of best fit forming an elliptical pattern. It is the extent to which the variables covary similarly at each value of the other variable. In other words, homoscedasticity is the degree to which the slope is consistent (maintains a straight-line relationship) in the observed data.

When the sample size is sufficiently large, the two variables are fairly normally distributed, and they demonstrate a linear relationship, the paired coordinates will tend to concentrate in the center at the intersection of the (joint) means of the two variables (see Figure 21.4). This indicates a **bivariate normal distribution**.

Correlation analysis requires matching data for two numeric (or ordinal) data points. They are not required to be in the same format. Other assumptions are covered in Section 21.5. Table 21.2 contains a dataset with 10 cases.

Let us plot the data. It stands to reason that hours studied is the independent variable so we assign it to the *x*-axis and the exam scores are placed on the *y*-axis. Figure 21.4 illustrates the plotted coordinates (data point to data point match) or **joint (bivariate) distribution**. The straight line running through the data points is the line of best fit. That is, it is calculated to bring as many data points as possible close to being on the line. It minimizes the distances of the data points from the line, which is the error or residual.

These data demonstrate a positive and strong correlation of .98 ($p < .001$), which has an effect size (r^2) of 97%, indicating that hours studying contributes to 97% of variance in test score. In plain English, how long a student studies affects 97% of student test performance as measured by the test score. This situation is straightforward. There is clearly a linear pattern.

Sometimes the independent variable is unclear. If that were the case here, we could frame the results conservatively as follows. Ninety-seven percent of the relationship (shared variance) between test grades and time spent studying can be explained by the sample data.

Table 21.2

Data for Hours Studying and Exam Scores

Student Name	Hours Studied	Exam Score
Ed	3.5	78
Kelsey	3.0	75
Monica	3.6	80
Nick	4.2	84
Rebecca*	**5.5**	**95**
Susan	4.3	83
Michael	5.0	90
Fred	4.5	85
Sandra	2.5	68
Ellen	4.0	80
Mean (Standard Deviation)	4.01 (.89)	81.80 (7.56)

Note: *Rebecca is identified in the graph. Hours studied are rounded to one decimal place and scores are based on 100.

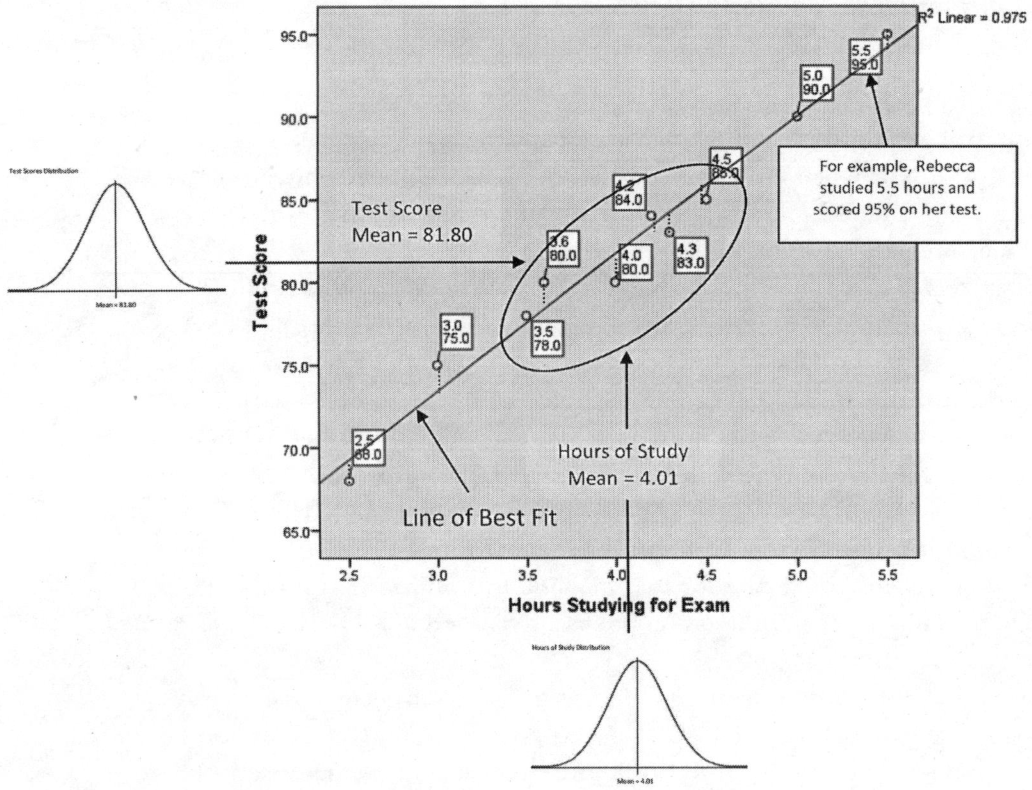

Figure 21.4

What follows is a review of other types of correlations, including the Spearman Rank Order Correlation, which can be used for ordinal categorical data and numeric data that do not meet some assumptions.

REAL WORLD SNAPSHOT

In a 2009 study by Skaalvik and Skaalvik entitled "Does School Context Matter? Relations with Teacher Burnout and Job Satisfaction," published in *Teaching and Teacher Education*, the associations between teachers' perception of school context (supervisory support, time pressure, relations with parents, and autonomy), teacher burnout (emotional exhaustion, reduced personal accomplishment, and depersonalization), and teacher job satisfaction were examined. Five hundred and sixty-three Norwegian teachers from elementary and middle schools participated in the study.

Some of the larger significant correlations ($p < .05$) were as follows: relations with parents and reduced sense of accomplishment (teacher burnout), $r = -.56$; time pressure and emotional exhaustion (teacher burnout), $r = .53$; emotional exhaustion and job satisfaction, $r = -.52$; reduced sense of accomplishment and job satisfaction, $r = -.41$. School size and years of teaching experience were not related to any of the variables.

These findings suggest that lack of relationships with student parents and increased time constraints relate to, and possibly contribute to, overall teacher burnout and less job satisfaction.

Ask yourself: What other variables might contribute to better understand these findings?

21.4 Types of Correlations

The three most widely used types of correlation analysis are the Pearson (r), Spearman (r^s), and Partial (r). The **Pearson correlation** is a parametric procedure used for numeric data and must meet the following assumptions: (1) each variable is fairly normally distributed; (2) each variable contains no outliers; (3) the variables share a linear association; and (4) the joint distribution is fairly normally distributed.

The **Spearman correlation** is a nonparametric test used when one or both variables are composed of ordinal categorical data or when numeric data do not meet the normality, linearity, and/or homoscedasticity assumptions, but are monotonic. In the case of ordinal data, if we wished to determine whether an association exists between ordered income categories and ordered education categories, we would use the Spearman procedure.

A **partial correlation** removes the influence of one or more designated variables from the correlation. For instance, we can study the association between income and professional experience while removing any influence of education. We can determine if there is a positive association between dog owner and high school student performance while removing the influence of household income so that the focus is on the two former variables. Since greater income can provide the environment and resources necessary to perform well in school independent of dog ownership, its effect must be removed. The SPSS Partial correlation analysis is limited to data treated as numeric. There are alternatives for categorical ordinal data which are beyond our discussion.

Squaring the Pearson or partial correlation gives us the variance explained or effect size. For example, if the correlation is .80, then the relationship between the variables explains $.80^2 = .64$ or 64% of their shared variance.

Last, we can control for the effects of one or more other variables on one of the two correlated variables by running a **semipartial correlation**. For instance, if we were interested in the correlation between education and income, the semipartial correlation tool would allow us to account for the influence of a third variable, such as experience on either income or education alone. In SPSS, this option is available through the "Regression" tab followed by the "Linear" option. After clicking the "Statistics" button, check the correlations box. We will not review this procedure in detail.

21.5 General Data Assumptions

Correlation analysis has a number of general assumptions.

- The sample data are representative of the target population.
- Each variable is either numeric, categorical ordinal, or in combination.
- Ideally, the sample sizes are equal.
- The rows must have matching or paired data, which are from the same case.
- Numeric data are approximately normally distributed (except for the Spearman correlation).
- Numeric data are linear, and categorical data are at least monotonic, thus, maintaining the same directionality.
- Numeric data are homoscedastic.
- The sample size is over 30.
- For numeric data, there are no outliers.

It is important to know that the normality assumption is crucial for significance testing and meeting linearity is vital for validity. Any association that is not linear is **curvilinear**. Curvilinear indicates a directional change in the slope (recall the rise over the run) of the line.

For the Pearson correlation, a bivariate normal distribution is required. This means that both variables are each normally distributed. The variance (slope) in the variables is approximately the same across bivariate (joint) combinations of the two variables, forming a straight-line relationship where the distribution is elliptical. These conditions meet the normality, linearity, and homoscedasticity assumptions.

The Shapiro-Wilk statistic is used to assess normality. The bivariate normal distribution is assessed visually by creating a scatter plot of the two variables. Again, if the scatter plot has an elliptical shape, then it is bivariate normal and meets the homoscedasticity assumption. Below are examples of positive and negative bivariate normal distributions. Many of the joint data points converge at the intersection of the variables' means.

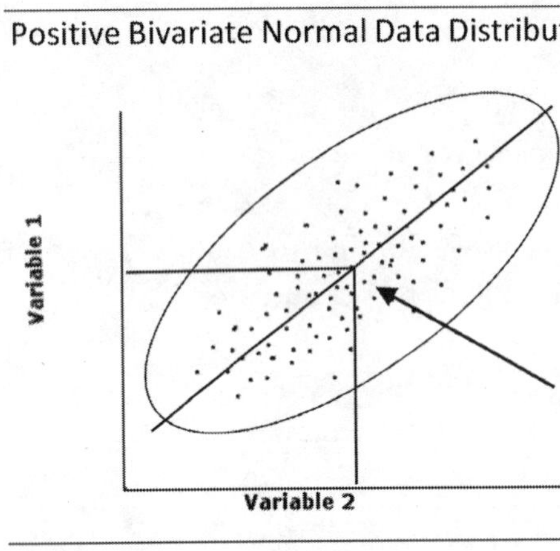

Figure 21.5

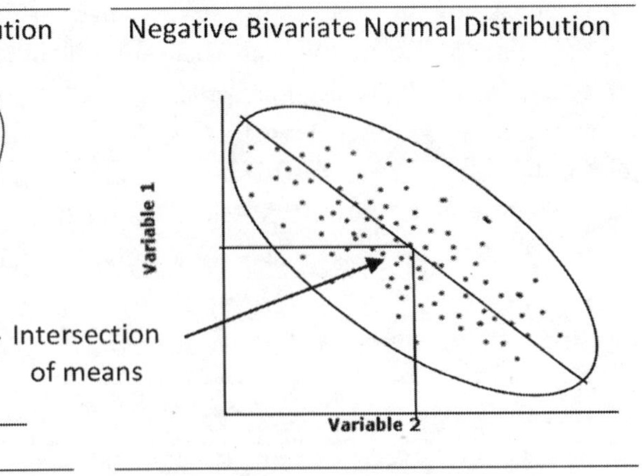

Figure 21.6

21.6 Examples Using SPSS: Step-by-Step Instructions

Using correlation analysis, the following examples examine for associations between numeric variables and between ordinal categorical variables.

Example 21.1: Pearson Correlation: The Significant Case

A nonprofit educational organization wishes to promote the benefits of a college/university education. A random sample of 575 professionals were surveyed about a number of topics, including their income in dollars and completed years of college or university. Is there a correlation between years of completed college and income? Alpha = .05. The name of the data file for this example is "Correlation Analysis Example 1 Data."

For the purposes of an SPSS introduction, we will focus on the basic steps.

Step 1: Open SPSS.

Locate the appropriate folder and data file, then highlight it. Next, click the "Open" button.

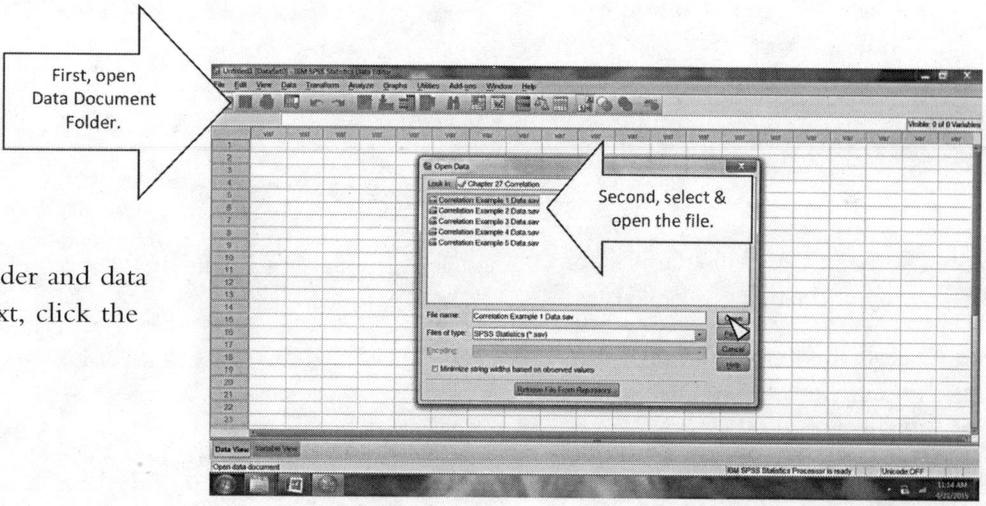

Figure 21.7

Step 2: First, we must screen the data for normal distribution. After the data file is open:

- Select the "Analyze" tab.
- Highlight "Descriptive Statistics."
- Click "Explore."

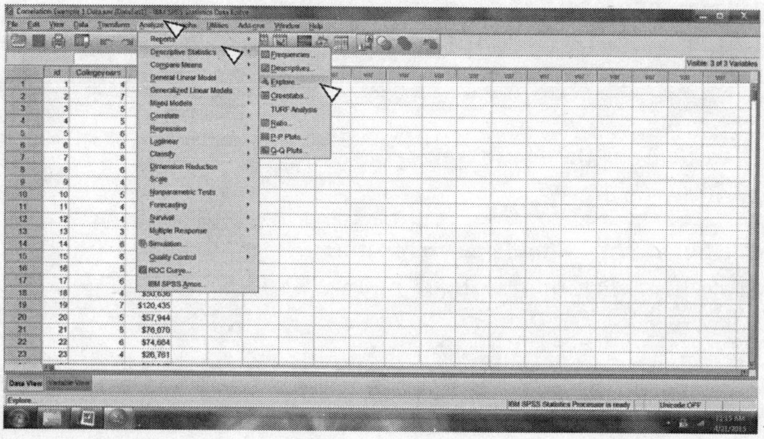

Figure 21.8

Step 3: The "Explore" window will open.

- Highlight the "Completed Years of College" and "Income in Dollars" variables and place them in the "Dependent List" box by clicking the "Arrow" button.
- Click the "Plots" button. In the "Explore: Plots" window:
  - Only check "None" in the box plot area.
  - Below that, check "Normality plots with tests."
  - Last, click the "Continue" button.
- Click the "OK" button. Output is generated.

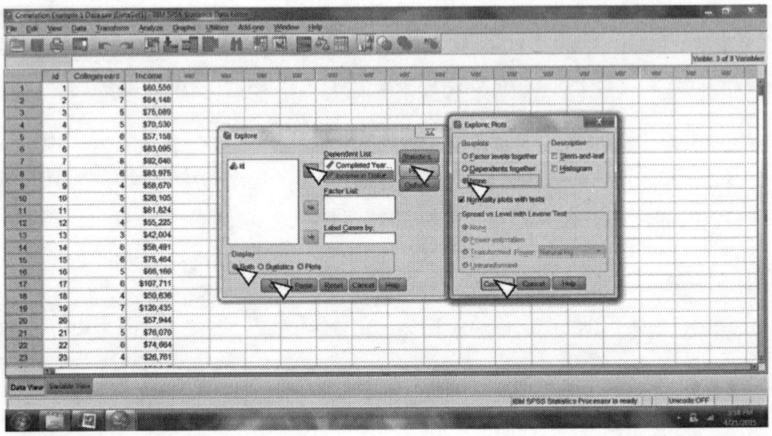

Figure 21.9

Step 4: Next, we will examine for linearity and bivariate normality.

- Select the "Graph" tab.
- Highlight "Legacy Dialogs."
- Click "Scatter/Dot."

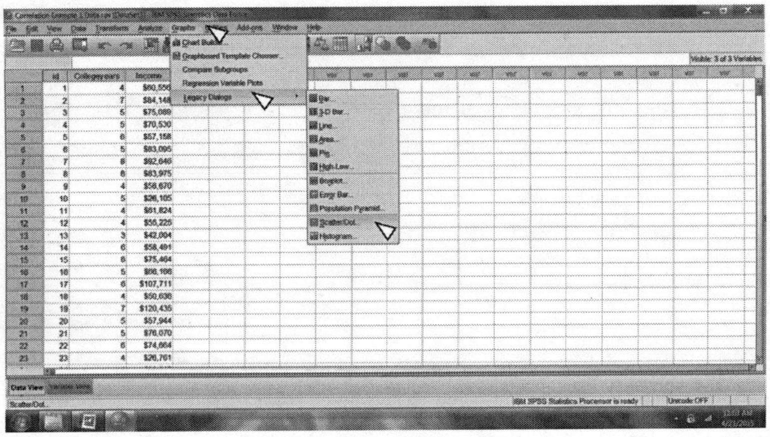

Figure 21.10

Step 5: After the "Scatter/Dot" window opens:

- Select the "Simple Scatter" option.
- Then, click the "Define" button.

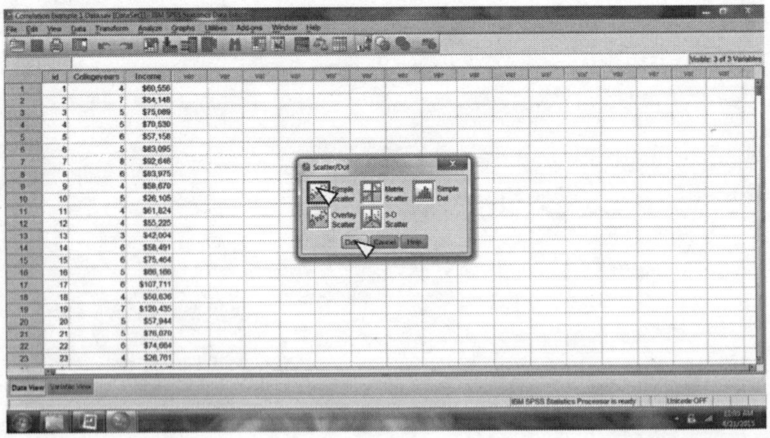

Figure 21.11

Step 6: The "Simple Scatterplot" window will open.

- Highlight and place one variable in the "Y-Axis" box by clicking the "Arrow" button.
- Place the other variable in the "X-Axis" box. If a variable is considered to be independent, it should be placed in the "X-Axis" box. However, this is not a requirement.
- Last, click the "OK" button. Output will be generated.

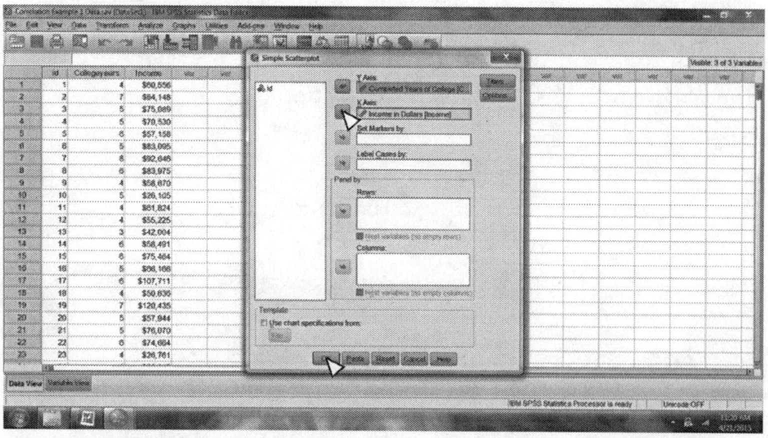

Figure 21.12

Step 7: Now it is time to run the correlation. In the data file:

- Select the "Analyze" tab.
- Highlight "Correlate."
- Click "Bivariate."

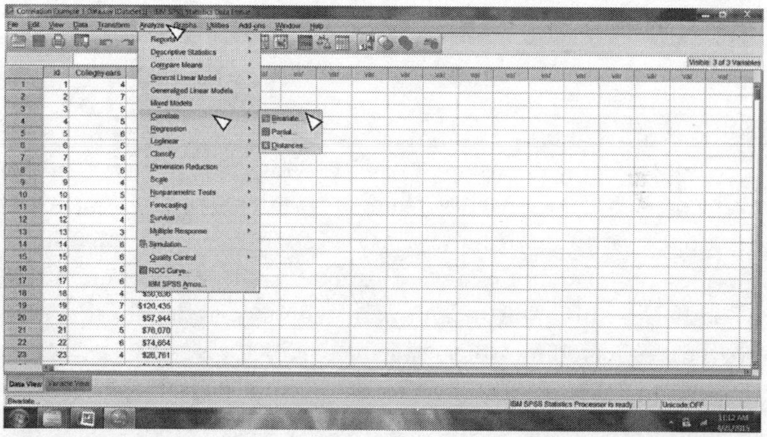

Figure 21.13

Step 8: When all of the numeric data assumptions are met, leave the default "Pearson Correlation Coefficient." However, if one variable is ordinal categorical, one or both variables are not normally distributed, or the variables are not bivariate normal, select the "Spearman Correlation Coefficient" option. For a partial correlation, one can add as many control variables as one wishes. In all three cases, more than two variables can be included in the correlation procedure producing a matrix table of correlations. In the "Correlation Coefficients" window:

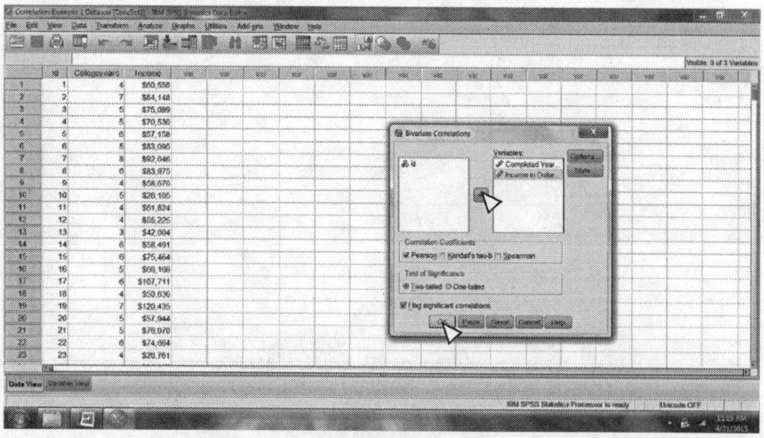

Figure 21.14

- Keep the Pearson default setting.
- Highlight the variables for your analysis, and then click the "Arrow" button so that they move into the "Variables" box.
- Last, click the "OK" button. Output will be generated.

Last, save the data and output files for your records.

SPSS Output Interpretation

We will focus on the tests for normality and correlation tables, as well as the joint distribution graph. Below is a discussion of the output.

Data Screening

The sample size is over 30. As rendered in Table 21.3, the Shapiro-Wilk statistics are p = .62 for Completed Years of College and p = .67 for Income in Dollars, which are both >.05, indicating that the samples approximate the normal distribution.

Table 21.3

Tests of Normality

	Kolmogorov-Smirnov[a]			Shapiro-Wilk		
	Statistic	df	Sig.	Statistic	df	Sig.
Completed Years of College	.024	575	.200*	.998	575	.629
Income in Dollars	.018	575	.200*	.998	575	.676

*. This is a lower bound of the true significance.

a. Lilliefors Significance Correction

"Sig" denotes a p-value of .629 for College Years and .676 for Income.

Non-normally distributed data increases the likelihood of producing unstable results. In the event of such an occurrence, there are a number of options. (1) More data can be collected with the hope that the distribution becomes fairly normal. (2) The Normal Q-Q Plot derived from the Descriptive/Explore analysis output could be examined to identify and aid in the removal of outliers, resulting in an approximately normal distribution (see Chapter 12 for a review of this procedure, including other available SPSS tools). (3) The "Spearman Correlation Coefficient" option can be used instead of running the "Pearson Correlation Coefficient." (4) The data can be transformed to normalize the distributions. If none of these solutions suffice, then include a caveat in the write-up.

The information in Figure 21.15 is used to assess linearity and homoscedasticity. A line and an elliptical shape have been imposed on the data. The joint data approximate linearity and the distribution is elliptical, which meets the homoscedasticity assumption.

Bivariate Distribution

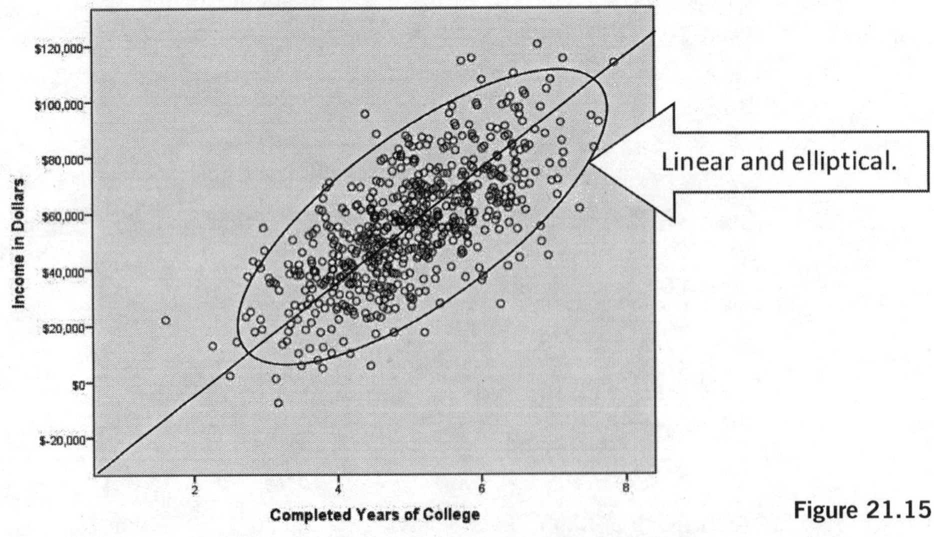

Figure 21.15

Pearson Correlation Analysis

The output in Table 21.4 contains the Pearson correlation, *p*-value, and sample size per variable. Because it is in matrix format, the table contains the information twice. For example, the correlation between A and B will be the same as the correlation between B and A. The positive correlation between completed years of college and income in dollars is meaningful and strong ($r = .68$, $p < .001$) assuming alpha = .05. In other words, there is a less than 1/1,000 probability that the correlation is by chance. Since the chance probability is < .001 < .05, the results are likely meaningful.

Table 21.4

Correlations

		Completed Years of College	Income in Dollars
Completed Years of College	Pearson Correlation	1	.689**
	Sig. (2-tailed)		.000
	N	575	575
Income in Dollars	Pearson Correlation	.689**	1
	Sig. (2-tailed)	.000	
	N	575	575

**. Correlation is significant at the 0.01 level (2-tailed).

The correlation is .689, Sig. is the p-value (<.001), and *N* is the sample size.

Additionally, the explained variance is $.68^2$ or $.68 \times .68 = .46$ or 46%. According to the sample data, 46% of the joint data points fall on the line of best fit. This tells us that 46% of the relationship between income and education is explained by the line, which is the shared variance.

In summary, based on the correlation and *p*-value, there is a strong and significant positive correlation between completed years of college and income in dollars. In most cases, as a person completes more years of college, that person's income increases. In some cases, someone who earns more may use some of that income to gain a degree. In both cases, the inverse may be true. However, there may be exceptions as well. Pearson correlation analysis addresses, on average, relationships consistent with drawing a representative sample of the target population.

Reporting Results

Write-Up

A Pearson product-moment correlation was run to determine whether an association exists between completed years of college and income in dollars. The data showed no violation of normality, linearity, or homoscedasticity. There was a statistically meaningful strong, positive correlation between completed years of college and income in dollars ($r = .68$, $N = 575$, $p < .001$). There is likely a relationship between education and income. The data explain 46% of the association between the two variables.

Example 21.2: Pearson Correlation: The Nonsignificant Case

A sports science program at a leading university wishes to determine if there is an association between an individual's perceptions of wellness and her/his reported amount of physical activity. A random sample of 100 individuals agreed to complete an online exercise questionnaire. Alpha = .05. The data file name is "Correlation Analysis Example 2 Data."

The analysis requires two variables: exercise reported as how many days per week: 0–7 days, and wellness reported on a 10-point scale: 1 = "not feeling well at all" to 10 = "couldn't feel better." We will skip the SPSS steps because they are identical to the first example.

SPSS Output Interpretation

Again, we focus on the tests for normality and correlation tables, as well as the joint distribution graph.

Data Screening

As depicted in Table 21.5, both Shapiro-Wilk statistics are greater than .05: Reported Days of Exercise During the Week (p = .90) and Self-Perceptions of Wellness (p = .13). Therefore, the variables meet the normality assumption.

Table 21.5

Tests of Normality

	Kolmogorov-Smirnov[a]			Shapiro-Wilk		
	Statistic	df	Sig.	Statistic	df	Sig.
Days/week exercise	.042	100	.200*	.993	100	.909
Reported wellness	.065	100	.200*	.980	100	.135

*. This is a lower bound of the true significance.

a. Lilliefors Significance Correction

"Sig" denotes a p-value of .909 for Exercise Days/Wk. and .135 Wellness Perceptions.

Figure 21.16 assesses whether the joint distribution of the two variables' data are linear and homoscedastic, which appears to be the case. A line and an elliptical shape have been imposed on the data to demonstrate these relationships.

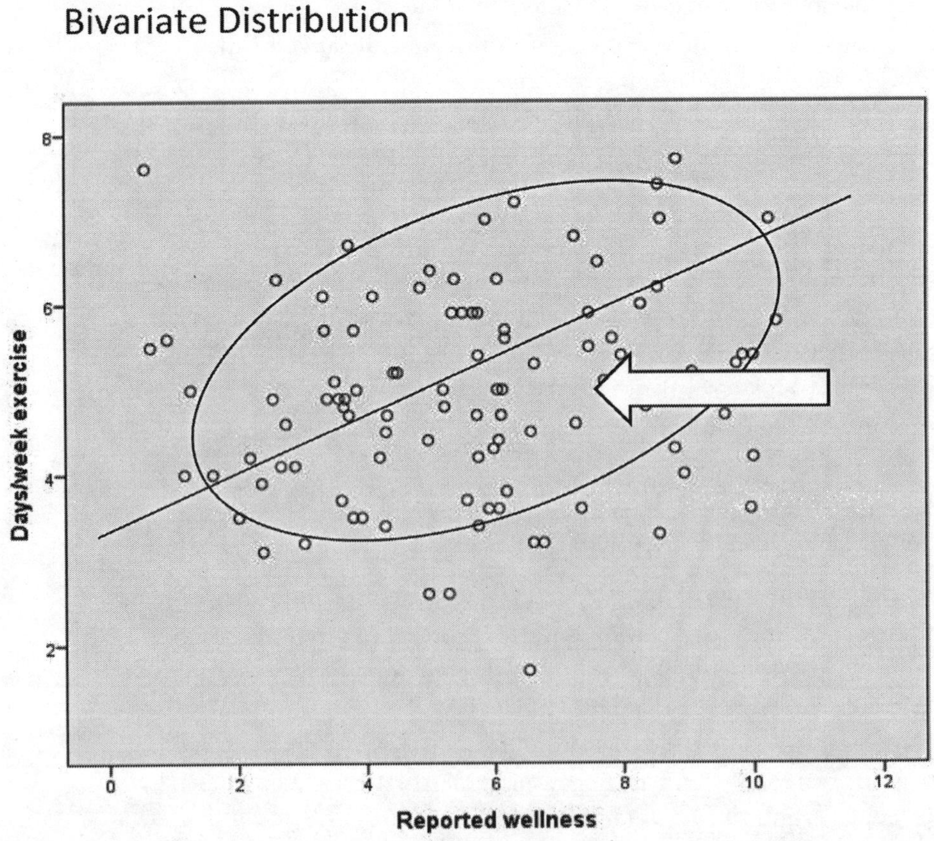

Figure 21.16

Pearson Correlation Analysis

The correlation between days/weeks of exercise and reported wellness is not significant ($r = .15$, $p = .12$).

Table 21.6

Correlations

		Days/week exercise	Reported wellness
Days/week exercise	Pearson Correlation	1	.154
	Sig. (2-tailed)		.125
	N	100	100
Reported wellness	Pearson Correlation	.154	1
	Sig. (2-tailed)	.125	
	N	100	100

The correlation is .154, Sig. is the p-value (.125), and *N* is the sample size.

In summary, based on the correlation and *p*-value, there is no meaningful association between days/weeks of exercise and self-perceptions of wellness.

Reporting Results

The r^2 is not reported because the correlation is not statistically significant.

Write-Up

A Pearson product-moment correlation was run to determine if an association exists between days/weeks of exercise and self-perceptions of wellness. The data showed no violation of normality, linearity, or homoscedasticity. There is no significant correlation between days/weeks of exercise and perceptions of wellness ($r = .15$, $N = 100$, $p = .12$). It is likely that feelings of wellness do not vary based on the number of exercise days.

Example 21.3: Spearman Correlation: Both Cases

A nonprofit educational organization wishes to promote the benefits of a college/university education. A random sample of 575 professionals were surveyed about a number of topics, including their income and completed college or university degree. Is there a correlation between the college degree attained and income categories? Alpha = .05. The data file name is "Correlation Analysis Example 3 Data."

Since reporting exact income is a sensitive issue for some survey respondents, the income question was formatted as ordered categories or income groups: \$0–\$25,000, \$25,001–\$50,000, \$50,001–\$75,000, \$75,001–\$100,000, \$100,001–\$125,000, and over \$125,001. Degree categories were established for the educational-level question: no degree, associates, bachelors, masters, and Ph.D. This example examines the two variables in Example 1 formatted as categorical data.

First, we used the Spearman correlation because the data are ordinal categorical. Second, we did not generate descriptives because the Spearman procedure is nonparametric. It does not depend on normality, linearity, or homoscedasticity.

SPSS Output Interpretation

Data Screening

The correlations table provides the basis for the assessment.

Spearman Correlation Analysis

Table 21.7 contains the correlation, level of significance, and sample size per variable analyzed. The correlation between college degree categories and income categories is significant, positive, and strong (r_s = .62, $p < .001$).

Table 21.7

Correlations

			College Degree	Income Group
Spearman's rho	College Degree	Correlation Coefficient	1.000	.627**
		Sig. (2-tailed)	.	.000
		N	575	575
	Income Group	Correlation Coefficient	.627**	1.000
		Sig. (2-tailed)	.000	.
		N	575	575

**. Correlation is significant at the 0.01 level (2-tailed).

The correlation is .627, Sig. is the p-value (<.001), and *N* is the sample size.

Additionally, the variance explained is $.62^2$ or 39%, indicating that according to the sample data, college degree and income share 39% of their variance. In summary, based on the correlation and *p*-value, there is a strong and significant positive correlation between these two variables.

Reporting Significant Results

Providing that category descriptions are not lengthy, include them in the write-up.

Write-Up

A Spearman correlation was run to determine whether an association exists between college degree (no degree, associates, bachelors, masters, and Ph.D.) and income group ($0–$25,000, $25,001–$50,000, $50,001–$75,000, $75,001–$100,000, $100,001–$125,000, and over $125,001). There was a statistically meaningful strong, positive correlation between the two variables (r^s = .62, N = 575, $p < .001$). There is likely a relationship between education and income. The data explain 39% of the association between education and income.

Reporting Nonsignificant Results

If the results were nonsignificant, the write-up would be as follows.

Write-Up

A Spearman correlation was run to determine whether an association exists between college degree (no degree, associates, bachelors, masters, and Ph.D.) and income group ($0–$25,000, $25,001–$50,000, $50,001–$75,000, $75,001–$100,000, $100,001–$125,000, and over $125,001). There was no significant correlation between the two variables (r^s = .09, N = 575, p = .395). Therefore, there is likely no relationship between college degree and income group.

Example 21.4: Partial Correlation: Both Cases

A think tank wants to examine recent assertions about the positive effects of lobster consumption on intellectual curiosity. A study pointed out a positive correlation between people enrolled in courses and lobster consumption. The available data for North America and South America span 40 years and include the number of people enrolled in at least one course, total lobster consumption by pounds per year, and economic growth as measured in GDP for the region. Based on this data, is there a relationship between lobster consumption and course enrollment, or might another factor contribute to this "relationship"? Alpha = .05. The data file name is "Correlation Analysis Example 4 Data."

The analysis requires three numeric variables that represent total numbers for the Americas: lobster consumption in pounds, number of people enrolled in at least one college course, and GDP as a measure of economic growth.

We can run a correlation analysis concurrently among pairs of variables, which is called a **multiple correlation**. This approach offers more of the data's story. A partial correlation provides a correlation between two variables that removes any potential influences from one or more other identified variables by controlling for them. Controlling for a variable in essence removes the variable's influence on the two variables in the analysis. We compare partial correlations to zero-order correlations in order to examine for differences. This will make more sense in the example below.

Because association between enrollments and lobster consumption may be driven by economic growth, we first run a Pearson correlation on all available data, followed by a partial correlation, focusing specifically on enrollments and lobster consumption, while removing the influence of economic growth (GDP). This approach will determine if it is economic growth rather than lobster consumption that is associated with enrollments in college.

SPSS Output Interpretation

We will focus on the tests for normality, correlations, and partial correlations output.

Data Screening

As depicted in Table 21.8, because all of the Shapiro–Wilk normality statistics are not significant (GDP, $p = .93$, lobster consumption, $p = .06$, and college enrollments, $p = .13$), the normality assumption is met.

Table 21.8

Tests of Normality

	Kolmogorov-Smirnov[a]			Shapiro-Wilk		
	Statistic	df	Sig.	Statistic	df	Sig.
Total GDP Rate for Western Hemisphere	.085	40	.200*	.988	40	.934
Lobster Consumption in Pounds	.135	40	.065	.948	40	.065
People Taking College/University Courses in Western Hemisphere	.105	40	.200*	.957	40	.131

*. This is a lower bound of the true significance.

a. Lilliefors Significance Correction

"Sig" denotes p-values for the three variables.

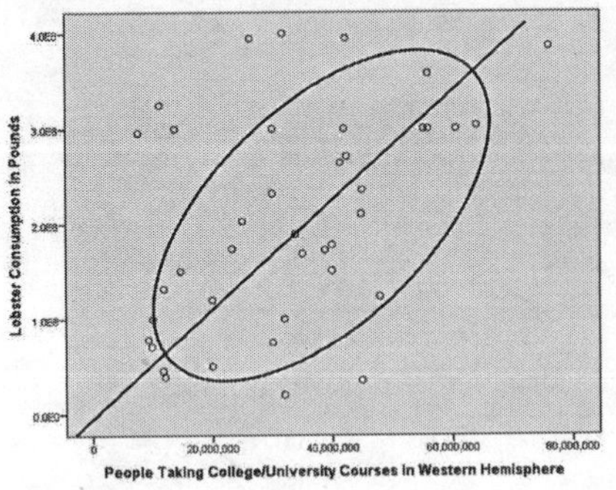

Figure 21.17

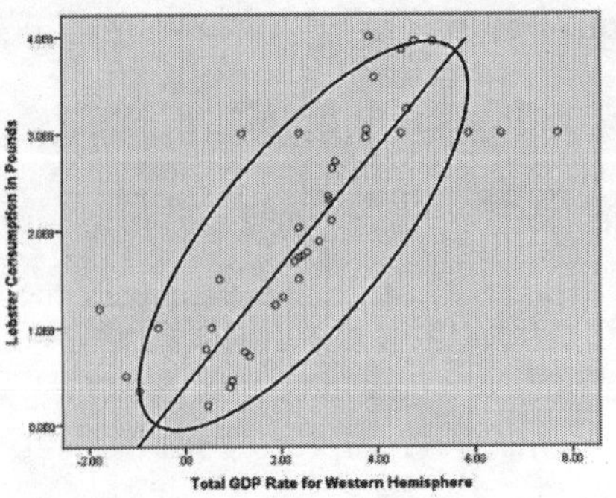

Figure 21.18

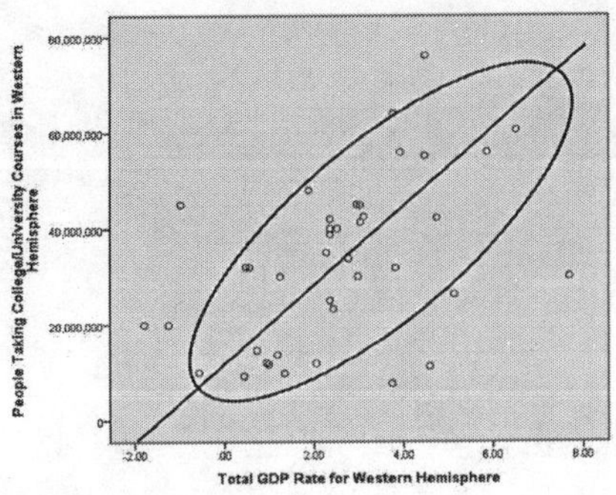

Figure 21.19

Figures 21.17–21.19 illustrate the joint distributions of the two variables and control variable. Figure 21.17 contains the variables of interest: lobster consumption and course enrollments. Figures 21.17–21.18 each contain one of the variables of interest and the control variable. The three plots contain all possible comparisons without being redundant. A line and an elliptical shape have been imposed on the distributions to assess the data assumptions.

There are a number of outliers that we will not address for the sake of brevity. Chapter 12 covers procedures for assessing and removing outliers. It is important to note that when the sample size is 40, few outliers can be removed in order to maintain over 30 cases.

Partial Correlation Analysis

First, we will run Pearson correlations on the three variables, followed by a partial correlation while controlling for GDP. There is a moderate positive correlation between lobster consumption and course enrollments ($r = .45$, $p = .003$) and a strong positive correlation between lobster consumption and GDP ($r = .79$, $p < .001$). Clearly, increased lobster consumption is associated with increased course enrollments and economic growth.

The correlation between course enrollments and GDP is .47 ($p = .002$), indicating that as the economy grows, so do course enrollments. This correlation is similar to that between lobster consumption and course enrollments. The stronger relationship among these variables appears to be between lobster consumption and GDP, and not course enrollments. A partial correlation will help clarify the relationship.

Table 21.9

Correlations

		Lobster Consumption in Pounds	People Taking College/University Courses in Western Hemisphere	Total GDP Rate for Western Hemisphere
Lobster Consumption in Pounds	Pearson Correlation	1	.455**	.798**
	Sig. (2-tailed)		.003	.000
	N	40	40	40
People Taking College/University Courses in Western Hemisphere	Pearson Correlation	.455**	1	.474**
	Sig. (2-tailed)	.003		.002
	N	40	40	40
Total GDP Rate for Western Hemisphere	Pearson Correlation	.798**	.474**	1
	Sig. (2-tailed)	.000	.002	
	N	40	40	40

**. Correlation is significant at the 0.01 level (2-tailed).

Table 21.11 reveals the results of a partial correlation where we removed the effects of GDP and focused on the association between lobster consumption and course enrollments only. We can see that there is no correlation between lobster consumption and course enrollments (r = .14, p = .38).

Table 21.10

Correlations

Control Variables			Lobster Consumption in Pounds	People Taking College/University Courses in Western Hemisphere
Total GDP Rate for Western Hemisphere	Lobster Consumption in Pounds	Correlation	1.000	.144
		Significance (2-tailed)	.	.381
		df	0	37
	People Taking College/University Courses in Western Hemisphere	Correlation	.144	1.000
		Significance (2-tailed)	.381	.
		df	37	0

In summary, based on a comparison of zero-order and partial correlations, it is likely that it is GDP that contributes to the variance in course enrollments and lobster consumption. The data suggest that eating lobsters does not contribute to intellectual curiosity. Inversely, intellectual pursuits appear to not drive a hunger for lobster consumption. These results imply that lobster, an expensive food, is consumed more when consumers are doing well financially. To a lesser degree, economic prosperity provides greater educational opportunities.

Reporting Nonsignificant Results

Write-Up

A partial correlation was run to determine whether an association exists between lobster consumption and course enrollments while removing the influence of economic growth as measured by GDP. The data over a 40-year period, which were provided for the Americas, showed no violation of normality, linearity, or homoscedasticity. There was no correlation found between lobster consumption and course enrollments (r = .14, N = 40, p = .38). It is likely that GDP and course enrollments are related, but not lobster consumption and enrollments.

Reporting Significant Results

If the results were significant, the write-up would be similar to the following.

Write-Up

A partial correlation was run to determine whether an association exists between lobster consumption and course enrollments while removing the influence of economic growth as measured by GDP. The data over a 40-year period, which were provided for the Americas, showed no violation of normality, linearity, or homoscedasticity. There was a statistically meaningful correlation found between lobster consumption and course enrollments (r = .54, N = 40, p < .001). It is likely that a relationship exists between these two variables. The data explain 29% of the association between them.

SUMMARY OF KEY CONCEPTS

- A correlation is the degree of covariance or association between two variables in terms of strength and directionality.
- A correlation analysis applies a numeric value from –1 to 1 on a linear and/or monotonic relationship between two variables.
- Correlations can be strong or weak and positive or negative, indicating that they differ in the same or opposite direction, respectively.
- Explained variance or the coefficient of determination is the correlation squared, which is the percentage of the joint data points that rest on the line of best fit. This measure describes what percentage of a variable's variance is explained (or predicted) by the variance in another variable.
- The amount of variance not explained by the line of best fit is the error, residual, and/or unexplained variance.
- Homoscedasticity is an important requirement when correlating numeric data. It is akin to equality of variance.
- The Pearson correlation is used when both variables are numeric and meet the numeric data assumptions.
- The Spearman correlation is used when one or both variables are ordinal categorical or when numeric data do not meet the normality, linearity, and homoscedasticity assumptions, but are monotonic.
- Partial correlations using numeric data account for the influence of other variables not part of the bivariate correlation.
- Conducting correlation analysis in SPSS involves a few short steps.
- Interpreting and reporting a significant or nonsignificant correlations is straightforward.

21.7 CORRELATION ANALYSIS APPLIED EXERCISES

21.1 What is a bivariate correlation?

21.2 What is a correlation?

21.3 What is an association between two variables?

21.4 Define covariance.

21.5 Define variance.

21.6 What is face validity?

21.7 Broadly define the term effect size.

21.8 What is the meaning of r^2?

21.9 What is variance explained or the explained variance?

21.10 What is a coefficient of determination?

21.11 What is unexplained variance in terms of explained variance?

21.12 Describe a zero-order correlation.

21.13 What is meant by the strength of a correlation?

21.14 What is meant by directionality of a correlation?

21.15 Describe a positive correlation.

21.16 Describe a negative correlation.

21.17 In correlation analysis, what is meant by a joint distribution?

21.18 Define linearity in the context of correlation analysis.

21.19 Define homoscedasticity.

21.20 What is statistical validity?

21.21 Describe bivariate normal distribution.

21.22 In short, what is a Pearson correlation?

21.23 When is it appropriate to use the Spearman correlation?

21.24 Broadly define a partial correlation.

21.25 Broadly define a semipartial correlation.

21.26 In one sentence, define or describe what is curvilinear.

21.27 What is a monotonic relationship?

21.28 Complex, a cable company, wishes to determine if there is an association between subscribers' reported amount of travel and interest in a new cable service that offers a full range of travel services. Are consumers more engaged in travel behavior more likely to show an interest in cable travel services? Data were collected from a random sample of 100. The two questions were as follows: "How would you report your amount of travel compared to people in general? 1 = I don't travel to 7 = I live to travel." "Would you be interested in a new cable service that offers a full range of travel services? 1 = I am not interested at all to 7 = Sign me up now." Explain your answer. Alpha = .05. Report results in the format provided in this chapter. The data file name is "Correlation Analysis Exercise 1 Data."

21.29 Previous research found that certain personality traits reduced job burnout in healthcare providers. Healthcare researchers are charged to explore this line of researcher further. Survey data were collected from 600 healthcare practitioners who were asked a number of questions. Two variables are of special interest. These are hardiness and burnout. Is increased hardiness associated with less burnout while accounting for age? "Hardiness" was measured using responses to self-perceptions of job commitment, sense of control over one's life, and high challenge questions. A composite sliding bar scale was formatted as 1 = "little hardiness" to 7 = "high hardiness." "Burnout" consisted of a composite sliding bar formatted as 1 = "not burned out at all" to 7 = "totally burned out." Age is in completed years of life. Explain your answer. Report results in the format provided in this chapter. Alpha = .05. The data file name is "Correlation Analysis Exercise 2 Data."

21.30 A human resources firm is charged with determining whether a relationship exists between compensation and job satisfaction. Pay data were collected from 286 workers representing all job functions so that pay is in dollars. Additionally, the same workers completed a short job satisfaction online sliding bar scale survey. The overall job satisfaction question "Are you satisfied with our job?" responses were anchored in a scale as follows: 1 = "not at all satisfied" to 9 = "completely satisfied." Is there an association between pay and job satisfaction? Explain your answer. Report results in the format provided in this chapter. Alpha = .05. The data file name is "Correlation Analysis Exercise 3 Data."

21.31 Researchers at a well-known nonprofit think tank wish to explore the relationship between hours spent playing video games and GPA (overall high school average). They recruited 520 high school juniors to participate in the online study after securing parental permission. The two variables (single-questions) of interest were "On average, how many hours a day do you play video games?" and "To the best of your knowledge, what is your GPA?" Both items were recorded using a sliding bar scale so that fractions could be provided. Is there an association between gaming and GPA? Explain your answer. Report results in the format provided in this chapter. Alpha = .05. The data file name is "Correlation Analysis Exercise 4 Data."

21.32 A macroeconomist for a large pharmaceutical company wished to confirm the relationship between drug price and units sold over one year for its 121 prescription drugs in order to determine if, on average, they are price-elastic. Price elasticity is a measure of how much prices can fluctuate (usually increase) before price changes significantly influence (decrease) demand for drugs. Prices are copayments after insurance coverage for a 30-day supply. Demand is measured by the number of 30-day orders placed. These drugs are prescribed for chronic illnesses and 30-day orders more accurately mimics real world conditions. Are these prescription drugs price elastic? Explain your answer. Report results in the format provided in this chapter. Alpha = .05. The data file name is "Correlation Analysis Exercise 5 Data."

Chapter 22

Single Linear Regression

LEARNING OBJECTIVES

To be able to:

- understand the purpose and describe what is single linear regression (SLR);
- describe the basic idea behind an SLR;
- understand the basic assumptions for SLR and how to assess them;
- describe the data screening process;
- understand and explain the components of a linear prediction equation and how it relates to the line of best fit and explained variance;
- learn how to interpret SLR results;
- understand how to determine values of the outcome variable from values of the predictor variable;
- learn how to run SLR in SPSS; and
- interpret and report significant and nonsignificant results in an easily understood manner.

22.1 Introduction to Single Linear Regression

In Chapter 21, we learned that a correlation allows us to discover the degree to which two variables relate to each other. Correlation provides information about the overall strength and direction of the relationship. **Single linear regression (SLR)**, commonly referred to as simple linear regression, extends correlation so that we can predict or estimate values of the dependent variable from the independent variable. It allows us to discover not only the strength and directionality of the relationship between two variables, but its precise nature as well. In regression, the dependent variable is the outcome and the independent variable is the predictor.

SLR uses the correlation between the variables to gain knowledge of the independent variable in order to predict the dependent variable. Larger correlations (greater shared variance) allow us to more accurately predict the outcome variable from values of the predictor variable. For example, we can use SLR to determine whether an elderly person's cognitive ability is at a level that would be predicted by age. Regression can be deployed to aid in diagnosing a host of medical conditions, such as AST or ALT, both predictors of liver damage. Linear regression is used in virtually every field of study and research.

SLR calculates a line of best fit expressed mathematically and based on the sample data. The prediction equation averages all the of sample data between the variables. The averages are used to develop a precise equation to predict unknown values of the outcome from a given value of the predictor. Like the Pearson correlation, and in order to provide an accurate picture of the relationship, the equation minimizes the distances between the data points and the line. Of the data points that do not fit the line, the distance from the observed data points to the line is the error or residual. It is the difference between what is the predicted joint data point and what is observed in the sample data. Thus, if a data point falls on the line, there is no error.

SLR helps us determine whether the changes between the predictor and outcome variables are consistent across bivariate data points so that they maintain the same relationship. From the equation, different values of the predictor can be used to project a corresponding on average outcome value. As we shall see, many of the SLR assumptions are similar to those of the Pearson correlation (see Chapter 21 for a review of these concepts).

Prediction vs. Cause and Effect

Although SLR can be used to predict values of a dependent variable from assigned values of an independent variable, it does not assure a cause and effect relationship. The actual cause(s) of covariance between two variables may rest in other variables. For example, let us say that we have data on Type II diabetes and amount of international travel. We run an SLR and find that the amount of international travel negatively predicts the tendency to develop Type II diabetes. Do we conclude that international travel reduces the incidence of Type II diabetes? Further examination reveals that those individuals who travel have the financial resources to afford healthcare insurance and healthy foods. Therefore, it is likely that financial resources, which provide the money to travel, also allows those travelers to purchase healthcare insurance and healthy foods, both contributing factors of lower rates of diabetes.

Cause and effect relationships must meet three requirements. First, the variables covary (correlate) so that they shift together in a systematic manner. Second, there is a time order to their relationship. In other words, the cause and effect make sense in the order in which they occur. Last, a nonspurious condition exists. In other words, the assumed effect is not brought about by some other cause not attributable to the predictor. Let us return to the diabetes example. Although there was a correlation between both tendency to not develop diabetes and travel, the order of the two variables is in question. Less "diabetes" may very well have come before travel. Additionally, the true cause of the relationship between the two variables was more likely money. As we can see, this example does not meet two out of the three requirements for causality.

Let us delve further into SLR, starting with the prediction model equation.

22.2 Prediction Model

The SLR equation or **prediction model** is a mathematical expression of the straight line of best fit based on the sample data. The value of the predictor is multiplied by its individual slopes and then the product is added to the *y*-intercept, resulting in a predicted outcome variable value given the assigned value to the predictor.

Keep in mind that extracting data is not perfect. There is naturally occurring variance, as well as variance from the sampling process. Nonetheless, the model minimizes the variation not explained by the line. For this reason, this type of regression is called the **least squares method**. Predictions cannot be **extrapolated**. That is, the model is only valid for the range of independent values in the sample data.

Statistically, we express the prediction model as follows:

$$Y_i = b_0 + b_1 X_i$$

where

Y_i = Y, the specific predicted value of the dependent variable when the independent variable takes on a specific value, i

b_0 = y-intercept, which is the value of the dependent variable when the independent variable is 0

b_1 = the slope of the line of best fit, which is the predicted unit amount of incremental change in the dependent variable as a result of a one-unit change (as measured) in the independent variable

X_i = a specific value of the independent variable for which there is a corresponding predicted dependent variable value (Y_i).

A joint data point or bivariate observation is the intersection of an X or independent variable observation with its corresponding Y or dependent variable observation. They are the joint distribution coordinates (X_i, Y_i). Therefore, for a given X, there is a corresponding Y. As we can see in Figure 22.1, some Y values are less than the prediction model projection while others are more. The distance of the bivariate distribution data points that are not on the line is the unexplained variance or error.

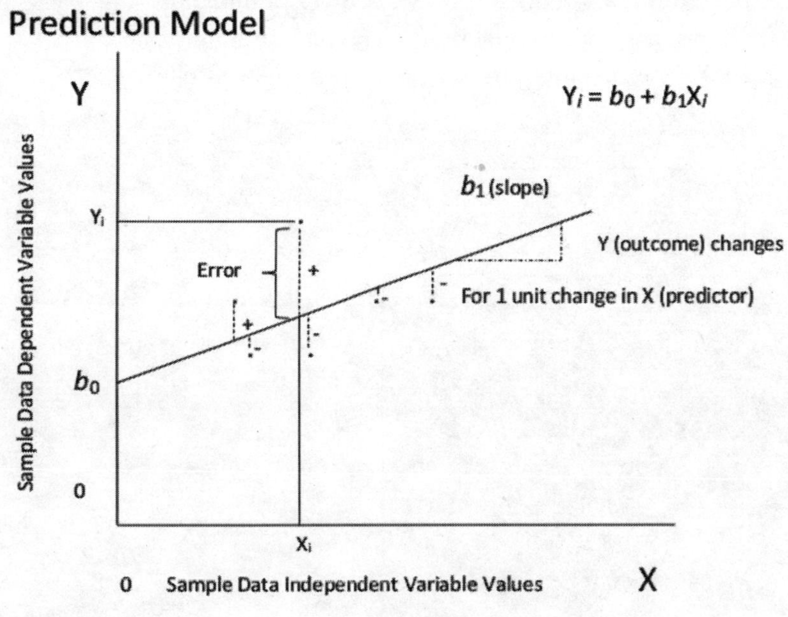

Figure 22.1

The b's are called the **regression coefficients** or **betas**. They are based on change in Y, the outcome. They can be **unstandardized** (b), which is in their original measurement, or **standardized** (β), which is based on one standard deviation. For now, we will refer to the unstandardized or original measurement values.

The line is oriented by the ***y*-intercept** (b_0) or predicted value of the outcome variable when the predictor variable (b_1) equals 0. It is the value of the outcome when the predictor is not present. Sometimes the y-intercept is 0 and many times it is not. For example, if we were to predict SAT math scores based on the number of math courses completed prior to college, the *y*-intercept would be 300 because everyone who completes the SAT automatically receives 300 points as a starting point. Most of reality is not so neat that a zero amount of something predicts a zero amount of something else. At the same time, many *y*-intercepts do not make sense. In either case, it is the required starting point needed to calculate a predicted outcome.

The regression coefficient, b_1, indicates the amount of incremental change in the dependent variable as a result of one unit of change in the independent variable's unit of measurement. It is incremental because it does not explicitly tell us anything about the *y*-intercept, but informs us about the nature of the predictability in the relationship between the predictor and the outcome variables. If the independent variable is measured in years, then the value for the dependent variable corresponds with one year change in the independent variable. For example, for each year of professional experience, an individual's salary, which is the dependent variable, will increase, on average, $1,000. It is said to be "on average" because usually the line is not a perfect fit. The b_1 (unit of change), or $1,000 in this case, is the **slope** of the line of best fit. More specifically, it is the incremental change in the dependent variable that corresponds with each unit change in the independent variable. Since the relationship is assumed to be linear, the covariance is constant or consistent throughout values of the predictor.

Applying the Prediction Model

Figure 22.2 depicts an illustration of SLR.

In this case, we analyze the relationship between horsepower and car price. The *y*-intercept (b_0) is –$12,012.00. It sets the initial starting point for the prediction line based on minimizing the residual. As we can see, horsepower affects car price. For every one unit of engine horsepower, the car's price increases incrementally by $212.00. The specific horsepower is the *X* value. The

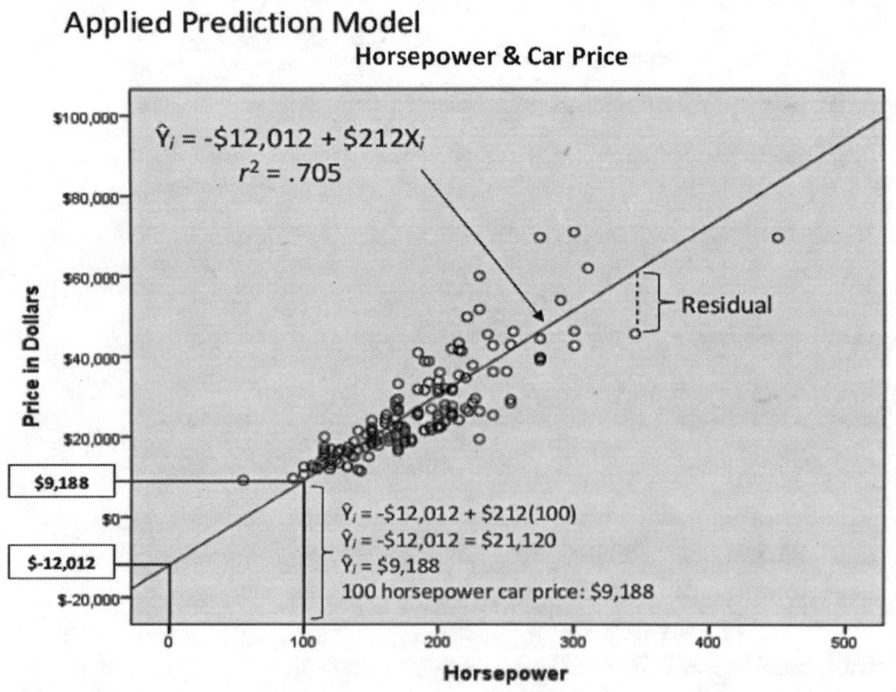

Figure 22.2

regression coefficient (b_1) is \$212.00, which is the slope of the line of best fit. It represents the variance in car price based on each horsepower unit in the engine.

Moreover, the r^2 or squared correlation is the coefficient of determination. Mathematically, it is the total of the squared variances explained by the line of best fit divided by all of the squared variances. Put differently, the r^2 is the percentage of the variance represented in the line or the variance explained by the line over the total variance: r^2 = regression sum of squares / total sum of squares. In this example, it is .705, which indicates that 70.5% of the change in car price is predicted by amount of horsepower. In SLR, the coefficient of determination is reported as a lower-case "*r*" square.

There is also the **adjusted r^2**, which is more useful for multiple linear regression analysis, as discussed in the next chapter. In SLR, a difference between r^2 and the adjusted r^2 suggests that the sample size may be insufficient. It serves more as a diagnostic statistic.

If we wished to determine car price for a given amount of horsepower, we return to the prediction line equation:

$$Y_i = b_0 + b_1X_i$$

$$\Downarrow$$

$$Y_i = -\$12{,}012 + \$212Xi$$

Based on the sample data, the price of a car with 200 horsepower ($X = 200$) would be:

$$Y_i = -\$12{,}012 + \$212Xi$$

$$Y_i = -\$12{,}012 + \$212(200)$$

$$Y_i = -\$12{,}012 + \$42{,}400$$

$$Y_i = \text{car price} = \$30{,}388$$

Standardized Regression Coefficients

SPSS output reports the standardized regression coefficients (β). They are based on standardizing the data so that they can be examined in terms of the ideal *z*-distribution. This is done by subtracting the sample mean from each observation and then dividing the result by the sample's standard deviation (see Chapter 11). SPSS does this calculation automatically. Both standardized and unstandardized betas are reported. Like the unstandardized coefficients, the β's indicate the variance in the dependent variable from the standardized distribution. It is interpreted as a result of one standard deviation in the independent variable. Thus, the standardized betas allow us see the relative influence of the independent variable on the dependent variable. It is more informative with multiple linear regression because multiple independent variables are compared in the same standardized measurement.

REAL WORLD SNAPSHOT

In a 2008 article published in *Industrial Health*, entitled "Self-Perceived Depression, Anxiety, Stress and Their Relationships with Psychosocial Job Factors in Male Automotive Assembly Workers," Edimansyah and colleagues surveyed 728 male automotive assembly workers about their perceptions of being depressed, anxious, and stressed at work, which served as the outcome variables for a series of single linear regression analyses where a number of job factors were the predictor variables.

The researchers found that the key significant predictors of self-perceptions of work related depression, anxiety, and stress were lack of social support, lack of coworker support, lack of supervisor support, as well as increased psychological job demands, job insecurity, and hazardous working conditions ($p > .001$). Depression and anxiety were also predicted by work-related physical exertion ($p < .01$).

Ask yourself: What other dependent variables might be predicted by job factors and why? What other work or non-work aspects would you consider?

22.3 Data Assumptions

There are a number of data assumptions required for SLR analysis. Some involve screening the independent and dependent variables separately and others involve examining them jointly. Thus, we have univariate and bivariate screening.

- The data are numeric.
- The sample size is over 30.
- The data are independent so that they come from different sampling elements.
- Each variable is approximately normally distributed.
- There is a linear relationship between the variables.
- The joint coordinates are approximately normally distributed (bivariate normal) so that the data are homoscedastic.
- Residuals are normally distributed, linear, and homoscedastic.

Testing Data Assumptions

The two variables are screened to determine whether they meet the data assumptions. If the normality, linear, and homoscedasticity assumptions are met, it is highly likely that the residuals as well do not violate the three conditions. Residual analysis can be basic or quite involved examining for detailed error patterns. What follows is a more basic approach.

The data are scale, interval, or ratio. For example, the data could be formatted in a Likert-type scale consisting of seven values: 1 = "strongly disagree" to 7 = "strongly agree;" SAT scores; and age, respectively.

The sample size is over 30 and we assume that they are independent unless informed otherwise.

The two variables each approximate the normal distribution and outliers do not exist. The Shapiro-Wilk test is used to assess univariate normality. Chapter 12 covers ways to detect and locate outliers using such tools as scatter plots and in particular the Normal Q-Q and simple dot plots. It is important to identify and remove outliers because these data can yield inaccurate results by calculating a line of best fit that minimizes large residual produced by outliers, and at the same time does not accommodate the vast majority of bivariate data points.

Bivariate normal distribution, linearity, and homoscedasticity are assessed by plotting the outcome variable on the y-axis and the predictor variable on the x-axis. If the data are linear and distributed in an oval shape with many points closer to the line of best fit and there is a concentration of data points near the intersection of the means of the two variables, then these assumptions are met. Homoscedasticity is the degree to which the variables covary similarly at each value of the predictor. In other words, it is the degree to which the slope remains consistent (keeps the straight-line pattern) in the observed data. Chapter 21 discusses the bivariate relationship. The bivariate scatter plot provides an opportunity to identify and remove outliers in both variables. Table 22.1 summarizes the required data screening assumptions and necessary stsistical tools to evaluate them.

Table 22.1

Data Screening

Assumption Screened	Data Screening (Predictor, Outcome, & Residuals)
✓ Numeric level data	✓ Scale, interval, & ratio data
✓ Sample size > 30	✓ Counted
✓ Normal distribution for each variable	✓ Shapiro-Wilk statistic, univariate scatter plots
✓ Normal joint distribution, linear relationship, & homoscedasticity for variables and residuals	✓ Bivariate scatter plot

Note: The listed screening options apply to numeric level data.

If the univariate and bivariate assumptions are met, it is likely that the residuals' assumptions will also be met. Therefore, the result of the variable screening serve as the basis for the residual analysis.

22.4 Examples Using SPSS: Step-by-Step Instructions

Using SPSS and significance testing, the SLR assumptions are assessed, and the specific relationship between the independent variable and the dependent variable can be uncovered, including predicting values for the dependent variable from the independent variable. The following two examples demonstrate significant and the nonsignificant cases.

Example 22.1: SLR: The Significant Case

A random sample of 575 professionals were surveyed and asked about their post-secondary educational level and gross annual income. The purpose of the study is to determine whether completed years of college predicts gross annual income. Alpha = .05. The name of the data file for this example is "SLR Example 1 Data."

The analysis requires two numeric variables: reported gross annual income in dollars and completed years of college or university. The following are the basic steps.

Step 1: Open SPSS.

Locate the appropriate folder and data file, then highlight it. Next, click the "Open" button.

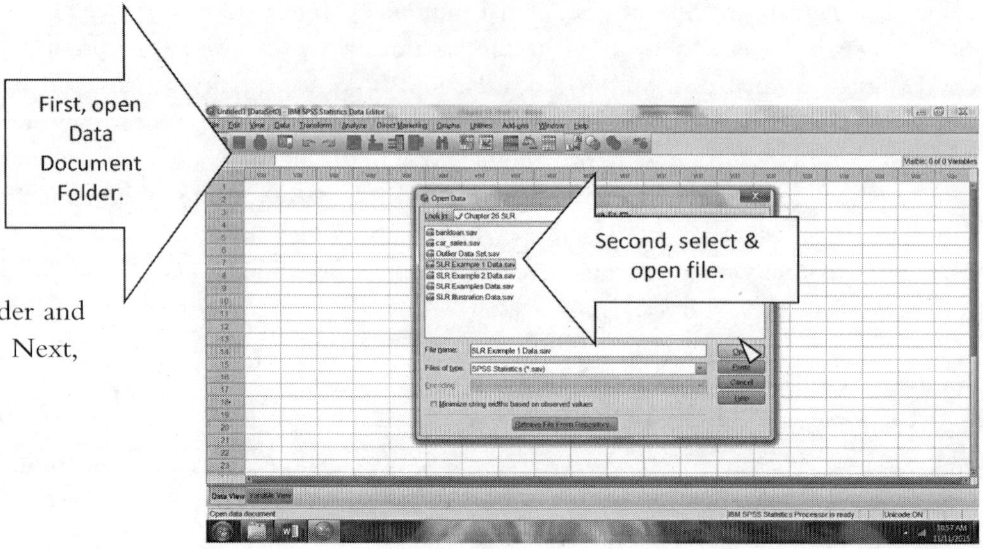

Figure 22.3

Step 2: First, we must screen the data for normal distribution.

- Select the "Analyze" tab.
- Highlight "Descriptive Statistics."
- Click "Explore."

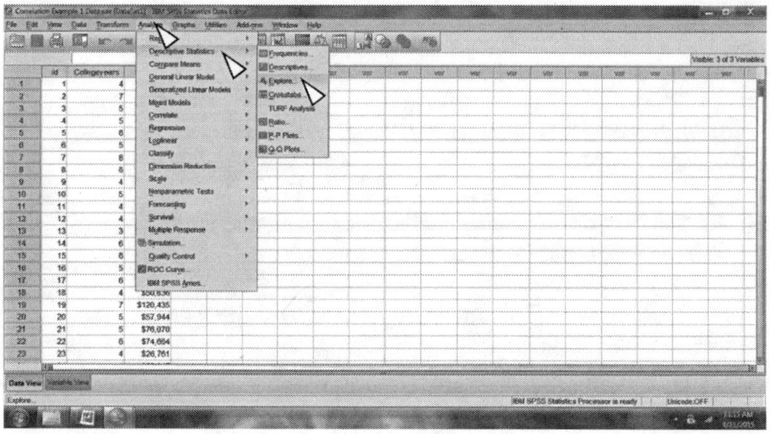

Figure 22.4

Step 3: After the "Explore" window opens:

- Highlight the "Completed Years of College" and "Income in Dollars" variables and place them in the "Dependent List" box by clicking the "Arrow" button.
- Click the "Plots" button. In the "Explore: Plots" window:
  - Only check "None" in the box plot area.
  - Below that, check "Normality plots with tests."
  - Click the "Continue" button.
- Last, click the "OK" button. Output is generated.

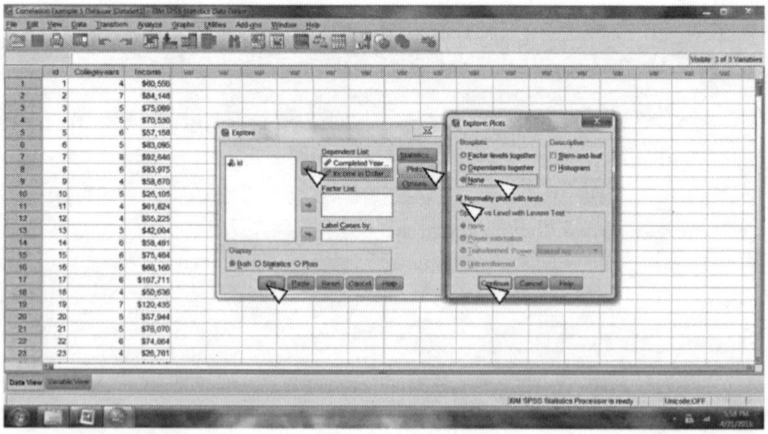

Figure 22.5

Step 4: Next, we will test the bivariate normal distribution, linearity, and homoscedasticity assumptions.

- Select the "Graph" tab.
- Highlight "Legacy Dialogs."
- Click "Scatter/Dot."

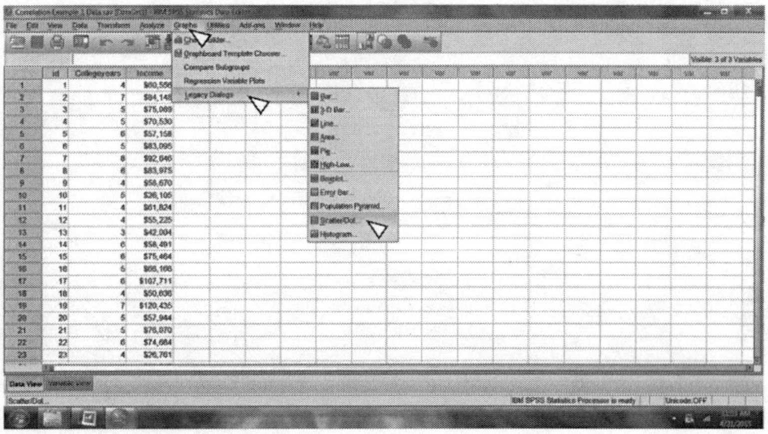

Figure 22.6

Step 5: In the "Scatter/Dot" window:

- Select the "Simple Scatter" option.
- Click the "Define" button.

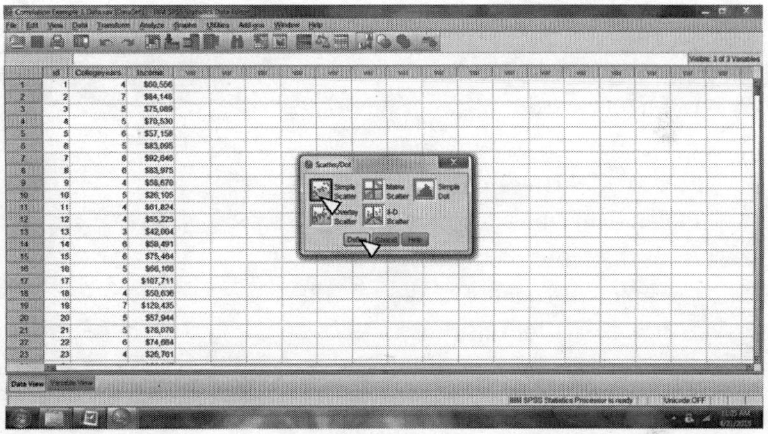

Figure 22.7

Step 6: After the "Simple Scatter Plot" window opens:

- Highlight and place "Income" (outcome variable) in the "Y-Axis" box by clicking the "Arrow" button.
- Place "Years of College" (predictor variable) in the "X-Axis" box. Optionally, a title can be added by clicking the "Title" button.
- Next, click the "OK" button. Output will be generated.

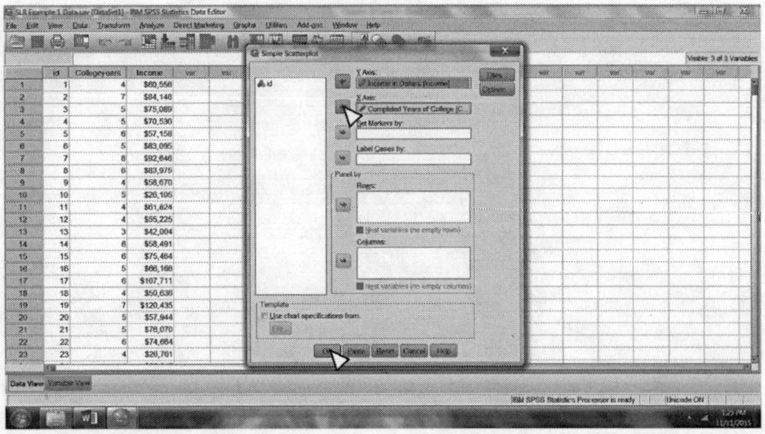

Figure 22.8

Step 7: Assuming that the data meet the pre-analysis screening, we now run SLR.

- Select the "Analyze" tab.
- Highlight "Regression."
- Click "Linear."

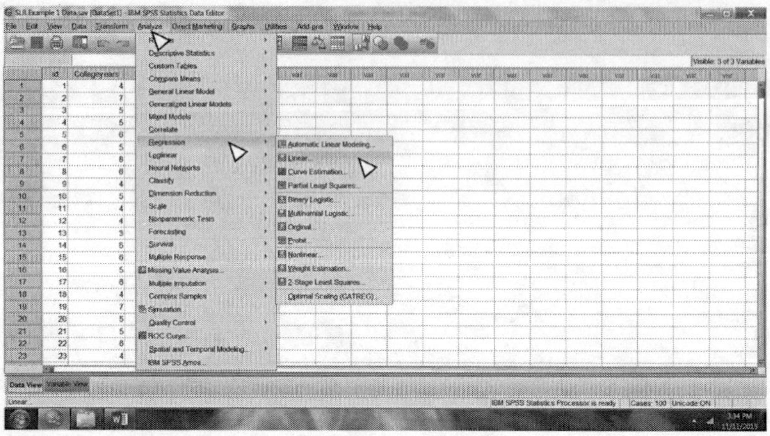

Figure 22.9

Step 8: After the "Linear Regression" opens:

- Highlight "Income" (the outcome or dependent variable) and then click the "Arrow" button for the "Dependent" box.
- Using the same technique, place "Completed Years of College" (the predictor variable) in the "Independent(s)" box.
- Last, click the "Statistics" button on the top-right-hand side of the window.

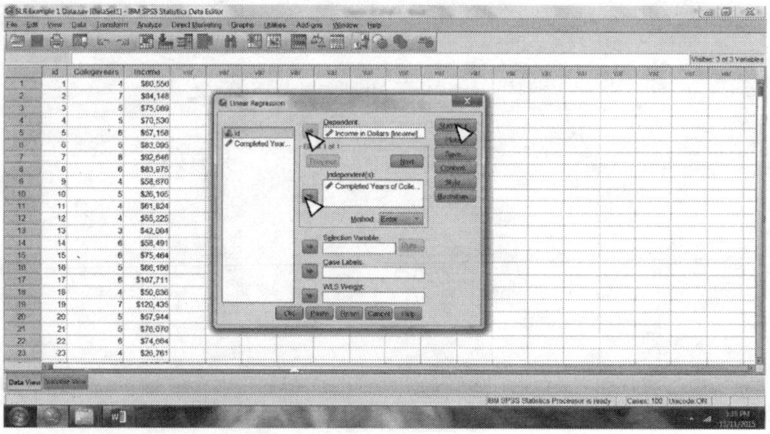

Figure 22.10

Step 9: The "Linear Regression Statistics" window will open.

- Make sure that the following options are checked off: "Estimates," "Confidence intervals," "Level(%): 95," "Model fit," and "Descriptives."
- Next, click the "Continue" button located on the bottom-left-hand corner of the window.
- Last, click the "OK" button located on the bottom-left-hand side of the "Linear Regression" window. Output is generated.

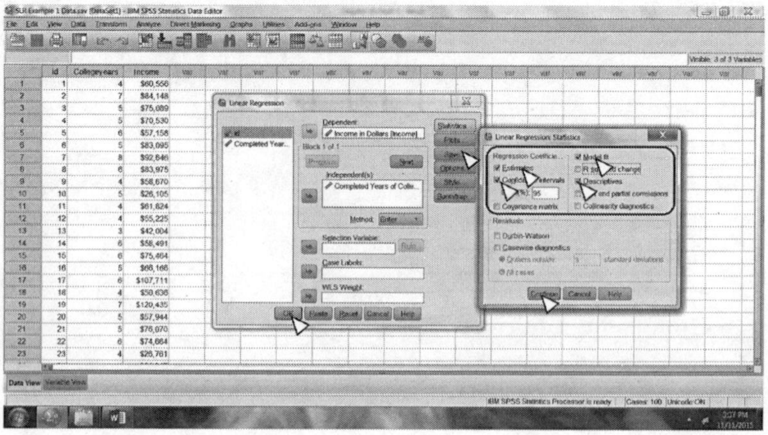

Figure 22.11

It is best to interpret this graph with the actual (regression) prediction equation line running through it. For this, we customize the scatter plot.

Step 10: Go to the output.

- Select the scatter plot where annual income is on the *y*-axis and years of college is on the *x*-axis.
- Right-click onto the scatter plot.
- When the window opens, select "Edit Content" and then "In Separate Window."

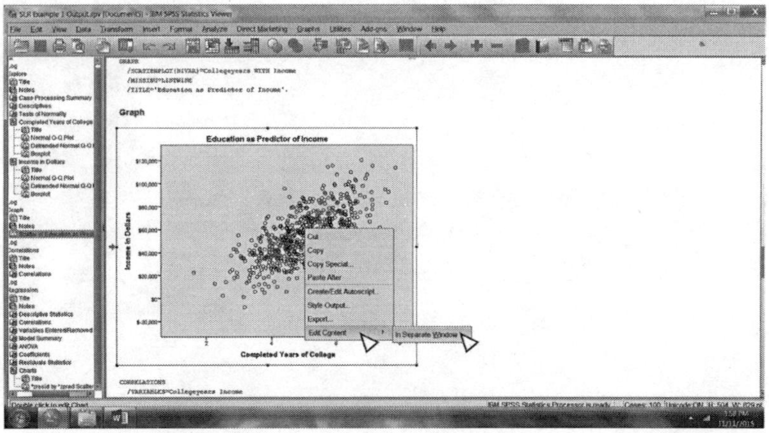

Figure 22.12

Step 11: After the "Chart Editor" window opens, select the "Add a Fit Line at Total" button, as depicted by a diagonal line and dots.

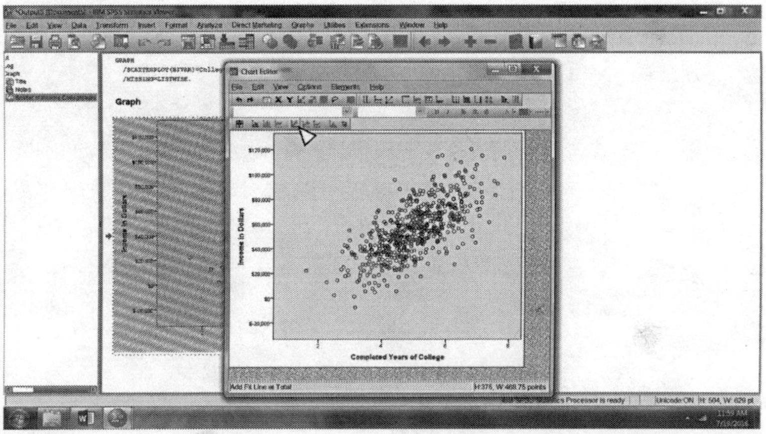

Figure 22.13

The "Properties" box and "Reference Line" tab will emerge. The model equation is located in the "Custom Equation" box.

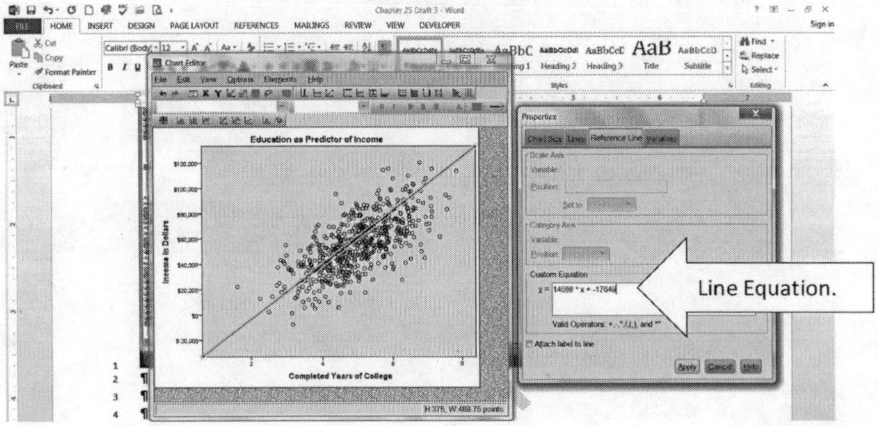

Figure 22.14

The line of best fit, its equation, and *r*-square appear in the bivariate data distribution.

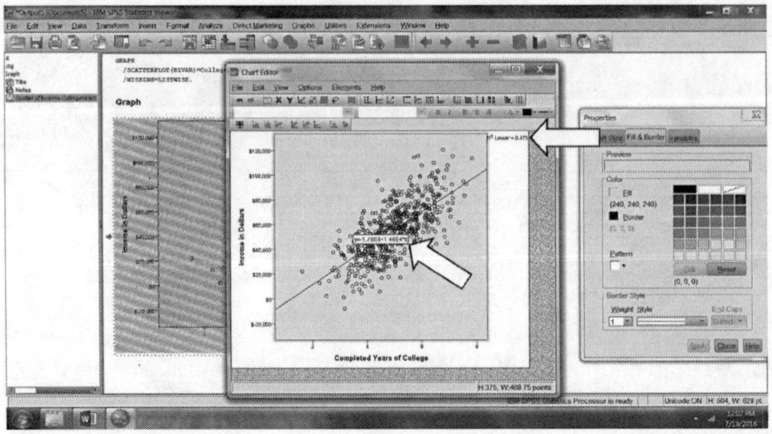

Figure 22.15

Step 12: Close the "Chart Editor" window.

- Click the "File" tab.
- Select the "Close" option.

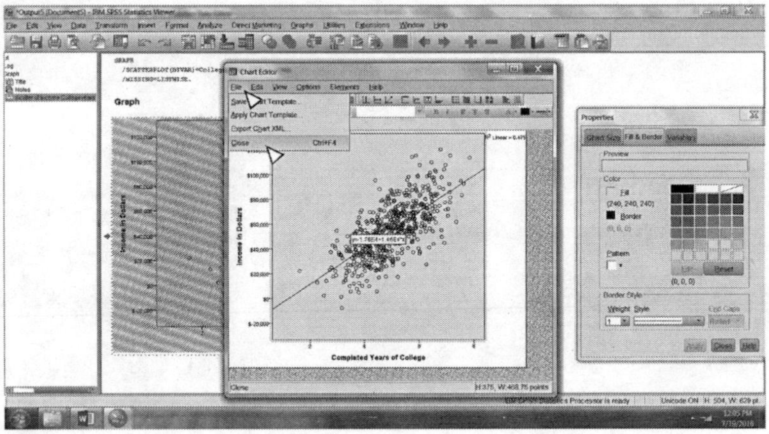

Figure 22.16

The enhanced graph now appears in the output.

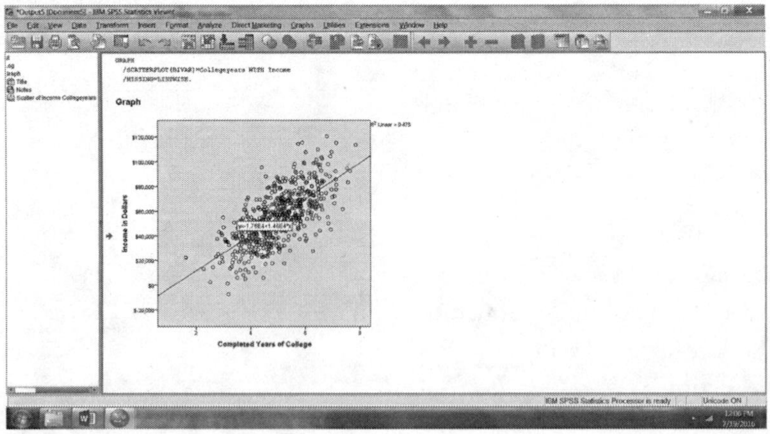

Figure 22.17

Be sure to save the data and output files for your records.

SPSS Output Interpretation

We will focus on the tests for normality table, bivariate distribution graph, ANOVA table, and, if the results are significant, the model summary and coefficients tables will be incorporated in the analysis. Below is a discussion of the output.

Data Screening

The data are numeric and meet the minimum size of over 30. Each case consists of data from a different person.

The Shapiro-Wilk statistic located in the tests for normality table indicates that completed years of college (p = .629) and income in dollars (p = .676) do not violate the normal distribution assumption. Both p-values are greater than alpha, which is .05. The probabilities of these findings being by chance are 62.9% and 67.6%, respectively, both representing nonsignificant results.

Table 22.2

Tests of Normality

	Kolmogorov-Smirnov[a]			Shapiro-Wilk		
	Statistic	df	Sig.	Statistic	df	Sig.
Completed Years of College	.024	575	.200*	.998	575	.629
Income in Dollars	.018	575	.200*	.998	575	.676

*. This is a lower bound of the true significance.

a. Lilliefors Significance Correction

"Sig" denotes a p-value of .629 for College Years and .676 for Income.

Non-normally distributed data increase the likelihood of producing inaccurate results. In the event of such an occurrence, we have a number of options. (1) We can collect more data with the hope that the distribution becomes normal. (2) We can examine the Normal Q-Q Plot derived from the Descriptive/Explore analysis output to identify and possibly remove outliers, which might then give us a fairly normal distribution (see Chapter 12 for a review of this procedure). (3) A data transformation can be implemented to normalize the data. (4) If none of these solutions suffices, include a caveat in the results write-up.

Figure 22.18 illustrates a bivariate normal distribution, including a superimposed oval circle. The distribution is linear as evidenced by visual inspection and the r^2 of 47.5%. Additionally, the joint values concentrate near the line close to where the means of both variables are located in the middle, which suggests a fairly normal distribution. Most of the data form an elliptical-like distribution, indicating homoscedasticity. There are a number of outliers that need to be removed before the analysis continues. Keep in mind, removing outliers yields a better-fitting and more accurate model. In this instance, let us assume that outliers were removed.

The variables meet the assumptions of bivariate normality, linearity, and homoscedasticity. Mathematically and by implication, the residuals meet these assumptions as well. Violations of linearity and homoscedasticity do not invalidate the results, but simply weaken them so that the full "effect" of the predictor on the outcome is not realized.

SLR Analysis

The ANOVA and model summary tables comprise the overall SLR goodness of fit statistics, which essentially is the output produced in correlation analysis. Starting with the ANOVA table, if this test is not significant, then we stop and conclude that there is no significant relationship between the two variables. In this example, the variable years of college and annual income have a significant relationship because $p < .001$. There is a low probability that this result is by chance.

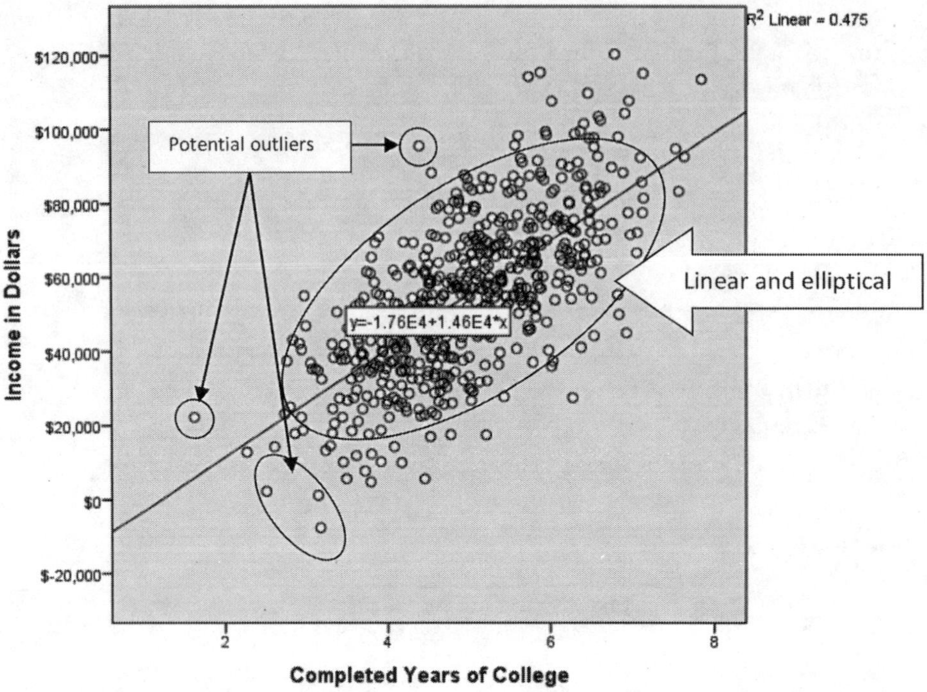

Figure 22.18

Table 22.3

ANOVA[a]

Model		Sum of Squares	df	Mean Square	F	Sig.
1	Regression	1.265E+11	1	1.265E+11	519.058	.000[b]
	Residual	1.396E+11	573	243686856.3		
	Total	2.661E+11	574			

a. Dependent Variable: Income in Dollars
b. Predictors: (Constant), Completed Years of College

Coefficient of determination: 1.265/2.661 = .475 = 47.5% = r^2.

There is less than a .000 probability that the SLR results are not meaningful. This risk is much less than our .05 probability of acceptable risk.

In the model summary table, the "R" is equal to the correlation between the predictor and outcome variables. When reporting, use the lower-case "*r*" for correlation analysis and SLR. In fact, the *r*-square or coefficient of determination are the same for correlation and SLR analyses because both consist of one independent and one dependent variable. In multiple linear regression, the "*r*" related statistics is represented by an upper-case "R" because there are multiple predictors.

The *p*-value in the ANOVA table ($p < .001$) pertains to "R" = .689, indicating that it is significant. The *r*-square is the percentage of variance in the outcome variable that can be explained by the predictor variable. In this case, 47.5% of the variance in annual income can be predicted by years of college completed. In SLR, the adjusted *r*-square corrects for small sample size. Here, they are virtually identical. The adjusted *r*-square can be informative in multiple linear regression, where it takes on additional significance and can be informative during the analysis, as we shall see. Typically, in SLR, the adjusted *r*-square is not reported.

Table 22.4

Model Summary[b]

Model	R	R Square	Adjusted R Square	Std. [illegible] of th[illegible]
1	.689[a]	.475	.474	[illegible]

a. Predictors: (Constant), Completed Years of Colle[illegible]

b. Dependent Variable: Income in Dollars

The r-square is .475 and the Adjusted R Square is .474 both close and thus indicating that the sample size is acceptable.

Table 22.5 is where we part from correlation analysis. This table provides both the unstandardized and standardized coefficients for the prediction model equation. Starting with the unstandardized model, for every year of college completed, annual income increases incrementally, on average, by \$14,598. The "Sig." column is the *p*-value, which is .000 and will always equal the *p*-value of the overall ANOVA *p*-value in the case of SLR because we have one predictor and outcome. The "Constant" item is the *y*-intercept, which is –\$17,649. It sets the initial starting point for the prediction line based on minimizing the residuals. It has no other purpose.

The standardized coefficient provides greater meaning when there is more than one predictor as in the case of multiple linear regression in which it provides the relative contribution of each predictor. It is defined as the change in the outcome variable measured in standard deviation units as a result of a one standard deviation change in the indicated predictor.

The last two columns are the lower and upper bounds of the 95% confidence interval for the independent coefficient. Thus, we are 95% confident that annual income will increase somewhere between \$13,339 and \$15,856 for every completed year of college. This statistic may or may not be reported in the write-up.

Table 22.5

When the predictor is 0, the outcome variable is -\$17,648.

For each one standard deviation in years in college, income increases on average .689 standard deviation.

P = .000 (*p*-value)

We are 95% confidence that each completed year of college increases income from \$13,339 to \$15,856.

Coefficients[a]

Model		Unstandardized Coefficients B	Unstandardized Coefficients Std. Error	Standardized Coefficients Beta	t	Sig.	95.0% Confidence Interval for B Lower Bound	95.0% Confidence Interval for B Upper Bound
1	(Constant)	17648.909	3270.231		-5.397	.00	-24072.011	-11225.807
	Completed Years of College	14598.024	640.746	.689	22.783	.000	13339.526	15856.523

a. Dependent Variable: Income in Dollars

For each 1 year of college, income increases on average by \$14,598.

Note that the standardized coefficient is equal to the correlation. This is so because SLR is a special case of regression where there are only one predictor and one outcome variable.

Reporting Results

Write-Up

A single linear regression was conducted on data collected from 575 participants in order to determine if education predicts income. A statistically meaningful regression equation was found ($F(1,573) = 519.058$, $p < .001$), with an R^2 of .475, indicating that 47.5% of the change in annual income can be explained by the change in years of college completed. Participants' predicted annual income was –$17,648 + $14,598 (Education) when education was measured in completed years of college. The annual income is likely to increase on average by $14,598 for each year of college completed.

Example 22.2: SLR: The Nonsignificant Case

Again, we focus on the tests for normality table, bivariate distribution graph, ANOVA table, and possibly the model summary and coefficients tables.

SPSS Output Interpretation

A random sample of 100 participants were surveyed and asked to report how many days per week they exercised, as well as to what extend they felt well. The purpose of the study is to determine whether days per week spent exercising could predict whether individuals felt well. Alpha = .05. The name of the data file for this example is "SLR Example 2 Data."

The analysis requires two numeric variables: reported days per week exercising and responses to a Likert-type perceived wellness scale (1 = "did not feel well" to 10 = "felt great"). We will skip the SPSS steps because they are identical to the first example.

Variable Data Screening

The data are numeric and we assume that the cases are independent. The sample size is 100.

The Shapiro-Wilk statistic indicates that days per week of exercise ($p = .909$) and reported wellness scores ($p = .135$) do not violate the normal distribution assumption. Both p-values are greater than .05.

Table 22.6

Tests of Normality

	Kolmogorov-Smirnov[a]			Shapiro-Wilk		
	Statistic	df	Sig.	Statistic	df	Sig.
Days/week exercise	.042	100	.200*	.993	100	.909
Reported wellness	.065	100	.200*	.980	100	.135

*. This is a lower bound of the true significance.

a. Lilliefors Significance Correction

However, as illustrated in Figure 22.19, the bivariate distribution displays a weak linear relationship. Only 2.4% of the bivariate data are on the line. The data do not represent an elliptical shape required to meet the homoscedasticity assumption.

Therefore, it is likely that days of exercise per week do not predict feelings of wellness. We will continue the analysis to confirm this conclusion.

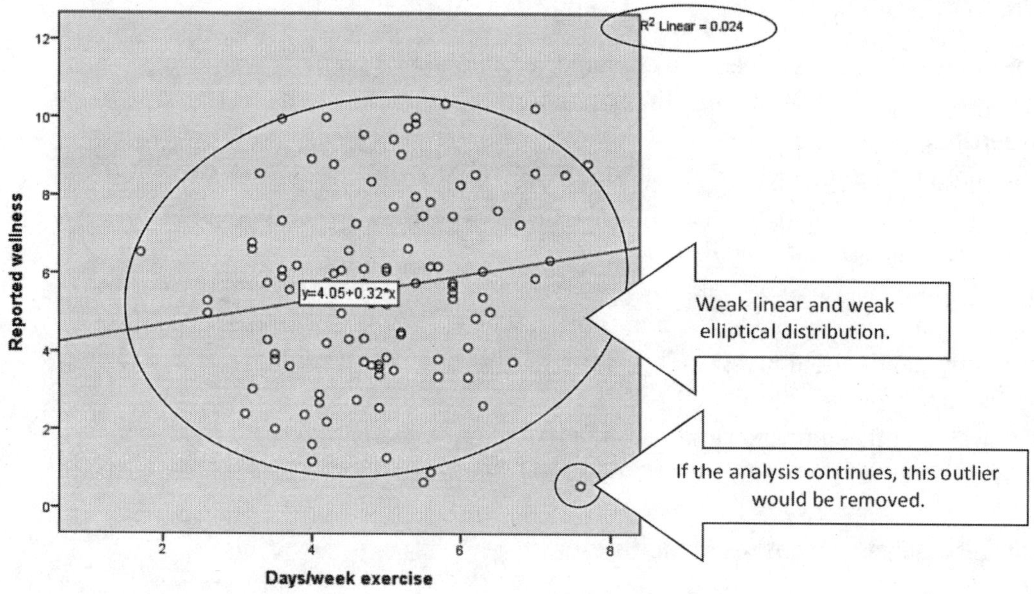

Figure 22.19

SLR Analysis

The ANOVA and model summary tables comprise the overall SLR goodness of fit statistics. Since $p = .125$, there is likely no relationship between exercise and feelings of wellness.

Table 22.7

ANOVA[a]

Model		Sum of Squares	df	Mean Square	F	Sig.
1	Regression	14.116	1	14.116	2.396	.125[b]
	Residual	577.283	98	5.891		
	Total	591.399	99			

a. Dependent Variable: Reported wellness

b. Predictors: (Constant), Days/week exercise

Coefficient of determination: 14.116/577.283 = .024 = 2.4% = r^2.

There is no point to continue because we now have all of the information required to assess and report our findings.

Reporting Results

Write-Up

A single linear regression was conducted on data collected from 100 participants in order to determine if the number of exercise days per week predicts feelings of well-being. No relationship was found between these two variables ($F(1,98) = 2.396$, $p = .125$). Therefore, it is likely that the number of days one exercises does not predict feelings of wellness.

SUMMARY OF KEY CONCEPTS

- SLR is a linear approach to predicting values of a outcome variable from a predictor variable.
- SLR minimizes the error from a line of best fit in order to mathematically express the predictability of a dependent variable.
- Bivariate data points not on the line of best fit contribute to model error.
- Normality, linearity, and homoscedasticity are SLR assumptions applied to each variable, their bivariate distribution, and their residuals.
- The coefficient of determination (the correlation squared or r^2) explains the percentage of the variation in the outcome variable predicted from the predictor.
- From the prediction equation, different specific values of the outcome variable can be predicted from the independent variable.
- The *y*-intercept is the value of the outcome variable when the predictor equals zero. It orients the line of best fit.
- Running SLR in SPSS is straightforward.
- Reporting significant and nonsignificant results are simple.

SINGLE LINEAR REGRESSION APPLIED EXERCISES

22.1 Generally, what is the purpose of single linear regression?

22.2 What is the prediction model in single linear regression?

22.3 What is extrapolation?

22.4 In general terms, define regression coefficient.

22.5 What is a beta?

22.6 What is an unstandardized beta (b)?

22.7 What is a standardized beta (β)?

22.8 What is the *y*-intercept (b_0)?

22.9 What is the slope in a linear regression equation?

22.10 Generally, what is the adjusted r^2?

22.11 Generally, what is the residual in SLR?

22.12 How do the independent and dependent variables relate to the predictor and outcome variables?

22.13 In SLR, why is the r^2 the same as would be the correlation squared of the same two variables?

22.14 What does SLR offer that is not provided by correlation analysis?

22.15 What are the general assumptions about SLR?

22.16 Can data not be correlated and yet meet the error assumptions of normal distribution, linearity, and homoscedasticity?

22.17 What is a predictor (variable)?

22.18 What is an outcome (variable)?

22.19 A random sample of 40 architects' records were examined in order to determine whether years of professional architecture experience predicts the square footage of building projects awarded to an architect. Run an SLR to discover if such a relationship exists.

Explain your answer. Report results in the format provided in this chapter. Alpha = .05. The name of the data file for this example is "SLR Exercise 1 Data."

22.20 Reported cases of diseases and healthcare funding data were collected for the 50 largest designated market areas in the United States. The aim of the study is to determine whether healthcare funding per 100 people predicts reported cases of diseases per 10,000 people. Explain your answer. Report results in the format provided in this chapter. Alpha = .05. The name of the data file for this example is "SLR Exercise 2 Data."

22.21 A marketing research firm was charged to determine the predictability of advertising expenditures on sales in the home healthcare field. Two hundred and sixty-five members of a national trade association agreed to have their data released to the research firm. To what extent does advertising predict sales? Explain your answer. Report results in the format provided in this chapter. Alpha = .05. The name of the data file for this example is "SLR Exercise 3 Data."

22.22 A company wishes to determine whether 265 employees' perceptions of their sense of control at work predicts how much time they spend going online at work for personal reasons. Control was measured using a self-determination theory instrument (perceived autonomy survey) and the online behavior data was providing by the IT department, which linked non-work activity to user by login credentials. Online activities were measured in hours per week. Control was self-reported using an online sliding bar scale ranging from 1 = "I have no control over what I do at work" to 7 = "I control all of what I do at work." Does a sense of control over one's work predict amount of time spent online for personal use at work? Explain your answer. Report results in the format provided in this chapter. Alpha = .05. The name of the data file for this example is "SLR Exercise 4 Data."

Chapter 23

Multiple Linear Regression

LEARNING OBJECTIVES

To be able to:

- understand the purpose and describe what is standard multiple linear regression (MLR);
- describe the idea behind MLR;
- understand the basic assumptions of MLR and how to assess them;
- describe the data screening process;
- understand and explain the components of a linear prediction equation and how they relate to the line of best fit and explained variance;
- learn how to interpret MLR results, including the adjusted R^2;
- understand how to determine values of the outcome variable from values of the predictor variable;
- learn how to run MLR in SPSS; and
- interpret and report significant and nonsignificant results in an easily understood manner.

23.1 Introduction to Multiple Linear Regression

In Chapter 22, we discussed single linear regression, in which we examined how an independent variable can predict or estimate values of a dependent variable. Much of what is covered in Chapter 22 applies to **multiple linear regression (MLR)** as well. So, what is MLR? It extends SLR to more than one predictor variable. MLR estimates the value or variance in the outcome variable from two or more predictors in the same model ($X_1 + Xk$). Often MLR allows us to explain more variation in the outcome variable because we incorporate more information owing to more than one predictor. For instance, we might examine if education, professional experience, and height predict annual income. We might study whether the age of machine operators, the age of their equipment, and whether the equipment is analog or digital predict productivity or number of defective parts per shift. Like single linear regression, MLR helps us determine whether the changes between the predictor and outcome variables are consistent across bivariate data points so that they maintain the same relationship.

23.2 Prediction Model

The prediction model follows the least squares method of regression, in which the error associated with the bivariate data points not on the line of best fit are minimized. Using this approach, and as illustrated in the equation below, the values of each predictor are multiplied by their individual slopes and then the products are added to the *y*-intercept, resulting in a predicted outcome variable value given the assigned value to each predictor (X_{1-ki}). In SPSS, the individual contribution of all of the predictors on the outcome variable are tallied to produce the overall statistics, as well as the individual predictor statistics. *P*-values for the overall test (overall *F*-test), as well as for the contribution of each predictor variable, are reported in the output:

$$Y_i = b_0 + b_1X_{1i} + b_2X_{2i} + b_3X_{3i} + \ldots + b_kX_{ki}$$

where

Y_i = *Y*, the specific predicted value of the outcome variable when the predictor variables take on specific values, *i*

b_0 = *Y*-intercept, which is the value of the outcome variable when the predictor variables are 0

b_1 = the slope of the line of best fit, which is the predicted unit amount of incremental change in the outcome variable as a result of a one-unit change (as measured) in the predictor variable, not considering variables $X_2, X_3, \ldots X_k$

b_2 = the slope of the line of best fit, which is the predicted unit amount of incremental change in the outcome variable as a result of a one-unit change (as measured) in the predictor variable, not considering $X_1, X_3, \ldots X_k$

b_3 = the slope of the line of best fit, which is the predicted unit amount of incremental change in the outcome variable as a result of a one-unit change (as measured) in the predictor variable, not considering $X_1, X_2, \ldots X_k$

b_k = the slope of the line of best fit, which is the predicted unit amount of incremental change in the outcome variable as a result of a one-unit change (as measured) in the predictor variable, not considering $X_1, X_2, X_3, \ldots X_{k-1}$

X_{ki} = additional predictor variable(s) for which there is a corresponding predicted outcome variable value(s) (Y_i), not considering other predictors

The effect of each predictor is measured alone. For example, let us assume that house price is predicted by the size and the age of the house, and that the *y*-intercept is zero. Each square foot of the house increases price on average by $200 and each year of house age decreases price on average by $500. For a 1,000 square foot home, the unique size contribution to price is $200,000. The unique contribution to price from house age depends on the age in years. Thus, given a 1,000 square foot home, a house that is 10 years old reduces the price by $5,000 so that the price now becomes $195,000. A 20-year-old house price decreases by $10,000 so that the price now becomes $190,000 for a 1,000 square foot house. Each predictor estimate focuses on its unique contribution to house price. The net effect of age on house price remains the same whether the house is 1,000 or 2,000 square feet. The price of a 2,000 square foot home that is 10 years old is (2,000 × $200) – (10 × $500) = $400,000 – $5,000 = $395,000. A 10-year-old house loses $5,000 in value no matter what the size of the house. Each predictor is independent of the other. Additionally, as covered in Chapter 22, the standardized regression coefficients allow us see the relative influence of the predictor variables on the outcome variable. SPSS reports unstandardized and standardized regression coefficients.

R-Square and Adjusted *R*-Square

The *R*-square ($\boldsymbol{R^2}$) is the **coefficient of multiple determination**, which is the percentage of variation in the outcome variable explained by the set of predictors in the model. The outcome is determined by multiple predictors. The overall *F*-test *p*-value pertains to the statistical significance level of the R^2, as well as the overall prediction model fit. These concepts are covered in the Examples section.

The adjusted *R*-square (R^2_{adj}) accounts for the contribution of each predictor and sample size. The R^2_{adj} can never be greater than R^2. It is deployed mostly as a diagnostic tool in order to develop an optimal prediction model. Predictors that do not make a meaningful contribution to the prediction model and/or an insufficiently small sample size can lower the R^2_{adj}. Typically, it is not reported.

REAL WORLD SNAPSHOT

In a 2014 article published in *Communication Research* entitled "The Relationships among Girls' Prosocial Video Gaming, Perspective-Taking, Sympathy, and Thoughts about Violence," Vieira used multiple linear regression to examine whether prosocial video games that promote social values and behaviors predict young girls' acceptance about certain types of violence.

In this study of 145 girls, ages 7–15, exposure to prosocial video games predicted greater empathy and sympathy toward others ($p < .001$). Less severe acts of violence prompted girls to consider the perpetrator's perspective as well, whereas severe violent actions left no room to consider the perpetrator's position and were summarily perceived as wrong. Further, the findings imply that it is easier to convince someone to do things that help others rather than to persuade someone to do something violent. In short, the results suggest that relationships exist among prosocial gaming exposure, empathy, sympathy, and assessments about various violent acts that vary by severity.

Ask yourself: What role might a girl's age play in this process? Do you think that "justified" violence might be more tolerable than violence for no apparent reason?

23.3 Data Assumptions

MLR assumptions are similar to SLR. The difference is that MLR incorporates more than one predictor variable. The same screening must be conducted for each predictor in conjunction with the outcome variable and, by extension, residuals.

- The data are numeric.
- The sample size is over 30.
- The data are independent so that they come from different sampling elements.
- Each variable is approximately normally distributed.
- There is a linear relationship between each predictor and the outcome variable.
- The joint coordinates are approximately normally distributed (bivariate normal) so that the data are homoscedastic for each predictor and the outcome variable.
- Residuals (error) are normally distributed, linear, and homoscedastic between each predictor and the outcome variable.

If the univariate and bivariate assumptions are met, it is likely that the residuals' assumptions will also be met. Therefore, the result of the variable screening serve as the basis for the residual analysis.

23.4 Examples Using SPSS: Step-by-Step Instructions

SPSS offers a number of approaches for how the predictors are calculated using the least squares method. The "Enter" option provides simultaneous or standard regression in which all predictors are processed simultaneously. There are other methods, such as stepwise and hierarchical, each with various options. Appendix G briefly discusses these approaches. The examples below use the "Enter" option.

Example 23.1: Multiple Linear Regression: The Significant Case

Three hundred and eighty-three adult clients from a local inner-city free mental health clinic agreed to release some of their records in an attempt to discover which variables contribute to whether individuals maintain long-term (over one year) therapy for chronic depression. The outcome variable is the number of annual therapy visits. The predictors are: (1) distance in miles to the clinic; (2) the initial assessment of depression severity based on a 10-point scale where 1 = least severe to 10 = most severe; and (3) self-perception of a support network formatted as 1 = no support to 10 = a great deal of support. Determine whether these variables predict the number of client visits per year to the clinic. Alpha = .05. The name of the data file for this example is "MLR Example 1 Data."

The following are the basic steps.

Step 1: Open SPSS.

Locate the appropriate folder and data file, then highlight it. Next, click the "Open" button.

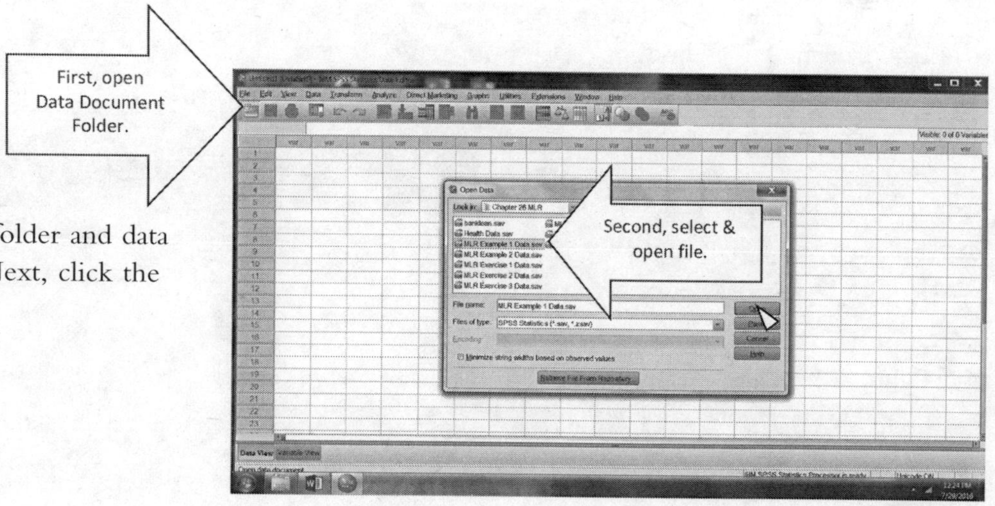

Figure 23.1

Step 2: After the data file opens, we will screen the data for normal distribution.

- Select the "Analyze" tab.
- Highlight "Descriptive Statistics."
- Click "Explore."

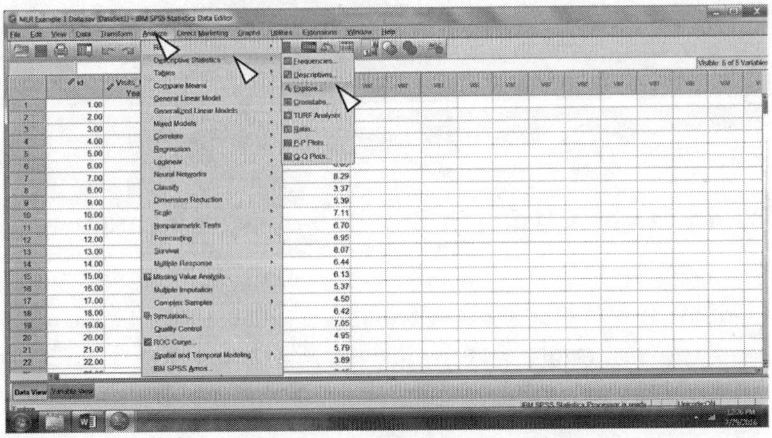

Figure 23.2

Step 3: After the "Explore" window opens:

- Highlight the "Miles to Clinic," "Initial Severity," and "Support Network" variables and place them in the "Dependent List" box by clicking the "Arrow" button.
- Click the "Plots" button.
- In the "Explore: Plots" window:
  - Only check "None" in the box plot area.
  - Below that, check "Normality plots with tests."
  - Click the "Continue" button.
- Last, click the "OK" button. Output is generated.

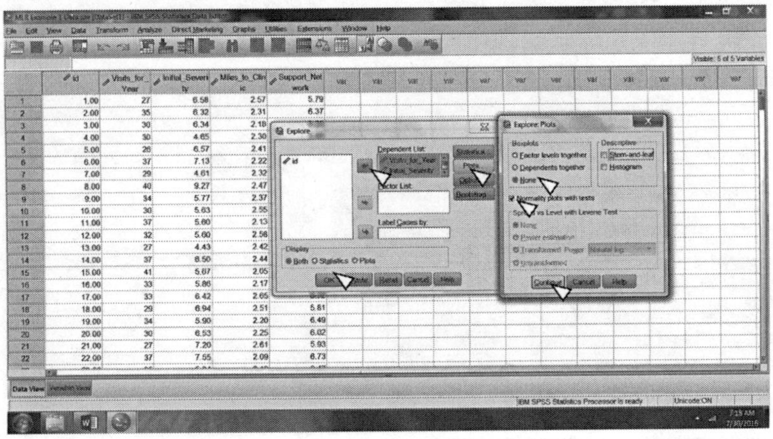

Figure 23.3

Step 4: Next, we will examine for linearity and homoscedasticity.

- Select the "Graph" tab.
- Highlight "Legacy Dialogs."
- Click "Scatter/Dot."

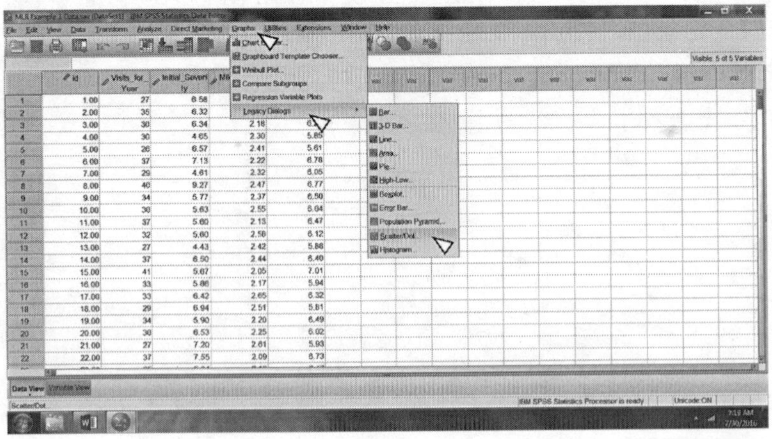

Figure 23.4

Step 5: The "Scatter/Dot" window will open.

- Select the "Simple Scatter" option.
- Click the "Define" button.

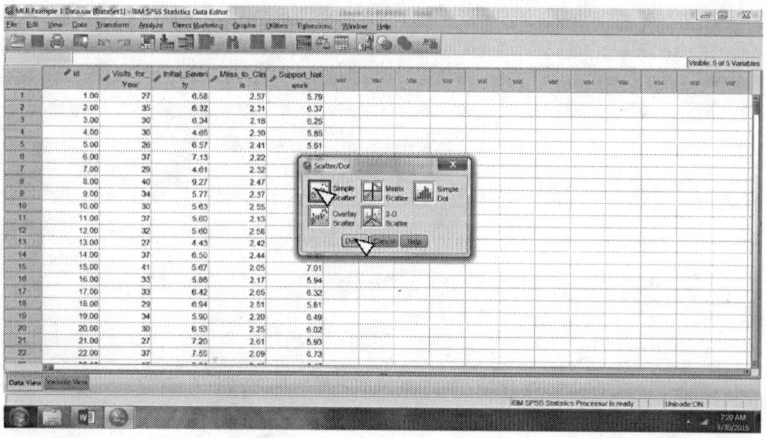

Figure 23.5

Step 6: After the "Single Scatterplot" window opens:

- Assign "Visits for Year" (outcome variable) to the "Y-Axis" box by highlighting it and then clicking the arrow button for the corresponding box.
- Assign "Initial Severity" (one of the predictor variables) to the "X-Axis" box. Optionally, a title can be added by clicking the "Title" button.
- Click the "OK" button. Output will be generated.

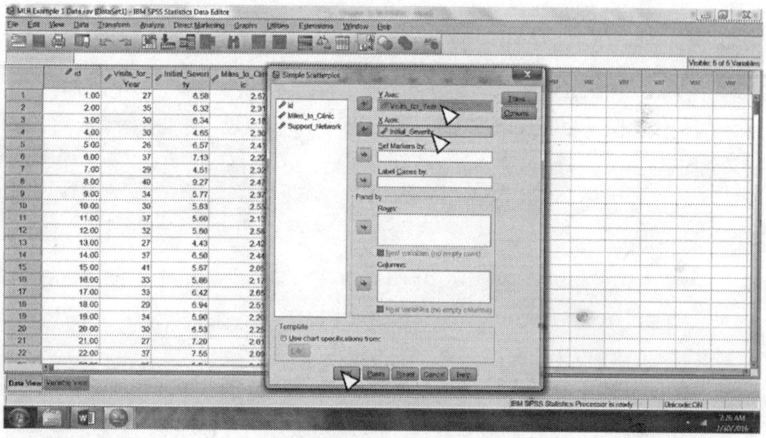

Figure 23.6

Step 7: Repeat the procedure by replacing the "Initial Severity" variable with the "Miles to Clinic" variable.

- Deselect "Initial Severity" by clicking the "Arrow" button and returning it to the variable list box on the left side of the window.
- Assign "Miles to Clinic" (the other predictor variable) to the "X-Axis" box.
- Click the "OK" button. Output will be generated.

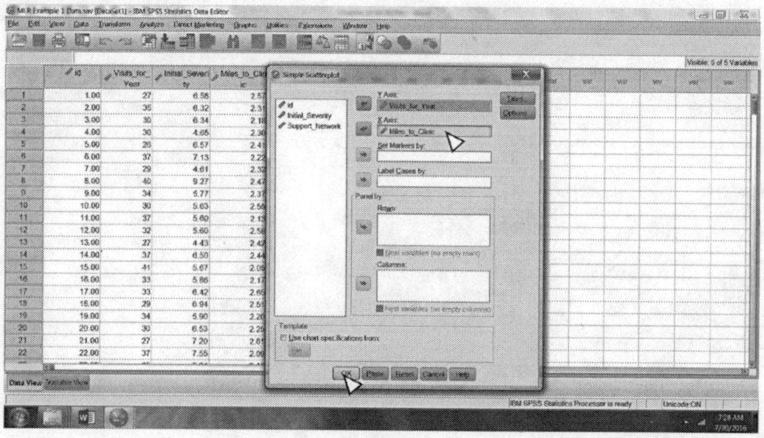

Figure 23.7

Follow the same procedure for the predictor "Support Network." Some statisticians would examine the data before proceeding to the regression analysis.

Step 8: To run MLR, do the following:

- Select the "Analyze" tab.
- Highlight "Regression."
- Select "Linear."

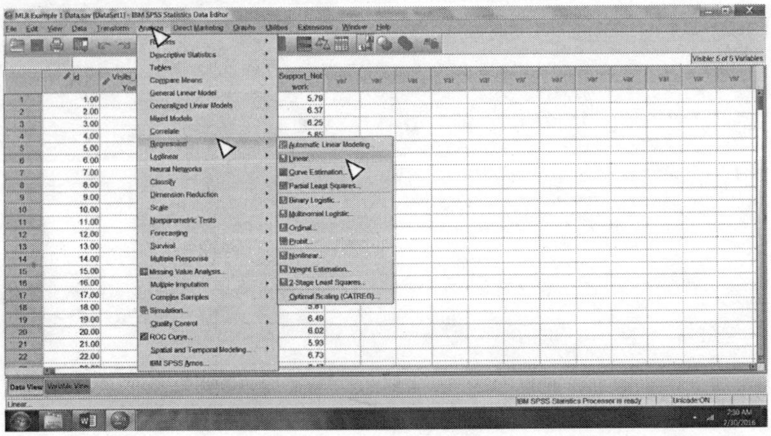

Figure 23.8

Step 9: After the "Linear Regression" window opens:

- Highlight "Visits for Year" (the outcome variable) and then click the "Arrow" button for the "Dependent" box.
- Using the same technique, place "Initial Severity," "Miles to Clinic," and "Support Network" in the "Independent(s)" box. We will leave the "Method: Enter" option unchanged, which will run all variables simultaneously.
- Last, click the "Statistics" button on the top-right-hand side of the window.

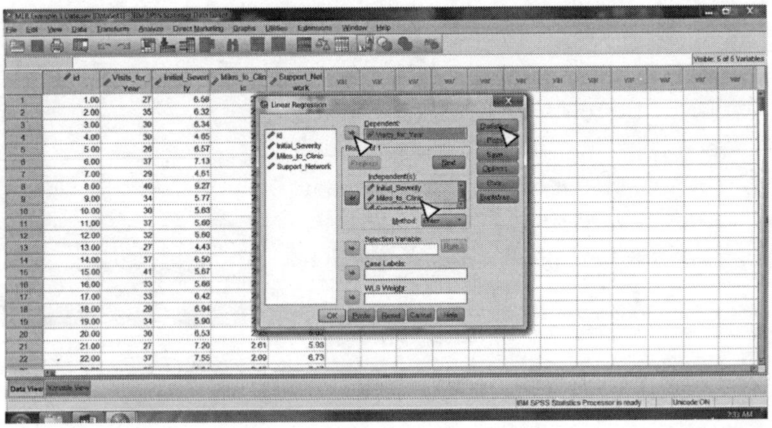

Figure 23.9

Step 10: After the "Linear Regression Statistics" window opens:

- Make sure that the following options are checked off: "Estimates," "Confidence intervals Level (%): 95," "Model fit," and "Descriptives."
- Next, click the "Continue" button located on the bottom-left-hand corner of the window.
- Last, select the "Plots" button located on the right-hand side of the "Linear Regression" window.

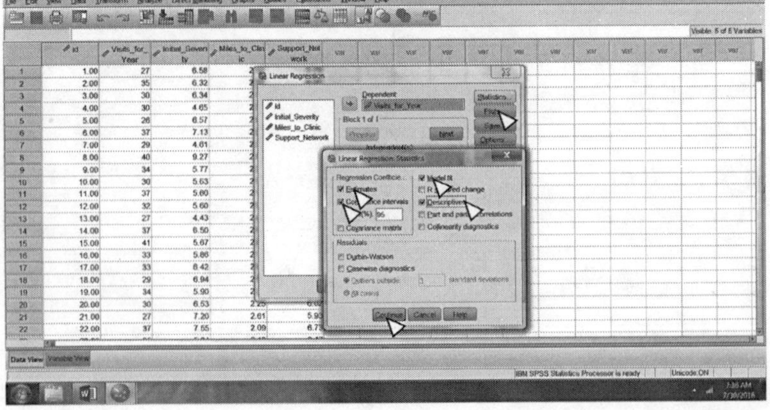

Figure 23.10

The graphs should be prepared following the procedures described in Steps 10–12 of Chapter 22 so that each graph displays its line of best fit and *r*-square.

SPSS Output Interpretation

We ran a **standard or simultaneous linear regression** where all predictor variables are run at once. The relevant output results are located in the tests for normality table, joint distribution (Visits for Year with Initial Severity, Miles to Clinic, and Support Network) graphs, ANOVA table, and, if findings are statistically meaningful, the model summary and coefficients tables. Below is a discussion of the output.

Data Screening

The data are numeric. Second, we assume that the cases are independent because each case consists of data from different customers. The sample size is 99.

The Shapiro-Wilk statistic located in the tests for normality table indicates that Visits for Year (p = .130), Initial Severity (p = .248), Miles to Clinic (p = .494) and Support Network (p = .619) do not violate the normal distribution assumption. The p-values are greater than alpha, which is .05. The probabilities of these findings being by chance are 13.0%, 24.8%, 49.4% respectively, and 61.9%, which are relatively high, and thus represent nonsignificant results.

Table 23.1

Tests of Normality

	Kolmogorov-Smirnov[a]			Shapiro-Wilk		
	Statistic	df	Sig.	Statistic	df	Sig.
Visits_for_Year	.057	383	.005	.994	383	.130
Initial_Severity	.028	383	.200*	.995	383	.248
Miles_to_Clinic	.033	383	.200*	.996	383	.494
Support_Network	.029	383	.200*	.997	383	.619

*. This is a lower bound of the true significance.

a. Lilliefors Significance Correction

"Sig" denotes the *p*-values of the four variables.

Had any variable not met the normality assumption, there are a number of corrective options, as discussed in Chapter 12.

Figure 23.11 illustrates the bivariate distributions along with the line of best fit and superimposed oval circle for the outcome variable with each predictor. The distributions are linear, as evidenced by visual inspection and the r^2's relative to Visits for Year, which is 29.0% for Initial Severity, 13.0% for Miles to Clinic, and 90.1% for Support Network. Additionally, the bivariate data points concentrate near the line close to where the means of the variables are located in the middle. This indicates bivariate normal distributions. In the three cases, most of the data form an elliptical-like distribution, indicating homoscedasticity. Should outliers be identified, they would be removed before the analysis continues. Keep in mind, removing outliers yields a better-fitting and thus more accurate model (see Appendix G).

Since the variables meet the assumptions of normality, linearity, and homoscedasticity, mathematically the residuals meet these assumptions as well. Violations of linearity and homoscedasticity do not invalidate the results, but simply weaken them so that the full "effect" of the predictors on the outcome is not realized.

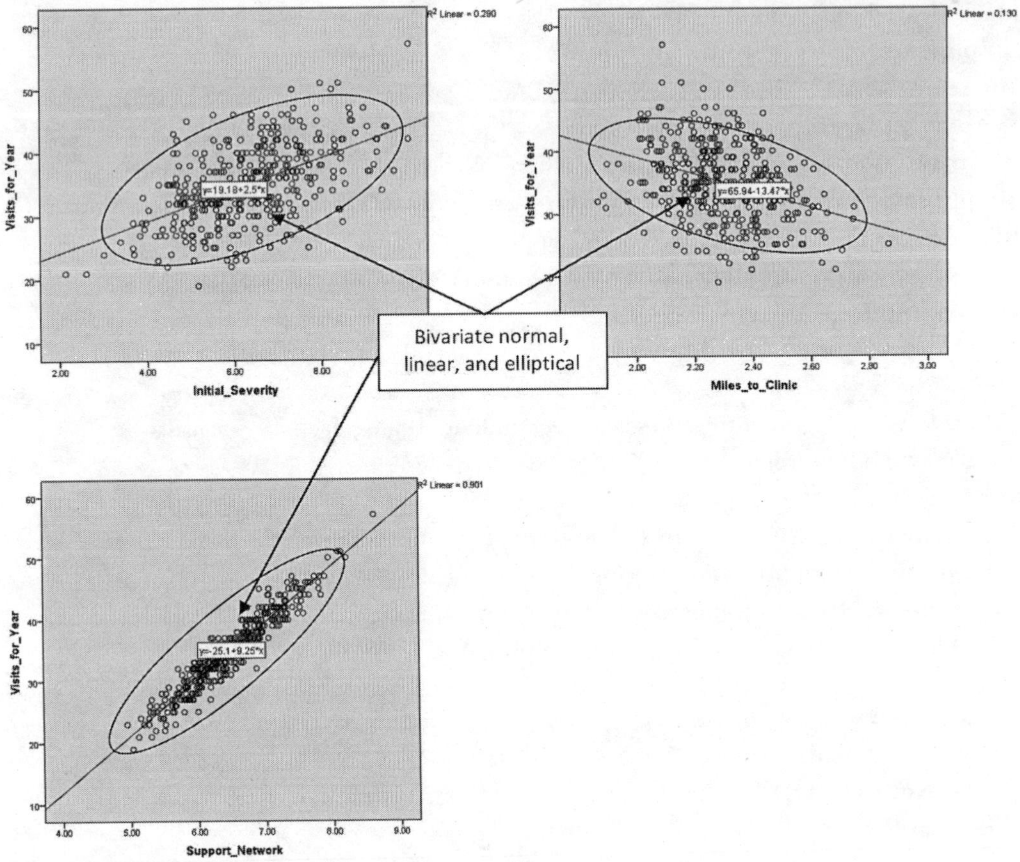

Figures 23.11

MLR Analysis

The ANOVA and model summary tables comprise the overall MLR goodness of fit statistics. It is how well the prediction line fits the data. The line is calculated in order to minimize the distances of points not on the line.

The ANOVA table is our starting point. If this test is not significant, then we stop and conclude that there is no statistically significant relationship between the predictors and the outcome variable. In this example, the predictors are initial severity of diagnosis, miles to clinic, and degree of supportive network. As we can see in the last column, there is a significant relationship because the *p*-value is .000. This indicates that there is a less than 1/1,000 probability that our results are by chance, which is less our acceptable .05 of probability risk. It is likely that at least one of the three independent variables significantly predicts number of clinic visits.

Table 23.2

ANOVA[a]

Model		Sum of Squares	df	Mean Square	F	Sig.
1	Regression	12713.655	3	4237.885	1225.792	.000[b]
	Residual	1310.303	379	3.457		
	Total	14023.958	382			

a. Dependent Variable: Visits_for_Year

b. Predictors: (Constant), Support_Network, Miles_to_Clinic, Initial_Severity

There is less than a .000 probability that the MLR results are by chance. This risk is much less than our .05 probability of acceptable risk.

Table 23.3 is the model summary information. In MLR, the "R" is equal to the total correlation between all of the predictors and the outcome variable. It is in upper case because there is more than one predictor. The *p*-value in the ANOVA table pertains to the three "R" statistics, which are .952, .907, and .906, indicating that they are significant. Ninety point seven percent of the variation in number of clinic visits are predicted by initial severity assessment, miles needed to travel to clinic, and degree of support network. The *R*-square and the adjusted *R*-square are very close, indicating that the predictors and sample size sufficiently contribute to the model.

Table 23.3

The R Square is .907 and the Adjusted R Square is .906 both are close and thus indicate that the number of predictors and sample size are optimal.

Model Summary

R	R Square	Adjusted R Square	Std. Error of the Estimate
.952[a]	.907	.906	1.859

dictors: (Constant), Support_Network, Miles_to_Clinic, nitial_Severity

Table 23.4 provides both the unstandardized and standardized regression coefficients for the prediction model equation. The effects are estimates or average variation in the outcome variable per predictor. As we shall see, some relationships may be negative, in which case the outcome and predictors move in opposite directions—one increases and the other decreases.

Starting with the unstandardized model, for every 1 point out of 10 in the initial severity assessment, the average number of clinic visits increases by .309 for the given year. For every mile traveled to visit the clinic, the average number of yearly visits decreases by 2.546. Last, for degree of support network as measured using a 10-point scale, the average number of annual visits increases by 8.686 for each reported point of support. The "Sig." column is the *p*-value for each predictor, which is .000 in each case. The "Constant" item is the *y*-intercept, which is −17.534. It sets the initial starting point for the prediction line based on minimizing the residual. It serves no other purpose. Its *p*-value has no meaning.

The standardized coefficients provide the relative contribution in standardized scores so that predictors can be compared along the same lines. They are defined as the change in the outcome variable measured in standard deviation units as a result of a one standard deviation change in the predictor.

The last two columns are the lower and upper bounds of the 95% confidence interval for the predictor coefficients. Thus, we are 95% confident that the annual number of clinic visits increase between .133 and .485 for initial severity per point. We are 95% confident that the number of annual clinic visits decrease from 1.278 to 3.814 for each travel mile required to reach the clinic. Finally, we are 95% confident that annual clinic visits will increase from 8.295 to 9.077 for each reported point in support network.

The support network variable is the key driver for number of annual visits. Perhaps a client's social network provides a supportive role that facilitates continued therapy on the part of the individual.

Table 23.4

For each one standard deviation in initial severity, the number of clinic visits increases by a .067 standard deviation.

For each 1 point of severity score, the number of clinic visits increases by .309.

For each one standard deviation in miles traveled to the clinic, the number of clinic visits decreases by a .068 standard deviation.

$P \leqslant .001$ (*p*-values).

We are 95% confidence that each point of initial severity, increases clinic visits from .133 to .485.

Coefficients[a]

Model		Unstandardized Coefficients		Standardized Coefficients			95.0% Confidence Interval for B	
		B	Std. Error	Beta	t	Sig.	Lower Bound	Upper Bound
1	(Constant)	-17.534	2.118		-8.278	.000	-21.698	-13.369
	Initial_Severity	.309	.089	.067	3.457	.001	.133	.485
	Miles_to_Clinic	-2.546	.645	-.068	-3.949	.000	-3.814	-1.278
	Support_Network	8.686	.199	.891	43.673	.000	8.295	9.077

a. Dependent Variable: Visits_for_Year

For each 1 mile commute to the clinic, the number of clinic visits decreases by 2.546.

For each 1 point representing increased social support, the number of clinic visits increases by 8.686.

For each one standard deviation in support network, the number of clinic visits increases by a .891 standard deviation.

We are 95% confidence that each mile needed to reach the clinic, decreases visits from 1.278 to 3.814.

We are 95% confidence that each support network point, increases visits from 8.295 to 9.077.

Reporting Results

Write-Up

A standard multiple linear regression was conducted on data collected from 383 clients in order to determine if the initial severity of clinical diagnosis, miles required to reach the mental health clinic regularly, and degree of personal support network explain the annual number of clinic visits. A statistically meaningful regression equation was found ($F(3,379) = 1{,}225.792$, $p < .001$), with an R^2 of .907 indicating that 90.7% of the variation in annual clinic visits can be predicted by the three variables. Predicted annual clinic visits was −17.534 + .309 (severity assessment) −2.546 (miles traveled to clinic) + 8.686 (degree of support network). It is likely that the average annual clinic visit increases .309 for each point of severity, decreases 2.546 for each mile traveled to the clinic, and increases 8.686 for each point of support network.

Example 23.2: Multiple Linear Regression: The Nonsignificant Case

A random sample of 525 participants were surveyed online and asked to report their level of optimism, motivation, feelings of helplessness, years of college completed, and income. The purpose of the study was to determine whether motivation, feelings of helplessness, years of college completed, and income predict perceptions of optimism. Alpha = .05. The name of the data file for this example is "MLR Example 2 Data."

Years of college was reported as years completed. Income was reported in dollars. Optimism and feelings of helplessness were reported on a 10-point sliding bar scale ranging from 0 = "I do not feel optimistic" or "I do not feel helpless at all" to 9 = "I am highly optimistic" or "I feel totally helpless," respectively. The level of general motivation was reported on a sliding bar scale from 1 to 9 from no motivation to highly motivated, respectively. The sliding bar allowed responses to two places to the right of the decimal point.

We will skip the SPSS steps because they are identical to the first example.

SPSS Output Interpretation

Again, the relevant output results are located in the tests for normality table, bivariate distribution (Optimism on Helplessness, Motivation, Years of College, and Income) graphs, ANOVA table, and, if findings are significant, the model summary and coefficients tables will be consulted.

Data Screening

The data are numeric. Second, each case consists of data from different participants, and are thus independent. The sample size is 525.

The tests for normality table indicates the Shapiro-Wilk statistic for the five variables. It is likely that the distributions do not violate the normal distribution assumption because Years of College (p = .383), Income (p = .491), Optimism (p = .092), Helplessness (p = .459), and Motivation (p = .862) are not significant.

Table 23.5

Tests of Normality

	Kolmogorov-Smirnov[a]			Shapiro-Wilk		
	Statistic	df	Sig.	Statistic	df	Sig.
Collegeyears	.041	525	.037	.997	525	.383
Income	.035	525	.168	.997	525	.491
Optimism	.028	525	.200*	.995	525	.092
Helplessness	.038	525	.069	.997	525	.459
Motivation	.023	525	.200*	.998	525	.862

*. This is a lower bound of the true significance.

a. Lilliefors Significance Correction

Figures 23.12–23.15 illustrate the bivariate distributions along with the line of best fit, r-squares, and superimposed circle for the outcome variable with each predictor. The distributions are not linear, as evidenced by visual inspection and the r^2's, which are essentially nonexistent. Additionally, the bivariate data points display somewhat of a concentration near the middle of line, indicating approximate bivariate normality, which is consistent with the Shapiro-Wilk statistics. In the four scatter plots, the distributions do not meet linearity and homoscedasticity. It is likely that MLR will not be significant. However, we will continue with the analysis.

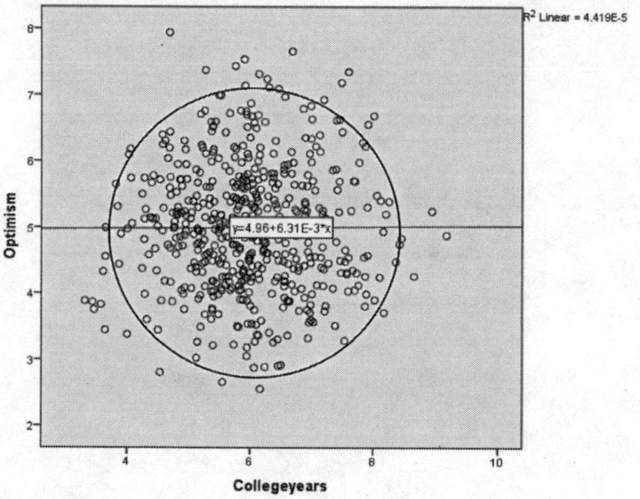

Figure 23.12

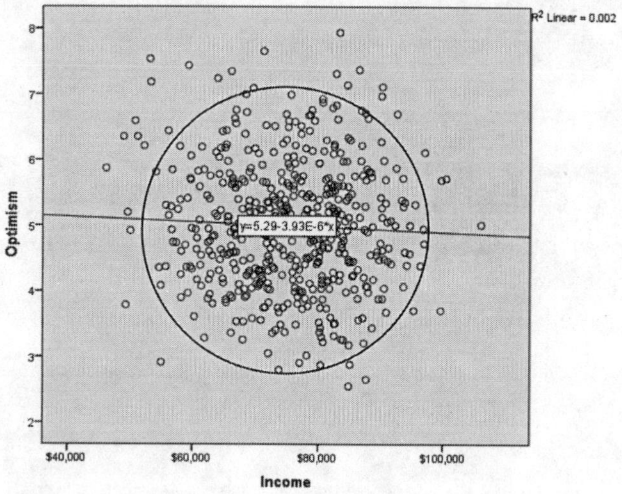

Figure 23.13

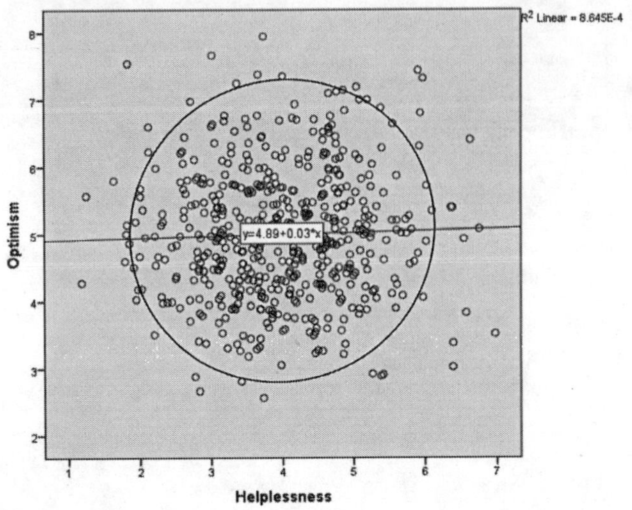

Figure 23.14

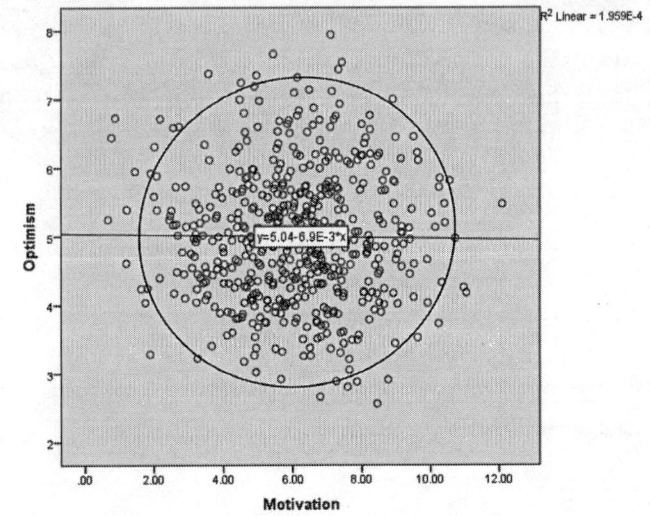

Figure 23.15

MLR Analysis

As we can see in the last column, there is no significant relationship between the predictors and the outcome variable because $p = .810$.

Table 23.6

ANOVA[a]

Model		Sum of Squares	df	Mean Square	F	Sig.
1	Regression	1.486	4	.371	.398	.810[b]
	Residual	485.291	520	.933		
	Total	486.777	524			

a. Dependent Variable: Optimism

b. Predictors: (Constant), Motivation, Collegeyears, Income, Helplessness

At this point, we stop and conclude that there is likely no relationship between the predictors and the outcome variable.

Reporting Results

Write-Up

A standard linear regression was conducted on data collected from 525 survey participants in order to determine whether helplessness, motivation, years of college, and income predict level of optimism. No relationships were found ($F(4,520) = .398$, $p = .810$). It is likely that these predictors do not explain variation in the level of reported optimism.

SUMMARY OF KEY CONCEPTS

- MLR is a linear approach to predicting values of an outcome variable from two or more predictor variables.
- MLR minimizes the error from a line of best fit in order to mathematically express the predictability of a dependent variable.
- Bivariate data points not on the line of best fit contribute to model error.
- Normality, linearity, and homoscedasticity are MLR assumptions that apply to each variable, their bivariate distribution, and their residuals.
- From the prediction equation, different outcome variable values can be predicted from the independent variables.
- The *y*-intercept is the value of the outcome variable when the predictors equal zero. It orients the line of best fit in a position that minimizes error.
- The adjusted *r*-square is an informative diagnostic tool.
- Running MLR in SPSS is straightforward.
- Interpreting and reporting significant and nonsignificant results are simple.

MULTIPLE LINEAR REGRESSION APPLIED EXERCISES

23.1 Generally, what is multiple linear regression (MLR)?

23.2 What is the basic idea behind the least squares method in regression?

23.3 What is the coefficient of multiple determination?

23.4 Define adjusted *R*-square (R^2_{adj}).

23.5 What is the basic idea behind standard or simultaneous linear regression?

23.6 An automobile consulting firm wishes to determine whether a luxury car's external appearance, price, advertised safety features, and miles per gallon (MPG) will influence the consumers' likelihood of buying such a vehicle in the future. Previous research suggests such a relationship. The study will examine the European luxury car market. The survey items were formatted in a 0–7 scale where consumers dragged a bar across increments of the scale. Seven hundred and fifty consumers participated in the mobile phone survey. Report your findings in the format provided in this chapter. Alpha = .05. Data file name: "MLR Exercise 1 Data."

23.7 For the month of January, a random sample of 250 customer records and corresponding surveys were used to determine the monthly cell phone bill, years with the current telephone company, percentage of telephone used for business, and household income. The researchers were charged with exploring whether these variables predict monthly cell phone sales as measured by the monthly cell phone bill. Report your findings in the format provided in this chapter. Alpha = .05. The name of the data file for this example is "MLR Exercise 2 Data."

23.8 An online survey was completed by 265 consumers concerning their reported consumer feelings, thoughts, and behaviors. The exploratory study's goal was to determine if impulse buying is predicted by seeing an ad for a product on TV, retailers setting discounts for the product, pre-purchase guilt for the product, and feeling sad before going shopping. Report your findings in the format provided in this chapter. Alpha = .05. The name of the data file for this example is "MLR Exercise 3 Data."

23.9 A random sample of 99 anonymous and random store sales transactions were collected in order to determine whether the dollar amount spent on CD purchases and/or the dollar amount of book purchases predicts special offer sales (promotional products). Report your findings in the format provided in this chapter. Alpha = .05. The name of the data file for this example is "MLR Exercise 4 Data."

23.10 A researcher wished to examine whether age (in years), years of education from 9th grade on (in completed years), and life satisfaction score (1 = "not satisfied with my life at all" to 5 = "totally satisfied with my life") predict thoughts (1 = " I will never go to jail again" to 5 = "I'll definitely go to jail again") about being re-incarcerated in adult men who were previously incarcerated at least twice for nonviolent offenses. The sample consisted of 478 adult men ages 25 to 50. Report your findings in the format provided in this chapter. Alpha = .05. The name of the data file for this example is "MLR Exercise 5 Data."

Appendices

Appendix A

Glossary

Addition rule. In probability statistics, this rule is used to determine the probability of one or another event occurring such as event A or event B. Since the events are assumed to be independent, the probability of one of the events taking place is calculated by simply adding together the probabilities of each occurring.

Adjusted r^2. This is an adjusted version of r^2, which is more useful for multiple linear regression analysis. It accounts for sample size and number of predictors.

Align (setting). The Align setting allows for data in the cells to be left, right, or center aligned.

Alpha. Also known as level of significance, this is the level of risk or threshold for assessing whether an effect is statistically significant or meaningful. It is set arbitrarily, but guided by standard conventions.

Association. This is a relationship between two variables. It does not indicate causality. It is equated with the term correlation.

Bar chart. This is a type of chart that depicts counts and percentages of those counts for each group within a categorical variable. The counts are depicted in vertical or horizontal bars, which can be colored. Both counts and percentages are reported. Bar charts make it easy to label, read, and understand categorical data, especially when there are more categories to compare.

Baseline count. The baseline count establishes the counts from which the subsequent counts are compared for differences.

Beta (b or β). This is another term for a regression coefficient.

Between-samples variance. This variance is between samples or groups and usually varies by categories within an independent variable.

Between-subjects analysis. An analysis that compares cases within one or more samples.

Big data. This term refers to massive amounts of data that are collected and analyzed quickly and regularly.

Binary data. These are dichotomous or nominal-level data that only have two possible outcomes. Binary data can also be viewed as the presence or absence of a condition. For examples,

"Do you like chocolate ice cream? Yes or No" or "The study was accurate: True or False." A binary formatted question provides the least amount of information; it is an "either one or the other" category.

Bivariate correlation. A bivariate correlation, represented by lower-case "*r*," measures the relationship between two variables. It is used to determine whether a linear (straight-line) relationship exists between two variables, as well as the strength and direction of that relationship.

Bivariate normal distribution. When the sample size is sufficiently large and the two variables are normally distributed and demonstrate a linear relationship, the paired coordinates will tend to concentrate in the center at the intersection of the (joint) means of the two variables. This indicates a bivariate normal distribution.

Bonferroni post hoc test. This is an appropriate post hoc test for all repeated measures analysis.

Brown-Forsythe test. This test is used in lieu of the ANOVA *F*-test statistic when we cannot assume equality of variance, equal sample sizes, and the distributions are close to violating normality.

Carry-over effect. This is a condition where any shared variance in a paired *t*-test can negate at least some of the treatment effect.

Case. A case is the individual record of data in the spreadsheet file located as a row and is composed of one or more variables (pieces of information).

Case row. This is an individual record of data or case.

Categorical variables. These variables consist of a set number of mutually exclusive characteristics or categories, which could be the simple presence or absence of a single attribute or one attribute from among multiple ones. They are measured by counting instances of the categories within each variable.

Causality relationship. This is a cause and effect relationship where change in at least one independent or predictor variable causes change in a dependent or outcome variable.

Ceiling effect. This effect results when data are skewed to the left, illustrating many high values.

Census. A type of research that collects data from virtually every member of the population under study.

Centering. Basic centering involves subtracting the variable mean from each observation in the variable in order to create a new centered variable ($XC = X - \bar{X}$).

Central Limit Theorem (CLT). The CLT states that a sample of means from randomly drawn samples will approach normal distribution as the (overall) sample size increases, whether or not the population from which the samples are drawn is normally distributed.

Central tendency. The extent to which data points concentrate around the mean (average) or center of the distribution. It is a measure of symmetry.

Chi-square goodness of fit significance test. This single sample test compares the (actually) observed and expected frequencies or counts for each category within a single categorical variable.

Chi-square probability distribution. This is a series of distributions that pertain to categorical data based on the number of groups or degrees of freedom within the categorical variable.

Chi-square probability set of distributions. This is a set of distributions based on the number of groups or degrees of freedom within the variable. "χ^2" is the chi-square symbol. They often, but not always, apply to categorical data.

Cluster (random) sampling. This sampling approach involves drawing data from natural clusters such as geopolitical locations such as states, company departments, neighborhood blocks, people who shop on certain days, and so forth. The clusters are mutually exclusive and collectively exhaustive subpopulations. The process usually involves the random selection of elements.

Cochran's Q test. This significance test is used to determine statistically significant differences among at least three measurement time points on the same sample using a categorical variable with two groups (categories).

Codebook. A codebook is the legend of all of the variable descriptions and values, including formatting. It provides operational definitions of the variables, which are the measurable definitions of variables. It serves as a reference that is handy when there are many variables that are not easily defined in terms of measurement.

Coefficient of determination. This is another term for the explained variance or r^2. This is the percentage of covariance shared by two variables.

Coefficient of Kurtosis. This statistic measures the degree of peakedness/flatness in a data distribution based on the variable's standard deviation.

Coefficient of multiple determination. This is the *R*-square (R^2) for MLR. It is the percentage of variation in the outcome variable explained by the set of predictors in the model.

Coefficient of skewness. This statistic measures the degree of symmetry in a variable's distribution based on the mean (the statistic can also be based on the median or mode).

Coefficient of variation (CV). This statistic represents the variable's standard deviation as a percentage of that variable's mean and is accurate when all of the values are positive.

Cohort study. This is a tracking study that focuses on a similar group of individuals who share a specific experience during the same time.

Column variable. This is the individual case data for a variable. All of the data values for a particular variable are organized by column.

Column (Width) (setting). Allows width adjustment by typing in a width value or setting using the spin control. It sets the column width in the Data View.

Complement rule. This rule involves variables with only two categories. It states that the sum of the probabilities of an event (one category) and its complement (the other category) must equal 1.00 or 100% of all possible outcomes.

Conceptual definition. This is an "idea" definition of something such as love, old age, wisdom, happiness, and effective leadership.

Conditional probability. This is the probability or chance of an event occurring within a subgroup of the sample space (total sample). It is based on the count of a category within a subset of the sample space.

Confidence interval. A confidence interval indicates the boundaries where a true population parameter lies based on a certain level of confidence expressed as a percentage. For instance, we are 95% confident that a mean is between 45 and 53.

Confidence interval (CI) estimate. A confidence interval estimate is a range of numbers constructed around a point estimate. For instance, we are 95% confident that a mean is between 45 and 53.

Content analysis. This type of analysis focuses on the examination of communication content. Behaviors, words, the relationships among words, themes, images, and the overall message are systematically studied.

Contingency table. This table depicts the relationship between two categorical variables each with two or more possible categorical values or responses.

Continuity Correction statistic. The Continuity Correction statistic is a conservative measure that adjusts for an insufficiently small sample size in a 2 × 2 chi-square analysis *only*.

Contrast analysis. This analysis is used to determine patterns across means.

Control variable. A variable that the researcher wants to account for so that it does not influence the relationship between and among the independent variable(s) and the dependent variable.

Convenience sampling. This method encompasses selecting readily available sampling elements. The elements are said to be convenient. Convenience sampling examples include students, coworkers, family members, and other social group members such as Facebook friends and Twitter followers.

Correlated samples *t*-test. This is another name for the paired *t*-test.

Correlation. A correlation, represented by lower-case "*r*," measures the degree to which a linear (straight-line) association or relationship exists between two variables based on the strength and direction of the relationship. A value from −1 to 1 represents a linear relationship or association between two variables. A correlation of −1 or 1 indicates a perfect linear relationship. A negative correlation reveals that the variables move in the opposite direction of each other and a positive correlation demonstrates that they move in the same direction. Correlations closer to −1 or 1 are stronger associations.

Correlation statistics. This is the analysis required in order to determine the strength and direction of a linear relationship between two variables known as a correlation. It does not indicate a cause and effect association. See the term correlation for details.

Counting process. The process by which categorical variables are measured by counting instances of the categories within it.

Counts or frequencies. These are the number of occurrences counted per category or grouping within a categorical variable. They can be represented as proportions or percentages in order to provide information about their relationship to other counts within the variable's categories.

Covariance. This is the degree to which two variables vary together.

Coverage error. Error that occurs when the sample does not represent a cross section of the target population, resulting in selection bias.

Cramer's *V*. This statistic, which is part of the chi-square test of independence, is the "correlation" between the two categorical variables.

Cross-sectional design. This design involves collecting data from a sample at a single point in time.

Crosstabs. Crosstabs is short for cross-tabulations table. It is a contingency table.

Crosstabs (cross-tabulations table) chi-square test of independence. The chi-square test of independence is a significance test that assesses whether there is a relationship between two categorical variables each with two or more categories.

Cumulative percentages. These percentages represent the increasing or cumulating percentage as each additional group's count is added to a subtotal.

Curvilinear. Any association or pattern in data that is not linear.

Data. Data are (datum is singular) the recorded individual measurements of variables. Data are the different values associated with a variable such as age in years (e.g. self-reported age by study participants), gender as women, men, and LGBTQ (e.g. self-reported gender by study participants), attitudes such as accepting or rejecting a brand, production output as in units, and so forth.

Data file. A file that stores data.

Data points. Data are (datum is singular) the recorded individual measurements of variables. Data are the different values associated with a variable such as age in years (e.g. self-reported age by study participants), gender as women, men, and LGBTQ (e.g. self-reported gender by study participants), attitudes such as accepting or rejecting a brand, production output as in units, and so forth.

Data View. This is one of two views in the SPSS data file that contains data in a spreadsheet format where the columns comprise variables and the rows consist of individual records of data.

Decimal (setting). The variable property setting for number of places to the right of the decimal point.

Degrees of freedom. The number of data points that can vary.

Dependent samples *t*-test. This is another name for the paired *t*-test.

Dependent variable. This variable changes because of change in the independent variable.

Descriptive statistics. Statistics that summarizes and describes sample data, which may be generalized to the population under study.

Dichotomous or binary pie chart. This is an image shaped as a circle, in which parts or slices are different colors representing the counts and percentages of those counts within each category of a variable. There are only two categories. The counts and frequencies are reported in the pie chart.

Directionality of a correlation. This refers to whether both variables in a correlation move in the same direction as they change. In other words, directionality indicates whether they increase together, decrease together, or move in the opposite direction from each other.

Disguised observation. The participants are unaware that they are being observed.

Dispersion. The spread of the data from the mean or degree to which values deviate from the mean. It is a measure of peakedness or flatness.

Disproportionate cluster sampling. This is a cluster sampling technique that maintains an equal number of elements per cluster despite the population segment size.

Disproportionate stratified sampling. The sample strata are not equal to their corresponding proportion in the total target population.

Distribution. This is where data values or measured observations fall when examined together as a variable.

Dummy coding. A dummy coded predictor measures the presence or absence of an attribute such as "yes" or "no"; "front-wheel drive" or "four-wheel drive"; "right" or "left" handed; and "aware" or "unaware." The presence of the attribute is usually coded "1" and its absence is coded "0."

Effect. This is a general term that refers to a meaningful statistical result of some kind that varies by procedure.

Effect size. This is a statistical measure of the degree to which one or more variables influences one or more other variables.

Element. The element is a specific source of data (individual unit) such as a specific person or piece of equipment. It is the basis of analysis.

Empirical Rule. This rule states that in a normal distribution, approximately 68% of the observations rest within one standard deviation from the mean, approximately 95% of the observations rest within two standard deviations, and 99.7% of the data rest within three standard deviations of the mean.

Epsilon. This value applies to Greenhouse-Geisser and Huynh-Feldt corrections for violation of the sphericity assumption and ranges from 0 to 1, with 1 indicating perfect sphericity. The correction applies to degrees of freedom and is automatically calculated in SPSS.

Equality of variance. Variance is the data's standard deviation squared. Equality of variance indicates whether the two samples share similar variance.

Equality of variance assumed. This is the SPSS output associated with the pooled two independent samples *t*-test.

Equality of variance not assumed. This is the SPSS output associated with the separate two independent samples *t*-test.

Error. Error is any deviation in sample data from the population of interest based on: (1) data collection methods; and (2) sources of data.

Exclusive range. This is the difference between the largest value and the smallest value of a data array. It does not include the endpoints.

Exhaustive. In the case of categorical variables, all categories are represented so that no counts are left out of the analysis.

Exogenous variable. These are often control or "outside" variables that are included in the analysis in order to determine whether they influence the dependent variable. They are not "created" by the researcher, but very well may influence study results. Examples are age, educational level, and ethnic background.

Expectation. This is an anticipated outcome.

Expectation-Maximization (EM) imputation. This imputation method employs a single imputation process and predicts missing values based among the variables' data patterns within each case. It is recommended for most missing value analyses and imputation.

Expected effect size. This is what we minimally expect to find, whether it involves means testing, categorical variable comparisons, correlations, or regression results.

Experimental design study. A design that introduces a condition in a laboratory or field (natural) setting and tests to determine if the condition affects the study participants or results in some way.

Expert sampling. This technique involves selecting participants (elements) who are available experts on the topic under study.

External validity. This is similar to generalizability. This type of validity is the extent to which findings from sample data can be applied to a larger population under study. It is only as valid as the degree to which the sample is representative of the population.

Extraneous variable. This is a variable external, but related to the study.

Extrapolation. This is the practice of predicting a dependent variable from an independent value that is beyond the range of the sample data.

Event. This is an outcome in which the probability of it occurring is known.

Face validity. This type of validity is the extent to which a finding or measurement is well founded and accurate based on common sense or face value.

Falsification. This is a process that tests the probability of a statement or hypothesis being untrue.

Field experiment. This experiment occurs in a natural setting because it is where the experimental treatment exists in real life.

Fisher exact test (two-sided). The Fisher exact test (two-sided) result is automatically generated for 2 × 2 chi-square analysis *only*. It is used to assess the chi-square test results if at least one category combination has an expected count less than 5, and may be reported in the write-up.

Flooring effect. This effect results when data are skewed to the right, denoting many low values.

Frequencies or counts. These are the number of occurrences counted per category or grouping within a categorical variable. They can be represented as proportions or percentages in order to provide information about their relationship to other counts within the variable's categories.

Frequency table. This is the general term for a table that depicts categorical data counts and percentages.

Games-Howell post hoc test. A test that determines where the paired differences lie among the ANOVA *F*-test groups when we cannot assume equality of variance.

General linear model (GLM) repeated measures. This is another name for one-way repeated measures ANOVA.

Grand mean. This is the mean or average of all of the data across samples (groups) of the variable being analyzed.

Greenhouse-Geisser. This overall repeated measures test is applicable when the sphericity assumption is not met and its epsilon value is less than .75.

Hawthorne effect. This effect is based on responses guided by participant perceptions of what they think the researcher wants them to answer or do in appreciation for the attention given them by the researcher.

Hierarchical linear regression. This type of linear regression allows us to enter variables as forced groups based on conceptual clusters for example.

Homoscedasticity. This refers to the degree of similarity in which the covariances of joint values or coordinates fit along the line of best fit. Normally, the distribution forms an elliptical pattern.

Huynh-Feldt. This overall repeated measures test is applicable when the sphericity assumption is not met and the Greenhouse-Geisser epsilon is equal to or greater than .75.

Hypothesis. This is a claim or statement that is tested through the process of falsification.

Imputation. Imputation is a process that allows us to replace missing values with predicted values, thus adding to statistical power (confidence in our results).

Inclusive range. This is the difference between the largest value and the smallest value of a data array, which includes the endpoints.

Independent event. The chance of an event occurring is independent of any other event taking place.

Independent variable. This kind of variable predicts change in another variable. In other words, it influences change in other variables. Its effects are measured so that a change or different condition in the independent variable affects or changes the dependent variable in some way.

Inferential statistics. Statistics that examines the relationships and nature between and among variables and helps us draw conclusions that can be generalized to the entire population under study, thus allowing us to reduce uncertainty in decision-making.

Interaction effect. This is the effect of two predictors acting together on an outcome variable. It is called so because the two independent variables interact and co-predict the outcome variable sometimes in ways unique to the additive effect of both predictors.

Interaction term (variable). This is a variable that comprises a combination of usually two but sometimes more than two independent variables. They have a combined effect on a dependent variable. The combined effects can be greater than or less than the sum of the predictors' effects operating separately on the dependent variable.

Interval variable. In the case of interval variables, we know the differences between the values of the characteristic measured. For instance, the difference between 1 and 2 is the same as the difference between 3 and 4, the difference between 5 and 6, and so forth. However, zero has no meaning and it does not equal nothing or the absence of the variable attribute; thus, relative to "zero," differences are not meaningful.

Joint counts (or joint frequencies). The data are set up in a contingency table and the marginal counts provide the expected counts that are compared with the combinations of categories, one each from the two variables, such as women who are 18–24 years old.

Joint (bivariate) distribution. This is the distribution of two variables plotted in a graph using the matched data points or coordinates of the variables. One variable is assigned the x-axis and the other the y-axis.

Joint probability. This is the probability or chance of two events occurring at the same time each from one of two categorical variables.

Kruskal-Wallis test. This test is a nonparametric alternative to the numeric-level data approaches to testing for differences among more than two means. It is not as powerful as the other tests, and consequently might not detect significant effects.

Kurtosis. This is the general measure of peakedness/flatness in a data distribution.

Label (setting). A label represents a variable name and provides more naming flexibility than the "Name" option.

Lab experiment. This experiment occurs in an artificial setting such as a controlled lab. It is highly structured, which makes it much easier to manage factors that can affect results.

Lab setting. This type of setting usually involves exposing research participants to an intervention or treatment in a managed environment that allows for the control of variables that might affect results.

Latent content analysis. In addition to action, word, and word co-occurrence counts, this type of content analysis has an interpretative component. For example, research might look for patterns in the relationships among television stereotypical roles and ethnic as well as gender background.

Least squares method. A regression method that minimizes the model variation not explained by the regression line of best fit.

Leptokurtic distribution. In terms of kurtosis, this distribution has a high peak that is thin and tall. The tails of the distribution are relatively short and heavy.

Level of alpha. This is the level of acceptable risk. It is usually less than .05, which means that the chance of findings not being statistically meaningful must be $\leqslant .05$ in order to detect effects.

Level of risk. This is the p-value or level of risk that we are willing to accept when concluding that a particular sample result is meaningful and not by chance alone.

Level of significance. Also known as alpha, this is the level of risk or threshold for assessing whether an effect is statistically significant or meaningful. It is set arbitrarily, but guided by standard conventions.

Levene test for equality of variance. This is a significance test that is used to assess equality of variance in two or more distributions.

Linear interpolation imputation. Linear interpolation replaces missing values using a linear interpolation formula, which is based on patterns detected in the data. The last value above (before) the missing value and the first value below (after) the missing value are used for the interpolation.

Linearity. This is a pattern in a joint distribution that maintains the same slope between two variables in a straight line. It occurs when the variance between two variables is constant in their respective directions.

Linear trend at point imputation. This imputation method replaces missing values with the linear trend for that point based on all values in the variable.

Listwise. The listwise (also called casewise) procedure is an option in many statistical procedures. Selecting this option simply removes all incomplete cases from the analysis, whether composed of numeric or categorical data.

Little's MCAR test. This test determines whether missing data are missing completely at random (MCAR). It requires at least two variables to detect a pattern.

Longitudinal design. This design usually entails collecting the same data from the same sample over a period of time (usually at least three times).

Lower-bound. This overall repeated measures test is applicable when the sphericity assumption is strongly violated. It is subject to a wide array of fluctuations. Since the introduction of the Greenhouse-Geisser and Huynh-Feldt tests, it is rarely used.

Main effect. Each predictor's influence alone is called a main effect.

Manifest content analysis. This is a content analysis methods that counts actions, words, and co-occurrence of words.

Manipulation. This is another word for an experimental condition.

Manipulation check. This is a test that determines whether the participants were aware of an experimental treatment.

Mann-Whitney *U* test. This is a two independent samples nonparametric test based on rank-ordering the data. It can be used when the data violate the normal distribution assumption. When the test is used to compare two means, equality of variance is not a consideration.

Marginal counts (or totals). The row and column totals are called marginal totals because they are located in the margins of the table.

Matched samples *t*-test. This is another name for the paired *t*-test.

Mauchly's significance test. This significance test is used to assess sphericity in repeated measures analysis.

McNemar chi-square test. This significance test is used to determine statistically significant differences among two measurement time points on the same sample using a categorical variable with two groups (categories).

McNemar test. This is a significance test that examines counts (and percentages of those counts) between the same cases or sample measured twice, usually using a Time 1 variable and a Time 2 variable, with two categories in the variable being measured.

McNemar-Bowker test. This is a significance test that examines counts (and percentages of those counts) between the same cases or sample measured twice, usually using a Time 1 variable and a Time 2 variable, with three or more identical categories in the variable being measured.

Mean. This is the average of a set of values or observations. It is calculated by summing all of the values in a set and then dividing the sum by the number of values. The mean often refers to the average value for a variable such as age or height.

Mean of nearby points imputation. The mean of nearby points imputes missing values with the mean of valid surrounding values.

Measurable definition. This is the way we measure the conceptual definition of a variable. For example, old age may be defined and measured by those individuals who are over 80 years old.

Measurable framework. The tools and formats that we use to collect and measure data.

Measure (setting). The Measure variable property indicates whether the level of data is numeric or categorical. There are three options in the pull-down menu. "Scale" is for numeric data. "Ordinal" is for ordinal categorical data. "Nominal" is for nominal categorical data, including binary.

Measurement error. This is error due to a flaw in data collection or measurement.

Measuring process. This process involves the systematic assignment of numbers to objects and their properties in order to facilitate the use statistics to study and describe concepts or objects and their relationships.

Mechanical observation. This type of observation requires a device rather than individual to record observations. The records are later analyzed. Observation may include video or audio recordings, Internet traffic and behavior, eyes-on-screen tracking, response latency devices, vehicle traffic counters, devices that record individual physiological responses, and so forth.

Median. This is the middle value of the cases ordered from smallest to largest.

Median of nearby points imputation. The median of nearby points replaces missing values with the median of the surrounding values.

Mesokurtic distribution. In terms of kurtosis, this is the normal distribution.

Missing at random (MAR). This is a condition in which missing values are not random, except within subsets where the missing values are random.

Missing completely at random (MCAR). This is a condition in which there is no pattern between any missing values and any values in the dataset.

Missing not at random (MNAR). In this situation, the missing values are not random, but demonstrate a pattern between the missing value and another value in the dataset.

Missing (setting). The Missing function can be used to code missing data with specific values.

Missing Value Analysis. This consists of a number of procedures used in order to determine whether missing data demonstrate a pattern.

Mixed research design. A research design that combines two or more other designs.

Mode. This is the value that appears most frequently in the variable. If there is no one value that appears most, then there is no mode. The data can have more than one mode, such as a bimodal or trimodal distribution.

Monotonic. This is a relationship where the degree of covariance may change, but maintains the same direction.

Multicollinearity. High correlations between or among predictors exhibit multicollinearity and can produce inaccurate linear regression results.

Multidimensional table. This kind of table contains two or more variables each with two or more categories so that there are joint counts. A multiple-dimensional table is also referred to as a contingency table.

Multiple category pie chart. This is an image shaped as a circle, in which parts or slices are different colors representing the counts and percentages of those counts within each category of the variable. There are more than two categories. The counts and frequencies are reported in the pie chart.

Multiple correlation. A multiple correlation compares the association between two or more pairs of variables together in an analysis producing a correlation matrix of these associations.

Multiple imputation (MI). This imputation technique accounts for all case values as well as selected variable values. It employs multiple imputations, which are set by the researcher. Generally no more than five imputations provide sufficient randomness. The average of the results is the replacement value.

Multiple linear regression (MLR). MLR extends SLR to more than one predictor variable. MLR estimates the value or variation in the outcome variable from two or more predictors together ($X_1 + Xk$). Often MLR allows us to explain more variation in the outcome variable because we incorporate more than one predictor, thus providing more information.

Multiplication rule. In probability statistics, this rule is used to determine the probability of two or more events occurring such as events A and B. Since the events are assumed to be independent, the probability is calculated by taking the cross-product of each probability (the probabilities are multiplied by each other).

Multistage cluster sampling. This cluster method draws elements from nested (populations within populations) data within clusters. For example, a researcher would sample companies, then departments within those companies or sample state voters, followed by county voters, and then municipal voters.

Mutually exclusive. In the case of categorical variables, categories do not overlap so that frequencies are not counted in two or more categories.

Naïve science. This is the popular perspective that anything that appears to be "common sense" true is true and unworthy of scientific verification.

Name (setting). This is the variable name. Name formatting is subject to restrictions.

Natural setting. The normal setting in which an experimental treatment occurs.

Negative correlation. A correlation that is $0 > r > -1$. It covaries in the opposite direction of the other variable.

Nominal-level data. These are categorical data with more than two categories, which do not demonstrate a natural order.

Nonparametric statistics. This is a type of probability statistics dependent on degrees of freedom (number of groups within the variable) and oftentimes based on rank ordered data. It is not based on the normal distribution.

Nonprobability sampling. This type of sampling is subjective and does not involve random selection, but is based on some other criterion.

Nonsampling random error. This error results from sources other than those ascribed to sampling. Some error may be caused by the intrinsic fluctuation of data and other error may be caused by the unit of measurement such as people, a chemical process, financial trends, weather conditions, or some other aspect of the measurement environment.

Nonsampling systematic error. This error demonstrates a pattern in the data not attributed to sampling. It is caused by the study design, some aspect of the study environment, and/or measurement error. The error follows a discernible pattern and is controllable.

Non-uniform probability distribution. These distributions are not uniform because each group within the categorical variable does not have an equal random chance of selection.

Normal distribution. This is a data distribution that is symmetrical like a bell-shaped curve.

Normality. This is a data distribution that is symmetrical like a bell-shaped curve.

Normal Q-Q Plot. This graphic places observations along a straight line that represents a perfect normal distribution.

Numeric data. Often called continuous data, numeric data can be Likert scale-level data, interval-level data, or ratio-level data.

Numeric variable. This variable comprises a level of some attribute measured in a sample. The measurements vary among data records. There are no predetermined selections or counts, unlike categorical variables. Data points are actual responses, measures, or observations. They are measured values.

Observational research design. This study design involves the observation, collecting, and recording of data from people, objects, and events in a systematic manner by human and/or mechanical methods.

Observations. These are the sample information that is collected.

Omnibus test. This is a general term applied to the overall significance of a statistical test.

One- or single-dimensional table. This table depicts a single categorical variable with two or more categories. It is also called a summary table.

One-stage cluster sampling. A sampling approach where all of the sampling frame clusters are identified and from which a random number of sampling elements are chosen.

One-way analysis of variances (one-way ANOVA) *F*-test. The one way analysis of variances (one-way ANOVA) *F*-test compares the means (averages) among more than two independent representative samples (groups) in order to determine the likelihood of at least one statistically significant difference between at least two of the samples.

One-way repeated measures ANOVA. Also called general linear model (GLM) repeated measures, this significance test is used to compare the means of measurements made more than twice on the same or related sample.

Ordinal categorical-level data. These data imply an order of magnitude to categories within the variable. There is an increase or decrease in intensity of something represented in the format of the data. An example would be class standing: freshman, sophomore, junior, and senior, where there is an inherent order to class standing implying greater school credits and being closer to graduating college.

Outcome. This is a dependent variable because it is predicted by an independent or predictor variable.

Outlier. This is an extreme value in a dataset because it is exceptionally less than or greater than the data mean. An outlier is located in the tail of a data distribution, which is three standard deviations or more away from the mean.

Outlier labeling rule. This technique for identifying and removing outliers is a multistep approach utilizing the 25th and 75th percentiles and a simple formula. It is an attempt to precisely identify and remove outliers.

Output file. This file, also known as the SPSS Output Viewer, contains data analysis output such as tables, graphs, and statistical information.

Paired-sample *t*-test. The paired-sample *t*-test usually compares the means (averages) between the same sample measured twice in order to determine if there is a likelihood of a statistically significant difference between both measurements.

Pairwise. The pairwise approach includes comparison where there are no missing values on an analysis-by-analysis basis, whether the data are numeric or categorical.

Panel study. This type of study entails collecting data from the same sample over time, whether they are persons, devices, records, or some other type of data source.

Parameter. This is a true measure of a target population based on a randomly drawn representative sample of that population.

Partial correlation. This correlation procedure removes the influence of one or more designated variables from the correlation.

Partial eta squared. This statistic indicates the percentage change in the data or an effect size related to or explained by a condition or an independent variable.

Pearson chi-square statistic. The Pearson chi-square statistic is the chi-square test used when there is a sufficient sample size in addition to meeting all of the data assumptions.

Pearson correlation. This type of correlation is a parametric procedure used for numeric data.

Percentages. These are the proportions or relative frequencies of counts or frequencies within the categories of a categorical variable. They are in relation to the entire sample size (sample space) or to a subset of the sample.

Person-to-person administered survey. This is a survey administered in-person by a researcher who directly asks the respondent questions in real time. The survey interview can be mediated by technology, such as telephone or digital devices, using applications such as Skype, Google Plus, and many more.

Personal observation. This observation method involves the researcher observing behavior without interacting with who or what is being observed.

Pie chart. This is an image shaped as a circle, in which parts or slices are different colors representing the counts and percentages of those counts within each category of the variable. The counts and frequencies are reported in the pie chart. As a best practice, a pie chart should contain no more than five to seven categories.

Platykurtic distribution. In terms of kurtosis, this distribution is flat (low peak) and spread out more than the normal distribution. Both tails are long.

Point estimate. A point estimate is the value of a single sample statistic such as a mean, median, correlation, proportion, and so forth.

Pooled two independent samples *t*-test. This significance *t*-test is used when two samples (groups) share similar distributions in the data to be compared.

Positive correlation. A positive correlation is $0 < r < 1$. This is when a variable covaries in the same direction of the other variable.

Post hoc significance testing. If the overall or omnibus test is statistically significant, then one of a variety of post hoc tests appropriate for the data's attributes can be used to identify specifically where the differences lie.

Post hoc testing. If an analysis of variance (ANOVA) is significant, a post hoc test is used to determine where the statistically significant differences are between samples. Post hoc testing is used when the analysis involves more than two samples.

Power analysis. This analysis is a statistical tool that calculates statistical power.

Prediction model. This is a mathematical expression of a straight line of best fit: $Yi = b_0 + b_1 Xi$.

Predictor. This is an independent variable because it predicts variance in the outcome (variable).

Probability. This is the chance of something occurring by random chance.

Probability sampling. This is a sampling approach that assures that each element has an equal chance of being chosen.

Probability statistics. This is a scientific and systematic approach for determining the chances of events occurring or results being meaningful based on the attributes of a representative sample.

Profile plot. This is a plot or graph for comparing statistics such as means or medians. It provides a visual depiction of potential patterns in statistical measures.

Proportionate cluster sampling. This cluster sampling method adjusts the sample cluster size according to the actual subpopulation size.

Proportionate stratified sampling. This type of stratified sampling consists of having sample strata sizes consistent with the corresponding target population proportions.

Proportions. These are the percentages or relative frequencies of counts or frequencies within the categories of a categorical variable. They are in relation to the entire sample size (sample space) or to a subset of the sample.

***P*-value.** This is the probability of an effect (value) occurring, assuming that the data are normally distributed. It is expressed as the probability percentage or random chance of occurrence.

Quota sampling. This sampling approach is similar to stratified random sampling; however, there is no random component. It involves two stages. First, categories of characteristics (like strata) are created to serve as the basis for groups. Second, the groups are assigned element quotas. These categories attempt to assure that the target population is represented in the sample.

r^2. This is the explained variance. The square of a correlation provides the percentage of the total covariance explained by the line of best fit. It is the variance that is shared between the two variables. It is the percentage of variance explained in a variable as a result of variability in a predictor variable.

Random. As it pertains to sampling, random denotes there is no pattern or order to selecting elements for a sample. Random sampling usually requires a sampling frame.

Random sampling. This is a sampling technique in which every element or data source has an equal chance of being selected.

Random sampling error. This error occurs when the sample selected is an imperfect representation of the population under study. The differences between the sample and population do not demonstrate a pattern, but are inherently random.

Range. This is the difference between the largest value and the smallest value.

Ratio variable. This variable is the most comprehensive and informative variable. All types of statistical analysis can be applied to ratio variables. Zero is a meaningful value; when the value of a variable equals zero, then there is nothing of that variable. It is absent. For example, zero income includes no income. Moreover, comparisons are clearly meaningful because we know the exact differences between the values of the characteristic measured along with a meaningful zero.

Regression coefficient. This is a beta in linear regression that relates to predicting a value in a dependent variable from a value in an independent variable. Specifically, the b_1 indicates the amount of incremental change in the dependent variable as a result of one unit of change in the independent variable's unit of measurement.

Reification. This is the process of taking something abstract, such as ideas, thoughts, and feelings, and making them concrete or measurable so that we can tell a story using numbers.

Related samples *t*-test. This is another name for the paired *t*-test.

Relative frequencies. These are the proportions or percentages of counts or frequencies within the categories of a categorical variable. They are in relation to the entire sample size (sample space) or to a subset of the sample.

Repeated measures *t*-test. This is another name for the paired *t*-test.

Research design. This is the strategy and plan that specifies the methods for collecting and analyzing data.

Research goal. This is what we intend to achieve and it guides the research process. Goals are inspired by a problem, challenge, or opportunity that requires data-driven decision-making.

Research objective. This is the means by which we achieve a goal. It is often stated as a research statement to be tested for its truth or falsity or as a research question to be answered.

Research question. This is an objective framed as a question to be answered.

Research statement. This is a claim or hypothesis that is tested through the process of falsification.

Residual. In the case of chi-square analysis, this is the difference between expected counts and observed counts.

Residual analysis. This analysis involves screening for error normality, linearity, and homoscedasticity after linear regression analysis is conducted.

Same samples *t*-test. This is another name for the paired *t*-test.

Sample. This is a relatively small representative number of a larger population selected for statistical analysis. The group is subject to statistical analysis with the intention of generalizing results to the population from which it was drawn.

Sample size. The sample size is the number of cases or elements in the sample. Given the required statistical power, anticipated minimum effect sizes, and alpha, we can determine the sample size.

Sampling. This is the process by which a representative small group or sample of a population of interest is selected for statistical analysis.

Sampling fraction. It is the desired sample size (n) divided by the population size (N): n/N. It is the proportion of the sample size compared to the population size.

Sampling frame. This is a data source list or list of elements that comprise a target population. Examples are telephone lists, email lists, Facebook friends, voter registration lists, other types of registration lists, property ownership lists, all the machinery output records from a manufacturing facility, lists of companies, and so forth.

Sampling frame error. This is a type of coverage error involving a difference between the actual target population and population as defined by the sampling frame.

Sample space. The categorical choices within a variable that consist of all possible outcomes, which can be represented in a table.

Sampling unit. The element is a specific source of data (individual unit) such as a specific person or piece of equipment. It is the basis of analysis. A sampling unit can also contain a set of elements.

Sampling with replacement. An element drawn for sampling is returned to the sampling frame (source) before another element is drawn so that the chances of elements being selected always remains the same.

Sampling without replacement. Once an element is drawn, it is not replaced, thus the chances for the remaining elements being drawn change.

Scale data. This level of data or variable is treated as interval-level data. Strictly speaking, scale response formats such as 1 = "strongly disagree" through 5 = "strongly agree," 1 = "less important" to 7 = "more important," or 1 = "the least" to 5 = "the most" are ordinal categorical-level data. However, research has shown that treating this type of response format as interval data is valid and reliable under many conditions (Carifio & Perla, 2007; Norman, 2010).

Scheffe post hoc test. A test that determines where the paired differences lie among the ANOVA *F*-test groups when the normality and equality of variances assumptions have been met. It can be used when there are unequal sample sizes.

Scientific notation. This is a way of reporting very large numbers or very small numbers in a shorthand form.

Self-administered survey. This is a survey completed by the respondents on their own time.

Semipartial correlation. This is a correlation that controls for the effects of one or more other variables on one of the two correlated variables.

Separate two independent samples *t*-test. This significance *t*-test is used when two samples (groups) do not share similar distributions in the data to be compared.

Series mean imputation. This imputation approach involves substituting the variable mean for all missing values.

Shapiro-Wilk test. This significance test is used to evaluate whether a data distribution approximates a normal distribution.

Significance testing. This is the statistical test that determines whether there is no difference or meaningful result based on the probability of the value occurring.

Sign test. In a paired *t*-test, if the data are not normally distributed and symmetrical, then the sign test option is appropriate in lieu of the Wilcoxon signed ranks test.

Simple dot plot. This plot represents data points where the data values are located on the horizontal axis and the frequencies of the values are located on the vertical axis

Simple outlier rule. This rule involves identifying outliers by examining data graphs and statistical measures such as the kurtosis and the skewness statistics as well as the Shapiro-Wilk test of normality.

Simple probability. This is the probability or chance of a single event occurring.

Simple random sampling. This is a sampling strategy where every element has a known and equal chance of being selected. Every element within a sample of a fixed size has the same chance of being selected as another element in a sample of the same size.

Single linear regression (SLR). This is commonly referred to as simple linear regression. It is a statistical technique used to predict the value of a dependent variable from the value of an independent variable.

Single sample *t*-test. This is a significance test that compares the mean of a single sample and a test value in order to determine if there is a difference between them.

Skewness. This statistical measure indicates the degree of symmetry in a data distribution.

Slope. This is the line of best fit, which is the rise over the run or the amount of change in the outcome as a result of one unit change in the predictor.

Snowball sampling. This sampling method is appropriate when it is difficult to reach the target population. The sensitive nature of both the data and the target population can make data collection challenging. In this approach, selected participants identify other potential participants.

Social desirability effects. This effect occurs when study respondents provide answers that are socially desirable even if they actually do not subscribe to those responses.

Spearman correlation. This nonparametric correlation procedure is used when one or both variables are composed of ordinal categorical data or when numeric data do not meet the normality and/or homoscedasticity assumptions.

Sphericity. It is the condition where the variances of the differences between all possible pairs of groups are similar. This test is used in repeated measures analysis.

Sphericity assumed. This overall repeated measures test is applicable when the sphericity assumption is met.

SPSS Output Viewer. This is the SPSS output file.

Standard deviation. It is a calculated statistical measure that applies to the sample and can be inferred to the target population. The sample standard deviation represents the typical (or standardized) difference between each sample variable between each observation and the mean. It allows us to determine the spread of the data distribution.

Standard deviation rule. This rule involves standardizing or converting the observations to their *z*-scores, rank-ordering the *z*-scores, and then removing outliers using the three standard deviation baseline.

Standardized beta (β). This is the regression coefficient expressed in terms of the *z*-distribution. It is calculated by subtracting the sample mean from each observation and then dividing the result by the sample standard deviation.

Standardized counts. These counts are the percentages of the counts of categories within variables as represented by their percentages of the total sample space (data set or some subset).

Standard or simultaneous linear regression. This is MLR where all predictor variables are run at once.

Standard normal distribution. Following the Empirical Rule, this represents a perfect normal distribution. It is also called the *z*-distribution.

Statistical error. In statistics, and especially numeric data, error is any deviation in sample data from the population of interest based on: (1) sources of data; and (2) data collection methods.

Statistical power. This is the level of confidence that we have for detecting a potential effect in sample data so that if an effect exists, it will be detected.

Statistics. This is a branch of applied mathematics that focuses on studying sample data that are representative of a specific population.

Stepwise linear regression. This type of linear regression allows for the predictor that contributes most to R^2 to be entered first and alone in the regression equation, thus creating Model 1. The automatic process repeats by entering a second predictor that makes the second largest contribution to R^2. Thus, there are two predictors and it is Model 2. However, in Model 2, if the predictor in Model 1 is not one of the top two contributors, then it is dropped in favor of the top two contributing predictors.

Stimulus. This is another word for an experimental condition.

Stratified random sampling. This sampling method encompasses segmenting the target population into subpopulations or strata based on homogenous characteristics important in the study using precise randomization procedures.

Strength of a correlation. The strength of a correlation is the degree to which the variables have similar variances. If the differences in the variables correspond perfectly, then the correlation will be −1 or 1. Less than perfect correlations will be between −1 and 1.

String data. Nominal categorical data recorded as words. For example, choices: "yes" or "no."

Structured observation. What is to be observed is specified.

Summary table. This table depicts a single categorical variable with two or more categories. It is also called a one- or single-dimensional table.

Survey design. This research design involves collecting data by directly questioning individuals.

Symmetric measures table. The symmetric measures table provides additional information about the relationship between two categorical variables. It is akin to a "correlation."

Syntax file. This file can be used to customize and specify statistical instructions to be executed in SPSS.

Systematic random sampling. This is a sampling strategy where every element has a known and equal chance of being selected. Every element within a sample of a fixed size has the same chance of being selected as another element in a sample of the same size. The method varies somewhat from simple random sampling. It is more random and more complex.

Systematic response error. This error pattern can result in a skewed response (data) distribution.

Systematic sampling error. Sampling error demonstrates a pattern in the data.

Target population. This is the entire population of interest.

***T*-distribution.** This is the sample distribution from which we infer to the target population. It approximates the *z*-distribution and is symmetrical, but varies slightly to account for sample fluctuations not present in a perfect distribution.

Tolerance. A measure of multicollinearity. It is a predictor variable's unique variance not accounted for by the other predictors.

Total variance. In ANOVA, total variance represents within and between variances.

Tracking study. This research design requires collecting data over time. Different samples are drawn from the same sampling frame (representative source or list from which sampling units are drawn such as an email list) so that response bias is minimized.

Treatment. The treatment is an independent variable of some type. It can be an intervention or experimental condition—all commonly referred to as the treatment. If there are differences between the before and after treatment measurements, then there is likely a treatment effect.

Treatment effect. If there is a statistically significant difference between paired data or between before and after treatment measurements, then there is a treatment effect.

Trimming. This technique for addressing outliers is based on the removal of a percentage of outliers at each tail of the distribution.

Tukey (HSD) post hoc test. A test that determines where the paired differences lie among the ANOVA *F*-test groups when the normality, equality of variances, and equal group sizes assumptions have been met.

Two-dimensional table. This kind of table contains two variables each with two categories so that there are joint counts. A two-dimensional table is also referred to as a contingency table.

Two independent samples *t*-test. The two independent samples *t*-test is a significance test that compares the means between two independent samples (groups) in order to determine if there is the likelihood of a statistically meaningful difference between them.

Type (setting). This is the variable format. Types include Numeric, Comma, Dollar, and String (labels composed of symbols, letters, and/or numbers and suitable for categorical data).

Undisguised observation. The participants are aware that they are being observed.

Unexplained variance. Since the explained variance is a percentage, then the unexplained variance or unaccounted for variance is $1 - r^2$. It is also called the coefficient of non-determination.

Uniform probability distributions. These distributions are uniform because each group within the categorical variable has an equal random chance of selection.

Univariate normal distribution. This distribution focuses on a single variable and whether the data in that variable is distributed in a bell-shaped curve.

Unstandardized beta (*b*). This is a regression coefficient in its original metric or scale.

Unstructured observation. What is to be observed is not specified.

Valid case. This is a count adjusted for missing sample data.

Validity. This is the extent to which a finding or measurement is well founded and accurate.

Valid percentage. This is a percentage adjusted for missing sample data.

Value. This is a piece of collected sample information.

Values (setting). The Values setting allows categories to be assigned numeric values.

Variable. A variable is a directly or indirectly observable characteristic or property of something that is measurable. It varies or changes particularly in relation to one or more other variables or in comparison to other observations or measurements of the same variable.

Variable View. This is one of two views in the SPSS data file that contains variable properties. The user can define the variable parameters or characteristics in this view.

Variance. A measure of the average variation in a variable's data. In other words, it is the average of the squared differences between each data point and its mean.

Variance explained. The percentage of the relationship between the two variables that can be explained by the sample data. It is the variance shared by two variables also referred to as r^2.

Variance inflation factor (VIF). VIF is the reciprocal of tolerance, which is a measure of multicollinearity.

Welch test. This test is used in lieu of the ANOVA *F*-test statistic when we cannot assume equality of variances and equal sample sizes.

Width (setting). The width setting pertains to the length of places to the right of the decimal point, which appears in the Data View.

Wilcoxon signed ranks test. This is a nonparametric test that can be used in place of the paired *t*-test when the difference(s) between the paired data are symmetrical but do not approximate the normal distribution.

Winsorizing. This outlier removal technique is similar to trimming with one major difference. In lieu of removing the lower and upper ends' outliers, the values are replaced with the first observation in the data that is not an outlier but next to the removed outlier.

Within-sample variance. This variance occurs within a single sample and represents random variance in ANOVA.

Within-subjects analysis. The focus of this type of analysis is on measuring change within the same individual data sources. For instance, a client participating in a new social support program is asked four times over one year if the program was helpful. The program's overall effectiveness is assessed based on a change in the sample's responses over time. The effect examined can be time or time in conjunction with a treatment.

Within-subjects design. A study in which the participants are measured more than once and the comparison is about change measured within the person based on more than one measurement.

Y-intercept (b_0). This is the predicted value of the dependent variable when the independent variable equals 0. The *y*-intercept orients the line of best fit.

Z-distribution. Following the Empirical Rule, this represents a perfect normal distribution. It is also called the standard normal distribution.

Zero-order correlation. This correlation measures the degree of association between two variables. It does not account for associations with other variables.

Z-score. This is a standardized observation based on the original value. A *z*-score is computed by subtracting the mean from the data point value and then dividing the result by the sample standard deviation.

Appendix B

Chapter Statistical Exercise Solutions

B.1 Chapter 1

1.1 Define statistics and be sure to cite general examples.

Answer: Statistics. This is a branch of applied mathematics that focuses on studying sample data that are representative of all possible data points of a specific population. Examples: A study sampling 18–24-year-olds about their choice for presidential candidates. A sample examining nursing job satisfaction.

1.2 What is a sample? Cite examples.

Answer: Sample. This is a relatively small representative number of a larger population selected for statistical analysis. Examples: A small group of social service clients. Ten fifth graders each from 12 schools.

1.3 Define descriptive statistics. Cite an example.

Answer: Descriptive statistics. Statistics that summarizes and describes sample data. Examples: The average age, educational level, ethnicity background, and gender of people enrolled in a health program or adult education program.

1.4 Define inferential statistics. Cite an example.

Answer: Inferential statistics. Statistics that examines the relationships between and among variables and helps us draw conclusions that can be generalized to the entire population under study, thus allowing us to reduce uncertainty in decision-making. Examples: The key factors associated with recidivism among teen boys. The modeling role of foster parents in encouraging education in children that reach 18 years old.

1.5 Are there cases where descriptive variables (or data) can be applied to inferential statistics? Explain your answer.

Answer: Descriptive statistics describes the characteristics or demographics of sample data that ideally represent a population being studied. For example, identifying a market segment may include summary data such as mean (average) age, gender, income ranges, educational level, ethnicity, and geographic location of primary residence. With the exception of age, which is a numeric variable in this case, these are categorical variables expressed in counts and percentages of counts.

Assume that we are marketers developing a number of clothing lines for various market segments. We may compare interest in the various clothing lines by demographic characteristics with the intention of identifying market segments that can be generalized or applied to the entire populations of the sample segments. This is where descriptive statistics can help us infer something about the population under study based on the sample data. For instance, women ages 24–35 in the North East of all ethnic groups, whose incomes range from $50,001 to $75,000, may prefer a median-priced clothing line focusing on quality, style, and variety. Other market segments would also be identified (or defined) by these variables.

Therefore, we can see that comparing demographic data or variables to our research goal/objective-oriented variables allows us to infer or generalize to the population under study. This process can be applied across many areas, such as medical research, operations management, organizational behavior, manufacturing, and so forth.

1.6 Define census data and provide examples. Under what study conditions would census data be appropriate (and easily available)?

Answer: Census. A type of research that collects data from virtually every member of the population under study. Studies where there is easy access to existing data and/or where the census data are relatively easy to collect owing to a limited population size. In the first case, online big data storage makes it easier for researchers and analysts to examine the entire population under study, such as all those who purchase a product at Amazon.com, for example. In the second case, if research involves some internal aspect of an organization such as asking all 10,000 employees their attitudes about a pension plan or studying the number of high-quality manufactured items in a company's production facilities throughout the world, then census data may be appropriate.

1.7 Explain what is naïve science.

Answer: Naïve science. This is the popular perspective that anything that appears to be "common sense" true is true and unworthy of scientific verification.

1.8 Is it possible to reify everything? Explain your reasoning.

Answer: Reification. This is the process of taking something abstract, such as ideas, thoughts, and feelings, and making them concrete or measurable so that we can tell a story using numbers. Some "things" are easier to make concrete than others. It is easier for us to reach agreement on what is "age" as opposed to what constitutes "love," an idea, an abstraction. The key point here is the degree of agreement, in terms of convention, as in the case of age measured in years, for example, and in terms of intersubjective agreement, as in the case of love as an idea with varied definitions. In both cases, a level of conceptual agreement is possible that thus informs how we measure the thing. As what we measure becomes more and more abstract, reification can become more and more challenging. However, it is difficult or nearly impossible to reify something that has no conceptual framework because there would be no frame of reference, and thus no informed way to measure the thing.

1.9 What is the relationship between a sample and a population?

Answer: When sample data represent a population under study, results from the sample can be inferred or generalized to the population. If the sample does not represent the target population, then the findings are limited to the sample.

1.10 Why does the U.S. Census Bureau collect census data rather than using sample data?

Answer: The U.S. Constitution mandates that a census be conducted every 10 years.

1.11 What is different today from data analysis in the past?

Answer: In the past, our data analyses were limited to after the fact studies, intentionality research, and some limited behavioral studies slicing away at bridging psychological and behavioral human activities. Collecting data was arduous and conducting accurate statistical analysis was time-consuming and laborious. Today, all of this has changed and continues to change. Statistics and the broader quantitative methodologies are now especially practical because of cost-effective advances in computer hardware and software, as well as the easy capture of online behaviors. We now have massive amounts of online psychological and behavioral data for analysis and the volume continues to grow at an accelerated rate. With big data and predictive analytics, we can integrate computer systems and statistics to analyze massive databases, which will allow us to develop predictive models for online and offline behaviors, sometimes in real time.

1.12 Why can sampling be more accurate than census data collection?

Answer: Sampling makes it easier to include individuals who are not easily accessible, whether they are undocumented workers or people living "off the grid."

B.2 Chapter 2

2.1 Define descriptive, correlation, and inferential statistics.

Answer: Descriptive statistics. Statistics that summarizes and describes sample data, which may be generalized to the population under study.

Correlation statistics. This is the analysis required in order to determine the strength and direction of a linear relationship between two variables known as a correlation. It does not indicate a cause and effect association. See the term correlation for details.

Inferential statistics. Statistics that examines the relationships and nature between and among variables and helps us draw conclusions that can be generalized to the entire population under study, thus allowing us to reduce uncertainty in decision-making.

2.2 Additionally, differentiate the three types of statistics by their key functions and provides examples of each.

Answer: Descriptive statistics describe the sample data, which can be applied to the population under study. For instance, percentage of sample by gender, average age, ethnicity, and educational level in the aggregate are descriptive. Correlation statistics examines for associations between two variables, but not cause and effect relationships. For example, there is a positive correlation between education and income. However, we do not know if education alone predicts greater income. It might be that those with more income may have the financial resources required to earn a degree. Again, correlation analysis simply reveals if a relationship exists, as well as the directionality and strength of that relationship (between two variables). Inferential statistics examines not just that a relationship exists between or among variables, but also the nature of those relationships. For instance, what personal attributes predict whether one will explore a career in criminal justice?

2.3 What is a correlation? What is an association?

Answer: Correlation. A value from −1 to 1 that represents a linear relationship or association between two variables. A correlation of −1 or 1 indicates a perfect linear relationship. A negative correlation reveals that the variables move in the opposite direction of each other and a positive correlation demonstrates that they move in the same direction. Correlations closer to −1 or 1 are stronger associations.

Association. This is a relationship between two variables. It does not indicate causality. It is equated with the term correlation.

2.4 Define and provide an example of external validity.

Answer: External validity. This is similar to generalizability. This type of validity is the extent to which findings from sample data can be applied to a larger population under study. It is only as valid as the degree to which the sample is representative of the population.

2.5 Which type of statistics is used to screen data? Explain your answer.

Answer: Descriptive statistics. Data from a given variable are described by their distribution as part of the data screening process, quite often using significance testing (see Chapter 11). For categorical variable data, the data are described in terms of counts and percentages of those counts in relation to the total count or sample space where there are required minimum frequencies per grouping. We can create various charts and tables that depict the data's characteristics, as discussed in Chapter 9. Numeric variable data are described in terms of the normal distribution.

2.6 Is a correlation typically a linear relationship between two variables? Explain your response.

Answer: A correlation analysis determines whether a linear relationship exists between two variables, as well as the strength and directionality of that relationship. It is not assumed to be a cause and effect relationship.

2.7 What is the focus of inferential statistics?

Answer: Inferential statistics is used to make conclusions and potential predictions about a population based on the analysis and evidence of data provided from a representative sample of that population. Inferential statistics focuses on the nature of the relationship between and among variables.

2.8 In the Pew study Real World Snapshot, what type of data are described? Explain your answer.

Answer: The data are categorical because the percentages are reported.

2.9 How do descriptive, correlation, and inferential statistics provide more and more information, respectively?

Answer: Descriptive statistics describes one or more of the population's general attributes. Correlation analysis determines whether a relationship exists between two variables. Inferential statistics examines the nature of the relationships between and among variables.

2.10 A new drug is being tested that can reverse the effects of Alzheimer's disease in certain patients. Researchers have sample data for 300 patients who have taken the drug over the minimum six-month period. The data include age, health condition, family history, blood type, sex, and a drug effectiveness score. From these data, provide types of descriptive, correlation, and inferential statistical analyses that can be conducted.

Answer: Descriptive statistics: Summary data, including age, blood type, sex, family history score, and effectiveness score, all define the typical patient.

Correlation statistics: Correlation between age and family history score, between family history score and effectiveness score, age and effectiveness score.

Inferential statistics: Summary data defining a typical patient (generalized to the population under study), statistically meaningful correlations applied to the population under study, and other analyses applied to the population, such as relationship between blood type and effectiveness score, sex and effectiveness score, and so forth.

B.3 Chapter 3

3.1 What is a variable? Provide three examples.

Answer: A variable is a directly or indirectly observable characteristic or property of something that is measurable. It varies or changes particularly in relation to one or more other variables or in comparison to other observations or measurements of the same variable. People vary and can be similar by age, income, motivation, attitude toward criminal justice, love toward an object or person, and so forth.

3.2 What is the conceptual definition of a variable? Provide examples.

Answer: The conceptual definition is an "idea" definition of something such as love, satisfaction, age, and education.

3.3 What is a measurable definition of a variable? Illustrate with examples.

Answer: The measurable definition is how we measure the conceptual definition, such as love or satisfaction using a Likert scale, age as life in number of years completed, and years of completed education or degrees earned.

3.4 When measuring the same phenomenon, can measurable definitions of variables (and conceptual definitions, for that matter) vary? If so, explain why.

Answer: Yes, they can vary. Sometimes we can measure a conceptual definition or variable through one or more measure. For example, a conceptual definition of love might include a nourishing relationship, mutual understanding, sacrifice, empathy, affection, sexual, and devotion. These components of love can be measured in different ways using different types of survey questions. They might also be measured by recording interactions between individuals who love each other. The point is that measures of love are informed by the conceptual definition or framework.

Likewise, we can have more than one conceptual definition of love, resulting in different but related ways of measuring. Definitions of love may vary and be less exhaustive as or more comprehensive and include more aspects of love than the example above. For another example, the standard for what constitutes defective manufactured parts may vary by customer, government regulation, and so forth. Yet the instrument used to measure quality remains the same. Therefore, the definition of defective part varies, but not the measure.

3.5 Define data and explain data in relation to variables. Illustrate your understanding with examples.

Answer: Data are (datum is singular) the recorded individual measurements of variables. Data are the different values associated with a variable, such as age in years reported by a sample of people, reported women, men, or LGBTQ gender identification, attitudes such as accepting or rejecting a political message, production output as in units, and so forth.

3.6 What components comprise a measurable framework?

Answer: The tools and formats that are used to collect and measure data are collectively called the measurable framework.

3.7 What are categorical variables? Provide some examples. Be sure to discuss the various types of categorical variables or levels of data.

Answer: Categorical variables consist of a set number of mutually exclusive characteristics or categories, which can be the simple presence or absence of a single variable attribute or a number of attributes within a variable. They are measured by counting instances of the categories within the variable. An example is "yes" and "no" responses to a question, which represents string data that can be coded as 2 = "yes" and 1 = "no." The categorical choices within a variable consist of all possible outcomes. It is called the sample space and can be represented in a table. For example, in a poll of 2,000 eligible voters, 50% (1,000 eligible voters) of respondents reported that they will vote for Candidate Brown, while 40% (800 eligible voters) intend to vote for Candidate White, and 7% (140 eligible voters) plan to vote for Candidate Green. Three percent (60 eligible voters) were undecided. These choices, their counts, and their percentages represent the sample space for this political poll.

Types of categorical variables:

1. Binary data, also called dichotomous or nominal-level data, only have two possible outcomes. They can also be viewed as the presence or absence of a condition.
2. Categorical data with more than two categories are called nominal-level data.
3. Ordinal categorical-level data or variables imply an order of magnitude to categories within the variable.

3.8 What are numeric variables? Provide some examples. Be sure to discuss the various types of numeric variables or levels of data.

Answer: A numeric variable comprises a level of some attribute measured in a sample. The measurements vary among data records and are part of a measuring process. This process involves the systematic assignment of numbers to objects and their properties in order to facilitate the use of statistics to study and describe concepts or objects and their relationships. There are no predetermined selections or counts, unlike categorical variables. Responses, measures, or observations are measured values. Age in number of years, income in dollars, height in inches, SAT scores, and the number of defective widgets produced in an eight-hour shift are examples of numeric data.

Types of numeric variables:

1. Ratio variables are the most comprehensive and informative level of data. All types of statistical analysis can be applied to ratio variables. Zero is a meaningful value; when the value of a variable equals zero, then there is nothing of that variable; it is absent. For example, zero income includes no income. Moreover, differences are clearly meaningful because we know the exact relationships between the values of the characteristic measured, including their relationship with zero.
2. In an interval variable, there are equal distances between the values of the characteristic measured. Put differently, the difference between 1 and 2 is the same as the difference between 3 and 4, the difference between 5 and 6, and so forth. However, zero has no meaning and it does not equal nothing or the absence of the variable attribute; thus, relative to "zero," differences are not meaningful. For example, a Fahrenheit temperature of zero has no meaning.
3. Scale data as interval variables. This is a special case usually involving survey-derived data. Strictly speaking, scale data formats such as 1 = "strongly disagree" through 5 = "strongly agree," 1 = "less important" to 7 = "more important," or 1 = "the least" to 5 = "the most" are ordinal categorical-level data. However, research has shown that treating this type of data format as interval data is valid and reliable under many conditions (Carifio & Perla, 2007; Norman, 2010).

3.9 Explain whether the following variables are categorical and/or numeric: mortgage amounts of randomly selected homeowners on the West Coast; political party affiliation; star mass in the Milky Way galaxy; temperatures along the equator; and the top three desirable product features by order of importance.

Answer: Mortgages (ratio), star mass (interval), and temperatures (interval) are numeric variables. Party affiliation is nominal categorical data and important product feature(s) are ordinal categorical data.

3.10 How might we conceptualize and measure attitudes of Brand Z sportswear?

Answer: We could conceptualize different aspects of attitude toward a brand. Attitude might capture perceptions of affordable prices, variety of styles, in vogue brand, quality of material, identification with the brand, and willingness to repeat purchase the brand. All of these together may constitute a favorable brand attitude. Measures might capture individual consumer attitudes of these aspects through a survey formatted in a scale ranging from 1 = none of the attribute (e.g. quality of material) to 5 = very much of the attribute (e.g. variety of styles). Each of these attributes could be examined individually and an average of these measures could represent overall attitude toward the brand.

3.11 What are string data? Provide an example.

Answer: Binary or nominal categorical choices can be recorded as words such as "yes" or "no," or favorite color such as "red," "white," "blue," "green," "black," or "brown."

3.12 What are counts or frequencies? Provide an example.

Answer: Counts or frequencies are the number of instances of a group within a categorical variable. For example, 100 people answer "yes," 60 people answer "no," and 40 people answer "maybe" for a total of 200.

3.13 What are relative frequencies? Provide an example.

Answer: Relative frequencies are the percentage of counts within a category based on the total count. For example, 50% of people answer "yes," 30% of people answer "no," and 20% of people answer "maybe" for a total of 100%.

3.14 Define a contingency table and provide an example.

Answer: A contingency table contains frequencies and percentage of grouping with a categorical variable by another categorical variable with groupings. For example:

Income Range by Gender Identification Frequencies

Income Range	Women	Men	LGBTQ	Total
Low Income	90 (51%)	65 (37%)	20 (12%)	175 (35%)
Middle Income	80 (39%)	100 (49%)	24 (12%)	204 (41%)
High Income	45 (37%)	37 (31%)	39 (32%)	121 (24%)
Total	215 (43%)	202 (40%)	83 (17%)	500 (100%)

Note: N = 500. Percentages are rounded.

3.15 What is a sample space?

Answer: The categorical choices within a variable consist of all possible outcomes. It is called the sample space and can be represented in a table.

3.16 What is a one-dimensional table? Provide a brief example.

Answer: A table is said to be a single- (or one-) dimensional table because it comprises only one variable. For example, see the table on the right.

Summary Count for Chocolate Ice Cream Preference

Response	Count	Percentage
Yes	120	60%
No	80	40%
Totals	200	100%

Note: N = 200

3.17 What is a two-dimensional table? Provide a brief example.

Answer: A table is said to be a two-dimensional table because it comprises two variables. For example:

Income Range by Gender Identification Frequencies

Income Range	Women	Men	LGBTQ	Total
Low Income	90 (51%)	65 (37%)	20 (12%)	175 (35%)
Middle Income	80 (39%)	100 (49%)	24 (12%)	204 (41%)
High Income	45 (37%)	37 (31%)	39 (32%)	121 (24%)
Total	215 (43%)	202 (40%)	83 (17%)	500 (100%)

Note: *N* = 500. Percentages are rounded.

3.18 What is the role of a meaningful zero in ratio-level data? Clearly explain your answer and provide an example.

Answer: Ratio variables are the most comprehensive and informative level of data. All types of statistical analysis can be applied to ratio variables. Zero is a meaningful value; when the value of a variable equals zero, then there is nothing of that variable; it is absent. For example, zero income includes no income. Moreover, differences are clearly meaningful because we know the exact relationships between the values of the characteristic measured, including their relationship with zero. For instance, one can say that a person who is 40 years old is twice the age of someone who is 20 years old. Likewise, the difference between 10 and 20 years old is the same as the difference between 60 and 70 years old, and the difference between 0 and 1 is as meaningful as the difference between 1 and 2. Examples of ratio variables are age, income, and state funding for nonprofit social services' programs in each of the 50 states.

3.19 What is scale-level data? Provide an example.

Answer: Scale data as interval variables. This is a special case usually involving survey-derived data. Strictly speaking, scale data formats such as 1 = "strongly disagree" through 5 = "strongly agree," 1 = "less important" to 7 = "more important," or 1 = "the least" to 5 = "the most" are ordinal categorical-level data. However, research has shown that treating this type of data format as interval data is valid and reliable under many conditions (Carifio & Perla, 2007; Norman, 2010).

3.20 Define a control variable.

Answer: A variable that the researcher wants to account for so that it does not influence the relationship between the independent variable(s) and the dependent variable is called a control variable.

3.21 If we wish to observe, measure, and analyze the relationship between consumer perceived Brand Z sportswear quality and consumer repeat purchases at retail bricks-and-mortar stores, what might we control for in this study? Identify at least three potential control variables.

Answer: There are a number of factors that could affect the relationship between perceived brand quality and repeat purchases of the brand. Some potential confounders are: store ambience, variety of selections, level of customer service, price points, brand loyalty (repeat purchases, positive attitude toward brand, and favorable word of mouth), availability of sales discounts, brand popularity, level of customer identification with the brand, and so forth.

3.22 What are independent and dependent variables? Explain their relationship. Be sure to provide an example.

Answer: An independent variable predicts change in another variable. Its effects are measured so that a change or different condition in the independent variable affects or changes the dependent variable in some way. For example, educational level and number of hours of work per week are two independent variables that might predict game hunting behaviors, which is the dependent variable. The dependent variable changes because of change in the independent variable. That is, the independent variable affects the dependent variable. In the example above, differences in amount of work per week and in educational level are thought to predict hunting behavior.

3.23 Define an interaction variable.

Answer: An interaction term is a variable that comprises a combination of usually two but sometimes more than two independent variables. They have a combined effect on a dependent variable. The collective effects can be more or less than the sum of the predictors' effects operating separately on the dependent variable.

3.24 Pair the following six variables into three interaction variables that make sense: lead time for responding to email; education; product Model X recall; relevant professional experience; advertising Model X; and effective interpersonal email communication. Explain their potential effects within the interaction.

Answer: The interaction pairs are: education/experience on salary and career advancement (positive relationship and potential synergy); Model X recall/advertising Model X (negative relationship and potential synergy); and effective email communication/lead time for responding to email (positive relationship and potential synergy).

B.4 Chapter 4

4.1 What is a data file?

Answer: It is the file that contains data.

4.2 In the SPSS data, define the "Data View" and the "Variable View" tabs.

Answer: The Data View contains the raw data, which are manually entered, in an existing SPSS data file, from another data file format, or imported from another source. The Variable View allows the SPSS user to define the variable parameters or characteristics. Data can also be exported to various spreadsheet formats.

4.3 What is the output file?

Answer: The output file, as the name suggests, contains data analysis output such as tables, graphs, and statistical information, which can be copied or exported. The output file also serves as a record of all activities conducted during an SPSS session.

4.4 What is a syntax file?

Answer: This file is used to code SPSS analysis, which allows for a customized analysis and output not typically available in the pull-down menu.

4.5 What is a case of data and where is it located?

Answer: It is an individual record located in the Data View as a row of data.

4.6 What is located in a data column?

Answer: The variable column contains data or observations about a specific variable. Each row within the column is the value for each case or observation.

4.7 Can variable names contain spaces?

Answer: No.

4.8 Can variable labels contain spaces?

Answer: Yes.

4.9 In the Variable View, what are the choices in the "Measure" option? Explain each option.

Answer: Scale is for numeric data, ordinal is for ordinal categorical data, and nominal is for nominal categorical data.

4.10 When opening or saving data files, what are the various formats available?

Answer: SPSS, Excel, text, dBase, and so forth.

4.11 When saving (or exporting) output files, what are some of the available formats?

Answer: SPSS, Word, PPT, and PDF.

4.12 Can SPSS data be cut and pasted to or from an SPSS data file?

Answer: Yes.

4.13 Can text files be opened in SPSS?

Answer: Yes.

4.14 What is a codebook? Provide examples.

Answer: A codebook is the legend of all of the variable descriptions and values, including formatting. It provides operational definitions of the variables, which are the measurable definitions of variables. It serves as a reference that is handy when there are many variables that are not easily defined in terms of measurement, and when variables are transformed (changed in some way). The transformation should be described in the codebook. In short, the codebook makes a daunting spreadsheet with many variables, cases, and numbers manageable.

4.15 Does SPSS have a codebook feature? If so, where is it located?

Answer: SPSS has a codebook option. It can be accessed by clicking: Analysis>Reports>Codebook.

4.16 How does one exit the data or output files?

Answer: Simply click on the "X" in the red box located in the top-right-hand corner of the screen or click the "File" tab and then the last option, which is "Exit." If related output or syntax files are open and have not been saved, the user will be prompted to save them.

4.17 What are the three basic SPSS file formats?

Answer: Data, syntax, and output.

4.18 What view allows for more variable information to be inputted?

Answer: The Variable View allows for more information.

4.19 In the "Variable View" tab, what types of data measurment (levels are data) are available?

Answer: Nominal, ordinal, and scale.

4.20 Refer to the codebook in this book. Create an SPSS data file based on the codebook. Where the codebook does not have coding, create your own coding scheme. Prepare the data file in the Variable View; however, do not enter any data in the Data View. Save the data file as a .sav file. Save your output file as a Word file. Name the files "Exercise 4.20 Data File Assignment" and "Exercise 4.20 Output File Assignment."

Answer: Students are required to submit the electronic SPSS data and output files via email or designated upload website.

B.5 Chapter 5

5.1 Define the term sample and provide two examples.

Answer: A representative small group of a population of interest. The group is subject to statistical analysis with the intention of generalizing results to the population from which it was drawn. For example, five students from each grade at a high school or 300 18–22-year-old college students from across the United States.

5.2 Define the process of sampling.

Answer: Sampling is the process by which a representative small group or sample of a population of interest is selected for statistical analysis. In other words, a representative sample must match key characteristics of the population under study because the statistical findings of the analyses will be applied to the population from which the sample was drawn.

5.3 Define the term target population and provide an example.

Answer: The target population is the entire population of interest. It must be clearly defined so that it informs the sampling strategy. It is defined by its characteristics. Its approximate size must be known as well. For example, every person over 65 years old in Canada.

5.4 Define the term element and provide three examples.

Answer: The targeted population consists of elements or individual units. The element serves as the basis of analysis. It is the data source, such as male student, restaurant chain, or a social services client.

5.5 Define a sampling unit.

Answer: Sometimes data are collected from a sampling unit, which is the element or contains a set of (unique) elements so that there may be more than one basis of analysis. For instance, data may be collected from children within households. The household is the sampling unit and the child is the element so that the children are studied in the context of household characteristics.

5.6 What is a sampling frame? Provide two examples.

Answer: A sampling frame is a data source or list of elements composed of the target population. Examples are telephone lists, email lists, Facebook friends, voter registration lists, other types of registration lists, property ownership lists, all the machinery output records from a manufacturing facility, lists of companies, and so forth.

5.7 What is sampling without replacement?

Answer: Sampling without replacement means that once you select a particular element, you cannot select it again. This approach affects the probability of selection.

5.8 What is sampling with replacement?

Answer: Sampling with replacement means that after you select a sampling unit, you return it to the frame where it might be selected again, which maintains the same probability of selection.

5.9 What is probability sampling? Provide two examples.

Answer: Probability sampling is an approach that assures that each element or sampling unit has an equal chance of being chosen. This method uses some form of random selection. Simple examples are picking one out of 10 names from a hat or selecting an ace of spades from a deck of 52 playing cards.

5.10 What does random denote in statistics?

Answer: Random denotes something that is not systematic nor has a pattern. It is arbitrary and usually includes a sampling frame.

5.11 Define central tendency. Explain your answer.

Answer: Central tendency is the extent to which data points concentrate around the mean (average) or center of the distribution. It is a measure of symmetry.

5.12 Define dispersion. Explain your answer.

Answer: Dispersion is the spread of the data from the mean or degree to which values deviate from the mean.

5.13 What is the relationship between central tendency and dispersion, and how do they relate to the shape of data's distribution?

Answer: The combination of two attributes determines the shape of data distribution. Thus, the assessment of these two characteristics is necessary in order to determine whether the data are normally distributed. These characteristics are central tendency and dispersion. Central tendency is the extent to which data points concentrate around the mean (average) or center of the distribution. It is a measure of symmetry. Dispersion is the spread of the data from the mean or degree to which values deviate from the mean. It is a measure of peakedness or flatness. Together, these attributes represent the shape of a variable's data distribution. Randomly selected data provide normal distribution and this allow for accurate probability statistical results.

5.14 Describe simple random sampling.

Answer: When utilizing simple random sampling, every sampling unit has a known and equal chance of being selected. Every sample of a fixed size has the same chance of being selected as another sample of the same size.

5.15 Describe systematic random sampling.

Answer: In the case of systematic random sampling, every element has a known and equal chance of being selected, as in the case of the simple random approach. However, for systematic random sampling, the methodology varies and is more complex than simple random sampling techniques, but manageable. This method attempts to overcome some of the pitfalls of simple random sampling by selecting elements from the full range of the population or sampling frame.

5.16 What is a sampling fraction?

Answer: It is the desired sample size divided by the population size or (n/N).

5.17 Describe cluster random sampling.

Answer: Cluster sampling often draws data from natural clusters, such as geopolitical locations like states, company departments, neighborhood blocks, people who shop on certain days, and so forth. The clusters are mutually exclusive and collectively exhaustive subpopulations.

5.18 Define one-stage cluster sampling.

Answer: This is a sampling technique that encompasses all of the cluster elements in the sample.

5.19 Describe multistage cluster sampling.

Answer: Multistage cluster sampling occurs when the sample is drawn from nested (populations within populations) data within clusters. For example, a researcher would sample companies, then departments within those companies or sample state voters, followed by county voters, and then municipal voters.

5.20 Describe proportionate cluster sampling.

Answer: Sampling can also account for subpopulation sizes, known as proportionate cluster sampling, where the samples are based on the population segment sizes.

5.21 Define disproportionate cluster sampling.

Answer: A sample can have an equal number of elements despite cluster size, which is called disproportionate cluster sampling.

5.22 What is a stratified random sample?

Answer: Stratified random sampling involves segmenting the target population into subpopulations or strata based on homogenous characteristics important in the study. These characteristics are called stratification variables and have different levels. Once the strata (or level) combinations are determined for each subpopulation, then a random representative sample is drawn from each.

5.23 What is a proportionate stratified sample?

Answer: If the population size of each stratum were known, then the strata sample sizes (n) could be adjusted to correspond with that of the population, which is called proportionate stratified sampling.

5.24 What is a disproportionate stratified sample?

Answer: A disproportionate stratified sampling approach is where each stratum is not equal to its proportion in the total target population.

5.25 What is a nonprobability sample?

Answer: Nonprobability sampling is a subjective sampling strategy that does not involve random selection, but is based on some other criterion. There are no assurances that each sampling unit has an equal chance of selection, the probability of selection is unknown, and the representativeness of the sample is left to the researcher rather than to an objective measure.

5.26 Describe convenience sampling and provide two examples.

Answer: Convenience sampling involves selecting sampling units based on convenience. Convenience sampling examples include students, coworkers, family members, and other social group members such as Facebook friends and Twitter followers. These elements are easy to access. There is no random component to selection and the sample often does not fully represent the population of interest.

5.27 Describe expert sampling and provide an example.

Answer: Expert sampling involving selecting elements who are available experts on the topic under study. For example, if a study goal is to predict when a likely cure for cancer will occur, the researcher may ask the leading oncologists and oncological researchers.

5.28 Define quota sampling and provide an example.

Answer: Quota sampling is a special case of expert sampling involving two stages. First, categories of characteristics (like strata) are created to serve as the basis for groups, including quotas for those groups. These categories attempt to assure that the target population is represented in the sample. Last, quotas (subsample sizes) are assigned to characteristics that are consistent with the target subpopulation sizes. For example, the sample consists of 60% women and 40% men because this represents the breakdown in the target population.

5.29 What is snowball sampling? Provide two examples.

Answer: Snowball sampling is appropriate when it is difficult to reach the target population. The sensitive nature of the data and the target population make data collection challenging. For instance, if the U.S. Census Bureau wanted to collect economic data on undocumented workers, it might use snowball sampling. The researchers would initially locate workers receptive to providing data and ask those workers to identify others who might be willing to "talk." The snowballing sampling method is effective to recruit victims of unreported domestic violence, workers who operate in some aspect of the underground economy, or people who live off the grid.

5.30 What is the optimal sampling method to collect numeric data from a population where subpopulation areas tend to be homogenous and have different sizes? We want to accurately generalize our findings to the entire population of interest. Explain your answer using appropriate terminology.

Answer: Proportionate stratified random sampling will assure that all subpopulations are represented in percentages that correspond with their population of interest proportions.

5.31 We wish to sample homeless people who suffer from substance abuse in order to collect data about their perspective on what type of social support might help them on the road to recovery. What sampling approach would you suggest and why?

Answer: Snowball sampling would be appropriate because this vulnerable population might be hesitant to participate unless a peer encourages another member of this group to do so. Trust needs to be established owing to the sensitive nature of the situation.

5.32 Cite and explain three examples where expert sampling would be appropriate.

Answer: Ph.D.s in law and/or attorneys polled on whether they think certain laws passed by Congress will stand the test of the U.S. Supreme Court. A vice president of manufacturing selecting several production facilities that she thinks is representative of her multinational company's typical production output. Top-level intelligence officers opinions on another country's intelligence capabilities.

5.33 Describe and explain a hypothetical cases deploying cluster sampling within an organization. Be sure to include the basis for clustering. Justify your hypothetical case.

Answer: Assume that sales have flattened inconsistently across sales districts and you wish to discover at least some determinants for the lack of growth so that you develop an online survey. In the past, responses from the sales force have been spotty and you suspect that some managers have actually discouraged feedback from salespersons. A multistage proportionate cluster-sampling approach would be appropriate. Clusters would be multilevel and sampling units would be randomly chosen. Sampling units would be sales region followed by sales districts and then salespersons. This approach would help uncover whether there are any sales patterns by region, district, or individual salesperson. It might be a regional or district issue predicted by certain associated characteristics, such as concentration of major competitor offering a new product. It might be management at a specific level. It might be a general economic trend.

B.6 Chapter 6

6.1 What is the Central Limit Theorem?

Answer: The Central Limit Theorem states that a sample of means from randomly drawn samples will approach normal distribution as the (overall) sample size increases, whether or not the population from which the samples are drawn is normally distributed.

6.2 What is a sample size? Provide one example.

Answer: The sample size is the number of cases or elements in the sample. Given the required statistical power, anticipated minimum effect sizes, and alpha, we can determine the sample size.

6.3 For categorical data, is there a minimum expected cell count? If so, what is it?

Answer: Yes, it is 5.

6.4 Generally, is sample size based on the total target population size? Explain your answer.

Answer: It is not because sample size is contingent upon drawing a random sample. In the case of numeric data, there is an assumption of normally distributed data, which allows for parametric statistical analysis.

6.5 What is an effect? Provide an example.

Answer: Effect is a general term that refers to a meaningful result of some kind from a statistical procedure. For example, a statistically significant difference between two sample means (averages) or a statistically significant correlation between two variables.

6.6 What is an expected effect size? Provide an example.

Answer: Expected effect sizes are what we minimally expect to find, whether it involves means testing, categorical variable comparisons, correlations, or regression results. For instance, a study strategy may target correlations of .30 or greater. Expected effects' sizes are often informed by previous research, expert advice, or target goals.

6.7 Is it possible to have a sample that is too large?

Answer: A very large sample size may yield such small statistically significant results that serve no practical purpose. Sometimes in very large samples, error can appear as an effect.

6.8 What is statistical power?

Answer: Statistical power is the level of confidence that we have for detecting a potential effect in sample data so that if it exists, it will be detected.

6.9 Describe the components of statistical power.

Answer: Statistical power is the level of confidence that we have for detecting a potential effect in sample data so that if an effect exists, it will be detected. Statistical power and the following three considerations are interdependent: (1) What potential effects do we hope to *minimally* detect?

(2) What is our acceptable level of risk known as alpha level? (3) Sample size. Knowing three out of four determines the fourth consideration.

6.10 What is alpha? Explain your answer.

Answer: Level of alpha is the level of acceptable risk. This is usually .05 or less, which means that the chance of findings not being statistically meaningful must be <.05 in order to detect effects. Depending on the study aim, alpha might increase or decrease. For example, at a nuclear power plant, a study that examines for serious reactor breaches might set alpha higher and perhaps at .20, which is a lower threshold of significance that increases the likelihood that the study will detect possible breaches. In this case, it is better to be safe than sorry, considering the consequences of such a breach. In less risky situations, setting alpha at the standard .05 is acceptable, such as in marketing and educational research. In sum, the circumstances and standard conventions of the subject matter or industry under study determine alpha.

6.11 Generally and briefly explain the concept of finite population correction.

Answer: In some cases, populations may be small, as in the case of organizational research where the organizational population of interest may be a few thousand or less. As a rule, samples should not consist of 10% or more of the target population because such a relatively large percentage overestimates the population variance. In such cases, a finite population correction is necessary.

6.12 What are some factors that inform how unequal sample sizes are addressed?

Answer: The influence of variable unequal sample sizes on statistical analysis varies. There are a number of factors that come into play. First, the approaches vary based on whether categorical or numeric data are analyzed. Second, measuring the same sample more than once for comparison would require equal sizes for each measurement. Third, the size of the samples to be compared can affect the analysis. Fourth, the degree of difference in the sizes is also a factor. Greater differences would be a cause for alarm.

Additionally, the decision to adjust for unequal sizes requires an assessment of the research situation. The study design, nature of the research, and number of variables are considerations. In light of these factors, some statisticians recommend deleting the extra cases using various strategies, and still others suggest doing nothing.

6.13 What is the name of the SPSS application provided to determine an appropriate sample size?

Answer: The application is called "IBM SPSS SamplePower 3."

6.14 What is the rule of thumb for estimating a standard deviation in normally distributed data?

Answer: If we assume that the data are normally distributed, there is a rule of thumb for estimating the standard deviation, which is dividing the range of the data by 4: Standard deviation = (maximum value – minimum value) / 4.

6.15 For what types of variables can an appropriate sample size be determined?

Answer: Sample size can be determined for categorical and numeric data.

6.16 In reporting the required sample size, what statistics are included?

Answer: The confidence level, anticipated minimum effect size, alpha, and sometimes other expected data attributes, depending on the statistical procedure, are reported.

6.17 What is a useful feature of SamplePower 3?

Answer: The analysis generates a test report that includes all of the required statistical power information.

6.18 A manufacturer wishes to know whether the diameter of its machined parts varies from 10 mm by sample testing output. The anticipated mean is 7.30 mm. In the past, the standard deviation was 6.50 mm. What sample size is necessary in order to be 90% confident in the sample results?

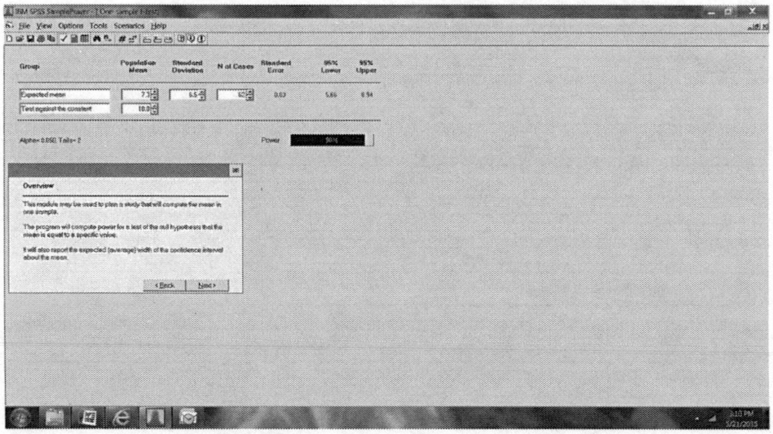

Answer: Sample size: 62.

6.19 You wish to determine if tuna is preferred more on the West Coast or East Coast in fine dining restaurants. Restaurant patrons will provide their preference by answering a question formatted in a five-point scale with responses ranging from 1 = "not preferred at all" to 5 = "preferred most or all of the time." The standard deviation will be 1 and the confidence level is 80%. What sample size is required? The minimum expected difference (effect) based on the five-point scale is .5 or scores 4.5 and 4.0.

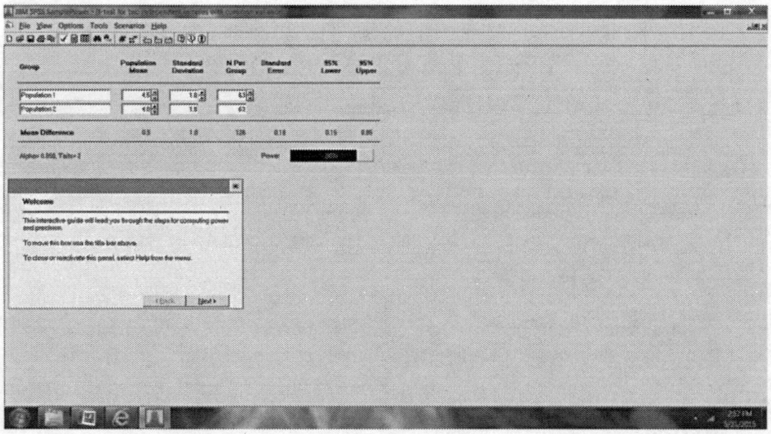

Answer: Sample size: 63 per coast sample.

6.20 Education researchers wish to determine whether household income, owning one or more dogs, and having educated parents will predict whether children will attend college. The anticipated minimum effect sizes are .10 for income, .10 for education, and .05 for dog ownership. The overall confidence level is 95%. What is the required sample size?

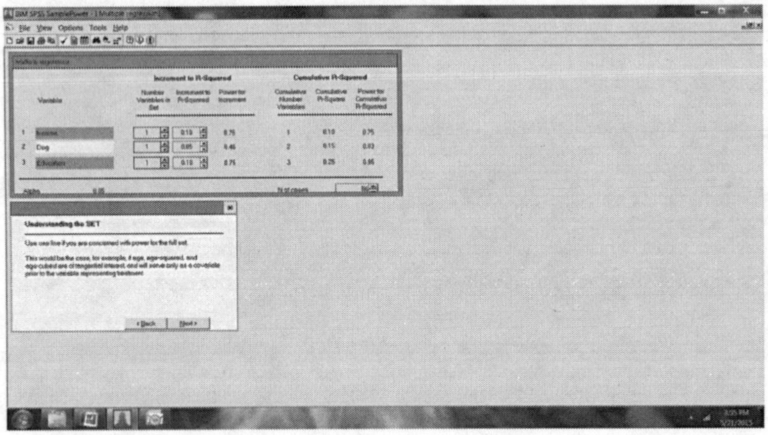

Answer: Sample size: 56.

B.7 Chapter 7

7.1 Define statistical error.

Answer: In statistics, and especially numeric data, error is any deviation in sample data from the population of interest based on: (1) sources of data; and (2) data collection methods.

7.2 Define random sampling error and provide one example.

Answer: This error occurs when the sample selected is an imperfect representation of the population under study. The differences between the sample and population do not demonstrate a pattern, but are inherently random. For example, political polls that deploy similar scientific or systematic sampling techniques often yield somewhat different results. Pollsters endeavor to minimize random sampling error so that they can produce accurate results.

7.3 Define systematic sampling error and provide one example.

Answer: Sampling error that demonstrates a pattern in the data as a result of sampling. For instance, consider a study examining national concerns about polluting the oceans. Drawing a sample from only the coastal areas as opposed to the central United States might result in systematic error because those participants residing in the coastal regions might be more sensitive to the topic, assuming that population concentration is not an issue. Determining national interest in photography from a sample frame consisting of membership to a photography website would likely yield an overestimate of interest.

7.4 What is coverage error?

Answer: Error that occurs when the sample does not represent a cross section of the target population, resulting in selection bias.

7.5 What is a systematic response error? Provide an example.

Answer: This error occurs when there is a pattern derived from sample elements, which can result in a skewed response (data) distribution. For example, a survey does not provide the full range of responses, which would be the case if a sample of children are tasked with reading a short story and then responding to comprehension questions. If the story is above their reading comprehension level, then most child readers will not grasp the full story, thus creating a response pattern.

7.6 What is a sampling frame error? Provide an example.

Answer: This is a type of coverage error involving a difference between the actual target population and population as defined by the sampling frame. For example, if a researcher wishes to run an opinion poll of all adults about a number of local social issues, drawing a sample solely from property ownership lists would result in sampling frame error because such lists would not include non-propriety-owning adults in the community.

7.7 What is a ceiling effect?

Answer: This effect results when data are skewed to the left, illustrating many high values, thus violating the normal distribution assumption. For instance, a survey in which the participants answer in a pattern of values in the higher end of a scale, thus the sample does not provide the full range of responses. If a sample of children are tasked with reading a short story and then respond to comprehension questions. If the story is below their reading comprehension level, then most readers will grasp the story and respond that they do understand the story, which creates a response pattern of mostly high scores.

7.8 What is a flooring effect?

Answer: This effect results when data are skewed to the right, denoting many low values, thus violating the normal distribution assumption. For example, a survey in which the participants answer in a pattern of values in the lower end of a scale, thus the sample does not provide the full range of responses. If a sample of children are tasked with reading a short story and then respond to comprehension questions. If the story is above their reading comprehension level, then most readers will not grasp the story and respond that they do not understand the story, which creates a response pattern of mostly low scores.

7.9 What is nonsampling random error? Provide an example.

Answer: This error results from sources other than those ascribed to sampling. Some error may be caused by the intrinsic fluctuation of data and other error may be caused by the unit of measurement, such as people, a chemical process, financial trends, weather conditions, or some other aspect of the measurement environment. For example, some survey questions may not have been clearly understood by some respondents, resulting in a wider range of responses. Alternatively, responses from survey participants may not be accurate because individuals might be compelled to provide socially acceptable responses to sensitive issues rather than deviate from what is perceived as acceptable answers, which then becomes a source of nonsampling random error.

7.10 Define nonsampling systematic error and provide an example.

Answer: This error demonstrates a pattern in the data not attributed to sampling. It is caused by the study design, some aspect of the study environment, and/or measurement error. The error follows a discernible pattern and is controllable. For instance, a measurement device that requires calibration over time would yield systematic inaccurate results such as a temperature reading that is consistently 2 degrees below the actual temperature.

7.11 Define measurement error and offer an example.

Answer: This is error due to a flaw in data collection or measurement. It is a type of nonsampling systematic error. For instance, a measurement device that requires calibration over time would yield systematic inaccurate results such as a temperature reading that is consistently 2 degrees below the actual temperature.

7.12 What is a social desirability effect? Provide an example.

Answer: This effect occurs when study respondents provide answers that are socially desirable even if they actually do not subscribe to those responses. This is especially the case when this issue is socially sensitive, such as reporting attitudes about specific lifestyles or behaviors, as well as personal value and religious beliefs.

7.13 What is the Hawthorne effect?

Answer: This effect is based on responses guided by participant perceptions of what they think the researcher wants them to answer or do in appreciation for the attention given them by the researcher.

7.14 What is problematic about the following question? "What is your party affiliation: Democrat, Republican, or Independent?"

Answer: Items must be exhaustive. What if the respondent were from another party? What if she were a Libertarian?

7.15 What is problematic about the following question? "What is your age range: 18–25, 25–45, 45–65, 65 and older?"

Answer: Items must be mutually exclusive. Participants whose ages are located at the end points have two choices, when they should have only one age category, which can provide inaccurate results and thus threaten validity.

7.16 What is problematic about the following scenario? Asking only progressive Democrats if they will vote for a conservative Republican.

Answer: Responses will be skewed in the direction of "no" responses and nonnormal distribution, which is a systematic response error. Thus, these findings cannot be generalized to the entire voting population.

7.17 What is the difference between sampling and nonsampling error?

Answer: Sampling error pertains to sample selection issues. Nonsampling error involves data collection methods and related considerations that can affect data collection, and thus the data.

7.18 What is the difference between random and systematic error?

Answer: Random error is natural and part of normal fluctuations. Systematic error involves error that demonstrates a pattern.

7.19 Explain how random fluctuations in data can appear to influence data trends. Cite the Real World Snapshot example.

Answer: Short-term fluctuations in climate change can mask a longer-term trend. Accounting for random error in trends can provide accurate data necessary for interpretation and data-driven decision-making.

7.20 Think of situations where people complete a survey. Such self-reported data can be subjective and not accurately represent a situation. Can you think of circumstances where this might be the case? How might you reduce these effects?

Answer: Survey research involving sexual behavior, reasons why a person desires a pay raise, drug use, and Web surfing for personal reasons while at work are such situations. There are instruments such as the social desirability scale and Hawthorne-related tools that can help tease out the subjective nature of responses. Additionally, other sources of information could be used to validate responses. In the pay raise example, employee human resources records and a supervisor interview about the employee might provide what is called concurrent validity, in addition to the employee survey response.

B.8 Chapter 8

8.1 What is the value to having nonrandom missing data?

Answer: Missing data that are not random may reveal valuable information. For instance, the lack of data for certain equipment production days may suggest that for those machinery units, there is a pattern of operation that requires identification and addressing in order to maximize production output. It could be that the machinery model, operator characteristics, training requirements, pattern of some aspect of maintenance, or even the practices of the supervisor, among other factors, influence production. Thus, the missing data can reveal a dynamic that is important in a study, which may not have been considered beforehand.

8.2 What is imputation?

Answer: Imputation is a process that allows us to replace missing values with predicted values, thus adding to statistical power (confidence in our results).

8.3 What is missing at random (MAR)?

Answer: This is a condition in which missing values are not random, except within subsets where the missing values are random.

8.4 What is missing completely at random (MCAR)?

Answer: This is a condition in which there is no pattern between any missing values and any values in the dataset.

8.5 What is missing not at random (MNAR)?

Answer: In this situation, the missing values are not at random, but demonstrate a pattern between the missing value and another value in the dataset.

8.6 What is listwise?

Answer: The listwise (also called casewise) procedure is an option in many statistical procedures. Selecting this option simply removes all incomplete cases from the analysis, whether composed of numeric or categorical data.

8.7 What is pairwise?

Answer: The pairwise approach includes comparison where there are no missing values on an analysis-by-analysis basis, whether the data are numeric or categorical.

8.8 Define series mean imputation.

Answer: This imputation approach involves substituting the variable mean for all missing values.

8.9 Define mean of nearby points imputation.

Answer: The mean of nearby points imputes missing values with the mean of valid surrounding values.

8.10 What is the median of nearby points imputation?

Answer: The median of nearby points replaces missing values with the median of the surrounding values.

8.11 Define linear interpolation imputation.

Answer: Linear interpolation replaces missing values using a linear interpolation formula, which is based on patterns detected in the data. The last value above (before) the missing value and the first value below (after) the missing value are used for the interpolation.

8.12 Define linear trend at point imputation.

Answer: This imputation method replaces missing values with the linear trend for that point based on all values in the variable.

8.13 What is expectation-maximization (EM) imputation?

Answer: This imputation method employs a single imputation process and predicts missing values based among the variables' data patterns within each case. It is recommended for most missing value analyses and imputation.

8.14 Define multiple imputation (MI).

Answer: This imputation technique accounts for all case values as well as selected variable values. It employs multiple imputations, which are set by the researcher. Generally, no more than five imputations provide sufficient randomness. The average of the results is the replacement value.

8.15 What options are available when a dataset has nonrandom missing data?

Answer: If there is a pattern in the data, some options are: (1) collect more data to increase the number of complete cases; (2) limit analysis to MAR subsets; (3) analyze the data listwise; or (4) provide a caveat in the write-up.

8.16 Why is adherence to the 5% rule important?

Answer: It is first important to acknowledge that the impact of missing data on statistics can be serious, leading to biased estimates of parameters, loss of information, decreased statistical power, increased standard errors, and weakened generalizability of findings. Most statistical procedures automatically eliminate cases with missing data, which can reduce statistical power. Consequently, results may not be meaningful because of a smaller sample size. A larger sample size with sufficient power might yield statistically significant effects not detected by a smaller size. Moreover, if the remaining complete sample is not random, results may not be accurate. Assuming a sufficiently large sample, removing no more than 5% of the missing data cases assures that it is random and maintains statistical power.

8.17 How might missing data have a negative impact on one's statistical analysis?

Answer: The impact of missing data on statistics can be serious, leading to biased estimates of parameters, loss of information, decreased statistical power, increased standard errors, and weakened generalizability of findings.

8.18 A dataset consists of three variables: social status of restaurant, service level, and average check (bill). The sample consists of 400 cases, some of which have missing values. First, determine if the missing values are numeric and MCAR. Second, determine whether the percentages of missing data are acceptable. Third, impute any missing values using EM. Last, report findings in the examples' format.

Answer: We assume that the missing data are numeric. Since Little's MCAR is p = .55, the missing values are assessed as MCAR. A p-value of .05 or less would indicate that the missing data are likely not MCAR, and thus are NMAR. The percentages of missing data per variable are well below 2% and the complete sample size is greater than 30.

EM Means[a]

SegmentbyStatus	ServiceLevel	AverageCheck
3.68	3.14	13.8980

a. Little's MCAR test: Chi-Square = 4.922, DF = 6, Sig. = .554

Univariate Statistics

	N	Mean	Std. Deviation	Missing		No. of Extremes[a]	
				Count	Percent	Low	High
SegmentbyStatus	397	3.69	1.983	3	.8	0	0
ServiceLevel	396	3.13	1.482	4	1.0	0	7
AverageCheck	396	13.8655	13.72612	4	1.0	0	30

a. Number of cases outside the range (Q1 - 1.5*IQR, Q3 + 1.5*IQR).

The imputed missing variables are available in the completed dataset named "Missing Data MCAR Exercise 1 COMPLETE."

Write-up: The sample size is 400. Little's MCAR was not meaningful (p = .55), indicating that the missing data did not follow a pattern. The percentage of missing values ranged from .8% to 1% (3–4 missing values/variable), well within the acceptable 2%. Expectation-maximization imputation was conducted, which provided a complete dataset.

8.19 This dataset consists of eight variables where PR professionals reported their preference for eight types of PR tasks. The sample consists of 255 cases, some of which have missing values. First, determine if the missing values are numeric and MCAR. Second, determine whether the percentages of missing data are acceptable. Third, impute any missing values using EM. Last, report findings in the proper format.

Answer: We assume that the missing data are numeric. Since Little's MCAR is p = 0.30, the missing values are assessed as NMAR. A p-value of .05 or less would indicate that the missing data are likely not MCAR, and thus are NMAR.

The percentages of missing data per variable are well below 2%. Since the missing value percentage is low and the sample size is 255 (greater than 30), we have the following options: (1) collect more data to increase the number of complete records (cases); (2) limit analysis to MAR subsets; (3) analyze the data listwise; and/or (4) provide a caveat in the write-up.

How to proceed will be informed by the required sample size, which will be determined using power analysis (see Chapter 8). However, it appears that the listwise procedure may be effective since the percentages of missing values are low. Researchers trained in advanced methods can discover unique patterns and replace missing data using approaches that account for missing value patterns.

EM Means[a]

q1	q2	q3	q4	q5	q6	q7	q8
4.722	4.316	4.712	4.702	4.566	4.143	4.345	4.520

a. Little's MCAR test: Chi-Square = 25.518, DF = 14, Sig. = .030

Univariate Statistics

	N	Mean	Std. Deviation	Missing		No. of Extremes[a,b]	
				Count	Percent	Low	High
q1	255	4.722	.5812	0	.0	.	.
q2	254	4.317	.8433	1	.4	10	0
q3	255	4.712	.6397	0	.0	.	.
q4	255	4.702	.5566	0	.0	63	0
q5	255	4.566	.6389	0	.0	4	0
q6	252	4.145	.8672	3	1.2	8	0
q7	255	4.345	.8300	0	.0	7	0
q8	255	4.520	.6827	0	.0	2	0

a. Number of cases outside the range (Q1 - 1.5*IQR, Q3 + 1.5*IQR).

b. . indicates that the inter-quartile range (IQR) is zero.

Write-up: For this dataset, a listwise procedure is recommended because there is the likelihood of missing value patterns (Little's MCAR, p = .030), the missing value rates are well below 2%, and the sample size will be 252, representing a small loss of data.

8.20 What is Little's MCAR Test?

Answer: Little's MCAR Test determines whether missing data are missing completely at random (MCAR). It requires at least two variables to detect a pattern.

B.9 Chapter 9

9.1 What is a sample frequency?

Answer: It is a tally or count that represents the number of occurrences of a category within a categorical variable.

9.2 What is a sample count?

Answer: It is a tally or frequency that represents the number of occurrences of a category within a categorical variable.

9.3 What is a sample proportion?

Answer: It is a percentage or relative frequency of a count or frequency within the categories of a categorical variable. It is in relation to the entire sample size (sample space) or to a subset of the sample.

9.4 What is a sample percentage?

Answer: It is a proportion or relative frequency of a count or frequency within the categories of a categorical variable. It is in relation to the entire sample size (sample space) or to a subset of the sample.

9.5 What is a relative frequency?

Answer: It is a proportion or percentage of a count or frequency within the categories of a categorical variable. It is in relation to the entire sample size (sampling space) or to a subset of the sample.

9.6 What is a contingency table? Provide a brief narrative example.

Answer: This is a table that represents the counts of two or more categorical variables each with two or more categories. The table suggests that one variable's categories may affect the outcome of another variable's counts. For example, such a table can represent educational level by gender.

9.7 What is a joint count?

Answer: This count represents the overlap of two categories. For instance, the number of women and those persons who are 18–24 years old is a joint count.

9.8 Describe a pie chart using an example.

Answer: This is an image shaped as a circle, in which parts or slices are different colors representing the counts and percentages of those counts within each category of the variable. The counts and frequencies are reported in the pie chart. As a best practice, a pie chart should contain no more than five to seven categories. For example, a pie chart consisting of a count of 200, where 52% are women and 48% men would provide these percentages as well as their counts, which would be 104 women and 96 men, respectively.

9.9 Describe a dichotomous pie chart using an example.

Answer: This is an image shaped as a circle, in which parts are shaped in different colors representing the counts and percentages of those counts within each category of the variable. There are only two categories. The counts and frequencies are reported in the pie chart. For example, a pie chart consisting of a count of 200 where 52% are right-handed and 48% are left-handed would provide these percentages as well as their counts, which would be 104 right-handed and 96 left-handed people, respectively.

9.10 Define the Complement Rule.

Answer: This rule involves variables with only two categories. It states that the sum of the probabilities of an event (one category) and its complement (the other category) must equal 1.00 or 100% of all possible outcomes.

9.11 Define a multiple category pie chart.

Answer: This is an image shaped as a circle, in which parts or slices are different colors representing the counts and percentages of those counts within each category of the variable. There are more than two categories. The counts and frequencies are reported in the pie chart.

9.12 What is a mode?

Answer: The mode is the most frequently appearing count in all of the categories within a variable. Variables can have more than one mode (bimodal or multimodal).

9.13 What is a bar chart?

Answer: This chart represents the counts and percentages of those counts for each category of a variable. The counts are depicted in vertical or horizontal bars, which can be colored. Both counts and percentages are reported. Bar charts make it easy to label, read, and understand categorical data, especially when there are more categories to compare.

9.14 What is a frequency table?

Answer: This is the general term for a table that depicts categorical data counts and percentages.

9.15 What is a cumulative percentage?

Answer: These percentages represent the increasing or cumulating percentage as each additional group's count is added to a subtotal.

9.16 What is a valid case?

Answer: This is a count adjusted for missing sample data.

9.17 What is a valid percentage?

Answer: This is a percentage adjusted for missing sample data.

9.18 Describe a summary table.

Answer: This table depicts a single categorical variable with two or more categories. It is also called a one- or single-dimensional table.

9.19 What is a one- or single-dimensional table?

Answer: This table depicts a single categorical variable with two or more categories. It is also called a summary table.

9.20 What is a multidimensional table?

Answer: This kind of table contains two or more variables each with two or more categories so that there are joint counts. A multiple-dimensional table is also referred to as a contingency table.

9.21 Describe a two-dimensional table.

Answer: This kind of table contains two variables each with two categories so that there are joint counts. A two-dimensional table is also referred to as a contingency table.

9.22 Define crosstabs.

Answer: This is a contingency table.

9.23 A pharma company ran a trial on a new cholesterol medication that lowers overall cholesterol within eight hours. One thousand and forty-eight patients with high cholesterol agreed to participate in the trial. Run descriptive statistics on the trial results based on the data available in the file. Provide a brief narrative and pie chart, including counts and percentages. The data file name is "Categorical Data Descriptives Exercise 1 Data."

Answer:

Output

Cholesterol

		Frequency	Percent	Valid Percent	Cumulative Percent
Valid	Normal	594	56.7	56.7	56.7
	High	454	43.3	43.3	100.0
	Total	1048	100.0	100.0	

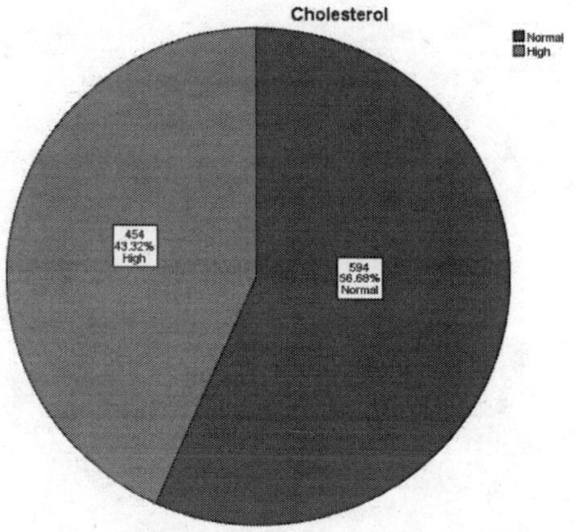

A trial study was conducted to test the effectiveness of a new quick-acting cholesterol drug. Of the 1,048 participants, 594 (56.7%) patients had normal cholesterol levels and 454 (43.3%) patients had high cholesterol. The following pie chart depicts the distribution.

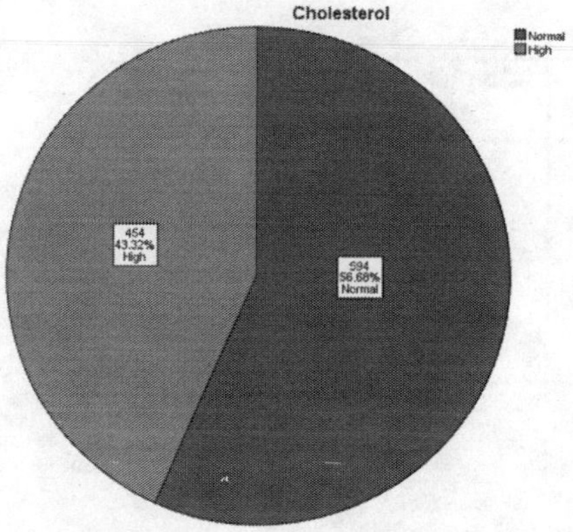

9.24 A hospital wished to determine how many patients were prescribed nitroglycerin over a given period. A sample of patient records was reviewed to discover whether they were prescribed nitroglycerin. Run descriptive statistics on the record results based on the data available in the file. Provide a brief narrative and table, including counts and percentages. The data file name is "Categorical Data Descriptive Exercise 2 Data."

Answer:

Output

Prescribed nitroglycerin

		Frequency	Percent	Valid Percent	Cumulative Percent
Valid	No	880	84.0	84.0	84.0
	Yes	168	16.0	16.0	100.0
	Total	1048	100.0	100.0	

A review of patient records study was conducted to determine the number of patients who were prescribed nitroglycerin over a given period. Of the 1,048 participants, 880 (84.0%) patients were not prescribed nitroglycerin and 168 (16.0%) patients were given nitroglycerin. The table below represents the distribution.

Patients Prescribed Nitroglycerin

Prescribed	Frequencies	Percentages
No	880	84.0%
Yes	168	16.0%
Total	700	100.0%

Note: "Yes" = Prescribed and "No" = Not prescribed. N = 1048.

9.25 A healthcare research firm conducted a study with 217 people diagnosed with various eating disorders. Run descriptive statistics on the distribution of the disorders based on the data available in the file. Provide a brief narrative and bar chart, including counts and percentages. The data file name is "Categorical Data Descriptive Exercise 3 Data."

Answer:

Output

Patient Diagnosis

		Frequency	Percent	Valid Percent	Cumulative Percent
Valid	Anorexia Nervosa	97	44.7	44.7	44.7
	Anorexia with Bulimia Nervosa	36	16.6	16.6	61.3
	Bullimia Nervosa after Anorexia	56	25.8	25.8	87.1
	Atypical Eating Disorder	28	12.9	12.9	100.0
	Total	217	100.0	100.0	

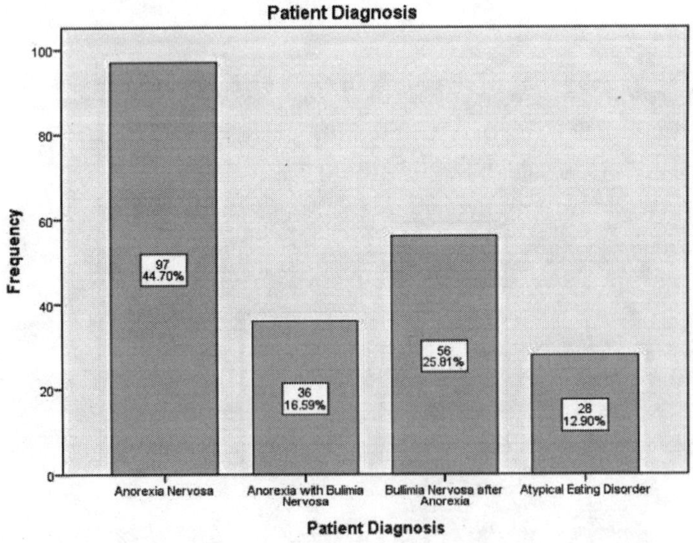

Write-up: A study was conducted on 217 patients in order to determine the distribution of eating disorder diagnoses. As depicted in the following bar chart, the diagnoses were as follows: 97 (44.70%) Anorexia Nervosa, 56 (25.81%) Bulimia Nervosa after Anorexia, 36 (16.59%) Anorexia with Bulimia, and 28 (12.90%) Atypical Eating Disorder.

B.10 Chapter 10

10.1 Define probability.

Answer: Probability is the chance of something occurring by random chance.

10.2 Define event and provide an example.

Answer: An event is an outcome (or potential categories within a categorical variable) based on counts and probabilities. For example, 6 out of 10 people at the fair are women or the category of people holding a bachelor's degree.

10.3 What is an independent event?

Answer: The chance of an event occurring is independent of any other event taking place.

10.4 What is sampling with replacement?

Answer: An element drawn for sampling is returned to the sampling frame (source) before another element is drawn so that the chances of elements being selected always remains the same.

10.5 What is sampling without replacement?

Answer: Once an element is drawn, it is not replaced. Thus, the chances of the remaining elements being drawn change.

10.6 Concerning categorical variables, what does mutually exclusive mean?

Answer: In the case of categorical variables, categories do not overlap so that counts are not counted in two or more categories.

10.7 In the case of categorical variables, define exhaustive.

Answer: In the case of categorical variables, all categories are represented so that no counts are left out of the analysis.

10.8 Define simple probability.

Answer: This is the probability or chance of a single event occurring.

10.9 Define joint probability.

Answer: This is the probability or chance of two events occurring at the same time each from one of two categorical variables.

10.10 Define conditional probability.

Answer: This is the probability or chance of an event occurring within a subgroup of the sample space (total sample). It is based on the count of a category within a subset of the sample space.

10.11 What is the Multiplication Rule?

Answer: In probability statistics, this rule is used to determine the probability of two or more events occurring such as events A and B. Since the events are assumed to be independent, the probability is calculated by taking the cross-product of each probability (the probabilities are multiplied by each other).

10.12 What is the Addition Rule?

Answer: In probability statistics, this rule is used to determine the probability of one or another event occurring such as event A or event B. Since the events are assumed to be independent, the probability of one of the events taking place is calculated by simply adding together the probabilities of each occurring.

10.13 The following are counts for home design preferences for potential homeowners:

Saltbox: 30
Raised Ranch: 105
Colonial: 100
Garrison: 25
Tutor: 50
Contemporary: 40
$N = 350$

What are the probabilities that potential homeowners will prefer each home design?

Answer: The probabilities of each outcome are as follows.

Saltbox: 30 (30 / 350 = .0857 = 8.57%)
Raised Ranch: 105 (105 / 350 = .30 = 30.00%)
Colonial: 100 (100 / 350 = .2857 = 28.58%)
Garrison: 25 (25 / 350 = .0714 = 7.14%)
Tutor: 50 (50 / 350 = .1428 = 14.29%)
Contemporary: 40 (40 / 350 = .1142 = 11.42%)
Total: 350 (350 / 350 = 1.00 = 100%)

10.14 Based on their undergraduate majors, students were asked about their intention to attend graduate school. There were two categorical variables. The first variable was about graduate school intention where respondents selected one of three possible answers: "No Intention," "Undecided," and "Intends to Go." The responses were categorized by major: "Healthcare," "Math/Science," "Engineering," "Business," and "Education." The following is the contingency table representing only frequency (count) data. Note that such a table would normally include relative frequencies (percentage proportions).

Interest in Graduate School by Major Category

Intent to Go to Graduate School	Healthcare	Math/Science	Engineering	Business	Education	Total
No Intention	8	13	23	29	7	80
Undecided	11	7	9	7	6	40
Intends to Go	12	10	10	8	40	80
Total	31	30	42	44	53	200

Note: N = 200.

Prepare a table that includes proportions. In narrative, indicate all of the simply, joint, and conditional probabilities. Be sure to interpret your results in plain English.

Answer:

Interest in Graduate School by Major Category

Intent to Go to Graduate School	Healthcare	Math/Science	Engineering	Business	Education	Total
No Intention	8 (4.0%)	13 (6.5%)	23 (11.5%)	29 (14.5%)	7 (3.5%)	80 (40.0%)
Undecided	11 (5.5%)	7 (3.5%)	9 (4.5%)	7 (3.5%)	6 (3.0%)	40 (20.0%)
Intends to Go	12 (6.0%)	10 (5.0%)	10 (5.0%)	8 (4.0%)	40 (20.0%)	80 (40.0%)
Total	31 (15.5%)	30 (15.0%)	42 (21.0%)	44 (22.0%)	53 (26.5%)	200 (100%)

Note: N = 200.

A simple probability is the total count of a categorical variable group based on the total sample space. Thus, the total sample space count is the denominator (bottom number of the fraction). The simple probabilities are as follows. Of the 200 participants, 80 (80 / 200 = .40 = 40.0%) have no intention of attending graduate school, 40 (20.0%) are undecided, and 80 (40.0%) intend to attend graduate school. The study consists of 31 (15.5%) Healthcare majors, 30 (15.0%) Math/Science majors, 42 (21.0%) Engineering majors, 44 (22.0%) Business majors, and 53 (26.5%) Education majors.

A joint probability is the total count of two or more categorical variable groups based on the total sample space count. The total sample space count is the denominator (bottom number of the fraction). The joint probabilities are as follows. Those respondents with no intention of attending graduate school and major are 8 (8 / 200 = .040 = 4.0%) Healthcare, 13 (6.5%) Math/Science, 23 (11.5%) Engineering, 29 (14.5%) Business, and 7 (3.5%) Education. Those respondents who are undecided about attending graduate school and major are 11 (5.5%) Healthcare, 7 (3.5%) Math/Science, 9 (4.5%) Engineering, 7 (3.5%) Business, and 6 (3.0%) Education. Those respondents who intent to attend graduate school and major are 12 (6.0%) Healthcare, 10 (5.0%) Math/Science, 10 (5.0%) Engineering, 8 (4.0%) Business, and 40 (20.0%) Education.

A conditional probability pertains to the probability of a subset of the total sample space. It is the total count of a categorical variable group within a subset of the total sample space. The denominator is the subtotal or total of the subset. Conditional probabilities are not clearly evident in the contingency table. They must be calculated from the information available in the table.

In this exercise, of those (given) in Healthcare (31), 8 out of 31 or 8 / 31 = .2580 = 25.80% have no intention to attend graduate school. Within the Healthcare majors, 35.48% are undecided and 38.70% intend to go to graduate school. Given Math/Science majors, the probabilities are 43.33%, 23.33%, and 33.33%, respectively. Within the Engineering subset, the probabilities are 54.76%, 21.42%, and 23.80%, respectively. Given Business majors, the probabilities are 65.90%, 15.09%, and 18.18%, respectively. Last, given Education majors, the probabilities are 13.20%, 11.32%, and 75.47%, respectively.

10.15 Why must categorical choices be mutually exclusive and exhaustive?

Answer: Mutually exclusive categories assure that categories do not overlap so that counts can be placed in more than one group, thus increasing accuracy. Exhaustive is important because it guarantees that all possible choices are available, thus increasing accuracy and confidence that results represent the target population.

10.16 What is the Complement Rule?

Answer: When there are two conditions, this means that the total probability for both events must equal 100% so that if the probability for one event is 60%, the other event's probability is 40%.

10.17 What is a marginal probability and why is it called so?

Answer: Simple probabilities are also called marginal probabilities because they occur in the margins.

10.18 Do conditional probabilities require information about marginal probabilities?

Answer: The marginal probabilities or counts are the denominator value for tabulating conditional probabilities.

10.19 When applying the Multiplication Rule to probability analysis, what is an important assumption?

Answer: The events must be independent.

10.20 What is the difference between the Multiplication Rule and the Addition Rule?

Answer: The Multiplication Rule provides the probability of two or more events occurring. The Addition Rule provides the probability of one or another event occurring.

B.11 Chapter 11

11.1 Define observations, data, and data points in statistical terms.

Answer: These are the sample information that is collected.

11.2 Define a statistical effect and provide an example.

Answer: This is a result, finding, or outcome derived from statistical analysis. An example would be a correlation or comparing two means in order to determine if they are similar.

11.3 What is a distribution?

Answer: This is where individual data values or measured observations fall when examined together as a variable.

11.4 What is a normal distribution?

Answer: This is a data distribution that is symmetrical like a bell-shaped curve.

11.5 What is a chi-square probability distribution?

Answer: This is a series of distributions that pertain to categorical data based on the number of groups (degrees of freedom = $n - 1$) within the categorical variable. "χ^2" is the chi-square symbol. The series often, but not always, applies to categorical data.

11.6 What is nonparametric statistics?

Answer: This is a type of probability statistics dependent on degrees of freedom (number of groups within the variable) and is oftentimes based on rank-ordered data. It does not require the normal distribution.

11.7 Define probability.

Answer: This is the chance of something occurring by random chance.

11.8 What is probability statistics?

Answer: This is a scientific and systematic approach for determining the chances of events occurring or results being meaningful based on the attributes of a representative sample.

11.9 What is the Central Limit Theorem?

Answer: The Central Limit Theorem states that a sample of means from randomly drawn samples will approach normal distribution as the (overall) sample size increases, whether or not the population from which the samples are drawn is normally distributed.

11.10 What is a standard deviation?

Answer: It is a calculated statistical measure that applies to the sample and can be inferred to the target population. The sample standard deviation represents the typical (or standardized) difference in a sample variable between each observation and the mean. It allows us to determine the spread of the data distribution. To calculate the sample standard deviation by hand requires the following steps:

- Compute the differences between each value and the mean of the values.
- Square each of the differences.
- Sum the squared differences.
- Divide the total squared differences by the sample size minus 1 ($N - 1$).
- Take the square root of what was divided, which is the sample standard deviation.

11.11 What is the Empirical Rule?

Answer: This rule states that in a normal distribution, approximately 68% of the observations rest within one standard deviation from the mean, approximately 95% of the observations rest within two standard deviations, and 99.7% of the data rest within three standard deviations of the mean.

11.12 What is the *z*-distribution?

Answer: Following the Empirical Rule, this represents a perfect normal distribution. It is also called the standard normal distribution.

11.13 What is the standard normal distribution?

Answer: Following the Empirical Rule, this represents a perfect normal distribution. It is also called the *z*-distribution.

11.14 What is a *z*-score?

Answer: This is a standardized observation based on the original value. A *z*-score is computed by subtracting the mean from the data point value and then dividing the result by the sample standard deviation.

11.15 What is the *t*-distribution?

Answer: This is the sample distribution from which we infer to the target population. It approximates the *z*-distribution and is symmetrical, but varies slightly to account for sample fluctuations not present in the perfect distribution.

11.16 What is significance testing?

Answer: This is the statistical test that determines whether there is no effect or a statistically meaningful effect based on the probability of the value occurring.

11.17 Define what is a *p*-value?

Answer: This is the probability of an effect (value) occurring, assuming that the data are normally distributed. It is expressed as the probability percentage or random chance of occurrence.

11.18 Relative to statistical analysis and *p*-values, what is the level of risk?

Answer: This is the *p*-value or level of risk that we are willing to accept when concluding that a particular sample result is meaningful and not by chance alone.

11.19 What is the level of significance?

Answer: Also known as alpha, this is the level of risk or threshold for assessing whether an effect is statistically significant or meaningful. It is set arbitrarily, but guided by standard conventions.

11.20 In statistics, what is alpha?

Answer: Also known as level of significance, this is the level of risk or threshold for assessing whether an effect is statistically significant or meaningful. It is set arbitrarily, but guided by standard conventions.

11.21 What are uniform probability distributions?

Answer: These distributions are uniform because each group within the categorical variable has an equal random chance of selection.

11.22 What are non-uniform probability distributions?

Answer: These distributions are not uniform because each group within the categorical variable does not have an equal random chance of selection.

11.23 Define degrees of freedom (*df*).

Answer: Degrees of freedom are the number of categories where counts can vary based on the total sample count.

11.24 When alpha or level of significance is .05, explain what *p*-values of .001 and .340 represent.

Answer: An alpha of .05 is the level of risk that is acceptable. It means that the probability of an effect occurring by chance must be less than .05 or 5% in order for results to be interpreted as meaningful or statistically significant. When p = .001, the chances of the result happening by chance are .001 or less, which is less than .05 and thus an acceptable level of risk. P = .001 is the probability of the effect not being meaningful, which is low and within the acceptable amount of risk. P = .001 is thus a meaningful or statistically significant result. On the other hand, when p = .340 and alpha is .05, the level of risk is not acceptable because there is a 34% of the result occurring by chance, which is too high (a level of risk). When p = .340, the results are not statistically significant; the results are not meaningful.

11.25 What do observations more than three standard deviations out in the distribution constitute and why?

Answer: In a normal distribution, observations that are three or more standard deviations in the distribution represent outliers. Normally, they constitute only .0026% of the observations and can alter results and the shape of the distribution because of their extreme nature. Typically, when screening data, outliers are removed unless there is a reason to consider them.

11.26 What is the basis for categorical data analysis?

Answer: This question can be answered in different ways. Categorical data result from a counting process and consists of frequencies or counts and percentages or proportions of those counts. The basic calculation involves comparing the expected with the sample observed values and then determining whether the difference(s) are statistically significant.

11.27 What is a parameter?

Answer: A parameter is a true measure of a target population based on a randomly drawn representative sample of that population.

11.28 What is a point estimate? Indicate examples.

Answer: A point estimate is the value of a single sample statistic such as a mean, median, correlation, proportion, and so forth.

11.29 What is a confidence interval estimate? Indicate examples.

Answer: A confidence interval estimate is a "range" of numbers constructed around a point estimate. For instance, we are 95% confident that a mean is between 45 and 53.

11.30 What is a confidence interval?

Answer: A confidence interval indicates the boundaries where a true population parameter lies based on a certain level of confidence expressed as a percentage.

11.31 What is (are) the relationship(s) between (among) confidence interval precision, level of confidence, and sample size?

Answer: Because of the Central Limit Theorem, a larger sample size allows for more normally distributed data, and thus less error, and narrow and more precise intervals. A greater level of confidence requires a wider interval in order to assure confidence.

B.12 Chapter 12

12.1 What is a univariate normal distribution? Provide an example.

Answer: This distribution focuses on a single variable and whether the data in that variable are distributed in a bell-shaped curve. Age or years of education distributed in a bell-shaped curve are examples of univariate normal distributions.

12.2 What is central tendency?

Answer: This is the extent to which data points concentrate around the mean (average) or center of the distribution. It is a measure of symmetry.

12.3 What is a mean?

Answer: This is the average value of the data comprising a variable.

12.4 What is the mean of the following data array: 21, 22, 2, 3, 6, 8, 12, 12, 12, 16, 18?

Answer: Mean = 12.

12.5 What is a median?

Answer: This is the middle value of the data ordered from smallest to largest.

12.6 What is the median from the following data array: 21, 22, 2, 3, 6, 8, 12, 12, 12, 16, 18, 20, 25, 22, 20?

Answer: Median = 16.

12.7 Define the term mode.

Answer: This is the value that appears most frequently in the variable. If there is no one value that appears most, then there is no mode. The data can have more than one mode, such as a bimodal or trimodal distribution.

12.8 Using the data in Question 12.6, what is the mode?

Answer: Mode = 12.

12.9 Define the term skew.

Answer: This statistical measure indicates whether there is an even number of values below and above the mean, and the degree to which the distribution is symmetrical.

12.10 Using the data in Question 12.6, what are the mean and median? What do they suggest about skew?

Answer: Mean = 14.60 and median = 16.00. These statistics suggest a left skew where there are more observations greater than the mean, but there are a few low outliers that draw the mean lower.

12.11 What is the coefficient of skewness?

Answer: This statistic measures the degree of symmetry in a distribution based on the mean (the statistic can also be based on the median or mode).

12.12 What is dispersion?

Answer: This statistical measure represents the spread of the data from the mean. It is the degree to which values deviate from the mean.

12.13 Define range in statistical terms.

Answer: This is the difference between the largest value and the smallest value in a data array.

12.14 What is an exclusive range?

Answer: It is the difference between the lowest value and the highest value in a data array.

12.15 What is an inclusive range?

Answer: It is the difference between the lowest value and highest value in a data array plus one.

12.16 What is a sample standard deviation?

Answer: This statistical measure represents the typical (standardized) difference in a sample data array between each value and its mean.

12.17 What is the coefficient of variation (CV)?

Answer: This is a statistic that represents the variable's standard deviation as a percentage of that variable's mean.

12.18 What is the coefficient of kurtosis?

Answer: This statistic measures the degree of peakedness/flatness in a distribution based on the variable's standard deviation.

12.19 What is kurtosis?

Answer: This is a general measure of peakedness/flatness in a distribution.

12.20 What is a mesokurtic distribution?

Answer: In terms of kurtosis, this is the normal distribution.

12.21 What is a leptokurtic distribution?

Answer: In terms of kurtosis, this distribution has a high peak that is thin and tall. The tails of the distribution are relatively short and heavy.

12.22 What is a platykurtic distribution?

Answer: In terms of kurtosis, this distribution is flat (low peak) and spread out more than the normal distribution. Both tails are long and relatively thick.

12.23 What is a Normal Q-Q Plot?

Answer: This graphic places observations along a straight line that represents a perfect normal distribution.

12.24 What is a simple dot plot?

Answer: This plot depicts the observations by frequencies in which a bell-shaped curve can be observed.

12.25 What is the Shapiro-Wilk test?

Answer: This significance test is used to evaluate whether a data distribution approximates a normal distribution.

12.26 What is the simple outlier rule?

Answer: This rule involves identifying outliers by examining graphed data and statistical measures such as the kurtosis and the skewness statistics, as well as the Shapiro-Wilk test of normality.

12.27 What is the standard deviation rule?

Answer: This rule involves standardizing or converting a set of observations to their *z*-scores, rank-ordering the *z*-scores, and then removing outliers using the three standard deviation baseline.

12.28 Define trimming.

Answer: This technique addresses outliers based on the removal of a percentage of them at each tail of the distribution.

12.29 What is winsorizing?

Answer: This outlier removal technique is similar to trimming with one major difference. In lieu of removing the lower and upper end outliers, the values are replaced with the first observation in the data that is not an outlier but next to the removed outlier.

12.30 Define the outlier labeling rule.

Answer: This technique identifies and removes outliers in a multistep approach, which utilizes the 25th and 75th percentiles and a simple formula. It is an attempt to precisely identify and remove outliers.

12.31 From the following dataset, determine the mean, median, mode, standard deviation, Coefficient of Variation, skewness, kurtosis, and the Shapiro-Wilk statistic: 10, 8, 2, 3, 9, 4, 5, 6, 5, 12, 1. Are the sample data normally distributed? Explain your response.

Answer:

Mean = 5.91
Median = 5.00
Mode = 5.00
Standard deviation = 3.47
Coefficient of Variation = 58.84%
Skewness = .35
Kurtosis = –.82
Shapiro-Wilk statistic: $p = .851$

The data appear to be fairly normally distributed. However, there is a small right skew where there are more observations less than the mean, but a few high outliers that draw the mean a bit higher. The kurtosis, although a bit flat, is within the normal area.

12.32 From the following dataset, determine the mean, median, mode, standard deviation, Coefficient of Variation, skewness, kurtosis, and the Shapiro-Wilk statistic: 42, 36, 25, 30, 25, 50, 52, 55, 60, 20, 18, 20. Are the sample data normally distributed? Explain your response.

Answer:

Mean = 36.08
Median = 33
Mode = 25
Standard deviation = 15.19
Coefficient of variation = 42.10%
Skewness = .31

Kurtosis = −1.57

Shapiro-Wilk statistic: $p = .17$

The data distribution is borderline normal. There is a small right skew where there are more observations less than the mean, but a few high outliers that draw the mean a bit higher. Additionally, the peak is more flat than a typical normal distribution.

12.33 What is the maximum percentage of outlier data that can be removed from a data array?

Answer: At most, no more than 10%.

12.34 The dataset consists of production in units for 500 machines worldwide. The data must be screened for normal distribution, and, if necessary, remove any outliers. Use the outlier labeling rule method. Alpha = .05. The SPSS file named "Outlier Exercise 1 Data" contains the data.

Answer:

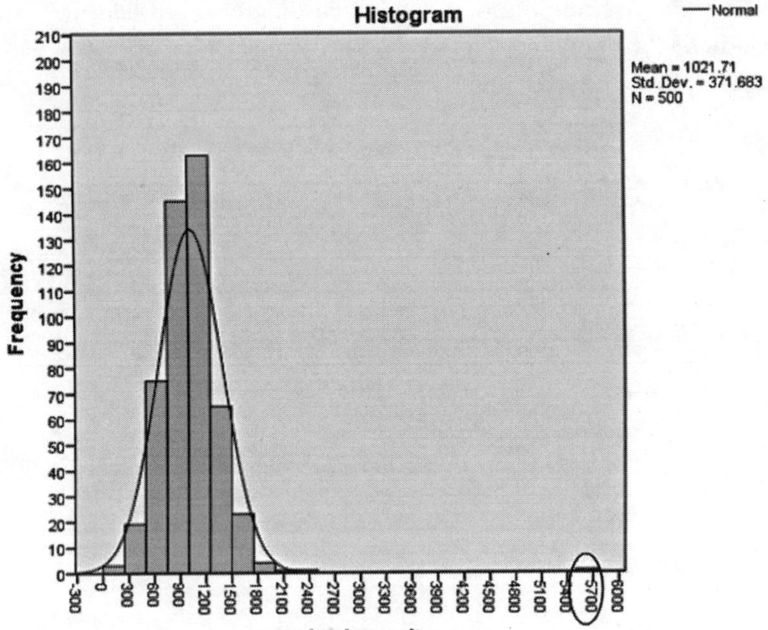

Descriptives

			Statistic	Std. Error
production_units	Mean		1021.71	16.622
	95% Confidence Interval for Mean	Lower Bound	989.05	
		Upper Bound	1054.37	
	5% Trimmed Mean		1009.73	
	Median		1012.00	
	Variance		138148.042	
	Std. Deviation		371.683	
	Minimum		81	
	Maximum		5696	
	Range		5615	
	Interquartile Range		384	
	Skewness		4.092	.109
	Kurtosis		49.502	.218

Tests of Normality

	Kolmogorov-Smirnov[a]			Shapiro-Wilk		
	Statistic	df	Sig.	Statistic	df	Sig.
production_units	.081	500	.000	.800	500	.000

a. Lilliefors Significance Correction

In this example, the calculations are as follows:

$$(1199.75 - 815.50) \times 1.50 = 576.38$$

where k (constant) = 1.50

Next, the lower and upper values are determined as follows:

$$(1199.75 + 576.38) = 1776.13$$

$$(815.50 - 576.38) = 239.12$$

Therefore, outliers are values that are 239.12 or less and 1,776.13 and greater.

Percentiles

		Percentiles						
		5	10	25	50	75	90	95
Weighted Average(Definition 1)	production_units	531.30	623.00	815.50	1012.00	1199.75	1420.90	1522.80
Tukey's Hinges	production_units			816.00	1012.00	1199.50		

In this case, the outliers include at least the five highest values and the three lowest extreme values.

Extreme Values

			Case Number	Value
production_units	Highest	1	500	5696
		2	499	2369
		3	498	2152
		4	497	1900
		5	496	1800
	Lowest	1	148	81
		2	491	96
		3	129	215
		4	347	266
		5	52	282

After the outliers are removed, the improved results are as follows:

Descriptives

			Statistic	Std. Error
production_units	Mean		1009.24	12.892
	95% Confidence Interval for Mean	Lower Bound	983.91	
		Upper Bound	1034.57	
	5% Trimmed Mean		1007.28	
	Median		1011.50	
	Variance		81767.511	
	Std. Deviation		285.950	
	Minimum		266	
	Maximum		1775	
	Range		1509	
	Interquartile Range		379	
	Skewness		.079	.110
	Kurtosis		-.248	.220

The distribution is now fairly normally distributed.

Tests of Normality

	Kolmogorov-Smirnov[a]			Shapiro-Wilk		
	Statistic	df	Sig.	Statistic	df	Sig.
production_units	.025	492	.200*	.996	492	.307

*. This is a lower bound of the true significance.

a. Lilliefors Significance Correction

The histogram does not appear to include any outliers.

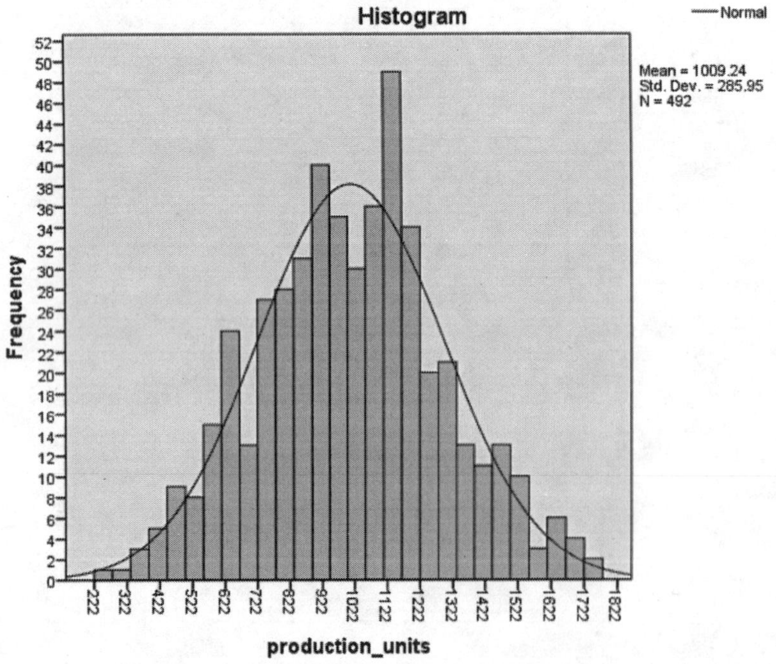

12.35 The dataset comprises 200 records of minutes to complete a task. The data must be screened for normal distribution, and, if necessary, remove any outliers. Use the simple outlier removal method. Alpha = .05. The SPSS file named "Outlier Exercise 2 Data" contains the data.

Answer: The data appear normally distribution (one outlier could be removed, as identified in the Normal Q-Q Plot).

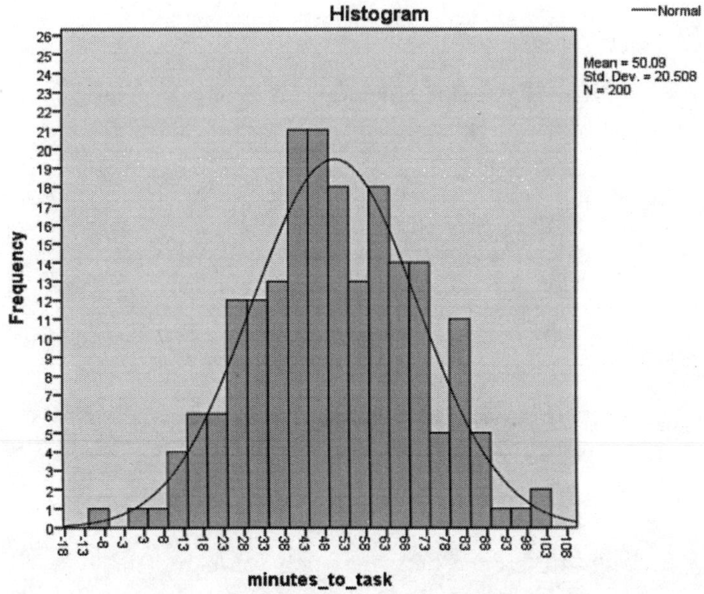

Descriptives

			Statistic	Std. Error
minutes_to_task	Mean		50.0950	1.45014
	95% Confidence Interval for Mean	Lower Bound	47.2354	
		Upper Bound	52.9546	
	5% Trimmed Mean		50.1833	
	Median		49.5000	
	Variance		420.579	
	Std. Deviation		20.50802	
	Minimum		-9.00	
	Maximum		99.00	
	Range		108.00	
	Interquartile Range		29.75	
	Skewness		-.055	.172
	Kurtosis		-.279	.342

Tests of Normality

	Kolmogorov-Smirnov[a]			Shapiro-Wilk		
	Statistic	df	Sig.	Statistic	df	Sig.
minutes_to_task	.037	200	.200*	.996	200	.905

*. This is a lower bound of the true significance.

a. Lilliefors Significance Correction

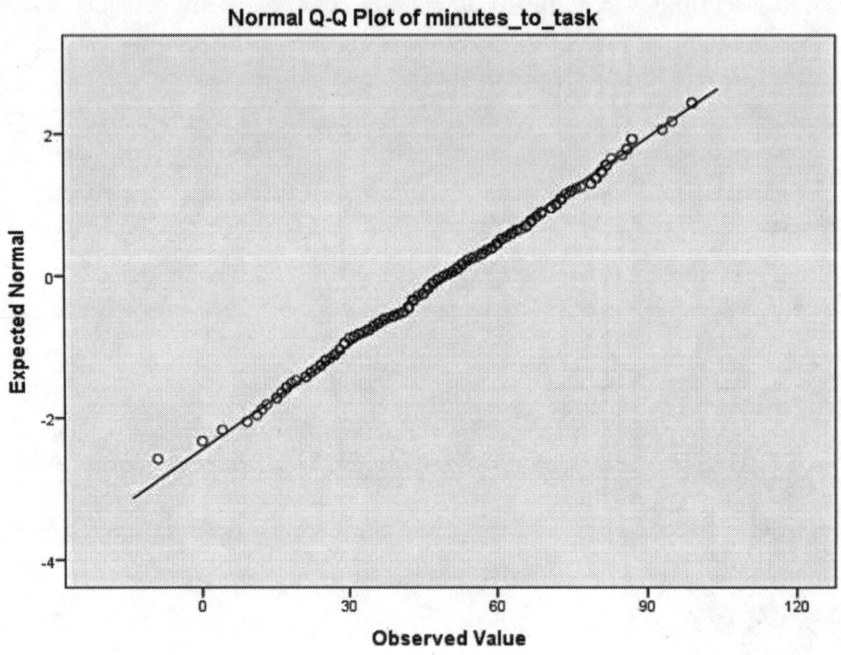

12.36 What is variance?

Answer: Variance is a measure of variation in which the difference between each value and the mean are squared and then summed. The summed total is then divided by the sample size minus 1.

B.13 Chapter 13

13.1 What is a chi-square goodness of fit test? Provide two examples.

Answer: This single sample test compares the observed (actual) and expected frequencies or counts for each category within a single categorical variable. For instance, counts and proportions of a sample's gender or preference for source of food protein such as meat, chicken, fish, or beans.

13.2 What is a between-subjects analysis? Offer one example.

Answer: An analysis that compares responses between participants or sources of data, such as preference for source of protein or choice for president.

13.3 In the context of a chi-square goodness of fit test, define residual.

Answer: In the case of chi-square analysis, this is the difference between expected counts and observed counts.

13.4 When conducting a chi-square goodness of fit analysis, what are the data assumptions?

Answer: The data assumptions are as follows:

- First, the sample is representative of the target population. For example, if 45–54-year-old middle-income men from the West Coast is the target population, then the sample must represent this targeted population or the findings will not be applicable to this group.
- Second, the sample must be randomly drawn as we covered in Chapter 5.
- Third, there must be a minimum of two categories so that comparison is possible.

- Fourth, the categories being compared must be independent of each other. In our examples, the categorical counts represent different respondents. Within the variable or attribute, there is only one selection. For instance, if persons are indicating preferred work shift over 24 hours and assuming 8-hour shifts, only one 8-hour shift can be so that there is only the presence of one category within the variable.
- Last, the expected counts for each category must be at least 1 and no more than 20% of the categories should have expected counts that are less than 5.

13.5 Although SPSS runs the chi-square, conceptually what are the required steps in the process?

Answer: (1) Determine the expected counts; (2) calculate the chi-square statistic; and (3) determine if the statistic is statistically significant.

13.6 How many samples and categories are involved when conducting a chi-square goodness of fit analysis?

Answer: The chi-square goodness of fit analysis must have one sample with at least two categories.

13.7 In terms of the expected counts, how are they determined?

Answer: There are two approaches. First, the default method assumes that each category within the variable is equally distributed (there is an equal number of counts for each category). Second, the expected count settings can be customized.

13.8 A manufacturing facility is considering reorganizing work hours and aims to survey employees on their preferred work shift: 1st, 2nd, or 3rd shift. There is a sample of 106 employees and it is assumed that each shift has an equal chance of being selected. Determine if there is a difference in desired work shift. Alpha is .05. The data file name is "Chi-Square Goodness of Fit Exercise 1 Data."

Answer: The table below reveals that 35.8% (38) of employees prefer to work first shift, 30.2% (32) prefer second shift, and 34.0% (36) like to work third shift. The total sample size is 106.

Preferred Work Shift

		Frequency	Percent	Valid Percent	Cumulative Percent
Valid	First Shift	38	35.8	35.8	35.8
	Second Shift	32	30.2	30.2	66.0
	Third Shift	36	34.0	34.0	100.0
	Total	106	100.0	100.0	

The table below contrasts the observed and expected counts. Equal counts were expected, as indicated by an expected count of 35.3 for each shift. The "Test Statistics" table below indicates whether the differences between the observed and expected counts are statistically meaningful.

Preferred Work Shift

	Observed N	Expected N	Residual
First Shift	38	35.3	2.7
Second Shift	32	35.3	-3.3
Third Shift	36	35.3	.7
Total	106		

Since the Pearson chi-square goodness of fit test has a *p*-value = .768, in all likelihood we can conclude that there is no overall meaningful difference between preferences for work shift. In other words, the results suggest that all employees are evenly split on preferred work shift.

Test Statistics

	Preferred Work Shift
Chi-Square	.528[a]
df	2
Asymp. Sig.	.768

a. 0 cells (.0%) have expected frequencies less than 5. The minimum expected cell frequency is 35.3.

A *p*-value of ⩾.05 indicates that the probability that these results are not meaningful is equal to or greater than 5 / 100. In this example, $p = .276$, which indicates that the probability of these findings being by chance alone is 27.6%. This is an unacceptable level of risk, especially since our alpha or level of risk is <.05. *P*-values that are equal to or higher than .001 are reported exactly to three places to the right of the decimal point (for example, .130 or .006). Clicking on the *p*-value in the SPSS output file will indicate the exact value in scientific notation, which is covered in Chapter 4.

13.9 Referring back to Exercise 13.8, assume that work shift preference varies such that specified expectations are that 53 (50%) prefer the first shift, 37 (35%) prefer the second shift, and 16 (15%) prefer the third shift. Do the data support these expectations? Alpha is .05. The data file name is "Chi-Square Goodness of Fit Exercise 2 Data."

Answer: The table reveals that 35.8% (38) of employees prefer the first shift, 30.2% (32) prefer the second shift, and 34.0% (36) like the third shift. The total sample size is 106.

Preferred Work Shift

		Frequency	Percent	Valid Percent	Cumulative Percent
Valid	First Shift	38	35.8	35.8	35.8
	Second Shift	32	30.2	30.2	66.0
	Third Shift	36	34.0	34.0	100.0
	Total	106	100.0	100.0	

The following table contrasts the observed and expected counts. The expected counts represent the specified percentages: 50% = 53, 35% = 37, and 15% = 16, which varies from the observed values based on the sample. The first and third shifts appear to have the greatest difference between specified expected and observed. The "Test Statistics" table below indicates whether the differences between the observed and specified expected counts are statistically meaningful.

Preferred Work Shift

	Observed N	Expected N	Residual
First Shift	38	53.0	-15.0
Second Shift	32	37.0	-5.0
Third Shift	36	16.0	20.0
Total	106		

Since the Pearson chi-square goodness of fit test has a *p*-value <.001, in all likelihood we can conclude that there is a meaningful difference between at least one specified expected count and observed count for the same shift.

Test Statistics

	Preferred Work Shift
Chi-Square	29.921[a]
df	2
Asymp. Sig.	.000

a. 0 cells (.0%) have expected frequencies less than 5. The minimum expected cell frequency is 16.0.

A *p*-value of <.05 indicates that the probability that these results are not meaningful is less than 5/100. In this example, $p < .001$, which indicates that the probability of these findings being by chance alone is very low. This risk is acceptable since our alpha or level of risk is <.05. *P*-values that are equal to or higher than .001 are reported exactly to three places to the right of the decimal point (for example, .130 or .006). Clicking on the *p*-value in the SPSS output file will indicate the exact value in scientific notation, which is covered in Chapter 4.

13.10 There are four political parties under study: Democrat, Republican, Independent, and Libertarian. A sample of 50 likely voters indicated which political party offers a presidential candidate who they are likely to support. Determine if there is a difference among the parties. There is an equal chance of selection. The data file name is "Chi-Square Goodness of Fit Exercise 3 Data."

Answer: A chi-square analysis testing evenly distributed counts revealed a nonsignificant finding. Thus, based on the test statistics below, there is likely no overall difference in party choice (p = .329). Thus, party choice likely does not vary.

Party Affiliation

		Frequency	Percent	Valid Percent	Cumulative Percent
Valid	Democrat	12	24.0	24.0	24.0
	Republican	10	20.0	20.0	44.0
	Independent	18	36.0	36.0	80.0
	Libertarian	10	20.0	20.0	100.0
	Total	50	100.0	100.0	

Test Statistics

	Party Affiliation
Chi-Square	3.440[a]
df	3
Asymp. Sig.	.329

a. 0 cells (0.0%) have expected frequencies less than 5. The minimum expected cell frequency is 12.5.

Party Affiliation

	Observed N	Expected N	Residual
Democrat	12	12.5	-.5
Republican	10	12.5	-2.5
Independent	18	12.5	5.5
Libertarian	10	12.5	-2.5
Total	50		

13.11 Taking the same data in Exercise 13.10, run the analysis again expecting the breakdown to be as follows: Democrat (16), Republican (15), Independent (13), and Libertarian (6). Is there a statistically significant difference among party affiliations? The data file name is "Chi-Square Goodness of Fit Exercise 4 Data."

Answer: A chi-square test examining the following distribution: Democrat (16), Republican (15), Independent (13), and Libertarian (6) revealed a nonsignificant finding (p = .064). Thus, based on the test statistics below, there is likely no overall difference in what was expected and what was observed in the sample data. Thus, party affiliation voting for president is likely to be as anticipated.

Party Affiliation

		Frequency	Percent	Valid Percent	Cumulative Percent
Valid	Democrat	12	24.0	24.0	24.0
	Republican	10	20.0	20.0	44.0
	Independent	18	36.0	36.0	80.0
	Libertarian	10	20.0	20.0	100.0
	Total	50	100.0	100.0	

Party Affiliation

	Observed N	Expected N	Residual
Democrat	12	16.0	-4.0
Republican	10	15.0	-5.0
Independent	18	13.0	5.0
Libertarian	10	6.0	4.0
Total	50		

Test Statistics

	Party Affiliation
Chi-Square	7.256[a]
df	3
Asymp. Sig.	.064

a. 0 cells (0.0%) have expected frequencies less than 5. The minimum expected cell frequency is 6.0.

13.12 Betterment Services offers group mental wellness counseling. Clients were required to attend sessions rotated during morning, afternoon, and evening times for a given day once per week. This format was for six months so that clients attended 26 sessions. A representative sample of 120 participants who experienced "positive affects" were asked to self-report which time of the day was most beneficial to their "feeling better." In order to force a choice, the specific answer format was morning, afternoon, or evening. Although not covered in this exercise, other factors were accounted for in the study. Determine if there is a difference in feelings of wellness based on time of the day assuming an equal distribution of answers. The data file name is "Chi-Square Goodness of Fit Exercise 5 Data."

Answer: A chi-square analysis testing evenly distributed counts revealed a significant finding. Thus, based on the test statistics below, there is likely a difference between at least one category's expected count and observed count ($p < .001$). Therefore, the wellness session time perceived effectiveness likely varies.

Time of Day Session

		Frequency	Percent	Valid Percent	Cumulative Percent
Valid	Morning	19	15.8	15.8	15.8
	Afternoon	72	60.0	60.0	75.8
	Evening	29	24.2	24.2	100.0
	Total	120	100.0	100.0	

Time of Day Session

	Observed N	Expected N	Residual
Morning	19	40.0	-21.0
Afternoon	72	40.0	32.0
Evening	29	40.0	-11.0
Total	120		

Test Statistics

	Time of Day Session
Chi-Square	39.650[a]
df	2
Asymp. Sig.	.000

a. 0 cells (0.0%) have expected frequencies less than 5. The minimum expected cell frequency is 40.0.

13.13 Using the data from Exercise 13.12, the researchers expect that of the 120 study participants, 50% (60) will feel better during the afternoon session, 30% (36) during the evening session, and 20% (24) during the morning session. Test this idea. The data file name is "Chi-Square Goodness of Fit Exercise 6 Data."

Answer: A chi-square test examining the following distribution: Morning (24), Afternoon (60), and Evening (36) revealed a nonsignificant finding. Thus, based on the test statistics below, there is likely no overall difference in what was expected and what was observed in the sample data (p = .091). The anticipated time of wellness session is likely as expected.

Time of Day Session

		Frequency	Percent	Valid Percent	Cumulative Percent
Valid	Morning	19	15.8	15.8	15.8
	Afternoon	72	60.0	60.0	75.8
	Evening	29	24.2	24.2	100.0
	Total	120	100.0	100.0	

Time of Day Session

	Observed N	Expected N	Residual
Morning	19	24.0	-5.0
Afternoon	72	60.0	12.0
Evening	29	36.0	-7.0
Total	120		

Test Statistics

	Time of Day Session
Chi-Square	4.803[a]
df	2
Asymp. Sig.	.091

a. 0 cells (0.0%) have expected frequencies less than 5. The minimum expected cell frequency is 24.0.

B.14 Chapter 14

14.1 What is the chi-square test of independence?

Answer: The chi-square test of independence is a significance test that assesses whether there is a relationship between two categorical variables each with two or more categories.

14.2 What is a crosstabs?

Answer: Crosstabs is short for cross-tabulations table. It is a contingency table.

14.3 What is a joint count?

Answer: The data are set up in a contingency table and the marginal counts provide the expected counts that are compared with the combinations of categories, one each from the two variables, which are called joint counts.

14.4 Define marginal totals.

Answer: The row and column totals are called marginal totals because they are located in the margins of the table.

14.5 What are standardized counts?

Answer: The percentages are the standardized (or relative) counts so that we can easily compare the counts' percentages of the different joint categories.

14.6 What is the Pearson chi-square statistic?

Answer: The Pearson chi-square statistic is the chi-square test used when there is a sufficient sample size in addition to meeting all of the data assumptions.

14.7 Define the continuity correction statistic.

Answer: The continuity correction statistic is a conservative measure that adjusts for an undersized sample size in a 2 × 2 chi-square analysis *only*.

14.8 What is the Fisher exact test (two-sided)?

Answer: The Fisher exact test (two-sided) result is automatically generated for 2 × 2 chi-square analysis only. It provides the basis for assessment and may be reported if at least one category combination has an expected count less than 5.

14.9 What are symmetric measures?

Answer: The symmetric measures table provides additional information about the relationship between age category and interest in private pension responses. It is akin to a "correlation."

14.10 Define Cramer's *V*.

Answer: This statistic, which can be generated as part of the chi-square test of independence output, is the "correlation" between the two categorical variables.

14.11 What is variance explained?

Answer: The variance explained is the percentage of the relationship between the two variables that can be explained by the sample data.

14.12 By hand, calculate the expected counts for the following contingency table.

Global Warming is Real	Political Party		
	Democrat	Republican	Total
Yes	160	75	235
No	15	100	115
Total	175	175	350

Note: We will assume a sample of 350.

Answer:

$$\text{Expected frequency} = \frac{(\text{Row total}) \times (\text{Column total})}{\text{Total sample size}}$$

Global Warming is Real	Political Party		
	Democrat	Republican	Total
Yes	Expected: 117.50	Expected: 117.50	235
No	Expected: 57.50	Expected: 57.50	115
Total	175	175	350

Note: We will assume a sample of 350.

14.13 By hand, calculate the chi-square statistic and what is the *df* for the data in Exercise 14.12.

Answer:

$$\chi^2_{STAT} = \sum_{\text{alt cells}} \frac{(O-E)^2}{E}$$

where

χ^2_{STAT}	=	the chi-square statistic
Σ	=	summation sign
O	=	observed count
E	=	expected count
χ^2	=	93.570
df	=	$(r-1) \times (c-1)$
	=	$(2-1=1) \times (2-1)$
	=	1

14.14 In narrative, explain why the differences between the observed and expected counts determine whether the two variables are related. Include the reasoning for the expected counts.

Answer: The expected counts are based on the total sample and the marginal totals in particular. What we would expect in the totals are thus expected in the observed joint counts. If the joint counts vary from the marginal counts, then the categories within a variable are driving the counts, indicating that there is a relationship between the variables.

14.15 Based on the following information in the table, determine the *df* and three missing counts.

Global Warming is Real	Political Party		
	Democrat	Republican	Total
Yes	?	150	470
No	?	?	230
Total	350	350	700

Note: We will assume a sample of 350.

Answer:

$$df = (r-1) \times (c-1)$$
$$= (2-1=1) \times (2-1)$$
$$= 1$$

Global Warming is Real	Political Party		
	Democrat	Republican	Total
Yes	350 – 30 = 320	150	470
No	230 – 200 = 30	350 – 150 = 200	230
Total	350	350	700

Note: We will assume a sample of 350.

After the Republican "Yes" count was set at 150, all other counts were predetermined.

14.16 What is the Pearson chi-square statistic for the data in Exercise 14.15?
Answer: $\chi^2 = 187.141$.

14.17 Conduct a crosstabs chi-square analysis to determine if there is a relationship between type of protein diet selection (soy or meat) and gender (woman or man). Do women or men prefer soy or meat as a protein source of food? Alpha = .05. Explain your answer. Report your results in the format covered in this book and, if necessary, include a table. Should it be necessary, include the Continuity Correction and/or Fisher Exact Test statistics, as well as providing any necessary solutions to problematic data. The data file name is "Chi-Square Independence Exercise 1 Data."

Answer:

Preferred Protein * Gender Crosstabulation

			Gender		
			Man	Woman	Total
Preferred Protein	Meat	Count	77	8	85
		Expected Count	50.4	34.6	85.0
		% within Gender	96.3%	14.5%	63.0%
		% of Total	57.0%	5.9%	63.0%
	Soy	Count	3	47	50
		Expected Count	29.6	20.4	50.0
		% within Gender	3.8%	85.5%	37.0%
		% of Total	2.2%	34.8%	37.0%
Total		Count	80	55	135
		Expected Count	80.0	55.0	135.0
		% within Gender	100.0%	100.0%	100.0%
		% of Total	59.3%	40.7%	100.0%

All expected counts are at least 5; therefore, the Pearson chi-square test is sufficient.

Chi-Square Tests

	Value	df	Asymp. Sig. (2-sided)	Exact Sig. (2-sided)	Exact Sig. (1-sided)
Pearson Chi-Square	93.302[a]	1	.000		
Continuity Correction[b]	89.831	1	.000		
Likelihood Ratio	106.763	1	.000		
Fisher's Exact Test				.000	.000
N of Valid Cases	135				

a. 0 cells (.0%) have expected count less than 5. The minimum expected count is 20.37.

b. Computed only for a 2x2 table

A sample size of 135 is sufficient, as evidenced by no difference between the Pearson chi-square and Continuity Correction *p*-values. The Pearson chi-square test indicates a significant relationship between gender and preferred protein diet ($p < .001$).

Symmetric Measures

		Value	Approx. Sig.
Nominal by Nominal	Phi	.831	.000
	Cramer's V	.831	.000
N of Valid Cases		135	

Cramer's *V*: Gender and preferred protein diet have a .831 ($p < .001$) correlation, which is significant and strong. Squaring the correlation ($r = .831 \times .831$) results in 69% variance explained, meaning that the data explains 69% of the relationship between gender and protein diet preference. The significant *p*-value is consistent with the significant Pearson chi-square statistic.

Write-up: Based on a representative sample of 135 participants consisting of 80 men and 55 women, a chi-square test of independence was calculated comparing the counts of those who prefer a meat protein diet as opposed to a soy protein diet by gender. A significant relationship was found between preferred protein diet and gender ($\chi^2(1) = 93.302$, $p < .001$), suggesting that one's gender influences one's preference for a protein diet. As depicted in the table, 96.3% of men preferred a meat protein diet, whereas 85.5% of women preferred a soy protein diet. The data explain nearly 69% ($p < .001$) of this relationship.

Protein Source	Men	Women	Total
Meat	77 (57.0%)	8 (5.9%)	85 (63.0%)*
Soy	3 (2.2%)	47 (34.8%)	50 (37.0%)
Total	80 (59.3%)	55 (40.7%)	135 (100%)

Note: ($\chi^2(1) = 93.302$, $p < .001$). Cramer's $V = .831$ ($p < .001$). $N = 135$. * Rounded.

14.18 Conduct a crosstabs chi-square analysis to determine if there is a relationship between working first or second shift and mood (positive or negative). Alpha = .05. Explain your answer. Report your results in the format covered in this book and, if necessary, include a table. Should it be necessary, include the Continuity Correction and/or Fisher Exact Test statistics, as well as providing any necessary solutions to problematic data. The data file name is "Chi-Square Independence Exercise 2 Data."

Answer:

Mood at Work * Work Shift Crosstabulation

			Work Shift		
			First	Second	Total
Mood at Work	Negative	Count	11	10	21
		Expected Count	10.7	10.3	21.0
		% within Work Shift	13.8%	13.0%	13.4%
		% of Total	7.0%	6.4%	13.4%
	Positive	Count	69	67	136
		Expected Count	69.3	66.7	136.0
		% within Work Shift	86.3%	87.0%	86.6%
		% of Total	43.9%	42.7%	86.6%
Total		Count	80	77	157
		Expected Count	80.0	77.0	157.0
		% within Work Shift	100.0%	100.0%	100.0%
		% of Total	51.0%	49.0%	100.0%

All expected counts are at least 5; therefore, the Pearson chi-square test is sufficient.

Chi-Square Tests

	Value	df	Asymp. Sig. (2-sided)	Exact Sig. (2-sided)	Exact Sig. (1-sided)
Pearson Chi-Square	.020[a]	1	.888		
Continuity Correction[b]	.000	1	1.000		
Likelihood Ratio	.020	1	.888		
Fisher's Exact Test				1.000	.538
N of Valid Cases	157				

a. 0 cells (.0%) have expected count less than 5. The minimum expected count is 10.30.

b. Computed only for a 2x2 table

A sample size of 157 is sufficient, as evidenced by consistent nonsignificance *p*-values for the Pearson chi-square (p = .888) and Continuity Correction (p = 1.00). Therefore, there is no relationship between work shift and mood state.

Symmetric Measures

		Value	Approx. Sig.
Nominal by Nominal	Phi	.011	.888
	Cramer's V	.011	.888
N of Valid Cases		157	

The Cramer's *V* (or correlation between work shift and mood state) is not significant, thus it cannot be used. Accordingly, the data indicate that there is no relationship between work shift and mood state. This is consistent with the Pearson chi-square statistic.

Write-up: Based on a representative sample of 157 participants consisting of 80 first shift workers and 77 second shift workers, a chi-square of independence was calculated comparing the counts of reported moods of workers by shift. A nonsignificant relationship was found ($\chi^2(1)$ = .020, p = .888). Therefore, there is likely no meaningful relationship between which shift one works and one's mood state.

14.19 Conduct a crosstabs chi-square analysis to determine if there is a relationship between college status (full-time or part-time) and preference for a statistics e-book or a statistics hard-copy book in a statistics course. Alpha = .05. Explain your answer. Report your results in the format covered in this book and, if necessary, include a table. Should it be necessary, include the Continuity Correction and/or Fisher Exact Test statistics, as well as providing any necessary solutions to problematic data. The data file name is "Chi-Square Independence Exercise 3 Data."

Answer:

Book Format Preference * College Status Crosstabulation

			College Status		Total
			Full-time	Part-time	
Book Format Preference	e-copy	Count	5	0	5
		Expected Count	3.0	2.0	5.0
		% within College Status	33.3%	0.0%	20.0%
		% of Total	20.0%	0.0%	20.0%
	Hardcopy	Count	10	10	20
		Expected Count	12.0	8.0	20.0
		% within College Status	66.7%	100.0%	80.0%
		% of Total	40.0%	40.0%	80.0%
Total		Count	15	10	25
		Expected Count	15.0	10.0	25.0
		% within College Status	100.0%	100.0%	100.0%
		% of Total	60.0%	40.0%	100.0%

One cell's expected count is <5; therefore, we should consider the Fisher's Exact Test. Moreover, since the sample size is small, we will consider the Continuity Correction test.

Chi-Square Tests

	Value	df	Asymp. Sig. (2-sided)	Exact Sig. (2-sided)	Exact Sig. (1-sided)
Pearson Chi-Square	4.167[a]	1	.041		
Continuity Correction[b]	2.344	1	.126		
Likelihood Ratio	5.925	1	.015		
Fisher's Exact Test				.061	.057
N of Valid Cases	25				

a. 2 cells (50.0%) have expected count less than 5. The minimum expected count is 2.00.

b. Computed only for a 2x2 table

Since one expected cell count is <5 and the sample size is small, we must consider the Continuity Correction test and Fisher's Exact Test. The Pearson chi-square test is significant at .041, assuming alpha is .05. However, the Continuity Correction test (p = .126) and Fisher's Exact Test (p = .061) are not significant. This represents an inconsistency between the Pearson chi-square (which is used under normal conditions), the Continuity Correction test (which adjusts for small sample size), and Fisher's Exact Test (which adjusts for cell counts less than 5 and small sample sizes). Therefore, we must be guided by the adjusted Continuity Correction and Fisher's Exact Test statistics and conclude that there is no significant relationship between college status and book format preference.

Symmetric Measures

		Value	Approx. Sig.
Nominal by Nominal	Phi	.408	.041
	Cramer's V	.408	.041
N of Valid Cases		25	

Because of the low expected cell count and small sample size, the Pearson chi-square and Cramer's V (or correlation between college status and preferred book format) statistics are not stable. The Continuity Correction and Fisher's Exact Test statistics, which are both not significant, therefore guide us. We conclude that there is no statistically meaningful relationship between college status and book format preference.

Write-up: Based on a representative sample of 25 participants consisting of 15 full-time and 10 part-time students, a chi-square test of independence was calculated comparing the counts of preference for statistics book format (hard copy or e-copy) based full-time or part-time college status. A nonsignificant relationship was found based on the Continuity Correction chi-square test ($\chi^2(1) = 2.344$, $p = .126$) and Fisher's Exact Test ($p = .061$). Therefore, there is likely no meaningful relationship between college status and book format preference.

14.20 Conduct a crosstabs chi-square analysis to determine if there is a relationship between pet ownership and college attendance. Alpha = .05. Explain your answer. Report your results in the format covered in this book and, if necessary, include a table. Should it be necessary, include the Continuity Correction and/or Fisher Exact Test statistics, as well as providing any necessary solutions to problematic data. The data file name is "Chi-Square Independence Exercise 4 Data."

Answer:

Attend College * Own Pet Crosstabulation

			Own Pet		
			No	Yes	Total
Attend College	No	Count	3	2	5
		Expected Count	2.3	2.7	5.0
		% within Own Pet	60.0%	33.3%	45.5%
		% of Total	27.3%	18.2%	45.5%
	Yes	Count	2	4	6
		Expected Count	2.7	3.3	6.0
		% within Own Pet	40.0%	66.7%	54.5%
		% of Total	18.2%	36.4%	54.5%
Total		Count	5	6	11
		Expected Count	5.0	6.0	11.0
		% within Own Pet	100.0%	100.0%	100.0%
		% of Total	45.5%	54.5%	100.0%

All expected cell counts are <5; therefore, we should consider the Fisher's Exact Test. Moreover, since the sample size is small, we will consider the Continuity Correction test.

Chi-Square Tests

	Value	df	Asymp. Sig. (2-sided)	Exact Sig. (2-sided)	Exact Sig. (1-sided)
Pearson Chi-Square	.782[a]	1	.376		
Continuity Correction[b]	.076	1	.782		
Likelihood Ratio	.790	1	.374		
Fisher's Exact Test				.567	.392
N of Valid Cases	11				

a. 4 cells (100.0%) have expected count less than 5. The minimum expected count is 2.27.

b. Computed only for a 2x2 table

The Pearson chi-square test is nonsignificant at $p = .376$, assuming alpha is .05. This is consistent with the Continuity Correction test ($p = .782$) and Fisher's Exact Test ($p = .567$), which are both not significant. All of the expected joint categories have counts that are less than 5. However, since all three test statistics are nonsignificant, we should report the Pearson chi-square statistic.

Symmetric Measures

		Value	Approx. Sig.
Nominal by Nominal	Phi	.267	.376
	Cramer's V	.267	.376
N of Valid Cases		11	

The Cramer's V (or correlation between work shift and mood state) is not significant, thus it cannot be used. Accordingly, the data indicate that there is no relationship between work shift and mood state. This is consistent with the three chi-square statistics.

Write-up: Based on a representative sample of 11 participants consisting of six pet owners and five non-pet owners, a chi-square of independence was calculated comparing the counts of those persons who attend and those persons who do not attend college based on whether they own pets. A non-significant relationship was found ($\chi^2(1) = .782$, $p = .376$). Therefore, we conclude that there is likely no significant relationship between pet ownership and whether one attends college.

B.15 Chapter 15

15.1 What is the McNemar chi-square significance test? Cite an example.

Answer: The McNemar chi-square significance test examines counts (and percentages of those counts) between the same cases or samples measured twice, usually using a Time 1 variable and a Time 2 variable, with two categories in the variable being measured. For instance, in order to measure recall, participants may be asked about their awareness of a major news topic, immediately after it occurs and then four weeks later.

15.2 What is the McNemar-Bowker chi-square significance test? Cite an example.

Answer: The McNemar-Bowker chi-square significance test examines counts (and percentages of those counts) between the same cases or samples measured twice, usually using a Time 1 variable and a Time 2 variable, with three or more categories in the variable being measured. For example, four groups of social service clients may be asked to rate their satisfaction with assistance provided to them after one month and later after six months of receiving services.

15.3 What is a within-subjects analysis? Cite an example.

Answer: Within-subjects analysis examines for differences in the same sample usually by collecting the same type of data two or more times. For example, typically, people may be surveyed about a topic before and after an intervention or treatment of sorts. The before intervention measurement provides a baseline from which to examine change after the intervention. The intervention can be, for example, a new method of teaching students or a sales pitch. The analysis would examine if the intervention caused a difference between the baseline data and the after intervention data. Likewise, time may simply be the effect such as studying whether people feel, think, or remember something differently over time.

15.4 In the McNemar chi-square test, what are the independent and dependent variables?

Answer: Either two time points or two time points in conjunction with some kind of treatment or intervention would be the independent variable. The dependent variable would be the categorical variable with groups such as yes or no, man or woman, right or wrong, and so forth.

15.5 In the McNemar-Bowker chi-square test, what are the independent and dependent variables?

Answer: Either two time points or two time points in conjunction with some kind of treatment or intervention would be the independent variable. The dependent variable would be the categorical variable with *more than two groups*, such as yes, no, or maybe; man, woman, or LGBTQ; right, wrong, or in the middle; and so forth.

15.6 Does a repeated counts analysis involve a dependent or independent sample? Explain your answer.

Answer: The sample is dependent in some way. Usually, the same sample provides data twice—once for the baseline and another time in order to examine variance or change between the two time points.

15.7 Why is it necessary to have an equal number of data cases per time point?

Answer: An equal number of cases per time period are necessary in order to have paired comparisons for the analysis. This type of analysis is limited to complete pairs for comparison so that if time 1 has 200 counts and time 2 has 125 counts, the analysis will be based on the corresponding 125 cases, which are the complete cases.

15.8 In the sleep education program Real World Snapshot, assuming alpha is .05, would an overall p-value of .02 still produce statistically significant results? Explain your response.

Answer: Since the acceptable level of risk is .05, any p-value $<.05$ is statistically significant. Any p-value less than .05 indicates that the probability of having such a result by chance is less than 5%, which is typically acceptable risk.

15.9 Protection Home Security (PHS) wants to test the effectiveness of its sales force. Six hundred potential customers were asked whether they were interested in PHS before and then after receiving a sales call from a PHS representative. Responses were "Yes" or "No." From the sample data, determine whether the sales call had a likely effect on consumers' interest in home security. Alpha is .05. The SPSS file named "2X Repeated Chi-Square Exercise 1 Data" contains the data for the analysis.

Answer: Based on a representative sample of 600 consumers, who were asked if they were interested in PHS home security products before and after they received a PHS sales call, a McNemar chi-square test was conducted. A significant difference in interest was found ($p < .001$). As depicted in the table, prior to the sales call, 23.8% ($n = 143$) consumers were interested. After the PHS sales call, 49.2% ($n = 295$) of those same consumers were interested in PHS products. Therefore, it is likely that the PHS sales call made a difference in interest in their home security systems.

Comparison of Interest in Home Security Systems Before and After the PHS Sales Call

Interest	Before Sales Call	After Sales Call
Yes	143 (23.8%)	295 (49.2%)
No	457 (76.2%)	305 (50.8%)
Total	600 (100.0%)	600 (100.0%)

Note: McNemar Chi-Square Test (p < .001). N = 600.

Interest in Home Security After Sales Call * Interest in Home Security Before Sales Call Crosstabulation

			Interest in Home Security Before Sales Call		
			No Interest	Interested	Total
Interest in Home Security After Sales Call	No Interest	Count	214	91	305
		% of Total	35.7%	15.2%	50.8%
	Interested	Count	243	52	295
		% of Total	40.5%	8.7%	49.2%
Total		Count	457	143	600
		% of Total	76.2%	23.8%	100.0%

Interest in Home Security Before Sales Call

		Frequency	Percent	Valid Percent	Cumulative Percent
Valid	No Interest	457	76.2	76.2	76.2
	Interested	143	23.8	23.8	100.0
	Total	600	100.0	100.0	

Interest in Home Security After Sales Call

		Frequency	Percent	Valid Percent	Cumulative Percent
Valid	No Interest	305	50.8	50.8	50.8
	Interested	295	49.2	49.2	100.0
	Total	600	100.0	100.0	

Chi-Square Tests

	Value	Exact Sig. (2-sided)
McNemar Test		.000[a]
N of Valid Cases	600	

a. Binomial distribution used.

15.10 Venus Tablets wants to test whether trial usage of its new tablet will increase interest in the device. One hundred and seventy consumers were surveyed about their interest in the tablet prior to using the product for 2 weeks. After the trial, they were again asked whether they were interested in the Venus tablet. Responses were framed as "Yes" or "No." Did the trial usage make a difference? Alpha is .05. The SPSS file named "2X Repeated Chi-Square Exercise 2 Data" contains the data for the analysis.

Answer: Based on a representative sample of 170 consumers, who were asked if they were interested in the Venus tablet before and after trial usage of the product, a McNemar chi-square test was conducted. A nonsignificant difference in interest was found (p = .607). Therefore, it is likely that the trial usage of the Venus tablet does not make a difference in product interest.

Tablet Interest After Trial Usage * Tablet Interest Prior to Trial Usage Crosstabulation

			Tablet Interest Prior to Trial Usage		
			Not Interested	Interested	Total
Tablet Interest After Trial Usage	Not Interested	Count	60	6	66
		% of Total	35.3%	3.5%	38.8%
	Interested	Count	9	95	104
		% of Total	5.3%	55.9%	61.2%
Total		Count	69	101	170
		% of Total	40.6%	59.4%	100.0%

Tablet Interest Prior to Trial Usage

		Frequency	Percent	Valid Percent	Cumulative Percent
Valid	Not Interested	69	40.6	40.6	40.6
	Interested	101	59.4	59.4	100.0
	Total	170	100.0	100.0	

Tablet Interest After Trial Usage

		Frequency	Percent	Valid Percent	Cumulative Percent
Valid	Not Interested	66	38.8	38.8	38.8
	Interested	104	61.2	61.2	100.0
	Total	170	100.0	100.0	

Chi-Square Tests

	Value	Exact Sig. (2-sided)
McNemar Test		.607[a]
N of Valid Cases	170	

a. Binomial distribution used.

15.11 Cornucopia Medical wants to test the feasibility of offering customized health insurance plans. The company asked 120 individuals about whether they were interested, not interested, or undecided (about their interest) in the product. They were then given information about Cornucopia's customized health insurance program. Then, they were asked again whether the plan interests them. Does providing information about customized health insurance plans likely increase interest in such products? Alpha is .05. The SPSS file named "2X Repeated Chi-Square Exercise 3 Data" contains the data for the analysis.

Answer: Based on a representative sample of 120 healthcare consumers, who were asked about their interest in customized healthcare insurance before reviewing materials about such plans, and who were again asked about their interest in the plans after a review of the materials, a McNemar-Bowker chi-square test was conducted. A significant difference was found among those who were interested, not interested, and undecided ($\chi^2(3) = 12.910$, $p = .005$), indicating that there was a meaningful difference between at least one of the three responses. Before reviewing the plans, the percentages of consumers interested were as follows: Interested = 16.7% ($n = 20$), Not Interested = 28.3% ($n = 34$), and Undecided = 55.0% ($n = 66$). After being informed about the plans, the breakdown was as follows: Interested = 37.5% ($n = 45$), Not Interested = 26.7% ($n = 32$), and Undecided = 35.8% ($n = 43$). It is likely that consumers who are informed about customized healthcare plans have a greater interest in the plans, especially if their initial position is interested or undecided. The table represents the level of interest.

Comparison of Interest in Customized healthcare Plans Before and After Reviewing Such Plans

Interest	Before a Review	After a Review
Interested	20 (16.7%)	45 (37.5%)
Not Interested	34 (28.3%)	32 (26.7%)
Undecided	66 (55.0%)	43 (35.8%)
Total	120 (100.0%)	120 (100.0%)

Note: McNemar-Bowker Chi-Square Test ($\chi^2(3) = 12.910$, $p = .005$). N = 120.

Interest in Customized Health Insurance After a Review of Programs * Interest in Customized Health Insurance Prior to Review of Programs Crosstabulation

			Interest in Customized Health Insurance Prior to Review of Programs			
			Not Interested	Undecided	Interested	Total
Interest in Customized Health Insurance After a Review of Programs	Not Interested	Count	16	14	2	32
		% of Total	13.3%	11.7%	1.7%	26.7%
	Undecided	Count	12	21	10	43
		% of Total	10.0%	17.5%	8.3%	35.8%
	Interested	Count	6	31	8	45
		% of Total	5.0%	25.8%	6.7%	37.5%
Total		Count	34	66	20	120
		% of Total	28.3%	55.0%	16.7%	100.0%

Interest in Customized Health Insurance Prior to Review of Programs

		Frequency	Percent	Valid Percent	Cumulative Percent
Valid	Not Interested	34	28.3	28.3	28.3
	Undecided	66	55.0	55.0	83.3
	Interested	20	16.7	16.7	100.0
	Total	120	100.0	100.0	

Interest in Customized Health Insurance After a Review of Programs

		Frequency	Percent	Valid Percent	Cumulative Percent
Valid	Not Interested	32	26.7	26.7	26.7
	Undecided	43	35.8	35.8	62.5
	Interested	45	37.5	37.5	100.0
	Total	120	100.0	100.0	

Chi-Square Tests

	Value	df	Asymptotic Significance (2-sided)
McNemar-Bowker Test	12.910	3	.005
N of Valid Cases	120		

B.16 Chapter 16

16.1 In general terms, define a single sample *t*-test?

Answer: This is a significance test that compares the mean of a single sample and a test value (often viewed as true population mean) in order to determine if there is a difference between them.

16.2 What is a confidence interval?

Answer: This is an estimated interval of a specific statistic where the true parameter is expected to exist with a certain level of confidence.

16.3 If a confidence interval of the difference between the sample mean and test value contains a zero, will the *p*-value of the single sample *t*-test be significant or nonsignificant? Explain your answer.

Answer: It will be nonsignificant because there is likely zero or no difference between the sample mean and the test value.

16.4 In a single sample *t*-test, if a confidence interval of the true mean contains the test value, will the single sample *t*-test results be significant or nonsignificant? Explain your answer.

Answer: If the confidence interval of the true mean contains the test value, then there is likely no difference between the sample mean and test value. Recall that the center of the interval is the sample mean where the width is, give or take, a specific value from the sample mean.

16.5 Pharma 1st wishes to test the efficacy of a new Alzheimer's disease drug on a group of Alzheimer's patients. The instrument was formatted using a response scale where 1 = "no apparent cognitive ability" to 12 = "no apparent cognitive impairment." These treatment-free patients were never administered this test by a licensed practitioner until now. However, previous research findings indicate that individuals in this age group who did not receive any type of treatment typically scored 9.13. Is there a difference between the sample intervention group average score and the typical no intervention 9.13 score (test value)? Alpha = .01. Explain your answer. Report results in the format provided in this book. Be sure to include the confidence interval. The data file name is "*T*-Test Single Sample Exercise 1 Data."

Answer: Using a single sample *t*-test, an analysis was run to determine if there is a (meaningful) cognitive difference between those patients who received the drug treatment and those do did not. Alpha = .01.

The sample size is greater than 30. The Shapiro-Wilk statistic located in the tests for normality table is p = .83, indicating that the sample is normally distributed.

Tests of Normality

	Kolmogorov-Smirnov[a]			Shapiro-Wilk		
	Statistic	df	Sig.	Statistic	df	Sig.
Cognitive Score: 1=no apparent cognitive ability TO 12=no apparent cognitive impairment	.042	165	.200*	.995	165	.831

*. This is a lower bound of the true significance.

a. Lilliefors Significance Correction

As we can see on the "One-Sample Statistics" table, 165 patients participated in this new Alzheimer's disease drug trial. The average cognitive score is 8.14 compared to a typical no treatment patient score of 9.13. The sample standard deviation is 3.01.

One-Sample Statistics

	N	Mean	Std. Deviation	Std. Error Mean
Cognitive Score: 1=no apparent cognitive ability TO 12=no apparent cognitive impairment	165	8.14	3.013	.235

The "One-Sample Test" table reveals that in all likelihood, there is a meaningful difference between the sample mean score of 8.14 and the text value of 9.13. Thus, those patients who received the drug intervention scored less on the cognitive test than those who did not receive the therapy. Since p < .001, which is less than .01 (.0 or 1 / 100 > .001 or 1/ 1,000), there is less than a .01 probability that our findings are not meaningful. The degrees of freedom are 165 – 1 = 164 so that 164 values can vary leaving the last or 165th to be determined by the previous 164 values. The difference between the sample mean and test value is –.989, where the greater test value is the point of reference, and hence a negative number (8.14 < 9.13) in this case.

We have a 95% confidence interval for the difference between the sample data mean of 8.14 and the test value of 9.13. This interval is the "range" of possible differences of the sample mean in relation to the test value. Based on the sample data, which we assume represents the population, we are 95% confident that the mean score for those individuals who take the new drug will be anywhere from .53 to 1.45 less than 9.13. The interval does not contain zero.

Based on the *p*-value and alpha, these findings are meaningful and can be generally applied to all those receiving the new drug.

One-Sample Test

	Test Value = 9.13					
					95% Confidence Interval of the Difference	
	t	df	Sig. (2-tailed)	Mean Difference	Lower	Upper
Cognitive Score: 1=no apparent cognitive ability TO 12=no apparent cognitive impairment	-4.218	164	.000	-.989	-1.45	-.53

In summary, assuming that the sample represents the effects of the new drug on patients and the sample data are normally distributed (see Chapter 12), there is an apparent cognitive capacity difference between drug treatment patients and those patients who did not received any type of treatment.

Write-up: A single sample *t*-test was conducted that compared the typical cognitive score for nonintervention Alzheimer's individuals to a current representative sample of 165 patients taking a new Alzheimer's drug. A significant difference was found ($t(164) = -4.21$, $p < .001$). It is likely that the treatment mean cognitive score of 8.14 ($SD = 3.01$) is not equal to those patients who have not had any type of intervention and scored on average 9.13. Thus, cognitive capacity varies between these two groups. Furthermore, we are 95% confident that the true mean cognitive score for patients taking the new Alzheimer's drug on average falls anywhere from 7.68 to 8.60.

(OR we can apply directionality)

A single sample *t*-test was conducted that compared the typical cognitive score for nonintervention Alzheimer's individuals to a current representative sample of 165 patients taking a new Alzheimer's drug. A significant difference was found ($t(164) = -4.21$, $p < .001$). It is likely that the treatment mean cognitive score of 8.14 ($SD = 3.01$) is lower than for those patients who have not had any type of intervention and scored on average 9.13. Thus, the Alzheimer's drug treatment patients scored less on the cognitive abilities test compared to the non-treatment patients. Furthermore, we are 95% confident that the true mean cognitive score for patients taking the new Alzheimer's drug on average falls anywhere between 7.68 and 8.60.

How might we interpret these findings? It might be that the drug actually diminishes cognitive capacity. Second, perhaps the sample patients had other health conditions that mitigated their cognitive capacity. Third, the treatment patients may have been at a more advanced stage of illness. Fourth, perhaps the cognitive instruments sufficiently varied so that accurate comparisons were difficult. There could be any number of factors that explain these results.

16.6 A professor has been recording student motivation in her highly popular yet demanding classes over a number of years using the same survey. Recently, she collected representative data from her current classes using the same survey. Responses were formatted as: 1 = "not motivated at all" to 7 = "highly motivated." She has an average of all previously collected data. To date, the mean motivation score is 6.12. Is there a difference between the collective previous samples of student motivation and the motivation of her current students? Alpha = .05. Explain your answer. Report results in the format provided in this book. Be sure to include the confidence interval. The data file name is "*T*-Test Single Sample Exercise 2 Data."

Answer: Using a single sample *t*-test, an analysis was run to determine if there is a meaningful difference in motivation between current students and collectively from those in previous classes. Alpha = .05.

The sample size is greater than 30. The Shapiro–Wilk statistic located in the tests for normality table is $p = .86$, indicating that the sample is normally distributed.

Tests of Normality

	Kolmogorov-Smirnov[a]			Shapiro-Wilk		
	Statistic	df	Sig.	Statistic	df	Sig.
1=not motivated TO 7= highly motivated	.091	60	.200*	.989	60	.860

*. This is a lower bound of the true significance.

a. Lilliefors Significance Correction

As we can see in the "One-Sample Statistics" table, 60 students participated in this motivational study. The average motivation score is 5.78, compared to previous classes, which averaged 6.12. The sample standard deviation is 1.94.

One-Sample Statistics

	N	Mean	Std. Deviation	Std. Error Mean
1=not motivated TO 7= highly motivated	60	5.78	1.941	.251

The "One-Sample Test" table reveals that in all likelihood, there is no meaningful difference between the sample of 5.78 and the test value of 6.12. In other words, current level of class reported motivation is likely not different from the collective mean score of all previously reported classes because $p = .18$, which is greater than .05. The degrees of freedom are $60 - 1 = 59$ so that 59 values can vary leaving the last or 60th value to be determined by the previous 59 values.

The difference between the sample mean and test value is –.336, where the greater test value is the point of reference, and hence a negative number (5.78 < 6.12) in this case.

We have a 95% confidence interval for the difference between the sample data mean of 5.78 and the test value of 6.12. This is the interval of possible differences between the sample mean in relation to the test value. We are 95% confident that current student motivation scores on average are anywhere from .84 below the previously reported 6.15 average score to .17 above 6.15, or we are 95% confident that the true population mean of motivation scores is between 5.31 and 6.32 (inclusively). This is so because the lower interval value is negative and the upper interval value is positive so that the interval goes from less than to greater than the test value, thus including zero. This is consistent with $p = .18$, a result that does not represent a meaningful finding. These findings can be applied to all of her current students providing that the sample truly represents her classes.

One-Sample Test

	Test Value = 6.12					
					95% Confidence Interval of the Difference	
	t	df	Sig. (2-tailed)	Mean Difference	Lower	Upper
1=not motivated TO 7= highly motivated	-1.341	59	.185	-.336	-.84	.17

In summary, based on the data, which we assume is normally distributed, these findings demonstrate that current student motivation is not likely different from the collective mean score of all previously reported classes.

Write-up: A single sample *t*-test was conducted that compared previous students' self-reported level of motivation to a current representative sample of 60 students. A nonsignificant difference was found ($t(59) = -1.34$, $p = .18$). It is likely that the current student mean motivation score of 5.78 ($SD = 1.94$) is not different from previous students' collective mean score of 6.12. Motivation has not changed. Furthermore, we are 95% confident that the true mean motivation score for current students is between 5.31 and 6.32.

16.7 In a production facility, the general manager suspects that the shoe production output of newer replacement machinery is different from the older replaced equipment average output. This may be the case because the new machinery requires additional adjustments and the operators require additional training and experience operating the new equipment. By the same token, the new equipment should produce more output than the older outdated machinery. The general manager directed her operations management research team to compare a sample of the current production output with the overall average of the older equipment's output. The overall average 24-hour production run on the old machinery was 1,200 pairs. Determine if there is a difference in output. Alpha = .05. Explain your answer. Report results in the format provided in this book. Be sure to include the confidence interval. The data file name is "*T*-Test Single Sample Exercise 3 Data."

Answer: Using a single sample *t*-test, we ran our analysis to determine if there is a meaningful difference in shoe production output between the older and newer machinery. Alpha = .05.

The sample size is 30; greater than 30 is preferred. The Shapiro-Wilk statistic located in the tests for normality table is $p = .24$, indicating that the sample is normally distributed.

Tests of Normality

	Kolmogorov-Smirnov[a]			Shapiro-Wilk		
	Statistic	df	Sig.	Statistic	df	Sig.
Production in Units	.101	30	.200*	.956	30	.245

*. This is a lower bound of the true significance.

a. Lilliefors Significance Correction

As we can see on the "One-Sample Statistics" table, 30 new machinery production output days were randomly selected. The average output in a 24-hour period is 1,070 pairs compared to the average old equipment output of 1,200 pairs. The sample standard deviation is 399 pairs. Since a complete pair of shoes is required to produce a unit for sale, we will round down.

One-Sample Statistics

	N	Mean	Std. Deviation	Std. Error Mean
Production in Units	30	1070.02	399.887	73.009

The "One-Sample Test" table reveals that there likely is no meaningful difference between the sample of 1,070 pairs and the test value of 1,200 pairs because p =.08. Therefore, there is an 8% probability that these findings are by chance, which is unacceptable risk when alpha is .05.

Based on the sample data, we are 95% confident that the likely mean production output for the new machinery will be between 279.30 pairs less than to 19.34 pairs greater than 1,200 pairs, which includes zero, meaning that there is no difference between the sample average and test value. We can also say that we are 95% confident that the true production mean is between 920 and 1219 pairs of shoes per 24-hour shift.

One-Sample Test

	Test Value = 1200					
					95% Confidence Interval of the Difference	
	t	df	Sig. (2-tailed)	Mean Difference	Lower	Upper
Production in Units	-1.780	29	.086	-129.981	-279.30	19.34

These findings demonstrate that at this stage of usage in their production "lives," the new equipment likely does not produce different production output compared to the old equipment.

Write-up: A single sample t-test was conducted to analyze whether there is a difference in productivity between old and new shoe (pairs) manufacturing machinery. The sample consisted of 30 representative new equipment 24-hour production runs. A nonsignificant difference was found ($t(29) = -1.78$, $p = .08$). It is likely that the current equipment average output of 1,070 pairs (SD = 399 pairs) for a 24-hour period is not different than the typical 1,200 pairs output of the old equipment. Thus, the new machinery does not produce different output. Furthermore, we are 95% confident that the new machinery production true average likely runs from 279.30 pairs less than to 19.34 pairs greater than 1,200 pairs per 24-hour shift.

16.8 Using a sample of those persons who completed its course, GOFORIT! wishes to determine whether students in general perform differently on the SAT for the first time after completing its SAT preparation course compared to first-time test takers who have no preparation. Based on past data, where students took the same format SAT for the first time and did not prepare for the test, test takers averaged 998 on their total Math/English scores. Determine whether those test takers who completed the SAT preparation class scored differently than the 998 previously reported average score. Alpha = .05. Explain your answer. Report results in the format provided in this book. Be sure to include the confidence interval. The data file name is "*T*-Test Single Sample Exercise 4 Data."

Answer: Using a single sample *t*-test, we ran our analysis to determine if there is a meaningful difference in first-time SAT scores by individuals who have not prepared for the test compared to those who have taken the GOFORIT! SAT preparation course. Alpha = .05.

The sample size is greater than 30. The Shapiro–Wilk statistic located in the tests for normality table is $p = .50$, indicating that the sample is normally distributed.

Tests of Normality

	Kolmogorov-Smirnov[a]			Shapiro-Wilk		
	Statistic	df	Sig.	Statistic	df	Sig.
SAT: Math & English	.021	738	.200*	.998	738	.503

*. This is a lower bound of the true significance.

a. Lilliefors Significance Correction

As we can see on the "One-Sample Statistics" table, 738 GOFORIT! SAT test takers participated in this study. The average Math/English SAT score is 1,101.60 compared to the unprepared test value of 998. The sample standard deviation is 191.51.

One-Sample Statistics

	N	Mean	Std. Deviation	Std. Error Mean
SAT: Math & English	738	1101.60	191.515	7.050

The "One-Sample Test" table reveals that in all likelihood, there is a meaningful difference between the GOFORIT! SAT test takers' mean score of 1,101.60 and the "unprepared" test takers' mean score of 998. This is so because $p < .001$, indicating that the probability of these results occurring by chance is less than .001.

Based on the sample data, we are 95% confident that GOFORIT! SAT test takers on average will score anywhere from 89.76 to 117.44 higher than the unprepared test takers. The interval does not contain zero. Likewise, we can state that we are 95% confident that the true mean SAT score for GOFORIT! test takers is between 1,087.76 and 1,115.44.

One-Sample Test

	Test Value = 998					
					95% Confidence Interval of the Difference	
	t	df	Sig. (2-tailed)	Mean Difference	Lower	Upper
SAT: Math & English	14.696	737	.000	103.600	89.76	117.44

In summary, these findings demonstrate that the GOFORIT! first-time test takers likely score differently compared to first-time unprepared test takers.

Write-up: A single sample *t*-test was conducted to analyze whether first-time SAT test takers who completed the GOFORIT! SAT preparation course scored differently compared to those first-time test takers who did not prepare for the test. The sample consisted of 738 GOFORIT! test takers. A significant difference was found ($t(737) = 14.69$, $p < .001$). It is likely that the GOFORIT! prepared first-time test takers' average score of 1,101.60 ($SD = 191.51$) is different than the unprepared first-time test takers' average SAT score of 998. Completing the GOFORIT! SAT preparation course results in different scores for first-time test takers who had no other test preparation. Furthermore, we are 95% confident that the GOFORIT! prepared first-time test taker Math/English SAT true mean score is anywhere from 1,087.76 to 1,115.44.

(OR we can apply directionality)

A single sample *t*-test was conducted to analyze whether first-time SAT test takers who completed the GOFORIT! SAT preparation course scored differently compared to those first-time test takers who did not prepare for the test. The sample consisted of 738 GOFORIT! test takers. A significant difference was found ($t(737) = 14.69$, $p < .001$). It is likely that the GOFORIT! prepared first-time test takers' average score of 1,101.60 ($SD = 191.51$) is greater than the unprepared first-time test takers' average SAT score of 998. Completing the GOFORIT! SAT preparation course results in higher scores on average for first-time test takers who had no other test preparation. Furthermore, we are 95% confident that the GOFORIT! prepared first-time test taker Math/English SAT true mean score is anywhere from 1,087.76 to 1,115.44.

B.17 Chapter 17

17.1 Define a two independent samples *t*-test. Provide an example.

Answer: The two independent samples *t*-test is a significance test that compares the means between two independent samples (groups) in order to determine if there is the likelihood of a statistically meaningful difference between them. For instance, we can measure age or income by gender (M/F).

17.2 What is equality of variance?

Answer: Variance is the data's standard deviation squared. Equality of variance indicates whether the two samples share similar variances or data spread.

17.3 What is the Levene test for equality of variance?

Answer: This is a significance test that is used to assess equality of variance in two or more distributions.

17.4 Define pooled two independent samples *t*-test.

Answer: This significance *t*-test is used when two samples (groups) share similar distributions in the data to be compared.

17.5 What is a separate two independent samples *t*-test?

Answer: This significance *t*-test is used when two samples (groups) do not share similar distributions in the data to be compared.

17.6 To what does the term "equality of variance assumed" refer?

Answer: This is the SPSS output associated with the pooled two independent samples *t*-test.

17.7 To what does the term "equality of variance not assumed" refer?

Answer: This is the SPSS output associated with the separate two independent samples *t*-test.

17.8 What is the Mann-Whitney *U* test?

Answer: This is a two independent samples nonparametric test based on rank-ordering the data. It can be used when the data violate the normal distribution assumption. When the test is used to compare two means, equality of variance is not a consideration.

17.9 A local hospital offered two 6-month weight management programs to individuals who were 40–60 pounds overweight. One hundred and forty-six clients enrolled and completed one of these two plans over a 6-month period. Among other information, weight loss data were collected over the 6-month period. There were 62 participants in the *Protein Focus* program and 84 participants in the *Calorie Factor* plan. Based on the data from the two samples, is there any evidence to suggest that one program is more effective than the other by the end of the 6-month program? Explain your answer. Report results in the format provided in this book. Be sure to include the confidence interval. Alpha = .05. The data file name is "*T*-Test 2 Independent Samples Exercise 1 Data."

Answer: The analysis requires two variables: a grouping variable (Protein Focus = 1 and Calorie Factor = 2) and a dependent variable (measured weight loss in pounds after 6 months).

The sample size is greater than 30. As depicted in the table below, we wish to examine the data for Protein Focus (p = .24) and for Calorie Factor (p = .16). Both Shapiro-Wilk statistics are greater than .05, indicating that the samples are normally distributed.

Tests of Normality

		Kolmogorov-Smirnov[a]			Shapiro-Wilk		
	Program	Statistic	df	Sig.	Statistic	df	Sig.
Weight Loss in lbs.	Protein Focus	.076	62	.200*	.975	62	.246
	Calorie Factor	.088	84	.154	.978	84	.160

*. This is a lower bound of the true significance.

a. Lilliefors Significance Correction

As we can see below, the total sample consists of 146 clients where respondents were not evenly split between the diet management plans. The Protein Focus mean reported pound loss is 24.07 and the standard deviation is 4.96 lbs. The Calorie Factor mean reported pound is 23.85 and the standard deviation is 3.33 lbs.

Group Statistics

	Program	N	Mean	Std. Deviation	Std. Error Mean
Weight Loss in lbs.	Protein Focus	62	24.07	4.968	.631
	Calorie Factor	84	23.85	3.339	.364

The output in the table below contains information about the equality of variances, the means' comparison of the weight management plans, and the 95% confidence interval for the difference between the two weight loss mean scores.

Independent Samples Test

		Levene's Test for Equality of Variances		t-test for Equality of Means						
									95% Confidence Interval of the Difference	
		F	Sig.	t	df	Sig. (2-tailed)	Mean Difference	Std. Error Difference	Lower	Upper
Weight Loss in lbs.	Equal variances assumed	17.653	.000	.316	144	.753	.217	.688	-1.143	1.577
	Equal variances not assumed			.298	100.261	.766	.217	.729	-1.228	1.662

The Levene test for equality of variance compared the data distributions between the two independent variables or samples. In this case, there is a meaningful difference between the shape of the two variables' data distribution because $p < .001$, which is less than our acceptable level of risk (alpha = .05). Therefore, we assume that the variances are not equal.

The corresponding two independent samples *t*-test for "equal variances not assumed" indicates that $p = .76$, which is not meaningful. Therefore, it is *likely* that there is no difference in weight loss over 6 months between the weight management programs.

We have a 95% confidence interval for the difference between the Protein Focus and Calorie Factor average weight loss. The point of reference is Protein Focus since it is the first sample in the comparison order. Based on the sample data, we are 95% confident that the Protein Focus true population average weight loss is anywhere from 1.22 lbs less than to 1.66 lbs greater than the sample average Calorie Factor weight loss.

Write-up: A two independent samples *t*-test was conducted that compared the average weight loss over 6 months between the Protein Focus and Calorie Factor weight management programs. A total of 146 clients participated, 62 from Protein Focus and 84 from Calorie Factor. A nonsignificant difference was found ($t(100.26) = -.298$, $p = .766$). There is no evidence to indicate that the average between Protein Focus ($M = 24.07$ [$SD = 4.96$]) and Calorie Factor ($M = 23.85$ [$SD = 3.33$]) varies. Thus, on average, there is likely no difference between weight loss programs. Furthermore, we are 95% confident that the true population average Protein Focus weight loss is between 1.22 lbs less than and 1.66 lbs more than the average Calorie Factor's weight loss.

17.10 Primary caregivers ($N = 57$), who were responsible for one or more minor children, and "empty nesters" ($N = 50$) were surveyed about their willingness to purchase delivered groceries online. Individuals responded to a scale question: 1 = "not at all willing" to 7 = "willing all of the time." Determine if there is a likely difference in responses between these two groups. Explain your answer. Report results in the format provided in this book. Be sure to include the confidence interval. Alpha = .05. The data file name is "*T*-Test 2 Independent Samples Exercise 2 Data."

Answer: The analysis requires two variables: a grouping variable (Primary Caregiver w/ minors = 1 and Empty Nesters = 2) and a dependent variable (scale data that measures interest in purchasing groceries online: 1 = "not at all willing" to 7 = "willing all the time").

The sample size is greater than 30. As depicted in the table below, we wish to examine the data for Empty Nesters ($p = .69$) and for w/ children ($p = .32$). Both Shapiro-Wilk statistics are greater than .05, indicating that the samples are normally distributed.

Tests of Normality

		Kolmogorov-Smirnov[a]			Shapiro-Wilk		
	Family Status	Statistic	df	Sig.	Statistic	df	Sig.
Interest in Online Grocery Shopping	empty nesters	.055	57	.200*	.985	57	.692
	with 1 or more minor children	.066	50	.200*	.974	50	.328

*. This is a lower bound of the true significance.

a. Lilliefors Significance Correction

As we can see below, the total sample consists of 107 heads of households where 57 were empty nesters and 50 were primary caregivers w/ minors. The empty nesters' mean reported willingness to buy groceries online is 4.15 ($SD = 1.02$). The primary caregiver w/ minors' mean reported willingness to purchase groceries online is 5.79 ($SD = .98$).

Group Statistics

	Family Status	N	Mean	Std. Deviation	Std. Error Mean
Interest in Online Grocery Shopping	empty nesters	57	4.15	1.027	.136
	with 1 or more minor children	50	5.79	.988	.140

The output in the table below contains information about the equality of variances, the means' comparison of the households, and the 95% confidence interval for the difference between the two mean scores.

Independent Samples Test

		Levene's Test for Equality of Variances		t-test for Equality of Means						
									95% Confidence Interval of the Difference	
		F	Sig.	t	df	Sig. (2-tailed)	Mean Difference	Std. Error Difference	Lower	Upper
Interest in Online Grocery Shopping	Equal variances assumed	.022	.882	-8.403	105	.000	-1.643	.196	-2.031	-1.255
	Equal variances not assumed			-8.424	104.080	.000	-1.643	.195	-2.030	-1.256

The Levene Test for Equality of Variance compared the data distributions between the two independent variables or samples. In our example, there is no meaningful difference between the shape of the two variables' data distribution because p = .88, which is greater than our acceptable level of risk (alpha = .05). Therefore, we assume that the variances are equal.

The corresponding two independent samples t-test for "equal variances assumed" indicates that $p < .001$, which is meaningful because .001 < .05. Therefore, it is likely that there is difference in willingness to buy groceries online between empty nesters and primary caregivers w/ minors.

We have a 95% confidence interval for the difference between the empty nesters' and primary caregiver w/ minors' willingness to shop online for groceries mean scores. The point of reference is empty nesters since it is the first sample in the comparison order. Based on the sample data, we are 95% confident that the empty nesters' true population average willingness to buy groceries online score is anywhere from 1.25 to 2.03 less than the average primary caregiver w/ minors average score of 5.79. In summary, based on the p-value and confidence interval, there is a very low probability that these results are by chance.

Write-up: A two independent samples t-test was conducted that compared the average willingness to buy groceries online between empty nesters and primary caregivers w/ minors. A total of 107 individuals participated; 57 were empty nesters, and 50 were primary caregivers w/ minors. A significant difference was found ($t(105) = -8.40$, $p < .001$). There is evidence to indicate that the willingness scores vary between empty nesters ($M = 4.15$ [$SD = 1.02$]) and primary caregivers w/ minors ($M = 5.79$ [SD = .98]). Thus, on average, there likely is a difference between these two groups. Furthermore, we are 95% confident that the true population average empty nester willingness to buy groceries online score anywhere from 1.25 to 2.03 less than the average primary caregiver w/ minors willingness score.

(OR we can apply directionality)

A two independent samples t-test was conducted that compared the average willingness to buy groceries online between empty nesters and primary caregivers w/ minors scores. A total of 107 individuals participated; 57 were empty nesters, and 50 were primary caregivers w/ minors. A significant difference was found ($t(105) = -8.40$, $p < .001$). There is evidence to suggest that, on average, empty nesters ($M = 4.15$ [$SD = 1.02$]) are less willing to buy groceries online compared to primary caregivers w/ minors ($M = 5.79$ [$SD = .98$]). Furthermore, we are 95% confident that the true population average empty nester willingness to buy groceries online score is anywhere from 1.25 to 2.03 less than the average primary caregiver w/ minors willingness score.

17.11 "Nursing" staff, including nurses, nursing assistants, and orderlies, sustain over 35,000 reported injuries per year. An occupational research firm seeks to discover the level of reported proper patient lifting and moving techniques employed by nursing staff based on whether they work in short-term hospital care facilities compared to long-term care nursing homes. Is there a difference between these two groups of healthcare workers? Five hundred nursing workers completed a survey, of which 235 worked in hospitals and 265 worked in long-term care nursing homes. The question of interest asked them if they employed proper patient lifting and moving techniques in order to minimize injury to themselves. Responses were anchored in the following format: 0 = "I do not use proper patient lifting and moving techniques" to 5 = "I always use proper patient lifting and moving techniques." Explain your answer. Report results in the format provided in this book. Be sure to include the confidence interval. Alpha = .05. The data file name is "*T*-Test 2 Independent Samples Exercise 3 Data."

Answer: The Shapiro–Wilk test of normality indicates that both samples do not violate the normal distribution assumption (Hospital staff, $p = .189$ and Nursing Home staff, $p = .845$).

Tests of Normality

		Kolmogorov-Smirnov[a]			Shapiro-Wilk		
	Level of Care	Statistic	df	Sig.	Statistic	df	Sig.
Proper Patient Moving Technique	Short-term Hospital	.053	235	.200*	.991	235	.189
	Long-term Nursing Home	.025	265	.200*	.997	265	.845

*. This is a lower bound of the true significance.

a. Lilliefors Significance Correction

The mean Hospital staffer ($N = 235$) score is 2.88 and the Nursing Home staffer mean ($N = 265$) score is 1.25. The 1.5× rule is not violated.

Group Statistics

	Level of Care	N	Mean	Std. Deviation	Std. Error Mean
Proper Patient Moving Technique	Short-term Hospital	235	2.88	.919	.060
	Long-term Nursing Home	265	1.25	.247	.015

The Levene test is significant at $p < .001$, indicating that the equality of variance assumption is not met. Therefore, we must use the "equal variances not assumed" results. Accordingly, on average, there is a meaningful difference between the reported usage of proper patient lifting and moving techniques ($p < .001$). The hospital staff average reported score is between 1.50 and 1.74 higher than the average nursing home staffer.

Independent Samples Test

		Levene's Test for Equality of Variances		t-test for Equality of Means						
									95% Confidence Interval of the Difference	
		F	Sig.	t	df	Sig. (2-tailed)	Mean Difference	Std. Error Difference	Lower	Upper
Proper Patient Moving Technique	Equal variances assumed	210.795	.000	27.709	498	.000	1.627	.059	1.512	1.742
	Equal variances not assumed			26.303	264.082	.000	1.627	.062	1.505	1.749

Write-up: A two independent samples *t*-test was conducted that compared the practice of proper patient lifting and moving scores from 500 nursing staff in hospitals ($N = 235$) and in nursing homes ($N = 265$). Staff responses ranged from 0 = "I do not use proper patient lifting/moving techniques" to 5 = "I always use proper patient lifting and moving techniques." A significant difference was found ($t(264) = 26.30$, $p < .001$). It is likely that the hospital staff average score of 2.88 (*SD* = .91) is different from the nursing home staff mean score of 1.25 (*SD* = .24). Thus, on average, hospital staff proper patient lifting/moving reported practices vary from those of nursing home staff. Furthermore, we are 95% confident that the hospital staff true population average score is between 1.50 to 1.74 higher than the nursing home staff average score.

(OR we can apply directionality)

A two independent samples *t*-test was conducted that compared the practice of proper patient lifting and moving scores from 500 nursing staff in hospitals (*N* = 235) and in nursing homes (*N* = 265). Staff responses ranged from 0 = "I do not use proper patient lifting/moving techniques" to 5 = "I always use proper patient lifting and moving techniques." A significant difference was found ($t(264) = 26.30$, $p < .001$). It is likely that the hospital staff average score of 2.88 (*SD* = .91) is greater than that of the nursing home staff mean score of 1.25 (*SD* = .24). Thus, on average, hospital staff report using proper patient lifting/moving practices more than their nursing home colleagues. Furthermore, we are 95% confident that the hospital staff true population average score is between 1.50 and 1.74 higher than the nursing home staff average score.

17.12 The total annual cost in dollars was calculated per individual inmate at federal prisons and at state prisons. The representative sample consisted of 500 federal inmates from various institutions throughout the USA and 500 state inmates from 40 states for a total sample size of 1,000. Determine if there is a difference in costs between federal inmates and the collective data on state inmates. Explain your answer. Report results in the format provided in this book. Be sure to include the confidence interval. Alpha = .05. The data file name is "*T*-Test 2 Independent Samples Exercise 4 Data."

Answer: The Shapiro-Wilk test of normality indicates that both samples do not violate the normal distribution assumption (federal inmates, $p = .676$, and state inmates, $p = .593$).

Tests of Normality

		Kolmogorov-Smirnov[a]			Shapiro-Wilk		
	Jurisdiction	Statistic	df	Sig.	Statistic	df	Sig.
Total Annual Cost Per Inmate	Federal	.026	500	.200*	.998	500	.676
	State	.031	500	.200*	.997	500	.593

*. This is a lower bound of the true significance.

a. Lilliefors Significance Correction

The mean federal prisoner annual cost is $34,081 and the annual cost per state prisoner is $32,119.

Group Statistics

	Jurisdiction	N	Mean	Std. Deviation	Std. Error Mean
Total Annual Cost Per Inmate	Federal	500	$34,081.4428	$4,871.29900	$217.85111
	State	500	$32,119.0612	$6,656.53548	$297.68932

The Levene test is significant at $p < .001$, indicating that the equality of variance assumption is not met. Therefore, we must use the "equal variances not assumed" results. Accordingly, on average, there is a meaningful difference between the annual cost to maintain a federal prisoner and the annual cost to maintain a state prisoner ($p < .001$). The federal prisoner costs on average between $1,238 and $2,686 more per year.

Independent Samples Test

		Levene's Test for Equality of Variances		t-test for Equality of Means						
									95% Confidence Interval of the Difference	
		F	Sig.	t	df	Sig. (2-tailed)	Mean Difference	Std. Error Difference	Lower	Upper
Total Annual Cost Per Inmate	Equal variances assumed	38.848	.000	5.320	998	.000	$1,962.38160	$368.88757	$1,238.49735	$2,686.26585
	Equal variances not assumed			5.320	914.347	.000	$1,962.38160	$368.88757	$1,238.41693	$2,686.34627

Write-up: A two independent samples *t*-test was conducted that compared the total annual cost to maintain a federal inmate ($N = 500$) and state inmate ($N = 500$). A significant difference was found ($t(914) = 5.32$, $p < .001$). It is likely that the typical cost to maintain a federal inmate (M = \$34,081 [SD = \$4,871]) is different from that of a state inmate (M = \$32,119 [SD = \$6,656]). Thus, on average, annual federal inmate costs vary from state annual inmate costs. Furthermore, we are 95% confident that the federal inmate true population average cost is between \$1,238 and \$2,686 higher than that of the state inmate.

(OR we can apply directionality)

A two independent samples *t*-test was conducted that compared the total annual cost to maintain a federal inmate ($N = 500$) and state inmate ($N = 500$). A significant difference was found ($t(914) = 5.32$, $p < .001$). It is likely that the typical cost to maintain a federal inmate (M = \$34,081 [SD = \$4,871]) is more than that of a state inmate (M = \$32,119 [SD = \$6,656]). Thus, on average, annual federal inmate costs are greater than that of a state inmate. Furthermore, we are 95% confident that the federal inmate true population average cost is between \$1,238 and \$2,686 higher than that of the state inmate.

17.13 A group of researchers studied whether the amount of open family dialogue related to whether children grew up to be more accepting of "justified" violence, such as war, capital punishment, and other forms of physical violence, for "good" reason. Two hundred and twenty-five adults 18–22 years old completed a survey. One hundred and twenty-five were classified as raised in "more open" dialogue families and 100 were grouped as reared in "less open" dialogue families. The participants were asked whether they thought that some situations warranted a physically violent response. Responses were framed in a seven-point scale: 1 = "violence is never justified" to 7 = "there are situations where violence is totally justified." Does the high or low level of family dialogue relate to support for physical violence under certain situations? Explain your answer. Report results in the format provided in this book. Be sure to include the confidence interval. Alpha = .05. The data file name is "*T*-Test 2 Independent Samples Exercise 5 Data."

Answer: The Shapiro-Wilk test of normality indicates that both samples do not violate the normal distribution assumption (Open Dialogue, $p = .616$, and Less Open Dialogue, $p = .909$).

Tests of Normality

		Kolmogorov-Smirnov[a]			Shapiro-Wilk		
	Open or Closed Dialogue	Statistic	df	Sig.	Statistic	df	Sig.
Justified Violence	Open Dialogue	.034	125	.200*	.991	125	.616
	Less Open Dialogue	.047	100	.200*	.993	100	.909

*. This is a lower bound of the true significance.

a. Lilliefors Significance Correction

The mean open dialogue score (N = 125) is 1.67 and the less open dialogue mean score (N = 100) is 1.98. The 1.5× rule is not violated.

Group Statistics

	Open or Closed Dialogue	N	Mean	Std. Deviation	Std. Error Mean
Justified Violence	Open Dialogue	125	1.67	.175	.016
	Less Open Dialogue	100	1.98	.518	.052

The Levene test is significant at $p < .001$, indicating that the equality of variance assumption is not met. Therefore, we must use the "equal variances not assumed" results. Accordingly, on average, there is a meaningful difference between assessments of justified violence between those people raised in open dialogue homes compared to those from less open dialogue families ($p <$ .001). The open dialogue family respondents were less likely to see any form of violence justified. Their scores were from .20 to .42 less on the scale.

Independent Samples Test

		Levene's Test for Equality of Variances		t-test for Equality of Means						
									95% Confidence Interval of the Difference	
		F	Sig.	t	df	Sig. (2-tailed)	Mean Difference	Std. Error Difference	Lower	Upper
Justified Violence	Equal variances assumed	88.751	.000	-6.320	223	.000	-.313	.050	-.411	-.216
	Equal variances not assumed			-5.781	117.136	.000	-.313	.054	-.420	-.206

Write-up: A two independent samples *t*-test was conducted that compared perceptions of some forms of violence as justifiable in open dialogue (N = 125) and less open dialogue (N = 100) families. A significant difference was found ($t(117) = -5.78$, $p < .001$). On average, it is likely than open dialogue family respondent (M = 1.67 [SD = .17]) scores about acceptable forms of violence are difference than those of less open dialogue respondent scores (M = 1.98 [SD = .51]). Thus, on average, open dialogue perceptions vary from less open dialogue perceptions. Furthermore, we are 95% confident that the open dialogue true population average perceptions about justified violence score is between .20 and .42 less than the less open scores based on a seven-point scale.

(OR we can apply directionality)

A two independent samples *t*-test was conducted that compared perceptions of some forms of violence as justifiable in open dialogue (N = 125) and less open dialogue (N = 100) families. A significant difference was found ($t(117) = -5.78$, $p < .001$). On average, it is likely than open dialogue family respondent (M = 1.67 [SD = .17]) scores about acceptable forms of violence are less than the less open dialogue respondents (M = 1.98 [SD = .51]). Thus, on average, open dialogue perceptions find justified violence as less acceptable compared to less open dialogue perceptions. Furthermore, we are 95% confident that the open dialogue true population average perceptions about justified violence as acceptable score is between .20 and .42 less than the less open scores based on a seven-point scale.

17.14 Two representative samples of undergraduate students eligible to vote were selected to indicate their likelihood to vote in the forthcoming presidential election. One sample viewed the last presidential debate of the major candidates and the other group did not view the debate. Each sample consisted of 175 students for a total of 350 participants. The question was formatted in a five-point scale as follows: 0 = "I do not intend to vote in the next presidential election" to 5 = "I absolutely intend to vote in the next presidential election." Did exposure to the final presidential debate relate to whether undergraduate students intend to vote in the presidential election? Explain your answer. Report results in the format provided in this book. Be sure to include the confidence interval. Alpha = .05. The data file name is "*T*-Test 2 Independent Samples Exercise 6 Data."

Answer: The Shapiro-Wilk test of normality indicates that both samples do not violate the normal distribution assumption (Viewed the Final Debate, $p = .419$, and Did Not View the Final Debate, $p = .090$).

Tests of Normality

		Kolmogorov-Smirnov[a]			Shapiro-Wilk		
	Debate Exposure	Statistic	df	Sig.	Statistic	df	Sig.
Intention to Vote	Viewed Complete Debate	.057	175	.200*	.992	175	.419
	Did Not View Debate	.044	175	.200*	.986	175	.090

*. This is a lower bound of the true significance.

a. Lilliefors Significance Correction

The mean score of those who viewed the debate is 3.01 and for those who did not view the debate it is 2.99. Each sample has 175 data records.

Group Statistics

	Debate Exposure	N	Mean	Std. Deviation	Std. Error Mean
Intention to Vote	Viewed Complete Debate	175	3.01	.673	.051
	Did Not View Debate	175	2.99	.654	.049

The Levene test is significant at $p < .833$, indicating that the equality of variance assumption is met. Therefore, we must use the "equal variances assumed" results. Accordingly, on average, there is no meaningful difference between intentionality to vote by whether students viewed the final debate ($p = .697$). Based on the scale, the intention to vote by those who viewed the debate is between .11 less than and .16 more than those who did not view the debate.

Write-up: A two independent samples *t*-test was conducted that compared the average intention to vote in the next presidential election between undergraduate students who watched the final presidential debate and those who did not watch the debate. A total of 350 students participated in the study, and they were evenly split between the two groups. A nonsignificant difference was found ($t(348) = .39$, $p = .69$). There is no evidence to suggest that watching the final debate ($M = 3.01$ [$SD = .673$]) or not watching it ($M = 2.99$ [$SD = .654$]) influenced voter intentionality. Furthermore, we are 95% confident that the true population average voter intentionality score for those exposed to the debate is anywhere from .11 less than to .16 greater than the mean score of those who did not watch the final debate.

B.18 Chapter 18

18.1 What is a one-way analysis of variances (one-way ANOVA) *F*-test? Provide an example.

Answer: The one-way analysis of variances (one-way ANOVA) *F*-test compares the means (averages) among more two independent representative samples (groups) in order to determine the likelihood of at least one statistically significant difference between at least two of the samples. For example, we may compare annual income across a full array of genders.

18.2 Generally, what is the ANOVA omnibus test?

Answer: The overall ANOVA *F*-test (including *F*-test statistic and *p*-value).

18.3 What is a post hoc test?

Answer: A test that determines where the paired differences lie among the ANOVA *F*-test groups.

18.4 Generally, what is within-sample variance?

Answer: This variance occurs within a single sample and represents random variance in ANOVA.

18.5 Generally, what is between-samples variance?

Answer: This variance is between samples or groups and usually varies by categories within an independent variable.

18.6 Generally, what is total variance?

Answer: In ANOVA, total variance represents the within and between variances.

18.7 What is a grand mean?

Answer: This is the mean or average of all of the data across samples (groups) of the variable being analyzed.

18.8 What is the Tukey (HSD) post hoc test?

Answer: A test that determines where the paired differences lie among the ANOVA *F*-test groups when the normality, equality of variances, and equal group sizes assumptions have been met.

18.9 What is the Scheffe post hoc test?

Answer: A test that determines where the paired differences lie among the ANOVA *F*-test groups when the normality and equality of variances assumptions have been met. It can be used when there are unequal sample sizes.

18.10 What is the Welch test?

Answer: This test is used in lieu of the ANOVA *F*-test statistic when we cannot assume equality of variances and equal sample sizes.

18.11 What is the Brown-Forsythe test?

Answer: This test is used in lieu of the ANOVA *F*-test statistic when we cannot assume equality of variance, equal sample sizes, and the distributions are close to violating normality.

18.12 When do we use the Games-Howell post hoc test?

Answer: A test that determines where the paired differences lie among the ANOVA *F*-test groups when we cannot assume equality of variance.

18.13 What is the Kruskal-Wallis test?

Answer: This test is a nonparametric alternative to the numeric-level data approaches to testing for differences among more than two means. It is not as powerful as the other tests, and consequently might not detect significant effects.

18.14 What tests should be utilized if equality of variances is not met and the sample sizes are unequal?

Answer: The Welch test for the overall assessment and the Games-Howell test for post hoc analysis.

18.15 What tests should be deployed if the sample sizes are not equal?

Answer: The one-way ANOVA *F*-test and the Scheffe post hoc test.

18.16 In ideal conditions, what tests should be used?

Answer: The one-way ANOVA *F*-test and the Tukey (HSD) post hoc test.

18.17 In ANOVA, what do the confidence intervals represent?

Answer: They represent an interval for a mean according to a specified level of confidence.

18.18 "We Sell," a sales/marketing company, wants to determine whether July monthly sales in dollars per salesperson varies by its three districts (Philadelphia, New York, and Boston). The last July sales figures are available for the analysis. Which district generates the most sales? Explain your answer. Report results in the format provided in this book. Be sure to include the confidence interval. Alpha = .05. The data file name is "One-Way ANOVA Exercise 1 Data."

Answer: The analysis requires two variables: a grouping variable (Philadelphia = 1, New York = 2, and Boston = 3) and a dependent variable (dollar sales generated in July per salesperson).

The sample sizes are each greater than 30. As depicted in the table, all Shapiro-Wilk statistics are not significant: Philadelphia (p = .41), NYC (p = .38), and Boston (p = .54), indicating that the samples meet the normal distribution assumption.

Tests of Normality

	Region	Kolmogorov-Smirnov[a]			Shapiro-Wilk		
		Statistic	df	Sig.	Statistic	df	Sig.
Salary	Philadelphia	.067	44	.200*	.974	44	.419
	NYC	.067	50	.200*	.976	50	.383
	Boston	.066	38	.200*	.975	38	.547

*. This is a lower bound of the true significance.

a. Lilliefors Significance Correction

The total sample consists of 132 salespersons. The sample sizes per region vary. The average scores, standard deviations, and 95% confidence interval for the mean sales per city are below.

Descriptives

Salary

	N	Mean	Std. Deviation	Std. Error	95% Confidence Interval for Mean		Minimum	Maximum
					Lower Bound	Upper Bound		
Philadelphia	44	$251,596.22	$39,449.381	$5,947.218	$239,602.51	$263,589.92	$186,940	$344,569
NYC	50	$267,488.58	$58,253.316	$8,238.263	$250,933.17	$284,043.99	$162,051	$391,675
Boston	38	$254,912.61	$43,367.012	$7,035.058	$240,658.23	$269,166.99	$156,547	$329,634
Total	132	$258,570.77	$48,599.387	$4,230.034	$250,202.75	$266,938.79	$156,547	$391,675

Below, the Levene test indicates that in all likelihood, the group variances or data distributions are not similar (p = .024).

Test of Homogeneity of Variances

Salary

Levene Statistic	df1	df2	Sig.
3.842	2	129	.024

Since the group sizes vary and the variances are not equal, we use the Welch test located in the robust tests of equality of means table in order to determine if there is at least one difference between regions. Since p = .29, we can conclude that it is likely that, on average, sales per salesperson do not vary by city. At this point, we stop further analysis.

ANOVA

Salary

	Sum of Squares	df	Mean Square	F	Sig.
Between Groups	6625242436	2	3312621218	1.411	.248
Within Groups	3.028E+11	129	2347160598		
Total	3.094E+11	131			

Robust Tests of Equality of Means

Salary

	Statistic[a]	df1	df2	Sig.
Welch	1.245	2	84.339	.293
Brown-Forsythe	1.477	2	122.494	.232

a. Asymptotically F distributed.

Write-up: A one-way ANOVA was conducted that compared 141 salespersons' July sales by Philadelphia (n = 44), New York City (n = 50), and Boston (n = 38). Since the sample sizes were not equal and equality of variances was not assumed, the Welch test was used. A nonsignificant difference was found, $F(2,84.33) = 1.24$, $p = .29$. It is likely that the average salesperson's sales do not vary by city. With 95% confidence, the true population mean sales amounts are Philadelphia: $239,602–$263,589, NYC: $250,933–$284,043, and Boston: $240,658–$269,166.

18.19 A local college wants to learn whether different faculty ranks (assistant, associate, and full professors) perceive that they are provided with the resources necessary to be effective teachers. The dean wishes to learn if the three faculty ranks share the same or vary on views about this topic. The key question answered by faculty was: "Do you think that the college provides you with sufficient resources to be an effective teacher?" **Answers** were formatted as follows: 1 = "I have no resources to help me be an effective teacher" to 10 = "I have more resources than I will ever need to help me be an effective teacher." Determine if there is a difference in perceptions based on the answer to this question. Explain your answer. Report results in the format provided in this book. Alpha = .05. Be sure to include the confidence interval. The data file name is "One-Way ANOVA Exercise 2 Data."

Answer: The analysis requires two variables: a grouping variable (Assistant Professor = 1, Associate Professor = 2, and Full Professor = 3) and a dependent variable (1 = "I have no resources to help me be an effective teacher" to 10 = "I have more resources than I will ever need to help me be an effective teacher").

Each sample size is greater than 30. As depicted in table below, all of the Shapiro-Wilk statistics are not significant: Assistant Professor (p = .41), Associate Professor (p = .35), and Full Professor (p = .17), indicating that the samples do not violate the normality assumption.

Tests of Normality

		Kolmogorov-Smirnov[a]			Shapiro-Wilk		
	Professor_Rank	Statistic	df	Sig.	Statistic	df	Sig.
Resource_Perceptions	Assistant Prof	.053	125	.200*	.989	125	.413
	Associate Prof	.077	98	.165	.985	98	.352
	Full Prof	.052	89	.200*	.980	89	.173

*. This is a lower bound of the true significance.

a. Lilliefors Significance Correction

The total sample consists of 312 professors. The professor type sample sizes vary. The average scores, standard deviations, and 95% confidence interval for the means are below.

Descriptives

Resource_Perceptions

	N	Mean	Std. Deviation	Std. Error	95% Confidence Interval for Mean		Minimum	Maximum
					Lower Bound	Upper Bound		
Assistant Prof	125	7.79	2.954	.264	7.26	8.31	1	15
Associate Prof	98	4.46	1.869	.189	4.08	4.83	0	9
Full Prof	89	4.18	1.657	.176	3.83	4.53	1	7
Total	312	5.71	2.870	.162	5.39	6.03	0	15

The Levene test indicates that in all likelihood, the professor type variances or data distributions are not similar ($p < .001$).

Test of Homogeneity of Variances

Resource_Perceptions

Levene Statistic	df1	df2	Sig.
15.838	2	309	.000

Since the group sizes vary and we cannot assume equality of variances, we use the Welch test located in the robust tests of equality of means table to determine if there is at least one difference between professor types. Since $p < .001$, we conclude that it is likely that, on average, professor perceived teaching support varies by rank. We must now explore where those specific differences exist.

Robust Tests of Equality of Means

Resource_Perceptions

	Statistic[a]	df1	df2	Sig.
Welch	70.254	2	205.993	.000
Brown-Forsythe	93.813	2	284.183	.000

a. Asymptotically F distributed.

Since the variances are not equal, we will use the Games-Howell post hoc test to discover the specific differences. As we can see below, based on the *p*-values (less than .001) and the asterisk comparisons, the Assistant Professor perceptions likely vary from the Associate and Full Professor types. The Assistant Professors reported having greater access to teaching resources.

Note that the 95% confidence interval for the difference between the means of Associate and Full Professors contains zero. This indicates that there is likely no difference between the two groups. Additionally, the 95% confidence interval for the mean reveals consistent results. That is to say, the intervals for Associate and Full Professors overlap, indicating no difference, whereas the interval for Assistant Professor does not overlap with either of the other two ranks.

Multiple Comparisons

Dependent Variable: Resource_Perceptions

	(I) Professor_Rank	(J) Professor_Rank	Mean Difference (I-J)	Std. Error	Sig.	95% Confidence Interval Lower Bound	95% Confidence Interval Upper Bound
Scheffe	Assistant Prof	Associate Prof	3.328*	.313	.000	2.56	4.10
		Full Prof	3.602*	.322	.000	2.81	4.39
	Associate Prof	Assistant Prof	-3.328*	.313	.000	-4.10	-2.56
		Full Prof	.274	.340	.723	-.56	1.11
	Full Prof	Assistant Prof	-3.602*	.322	.000	-4.39	-2.81
		Associate Prof	-.274	.340	.723	-1.11	.56
Games-Howell	Assistant Prof	Associate Prof	3.328*	.325	.000	2.56	4.09
		Full Prof	3.602*	.317	.000	2.85	4.35
	Associate Prof	Assistant Prof	-3.328*	.325	.000	-4.09	-2.56
		Full Prof	.274	.258	.539	-.34	.88
	Full Prof	Assistant Prof	-3.602*	.317	.000	-4.35	-2.85
		Associate Prof	-.274	.258	.539	-.88	.34

*. The mean difference is significant at the 0.05 level.

Write-up: A one-way ANOVA was conducted that compared 312 professors' perceptions of access to teaching support by rank. Since the sample sizes were not equal and equality of variances was not assumed, the Welch test was used. A significant difference was found, $F(2,205.99) = 70.25$, $p < .001$. Assistant Professor ($M = 7.79$, $SD = 2.95$) perceptions were likely different from those of Associate Professors ($M = 4.46$, $SD = 1.86$, $p < .001$) and Full Professors ($M = 4.18$, $SD = 1.65$, p < .001). However, no differences were found between the other two ranks. The table summarizes the results, including confidence intervals for the true population means.

Table
Perceptions of Teaching Support by Rank ANOVA

Professor Rank	Teaching Support *Mean* (*SD*)	95% Confidence Interval for the Mean
Assistant Professor (*n* = 125)	7.79 (2.95)	7.26 – 8.31
Associate Professor (*n* = 98)	4.46 (1.86)	4.08 – 4.83
Full Professor (*n* = 89)	4.18 (1.65)	3.83 – 4.53

Note: $F(2,205.99) = 70.25$, $p < .001$). Scheffe post hoc test was used. $N = 312$.

(OR we can apply directionality.)

A one-way ANOVA was conducted that compared 312 professors' perceptions of access to teaching support by rank. Since the sample sizes were not equal and equality of variances was not assumed, the Welch test was used. A significant difference was found, $F(2,205.99) = 70.25$, $p < .001$. Assistant Professor ($M = 7.79$, $SD = 2.95$) perceptions were likely to report greater access to teaching resources compared to those of Associate Professors ($M = 4.46$, $SD = 1.86$, $p < .001$) and Full Professors ($M = 4.18$, $SD = 1.65$, $p < .001$). However, no differences were found between the other two ranks. The table summarizes the results including confidence intervals for the true population means.

18.20 Shoe ($n = 525$), Technology ($n = 476$), Food ($n = 525$), and Major Appliance ($n = 453$) retailers were surveyed about their assessment of the economy. They responded to a question that asked: "Are you optimistic about the current economic conditions?" 1 = "not optimistic at all" to 5 = "very optimistic" was the answer format. Determine if there is any difference in level of economic optimism by these four retail sectors. Explain your answer. Report results in the format provided in this book. Be sure to include the confidence interval. Alpha = .05. The data file name is "One-Way ANOVA Exercise 3 Data."

Answer: There are two variables. The grouping or sample variable is coded into four categories, one for each retail sector: 1 = Shoe, 2 = Technology, 3 = Food, and 4 = Major Appliances, which is the independent variable. The dependent variable is the level of optimism, which is coded from 1 to 5, with 5 indicating more economic optimism.

The table below reveals the descriptives. The sample sizes are not equal. Upon a cursory inspection of the standard deviations, they equality of variances assumption may be violated.

Descriptives

1=not optimistic,5=very optimistic

	N	Mean	Std. Deviation	Std. Error	95% Confidence Interval for Mean		Minimum	Maximum
					Lower Bound	Upper Bound		
Shoe Retailer	525	3.29	.499	.022	3.25	3.33	2	5
Technology Retailer	476	3.38	1.041	.048	3.28	3.47	0	6
Food Retailer	525	3.24	.208	.009	3.23	3.26	3	4
Major Appliances Retailer	453	2.35	.479	.023	2.31	2.40	1	4
Total	1979	3.08	.743	.017	3.05	3.12	0	6

All four samples meet the normality assumption because Shapiro-Wilk p-values are .277 to .633.

Tests of Normality

	Retailer	Kolmogorov-Smirnov[a]			Shapiro-Wilk		
		Statistic	df	Sig.	Statistic	df	Sig.
Optimistic	Shoe Retailer	.032	525	.200*	.996	525	.277
	Technology Retailer	.029	476	.200*	.997	476	.432
	Food Retailer	.024	525	.200*	.997	525	.323
	Major Appliances Retailer	.029	453	.200*	.997	453	.630

*. This is a lower bound of the true significance.

a. Lilliefors Significance Correction

Since $p < .001$, the equality of variances assumption is not met.

Test of Homogeneity of Variances

1=not optimistic,5=very optimistic

Levene Statistic	df1	df2	Sig.
273.388	3	1975	.000

Because the samples are normally distributed and the variances are not similar, the Welch test located in the robust tests of equality of means table will be the basis of the overall assessment. Note that the Welch test, along with the ANOVA and Brown-Forsythe test, are all significant at $p < .001$.

ANOVA

1=not optimistic,5=very optimistic

	Sum of Squares	df	Mean Square	F	Sig.
Between Groups	319.054	3	106.351	272.194	.000
Within Groups	771.668	1975	.391		
Total	1090.722	1978			

Robust Tests of Equality of Means

1=not optimistic,5=very optimistic

	Statistic[a]	df1	df2	Sig.
Welch	474.902	3	941.716	.000
Brown-Forsythe	262.649	3	945.337	.000

a. Asymptotically F distributed.

Since the variances vary, the Games-Howell post hoc test is used. The Major Appliances retailers' level of optimism significantly varies from the other three sectors (all at $p < .001$). The Technology and Food sectors vary as well ($p = .031$).

Multiple Comparisons

Dependent Variable: 1=not optimistic,5=very optimistic

Games-Howell

(I) Retailer	(J) Retailer	Mean Difference (I-J)	Std. Error	Sig.	95% Confidence Interval Lower Bound	Upper Bound
Shoe Retailer	Technology Retailer	-.088	.052	.340	-.22	.05
	Food Retailer	.046	.024	.211	-.01	.11
	Major Appliances Retailer	.937*	.031	.000	.86	1.02
Technology Retailer	Shoe Retailer	.088	.052	.340	-.05	.22
	Food Retailer	.133*	.049	.031	.01	.26
	Major Appliances Retailer	1.025*	.053	.000	.89	1.16
Food Retailer	Shoe Retailer	-.046	.024	.211	-.11	.01
	Technology Retailer	-.133*	.049	.031	-.26	-.01
	Major Appliances Retailer	.891*	.024	.000	.83	.95
Major Appliances Retailer	Shoe Retailer	-.937*	.031	.000	-1.02	-.86
	Technology Retailer	-1.025*	.053	.000	-1.16	-.89
	Food Retailer	-.891*	.024	.000	-.95	-.83

*. The mean difference is significant at the 0.05 level.

We can say that it is likely that level of economic optimism varies by retail sector especially the major appliances retailers compared to the others.

Write-up: A one-way ANOVA was conducted that compared 1,979 retailers' level of optimism about the economy based on a five-point scale from 1 = "not optimistic at all" to 5 = "very optimistic." Since the sample sizes were not equal and equality of variances was not assumed, the Welch test was used. A significant difference was found, $F(3,941.71) = 474.90$, $p < .001$. Major Appliances retailers ($M = 2.35$, $SD = .479$, $p < .001$) were likely different from Shoe retailers ($M = 3.29$, $SD = .499$), Technology retailers ($M = 3.38$, $SD = 1.04$), and Food retailers ($M = 3.24$, $SD = .208$). There was also a difference between Food and Technology retailers ($p = .031$). The table below summarizes the results including the true population mean confidence intervals.

Perceptions of Teaching Support by Rank ANOVA

Retail Sector	Optimism *Mean* (*SD*)	95% Confidence Interval for the True Mean
Shoe (*n* = 525)	3.29 (.499)	3.25 – 3.33
Technology (*n* = 476)*	3.38 (1.04)	3.28 – 3.47
Food (*n* = 525)*	3.24 (.208)	3.23 – 3.26
Major Appliances (*n* = 453)*	2.35 (.479)	2.31 – 2.40

Note: $F(3,941.71) = 474.90$, $p < .001$). *The Games-Howell post hoc test was used. $N = 1979$.

(OR we can apply directionality.)

A one-way ANOVA was conducted that compared 1,979 retailers' level of optimism about the economy based on a five-point scale from 1 = "not optimistic at all" to 5 = "very optimistic." Since the sample sizes were not equal and equality of variances was not assumed, the Welch test was used. A significant difference was found, $F(3{,}941.71) = 474.90$, $p < .001$. Major Appliances retailers ($M = 2.35$, $SD = .479$, $p < .001$) were likely less optimistic compared to Shoe retailers ($M = 3.29$, $SD = .499$), Technology retailers ($M = 3.38$, $SD = 1.04$), and Food retailers ($M = 3.24$, $SD = .208$). Food retailers were less optimistic than Technology retailers ($p = .031$). The table below summarizes the results including the true population mean confidence intervals.

18.21 An Italian automobile manufacturer launched a new line of three fuel-efficient midsized vehicles. Data was collected from 50 cars of each brand, which are the Avanti, Forte, and Pronto. Determine whether there is a difference in gas mileage as measured in miles per gallon of gas. Explain your answer. Report results in the format provided in this book. Be sure to include the confidence interval. Alpha = .05. The data file name is "One-Way ANOVA Exercise 4 Data."

Answer: There are two variables. The grouping or sample variable is coded into three categories, one for each car model: 1 = Avanti, 2 = Forte, and 3 = Pronto, which is the independent variable. The dependent variable is miles per gallon of gas.

The table below reveals the descriptives. The sample sizes are equal. Upon a cursory inspection of the standard deviations, the equality of variances assumption appears to be met.

Descriptives

Miles per Gallon

	N	Mean	Std. Deviation	Std. Error	95% Confidence Interval for Mean Lower Bound	95% Confidence Interval for Mean Upper Bound	Minimum	Maximum
Avanti	50	35.4041	5.14212	.72721	33.9427	36.8655	27.12	46.82
Forte	50	35.6659	3.88355	.54922	34.5622	36.7696	28.64	43.94
Pronto	50	35.6253	4.70585	.66551	34.2880	36.9627	25.38	44.09
Total	150	35.5651	4.57726	.37373	34.8266	36.3036	25.38	46.82

All three samples meet the normality assumption because Shapiro-Wilk p-values are .155 to .469.

Tests of Normality

	Car Model	Kolmogorov-Smirnov[a] Statistic	df	Sig.	Shapiro-Wilk Statistic	df	Sig.
Miles per Gallon	Avanti	.077	50	.200*	.966	50	.155
	Forte	.067	50	.200*	.976	50	.383
	Pronto	.084	50	.200*	.978	50	.469

*. This is a lower bound of the true significance.

a. Lilliefors Significance Correction

Since the level test is $p = .119$, the equality of variances assumption is met.

Test of Homogeneity of Variances

Miles per Gallon

Levene Statistic	df1	df2	Sig.
2.163	2	147	.119

Because the data are normal and there are similar variances, we turn to the ANOVA *F*-test, which is not significant at $p = .954$. Therefore, there is no need for further analysis. The vehicles likely do not vary in miles per gallon of gas.

ANOVA

Miles per Gallon

	Sum of Squares	df	Mean Square	F	Sig.
Between Groups	1.985	2	.993	.047	.954
Within Groups	3119.756	147	21.223		
Total	3121.741	149			

Write-up: A one-way ANOVA was conducted that compared 150 vehicles' gas mileage, of which there were three models: Avanti, Forte, and Pronto models (50 records for each car). A nonsignificant difference was found, $F(2,147) = .047$, $p = .95$. It is likely that the average mileage per gallon of gas does not vary by model. With 95% confidence, the true population mean miles per gallon are Avanti: 33.94–36.86, Forte: 34.56–36.76, and Pronto: 34.28–36.30.

B.19 Chapter 19

19.1 What is a paired *t*-test?

Answer: The paired-sample *t*-test usually compares the means (averages) between the same sample measured twice in order to determine if there is the likelihood of a statistically significant difference between both measurements.

19.2 What are other names for the paired *t*-test?

Answer: They are the dependent samples *t*-test, related samples *t*-test, same samples *t*-test, repeated measures *t*-test, matched samples *t*-test, and correlated samples *t*-test.

19.3 Define treatment. Cite an example.

Answer: The treatment is an independent variable of some type. It can be an intervention or experimental condition—all commonly referred to as the treatment. If there is a difference between the measures of the two time points, then there is likely a treatment effect. For example, students' knowledge about a topic can be measured before completing a course and then after completing the course in order to discover any changes in topical knowledge.

19.4 What is a carry-over effect? Cite an example.

Answer: This is a condition where any shared variance in a paired *t*-test can negate at least some of the treatment effect. For instance, taking the GREs or SATs multiple times will generally result in score improvement owing to familiarity.

19.5 What is the Wilcoxon signed ranks test?

Answer: This is a nonparametric test that can be used in place of the paired *t*-test when the difference(s) between the paired data are symmetrical but do not approximate the normal distribution.

19.6 What is a sign test?

Answer: In a paired *t*-test, if the data are not normally distributed and are not symmetrical, then the sign test option is appropriate in lieu of the Wilcoxon test.

19.7 Free-Air is a new asthma preventative medication in trials. At the onset of an asthmatic attack, an individual takes two puffs, which prevent a full asthmatic episode. Asthmatic attack data were collected for six months from patients who never used any type of medicine. The same patients provided data while using Free-Air for six months. Researchers must determine whether Free-Air is effective at reducing full asthmatic episodes. Explain your answer. Report results in the format provided in this book. Alpha = .05. Be sure to include the 95% confidence interval. The data file name is "*T*-Test Paired-Sample Exercise 1 Data."

Answer: The analysis requires three variables: the number of full asthmatic episodes prior to Free-Air usage, the number of full asthmatic episodes after using Free-Air for a six-month period, and a "difference" variable.

As depicted in the table, the difference data approximate the normal distribution because the Shapiro-Wilk *p*-value is .493, which is not significant.

Tests of Normality

	Kolmogorov-Smirnov[a]			Shapiro-Wilk		
	Statistic	df	Sig.	Statistic	df	Sig.
Difference	.049	150	.200*	.991	150	.493

*. This is a lower bound of the true significance.

a. Lilliefors Significance Correction

As we can see in the table below, the total sample consists of 150 patients' data for pre-Free-Air and Free-Air usage number of full asthmatic episodes. The pre-Free-Air number of full asthmatic attacks mean is 6.06 with a standard deviation of 1.92. The Free-Air number of full asthmatic attacks mean is 2.99 with a standard deviation of 1.04.

Paired Samples Statistics

		Mean	N	Std. Deviation	Std. Error Mean
Pair 1	Pre Free Air Number of Episodes	6.06	150	1.925	.157
	With Free Air Number of Episodes	2.99	150	1.041	.085

The "Paired-Samples Correlations" table indicates the level of relatedness between the paired cases. In this analysis, the correlation (*r*) is −.046 and is not statistically significant (p = .579). Therefore, there is no pattern in the paired data.

Paired Samples Correlations

		N	Correlation	Sig.
Pair 1	Pre Free Air Number of Episodes & With Free Air Number of Episodes	150	-.046	.579

The "Paired-Sample Test" table indicates that, in all likelihood, there is a meaningful difference between the average number of full asthmatic episodes prior to Free-Air usage (M = 6.06) and while using Free-Air (M = 2.99), $p < .001$.

Paired Samples Test

		Paired Differences					t	df	Sig. (2-tailed)
					95% Confidence Interval of the Difference				
		Mean	Std. Deviation	Std. Error Mean	Lower	Upper			
Pair 1	Pre Free Air Number of Episodes - With Free Air Number of Episodes	3.070	2.230	.182	2.710	3.429	16.860	149	.000

Furthermore, we are 95% confident that the true population average pre-Free-Air mean (M = 5.64) is anywhere from 2.71 to 3.42 greater than the true population mean for Free-Air usage (M = 3.32).

Notice that the lower and upper interval values are positive so that the interval only represents the before-training greater number of defects compared to the after-training number of defects, which does not include the possibility of a zero or no difference.

Therefore, assuming that the data represent the typical pre- and during-Free-Air patients, the patients using Free-Air likely have fewer full asthmatic episodes compared to patients not taking medication.

Write-up: A paired-sample *t*-test was conducted that compared the number of reported full asthmatic episodes over six months for patients who did not use asthma medication with those same patients using Free-Air for six months. There were 150 patients. The no medication true population mean is 6.06 full episodes (SD = 1.92) and the Free-Air true population mean is 2.99 full episodes (SD = 1.04). A significant difference was found ($t(149) = 16.86$, $p < .001$). It is likely that there is a difference between the number of episodes for patients not taking any medication as opposed to those same patients using Free-Air. Furthermore, we are 95% confident that when patients do not use medication, they will, on average, have anywhere from 2.71 to 3.42 more episodes compared to those who use Free-Air.

(OR we can apply directionality)

A paired-sample *t*-test was conducted that compared the number of reported full asthmatic episodes over six months for patients who did use asthma medication with those same patients using Free-Air for six months. There were 150 patients. The no medication true population mean is 6.06 full episodes (SD = 1.92) and the Free-Air true population mean is 2.99 episodes (SD = 1.04). A significant difference was found ($t(149) = 16.86$, $p < .001$). It is likely that when patients do not use Free-Air, they experience more full asthmatic episodes compared to when they use Free-Air. Furthermore, we are 95% confident that patients who do not use medication, on average, have anywhere from 2.71 to 3.42 more episodes compared to the those who use Free-Air.

"*SD*" denotes standard deviation. The "*t*" is the *t*-test statistic. The "(149)" represents the degree of freedom (*df*), which is the number of data points that can vary. Its formula is $n - 1$ because there is one sample. In our case, it is $150 - 1 = 149 = df$. $P < .001$ indicates a statistically significant finding. The likelihood of this result occurring by chance is less than 1/1,000 or .1%.

19.8 A local hospital offered a six-month weight management program to individuals who were 40–60 pounds overweight. Clients enrolled and completed the *Protein Focus* program over a six-month period. Among other information, client weight in pounds was collected before and after the six-month period. Based on the data from the sample, is there any evidence to suggest that *Protein Focus* is effective as a six-month program? Explain your answer. Report results in the format provided in this book. Be sure to include the 95% confidence interval. Alpha = .05. The data file name is "*T*-Test Paired-Sample Exercise 2 Data."

Answer: The analysis requires three variables: recorded client weights before starting the Protein Focus program, the same clients' weights after completing the six-month program, and a "difference" variable.

The sample size is greater than 30. As depicted in the table below, according to the Shapiro-Wilk test (p = .117), the "difference" variable approximates the normal distribution.

Tests of Normality

	Kolmogorov-Smirnov[a]			Shapiro-Wilk		
	Statistic	df	Sig.	Statistic	df	Sig.
Difference	.103	50	.200*	.963	50	.117

*. This is a lower bound of the true significance.

a. Lilliefors Significance Correction

The total sample consists of 50 clients who were weighed before and six months after completing the program. The before-program mean weight is 227.12 lbs with a standard deviation of 21.21 lbs. The after-program mean weight is 228.72 lbs with a standard deviation of 20.47 lbs.

Paired Samples Statistics

		Mean	N	Std. Deviation	Std. Error Mean
Pair 1	Before Protein Focus	227.12	50	21.218	3.001
	6 mths After Protein Focus	228.72	50	20.472	2.895

As depicted in the "Paired-Samples Correlations" Table, $r = -.22$, which is a small and not significant correlation ($p = .12$). This finding reveals that awareness scores do not maintain the same pattern between the paired data.

Paired Samples Correlations

		N	Correlation	Sig.
Pair 1	Before Protein Focus & 6 mths After Protein Focus	50	-.222	.122

As the "Paired-Sample Test" table reveals, there is not a meaningful difference between the before-program (M = 227.12) and after-program (M = 228.72) average weight loss because p = .729. Therefore, assuming that the samples represent typical before- and after-program weight loss, it is likely that the program had no effect on weight loss.

Paired Samples Test

		Paired Differences					t	df	Sig. (2-tailed)
					95% Confidence Interval of the Difference				
		Mean	Std. Deviation	Std. Error Mean	Lower	Upper			
Pair 1	Before Protein Focus - 6 mths After Protein Focus	-1.607	32.586	4.608	-10.868	7.654	-.349	49	.729

We are 95% confident that the true population average before-program mean weight (M = 227.12) is anywhere from 10.86 lbs below to 7.65 lbs above the after-program true population mean weight (M = 228.72). Notice that the lower interval value is negative and the upper interval value is positive, which includes the possibility of a zero or no difference, a finding consistent with $p = .72$.

In summary, based on the p-value and confidence interval, there is a very low probability that these results are statistically significant. These findings can be applied to all before-program and after-program clients providing that the sample truly represents the target population.

Write-up: A paired-sample t-test was conducted that examined the effectiveness of a six-month weight management program on 50 clients who were 40–60 pounds overweight. Client weight was recorded before the start of the program and at its completion. A nonsignificant difference was found ($t(49) = 1.745$, $p = .087$). There is no evidence to indicate that the before-program mean weight of 227.12 lbs (SD = 21.21 lbs) varies from the after-program mean weight of 228.72 lbs (SD = 20.47 lbs). Thus, it is likely that the Protein Focus program had no effect on weight loss. Furthermore, we are 95% confident that the true population average before-program weight is between 10.86 lbs less than and 7.65 lbs greater than the true population average after-program weight.

The "(49)" represents the degree of freedom (*df*), which is the number of data points that can vary. Its formula is $n - 1$ because there is one sample. In our case, it is $50 - 1 = 49 = df$. The t-test statistic is –.34. "*SD*" denotes standard deviation.

19.9 Two hundred drivers were asked to do their normal weekly driving using two different gasoline brands. They were to receive a full tank of gas at the beginning of the week, and at the end of the week the amount of gas consumed would be measured along with the miles traveled. A week later, the gas tank would be drained and replaced with the second brand of gas, where the procedure would be repeated. Determine whether Brand A or Brand B offered greater gas mileage. Explain your answer. Report results in the format provided in this book. Be sure to include the 95% confidence interval. Alpha = .05. The data file name is "*T*-Test Paired-Sample Exercise 3 Data."

Answer: The analysis requires three variables: the gas mileage from Brand A, the gas mileage from Brand B, and the difference between both brands' scores.

The difference data do not violate the normal distribution assumption because the Shapiro-Wilk statistic was not significant ($p = .430$); thus, the data approximate normality.

Tests of Normality

	Kolmogorov-Smirnov[a]			Shapiro-Wilk		
	Statistic	df	Sig.	Statistic	df	Sig.
Difference	.040	200	.200*	.993	200	.430

*. This is a lower bound of the true significance.

a. Lilliefors Significance Correction

The Brand A gas averaged 35.30 miles per gallon (SD = 4.70) and Brand B averaged 27.99 miles per gallon (SD = 3.97).

Paired Samples Statistics

		Mean	N	Std. Deviation	Std. Error Mean
Pair 1	Brand_A	35.3049	200	4.70282	.33254
	Brand_B	27.9921	200	3.97263	.28091

The paired data were not correlated ($r = .004$, $p = .955$).

Paired Samples Correlations

		N	Correlation	Sig.
Pair 1	Brand_A & Brand_B	200	.004	.955

There was a statistically significant difference in gas mileage ($p < .001$). It is likely that the brand mileage varies. The average difference is 7.31 miles per gallon. We are 95% confident that

Brand A's true population mean miles per gallon is 6.46–8.16 greater than Brand B's true mean average. The difference standard deviation is 6.14 miles per gallon.

Paired Samples Test

		Paired Differences					t	df	Sig. (2-tailed)
					95% Confidence Interval of the Difference				
		Mean	Std. Deviation	Std. Error Mean	Lower	Upper			
Pair 1	Brand_A - Brand_B	7.31283	6.14396	.43444	6.45613	8.16953	16.833	199	.000

Write-up: A paired-sample *t*-test was conducted that compared the amount of miles per gallon of gas for 200 drivers that used two brands of gas. Brand A's mileage was 35.30 (*SD* = 4.70) and Brand B's mileage was 27.99 (*SD* = 3.97). A significant difference was found ($t(199)$ = 16.83, $p < .001$). It is likely that the brands vary in miles per gallon of gas. Furthermore, we are 95% confident that Brand A's true population average is 6.46 to 8.16 miles per gallon more than the true population average for Brand B.

(OR we can apply directionality)

A paired-sample *t*-test was conducted that compared the amount of miles per gallon of gas for 200 drivers that used two brands of gas. Brand A's mileage was 35.30 (*SD* = 4.70) and Brand B's mileage was 27.99 (*SD* = 3.97). A significant difference was found ($t(199)$ = 16.83, $p < .001$). It is likely that Brand A gets more miles per gallon compared to Brand B. Furthermore, we are 95% confident that Brand A's true population average is 6.46 to 8.16 miles per gallon more than the true population average for Brand B.

19.10 Referring back to Exercise 19.9, was there a difference in the miles traveled between the two weeks? Explain your answer. Report results in the format provided in this book. Be sure to include the 95% confidence interval. Alpha = .05. The data file name is "*T*-Test Paired-Sample Exercise 4 Data."

Answer: The analysis requires three variables: the miles traveled while using Brand A (week 1), the miles traveled while using Brand B (week 2), and the difference between both weeks.

The difference between the two miles traveled points did not violate the normal distribution assumption because the Shapiro-Wilk statistic was not significant (p = .823).

Tests of Normality

	Kolmogorov-Smirnov[a]			Shapiro-Wilk		
	Statistic	df	Sig.	Statistic	df	Sig.
Difference	.044	200	.200*	.996	200	.823

*. This is a lower bound of the true significance.

a. Lilliefors Significance Correction

The miles traveled the first week were 450.38 (*SD* = 9.78) and the second week were 449.12 (*SD* = 12.98).

Paired Samples Statistics

		Mean	N	Std. Deviation	Std. Error Mean
Pair 1	First_Week	450.3877	200	9.78541	.69193
	Second_Week	449.1257	200	12.98403	.91811

The paired data were not correlated (r = .050, p = .486).

Paired Samples Correlations

		N	Correlation	Sig.
Pair 1	First_Week & Second_Week	200	.050	.486

The mean difference was 1.26 miles and the standard deviation was 15.86. Because p = .262, it is likely that miles traveled per week do not vary. We are 95% confident that the miles for week 1 are between .95 less and 3.47 greater than the miles traveled for week 2.

Paired Samples Test

		Paired Differences					t	df	Sig. (2-tailed)
					95% Confidence Interval of the Difference				
		Mean	Std. Deviation	Std. Error Mean	Lower	Upper			
Pair 1	First_Week - Second_Week	1.26192	15.86671	1.12195	-.95051	3.47435	1.125	199	.262

Write-up: A paired-sample t-test was conducted that examined whether miles traveled by 200 drivers varied from week 1 to week 2. A nonsignificant difference was found (t(199) = 1.125, p = .262). There is no evidence to indicate that drivers varied their miles traveled between the two weeks. Furthermore, we are 95% confident that the true population average miles traveled for week 1 (M = 450.38, SD = 9.78) is between .95 miles less than and 3.47 miles more than the true population mean for week two (M = 449.12, SD = 12.98).

19.11 Father and mother dyads were asked whether they believed that communication between them and their children, ages 3–17, was open and easily flowed bidirectionally. Two hundred and fifty parental dyads participated by completing an online survey. The question was framed as follows: "Is there open communication between you and your children so that everyone has the opportunity to easily express him/herself openly in a family setting?" 0 = "Not at all open for everyone" to 5 = "Everyone can say what he/she wants." Based on this question, do parents have similar views about whether they have an open communication family? Explain your answer. Report results in the format provided in this book. Be sure to include the 95% confidence interval. Alpha = .05. The data file name is "*T*-Test Paired-Sample Exercise 5 Data."

Answer: According to the Shapiro-Wilk test (p < .001), the difference data do not approximate normality. Therefore, we must consult the skewness statistic to determine whether the data are symmetrical.

Tests of Normality

	Kolmogorov-Smirnov[a]			Shapiro-Wilk		
	Statistic	df	Sig.	Statistic	df	Sig.
Difference	.158	250	.000	.950	250	.000

a. Lilliefors Significance Correction

Since the skewness statistic (.199) is between −1.00 and 1.00, the data approximate symmetry. Thus, we can apply the Wilcoxon test to determine whether the parental responses vary.

Descriptives

			Statistic	Std. Error
Difference	Mean		.0360	.08986
	95% Confidence Interval for Mean	Lower Bound	-.1410	
		Upper Bound	.2130	
	5% Trimmed Mean		.0089	
	Median		.0000	
	Variance		2.019	
	Std. Deviation		1.42084	
	Minimum		-3.00	
	Maximum		4.00	
	Range		7.00	
	Interquartile Range		2.00	
	Skewness		.199	.154
	Kurtosis		-.046	.307

The fathers' mean score is 3.49 (*SD* = .96) and the mothers' mean score is 3.46 (*SD* = 1.05).

Descriptive Statistics

	N	Mean	Std. Deviation	Minimum	Maximum
Father	250	3.4960	.96213	.00	5.00
Mother	250	3.4600	1.05301	.00	5.00

The Wilcoxon Sign Ranks Test is not significant (p = .891), indicating that there is not a likely difference between parental scores on family communication openness.

Test Statistics[a]

	Mother - Father
Z	-.138[b]
Asymp. Sig. (2-tailed)	.891

a. Wilcoxon Signed Ranks Test

b. Based on positive ranks.

Write-up: A paired-sample t-test was conducted that examined whether fathers and mothers differed in their perceptions of open family communication with their children. A nonsignificant Wilcoxon signed ranks test difference was found ($Z = -.138$, $p = .891$). There is no evidence to suggest that fathers' (M = 3.49, SD = .96) and mothers' (M = 3.46, SD = 1.05) scores vary in their perceptions of open family communication.

19.12 A sample of 120 clients from Balanced Health participated in a pilot study designed to increase knowledge about mental health challenges and raise awareness about behavioral wellness options. Clients completed an online baselines survey that measured their knowledge about mental health and behavioral choices. They were then provided with weekly website links over a three-week period followed by their completing another survey that measured their knowledge and awareness levels. Did the website links increase client knowledge about mental health and behavioral choices? Scores for both surveys were based on 100 points. Explain your answer. Report results in the format provided in this book. Be sure to include the 95% confidence interval. Alpha = .05. The data file name is "*T*-Test Paired-Sample Exercise 6 Data."

Answer: According to the Shapiro-Wilk statistic (p = .122), the difference data do not violate the normality assumption.

Tests of Normality

	Kolmogorov-Smirnov[a]			Shapiro-Wilk		
	Statistic	df	Sig.	Statistic	df	Sig.
Difference	.075	120	.094	.983	120	.122

a. Lilliefors Significance Correction

The mean baseline score was 50.94 (SD = 9.47) and after viewing the videos, the mean knowledge score was 85.49 (SD = 6.03).

Paired Samples Statistics

		Mean	N	Std. Deviation	Std. Error Mean
Pair 1	Baseline	50.9444	120	9.47004	.86449
	After_Viewing	85.4934	120	6.03944	.55132

The paired data were not correlated (r = –.004, p = .968).

Paired Samples Correlations

		N	Correlation	Sig.
Pair 1	Baseline & After_Viewing	120	-.004	.968

Because $p < .001$, the level of mental health knowledge likely changed (increased) after the clients viewed the online videos. The baseline scores were, on average, 34.54 points less than the after video scores. The standard deviation of the mean difference was 11.25 points. We are 95% confident that the true population mean baseline score was 32.51 to 36.58 points less than the after viewing scores, or we can also say that after viewing the videos, the true population mean knowledge scores increased from 32.51 to 36.58 points out of 100.

Paired Samples Test

		Paired Differences							
					95% Confidence Interval of the Difference				
		Mean	Std. Deviation	Std. Error Mean	Lower	Upper	t	df	Sig. (2-tailed)
Pair 1	Baseline - After_Viewing	-34.54899	11.25085	1.02706	-36.58267	-32.51531	-33.639	119	.000

Write-up: A paired-sample t-test was conducted that compared the amount of mental health knowledge in 120 clients before and after their participation in an online awareness program. The pre-participation knowledge score was 50.94 (SD = 9.47) and post-participation score was 85.49 (SD = 6.03). A significant difference was found ($t(199) = -33.63$, $p < .001$). It is likely that the awareness program had an effect on client knowledge about mental health. Furthermore, we are 95% confident that the true population average score is 32.51 to 36.58 points higher than the true population mean score of clients before program participation.

(OR we can apply directionality)

A paired-sample t-test was conducted that compared the amount of mental health knowledge in 120 clients before and after their participation in an online awareness program. The pre-participation knowledge score was 50.94 (SD = 9.47) and post-participation score was 85.49

(*SD* = 6.03). A significant difference was found ($t(199) = -33.63$, $p < .001$). It is likely that the awareness program increase client knowledge about mental health. Furthermore, we are 95% confident that the true population average score is 32.51 to 36.58 points higher than the true population mean score of clients before program participation.

B.20 Chapter 20

20.1 What is a one-way repeated measures ANOVA?

Answer: Also called general linear model (GLM) repeated measures, this significance test is used to compare the means of measurements made more than twice on the same or related samples.

20.2 What is a general linear model (GLM) repeated measures?

Answer: This is another name for one-way repeated measures ANOVA.

20.3 In repeated measures, what is the overall repeated measures test?

Answer: This is a general term applied to the overall significance of the repeated measures statistical test. It is assessed using the *p*-value.

20.4 What is a post hoc significance testing?

Answer: If the overall or omnibus test is statistically significant, then one of a variety of post hoc tests appropriate for the data's attributes can be used to identify specifically where the differences lie.

20.5 Conceptually, define sphericity.

Answer: It is the condition where the variances of the differences between all possible pairs of groups are similar. This test is used in repeated measures analysis.

20.6 What is the purpose of Mauchly's significance test?

Answer: This significance test is used to assess sphericity in repeated measures analysis.

20.7 Conceptually, what is the sphericity assumed test?

Answer: This overall repeated measures test is applicable when the sphericity assumption is met.

20.8 What is the Greenhouse-Geisser statistic?

Answer: This overall repeated measures test is applicable when the sphericity assumption is not met and its epsilon value is less than .75.

20.9 Define epsilon in the context of repeated measures analysis.

Answer: This value applies to Greenhouse-Geisser and Huynh-Feldt corrections for violation of the sphericity assumption and ranges from 0 to 1, with 1 indicating perfect sphericity. The corrections apply to degrees of freedom and are automatically calculated in SPSS.

20.10 What is the Huynh-Feldt test in general?

Answer: This overall repeated measures test is applicable when the sphericity assumption is not met and the Greenhouse-Geisser epsilon is equal to or greater than .75.

20.11 What is the lower-bound in the context of repeated measures?

Answer: This overall repeated measures test is applicable when the sphericity assumption is strongly violated. It is subject to a wide array of fluctuations. After the introduction of the Greenhouse-Geisser and Huynh-Feldt tests, it is rarely used.

20.12 Generally, what is the Bonferroni post hoc test?

Answer: This is an appropriate post hoc test for all repeated measures analysis.

20.13 Regarding repeated measures, what is a partial eta squared?

Answer: This statistic indicates the percentage change in the data or an effect size related to a condition.

20.14 Pertaining to repeated measures, what is contrast analysis?

Answer: This analysis is used to determine patterns across means.

20.15 Generally, what is a profile plot?

Answer: This is a plot or graph comparing statistics such as means or medians. It provides a visual depiction of potential patterns in statistical measures.

20.16 Once data have been screened for normality, what are the basic steps required to conduct a one-way repeated measures ANOVA?

Answer: The following steps are needed:

- The variables are screened for paired comparisons' differences equality of variance in order to select the proper overall test
- If the overall test is significant, post hoc analysis is appropriate.
- Whether or not the omnibus test is meaningful, examining trends in the means using profile plotting and contrast analysis may be informative.

20.17 A study followed the holiday spending of 380 families over three seasons. The same families, whose average annual household income was reported from $0 to $75,000, were asked how much they spent on holiday gifts for seasons 2013, 2014, and 2015. Were there differences in spending, and, if so, were there any patterns? Explain your answer. Report results in the format provided in this book. Alpha = .05. The data file name is "GLM Repeated Measures Exercise 1 Data."

Answer: Data screening using the Shapiro–Wilk test for normal distribution reveals that the data are approximately normally distributed because all p-values are >.05.

Tests of Normality

	Kolmogorov-Smirnov[a]			Shapiro-Wilk		
	Statistic	df	Sig.	Statistic	df	Sig.
2013 Holiday Spending	.034	380	.200*	.998	380	.841
2014 Holiday Spending	.033	380	.200*	.996	380	.397
2015 Holiday Spending	.043	380	.090	.996	380	.459

*. This is a lower bound of the true significance.

a. Lilliefors Significance Correction

Mauchly's Test of Sphericity indicates that there is equality of variance in the paired comparison differences because $p = .481$.

Mauchly's Test of Sphericity[a]

Measure: MEASURE_1

Within Subjects Effect	Mauchly's W	Approx. Chi-Square	df	Sig.	Epsilon[b] Greenhouse-Geisser	Huynh-Feldt	Lower-bound
HolidaySpending	.996	1.462	2	.481	.996	1.000	.500

Tests the null hypothesis that the error covariance matrix of the orthonormalized transformed dependent variables is proportional to an identity matrix.

a. Design: Intercept
Within Subjects Design: HolidaySpending

b. May be used to adjust the degrees of freedom for the averaged tests of significance. Corrected tests are displayed in the Tests of Within-Subjects Effects table.

Since Mauchly's Test of Sphericity is not significant, we apply the "sphericity assumed" statistics to this analysis. The omnibus test reveals that there is likely no difference in holiday spending from 2013 to 2015 by the families because $p = .352$.

Tests of Within-Subjects Effects

Measure: MEASURE_1

Source		Type III Sum of Squares	df	Mean Square	F	Sig.	Partial Eta Squared
HolidaySpending	Sphericity Assumed	72635.170	2	36317.585	1.044	.352	.003
	Greenhouse-Geisser	72635.170	1.992	36457.771	1.044	.352	.003
	Huynh-Feldt	72635.170	2.000	36317.585	1.044	.352	.003
	Lower-bound	72635.170	1.000	72635.170	1.044	.308	.003
Error(HolidaySpending)	Sphericity Assumed	26364058.24	758	34781.079			
	Greenhouse-Geisser	26364058.24	755.085	34915.334			
	Huynh-Feldt	26364058.24	758.000	34781.079			
	Lower-bound	26364058.24	379.000	69562.159			

The plots of the spending for each of the three years suggest a linear effect. Thus, we will examine the contrasts test.

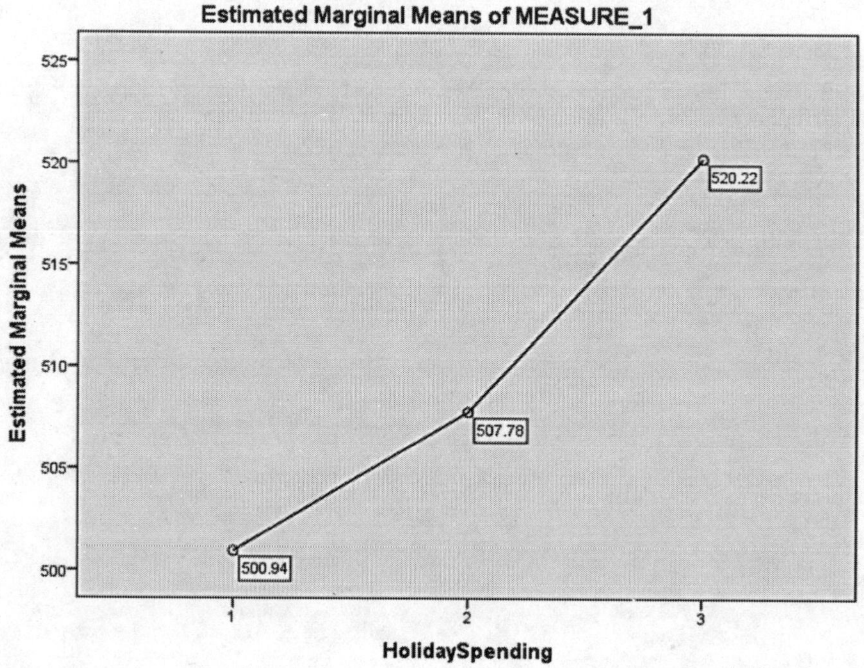

Since the contrasts tests are not significant (>.05), there is no meaningful (linear) pattern in spending over time.

Tests of Within-Subjects Contrasts

Measure: MEASURE_1

Source	HolidaySpending	Type III Sum of Squares	df	Mean Square	F	Sig.	Partial Eta Squared
HolidaySpending	Linear	70644.827	1	70644.827	2.163	.142	.006
	Quadratic	1990.343	1	1990.343	.054	.816	.000
Error(HolidaySpending)	Linear	12377762.51	379	32659.004			
	Quadratic	13986295.74	379	36903.155			

Write-up: A repeated measures ANOVA determined that the amount of holiday spending from 2012 to 2015 in families with household income $0–$75,000 does not statistically differ by year ($F(2,758) = 1.044$, $p = .352$).

20.18 A new on-demand video stream company wanted to test the brand awareness effectiveness of its new ad format. An advertising customer purchased space over a four-week period to run ads. The video streaming company had a list of opt-in regular subscribers who agreed to answer a short survey about their "viewing habits" over four weeks. The question was formatted in a scale where 1 = "not aware at all of Brand A" to 10 = "totally aware of Brand A." The survey was distributed immediately before the campaign and then after each of four weeks so that there were five data collection points from the same participants. Nine hundred and twenty-five subscribers provided a complete dataset. Did the ad campaign increase brand awareness? If so, what was the nature of the awareness effect? Explain your answer. Report results in the format provided in this book. Alpha = .05. The data file name is "GLM Repeated Measures Exercise 2 Data."

Answer: Data screening using the Shapiro–Wilk test for normal distribution reveals that the data are approximately normally distributed because all p-values are > .05.

Tests of Normality

	Kolmogorov-Smirnov[a]			Shapiro-Wilk		
	Statistic	df	Sig.	Statistic	df	Sig.
Precampaign	.023	925	.200*	.999	925	.707
Week1	.015	925	.200*	.999	925	.788
Week2	.017	925	.200*	.999	925	.843
Week3	.015	925	.200*	.999	925	.990
Postcampaign	.027	925	.119	.998	925	.405

*. This is a lower bound of the true significance.

a. Lilliefors Significance Correction

Mauchly's Test of Sphericity indicates that there is equality of variance in the comparison differences because $p = .480$.

Mauchly's Test of Sphericity[a]

Measure: MEASURE_1

Within Subjects Effect	Mauchly's W	Approx. Chi-Square	df	Sig.	Epsilon[b] Greenhouse-Geisser	Huynh-Feldt	Lower-bound
Awareness	.991	8.544	9	.480	.995	1.000	.250

Tests the null hypothesis that the error covariance matrix of the orthonormalized transformed dependent variables is proportional to an identity matrix.

a. Design: Intercept
Within Subjects Design: Awareness

b. May be used to adjust the degrees of freedom for the averaged tests of significance. Corrected tests are displayed in the Tests of Within-Subjects Effects table.

Since Mauchly's Test of Sphericity is not significant, we apply the "sphericity assumed" statistics to this analysis, which reveals a significant finding ($p < .001$). There is at least one difference in brand awareness between at least two measurement points.

Tests of Within-Subjects Effects

Measure: MEASURE_1

Source		Type III Sum of Squares	df	Mean Square	F	Sig.	Partial Eta Squared
Awareness	Sphericity Assumed	2455.244	4	613.811	6880.717	.000	.882
	Greenhouse-Geisser	2455.244	3.982	616.650	6880.717	.000	.882
	Huynh-Feldt	2455.244	4.000	613.811	6880.717	.000	.882
	Lower-bound	2455.244	1.000	2455.244	6880.717	.000	.882
Error(Awareness)	Sphericity Assumed	329.711	3696	.089			
	Greenhouse-Geisser	329.711	3678.984	.090			
	Huynh-Feldt	329.711	3696.000	.089			
	Lower-bound	329.711	924.000	.357			

The pairwise comparisons yield where the specific differences are located. All five measures of awareness over time were significantly different from each other ($p < .001$). The paired comparison confidence intervals are also reported. Since all matched pairs are significant, none of the difference intervals contain zero.

Pairwise Comparisons

Measure: MEASURE_1

(I) Awareness	(J) Awareness	Mean Difference (I-J)	Std. Error	Sig.[b]	95% Confidence Interval for Difference[b] Lower Bound	Upper Bound
1	2	-.303*	.014	.000	-.342	-.265
	3	-.808*	.014	.000	-.848	-.768
	4	-1.408*	.014	.000	-1.446	-1.369
	5	-2.006*	.014	.000	-2.044	-1.967
2	1	.303*	.014	.000	.265	.342
	3	-.504*	.014	.000	-.543	-.466
	4	-1.104*	.014	.000	-1.144	-1.064
	5	-1.702*	.014	.000	-1.741	-1.664
3	1	.808*	.014	.000	.768	.848
	2	.504*	.014	.000	.466	.543
	4	-.600*	.014	.000	-.639	-.560
	5	-1.198*	.014	.000	-1.236	-1.159
4	1	1.408*	.014	.000	1.369	1.446
	2	1.104*	.014	.000	1.064	1.144
	3	.600*	.014	.000	.560	.639
	5	-.598*	.014	.000	-.637	-.559
5	1	2.006*	.014	.000	1.967	2.044
	2	1.702*	.014	.000	1.664	1.741
	3	1.198*	.014	.000	1.159	1.236
	4	.598*	.014	.000	.559	.637

Based on estimated marginal means

*. The mean difference is significant at the .05 level.

b. Adjustment for multiple comparisons: Bonferroni.

The means plot appears to demonstrate a linear effect where each time awareness is measured, it increases, thus representing a growing effect of the ad campaign.

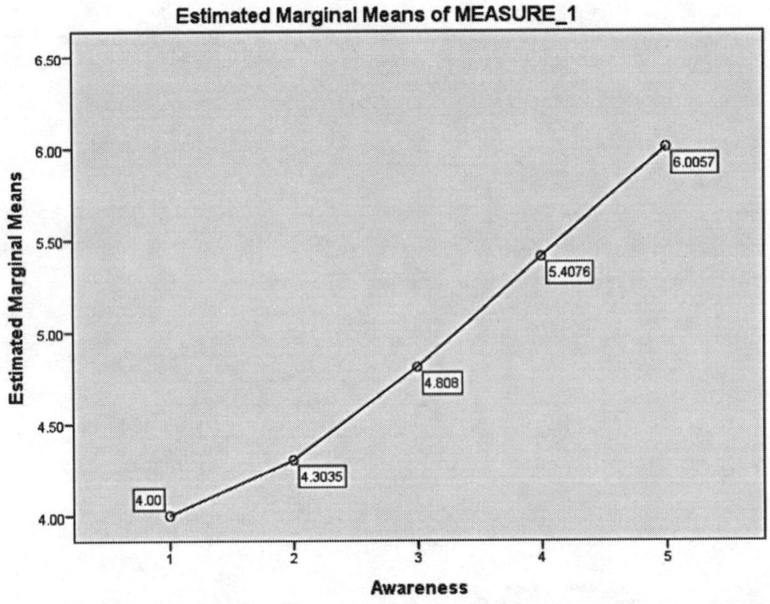

The linear, quadratic, and cubic contrasts tests were meaningful. For the linear effect, the partial eta squared, which is 96.8%, is larger than those for the quadratic and cubic effects. Clearly, 96.8% of the pattern in the data is linear. The trend is linear.

Tests of Within-Subjects Contrasts

Measure: MEASURE_1

Source	Awareness	Type III Sum of Squares	df	Mean Square	F	Sig.	Partial Eta Squared
Awareness	Linear	2420.505	1	2420.505	27553.425	.000	.968
	Quadratic	30.949	1	30.949	349.812	.000	.275
	Cubic	3.789	1	3.789	39.667	.000	.041
	Order 4	.001	1	.001	.014	.907	.000
Error(Awareness)	Linear	81.171	924	.088			
	Quadratic	81.749	924	.088			
	Cubic	88.261	924	.096			
	Order 4	78.530	924	.085			

Write-up: A repeated measures ANOVA determined that the true population mean brand awareness score statistically differed over time during the four-week ad campaign (F(1, 924) = 27,553.425, $p < .001$). The ad campaign explained 96.8% of the change in brand awareness. Bonferroni comparisons revealed that Week 1 awareness likely increased (M = 4.304, $p < .001$) over pre-campaign awareness (M = 4.000) and that Week 2 awareness (M = 4.808, $p < .001$) was greater than Week 1 awareness. Week 3 awareness (M = 5.408, $p < .001$) was greater than Week 2 awareness. The post-campaign awareness (M = 6.006, $p < .001$) was greater than Week 3 awareness. Consistent with these findings, the data indicate a significant linear (F(1,924) = 27,533.505, $p < .001$) effect where awareness increased over the course of the ad campaign.

20.19 A medical research firm received a grant to determine if the color of nurses' uniforms affected patient moods. A local hospital agreed to ask patients to participant in this study. The patients did not have life-threatening illnesses. Fifty-five of the participants completed the five tablet-based "mood" surveys. The responses were formatted in a smiley face pull bar scale from 1 = "I'm in a very sad mood" to 5 = "I'm in a great mood," including increments between 1 and 5 in order to increase reliability. The study transpired over five days. The nurses wore the same style uniform only the color varied as follows: Day 1 = Whatever uniform the nurse typically wore, Day 2 = Green, Day 3 = Navy Blue, Day 4 = White, and Day 5 = Beige. Is uniform color related to patient mood? Explain your answer. Report results in the format provided in this book. Alpha = .05. The data file name is "GLM Repeated Measures Exercise 3 Data."

Answer: There are five variables representing the five measurement times, one for each color of uniform for the given day. The uniform color is the independent variable. Since the Shapiro-Wilk statistics for the five variables are greater than .05, they do not violate the normality assumption.

Tests of Normality

	Kolmogorov-Smirnov[a]			Shapiro-Wilk		
	Statistic	df	Sig.	Statistic	df	Sig.
Day1	.113	55	.077	.975	55	.316
Day2	.109	55	.156	.971	55	.215
Day3	.099	55	.200*	.975	55	.296
Day4	.079	55	.200*	.983	55	.640
Day5	.093	55	.200*	.961	55	.071

*. This is a lower bound of the true significance.

a. Lilliefors Significance Correction

The descriptives table provides the means and standard deviations for each of the five days' mean scores. Day 3: Navy Blue uniform appears to have the highest positive mood score.

Descriptive Statistics

	Mean	Std. Deviation	N
Day1	3.4840	.30011	55
Day2	3.4464	.32581	55
Day3	4.1261	.36936	55
Day4	3.5025	.60002	55
Day5	3.4386	.44138	55

The sphericity assumption is not met because $p < .001$. Since the Greenhouse-Geisser epsilon is $< .75$, it is the applicable statistic for the overall test.

Mauchly's Test of Sphericity[a]

Measure: MEASURE_1

					Epsilon[b]		
Within Subjects Effect	Mauchly's W	Approx. Chi-Square	df	Sig.	Greenhouse-Geisser	Huynh-Feldt	Lower-bound
Color_Uniform_Day	.458	40.906	9	.000	.719	.764	.250

Tests the null hypothesis that the error covariance matrix of the orthonormalized transformed dependent variables is proportional to an identity matrix.

a. Design: Intercept
Within Subjects Design: Color_Uniform_Day

b. May be used to adjust the degrees of freedom for the averaged tests of significance. Corrected tests are displayed in the Tests of Within-Subjects Effects table.

The Greenhouse-Geisser statistic is $p < .001$, indicating a significant result or main effect. It is likely that 34.6% of mood is predicted by the color of the nurse's uniform. As we shall see shortly, it is the navy blue color that makes the difference.

Tests of Within-Subjects Effects

Measure: MEASURE_1

Source		Type III Sum of Squares	df	Mean Square	F	Sig.	Partial Eta Squared
Color_Uniform_Day	Sphericity Assumed	19.218	4	4.804	28.537	.000	.346
	Greenhouse-Geisser	19.218	2.875	6.684	28.537	.000	.346
	Huynh-Feldt	19.218	3.054	6.292	28.537	.000	.346
	Lower-bound	19.218	1.000	19.218	28.537	.000	.346
Error (Color_Uniform_Day)	Sphericity Assumed	36.366	216	.168			
	Greenhouse-Geisser	36.366	155.272	.234			
	Huynh-Feldt	36.366	164.930	.220			
	Lower-bound	36.366	54.000	.673			

Day 3: Navy Blue uniform is significantly different from all other days at $p < .001$. The table also produced the 95% confidence interval for differences between the paired comparisons. All of Day 3's intervals are greater than the other four days. Essentially, 34.6% of reason for mood change is attributable to the navy blue uniforms.

Pairwise Comparisons

Measure: MEASURE_1

(I) Color_Uniform_Day	(J) Color_Uniform_Day	Mean Difference (I-J)	Std. Error	Sig.[b]	95% Confidence Interval for Difference[b] Lower Bound	Upper Bound
1	2	.038	.053	1.000	-.118	.194
	3	-.642*	.063	.000	-.825	-.459
	4	-.018	.082	1.000	-.259	.222
	5	.045	.075	1.000	-.173	.264
2	1	-.038	.053	1.000	-.194	.118
	3	-.680*	.062	.000	-.862	-.498
	4	-.056	.096	1.000	-.337	.225
	5	.008	.076	1.000	-.214	.229
3	1	.642*	.063	.000	.459	.825
	2	.680*	.062	.000	.498	.862
	4	.624*	.100	.000	.330	.917
	5	.688*	.062	.000	.505	.870
4	1	.018	.082	1.000	-.222	.259
	2	.056	.096	1.000	-.225	.337
	3	-.624*	.100	.000	-.917	-.330
	5	.064	.097	1.000	-.219	.347
5	1	-.045	.075	1.000	-.264	.173
	2	-.008	.076	1.000	-.229	.214
	3	-.688*	.062	.000	-.870	-.505
	4	-.064	.097	1.000	-.347	.219

Based on estimated marginal means

*. The mean difference is significant at the .05 level.

b. Adjustment for multiple comparisons: Bonferroni.

The profile plot depicts the same result as the Bonferroni post hoc test.

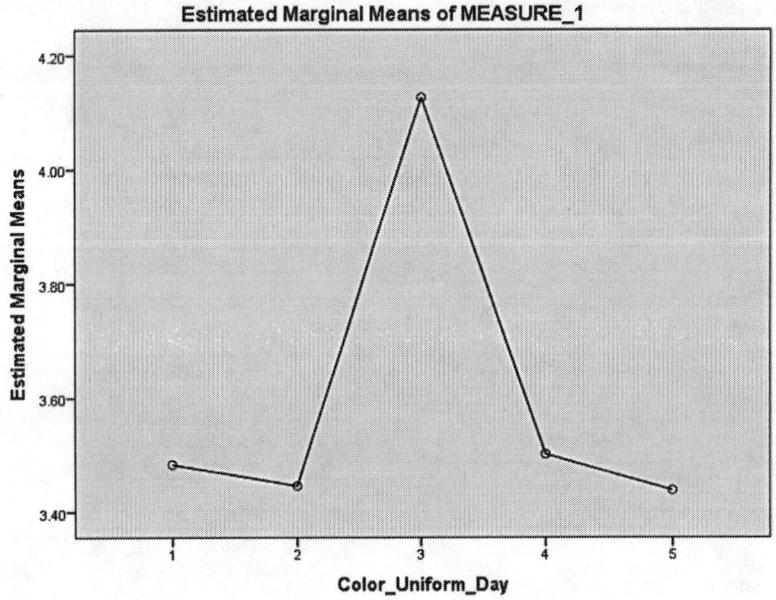

A quadratic pattern in the means appears to exist ($p < .001$). The partial eta squared is .616. In others, the means' data pattern explains 61.6% of the quadratic shape.

Tests of Within-Subjects Contrasts

Measure: MEASURE_1

Source	Color_Uniform_Day	Type III Sum of Squares	df	Mean Square	F	Sig.	Partial Eta Squared
Color_Uniform_Day	Linear	.007	1	.007	.038	.847	.001
	Quadratic	7.223	1	7.223	86.470	.000	.616
	Cubic	.137	1	.137	.594	.444	.011
	Order 4	11.852	1	11.852	64.702	.000	.545
Error (Color_Uniform_Day)	Linear	9.525	54	.176			
	Quadratic	4.510	54	.084			
	Cubic	12.439	54	.230			
	Order 4	9.891	54	.183			

Write-up: A repeated measures ANOVA with a Greenhouse-Geisser correction determined that the reported 55 patient mood differs over time according to the color of the nurse's uniform (F(2.875, 155.272) = 28.537, $p < .001$). Uniform color explained 34.6% of the change in patient mood. Bonferroni comparisons revealed that Day 3 (Navy Blue, M = 4.126, SD = .369, $p <$ .001) likely increases patient mood over the other colors Day 1 (normal color, M = 3.348, SD = .300), Day 2 (Green, M = 3.446, SD = .325), Day 4 (White, M = 3.3502, SD = .600), and Day 5 (Beige, M = 3.438, SD = .441). It is likely that patient mood elevates when the attending nurse wears a navy blue uniform. None of the other uniform colors made a difference.

20.20 At an afternoon session, 138 high school juniors were surveyed about their knowledge on the three branches of the U.S. federal government and how they are organized in providing checks and balances. After completing the survey, they immediately attended a two-hour workshop that consisted of a PowerPoint lecture by a teacher on the three branches followed by some related small group activities. At the end of the session, they were administered the same survey. Three weeks later, they completed the same survey once more. Each survey was based on 100 points. Did student knowledge increase over the short term and was it sustained three weeks later? Explain your answer. Report results in the format provided in this book. Alpha = .05. The data file name is "GLM Repeated Measures Exercise 4 Data."

Answer: There are three variables and the treatments are the workshop and time.

Tests of Normality

	Kolmogorov-Smirnov[a]			Shapiro-Wilk		
	Statistic	df	Sig.	Statistic	df	Sig.
Pre_Workshop	.073	138	.070	.989	138	.365
Immediately_After	.049	138	.200*	.989	138	.357
Three_Weeks	.073	138	.067	.989	138	.362

*. This is a lower bound of the true significance.

a. Lilliefors Significance Correction

The Shapiro–Wilk statistic indicates that the three variables do not violate the normality assumption. The means and standard deviations are below. The three means appear to vary, especially immediately after the workshop.

Descriptive Statistics

	Mean	Std. Deviation	N
Pre_Workshop	49.77	6.502	138
Immediately_After	92.16	6.352	138
Three_Weeks	85.04	6.279	138

Since the Mauchly's test is $p = .139$, the sphericity assumption is met.

Mauchly's Test of Sphericity[a]

Measure: MEASURE_1

					Epsilon[b]		
Within Subjects Effect	Mauchly's W	Approx. Chi-Square	df	Sig.	Greenhouse-Geisser	Huynh-Feldt	Lower-bound
Knowledge	.971	3.954	2	.139	.972	.986	.500

Tests the null hypothesis that the error covariance matrix of the orthonormalized transformed dependent variables is proportional to an identity matrix.

a. Design: Intercept
Within Subjects Design: Knowledge

b. May be used to adjust the degrees of freedom for the averaged tests of significance. Corrected tests are displayed in the Tests of Within-Subjects Effects table.

The sphericity assumed statistic is $p < .001$, which is significant. The workshop and over time conditions explain 92.6% of the variance in scores.

Tests of Within-Subjects Effects

Measure: MEASURE_1

Source		Type III Sum of Squares	df	Mean Square	F	Sig.	Partial Eta Squared
Knowledge	Sphericity Assumed	142232.483	2	71116.242	1717.998	.000	.926
	Greenhouse-Geisser	142232.483	1.944	73153.840	1717.998	.000	.926
	Huynh-Feldt	142232.483	1.972	72130.732	1717.998	.000	.926
	Lower-bound	142232.483	1.000	142232.483	1717.998	.000	.926
Error(Knowledge)	Sphericity Assumed	11342.184	274	41.395			
	Greenhouse-Geisser	11342.184	266.368	42.581			
	Huynh-Feldt	11342.184	270.146	41.985			
	Lower-bound	11342.184	137.000	82.790			

All three time points are statistically significant from each other. The difference confidence intervals reveal the same tale. There are no zero differences.

Pairwise Comparisons

Measure: MEASURE_1

(I) Knowledge	(J) Knowledge	Mean Difference (I-J)	Std. Error	Sig.[b]	95% Confidence Interval for Difference[b]	
					Lower Bound	Upper Bound
1	2	-42.391*	.721	.000	-44.139	-40.644
	3	-35.275*	.833	.000	-37.294	-33.256
2	1	42.391*	.721	.000	40.644	44.139
	3	7.116*	.766	.000	5.260	8.972
3	1	35.275*	.833	.000	33.256	37.294
	2	-7.116*	.766	.000	-8.972	-5.260

Based on estimated marginal means

*. The mean difference is significant at the .05 level.

b. Adjustment for multiple comparisons: Bonferroni.

The profile plot appears to demonstrate a quadratic function.

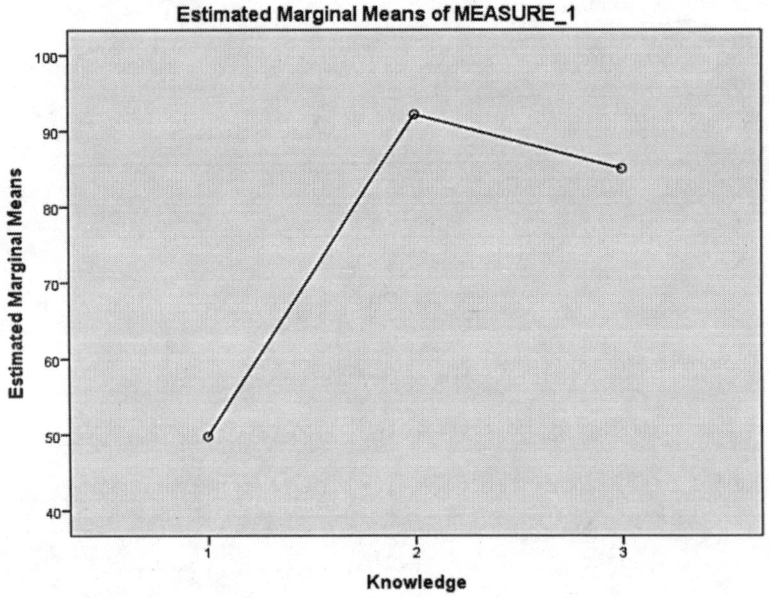

In fact, based on the contrasts results ($p < .001$), the plot is both quadratic and linear. The linear component suggests the workshop immediate effect and the quadratic pattern illustrates an attentuating effect over time. Nearly 93% each of the linear and quadratic patterns are explained by the means' data.

Tests of Within-Subjects Contrasts

Measure: MEASURE_1

Source	Knowledge	Type III Sum of Squares	df	Mean Square	F	Sig.	Partial Eta Squared
Knowledge	Linear	85860.232	1	85860.232	1793.181	.000	.929
	Quadratic	56372.251	1	56372.251	1614.874	.000	.922
Error(Knowledge)	Linear	6559.768	137	47.882			
	Quadratic	4782.415	137	34.908			

Write-up: A repeated measures ANOVA determined that a school workshop attended by 138 high school juniors led to a significant increase in their knowledge about the workings of the three branches of government ($F(2, 274) = 1{,}717.998$, $p < .001$). The workshop explained 92.6% of the change in knowledge. Based on 100 points, Bonferroni comparisons revealed differences among all paired comparisons at $p < .001$ of the three measurement points: pre-workshop ($M = 49.77$, $SD = 6.502$), immediately after the workshop ($M = 92.16$, $SD = 6.352$), and three weeks later ($M = 85.04$, $SD = 6.279$).

B.21 Chapter 21

21.1 What is a bivariate correlation?

Answer: A bivariate correlation, represented by lower-case "*r*," measures the degree of association or extent of the relationship between two variables. It is used to determine whether a linear (straight-line) relationship between two variables exists, as well as the strength and direction of that relationship.

21.2 What is a correlation?

Answer: A correlation, represented by lower-case "*r*," measures the degree to which a linear (straight-line) association or relationship exists between two variables based on the strength and direction of the relationship.

21.3 What is an association between two variables?

Answer: A relationship between two variables is known as an association.

21.4 Define covariance.

Answer: This is the degree to which two variables vary together.

21.5 Define variance.

Answer: Variance is a measure of variation in which the difference between each value and the mean are squared and then summed. The summed total is then divided by the sample size minus 1.

21.6 What is face validity?

Answer: This type of validity is the extent to which a finding or measurement is well founded and accurate based on common sense or face value.

21.7 Broadly define the term effect size.

Answer: This is a statistical measure of the degree to which one or more variables influences one or more other variables.

21.8 What is the meaning of r^2?

Answer: This is the explained variance. The square of a correlation provides the percentage of the total covariance explained by the line of best fit. It is the variance that is share between the two variables. It is the percentage of variance explained in a variable as a result of variability in a predictor variable.

21.9 What is variance explained or the explained variance?

Answer: This is the percentage of covariance shared by two variables. It is the r^2.

21.10 What is a coefficient of determination?

Answer: This is another term for the explained variance or r^2. This is the percentage of covariance shared by two variables.

21.11 What is unexplained variance in terms of explained variance?

Answer: Since the explained variance is a percentage, then the unexplained variance or unaccounted for variance is $1 - r^2$. It is also called the coefficient of nondetermination.

21.12 Describe a zero-order correlation.

Answer: This correlation measures the degree of association between two variables. It does not account for associations with other variables in relation to the two correlation variables.

21.13 What is meant by the strength of a correlation?

Answer: The strength of a correlation is the degree to which the variables have similar variances. If the differences in the variables corresponds perfectly, then the correlation will be −1 or 1. Less than perfect correlations will be between −1 and 1.

21.14 What is meant by directionality of a correlation?

Answer: This refers to whether both variables in a correlation move in the same direction as they change. In other words, directionality indicates whether they increase together, decrease together, or move in the opposite direction from each other.

21.15 Describe a positive correlation.

Answer: A positive correlation is $0 < r \leqslant 1$. It covaries in the same direction of the other variable.

21.16 Describe a negative correlation.

Answer: A correlation that is $0 > r \geqslant -1$. It covaries in the opposite direction of the other variable.

21.17 In correlation analysis, what is meant by a joint distribution?

Answer: This is the distribution of two variables plotted in a graph using the matched data points or coordinates of the variables. One variable is assigned the x-axis and the other the y-axis.

21.18 Define linearity in the context of correlation analysis.

Answer: This is a pattern in a joint distribution that maintains the same slope between two variables in a straight line. It occurs when the variance between two variables is constant in their respective directions.

21.19 Define homoscedasticity.

Answer: This refers to the degree of similarity in which the covariances of joint values or coordinates fit along the line of best fit. The distribution forms an elliptical pattern.

21.20 What is statistical validity?

Answer: This is the extent to which a finding or measurement is well founded and accurate.

21.21 Describe bivariate normal distribution.

Answer: When the sample size is sufficiently large and the two variables are normally distributed and demonstrate a linear relationship, the paired coordinates will tend to concentrate in the center at the intersection of the (joint) means of the two variables. This indicates a bivariate normal distribution.

21.22 In short, what is a Pearson correlation?

Answer: This type of correlation is a parametric procedure used for numeric data.

21.23 When is it appropriate to use the Spearman correlation?

Answer: This nonparametric correlation procedure is used when one or both variables are composed of ordinal categorical data or when numeric data do not meet the normality and/or homoscedasticity assumptions.

21.24 Broadly define a partial correlation.

Answer: This correlation procedure removes the influence of one or more designated variables from the correlation.

21.25 Broadly define a semipartial correlation.

Answer: This is a correlation that controls for the effects of one or more other variables on one of the two correlated variables.

21.26 In one sentence, define or describe what is curvilinear.

Answer: Any association or pattern in data that is not linear.

21.27 What is a monotonic relationship?

Answer: This means that the degree of covariance may change in a relationship but it will maintain the same direction.

21.28 Complex, a cable company, wishes to determine if there is an association between subscribers' reported amount of travel and interest in a new cable service that offers a full range of travel services. Are consumers more engaged in travel behavior more likely to show an interest in cable travel services? Data were collected from a random sample of 100. The two questions were as follows: "How would you report your amount of travel compared to people in general? 1 = I don't travel to 7 = I live to travel." "Would you be interested in a new cable service that offers a full range of travel services? 1 = I am not interested at all to 7 = Sign me up now." Explain your answer. Alpha = .05. Report results in the format provided in this book. The data file name is "Correlation Analysis Exercise 1 Data."

Answer:

Tests of Normality

	Kolmogorov-Smirnov[a]			Shapiro-Wilk		
	Statistic	df	Sig.	Statistic	df	Sig.
Reported Travel	.069	100	.200*	.983	100	.214
Interest in Service	.060	100	.200*	.988	100	.495

*. This is a lower bound of the true significance.

a. Lilliefors Significance Correction

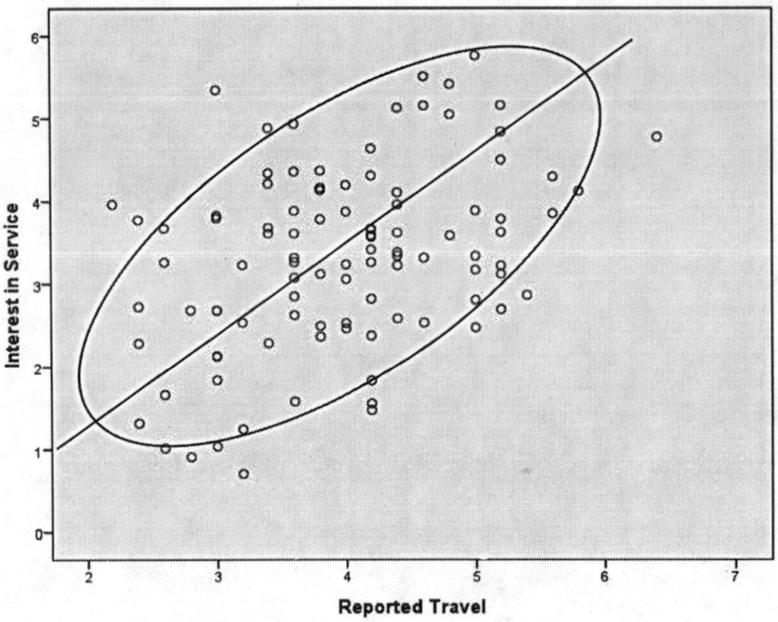

Correlations

		Reported Travel	Interest in Service
Reported Travel	Pearson Correlation	1	.395**
	Sig. (2-tailed)		.000
	N	100	100
Interest in Service	Pearson Correlation	.395**	1
	Sig. (2-tailed)	.000	
	N	100	100

**. Correlation is significant at the 0.01 level (2-tailed).

The data are normally distributed, linear, and bivariate normal. The Pearson correlation (r = .39, p < .001) is positive, moderate, and meaningful (the p-value is less than .05). The Complex customers who reported greater travel were more interested in the new cable travel service. These variables share 15% of their variance. We assume that the sample is representative of the typical Complex customer.

Write-up: A Pearson product-moment correlation was run to determine whether an association exists between Complex customers' reported travel habits and their interest in a new cable travel service. The data showed no violation of normality, linearity, or bivariate normality. There was a moderate, positive correlation between customers' reported travel habits and their interest in a new cable travel service (r = .39, N = 100, p < .001). It is likely that customers who travel more report greater interest in the travel service. The data explain 15% of the association between the two variables.

21.29 Previous research found that certain personality traits reduced job burnout in healthcare providers. Healthcare researchers are charged to explore this line of researcher further. Survey data were collected from 600 healthcare practitioners who were asked a number of questions. Two variables are of special interest. These are hardiness and burnout. Is increased hardiness associated with less burnout while accounting for age? "Hardiness" was measured using a number of job commitment, sense of control over one's life, and high challenge questions. The composite sliding bar scale was formatted as 1 = "little hardiness" to 7 = "high hardiness." "Burnout" consisted of emotional exhaustion, lack of personal accomplishment, and depersonalization questions. The composite sliding bar scale was formatted as 1 = "not burned out at all" to 7 = "totally burned out." Age is in completed years of life. Explain your answer. Report results in the format provided in this book. Alpha = .05. The data file name is "Correlation Analysis Exercise 2 Data."

Answer: The variables do not violate the normality assumption because all Shapiro-Wilk p-values are greater than .05.

Tests of Normality

	Kolmogorov-Smirnov[a]			Shapiro-Wilk		
	Statistic	df	Sig.	Statistic	df	Sig.
Age	.022	600	.200*	.998	600	.710
Hardiness	.024	600	.200*	.998	600	.861
Burnout	.037	600	.044	.996	600	.200

*. This is a lower bound of the true significance.

a. Lilliefors Significance Correction

Based on the scatter plot below, the data appear linear and homoscedastic (elliptical shape of the data points).

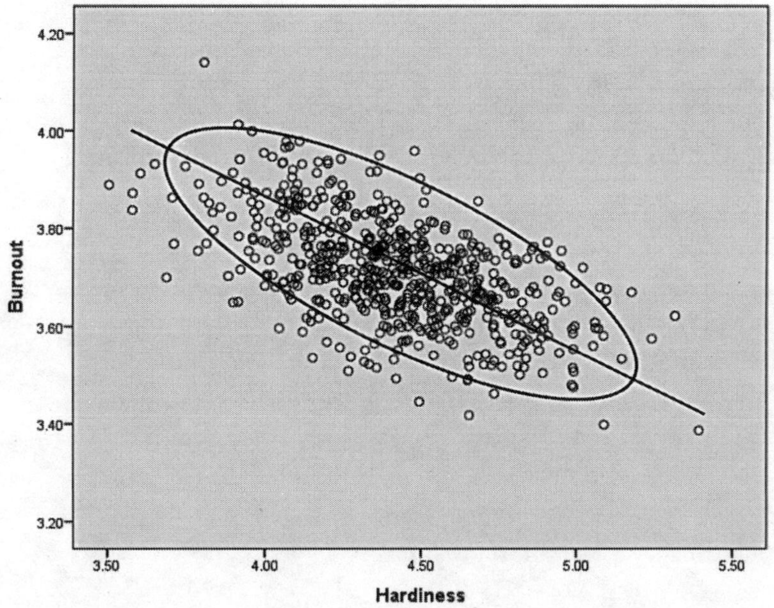

Based on the zero-order and partial correlations (controlling for age), age does not have an effect on the significant ($p < .001$), strong, and negative correlation between hardiness and burnout. It appears that greater hardiness is associated with less burnout. Further, the line of best fit explains 33.75% of their covariance or shared variance. It is likely that nearly 34% of the variance in burnout can be explained by the degree of hardiness in the healthcare provider's personality.

Correlations

		Age	Hardiness	Burnout
Age	Pearson Correlation	1	-.022	-.011
	Sig. (2-tailed)		.592	.782
	N	600	600	600
Hardiness	Pearson Correlation	-.022	1	-.581**
	Sig. (2-tailed)	.592		.000
	N	600	600	600
Burnout	Pearson Correlation	-.011	-.581**	1
	Sig. (2-tailed)	.782	.000	
	N	600	600	600

**. Correlation is significant at the 0.01 level (2-tailed).

Correlations

Control Variables			Hardiness	Burnout
Age	Hardiness	Correlation	1.000	-.581
		Significance (2-tailed)	.	.000
		df	0	597
	Burnout	Correlation	-.581	1.000
		Significance (2-tailed)	.000	.
		df	597	0

Write-up: A Pearson product-moment correlation was run to determine whether an association exists between a hardy personality and healthcare provider job burnout. The data showed no violation of normality, linearity, or bivariate normality. There was a strong, negative correlation between hardiness and burnout ($r = -.58$, $N = 600$, $p < .001$). It is likely that those providers who self-report high levels of hardiness will not experience as much job burnout. The data explain 33.75% of the association between the two variables.

21.30 A human resources firm is charged with determining whether a relationship exists between compensation and job satisfaction. Pay data in dollars were collected from 286 workers representing all job functions. Additionally, the same workers completed a short job satisfaction online sliding bar scale survey. The overall job satisfaction question "Are you satisfied with our job?" responses were anchored in a scale as follows: 1 = "not at all satisfied" to 9 = "completely satisfied." Is there an association between pay and job satisfaction? Explain your answer. Report results in the format provided in this book. Alpha = .05. The data file name is "Correlation Analysis Exercise 3 Data."

Answer: The variables do not violate the normality assumption because all Shapiro-Wilk p-values are greater than .05.

Tests of Normality

	Kolmogorov-Smirnov[a]			Shapiro-Wilk		
	Statistic	df	Sig.	Statistic	df	Sig.
Pay	.055	286	.036	.994	286	.298
Job_Satisfaction	.037	286	.200*	.993	286	.207

*. This is a lower bound of the true significance.

a. Lilliefors Significance Correction

Based on the scatter plot below, the data do not appear linear or homoscedastic. A line cannot be drawn through the data to indicate a linear association and the data do not form an elliptical shape. Thus, these assumptions are violated. In all likelihood, there is no correlation between them.

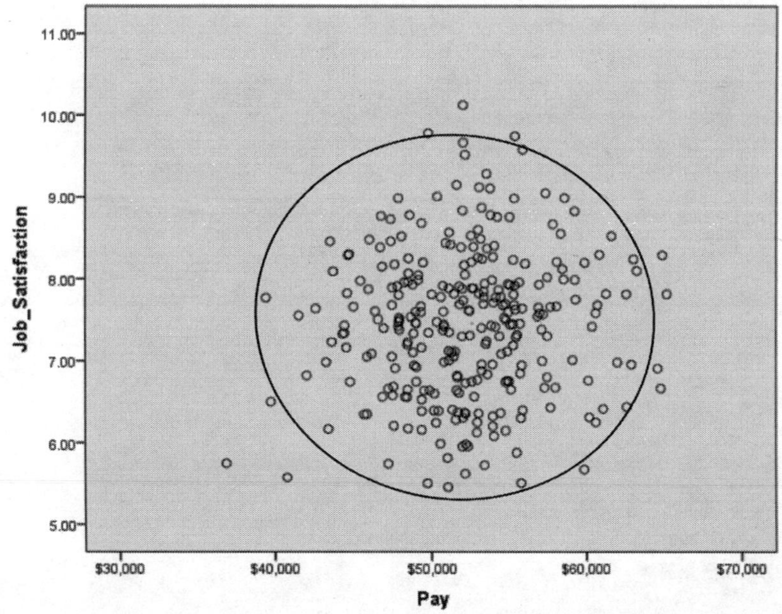

At this point, we would stop. However, let us run a Pearson correlation to examine the results. Since $p = .167$, which is greater than .05, there is no significant correlation between pay and job satisfaction, which is what we suspected after screening the data.

Correlations

		Pay	Job_Satisfaction
Pay	Pearson Correlation	1	.082
	Sig. (2-tailed)		.167
	N	286	286
Job_Satisfaction	Pearson Correlation	.082	1
	Sig. (2-tailed)	.167	
	N	286	286

21.31 Researchers at a well-known nonprofit think tank wish to explore the relationship between hours spent playing video games and GPA (overall high school average). They recruited 520 high school juniors to participate in the online study after securing parental permission. The two variables (single-item questions) of interest were "On average, how many hours a day do you play video games?" and "To the best of your knowledge, what is your GPA?" Both items were recorded using a sliding bar scale so that fractions could be provided. Is there an association between gaming and GPA? Explain your answer. Report results in the format provided in this book. Alpha = .05. The data file name is "Correlation Analysis Exercise 4 Data."

Answer: The variables do not violate the normality assumption because all Shapiro-Wilk *p*-values are greater than .05.

Tests of Normality

	Kolmogorov-Smirnov[a]			Shapiro-Wilk		
	Statistic	df	Sig.	Statistic	df	Sig.
GPA	.026	520	.200*	.998	520	.674
Gaming_Hours	.026	520	.200*	.998	520	.653

*. This is a lower bound of the true significance.

a. Lilliefors Significance Correction

Based on the scatter plot below, the data appear linear and homoscedastic (elliptical shape of the data points).

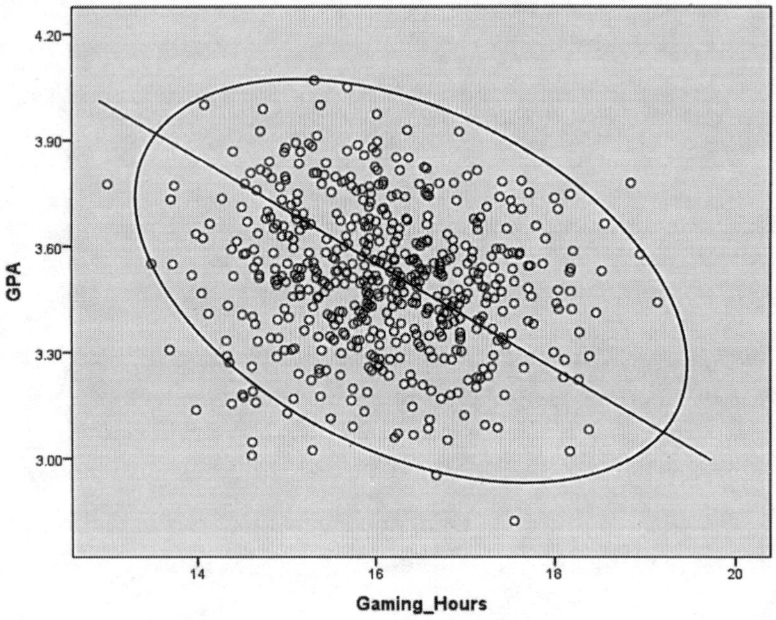

According to the Pearson correlation, there is a weak negative and significant ($p < .001$) relationship between hours spent gaming and high school GPA. Further, the line of best fit explains 2.1% of their covariance or shared variance. It is likely that nearly 2.1% of the variance in GPA can be explained by hours spent gaming. Although it is a small effect, hours spent gaming explain some variance (change) in GPA.

Correlations

		Gaming_Hours	GPA
Gaming_Hours	Pearson Correlation	1	-.145**
	Sig. (2-tailed)		.001
	N	520	520
GPA	Pearson Correlation	-.145**	1
	Sig. (2-tailed)	.001	
	N	520	520

**. Correlation is significant at the 0.01 level (2-tailed).

Write-up: A Pearson product-moment correlation was run to determine whether an association exists between hours spent gaming and high school GPA. The data showed no violation of normality, linearity, or bivariate normality. There was a weak, negative correlation between hours spent gaming and GPA ($r = -.14$, $N = 520$, $p < .001$). It is likely that juniors who spend more time gaming will have a slightly lower GPA. The data explain 2.1% of the association between the two variables.

21.32 A macroeconomist for a large pharmaceutical company wished to confirm the relationship between drug price and units sold over one year for its 121 prescription drugs in order to determine if, on average, they are price-elastic. Price elasticity is a measure of how much prices can fluctuate (usually increase) before price changes significantly influence (decrease) demand for drugs. Prices are copayments after insurance coverage for a 30-day supply. Demand is measured by the number of 30-day supply orders placed. These drugs are prescribed for chronic illnesses and 30-day orders more accurately mimics real world conditions. Are these prescription drugs price elastic? Explain your answer. Report results in the format provided in this book. Alpha = .05. The data file name is "Correlation Analysis Exercise 5 Data."

Answer: The variables do not violate the normality assumption because all Shapiro-Wilk *p*-values are greater than .05.

Tests of Normality

	Kolmogorov-Smirnov[a]			Shapiro-Wilk		
	Statistic	df	Sig.	Statistic	df	Sig.
Drug_Copay	.037	121	.200*	.994	121	.895
Orders	.051	121	.200*	.993	121	.809

*. This is a lower bound of the true significance.

a. Lilliefors Significance Correction

Based on the scatter plot below, the data appear linear and homoscedastic (elliptical shape of the data points).

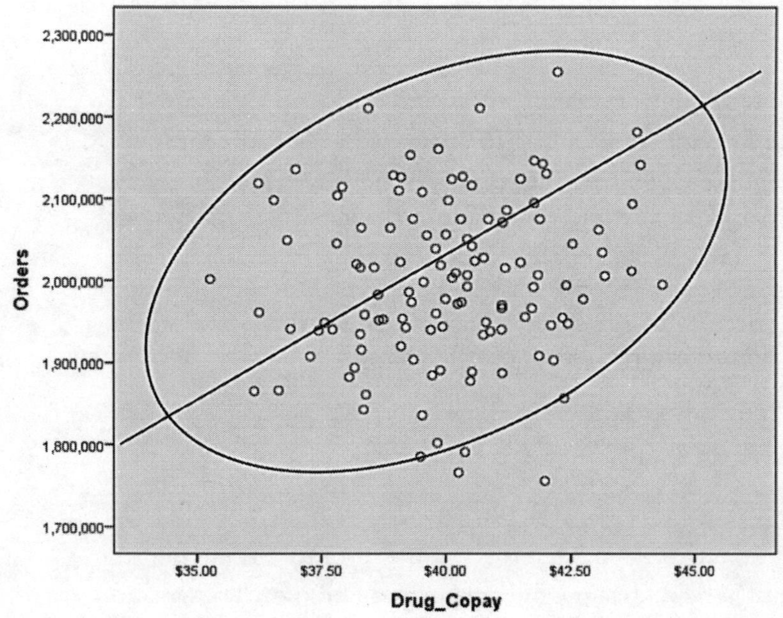

The Pearson correlation (r = .13) reveals a nonsignificant association because p = .15. It is likely that there is no relationship between drug copayments and number of orders.

Correlations

		Drug_Copay	Orders
Drug_Copay	Pearson Correlation	1	.130
	Sig. (2-tailed)		.155
	N	121	121
Orders	Pearson Correlation	.130	1
	Sig. (2-tailed)	.155	
	N	121	121

Write-up: A Pearson product-moment correlation was run to determine if an association exists between drug copayments and number of orders placed. The data showed no violation of normality, linearity, or homoscedasticity. There is no significant correlation between the two variables (r = .13, N = 100, p = .15). It is likely that the number of orders does not vary based on the amount of the drug copayment.

B.22 Chapter 22

22.1 Generally, what is the purpose of single linear regression?

Answer: This type of regression is commonly referred to as simple linear regression. It is a statistical technique used to predict the value of a dependent variable from the value of an independent variable.

22.2 What is the prediction model in single linear regression?

Answer: This is a mathematical expression of the straight line of best fit: $Y_i = b_0 + b_1 Xi$.

22.3 What is extrapolation?

Answer: This is the practice of predicting a dependent variable from an independent value that is beyond the range of the sample data.

22.4 In general terms, define regression coefficient.

Answer: This is a beta in the regression line equation that relates to predicting a value in a dependent variable from a value in an independent variable. Specifically, the b_1 indicates the amount of incremental change in the dependent variable as a result of one unit of change in the independent variable's unit of measurement.

22.5 What is a beta?

Answer: Beta (b or β). This is another term for a regression coefficient.

22.6 What is an unstandardized beta (b)?

Answer: This is a regression coefficient in its original metric or measurement.

22.7 What is a standardized beta (β)?

Answer: This is the regression coefficient expressed in terms of the z-distribution. For the z-distribution, each observation is calculated by subtracting the sample mean from each observation and then dividing the sum by the sample standard deviation.

22.8 What is the y-intercept (b_0)?

Answer: This is the predicted value of the dependent variable when the independent variable equals 0. The y-intercept orients the line of best fit.

22.9 What is the slope in a linear regression equation?

Answer: This is the line of best fit, which is the rise over the run or the amount of change (variance) in the outcome as a results of one unit change in the predictor.

22.10 Generally, what is the adjusted r^2?

Answer: This is an adjusted version of r^2, which is more useful for multiple linear regression analysis. It accounts for sample size and number of predictors.

22.11 Generally, what is the residual in SLR?

Answer: Residual is the variance not accounted for by the line of best fit.

22.12 How do the independent and dependent variables relate to the predictor and outcome variables?

Answer: The independent variable is the predictor and the dependent variable is the outcome or response variable.

22.13 In SLR, why is the r^2 the same as the squared correlation of two variables?

Answer: This is so because there are only two variables in the analysis.

22.14 What does SLR offer that is not provided by correlation analysis?

Answer: SLR allows us to predict specific values of the outcome, on average, based on specific values of the predictor. Correlation analysis only provides information about the overall strength and direction of the relationship, and not the prediction of specific values of the designated outcome variable.

22.15 What are the general assumptions about SLR?

Answer:

1. The data are numeric.
2. The sample size is over 30.
3. The data are independent so that they come from different sampling elements.
4. Each variable is approximately normally distributed.
5. There is a linear relationship between the variables.
6. The joint coordinates are approximately normally distributed (bivariate normal).
7. The bivariate data are homoscedastic.
8. Residuals are normally distributed, linear, and homoscedastic.

22.16 Can data not be correlated and yet meet the error assumptions of normal distribution, linearity, and homoscedasticity?

Answer: These assumptions apply to the residuals and assure whether a significant linear relationship between variables is accurate. Two variables may be at best weakly correlated, but their bivariate relationship may be consistent across the their distribution. This would be the case in a curvilinear relationship.

22.17 What is a predictor (variable)?

Answer: This is an independent variable because it predicts variance in the outcome (variable).

22.18 What is an outcome (variable)?

Answer: This is a dependent variable because it is predicted by an independent or predictor variable.

22.19 A random sample of 40 architects' records were examined in order to determine whether years of professional architecture experience predicts the square footage of building projects awarded to an architect. Run an SLR to discover if such a relationship exists. Explain your answer. Report results in the format provided in this book. Alpha = .05. The name of the data file for this example is "SLR Exercise 1 Data."

Answer: The Shapiro-Wilk test of normality reveals that both "Years of Architectural Experience" (p = .061) and "Square Footage" (p = .537) of architectural projects do not violate the normal distribution assumption because both p-values are greater than .05.

Tests of Normality

	Kolmogorov-Smirnov[a]			Shapiro-Wilk		
	Statistic	df	Sig.	Statistic	df	Sig.
Years of Experience of Architect	.170	40	.005	.947	40	.061
Square Footage	.085	40	.200*	.976	40	.537

*. This is a lower bound of the true significance.

a. Lilliefors Significance Correction

The scatter plot below does not depict a linear or elliptical pattern. R-square is virtually nonexistent. There does not appear to be a linear relationship between the predictor variable or years of architectural experience and the outcome variable or square footage of architectural projects. The data are only slightly oval-shaped.

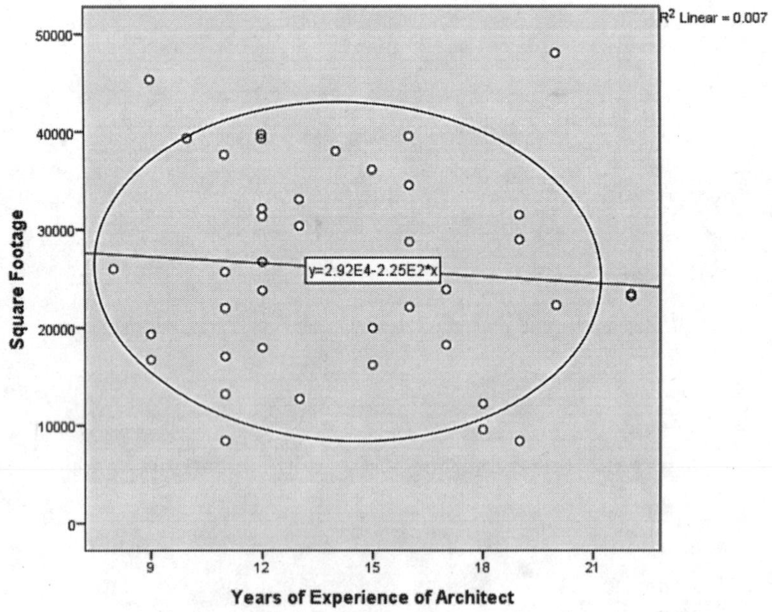

The ANOVA table comprises the overall SLR goodness of fit statistic. It is how well the prediction line fits the data. The line is calculated in order to minimize the distances of points not on the line.

The table reveals $p = .616$. Since $.616 > .05$, the results do not reveal a statistically significant relationship between the predictor (years of architectural experience) and outcome (square footage of architectural projects). No further analysis is required.

ANOVA[a]

Model		Sum of Squares	df	Mean Square	F	Sig.
1	Regression	27948143.74	1	27948143.74	.256	.616[b]
	Residual	4156161154	38	109372661.9		
	Total	4184109297	39			

a. Dependent Variable: Square Footage

b. Predictors: (Constant), Years of Experience of Architect

Write-up: A single linear regression was conducted on data collected from 40 architects in order to determine if the number of architectural years of experience predicts the square footage of architectural projects assigned to the architect. No relationship was found between these two variables ($F(1,38) = .256$, $p = .616$). It is likely that years of experience do not predict the size of the job assignment.

22.20 Reported cases of diseases and healthcare funding data were collected for the 50 largest designated market areas in the United States. The aim of the study is to determine whether healthcare funding per 100 people predicts reported cases of diseases per 10,000 people. Explain your answer. Report results in the format provided in this book. Alpha = .05. The name of the data file for this example is "SLR Exercise 2 Data."

Answer: The Shapiro-Wilk test of normality reveals that both "Reported Diseases" ($p = .913$) and "Healthcare Funding" ($p = .068$) do not violate the univariate normality assumption because both *p*-values are greater than .05.

Tests of Normality

	Kolmogorov-Smirnov[a]			Shapiro-Wilk		
	Statistic	df	Sig.	Statistic	df	Sig.
Reported diseases (rate per 10,000)	.070	50	.200*	.989	50	.913
Health care funding (amount per 100)	.070	50	.200*	.957	50	.068

*. This is a lower bound of the true significance.

a. Lilliefors Significance Correction

The scatter plot reveals a linear relationship ($r^2 = .543$) between the variables and somewhat of an elliptical pattern in the bivariate distribution. Thus, the data appear to have a linear and homoscedastic relationship. This conclusion also applies to the residuals.

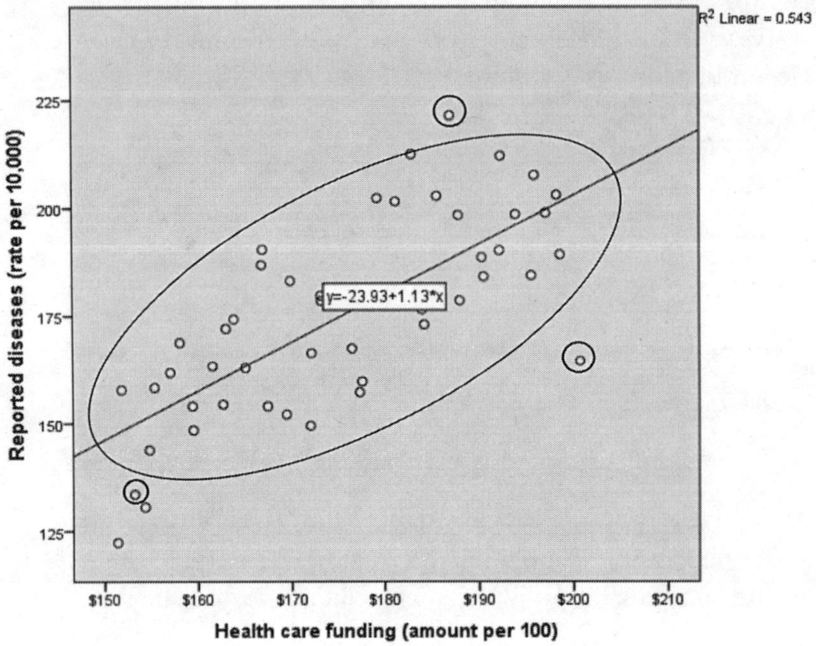

The scatter plot reveals four apparent outliers that would be removed using one of the techniques covered in Chapter 12, which is suggested prior to conducting further analysis. We will focus on the additional analysis.

The ANOVA and model summary tables comprise the overall SLR goodness of fit statistic. It is how well the prediction line fits the data. The line is calculated in order to minimize the distances of points not on the line. In this case, the SLR model is significant because $p < .001$.

ANOVA[a]

Model		Sum of Squares	df	Mean Square	F	Sig.
1	Regression	13308.743	1	13308.743	57.092	.000[b]
	Residual	11189.236	48	233.109		
	Total	24497.979	49			

a. Dependent Variable: Reported diseases (rate per 10,000)

b. Predictors: (Constant), Health care funding (amount per 100)

The *r*-square is the percentage of change in the outcome variable accounted for in the predictor. In this instance, healthcare funding is responsible for 54.3% of the variance in reported diseases.

Model Summary[b]

Model	R	R Square	Adjusted R Square	Std. Error of the Estimate
1	.737[a]	.543	.534	15.268

a. Predictors: (Constant), Health care funding (amount per 100)

b. Dependent Variable: Reported diseases (rate per 10,000)

The coefficients table represents the specific linear influence of the predictor on the outcome. For every dollar spent on healthcare funding per 100 people, there is an incremental increase in reported cases of disease of 1.134 per 100,000 people. At first, one might think that spending more on healthcare increases the incidence of disease. However, with more healthcare funding, there is the likelihood that more people will seek healthcare. This, in turn, results in an increase in the reporting of treatment and incidences of disease that likely would not have been recorded had there not been an increase in healthcare services provided.

The last two columns are the lower and upper bounds of the 95% confidence interval for the data. Thus, we are 95% confident that reported cases of diseases will increase somewhere between .832 and 1.436 per 100,000 people for every healthcare funding dollar spent per 100 people.

Coefficients[a]

Model		Unstandardized Coefficients B	Unstandardized Coefficients Std. Error	Standardized Coefficients Beta	t	Sig.	95.0% Confidence Interval for B Lower Bound	95.0% Confidence Interval for B Upper Bound
1	(Constant)	-23.926	26.438		-.905	.370	-77.083	29.232
	Health care funding (amount per 100)	1.134	.150	.737	7.556	.000	.832	1.436

a. Dependent Variable: Reported diseases (rate per 10,000)

Write-up: A single linear regression was conducted on data collected from the 50 largest designated market areas in the United States in order to determine whether healthcare funding per 100 people predicts reported cases of diseases per 10,000 people. A statistically meaningful regression equation was found ($F(1,48) = 57.092$, $p < .001$), with an R^2 of .543 indicating that 54.3% of the change in reported diseases can be explained by the change in healthcare funding. The number of reported diseases was –23.926 + 1.134 (healthcare funding) when healthcare was measured in one dollar spent per 100 people. The average reported number of reported cases of disease per 100,000 people is likely to increase by 1.134 for each dollar increase in healthcare funding.

22.21 A marketing research firm was charged to determine the predictability of advertising expenditures on sales in the home healthcare field. Two hundred and sixty-five members of a national trade association agreed to have their data released to the research firm. To what extent does advertising predict sales? Explain your answer. Report results in the format provided in this book. Alpha = .05. The name of the data file for this example is "SLR Exercise 3 Data."

Answer: Both advertising ($p = .667$) and sales ($p = .887$) meet the normality assumption based on the Shapiro-Wilk statistic. They are each greater than alpha, which is .05.

Tests of Normality

	Kolmogorov-Smirnov[a] Statistic	Kolmogorov-Smirnov[a] df	Kolmogorov-Smirnov[a] Sig.	Shapiro-Wilk Statistic	Shapiro-Wilk df	Shapiro-Wilk Sig.
Advertising	.036	265	.200*	.996	265	.667
Sales	.032	265	.200*	.997	265	.887

*. This is a lower bound of the true significance.

a. Lilliefors Significance Correction

The bivariate distribution does not appear linear ($r^2 = .002$) or homoscedastic (oval-shaped distribution along the line).

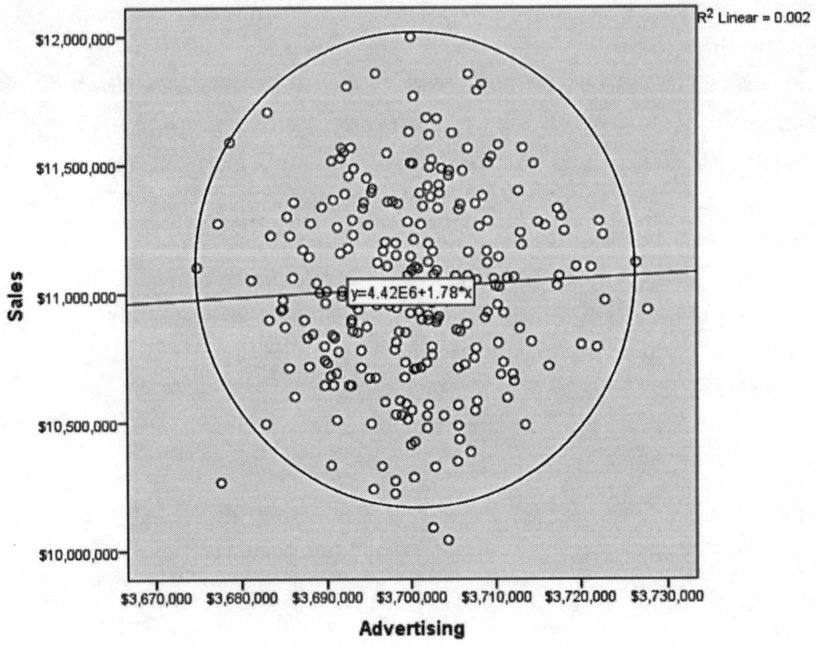

As suspected, because of the scatter plot, there is likely no relationship between advertising and sales because the overall *p*-value is not significant ($p = .456$). No further analysis is required.

ANOVA[a]

Model		Sum of Squares	df	Mean Square	F	Sig.
1	Regression	7.363E+10	1	7.363E+10	.557	.456[b]
	Residual	3.475E+13	263	1.321E+11		
	Total	3.483E+13	264			

a. Dependent Variable: Sales

b. Predictors: (Constant), Advertising

Write-up: A single linear regression was conducted on data collected from 265 companies in order to determine if dollars spent annually on advertising predict annual sales. No relationship was found between these two variables ($F(1,263) = .557$, $p = .456$). It is likely that advertising spending does not impact sales.

22.22 A company wishes to determine whether 265 employees' perceptions of their sense of control at work predicts how much time they spend going online at work for personal reasons. Control was measured using a self-determination theory instrument (perceived autonomy survey) and the online behavior data was providing by the IT department, which linked non-work activity to user by login credentials. Online activities were measured in hours per week. Control was self-reported using an online sliding bar scale ranging from 1 = "I have no control over what I do at work" to 7 = "I control all of what I do at work." Does a sense of control over one's work predict amount of online activities for personal use at work? Explain your answer. Report results in the format provided in this book. Alpha = .05. The name of the data file for this example is "SLR Exercise 4 Data."

Answer: According to the Shapiro-Wilk statistic, the control (p = .917) and hours online (p = .833) variables approximate the normal distribution.

Tests of Normality

	Kolmogorov-Smirnov[a]			Shapiro-Wilk		
	Statistic	df	Sig.	Statistic	df	Sig.
Control	.033	265	.200*	.997	265	.917
Hours_Online	.038	265	.200*	.997	265	.833

*. This is a lower bound of the true significance.

a. Lilliefors Significance Correction

Although demonstrating homoscedasticity in the oval-like distribution, the brivariate distribution indicates a weak negative linear relationship (r^2 = .057). There are a few outliers that should be removed (see Chapter 12). These results suggest that the normality, linear, and homoscedasticity requirements have been met for the variables and their residuals.

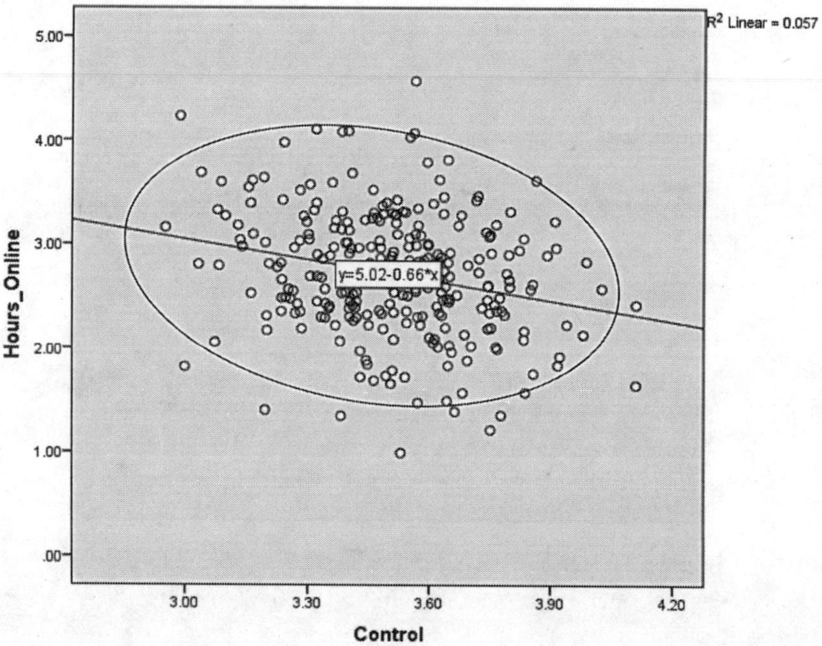

The ANOVA and model summary tables comprise the overall SLR goodness of fit statistic. It is how well the prediction line fits the data. The line is calculated in order to minimize the distances of points from the line. In this case, the SLR model is significant because $p < .001$.

ANOVA[a]

Model		Sum of Squares	df	Mean Square	F	Sig.
1	Regression	5.342	1	5.342	15.884	.000[b]
	Residual	88.450	263	.336		
	Total	93.793	264			

a. Dependent Variable: Hours_Online

b. Predictors: (Constant), Control

The R-square is the percentage of change in the outcome variable accounted for in the predictor. In this instance, a sense of control is responsible for only 5.7% of the variance in online activity for personal reasons at work. This is weak but significant explained variance.

Model Summary

Model	R	R Square	Adjusted R Square	Std. Error of the Estimate
1	.239[a]	.057	.053	.57993

a. Predictors: (Constant), Control

The coefficients table represents the specific linear influence of the predictor on the outcome. In this case, for every one point out of seven increase sense of control, there is an incremental decrease of .657 of an hour in personal Web surfing at work per week.

The last two columns are the lower and upper bounds of the 95% confidence interval for the data. Thus, we are 95% confident that amount of Web surfing for personal reasons at work will decrease somewhere between .332 and .981 hours per week for each 1 point increase in reported control.

Coefficients[a]

Model		Unstandardized Coefficients		Standardized Coefficients	t	Sig.	95.0% Confidence Interval for B	
		B	Std. Error	Beta			Lower Bound	Upper Bound
1	(Constant)	5.018	.580		8.655	.000	3.876	6.159
	Control	-.657	.165	-.239	-3.986	.000	-.981	-.332

a. Dependent Variable: Hours_Online

Write-up: A single linear regression was conducted on data collected from 265 employees of a company that wished to determine whether a sense of control at work predicts the amount of time employees spend at the company surfing the Web for personal reasons. A statistically meaningful regression equation was found ($F(1,263) = 15.884$, $p < .001$), with an R^2 of .057 indicating that 5.7% of the change in work activity can be explained by a sense of control at work. The amount of time measured in hours per week was 5.018 – .657 (control). The true population average reported hours per week spent Web surfing is likely to decrease by .657 hours for each point of perceived control.

B.23 Chapter 23

23.1 Generally, what is multiple linear regression (MLR)?

Answer: MLR extends SLR to more than one predictor variable. MLR estimates the value or variation in the outcome variable from two or more predictors together ($X_1 + Xk$). Often MLR allows us to explain more variation in the outcome variable because we incorporate more than one predictor, thus providing more information.

23.2 What is the basic idea behind the least squares method in regression?

Answer: This is an approach to regression that minimizes the amount of error in the line of best fit.

23.3 What is the coefficient of multiple determination?

Answer: This is the *R*-square (R^2) for MLR. It is the percentage of variation in the outcome variable explained by the set of predictors in the model.

23.4 Define adjusted *R*-square (R^2_{adj}).

Answer: This statistic accounts for the contribution of each predictor and sample size when calculating the *r*-square.

23.5 What is the basic idea behind standard or simultaneous linear regression?

Answer: This is MLR where all predictor variables are run at once.

23.6 An automobile consulting firm wishes to determine whether a luxury car's external appearance, price, advertised safety features, and miles per gallon (MPG) will influence the consumers' likelihood of buying such a vehicle in the future. Previous research suggests such a relationship. The study will examine the European luxury car market. The survey items were formatted in a 0–7 scale where consumers dragged a bar across increments of the scale. Seven hundred and fifty consumers participated in the mobile phone survey. Report your findings in the format provided in this book. Alpha = .05. Data file name: "MLR Exercise 1 Data."

Answer: The Shapiro-Wilk normality statistic indicates that all of the variables do not violate the normal distribution assumption because they are all greater than .05.

Tests of Normality

	Kolmogorov-Smirnov[a]			Shapiro-Wilk		
	Statistic	df	Sig.	Statistic	df	Sig.
LikelyBuy	.025	750	.200*	.999	750	.875
Look	.019	750	.200*	.997	750	.163
Price	.020	750	.200*	.999	750	.896
Safety	.021	750	.200*	.999	750	.938
MPG	.031	750	.085	.998	750	.371

*. This is a lower bound of the true significance.

a. Lilliefors Significance Correction

The following bivariate scatter plots do not depict linearity and homoscedasticity. The *r*-square statistics, which are virtually nonexistent, support nonlinearity and the distributions do not display oval shapes, but are circular. There are a number of outliers.

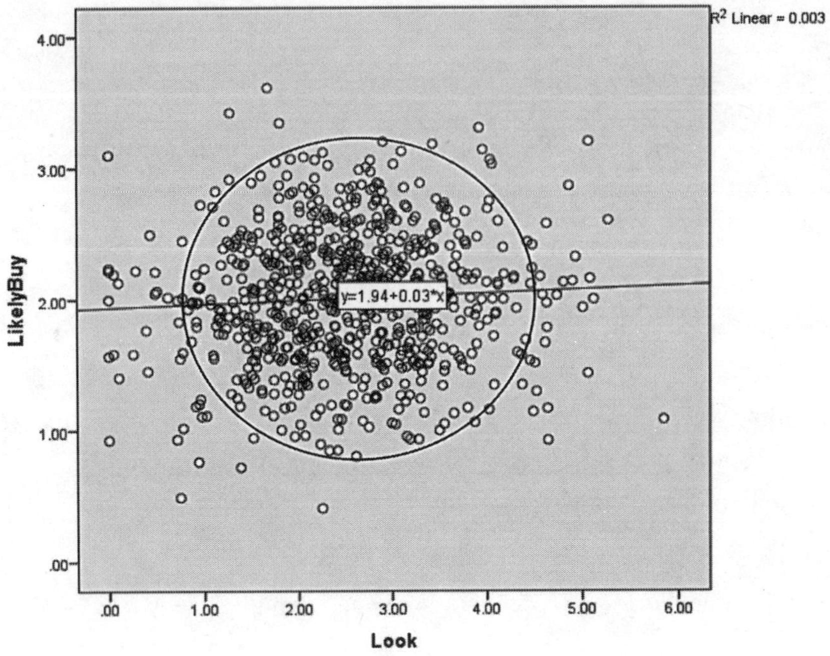
R² Linear = 0.003
4.00
3.00
2.00
1.00
.00
LikelyBuy
y=1.94+0.03*x
.00
1.00
2.00
3.00
4.00
5.00
6.00
Look

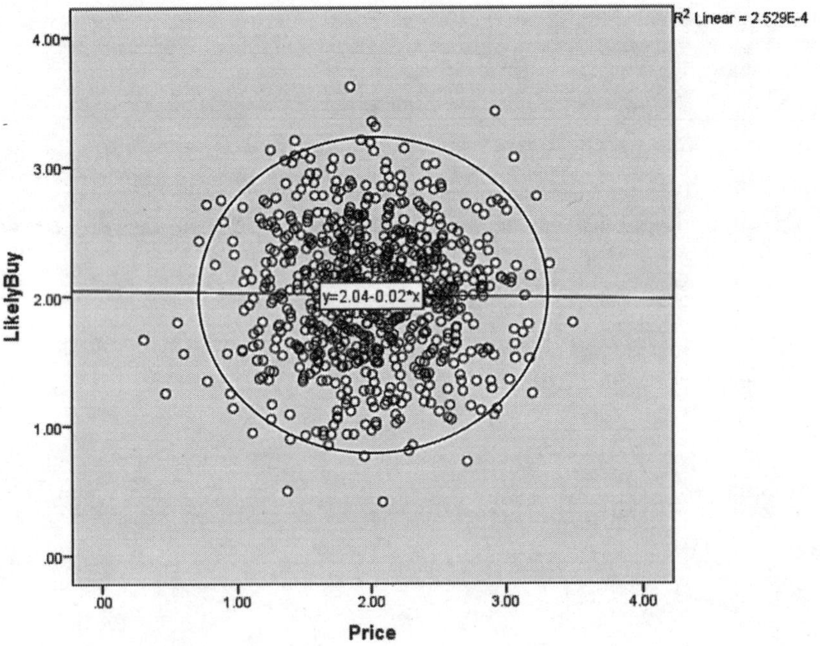
R² Linear = 2.529E-4
4.00
3.00
2.00
1.00
.00
LikelyBuy
y=2.04-0.02*x
.00
1.00
2.00
3.00
4.00
Price

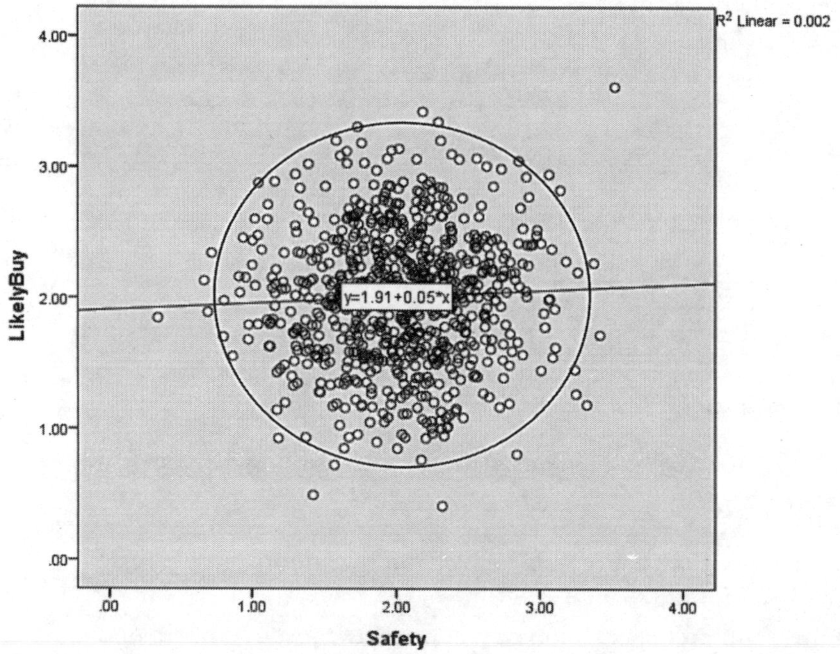
R² Linear = 0.002
y=1.91+0.05*x
LikelyBuy
Safety
.00
1.00
2.00
3.00
4.00

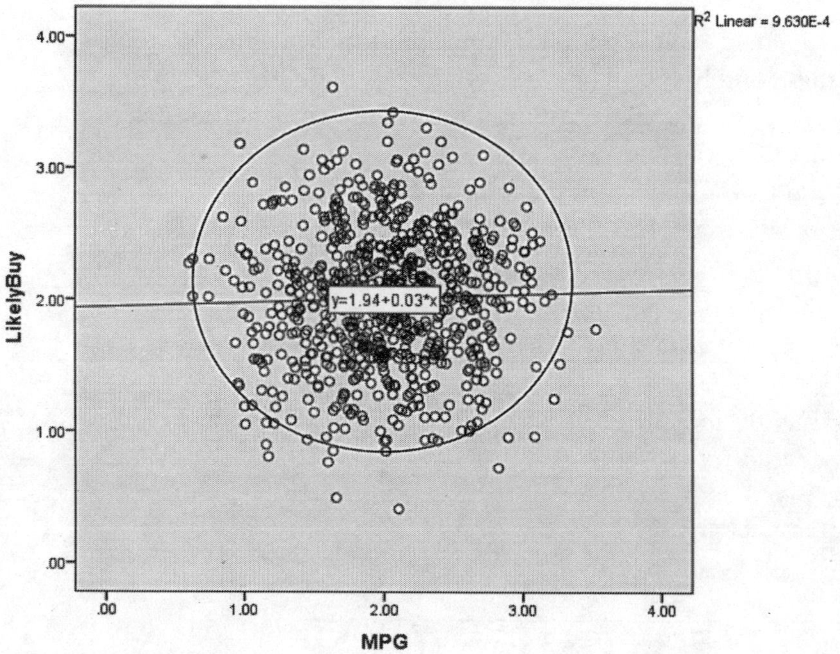
R² Linear = 9.630E-4
y=1.94+0.03*x
LikelyBuy
MPG
.00
1.00
2.00
3.00
4.00

The overall regression is not meaningful because $p = .276 > .05$, indicating an unacceptable level of risk or chance occurrence higher than what is acceptable. Therefore, it is likely that the independent variables do not predict intention to purchase a vehicle.

ANOVA[a]

Model		Sum of Squares	df	Mean Square	F	Sig.
1	Regression	1.341	4	.335	1.281	.276[b]
	Residual	194.997	745	.262		
	Total	196.338	749			

a. Dependent Variable: LikelyBuy

b. Predictors: (Constant), MPG, Look, Price, Safety

We stop here because the model indicates that there is no relationship between the predictors and the outcome variable.

Write-up: A standard multiple linear regression was conducted on mobile phone survey data collected from 750 European luxury car consumers in order to determine whether external car design, price, advertised safety features, and miles per gallon of fuel predicts consumer likelihood to buy a car. No relationships were found ($F(4,745) = 1.281$, $p = .276$). It is likely that these considerations do not predict car purchases.

23.7 For the month of January, a random sample of 250 customer records and corresponding surveys were used to determine the monthly cell phone bill, years with the current telephone company, percentage of telephone used for business, and household income. The researchers were charged with exploring whether these variables predict monthly cell phone sales as measured by the monthly cell phone bill. Report your findings in the format provided in this book. Alpha = .05. The name of the data file for this example is "MLR Exercise 2 Data."

Answer: The analysis requires four numeric variables. The monthly cell phone bill is measured in dollars. Length with the current telephone company is measured in years. The proportion of phone usage devoted to business activities is measured as a percentage. Household income is measured in dollars.

The Shapiro-Wilk normality statistic indicates that all of the variables do not violate the normal distribution assumption because they are all greater than .05.

Tests of Normality

	Kolmogorov-Smirnov[a]			Shapiro-Wilk		
	Statistic	df	Sig.	Statistic	df	Sig.
Monthly Cell Phone Bill	.037	250	.200*	.995	250	.673
Years using our service	.034	250	.200*	.997	250	.916
Percentage used for business	.031	250	.200*	.995	250	.635
Household income	.043	250	.200*	.996	250	.791

*. This is a lower bound of the true significance.

a. Lilliefors Significance Correction

The following bivariate scatter plots depict approximate bivariate normality, linearity, and homoscedasticity. The data are concentrated near the center of the line, r-square statistics are small (which indicates weak linearity), and the distributions display oval-like shapes. There are a number of outliers.

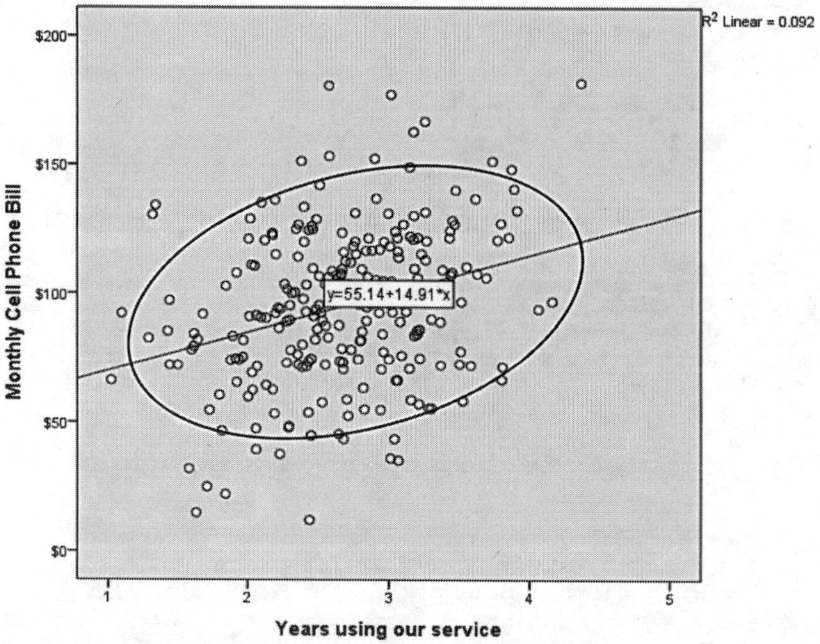
$200
$150
$100
$50
$0
Monthly Cell Phone Bill
1
2
3
4
5
Years using our service
R² Linear = 0.092
y=55.14+14.91*x

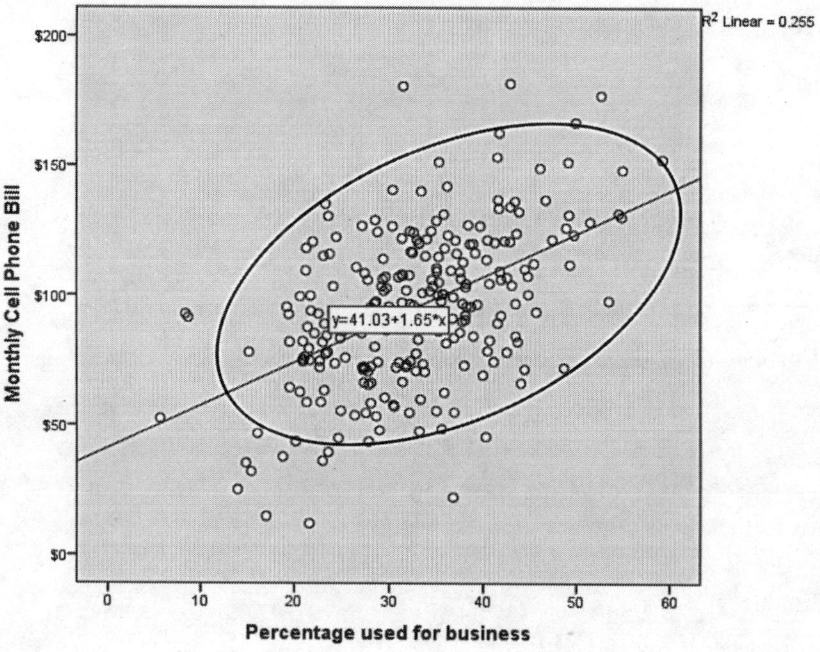
$200
$150
$100
$50
$0
Monthly Cell Phone Bill
0
10
20
30
40
50
60
Percentage used for business
R² Linear = 0.255
y=41.03+1.65*x

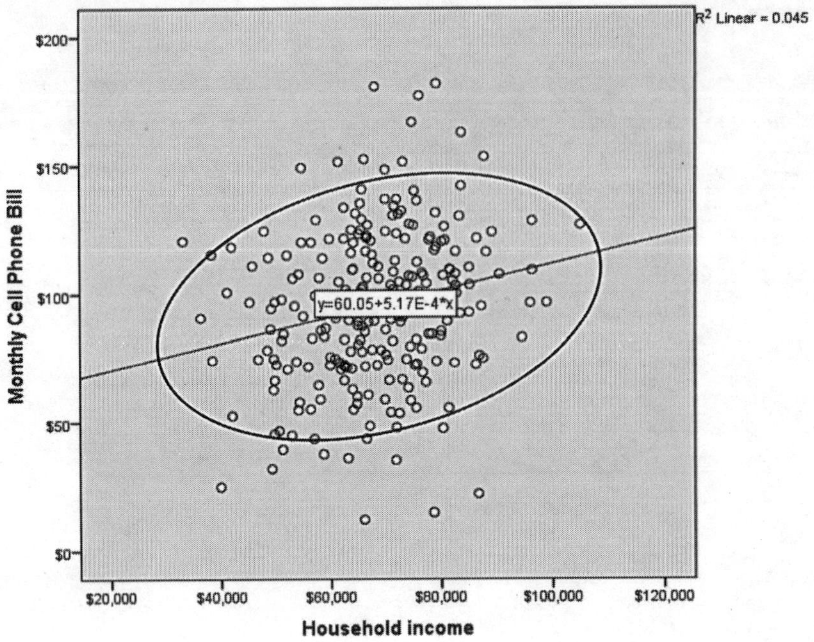

The overall regression is significant because $p < .001$, which is less than .05. The probability of achieving these results by chance is very low, indicating an acceptable level of risk. Therefore, it is likely that at least one of the independent variables predicts monthly cell phone usage.

ANOVA[a]

Model		Sum of Squares	df	Mean Square	F	Sig.
1	Regression	62380.805	3	20793.602	32.528	.000[b]
	Residual	157255.393	246	639.250		
	Total	219636.198	249			

a. Dependent Variable: Monthly Cell Phone Bill

b. Predictors: (Constant), Household income, Percentage used for business, Years using our service

The predictor(s) explain 28.4% of the variation in monthly cell phone use. There is approximately a 1% difference between the *r*-square and adjusted *r*-square.

Model Summary

Model	R	R Square	Adjusted R Square	Std. Error of the Estimate
1	.533[a]	.284	.275	$25.283

a. Predictors: (Constant), Household income, Percentage used for business, Years using our service

Years using the company and percentage used for business are significant regression coefficients (predictors), which is not the case for household income. Each year using the company adds $7.31 to the monthly cell phone bill and for each percentage of usage for business adds

$1.44 to the bill. Again, household income played no role, which probably contributed to the adjusted *r*-square value.

Coefficients[a]

Model		Unstandardized Coefficients		Standardized Coefficients			95.0% Confidence Interval for B	
		B	Std. Error	Beta	t	Sig.	Lower Bound	Upper Bound
1	(Constant)	15.884	10.681		1.487	.138	-5.153	36.922
	Years using our service	7.315	2.837	.149	2.578	.011	1.727	12.903
	Percentage used for business	1.447	.189	.442	7.671	.000	1.075	1.818
	Household income	.000	.000	.075	1.328	.185	.000	.000

a. Dependent Variable: Monthly Cell Phone Bill

The MLR was run again without household income. The overall test was significant ($p < .001$).

ANOVA[a]

Model		Sum of Squares	df	Mean Square	F	Sig.
1	Regression	61253.449	2	30626.724	47.763	.000[b]
	Residual	158382.749	247	641.226		
	Total	219636.198	249			

a. Dependent Variable: Monthly Cell Phone Bill

b. Predictors: (Constant), Percentage used for business, Years using our service

The predictor(s) explain 27.9% of the variation in monthly cell phone use. Notice that the adjusted *r*-square is now closer to the *r*-square.

Model Summary

Model	R	R Square	Adjusted R Square	Std. Error of the Estimate
1	.528[a]	.279	.273	$25.322

a. Predictors: (Constant), Percentage used for business, Years using our service

Each year using the company adds $8.00 to the monthly cell phone bill and for each percentage of usage for business adds $1.48 to the bill. The later model is more accurate and more informative.

Coefficients[a]

Model		Unstandardized Coefficients		Standardized Coefficients			95.0% Confidence Interval for B	
		B	Std. Error	Beta	t	Sig.	Lower Bound	Upper Bound
1	(Constant)	24.972	8.213		3.040	.003	8.795	41.149
	Years using our service	8.003	2.793	.163	2.865	.005	2.501	13.505
	Percentage used for business	1.489	.186	.455	8.002	.000	1.123	1.856

a. Dependent Variable: Monthly Cell Phone Bill

Write-up: A standard multiple linear regression was conducted on data collected from 250 customer records and corresponding surveys to determine whether the monthly cell phone bill can be estimated from customer years with the current telephone company, percentage of telephone used for business, and household income. A statistically meaningful regression equation was found ($F(2,247) = 47.763$, $p < .001$), with an R^2 of .279 indicating that 27.9% of the variation in the monthly cell phone bill is predicted by years with the current telephone company and percentage of telephone used for business. Household income has no effect. Predicted monthly cell phone bill was \$24.97 + \$8.00 (years with cell phone company) + \$1.48 (percentage of phone used for business). It is likely that the monthly cell phone bill increases, on average, \$8.00 for each year of service with the current provider and \$1.48 for each percentage of the phone used for business.

23.8 An online survey was completed by 265 consumers concerning their reported consumer feelings, thoughts, and behaviors. The exploratory study's goal was to determine if impulse buying is predicted by seeing an ad for a product on TV, retailer set discounts for the product, pre-purchase guilt for the product, and feeling sad before going shopping. Report your findings in the format provided in this book. Alpha = .05. The name of the data file for this example is "MLR Exercise 3 Data."

Answer: The analysis requires five numeric variables anchored in a scale ranging from 0 to 7 where respondents drag a bar to the desired response for impulse buying, seeing the product on TV commercials, pre-purchase guilt, in-store ads indicating that the product is on sale, and pre-purchase feelings of sadness. Zero indicates no presence of the variable being measured and 7 indicates a substantial presence of the variable.

The Shapiro-Wilk normality statistic indicates that all of the variables do not violate the normal distribution assumption because they are all greater than .05.

Tests of Normality

	Kolmogorov-Smirnov[a]			Shapiro-Wilk		
	Statistic	df	Sig.	Statistic	df	Sig.
Impulse_Buying	.038	265	.200*	.996	265	.639
Discount_Price	.063	265	.013	.995	265	.548
Prepurchase_Guilt	.040	265	.200*	.994	265	.426
Pre_Buy_Sadness	.042	265	.200*	.996	265	.677
See_TVad	.030	265	.200*	.996	265	.790

*. This is a lower bound of the true significance.

a. Lilliefors Significance Correction

The following bivariate scatter plots depict the degree of normality, linearity, and homoscedasticity. Only "See TVad" and "Prepurchase Sadness" do not violate the three assumptions. For these two variables, the distributions are concentrated near the center of the line, *r*-square statistics support the linear patterns, and the distributions display oval-like shapes. There are a number of outliers.

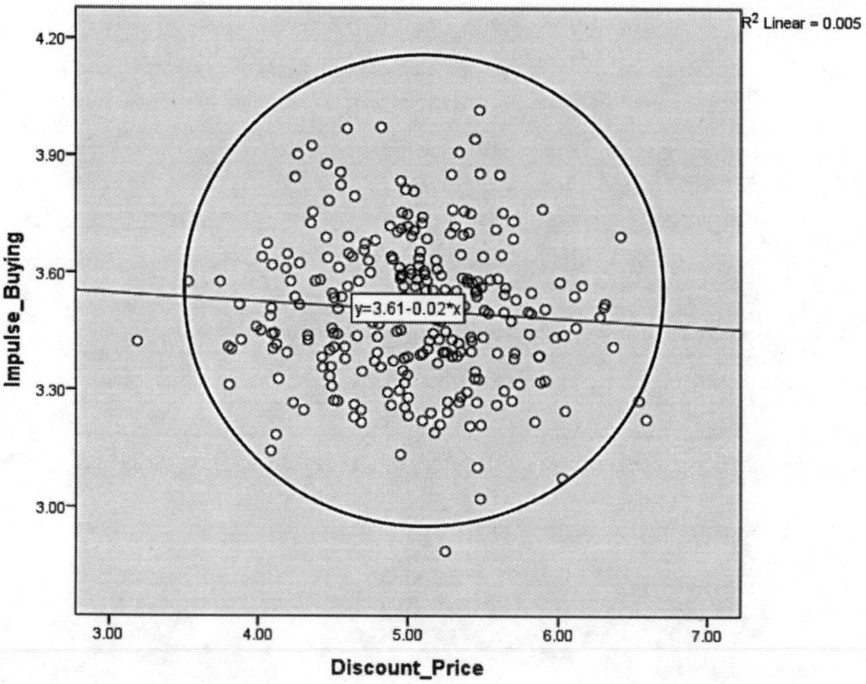
R^2 Linear = 0.005
4.20
3.90
3.60
3.30
3.00
Impulse_Buying
y=3.61-0.02*x
3.00
4.00
5.00
6.00
7.00
Discount_Price

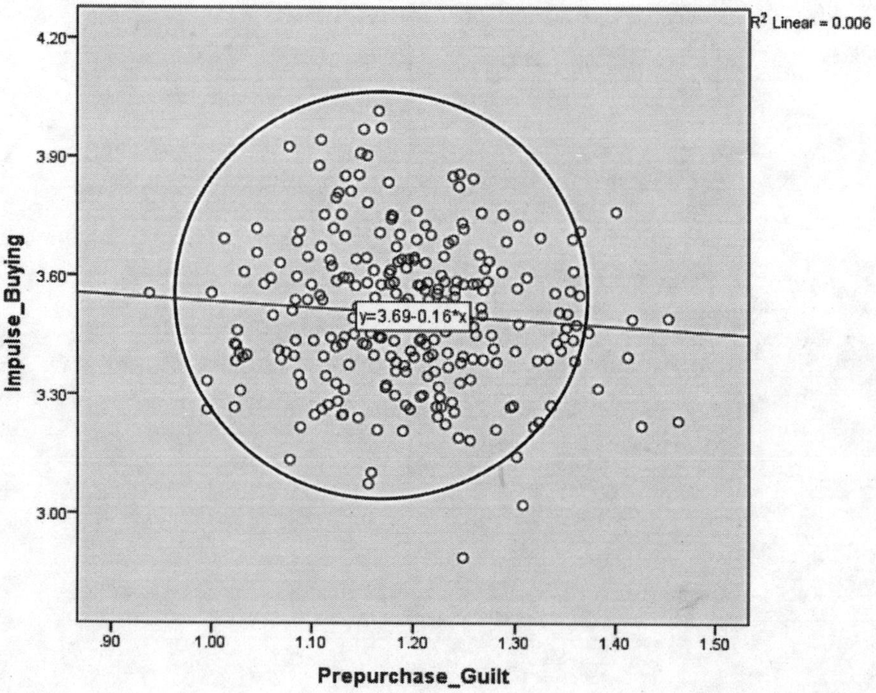
R^2 Linear = 0.006
4.20
3.90
3.60
3.30
3.00
Impulse_Buying
y=3.69-0.16*x
.90
1.00
1.10
1.20
1.30
1.40
1.50
Prepurchase_Guilt

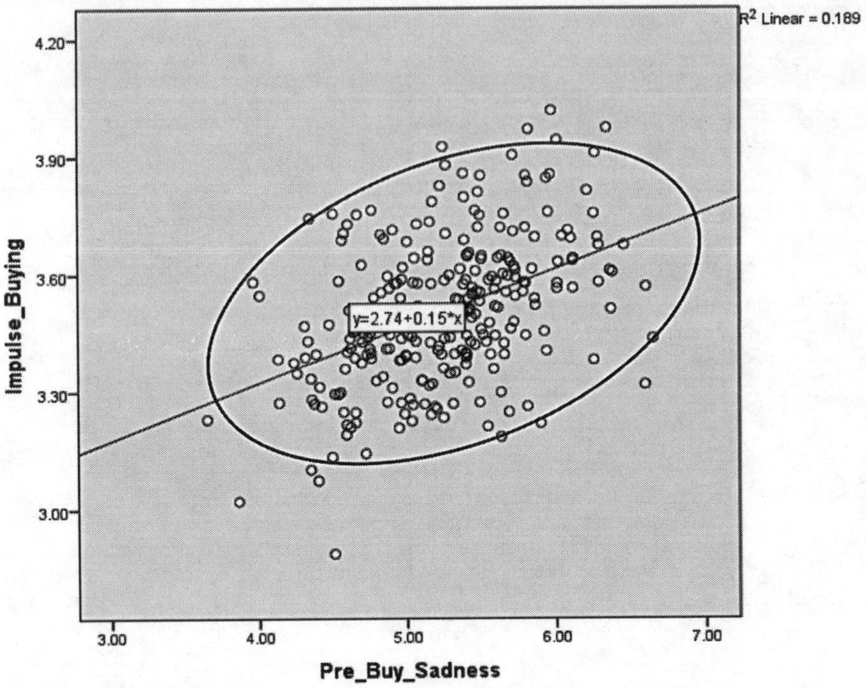
R2 Linear = 0.189
4.20
3.90
3.60
3.30
3.00
Impulse_Buying
y=2.74+0.15*x
3.00
4.00
5.00
6.00
7.00
Pre_Buy_Sadness

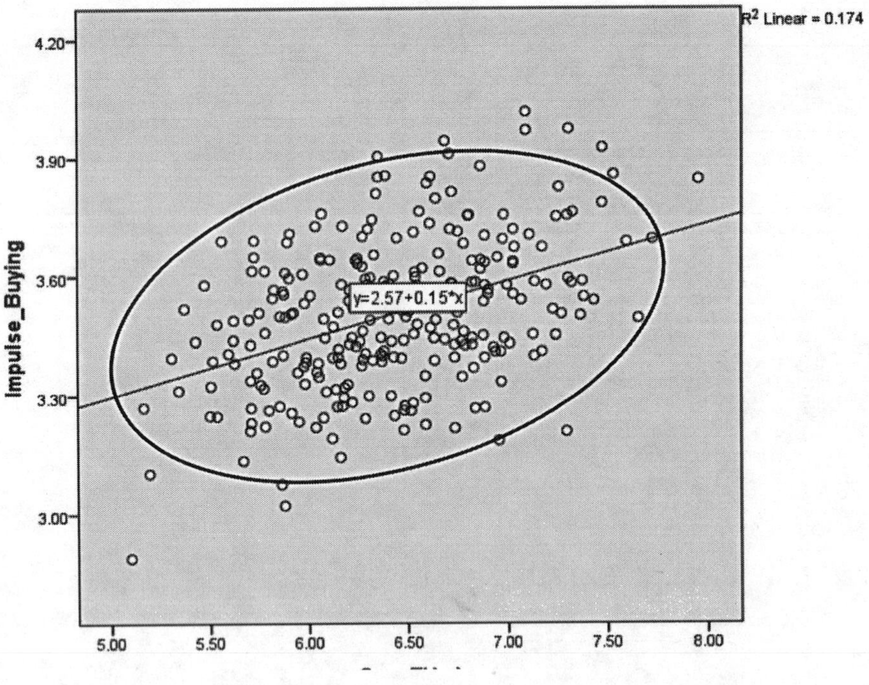
R2 Linear = 0.174
4.20
3.90
3.60
3.30
3.00
Impulse_Buying
y=2.57+0.15*x
5.00
5.50
6.00
6.50
7.00
7.50
8.00

Since "See TVad" and "Prepurchase Sadness" met the assumptions, the analysis was run with those two predictors. The model was significant because $p < .001$.

ANOVA[a]

Model		Sum of Squares	df	Mean Square	F	Sig.
1	Regression	2.862	2	1.431	59.138	.000[b]
	Residual	6.340	262	.024		
	Total	9.201	264			

a. Dependent Variable: Impulse_Buying

b. Predictors: (Constant), See_TVad, Pre_Buy_Sadness

"See TVad" and "Prepurchase Sadness" explain 31.1% of the variation in impulse buying.

Model Summary

Model	R	R Square	Adjusted R Square	Std. Error of the Estimate
1	.558[a]	.311	.306	.15555

a. Predictors: (Constant), See_TVad, Pre_Buy_Sadness

Both predictors were significant at $p > 001$. For each 1 out of 7 points reported for prepurchase sadness, reported impulsive buying increased by .126 and for those who reported seeing TV ads for a products, reported impulse buying increased by .123.

Coefficients[a]

Model		Unstandardized Coefficients		Standardized Coefficients	t	Sig.	95.0% Confidence Interval for B	
		B	Std. Error	Beta			Lower Bound	Upper Bound
1	(Constant)	2.049	.136		15.075	.000	1.782	2.317
	Pre_Buy_Sadness	.126	.017	.375	7.218	.000	.092	.161
	See_TVad	.123	.018	.354	6.815	.000	.088	.159

a. Dependent Variable: Impulse_Buying

Write-up: A standard multiple linear regression was conducted on data collected from 265 consumer surveys to determine whether impulse buying can be estimated from product ads viewed on TV, discounted prices, degree of prepurchase guilt, and prepurchase sadness. A statistically meaningful regression equation was found ($F(2,262) = 59.138$, $p < .001$), with an R^2 of .331, indicating that 33.1% of the variation in impulse buying is predicted by seeing product ads on TV and prepurchase feelings of sadness. The other variables had no effect. Predicted monthly cell phone bill was 2.04 + .126 (Prepurchase Sadness) + .123 (Seen in TV Ad). It is likely that reported impulse buying increases, on average, .126 for each reported 1.00 point in prepurchase sadness and increases .123 for each reported 1.00 point in seeing product ads on TV.

23.9 A random sample of 99 anonymous and random store sales transactions were collected in order to determine whether the dollar amount spent on CD purchases and/or the dollar amount of book purchases predicts special offer sales (promotional products). Report your findings in the format provided in this book. Alpha = .05. The name of the data file for this example is "MLR Exercise 4 Data."

Answer: The analysis requires three numeric variables recorded in dollars: reported CD purchases, book purchases, and special offer sales. The Shapiro-Wilk normality statistics indicate that all of the variables do not violate the normal distribution assumption because they are all greater than .05.

Tests of Normality

	Kolmogorov-Smirnov[a]			Shapiro-Wilk		
	Statistic	df	Sig.	Statistic	df	Sig.
Special offer purchases	.063	99	.200*	.988	99	.493
CD purchases	.072	99	.200*	.982	99	.180
Book purchases	.058	99	.200*	.993	99	.881

*. This is a lower bound of the true significance.

a. Lilliefors Significance Correction

"CD Purchases" and "Book Purchases" do not violate the bivariate normality, linearity, and homoscedasticity assumptions. For these two variables, the distributions are concentrated near the center of the line, *r*-square statistics support the linear patterns, and the distributions display oval-like shapes.

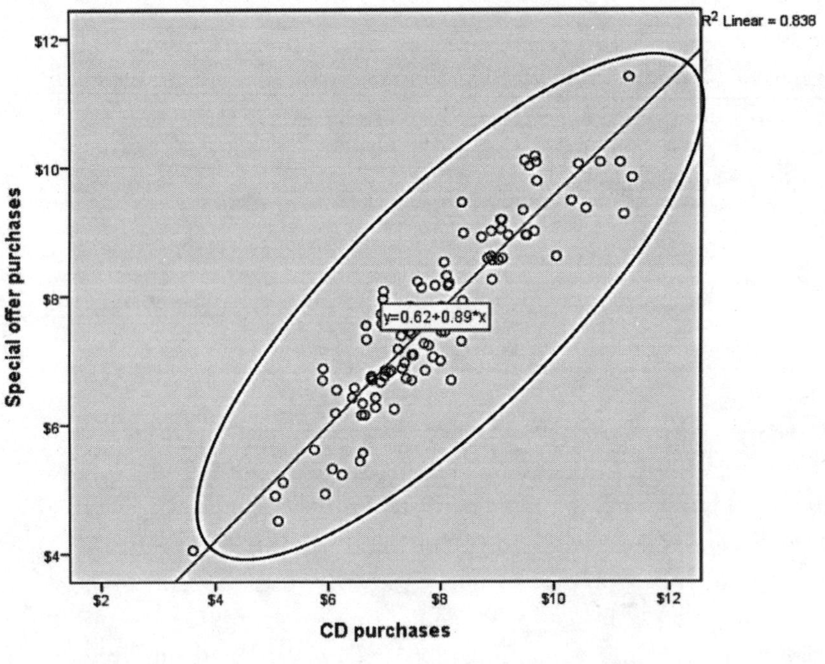

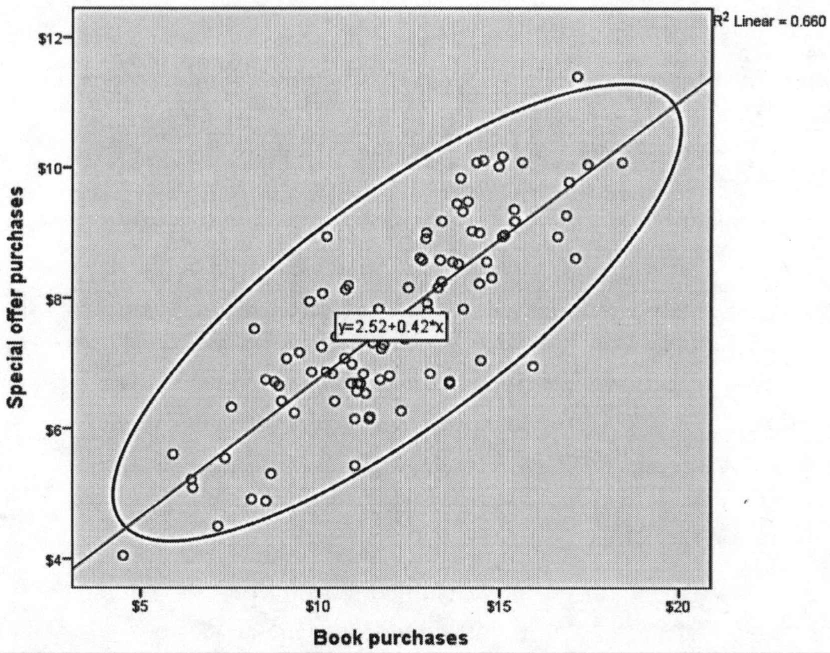

The model is significant because $p < .001$. This suggests special offer sales are explained by the variation or amount of CD and book purchases because the probably of having such results by chance are very low (less than 1/1,000).

ANOVA[a]

Model		Sum of Squares	df	Mean Square	F	Sig.
1	Regression	179.333	2	89.666	290.870	.000[b]
	Residual	29.594	96	.308		
	Total	208.926	98			

a. Dependent Variable: Special offer purchases

b. Predictors: (Constant), Book purchases, CD purchases

CD and book purchases explain 85.8% of the variation in special offer sales.

Model Summary

Model	R	R Square	Adjusted R Square	Std. Error of the Estimate
1	.926[a]	.858	.855	$0.555

a. Predictors: (Constant), Book purchases, CD purchases

As expected, both predictors are significant at $p < .001$. On average, every dollar spent on CDs generates 71.2¢ in special offer purchases and every dollar spent on books results in an average sale of 12.2¢ for special offer items.

Coefficients[a]

Model		Unstandardized Coefficients B	Std. Error	Standardized Coefficients Beta	t	Sig.	95.0% Confidence Interval for B Lower Bound	Upper Bound
1	(Constant)	.568	.301		1.889	.062	-.029	1.164
	CD purchases	.712	.061	.730	11.602	.000	.590	.833
	Book purchases	.122	.033	.234	3.712	.000	.057	.188

a. Dependent Variable: Special offer purchases

Write-up: A standard multiple linear regression was conducted on data collected from 99 sales transactions in order to determine if gift purchases and book purchases predict sales of special offered products. A statistically meaningful regression equation was found ($F(2,96) = 290.870$, $p < .001$), with an R^2 of .858, indicating that 85.8% of the variation in special offer sales can be predicted by CD and book sales. Predicted special offer sales was 56.8¢ + 71.2¢ (gift purchases) + 12.2¢ (book purchases). It is likely that the average special offer sale increases 71.2¢ for each dollar spent on CDs and increases 12.2¢ for each dollar spent on books.

23.10 A researcher wished to examine whether age (in years), years of education from 9th grade on (in completed years), and life satisfaction score (1 = "not satisfied with my life at all" to 5 = "totally satisfied with my life") predict thoughts (1 = " I will never go to jail again" to 5 = "I'll definitely go to jail again") about being re-incarcerated again in adult men who were previously incarcerated at least twice for nonviolent offenses. The sample consisted of 478 adult men ages 25 to 50. Report your findings in the format provided in this book. Alpha = .05. The name of the data file for this example is "MLR Exercise 5 Data."

Answer: The Shapiro-Wilk normality statistic indicates that all of the variables do not violate the normal distribution assumption because they are all greater than .05.

Tests of Normality

	Kolmogorov-Smirnov[a] Statistic	df	Sig.	Shapiro-Wilk Statistic	df	Sig.
Education	.026	478	.200*	.996	478	.300
Life_Satisfaction	.034	478	.200*	.996	478	.372
Reincarceration	.033	478	.200*	.998	478	.931

*. This is a lower bound of the true significance.

a. Lilliefors Significance Correction

The following bivariate scatter plots do not depict linearity and homoscedasticity. The *r*-square statistics, which are virtually nonexistent, support nonlinearity and the distributions do not display oval shapes, but are circular. There are a number of outliers.

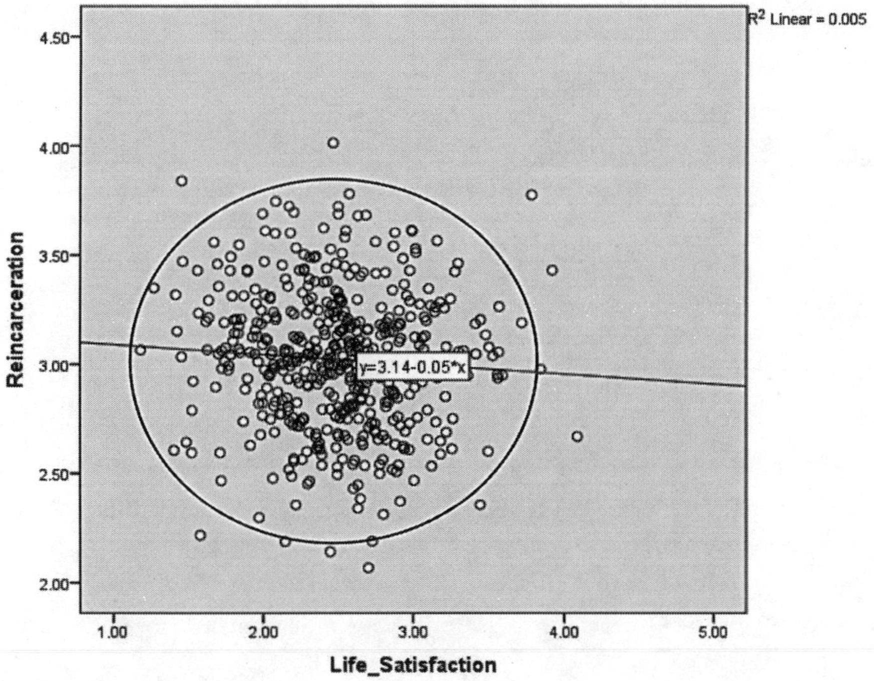
R² Linear = 0.005
4.50
4.00
3.50
3.00
2.50
2.00
Reincarceration
y=3.14-0.05*x
1.00
2.00
3.00
4.00
5.00
Life_Satisfaction

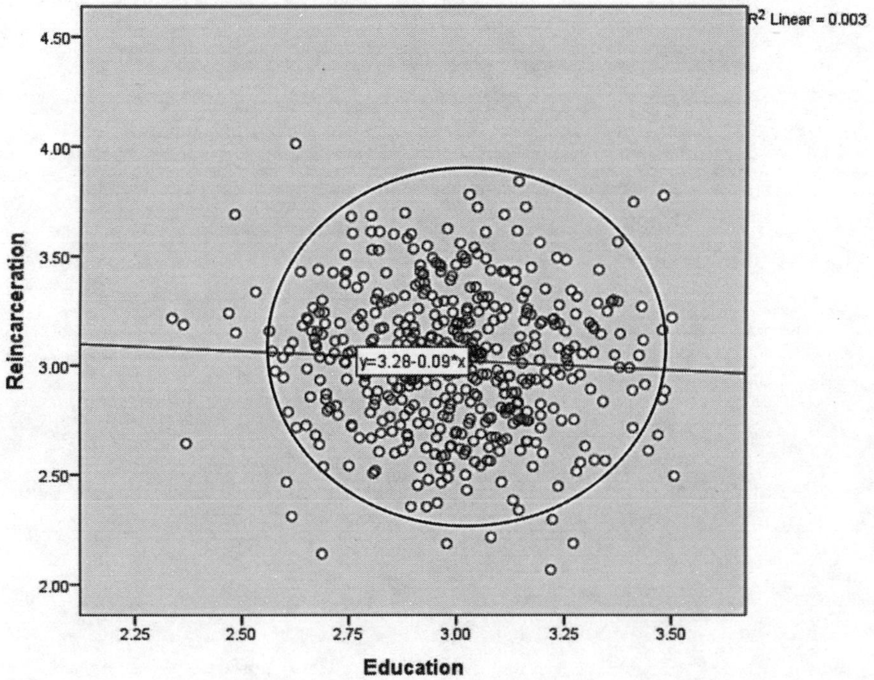
R² Linear = 0.003
4.50
4.00
3.50
3.00
2.50
2.00
Reincarceration
y=3.28-0.09*x
2.25
2.50
2.75
3.00
3.25
3.50
Education

We will consult the overall ANOVA results because it contains information required for reporting.

ANOVA[a]

Model		Sum of Squares	df	Mean Square	F	Sig.
1	Regression	.348	2	.174	1.739	.177[b]
	Residual	47.573	475	.100		
	Total	47.921	477			

a. Dependent Variable: Reincarceration

b. Predictors: (Constant), Life_Satisfaction, Education

Write-up: A standard multiple linear regression was conducted on self-reported data from 478 recidivists. Years of education and feelings of life satisfaction were included in order to determine if they predicted participant perceptions of being eventually re-incarcerated. No relationships were found ($F(2,475) = 1.739$, $p = .177$). It is likely that education and satisfaction do not predict the recidivists' thoughts about being re-incarcerated.

Appendix C

Case Studies and Solutions

C.1 Case Study Questions

Financial Attributes

This survey study includes responses from 752 participants in working-class neighborhoods representing a cross section of the Canadian and U.S. population. Its aim is to examine the relations between reported age, income, monthly mortgage or rent payments, number of persons residing in the household, whether the respondent has a pension other than Social Security, and level of education.

Please explain all of your responses and answer the study questions in the proper reporting format as covered in this textbook. Alpha is .05. The data file name is "Financial Case Study Data."

(1) Provide descriptive statistics for the study variables. Where appropriate, include means, standard deviations, frequencies, and pie charts (category labels and depict percentages).
(2) Study the numeric data for normal distribution.
(3) Are there differences in age, respondent income, monthly mortgage or rent, and number of family members by educational level?
(4) Are there any associations among the study variables?
(5) Overall, what do these findings suggest?

Gift Shop Customers

This case study consists of 200 completed surveys from the typical customer of a local gift shop chain consisting of three stores. The questionnaire collected data about age, typical sale transaction amount, and preferences for physical store shopping, online store shopping, greeting cards, and gifts. The preference questions were formatted in a 0- to 9-point sliding bar scale, with values closer to 9 expressing greater preference. Age was in years and typical sales amount in dollars. The stores are identified as #1–#3.

Please explain all of your responses and answer the study questions in the proper reporting format as covered in this textbook. Alpha is .05. The data file name is "Gift Shops Case Study Data."

(1) Provide the overall means and standard deviations of all study variables.
(2) Are the variables normally distributed? Provide the appropriate statistics.

(3) Do the customer age and sales transaction vary by store location? Explain your results.
(4) Do preferences for physical store shopping, online store shopping, greeting cards, and gifts vary by store? If so, where do the differences lie?
(5) Is there a correlation between age and amount spent in the gift store?
(6) Based on the sample and your analyses, what is your overall impression of these variables on years at current residence?

Health Issues

This case study consists of 500 patients who participated in completing a health-related habits questionnaire. Typically, these respondents smoke, have health issues, and face weight management challenges. The focus of the study is to examine for *age-related effects*. Please answer the following study questions in the proper reporting format as covered in this textbook. Alpha is .05. The data file name is "Health Case Study Data."

(1) Describe and screen the sample data. What is the average age of the study participant? What is the sex breakdown? What is the breakdown by location? Remember that these are descriptive statistics. Describe your results.
(2) Are there meaningful differences within smoking status and within each physical activity measure? Explain your output.
(3) Examine for meaningful differences in age by sex, smoking status, types of vitamins or supplements taken, level of physical activity, moving around activity, and lifting activity. Explain your results.
(4) Is there a meaningful difference in smoking status by region of the country? Explain your results.
(5) Is there a difference in moderate activity by sex? Explain your answer.
(6) Based on the sample and your analyses, what is your overall impression of health activities in this population?

Moving Services

This case study consists of 5,000 cases of residents who completed a questionnaire designed to discover factors that might affect the amount of years one lives at a place. An independent movers' association commissioned a consulting firm specializing in the service sector to conduct the research. Please explain your responses and answer the study questions in the proper reporting format as covered in this textbook. Alpha is .05. The data file name is "Moving Services Case Study Data."

(1) Describe and screen the sample data. What is the average age (in years) of the study participants? What is the binary gender breakdown? What are the breakdowns by household income and education categories? Remember that these are descriptive statistics. Describe your results.
(2) Examine years at current address, residential zones, hometown size, home status, and building types, all by retirement status. Discuss your findings.
(3) Expert assessments and previous research suggest that a number of variables may contribute to how long people remain at a residence before moving. Examine for correlations between "years at current address" and each of the following variables: age, years of education, years with current employer, household income, number of people in household, hours spent watching TV/week, amount spent on primary credit card during the last month,

amount spent on secondary credit card during the last month, and job satisfaction. Explain your results.

(4) Based on any significant results in Question 3, run a regression where years at current residence is the outcome variable. Explain your results.

(5) Based on the sample and your analyses, what is your overall impression of these variables on years at current residence?

Sample Size Matters

You are charged with preparing the requirements for a number of statistical studies and analyses. Download a free trial copy of SamplePower3 and determine the appropriate sample sizes for the following analyses. In cases in which sample sizes are less than 30, assume a minimum of 31. In all cases, alpha is .05. Please answer the following questions in the proper reporting format as covered in this textbook.

(1) We wish to determine the average age of a typical human services client. Assume that it is 38 years old and we want to know if it is different from 45 years old, which is the cutoff age for the program under study. The standard deviation is 10 years and the required statistical power is 95%. What is the optimal sample size?

(2) The state wishes to determine whether the state mean household income of $52,000 (standard deviation = $20,000) significantly differs from its most affluent community's suspected mean household income of $65,000 (standard deviation = $25,000). The required statistical power is 80%. What is the necessary sample size?

(3) The state wishes to determine whether the state mean household (HH) income of $52,000 significantly differs from its most affluent community's suspected mean HH income of $65,000. They have a similar standard deviation, which is $25,000. The required statistical power is 90%. A difference of $2,000 would be meaningful. What is the necessary sample size?

(4) This study will involve measuring weight loss from those individuals participating in a two-week revised diet program. The persons will be weighed before and after the diet. Previous records indicate a mean loss of 4 pounds for those who completed the program. The revised diet plan is expected to yield a loss (difference) of 5 pounds. What is the appropriate sample size?

(5) Candidate A's staff wishes to survey whether their candidate has more than 50% of the vote. They want to detect at least 55% support. Assuming power is 85%, what sample size is required?

(6) This study plans to examine the association between violent video gaming and individuals' tendency to assess some forms of violence as justified. The minimum expected correlation is .25. Power is 95%. What is a sufficient sample size?

(7) A study plans to examine the average length of residency in three areas (groups). The standard deviation is 2 years and power is 85%. The expected effect size is .40, which is the change in the data explained by the groups. What is the required sample size?

(8) This study's aim is to determine whether education, experience, and company growth predict employee salary. The minimum explained variance is 20% and power is 90%. What is the necessary sample size?

Violent Crime Recidivism

The sample data for this case study consist of the criminal records of 5,687 offenders who were examined to determine if there were any relationships among a number of record variables that contributed to or reduced the rate of recidivism among offenders. Please explain all of your responses and answer the study questions in the proper reporting format as covered in this textbook. Alpha is .05. The data file name is "Recidivism Case Study Data."

(1) Describe and screen the sample data. Conduct descriptive and screening statistical analysis for the following variables: age in years, gender, marital status, SES, educational level, and employment status.
(2) Is there a relationship between the first violent crime and the second? Is there a relationship between the severity of the first crime and the second's severity?
(3) Is there a relationship between those offenders exposed to rehabilitation and the second offense? Is there a relationship between those offenders exposed to rehabilitation and a second arrest?
(4) Are there associations among SES, educational level, severity of first crime, and severity of second crime?
(5) Is age correlated with crime severity?
(6) What can you conclude from your findings?

What Motivates Students to Perform

In an effort to understand what motivates students to do well in school, motivational data were collected from 1,000 undergraduate junior and senior level female and male students from across the United States. With self-determination theory serving as a framework, students were asked about whether they enjoyed their academic studies, had a sense of control of their academic activities, felt competent about their academic performance, and could relate to and had meaningful relationships with others in their college or university. These variables are believed to drive motivation to do well in college. Additionally, students reported the degree to which they were required to use math in courses. The dependent variable was student-reported GPA (overall grade average at the time of the study). The study aim was to determine whether and to what extent enjoyment, control, competence, relatedness, and level of math estimate academic performance as measured by GPA.

GPA is coded using a 4.00 scale. Age is reported in years. Gender is coded 1 = men and 2 = women. All of the other variables are formatted in a nine-point sliding scale from 1 to 9, where a higher score represents more of the variable attribute. The bar sliding scale allows for selections two places to the right of the decimal point. Please explain your responses and answer the study questions in the proper reporting format as covered in this textbook. Alpha is .05. The data file name is "Student Motivation Study Data."

(1) Provide descriptive statistics for all numeric variables as well as percentage breakdown by gender.
(2) Screen the data (all variables) for univariate normal distribution. Report any violations of the normality assumption.
(3) Before analyzing the data in the aggregate, examine for gender effects.
(4) Based on the results in Question 3, run bivariate data screening to examine for bivariate normality, linearity, and homoscedasticity.
(5) Based on the results in Question 3, run a MLR.
(6) Interpret the MLR results.

Psychological Effects of the Workplace

In an effort to understand and reduce employee stress, a major corporation surveyed a cross section of 500 employees. The study aim was to determine whether and to what extent employee age, salary, education, the informal company support network, and perceptions of job insecurity explain overall employee self-perceived depression, anxiety, and stress.

Age is reported in years. Salary is reported in dollars annually. Education is formatted in years completed, allowing for partial years. Workplace support network is formatted in a five-point scale, ranging from 0 = no support to 5 = great deal of support. Job insecurity is formatted in a seven-point scale, ranging from 0 = no job insecurity to 7 = complete job insecurity. Anxiety and stress are formatted in a 10-point scale, from 0 = no anxiety or stress to 10 = completely anxious or stressed. Overall depression is anchored in a five-point scale, from 0 = not depressed at all to 5 = deeply depressed. These measures are self-perceptions of the attributes and do not necessarily meet the clinical definitions of the conditions.

Please explain your responses and answer the study questions in the proper reporting format as covered in this textbook. Alpha is .05. The data file name is "Workplace Study Data."

(1) Screen all of the variables for normal distribution. Report each variable mean and standard deviation score. Interpret the results. Do all of the variables meet the normality assumption according to the Shapiro-Wilk statistic? What are their *p*-values?
(2) Consider overall depression, anxiety, and stress as outcome variables. Run bivariate screening of each outcome variable with age, salary, education, the informal company support network, and perceptions of job insecurity. Interpret the results.
(3) Run three separate MLRs for each of the outcome variables. Interpret each model.
(4) Which model is most appropriate and why?

C.2 Case Study Solutions

Financial Attributes

This case study is meant to delve into real world situations, sometimes with imperfect information where alternative courses of action are viable. Interpretation of the results may vary based on different perspectives and topical expertise. The following are possible responses.

This survey study includes responses from 752 participants in working-class neighborhoods representing a cross section of the Canadian and U.S. population. Its aim is to examine the relations between reported age, income, monthly mortgage or rent payments, number of persons residing in the household, whether the respondent has a pension other than Social Security, and level of education.

Please explain all of your responses and answer the study questions in the proper reporting format as covered in this textbook. Alpha is .05. The data file name is "Financial Case Study Data."

(1) Provide descriptive statistics for the study variables. Where appropriate, include means, standard deviations, frequencies, and pie charts (category labels and depict percentages).

Below are the numeric variable descriptives, as well as frequency tables and pie charts for the categorical variables.

Descriptive Statistics

	N	Mean	Std. Deviation
Age	752	38.0788	5.12616
Respondent_Income	752	$42,077.91	$3,976.286
Monthly_Mortg_or_rent	752	$1,051.36	$100.046
Members	752	2.97	.403
Valid N (listwise)	752		

Education

		Frequency	Percent	Valid Percent	Cumulative Percent
Valid	up to HS/technical	22	2.9	2.9	2.9
	some college	567	75.4	75.4	78.3
	bachelors	160	21.3	21.3	99.6
	masters	3	.4	.4	100.0
	Total	752	100.0	100.0	

Pension

		Frequency	Percent	Valid Percent	Cumulative Percent
Valid	No	697	92.7	92.7	92.7
	Yes	55	7.3	7.3	100.0
	Total	752	100.0	100.0	

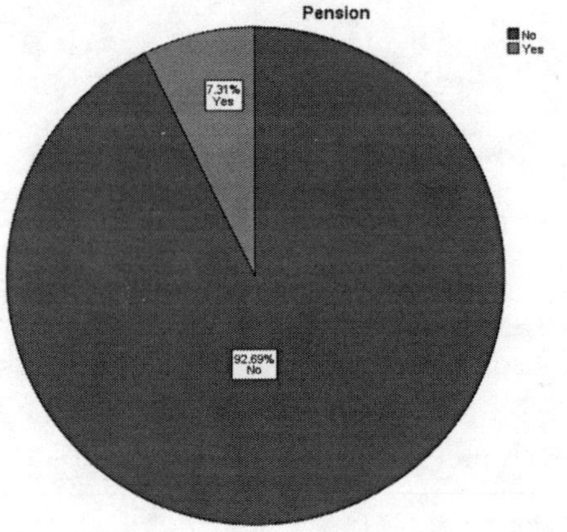

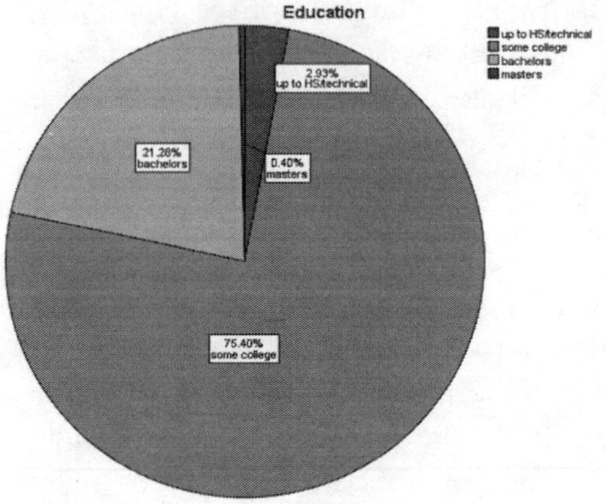

(2) Study the numeric data for normal distribution.

It is likely that age, respondent income, and monthly mortgage or rent payment do not violate the normality assumption because their Shapiro-Wilk statistics are greater than .05. Thus, the chances that the distributions do not vary from normality are above the acceptable risk level. The *p*-values range from .151 to .903. However, number of household members does not meet the normal distribution assumption ($p < .001$).

Tests of Normality

	Kolmogorov-Smirnov[a]			Shapiro-Wilk		
	Statistic	df	Sig.	Statistic	df	Sig.
Age	.025	752	.200*	.999	752	.849
Respondent_Income	.023	752	.200*	.997	752	.151
Monthly_Mortg_or_rent	.019	752	.200*	.999	752	.903
Members	.458	752	.000	.483	752	.000

*. This is a lower bound of the true significance.

a. Lilliefors Significance Correction

(3) Are there differences in age, respondent income, monthly mortgage or rent, and number of family members by educational level?

Descriptives

		N	Mean	Std. Deviation	Std. Error	95% Confidence Interval for Mean		Minimum	Maximum
						Lower Bound	Upper Bound		
Age	up to HS/technical	22	37.0812	4.91771	1.04846	34.9008	39.2616	27.28	48.99
	some college	567	38.1116	5.16421	.21688	37.6856	38.5376	22.08	54.14
	bachelors	160	38.1708	4.96662	.39265	37.3953	38.9463	27.26	51.06
	masters	3	34.2884	8.45112	4.87925	13.2947	55.2822	28.84	44.02
	Total	752	38.0788	5.12616	.18693	37.7118	38.4458	22.08	54.14
Respondent_Income	up to HS/technical	22	$32,922.05	$1,508.724	$321.661	$32,253.12	$33,590.98	$28,685	$34,943
	some college	567	$40,881.17	$2,523.734	$105.987	$40,673.00	$41,089.35	$34,995	$44,984
	bachelors	160	$47,336.89	$2,011.450	$159.019	$47,022.83	$47,650.96	$44,992	$53,096
	masters	3	$54,925.27	$801.308	$462.635	$52,934.71	$56,915.83	$54,000	$55,388
	Total	752	$42,077.91	$3,976.286	$145.000	$41,793.26	$42,362.56	$28,685	$55,388
Monthly_Mortg_or_rent	up to HS/technical	22	$1,023.24	$92.495	$19.720	$982.23	$1,064.25	$857	$1,186
	some college	567	$1,050.13	$99.782	$4.190	$1,041.90	$1,058.36	$712	$1,348
	bachelors	160	$1,057.16	$99.738	$7.885	$1,041.58	$1,072.73	$793	$1,294
	masters	3	$1,181.03	$151.848	$87.670	$803.82	$1,558.24	$1,010	$1,300
	Total	752	$1,051.36	$100.046	$3.648	$1,044.20	$1,058.52	$712	$1,348

The one-way ANOVA results reveal that it is likely that respondent income varies by educational level ($p < .001$). Moreover, income does not meet the equality of variance assumption. Therefore, we will consult the Game-Howell post hoc test paired comparisons.

ANOVA

		Sum of Squares	df	Mean Square	F	Sig.
Age	Between Groups	66.959	3	22.320	.849	.467
	Within Groups	19667.479	748	26.293		
	Total	19734.438	751			
Respondent_Income	Between Groups	7576572528	3	2525524176	439.592	.000
	Within Groups	4297374212	748	5745152.689		
	Total	1.187E+10	751			
Monthly_Mortg_or_rent	Between Groups	74077.011	3	24692.337	2.482	.060
	Within Groups	7442778.292	748	9950.238		
	Total	7516855.303	751			

Test of Homogeneity of Variances

	Levene Statistic	df1	df2	Sig.
Age	.934	3	748	.424
Respondent_Income	10.027	3	748	.000
Monthly_Mortg_or_rent	.383	3	748	.765

The comparisons indicate that all income levels vary by educational level. The *p*-values range from less than .001 to .004.

Multiple Comparisons

Dependent Variable: Respondent_Income
Games-Howell

(I) Education	(J) Education	Mean Difference (I-J)	Std. Error	Sig.	95% Confidence Interval Lower Bound	Upper Bound
up to HS/technical	some college	-$7,959.124*	$338.672	.000	-$8,888.70	-$7,029.55
	bachelors	-$14,414.846*	$358.822	.000	-$15,386.59	-$13,443.10
	masters	-$22,003.224*	$563.469	.000	-$24,217.77	-$19,788.68
some college	up to HS/technical	$7,959.124*	$338.672	.000	$7,029.55	$8,888.70
	bachelors	-$6,455.722*	$191.103	.000	-$6,949.31	-$5,962.14
	masters	-$14,044.099*	$474.621	.002	-$16,995.09	-$11,093.11
bachelors	up to HS/technical	$14,414.846*	$358.822	.000	$13,443.10	$15,386.59
	some college	$6,455.722*	$191.103	.000	$5,962.14	$6,949.31
	masters	-$7,588.378*	$489.202	.004	-$10,307.67	-$4,869.08
masters	up to HS/technical	$22,003.224*	$563.469	.000	$19,788.68	$24,217.77
	some college	$14,044.099*	$474.621	.002	$11,093.11	$16,995.09
	bachelors	$7,588.378*	$489.202	.004	$4,869.08	$10,307.67

*. The mean difference is significant at the 0.05 level.

Since number of household members did not meet the normal distribution assumption, a nonparametric test was conducted. The Kruskal-Wallis statistic was significant ($p < .001$). Post hoc testing is available in the nonparametric tests options.

Descriptive Statistics

	N	Mean	Std. Deviation	Minimum	Maximum
Members	752	2.97	.403	1	4
Education	752	4.1915	.47075	3.00	6.00

Test Statistics[a,b]

	Members
Chi-Square	39.005
df	3
Asymp. Sig.	.000

a. Kruskal Wallis Test
b. Grouping Variable: Education

(4) Is there an association between the study variables?

Respondent income is positively associated with those individuals who have a pension ($r = .451$) and education ($r = .749$). Income is negatively correlated with number of household members ($r = -.174$). Pension ($r = -.321$) and education ($r = -.156$) are negatively related to number of family members. Level of education and pension are positively correlated ($r = .514$). All reported correlations are at $p < .01$.

Correlations

			Respondent_Income	Monthly_Mortg_or_rent	Age	Members	Pension	Education
Spearman's rho	Respondent_Income	Correlation Coefficient	1.000	.031	.052	-.174**	.451**	.749**
		Sig. (2-tailed)	.	.396	.154	.000	.000	.000
		N	752	752	752	752	752	752
	Monthly_Mortg_or_rent	Correlation Coefficient	.031	1.000	-.026	.016	-.003	.060
		Sig. (2-tailed)	.396	.	.484	.671	.935	.102
		N	752	752	752	752	752	752
	Age	Correlation Coefficient	.052	-.026	1.000	.035	-.005	.007
		Sig. (2-tailed)	.154	.484	.	.342	.890	.851
		N	752	752	752	752	752	752
	Members	Correlation Coefficient	-.174**	.016	.035	1.000	-.321**	-.156**
		Sig. (2-tailed)	.000	.671	.342	.	.000	.000
		N	752	752	752	752	752	752
	Pension	Correlation Coefficient	.451**	-.003	-.005	-.321**	1.000	.514**
		Sig. (2-tailed)	.000	.935	.890	.000	.	.000
		N	752	752	752	752	752	752
	Education	Correlation Coefficient	.749**	.060	.007	-.156**	.514**	1.000
		Sig. (2-tailed)	.000	.102	.851	.000	.000	.
		N	752	752	752	752	752	752

**. Correlation is significant at the 0.01 level (2-tailed).

(5) What do these overall findings suggest?

The analysis suggests the following findings:

- The average age of respondent is 38 years old (standard deviation = 5.12 years).
- The mean respondent income is $42,077.
- The average monthly mortgage or rent payment is $1,051.
- Approximately three persons reside in the respondent's household.
- Seventy-five point four percent have some college education.
- Nearly 93% have no pension other than Social Security.
- Those participants with greater education earn more.
- The data suggest that respondents with less education (and, by implication, less income) have more individuals residing in the same household. People might be sharing living expenses.

Providing that the sample represents the target population, these findings can be applied to the target population.

Gift Shop Customers

This case study is meant to delve into real world situations, sometimes with imperfect information where alternative courses of action are viable. Interpretation of the results may vary based on different perspectives and topical expertise. The following are possible responses.

This case study consists of 200 completed surveys from the typical customer of a local gift shop chain consisting of three stores. The questionnaire collected data about age, typical sale transaction amount, and preferences for physical store shopping, online store shopping, greeting cards, and gifts. The preference questions were formatted in a 0- to 9-point sliding bar scale, with values closer to 9 expressing greater preference. Age was in years and typical sales amount in dollars. The stores are identified as #1–#3.

Please explain all of your responses and answer the study questions in the proper reporting format as covered in this textbook. Alpha is .05. The data file name is "Gift Shops Case Study Data."

(1) Provide the overall means and standard deviations of all study variables.

The following depicts the overall means and standard deviations:

Descriptive Statistics

	N	Mean	Std. Deviation
Gifts	200	5.0113	1.04969
Online_Store	200	5.0588	1.00044
Cards	200	5.0649	.99576
Age	200	50.7758	15.17827
Typical_Sale	200	$18.08	$1.512
Physical_Store	200	3.5578	1.54317
Valid N (listwise)	200		

(2) Are the variables normally distributed? Provide the appropriate statistics.

Since all of the Shapiro-Wilk statistics are not significant, they do not violate the normality assumption. The chances that the distributions do not vary from normality are well above .05 or the acceptable risk level. The *p*-values range from .392 to .839.

Tests of Normality

	Kolmogorov-Smirnov[a]			Shapiro-Wilk		
	Statistic	df	Sig.	Statistic	df	Sig.
Gifts	.046	200	.200*	.992	200	.392
Online_Store	.045	200	.200*	.995	200	.701
Cards	.040	200	.200*	.996	200	.839
Age	.040	200	.200*	.993	200	.427
Typical_Sale	.047	200	.200*	.994	200	.549
Physical_Store	.040	200	.200*	.993	200	.436

*. This is a lower bound of the true significance.

a. Lilliefors Significance Correction

(3) Do the customer age and sales transaction vary by store location? Explain your results.

Since the overall ANOVA statistics for "Age" and "Typical Sales Amount" are each significant ($p < .001$), there is at least one likely difference in age as well as in sales transaction amount between at least two out of the three stores.

Descriptives

		N	Mean	Std. Deviation	Std. Error	95% Confidence Interval for Mean		Minimum	Maximum
						Lower Bound	Upper Bound		
Age	1	37	33.9112	12.36295	2.03246	29.7892	38.0332	18.00	60.78
	2	99	57.7484	13.32024	1.33873	55.0918	60.4051	30.02	91.61
	3	64	49.7398	10.94727	1.36841	47.0052	52.4743	30.90	84.23
	Total	200	50.7758	15.17827	1.07327	48.6593	52.8922	18.00	91.61
Typical_Sale	1	37	$16.43	$1.189	$0.195	$16.04	$16.83	$15	$19
	2	99	$18.80	$1.336	$0.134	$18.53	$19.06	$16	$22
	3	64	$17.94	$1.103	$0.138	$17.66	$18.21	$16	$21
	Total	200	$18.08	$1.512	$0.107	$17.87	$18.30	$15	$22

ANOVA

		Sum of Squares	df	Mean Square	F	Sig.
Age	Between Groups	15405.175	2	7702.588	49.848	.000
	Within Groups	30440.450	197	154.520		
	Total	45845.625	199			
Typical_Sale	Between Groups	152.347	2	76.174	49.613	.000
	Within Groups	302.464	197	1.535		
	Total	454.811	199			

The variances meet the equality of variance assumption.

Test of Homogeneity of Variances

	Levene Statistic	df1	df2	Sig.
Age	2.044	2	197	.132
Typical_Sale	2.015	2	197	.136

Because there are unequal sample sizes per store and the equality of variance assumption is met, we are guided by the Scheffe post hoc test. All paired comparisons are significant, which indicates that it is likely that age and typical sales amount vary by store location.

Multiple Comparisons

Dependent Variable		(I) Store_Location	(J) Store_Location	Mean Difference (I-J)	Std. Error	Sig.	95% Confidence Interval Lower Bound	95% Confidence Interval Upper Bound
Age	Scheffe	1	2	-23.83723*	2.39521	.000	-29.7450	-17.9295
			3	-15.82857*	2.56722	.000	-22.1605	-9.4966
		2	1	23.83723*	2.39521	.000	17.9295	29.7450
			3	8.00866*	1.99379	.000	3.0910	12.9263
		3	1	15.82857*	2.56722	.000	9.4966	22.1605
			2	-8.00866*	1.99379	.000	-12.9263	-3.0910
	Games-Howell	1	2	-23.83723*	2.43374	.000	-29.6664	-18.0081
			3	-15.82857*	2.45019	.000	-21.6993	-9.9578
		2	1	23.83723*	2.43374	.000	18.0081	29.6664
			3	8.00866*	1.91435	.000	3.4775	12.5398
		3	1	15.82857*	2.45019	.000	9.9578	21.6993
			2	-8.00866*	1.91435	.000	-12.5398	-3.4775
Typical_Sale	Scheffe	1	2	-$2.363*	$0.239	.000	-$2.95	-$1.77
			3	-$1.506*	$0.256	.000	-$2.14	-$0.87
		2	1	$2.363*	$0.239	.000	$1.77	$2.95
			3	$0.857*	$0.199	.000	$0.37	$1.35
		3	1	$1.506*	$0.256	.000	$0.87	$2.14
			2	-$0.857*	$0.199	.000	-$1.35	-$0.37
	Games-Howell	1	2	-$2.363*	$0.237	.000	-$2.93	-$1.80
			3	-$1.506*	$0.239	.000	-$2.08	-$0.93
		2	1	$2.363*	$0.237	.000	$1.80	$2.93
			3	$0.857*	$0.192	.000	$0.40	$1.31
		3	1	$1.506*	$0.239	.000	$0.93	$2.08
			2	-$0.857*	$0.192	.000	-$1.31	-$0.40

*. The mean difference is significant at the 0.05 level.

(4) Do preferences for physical store shopping, online store shopping, greeting cards, and gifts vary by store? If so, where do the differences lie?

Descriptives

		N	Mean	Std. Deviation	Std. Error	95% Confidence Interval for Mean		Minimum	Maximum
						Lower Bound	Upper Bound		
Gifts	1	37	5.3476	1.06683	.17539	4.9919	5.7033	3.16	7.75
	2	99	4.8611	1.04727	.10525	4.6522	5.0700	2.43	7.25
	3	64	5.0492	1.01027	.12628	4.7968	5.3016	2.78	7.34
	Total	200	5.0113	1.04969	.07422	4.8649	5.1577	2.43	7.75
Online_Store	1	37	5.4088	.92183	.15155	5.1015	5.7162	3.60	7.50
	2	99	4.9154	.96863	.09735	4.7222	5.1086	2.52	6.99
	3	64	5.0782	1.05443	.13180	4.8148	5.3416	2.86	7.20
	Total	200	5.0588	1.00044	.07074	4.9193	5.1983	2.52	7.50
Cards	1	37	5.3808	1.09683	.18032	5.0151	5.7465	3.55	7.82
	2	99	5.0162	.95058	.09554	4.8266	5.2057	1.83	7.40
	3	64	4.9576	.98229	.12279	4.7122	5.2030	2.76	6.82
	Total	200	5.0649	.99576	.07041	4.9260	5.2037	1.83	7.82
Physical_Store	1	37	1.8560	1.25904	.20698	1.4362	2.2757	.06	5.35
	2	99	4.2528	1.37204	.13789	3.9792	4.5265	1.27	7.67
	3	64	3.4666	1.10429	.13804	3.1907	3.7424	1.67	7.04
	Total	200	3.5578	1.54317	.10912	3.3426	3.7730	.06	7.67

All variables meet the equality of variance assumptions.

Test of Homogeneity of Variances

	Levene Statistic	df1	df2	Sig.
Gifts	.253	2	197	.777
Online_Store	.737	2	197	.480
Cards	.642	2	197	.528
Physical_Store	1.428	2	197	.242

Online store preference ($p = .036$) and physical store preference ($p < .001$) indicate a likely difference by store location. There is least one difference between two stores for online and for physical stores.

ANOVA

		Sum of Squares	df	Mean Square	F	Sig.
Gifts	Between Groups	6.510	2	3.255	3.014	.051
	Within Groups	212.757	197	1.080		
	Total	219.267	199			
Online_Store	Between Groups	6.593	2	3.296	3.372	.036
	Within Groups	192.584	197	.978		
	Total	199.177	199			
Cards	Between Groups	4.665	2	2.332	2.385	.095
	Within Groups	192.652	197	.978		
	Total	197.316	199			
Physical_Store	Between Groups	155.516	2	77.758	48.114	.000
	Within Groups	318.375	197	1.616		
	Total	473.891	199			

The Scheffe post hoc test reveals that the difference online store preference is likely between Stores 1 (M = 5.40, SD = .92) and 2 (M = 4.91, SD = .96). Store 3 (M = 5.07, SD = 1.05) does not differ from Stores 1 or 2. In terms of preference for a physical store, respondents from all three stores are significantly different: Store 1 (M = 1.85, SD = 1.25), Store 2 (M = 4.25, SD = 1.37), and Store 3 (M = 3.46, SD = 1.10).

Multiple Comparisons

Dependent Variable		(I) Store_Location	(J) Store_Location	Mean Difference (I-J)	Std. Error	Sig.	95% Confidence Interval	
							Lower Bound	Upper Bound
Gifts	Scheffe	1	2	.48652	.20024	.055	-.0074	.9804
			3	.29843	.21462	.382	-.2309	.8278
		2	1	-.48652	.20024	.055	-.9804	.0074
			3	-.18809	.16668	.530	-.5992	.2230
		3	1	-.29843	.21462	.382	-.8278	.2309
			2	.18809	.16668	.530	-.2230	.5992
	Games-Howell	1	2	.48652	.20454	.053	-.0043	.9774
			3	.29843	.21612	.356	-.2188	.8156
		2	1	-.48652	.20454	.053	-.9774	.0043
			3	-.18809	.16440	.489	-.5776	.2014
		3	1	-.29843	.21612	.356	-.8156	.2188
			2	.18809	.16440	.489	-.2014	.5776
Online_Store	Scheffe	1	2	.49342*	.19051	.037	.0235	.9633
			3	.33062	.20420	.272	-.1730	.8343
		2	1	-.49342*	.19051	.037	-.9633	-.0235
			3	-.16280	.15859	.591	-.5539	.2283
		3	1	-.33062	.20420	.272	-.8343	.1730
			2	.16280	.15859	.591	-.2283	.5539
	Games-Howell	1	2	.49342*	.18012	.021	.0618	.9251
			3	.33062	.20085	.232	-.1486	.8099
		2	1	-.49342*	.18012	.021	-.9251	-.0618
			3	-.16280	.16386	.582	-.5514	.2258
		3	1	-.33062	.20085	.232	-.8099	.1486
			2	.16280	.16386	.582	-.2258	.5514
Cards	Scheffe	1	2	.36464	.19055	.163	-.1053	.8346
			3	.42321	.20423	.120	-.0805	.9269
		2	1	-.36464	.19055	.163	-.8346	.1053
			3	.05857	.15861	.934	-.3326	.4498
		3	1	-.42321	.20423	.120	-.9269	.0805
			2	-.05857	.15861	.934	-.4498	.3326
	Games-Howell	1	2	.36464	.20406	.183	-.1263	.8556
			3	.42321	.21815	.135	-.0994	.9458
		2	1	-.36464	.20406	.183	-.8556	.1263
			3	.05857	.15558	.925	-.3102	.4274
		3	1	-.42321	.21815	.135	-.9458	.0994
			2	-.05857	.15558	.925	-.4274	.3102
Physical_Store	Scheffe	1	2	-2.39686*	.24496	.000	-3.0010	-1.7927
			3	-1.61060*	.26255	.000	-2.2582	-.9630
		2	1	2.39686*	.24496	.000	1.7927	3.0010
			3	.78626*	.20390	.001	.2833	1.2892
		3	1	1.61060*	.26255	.000	.9630	2.2582
			2	-.78626*	.20390	.001	-1.2892	-.2833
	Games-Howell	1	2	-2.39686*	.24871	.000	-2.9924	-1.8013
			3	-1.61060*	.24879	.000	-2.2068	-1.0144
		2	1	2.39686*	.24871	.000	1.8013	2.9924
			3	.78626*	.19511	.000	.3245	1.2480
		3	1	1.61060*	.24879	.000	1.0144	2.2068
			2	-.78626*	.19511	.000	-1.2480	-.3245

*. The mean difference is significant at the 0.05 level.

(5) Is there a correlation between age and amount spent in the gift store?

There is a very strong correlation between age and typical transaction dollar amount ($r = .991$, $p < .001$).

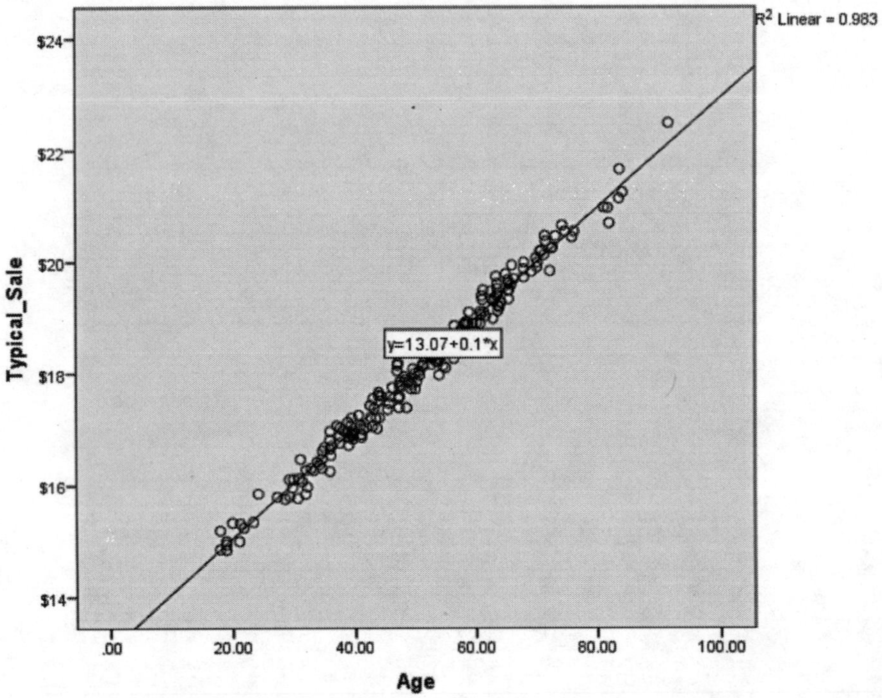

Correlations

		Age	Typical_Sale
Age	Pearson Correlation	1	.991**
	Sig. (2-tailed)		.000
	N	200	200
Typical_Sale	Pearson Correlation	.991**	1
	Sig. (2-tailed)	.000	
	N	200	200

**. Correlation is significant at the 0.01 level (2-tailed).

(6) Based on the sample and your analyses, what is your overall impression of these variables on years at current residence?

The typical gift shop customer is nearly 50 years old and spends, on average, $18.00 each time he/she visits the store. Older customers tend to spend more and mostly shop at Store 2. The older Store 2 customers prefer to shop in a physical store rather than online, which is contrary to the common younger Store 1 customer.

Providing that the sample represents the target population, these findings can be applied to the population.

Health Issues

This case study is meant to delve into real world situations, sometimes with imperfect information where alternative courses of action are viable. Interpretation of the results may vary based on different perspectives and topical expertise. The following are possible responses.

This case study consists of 500 patients who participated in completing a health-related habits questionnaire. Typically, these respondents smoke, have health issues, and face weight management challenges. The focus of the study is to examine for *age-related effects*. Please answer the following study questions in the proper reporting format as covered in this textbook. Alpha is .05. The data file name is "Health Case Study Data."

(1) Describe and screen the sample data. What is the average age of the study participant? What is the sex breakdown? What is the breakdown by location? Remember that these are descriptive statistics. Describe your results.

The age data do not approximate the normal distribution because the Shapiro–Wilk test is $p <$ .001.

Tests of Normality

	Kolmogorov-Smirnov[a]			Shapiro-Wilk		
	Statistic	df	Sig.	Statistic	df	Sig.
Age	.077	500	.000	.960	500	.000

a. Lilliefors Significance Correction

The average age is 47.34 years old and the standard deviation is 17.71 years.

Descriptives

			Statistic	Std. Error
Age	Mean		47.34	.792
	95% Confidence Interval for Mean	Lower Bound	45.79	
		Upper Bound	48.90	
	5% Trimmed Mean		46.91	
	Median		45.00	
	Variance		313.833	
	Std. Deviation		17.715	
	Minimum		18	
	Maximum		85	
	Range		67	
	Interquartile Range		27	
	Skewness		.378	.109
	Kurtosis		-.843	.218

There are 220 (44.0%) men and 280 (56.0%) women.

Sex

		Frequency	Percent	Valid Percent	Cumulative Percent
Valid	Male	220	44.0	44.0	44.0
	Female	280	56.0	56.0	100.0
	Total	500	100.0	100.0	

The breakdown by region of the country is as follows:

Region

		Frequency	Percent	Valid Percent	Cumulative Percent
Valid	Northeast	95	19.0	19.0	19.0
	Midwest	105	21.0	21.0	40.0
	South	200	40.0	40.0	80.0
	West	100	20.0	20.0	100.0
	Total	500	100.0	100.0	

(2) Are there meaningful differences within smoking status and within each physical activity measure? Explain your output.

Chi-square tests for smoking frequency, as well as vigorous, moderate, and strength activities, all were significant at $p < .001$. The category amounts of the these activities varied within the variables.

Test Statistics

	Smoking frequency	Freq vigorous activity (times per wk)	Freq moderate activity (times per wk)	Freq strength activity (times per wk)
Chi-Square	65.797[a]	692.419[b]	576.497[c]	834.488[d]
df	2	2	2	2
Asymp. Sig.	.000	.000	.000	.000

a. 0 cells (0.0%) have expected frequencies less than 5. The minimum expected cell frequency is 75.7.

b. 0 cells (0.0%) have expected frequencies less than 5. The minimum expected cell frequency is 160.7.

c. 0 cells (0.0%) have expected frequencies less than 5. The minimum expected cell frequency is 162.3.

d. 0 cells (0.0%) have expected frequencies less than 5. The minimum expected cell frequency is 164.0.

Below are the tables that depict the likely differences. The major difference is between nonsmokers and moderate smokers. Those persons who do not engage in vigorous activity are clearly different than those who participate in some form of vigorous activity. Essentially, the same pattern emerges for other types of activities.

Smoking frequency

	Observed N	Expected N	Residual
Every day	95	75.7	19.3
Some days	19	75.7	-56.7
Not at all	113	75.7	37.3
Total	227		

Freq vigorous activity (times per wk)

	Observed N	Expected N	Residual
Less than once per week	24	160.7	-136.7
Never	25	160.7	-135.7
Unable to do vig activity	433	160.7	272.3
Total	482		

Freq moderate activity (times per wk)

	Observed N	Expected N	Residual
Less than once per week	31	162.3	-131.3
Never	44	162.3	-118.3
Unable to do moderate activity	412	162.3	249.7
Total	487		

Freq strength activity (times per wk)

	Observed N	Expected N	Residual
Less than once per week	8	164.0	-156.0
Never	18	164.0	-146.0
Unable to do strength activity	466	164.0	302.0
Total	492		

(3) Examine for meaningful differences in age by sex, smoking status, types of vitamins or supplements taken, level of physical activity, moving around activity, and lifting activity. Explain your results.

Since age does not meet the normality assumption, nonparametric tests were conducted using the Mann-Whitney *U* test. The nonparametric tests are not as sensitive to differences as are parametric statistics. Although below only represents the nonparametric output, the SPSS output file contains both nonparametric and parametric results for those readers who wish to compare the results.

It is likely that age does not vary by sex ($p = .421$).

Test Statistics[a]

	Age
Mann-Whitney U	29511.000
Wilcoxon W	53821.000
Z	-.804
Asymp. Sig. (2-tailed)	.421

a. Grouping Variable: Sex

Group Statistics

	Sex	N	Mean	Std. Deviation	Std. Error Mean
Age	Male	220	46.15	15.908	1.073
	Female	280	48.28	18.991	1.135

It is likely that age varies by smoking status ($p < .001$).

Test Statistics[a,b]

	Age
Chi-Square	35.880
df	2
Asymp. Sig.	.000

a. Kruskal Wallis Test

b. Grouping Variable: Smoking frequency

Descriptives

Age

	N	Mean	Std. Deviation	Std. Error	95% Confidence Interval for Mean		Minimum	Maximum
					Lower Bound	Upper Bound		
Every day	95	42.77	14.478	1.485	39.82	45.72	18	81
Some days	19	43.95	15.138	3.473	36.65	51.24	18	75
Not at all	113	56.04	15.592	1.467	53.14	58.95	23	85
Total	227	49.48	16.400	1.089	47.33	51.62	18	85

It is likely that age varies by vitamins/minerals usage ($p = .004$).

Test Statistics[a]

	Age
Mann-Whitney U	23844.000
Wilcoxon W	52285.000
Z	-2.844
Asymp. Sig. (2-tailed)	.004

a. Grouping Variable: Vitamin/mineral supplmnts-past 12 months

Group Statistics

	Vitamin/mineral supplmnts-past 12 months	N	Mean	Std. Deviation	Std. Error Mean
Age	Yes	236	49.21	16.810	1.094
	No	238	45.18	18.235	1.182

The significance test could not be conducted on age by multiple vitamins usage because the "No" category has a zero value so there is nothing to compare.

Ranks

	Take any multi-vitamins in past 12 months	N	Mean Rank	Sum of Ranks
Age	Yes	341	171.00	58311.00
	No	0[a]	.00	.00
	Total	341		

a. Mann-Whitney Test cannot be performed on empty groups.

It is likely that age does not vary by herbal supplements usage ($p = .701$).

Group Statistics

	Take herbal supplements during past 12 months	N	Mean	Std. Deviation	Std. Error Mean
Age	Yes	81	45.78	14.883	1.654
	No	393	47.46	18.134	.915

Test Statistics[a]

	Age
Mann-Whitney U	15486.000
Wilcoxon W	18807.000
Z	-.384
Asymp. Sig. (2-tailed)	.701

a. Grouping Variable: Take herbal supplements during past 12 months

As one might expect, age does vary by reported vigorous activities ($p = .001$). As depicted below, it is likely that older individuals are unable to engage in vigorous activities.

Descriptives

Age

	N	Mean	Std. Deviation	Std. Error	95% Confidence Interval for Mean		Minimum	Maximum
					Lower Bound	Upper Bound		
Less than once per week	24	39.17	14.254	2.910	33.15	45.19	18	73
Never	25	38.04	12.555	2.511	32.86	43.22	18	68
Unable to do vig activity	433	48.71	17.985	.864	47.01	50.41	18	85
Total	482	47.68	17.818	.812	46.08	49.27	18	85

Test Statistics[a,b]

	Age
Chi-Square	13.741
df	2
Asymp. Sig.	.001

a. Kruskal Wallis Test

b. Grouping Variable: Freq vigorous activity (times per wk)

It is likely that there is no difference in age by reported level of moderate activities (p = .693).

Descriptives

Age

	N	Mean	Std. Deviation	Std. Error	95% Confidence Interval for Mean Lower Bound	95% Confidence Interval for Mean Upper Bound	Minimum	Maximum
Less than once per week	31	46.00	13.089	2.351	41.20	50.80	24	77
Never	44	44.77	15.602	2.352	40.03	49.52	18	82
Unable to do moderate activity	412	47.73	18.145	.894	45.98	49.49	18	85
Total	487	47.36	17.646	.800	45.78	48.93	18	85

Test Statistics[a,b]

	Age
Chi-Square	.733
df	2
Asymp. Sig.	.693

a. Kruskal Wallis Test

b. Grouping Variable: Freq moderate activity (times per wk)

As shown below, it is likely that older individuals are unable to engage in strength activities (p = .014).

Descriptives

Age

	N	Mean	Std. Deviation	Std. Error	95% Confidence Interval for Mean Lower Bound	95% Confidence Interval for Mean Upper Bound	Minimum	Maximum
Less than once per week	8	37.88	11.886	4.202	27.94	47.81	21	53
Never	18	37.44	14.009	3.302	30.48	44.41	18	70
Unable to do strength activity	466	47.94	17.843	.827	46.31	49.56	18	85
Total	492	47.39	17.768	.801	45.82	48.96	18	85

Test Statistics[a,b]

	Age
Chi-Square	8.484
df	2
Asymp. Sig.	.014

a. Kruskal Wallis Test

b. Grouping Variable: Freq strength activity (times per wk)

Concerning movement activities, and as illustrated in the table below, it is likely that older people tend to sit most of the day, whereas younger people tend to stand most of the day (p = .005).

Descriptives

Age

	N	Mean	Std. Deviation	Std. Error	95% Confidence Interval for Mean		Minimum	Maximum
					Lower Bound	Upper Bound		
SIT during MOST of the day	178	50.51	18.983	1.423	47.70	53.32	18	85
STAND during MOST of the day	65	42.49	13.561	1.682	39.13	45.85	20	79
WALK AROUND MOST of the day	226	45.86	17.173	1.142	43.61	48.11	18	85
Total	469	47.16	17.645	.815	45.56	48.76	18	85

Test Statistics[a,b]

	Age
Chi-Square	10.556
df	2
Asymp. Sig.	.005

a. Kruskal Wallis Test

b. Grouping Variable: Daily activities, moving around

Again, as expected, older people are likely unable to carry things, especially heavy objects (p = .007). Younger individuals report lifting heavier objects. See the tables below.

Descriptives

Age

	N	Mean	Std. Deviation	Std. Error	95% Confidence Interval for Mean		Minimum	Maximum
					Lower Bound	Upper Bound		
NOT lift or carry things very often	129	50.33	17.442	1.536	47.29	53.37	18	85
LIFT or carry LIGHT loads	165	47.67	18.414	1.434	44.84	50.50	18	85
LIFT or carry MODERATE loads	133	43.58	15.622	1.355	40.90	46.26	18	82
LIFT or carry HEAVY loads	32	40.63	15.237	2.694	35.13	46.12	18	75
Unable to lift or carry loads	13	66.31	14.574	4.042	57.50	75.11	37	85
Other	2	29.00	11.314	8.000	-72.65	130.65	21	37
Total	474	47.20	17.597	.808	45.61	48.79	18	85

Test Statistics[a,b]

	Age
Chi-Square	9.965
df	2
Asymp. Sig.	.007

a. Kruskal Wallis Test

b. Grouping Variable: Daily activities, lifting or carrying

(4) Is there a meaningful difference in smoking status by region of the country? Explain your results.

It is likely that smoking status varies by region of the country ($p = .047$). Three cells have less than the minimum five expected counts each, which indicates that our results may not be accurate. It would be prudent to collect more data to achieve the minimum expected counts. Assuming that we cannot collect more data, the write-up would include a statement indicating that since the minimum expected counts were not reached, the result may not be accurate.

Region

		Frequency	Percent	Valid Percent	Cumulative Percent
Valid	Northeast	95	19.0	19.0	19.0
	Midwest	105	21.0	21.0	40.0
	South	200	40.0	40.0	80.0
	West	100	20.0	20.0	100.0
	Total	500	100.0	100.0	

Smoking frequency

		Frequency	Percent	Valid Percent	Cumulative Percent
Valid	Every day	95	19.0	41.9	41.9
	Some days	19	3.8	8.4	50.2
	Not at all	113	22.6	49.8	100.0
	Total	227	45.4	100.0	
Missing	System	273	54.6		
Total		500	100.0		

Chi-Square Tests

	Value	df	Asymptotic Significance (2-sided)
Pearson Chi-Square	12.787[a]	6	.047
Likelihood Ratio	13.184	6	.040
Linear-by-Linear Association	.990	1	.320
N of Valid Cases	227		

a. 3 cells (25.0%) have expected count less than 5. The minimum expected count is 3.43.

Symmetric Measures

		Value	Approximate Significance
Nominal by Nominal	Phi	.237	.047
	Cramer's V	.168	.047
N of Valid Cases		227	

Since the counts vary by region, we focus on counts or percentages within each region. It is likely that there are more smokers in the South and less in the Northeast. The table below represents all of the counts.

Smoking frequency * Region Crosstabulation

			Region				
			Northeast	Midwest	South	West	Total
Smoking frequency	Every day	Count	13	19	50	13	95
		Expected Count	17.2	19.7	40.6	17.6	95.0
		% within Region	31.7%	40.4%	51.5%	31.0%	41.9%
		% of Total	5.7%	8.4%	22.0%	5.7%	41.9%
	Some days	Count	2	2	11	4	19
		Expected Count	3.4	3.9	8.1	3.5	19.0
		% within Region	4.9%	4.3%	11.3%	9.5%	8.4%
		% of Total	0.9%	0.9%	4.8%	1.8%	8.4%
	Not at all	Count	26	26	36	25	113
		Expected Count	20.4	23.4	48.3	20.9	113.0
		% within Region	63.4%	55.3%	37.1%	59.5%	49.8%
		% of Total	11.5%	11.5%	15.9%	11.0%	49.8%
Total		Count	41	47	97	42	227
		Expected Count	41.0	47.0	97.0	42.0	227.0
		% within Region	100.0%	100.0%	100.0%	100.0%	100.0%
		% of Total	18.1%	20.7%	42.7%	18.5%	100.0%

(5) Is there a difference in moderate activity by sex? Explain your answer.

There is no difference in moderate activity by sex because $p = .408$, which is not significant.

Sex

		Frequency	Percent	Valid Percent	Cumulative Percent
Valid	Male	220	44.0	44.0	44.0
	Female	280	56.0	56.0	100.0
	Total	500	100.0	100.0	

Freq moderate activity (times per wk)

		Frequency	Percent	Valid Percent	Cumulative Percent
Valid	Less than once per week	31	6.2	6.4	6.4
	Never	44	8.8	9.0	15.4
	Unable to do moderate activity	412	82.4	84.6	100.0
	Total	487	97.4	100.0	
Missing	System	13	2.6		
Total		500	100.0		

Chi-Square Tests

	Value	df	Asymptotic Significance (2-sided)
Pearson Chi-Square	1.794[a]	2	.408
Likelihood Ratio	1.807	2	.405
Linear-by-Linear Association	.040	1	.841
N of Valid Cases	487		

a. 0 cells (0.0%) have expected count less than 5. The minimum expected count is 13.69.

Symmetric Measures

		Value	Approximate Significance
Nominal by Nominal	Phi	.061	.408
	Cramer's V	.061	.408
N of Valid Cases		487	

Freq moderate activity (times per wk) * Sex Crosstabulation

			Sex		
			Male	Female	Total
Freq moderate activity (times per wk)	Less than once per week	Count	16	15	31
		Expected Count	13.7	17.3	31.0
		% within Sex	7.4%	5.5%	6.4%
		% of Total	3.3%	3.1%	6.4%
	Never	Count	16	28	44
		Expected Count	19.4	24.6	44.0
		% within Sex	7.4%	10.3%	9.0%
		% of Total	3.3%	5.7%	9.0%
	Unable to do moderate activity	Count	183	229	412
		Expected Count	181.9	230.1	412.0
		% within Sex	85.1%	84.2%	84.6%
		% of Total	37.6%	47.0%	84.6%
Total		Count	215	272	487
		Expected Count	215.0	272.0	487.0
		% within Sex	100.0%	100.0%	100.0%
		% of Total	44.1%	55.9%	100.0%

(6) Based on the sample and your analyses, what is your overall impression of health activities in this target population?

The following are the general results:

- The average respondent was 47 years old.
- There were more women participants.
- Forty percent of respondents were from the South.
- Based on within regions, as a percentage, people in the South tended to smoke more.
- Half of the respondents smoked to some degree and tended to be younger.
- Those who did not smoke were older, took vitamins, and did little vigorous exercise or strength activities.
- Younger people were more active.
- There was no difference in moderate activity by age.
- The older participants reported sitting most of the day and lifting less.

In conclusion, older participants were likely to be more conscious of their health and limitations. They took some measures to assure a healthy lifestyle.

Providing that the sample represents the target population, these findings can be applied to the population.

Moving Services

This case study is meant to delve into real world situations, sometimes with imperfect information where alternative courses of action are viable. Interpretation of the results may vary based on different perspectives and topical expertise. The following are possible responses.

This case study consists of 5,000 cases of residents who completed a questionnaire designed to discover factors that might affect the amount of years one lives at a place. An independent movers' association commissioned a consulting firm specializing in the service sector to conduct the research. Please explain your responses and answer the study questions in the proper reporting format as covered in this textbook. Alpha is .05. The data file name is "Moving Services Case Study Data."

(1) Describe and screen the sample data. What is the average age (in years) of the study participants? What is the binary gender breakdown? What are the breakdowns by household income and education categories? Remember that these are descriptive statistics. Describe your results.

The average study participant is nearly 47 years old and the standard deviation is 17.70 years.

Descriptives

			Statistic	Std. Error
Age in years	Mean		46.94	.250
	95% Confidence Interval for Mean	Lower Bound	46.45	
		Upper Bound	47.43	
	5% Trimmed Mean		46.79	
	Median		46.00	
	Variance		313.407	
	Std. Deviation		17.703	
	Minimum		18	
	Maximum		79	
	Range		61	
	Interquartile Range		30	
	Skewness		.097	.035
	Kurtosis		-1.174	.069

The age data do not meet the normal distribution assumption because the Shapiro-Wilk statistic is significant at $p < .001$.

Tests of Normality

	Kolmogorov-Smirnov[a]			Shapiro-Wilk		
	Statistic	df	Sig.	Statistic	df	Sig.
Age in years	.073	5000	.000	.955	5000	.000

a. Lilliefors Significance Correction

As can be seen below, the gender is approximately equally distributed.

Gender

		Frequency	Percent	Valid Percent	Cumulative Percent
Valid	Male	2449	49.0	49.0	49.0
	Female	2551	51.0	51.0	100.0
	Total	5000	100.0	100.0	

Nearly 63% reported incomes up to $49,000. Seven point eight percent of the respondents were in the $125,000+ category.

Income category

		Frequency	Percent	Valid Percent	Cumulative Percent
Valid	Under $25,000	1330	26.6	26.6	26.6
	$25,000 - $49,000	1793	35.9	35.9	62.5
	$50,000 - $74,000	819	16.4	16.4	78.8
	$75,000 - $124,000	668	13.4	13.4	92.2
	$125,000+	390	7.8	7.8	100.0
	Total	5000	100.0	100.0	

Nearly 51% had a high school degree or less. Just over 22% reported holding a four-year college degree.

Level of education

		Frequency	Percent	Valid Percent	Cumulative Percent
Valid	Did not complete high school	953	19.1	19.1	19.1
	High school degree	1571	31.4	31.4	50.5
	Some college	1002	20.0	20.0	70.5
	College degree	1113	22.3	22.3	92.8
	Post-undergraduate degree	361	7.2	7.2	100.0
	Total	5000	100.0	100.0	

(2) Examine years at current address, residential zones, hometown size, home status, and building types, all by retirement status. Discuss your findings.

Since the years data violate the normality assumption, we use the nonparametric test. Below are the results for such a test. The Mann-Whitney U test is significant ($p < .001$). It is likely that there is a significant difference in years at current address by retirement status. See the tables below.

Group Statistics

	Retired	N	Mean	Std. Deviation	Std. Error Mean
Years at current address	No	4268	14.29	11.129	.170
	Yes	732	28.60	12.232	.452

Test Statistics[a]

	Age in years
Mann-Whitney U	152882.500
Wilcoxon W	9262928.500
Z	-39.060
Asymp. Sig. (2-tailed)	.000

a. Grouping Variable: Retired

There is a significant difference in residency zone by retirement status ($p = .020$). It is likely that the major difference is between Zones 1 and 5.

Chi-Square Tests

	Value	df	Asymptotic Significance (2-sided)
Pearson Chi-Square	11.623[a]	4	.020
Likelihood Ratio	11.432	4	.022
Linear-by-Linear Association	10.811	1	.001
N of Valid Cases	5000		

a. 0 cells (0.0%) have expected count less than 5. The minimum expected count is 138.06.

Symmetric Measures

		Value	Approximate Significance
Nominal by Nominal	Phi	.048	.020
	Cramer's V	.048	.020
N of Valid Cases		5000	

Crosstab

			Retired		
			No	Yes	Total
Geographic indicator	Zone 1	Count	840	179	1019
		Expected Count	869.8	149.2	1019.0
		% within Geographic indicator	82.4%	17.6%	100.0%
		% of Total	16.8%	3.6%	20.4%
	Zone 2	Count	853	152	1005
		Expected Count	857.9	147.1	1005.0
		% within Geographic indicator	84.9%	15.1%	100.0%
		% of Total	17.1%	3.0%	20.1%
	Zone 3	Count	840	141	981
		Expected Count	837.4	143.6	981.0
		% within Geographic indicator	85.6%	14.4%	100.0%
		% of Total	16.8%	2.8%	19.6%
	Zone 4	Count	816	127	943
		Expected Count	804.9	138.1	943.0
		% within Geographic indicator	86.5%	13.5%	100.0%
		% of Total	16.3%	2.5%	18.9%
	Zone 5	Count	919	133	1052
		Expected Count	898.0	154.0	1052.0
		% within Geographic indicator	87.4%	12.6%	100.0%
		% of Total	18.4%	2.7%	21.0%
Total		Count	4268	732	5000
		Expected Count	4268.0	732.0	5000.0
		% within Geographic indicator	85.4%	14.6%	100.0%
		% of Total	85.4%	14.6%	100.0%

It is likely that hometown size varies by retirement status ($p < .001$).

Chi-Square Tests

	Value	df	Asymptotic Significance (2-sided)
Pearson Chi-Square	29.554[a]	4	.000
Likelihood Ratio	30.292	4	.000
Linear-by-Linear Association	24.207	1	.000
N of Valid Cases	4998		

a. 0 cells (0.0%) have expected count less than 5. The minimum expected count is 110.57.

Symmetric Measures

		Value	Approximate Significance
Nominal by Nominal	Phi	.077	.000
	Cramer's V	.077	.000
N of Valid Cases		4998	

Compared to what would be expected, retirees tend to reside in larger populated areas. Perhaps they live in larger communities that can provide adequate healthcare and living quarters.

Crosstab

			Retired		
			No	Yes	Total
Size of hometown	> 250,000	Count	1178	252	1430
		Expected Count	1220.9	209.1	1430.0
		% within Size of hometown	82.4%	17.6%	100.0%
		% of Total	23.6%	5.0%	28.6%
	50,000-249,999	Count	881	174	1055
		Expected Count	900.7	154.3	1055.0
		% within Size of hometown	83.5%	16.5%	100.0%
		% of Total	17.6%	3.5%	21.1%
	10,000-49,999	Count	774	122	896
		Expected Count	765.0	131.0	896.0
		% within Size of hometown	86.4%	13.6%	100.0%
		% of Total	15.5%	2.4%	17.9%
	2,500-9,999	Count	772	89	861
		Expected Count	735.1	125.9	861.0
		% within Size of hometown	89.7%	10.3%	100.0%
		% of Total	15.4%	1.8%	17.2%
	< 2,500	Count	662	94	756
		Expected Count	645.4	110.6	756.0
		% within Size of hometown	87.6%	12.4%	100.0%
		% of Total	13.2%	1.9%	15.1%
Total		Count	4267	731	4998
		Expected Count	4267.0	731.0	4998.0
		% within Size of hometown	85.4%	14.6%	100.0%
		% of Total	85.4%	14.6%	100.0%

There is a significant relationship between rent/own status and retirement status ($p < .001$). It is likely that retirees rent rather than own their residencies. See the tables below.

Chi-Square Tests

	Value	df	Asymptotic Significance (2-sided)	Exact Sig. (2-sided)	Exact Sig. (1-sided)
Pearson Chi-Square	42.612[a]	1	.000		
Continuity Correction[b]	42.073	1	.000		
Likelihood Ratio	41.542	1	.000		
Fisher's Exact Test				.000	.000
Linear-by-Linear Association	42.604	1	.000		
N of Valid Cases	5000				

a. 0 cells (0.0%) have expected count less than 5. The minimum expected count is 270.25.

b. Computed only for a 2x2 table

Symmetric Measures

		Value	Approximate Significance
Nominal by Nominal	Phi	-.092	.000
	Cramer's V	.092	.000
N of Valid Cases		5000	

Crosstab

			Retired		
			No	Yes	Total
Home Status	Rent	Count	1497	349	1846
		Expected Count	1575.7	270.3	1846.0
		% within Home Status	81.1%	18.9%	100.0%
		% of Total	29.9%	7.0%	36.9%
	Own	Count	2771	383	3154
		Expected Count	2692.3	461.7	3154.0
		% within Home Status	87.9%	12.1%	100.0%
		% of Total	55.4%	7.7%	63.1%
Total		Count	4268	732	5000
		Expected Count	4268.0	732.0	5000.0
		% within Home Status	85.4%	14.6%	100.0%
		% of Total	85.4%	14.6%	100.0%

It is likely that residency building type varies by retirement status ($p < .001$).

Chi-Square Tests

	Value	df	Asymptotic Significance (2-sided)
Pearson Chi-Square	63.544[a]	3	.000
Likelihood Ratio	61.423	3	.000
Linear-by-Linear Association	15.877	1	.000
N of Valid Cases	5000		

a. 0 cells (0.0%) have expected count less than 5. The minimum expected count is 42.75.

Symmetric Measures

		Value	Approximate Significance
Nominal by Nominal	Phi	.113	.000
	Cramer's V	.113	.000
N of Valid Cases		5000	

Most of the homeowners are not retirees. Of the retirees that own their home, the greatest percentage are mobile and multiple-family homes. They do not tend to reside in single-family homes.

Crosstab

			Retired		
			No	Yes	Total
Building type	Single-family	Count	1988	258	2246
		Expected Count	1917.2	328.8	2246.0
		% within Building type	88.5%	11.5%	100.0%
		% of Total	39.8%	5.2%	44.9%
	Multiple-Family	Count	1254	300	1554
		Expected Count	1326.5	227.5	1554.0
		% within Building type	80.7%	19.3%	100.0%
		% of Total	25.1%	6.0%	31.1%
	Condominium/Townhouse	Count	799	109	908
		Expected Count	775.1	132.9	908.0
		% within Building type	88.0%	12.0%	100.0%
		% of Total	16.0%	2.2%	18.2%
	Mobile Home	Count	227	65	292
		Expected Count	249.3	42.7	292.0
		% within Building type	77.7%	22.3%	100.0%
		% of Total	4.5%	1.3%	5.8%
Total		Count	4268	732	5000
		Expected Count	4268.0	732.0	5000.0
		% within Building type	85.4%	14.6%	100.0%
		% of Total	85.4%	14.6%	100.0%

(3) Expert assessments and previous research suggest that a number of variables may contribute to how long people remain at a residence before moving. Examine for correlations between "years at current address" and each of the following variables: age, years of education, years with current employer, household income, number of people in household, hours spent watching TV/week, amount spent on primary credit card during the last month, amount spent on secondary credit card during the last month, and job satisfaction. Explain your results.

Among the significant correlations, age is associated with many of the variables. There are correlations between age and: years at current address, years with current employer, number of people in household, and job satisfaction, which all appear to make sense. Years with current employer is correlated with years at current address, suggesting that perhaps commute may play a role in this relationship.

Correlations

		Years at current address	Age in years	Years of education	Years with current employer	Household income	Number of people in household (inc respondent)	Hours spent watching TV last week	Amount spent on primary card last month	Amount spent on secondary card last month	Job satisfaction
Years at current address	Pearson Correlation	1	.821**	-.053**	.601**	.239**	-.235**	-.008	.068**	.060**	.348**
	Sig. (2-tailed)		.000	.000	.000	.000	.000	.574	.000	.000	.000
	N	5000	5000	5000	5000	5000	5000	5000	5000	5000	5000
Age in years	Pearson Correlation	.821**	1	-.091**	.703**	.195**	-.333**	-.036*	.031*	.027	.413**
	Sig. (2-tailed)	.000		.000	.000	.000	.000	.010	.028	.057	.000
	N	5000	5000	5000	5000	5000	5000	5000	5000	5000	5000
Years of education	Pearson Correlation	-.053**	-.091**	1	-.211**	.177**	.022	-.005	.099**	.059**	-.079**
	Sig. (2-tailed)	.000	.000		.000	.000	.118	.745	.000	.000	.000
	N	5000	5000	5000	5000	5000	5000	5000	5000	5000	5000
Years with current employer	Pearson Correlation	.601**	.703**	-.211**	1	.324**	-.244**	-.011	.082**	.088**	.461**
	Sig. (2-tailed)	.000	.000	.000		.000	.000	.424	.000	.000	.000
	N	5000	5000	5000	5000	5000	5000	5000	5000	5000	5000
Household income	Pearson Correlation	.239**	.195**	.177**	.324**	1	-.068**	.051**	.359**	.319**	.229**
	Sig. (2-tailed)	.000	.000	.000	.000		.000	.000	.000	.000	.000
	N	5000	5000	5000	5000	5000	5000	5000	5000	5000	5000
Number of people in household (inc respondent)	Pearson Correlation	-.235**	-.333**	.022	-.244**	-.068**	1	.030*	-.006	-.011	-.160**
	Sig. (2-tailed)	.000	.000	.118	.000	.000		.035	.668	.428	.000
	N	5000	5000	5000	5000	5000	5000	5000	5000	5000	5000
Hours spent watching TV last week	Pearson Correlation	-.008	-.036*	-.005	-.011	.051**	.030*	1	.038**	.016	-.006
	Sig. (2-tailed)	.574	.010	.745	.424	.000	.035		.007	.245	.696
	N	5000	5000	5000	5000	5000	5000	5000	5000	5000	5000
Amount spent on primary card last month	Pearson Correlation	.068**	.031*	.099**	.082**	.359**	-.006	.038**	1	.593**	.067**
	Sig. (2-tailed)	.000	.028	.000	.000	.000	.668	.007		.000	.000
	N	5000	5000	5000	5000	5000	5000	5000	5000	5000	5000
Amount spent on secondary card last month	Pearson Correlation	.060**	.027	.059**	.088**	.319**	-.011	.016	.593**	1	.051**
	Sig. (2-tailed)	.000	.057	.000	.000	.000	.428	.245	.000		.000
	N	5000	5000	5000	5000	5000	5000	5000	5000	5000	5000
Job satisfaction	Pearson Correlation	.348**	.413**	-.079**	.461**	.229**	-.160**	-.006	.067**	.051**	1
	Sig. (2-tailed)	.000	.000	.000	.000	.000	.000	.696	.000	.000	
	N	5000	5000	5000	5000	5000	5000	5000	5000	5000	5000

**. Correlation is significant at the 0.01 level (2-tailed).

*. Correlation is significant at the 0.05 level (2-tailed).

(4) Based on any significant results in Question 3, run a regression where years at current residence is the outcome variable. Explain your results.

Best practice dictates that we first screen the data before running regression. In this case, we will assume that the data meet the assumptions.

Outcome variable: Years at current residence.

Predictors: Age, years of education, years with current employer, household income, number of people in household, amount spent on primary credit card during the last month, amount spent on secondary credit card during the last month, and job satisfaction.

The regression model is significant ($p < .001$) and explains 68.3% of the variance in years at current address.

ANOVA[a]

Model		Sum of Squares	df	Mean Square	F	Sig.
1	Regression	523137.085	8	65392.136	1345.316	.000[b]
	Residual	242598.865	4991	48.607		
	Total	765735.950	4999			

a. Dependent Variable: Years at current address

b. Predictors: (Constant), Job satisfaction, Amount spent on secondary card last month, Years of education, Number of people in household (inc respondent), Household income, Age in years, Amount spent on primary card last month, Years with current employer

Model Summary

Model	R	R Square	Adjusted R Square	Std. Error of the Estimate
1	.827[a]	.683	.683	6.972

a. Predictors: (Constant), Job satisfaction, Amount spent on secondary card last month, Years of education, Number of people in household (inc respondent), Household income, Age in years, Amount spent on primary card last month, Years with current employer

However, a number of variables do not have significant regression coefficients. Interestingly, in this case, the adjusted *r*-square does not vary. This is unusual, but does occur. We know that the age variable is not normally distributed and that we have not screened the data. Consider screening the data to determine if there is a possible connection between the data characteristics and the inconsistent adjusted *r*-square result.

Coefficients[a]

Model		Unstandardized Coefficients		Standardized Coefficients	t	Sig.	95.0% Confidence Interval for B	
		B	Std. Error	Beta			Lower Bound	Upper Bound
1	(Constant)	-12.853	.632		-20.352	.000	-14.091	-11.615
	Age in years	.565	.008	.808	69.032	.000	.549	.581
	Years of education	.041	.032	.011	1.295	.195	-.021	.104
	Years with current employer	.032	.016	.025	2.034	.042	.001	.063
	Household income	1.537E-5	.000	.069	7.327	.000	.000	.000
	Number of people in household (inc respondent)	.383	.075	.043	5.118	.000	.236	.530
	Amount spent on primary card last month	.001	.001	.012	1.132	.258	.000	.002
	Amount spent on secondary card last month	.001	.001	.007	.710	.478	-.001	.002
	Job satisfaction	-.055	.082	-.006	-.665	.506	-.215	.106

a. Dependent Variable: Years at current address

If the data met the assumptions, we would rerun the model without the nonsignificant predictors, which is what we did here.

ANOVA[a]

Model		Sum of Squares	df	Mean Square	F	Sig.
1	Regression	522843.973	4	130710.993	2688.032	.000[b]
	Residual	242891.978	4995	48.627		
	Total	765735.950	4999			

a. Dependent Variable: Years at current address

b. Predictors: (Constant), Number of people in household (inc respondent), Household income, Age in years, Years with current employer

Model Summary

Model	R	R Square	Adjusted R Square	Std. Error of the Estimate
1	.826[a]	.683	.683	6.973

a. Predictors: (Constant), Number of people in household (inc respondent), Household income, Age in years, Years with current employer

We now have another nonsignificant predictor. Repeat the procedure without years with current employer.

Coefficients[a]

Model		Unstandardized Coefficients		Standardized Coefficients			95.0% Confidence Interval for B	
		B	Std. Error	Beta	t	Sig.	Lower Bound	Upper Bound
1	(Constant)	-12.146	.406		-29.897	.000	-12.942	-11.349
	Age in years	.564	.008	.807	69.999	.000	.549	.580
	Years with current employer	.024	.015	.019	1.632	.103	-.005	.053
	Household income	1.739E-5	.000	.078	9.253	.000	.000	.000
	Number of people in household (inc respondent)	.383	.075	.043	5.125	.000	.237	.530

a. Dependent Variable: Years at current address

The model and all predictors are significant.

ANOVA[a]

Model		Sum of Squares	df	Mean Square	F	Sig.
1	Regression	522714.441	3	174238.147	3581.962	.000[b]
	Residual	243021.509	4996	48.643		
	Total	765735.950	4999			

a. Dependent Variable: Years at current address

b. Predictors: (Constant), Number of people in household (inc respondent), Household income, Age in years

Model Summary

Model	R	R Square	Adjusted R Square	Std. Error of the Estimate
1	.826[a]	.683	.682	6.974

a. Predictors: (Constant), Number of people in household (inc respondent), Household income, Age in years

For each year of age, years at current address incrementally increase by .573 of a year. Household income contributes very little to years at current address, yet it is significant. For each person in the household, years at current residence incrementally increase .382 of a year.

Coefficients[a]

Model		Unstandardized Coefficients		Standardized Coefficients			95.0% Confidence Interval for B	
		B	Std. Error	Beta	t	Sig.	Lower Bound	Upper Bound
1	(Constant)	-12.363	.384		-32.199	.000	-13.115	-11.610
	Age in years	.573	.006	.820	95.339	.000	.561	.585
	Household income	1.821E-5	.000	.082	10.057	.000	.000	.000
	Number of people in household (inc respondent)	.382	.075	.043	5.102	.000	.235	.528

a. Dependent Variable: Years at current address

(5) Based on the sample and your analyses, what is your overall impression of these variables on years at current residence?

- The average age of respondents is nearly 47 years old.
- The gender split was roughly 50% women and 50% men.
- Nearly 63% reported incomes up to $49,000. Nearly 79% have a household income no more than $74,000. Seven point eight percent of the respondents were in the $125,000+ category.
- Fifty-one percent have at most a high school degree and 22% hold bachelor's degrees.
- Compared to what would be expected, retirees tend to live in larger populated communities.
- Most of the homeowners are not retirees. Of the retirees that own their home, the greatest percentage are mobile and multiple-family homes. They do not tend to reside in single-family homes.
- Retirees are likely to not move, especially if someone resides with them.

In sum, retirees tend to make do with their resources. They reside in larger communities where elder-care resources are available. Retirees likely rent an apartment, and when they do own a residence, it is a mobile or multiple-family home. They are less likely to reside in a single-family home. Multiple-family homes can accommodate a variety of conditions and elder needs.

Providing that the sample represents the target population, these findings can be applied to the population.

Sample Size Matters

These case study exercises are meant to delve into real world situations, sometimes with imperfect information where alternative courses of action are viable. Choices made may vary based on different perspectives and topical expertise. The following are possible responses.

You are charged with preparing the requirements for a number of statistical studies and analyses. Download a free trial copy of SamplePower3 and determine the appropriate sample sizes for the following analyses. In cases in which sample sizes are less than 30, assume a minimum of 31. In all cases, alpha is .05. Please answer the following questions in the proper reporting format as covered in this textbook.

(1) We wish to determine the average age of a typical human services client. Assume that it is 38 years old and we want to know if it is different from 45 years old, which is the cutoff age for the program under study. The standard deviation is 10 years and the required statistical power is 95%. What is the optimal sample size?

With the proposed sample size of 29 cases, the study will have power of 94.8% to yield a statistically significant result. The sample size of 29 is changed to 31.

This computation assumes that the population from which the sample will be drawn has a mean of 38.1 years old with a standard deviation of 10.0 years old. The observed value will be tested against a theoretical value of 45.0 years old.

Additionally, an observed mean of 38.1 years old would be reported with a 95.0% confidence interval of 34.34 to 41.86.

The precision estimated here is the median precision. Precision will vary as a function of the observed standard deviation (as well as sample size).

(2) The state wishes to determine whether the state mean household income of $52,000 (standard deviation = $20,000) significantly differs from its most affluent community's suspected mean household income of $65,000 (standard deviation = $25,000). The required statistical power is 80%. What is the necessary sample size?

The goal of the proposed study is to detect whether two population means are equal (or not equal). With a proposed sample size of 49 for each of the two groups, the study will have power of 80.3% to yield a statistically significant result.

This computation assumes that the mean difference is –$13,000.0 (corresponding to means of $52,000 vs. $65,000) and the common within-group standard deviation is $22,638.5 (based on standard deviation estimates of $20,000 and $25,000).

(3) The state wishes to determine whether the state mean household (HH) income of $52,000 significantly differs from its most affluent community's suspected mean HH income of $65,000. They have a similar standard deviation, which is $25,000. The required statistical power is 90%. A difference of $2,000 would be meaningful. What is the necessary sample size?

This study will have power of 90% to show that the mean HH income for the affluent community is at least as high as the mean income for the state overall. This assumes that the HH income means for the state and affluent populations are $52,000 and $65,000, with a common within-group standard deviation of $25,000, that a difference of $2,000 or less is unimportant, that the sample size in the two groups will be 48 each, and that alpha (one-tailed test) is set at .05.

(4) This study will involve measuring weight loss from those individuals participating in a two-week revised diet program. The persons will be weighed before and after the diet. Previous records indicate a mean loss of 4 pounds for those who completed the program. The revised diet plan is expected to yield a loss (difference) of 5 pounds. What is the appropriate sample size?

With the proposed sample size of 50 pairs of cases, the study will have power of 89.6% to yield a statistically significant result. This computation assumes that the population from which the sample will be drawn has a mean difference of 5.0 pounds with a standard deviation of 2.2 pounds. The observed value will be tested against a theoretical value of a 4.0 pound difference.

(5) Candidate A's staff wishes to survey whether their candidate has more than 50% of the vote. They want to detect at least 55% support. Assuming power is 85%, what sample size is required?

This proposed study is to test that the proportion positive in the population is 0.50. With the proposed sample size of 890, the study will have power of 84.8% to yield a statistically significant result. This computation assumes that the proportion positive in the population is 0.55. The observed value will be tested against a theoretical value of 0.50.

This effect was selected as the smallest effect that would be important to detect, in the sense that any smaller effect would not be of substantive significance. It is also assumed that this effect size is reasonable given the circumstances and/or any study objectives.

(6) This study plans to examine the association between violent video gaming and individuals' tendency to assess some forms of violence as justified. We wish to detect a minimum correlation of .25. Power is 95%. What is a sufficient sample size?

With the proposed sample size of 200, the study will have power of 95.3% to yield a statistically significant result. This computation assumes that the correlation in the population is .25. The observed value will be tested against a theoretical value of .00. Moreover, an observed correlation of .25 would be reported with a 95% confidence interval of .12 to .38.

(7) A study plans to examine the average length of residency in three areas (groups). The standard deviation is 2 years and power is 85%. The expected effect size is .40, which is the change in the data explained by the groups. What is the required sample size?

This power analysis is for a one-way analysis of variance with three levels. The study will include 24 cases per cell for a total of 72 cases. The effect size (f) is 0.40, which yields power of 0.85.

(8) This study's aim is to determine whether education, experience, and company growth predict employee salary. The minimum explained variance is 20% and power is 90%. What is the necessary sample size?

The MLR model will include three variables in the set of interest, which will yield an *r*-square of .20. With the given sample size of 60, the study will have power of .90.

This effect was selected as the smallest effect that would be important to detect, in the sense that any smaller effect would not be of substantive significance. It is also assumed that the effect size is reasonable in this field of study.

Violent Crime Recidivism

This case study is meant to delve into real world situations, sometimes with imperfect information where alternative courses of action are viable. Interpretation of the results may vary based on different perspectives and topical expertise. The following are possible responses.

The sample data for this case study consist of the criminal records of 5,687 offenders who were examined to determine if there were any relationships among a number of record variables that contributed to or reduced the rate of recidivism among offenders. Please explain all of your responses and answer the study questions in the proper reporting format as covered in this textbook. Alpha is .05. The data file name is "Recidivism Case Study Data."

(1) Describe and screen the sample data. Conduct descriptive and screening statistical analysis for the following variables: age in years, gender, marital status, SES, educational level, and employment status.

The total sample size is 5,687. The mean age is 29.69 years and the standard deviation is 10.80.

Tests of Normality

	Kolmogorov-Smirnov[a]		
	Statistic	df	Sig.
Age in years	.146	5687	.000

a. Lilliefors Significance Correction

Descriptives

				Statistic	Std. Error
Age in years	Mean			29.69	.143
	95% Confidence Interval for Mean		Lower Bound	29.41	
			Upper Bound	29.97	
	5% Trimmed Mean			28.95	
	Median			26.00	
	Variance			116.834	
	Std. Deviation			10.809	
	Minimum			18	
	Maximum			59	
	Range			41	
	Interquartile Range			16	
	Skewness			.878	.032
	Kurtosis			-.320	.065

In the sample, the gender breakdown is 85.1% men and 14.9% women.

Binary Gender

		Frequency	Percent	Valid Percent	Cumulative Percent
Valid	Male	4838	85.1	85.1	85.1
	Female	849	14.9	14.9	100.0
	Total	5687	100.0	100.0	

Of the respondents, 42.4% are married and 57.6% are unmarried.

Marital status

		Frequency	Percent	Valid Percent	Cumulative Percent
Valid	Unmarried	3273	57.6	57.6	57.6
	Married	2414	42.4	42.4	100.0
	Total	5687	100.0	100.0	

The social status is 32.9% for lower SES, 36.8% for middle SES, and 30.3% for upper SES.

Social status

		Frequency	Percent	Valid Percent	Cumulative Percent
Valid	Lower class	1869	32.9	32.9	32.9
	Middle class	2092	36.8	36.8	69.7
	Upper class	1726	30.3	30.3	100.0
	Total	5687	100.0	100.0	

Below are the counts and percentages by educational level.

Level of education

		Frequency	Percent	Valid Percent	Cumulative Percent
Valid	Did not complete high school	1106	19.4	19.4	19.4
	High school degree	2944	51.8	51.8	71.2
	College degree	1440	25.3	25.3	96.5
	Post-undergraduate degree	197	3.5	3.5	100.0
	Total	5687	100.0	100.0	

Below is the employment status breakdown.

Employed

		Frequency	Percent	Valid Percent	Cumulative Percent
Valid	No	2154	37.9	37.9	37.9
	Yes	3533	62.1	62.1	100.0
	Total	5687	100.0	100.0	

(2) Is there a relationship between the first violent crime and the second? Is there a relationship between the severity of the first crime and the second's severity?

Use the valid percentages unless otherwise advised. See the tables below.

Violent first crime

		Frequency	Percent	Valid Percent	Cumulative Percent
Valid	No	5277	92.8	92.8	92.8
	Yes	410	7.2	7.2	100.0
	Total	5687	100.0	100.0	

Violent second crime

		Frequency	Percent	Valid Percent	Cumulative Percent
Valid	No	1549	27.2	92.5	92.5
	Yes	125	2.2	7.5	100.0
	Total	1674	29.4	100.0	
Missing	System	4013	70.6		
Total		5687	100.0		

Chi-Square Tests

	Value	df	Asymptotic Significance (2-sided)	Exact Sig. (2-sided)	Exact Sig. (1-sided)
Pearson Chi-Square	210.285[a]	1	.000		
Continuity Correction[b]	205.856	1	.000		
Likelihood Ratio	132.022	1	.000		
Fisher's Exact Test				.000	.000
Linear-by-Linear Association	210.159	1	.000		
McNemar Test				.001[c]	
N of Valid Cases	1674				

a. 0 cells (0.0%) have expected count less than 5. The minimum expected count is 12.77.

b. Computed only for a 2x2 table

c. Binomial distribution used.

Symmetric Measures

		Value	Approximate Significance
Nominal by Nominal	Phi	.354	.000
	Cramer's V	.354	.000
N of Valid Cases		1674	

Since the two samples or groups are related, we use the McNemar test statistic. There is a significant relationship between first violent crime and the second (p = .001). It is likely that those who committed a first violent crime will likely commit a second. The first violent act results were: no = 92.8% and yes = 7.2% and the second violent act: no = 92.5% and yes = 7.5%, which represents a pattern.

Violent second crime * Violent first crime Crosstabulation

			Violent first crime		
			No	Yes	Total
Violent second crime	No	Count	1438	111	1549
		Expected Count	1390.8	158.2	1549.0
		% within Violent second crime	92.8%	7.2%	100.0%
		% of Total	85.9%	6.6%	92.5%
	Yes	Count	65	60	125
		Expected Count	112.2	12.8	125.0
		% within Violent second crime	52.0%	48.0%	100.0%
		% of Total	3.9%	3.6%	7.5%
Total		Count	1503	171	1674
		Expected Count	1503.0	171.0	1674.0
		% within Violent second crime	89.8%	10.2%	100.0%
		% of Total	89.8%	10.2%	100.0%

Again, because the two samples or groups are related, we use the McNemar test statistic. There is a significant relationship between the first crime and the second (p = .001). The same pattern emerges between the severity of the crimes where there are fewer severe crimes and more less severe crimes. Use the valid percentages unless otherwise advised. See the tables below.

Severity of first crime

		Frequency	Percent	Valid Percent	Cumulative Percent
Valid	Class B misdemeanor	1982	34.9	34.9	34.9
	Class A misdemeanor	1615	28.4	28.4	63.2
	Class C felony	1110	19.5	19.5	82.8
	Class B felony	722	12.7	12.7	95.5
	Class A felony	258	4.5	4.5	100.0
	Total	5687	100.0	100.0	

Severity of second crime

		Frequency	Percent	Valid Percent	Cumulative Percent
Valid	Class B misdemeanor	510	9.0	30.5	30.5
	Class A misdemeanor	422	7.4	25.2	55.7
	Class C felony	316	5.6	18.9	74.6
	Class B felony	265	4.7	15.8	90.4
	Class A felony	161	2.8	9.6	100.0
	Total	1674	29.4	100.0	
Missing	System	4013	70.6		
Total		5687	100.0		

Chi-Square Tests

	Value	df	Asymptotic Significance (2-sided)
Pearson Chi-Square	336.927[a]	16	.000
Likelihood Ratio	321.411	16	.000
Linear-by-Linear Association	292.918	1	.000
McNemar-Bowker Test	71.609	10	.000
N of Valid Cases	1674		

a. 0 cells (0.0%) have expected count less than 5. The minimum expected count is 6.83.

Symmetric Measures

		Value	Approximate Significance
Nominal by Nominal	Phi	.449	.000
	Cramer's V	.224	.000
N of Valid Cases		1674	

Severity of second crime * Severity of first crime Crosstabulation

			Severity of first crime					
			Class B misdemeanor	Class A misdemeanor	Class C felony	Class B felony	Class A felony	Total
Severity of second crime	Class B misdemeanor	Count	284	128	73	21	4	510
		Expected Count	177.0	132.5	111.8	67.0	21.6	510.0
		% within Severity of second crime	55.7%	25.1%	14.3%	4.1%	0.8%	100.0%
		% of Total	17.0%	7.6%	4.4%	1.3%	0.2%	30.5%
	Class A misdemeanor	Count	150	126	97	42	7	422
		Expected Count	146.5	109.7	92.5	55.5	17.9	422.0
		% within Severity of second crime	35.5%	29.9%	23.0%	10.0%	1.7%	100.0%
		% of Total	9.0%	7.5%	5.8%	2.5%	0.4%	25.2%
	Class C felony	Count	81	90	79	53	13	316
		Expected Count	109.7	82.1	69.3	41.5	13.4	316.0
		% within Severity of second crime	25.6%	28.5%	25.0%	16.8%	4.1%	100.0%
		% of Total	4.8%	5.4%	4.7%	3.2%	0.8%	18.9%
	Class B felony	Count	52	62	79	54	18	265
		Expected Count	92.0	68.9	58.1	34.8	11.2	265.0
		% within Severity of second crime	19.6%	23.4%	29.8%	20.4%	6.8%	100.0%
		% of Total	3.1%	3.7%	4.7%	3.2%	1.1%	15.8%
	Class A felony	Count	14	29	39	50	29	161
		Expected Count	55.9	41.8	35.3	21.2	6.8	161.0
		% within Severity of second crime	8.7%	18.0%	24.2%	31.1%	18.0%	100.0%
		% of Total	0.8%	1.7%	2.3%	3.0%	1.7%	9.6%
Total		Count	581	435	367	220	71	1674
		Expected Count	581.0	435.0	367.0	220.0	71.0	1674.0
		% within Severity of second crime	34.7%	26.0%	21.9%	13.1%	4.2%	100.0%
		% of Total	34.7%	26.0%	21.9%	13.1%	4.2%	100.0%

(3) Is there a relationship between those offenders exposed to rehabilitation and the second offense?

There is a significant relationship between initial rehabilitation and second arrest ($p < .001$). Those who received rehabilitation tended not to be arrested a second time.

Received rehabilitation

		Frequency	Percent	Valid Percent	Cumulative Percent
Valid	No	4074	71.6	71.6	71.6
	Yes	1613	28.4	28.4	100.0
	Total	5687	100.0	100.0	

Second arrest

		Frequency	Percent	Valid Percent	Cumulative Percent
Valid	No	4013	70.6	70.6	70.6
	Yes	1674	29.4	29.4	100.0
	Total	5687	100.0	100.0	

Chi-Square Tests

	Value	df	Asymptotic Significance (2-sided)	Exact Sig. (2-sided)	Exact Sig. (1-sided)
Pearson Chi-Square	12.971[a]	1	.000		
Continuity Correction[b]	12.739	1	.000		
Likelihood Ratio	13.168	1	.000		
Fisher's Exact Test				.000	.000
Linear-by-Linear Association	12.969	1	.000		
N of Valid Cases	5687				

a. 0 cells (0.0%) have expected count less than 5. The minimum expected count is 474.80.

b. Computed only for a 2x2 table

Symmetric Measures

		Value	Approximate Significance
Nominal by Nominal	Phi	-.048	.000
	Cramer's V	.048	.000
N of Valid Cases		5687	

Second arrest * Received rehabilitation Crosstabulation

			Received rehabilitation		
			No	Yes	Total
Second arrest	No	Count	2819	1194	4013
		Expected Count	2874.8	1138.2	4013.0
		% within Second arrest	70.2%	29.8%	100.0%
		% of Total	49.6%	21.0%	70.6%
	Yes	Count	1255	419	1674
		Expected Count	1199.2	474.8	1674.0
		% within Second arrest	75.0%	25.0%	100.0%
		% of Total	22.1%	7.4%	29.4%
Total		Count	4074	1613	5687
		Expected Count	4074.0	1613.0	5687.0
		% within Second arrest	71.6%	28.4%	100.0%
		% of Total	71.6%	28.4%	100.0%

(4) Are there associations among SES, educational level, severity of first crime, and severity of second crime?

There is a positive medium correlation between the first and second crime's severity ($r_s = .407$, $p < .001$) and a weak negative correlation between level of education and social status ($r_s = -.033$, $p = .014$).

Correlations

			Social status	Level of education	Severity of first crime	Severity of second crime
Spearman's rho	Social status	Correlation Coefficient	1.000	-.033*	.000	.000
		Sig. (2-tailed)	.	.014	.973	.998
		N	5687	5687	5687	1674
	Level of education	Correlation Coefficient	-.033*	1.000	.016	-.017
		Sig. (2-tailed)	.014	.	.232	.493
		N	5687	5687	5687	1674
	Severity of first crime	Correlation Coefficient	.000	.016	1.000	.407**
		Sig. (2-tailed)	.973	.232	.	.000
		N	5687	5687	5687	1674
	Severity of second crime	Correlation Coefficient	.000	-.017	.407**	1.000
		Sig. (2-tailed)	.998	.493	.000	.
		N	1674	1674	1674	1674

*. Correlation is significant at the 0.05 level (2-tailed).

**. Correlation is significant at the 0.01 level (2-tailed).

(5) Is age correlated with crime severity?

There is no correlation between age and crime severity.

Correlations

			Age category	Severity of first crime	Severity of second crime
Spearman's rho	Age category	Correlation Coefficient	1.000	-.019	.009
		Sig. (2-tailed)	.	.142	.706
		N	5687	5687	1674
	Severity of first crime	Correlation Coefficient	-.019	1.000	.407**
		Sig. (2-tailed)	.142	.	.000
		N	5687	5687	1674
	Severity of second crime	Correlation Coefficient	.009	.407**	1.000
		Sig. (2-tailed)	.706	.000	.
		N	1674	1674	1674

**. Correlation is significant at the 0.01 level (2-tailed).

(6) What can you conclude from your findings?

- The average respondent age is 29.69 years (standard deviation = 10.80 years).
- Men comprised 85.1% of participants and 14.9% were women.
- The majority of participants were not married.
- SES was unremarkable.
- 71.1% received education through high school.
- Their employment rate was 62.1%.
- First time violent offenders were likely to commit another violent crime.
- The crime severity pattern remained the same, with most crimes being minor.
- Rehabilitation after the first crime tended to reduce the probability of a second arrest.

In conclusion, most offenders were men and not married. Many did not attend college and the majority worked. The violent offenders were likely to commit subsequent violent crimes. Generally, offenders tended to maintain a pattern of less severe crimes. Early intervention appeared to reduce the rate of second arrests.

Providing that the sample represents the target population, these findings can be applied to the population.

What Motivates Students to Perform

This case study is meant to delve into real world situations, sometimes with imperfect information where alternative courses of action are viable. Interpretation of the results may vary based on different perspectives and topical expertise. The following are possible responses.

In an effort to understand what motivates students to do well in school, motivational data were collected from 1,000 undergraduate junior and senior level female and male students from across the United States. With self-determination theory serving as a framework, students were asked about whether they enjoyed their academic studies, had a sense of control of their academic activities, felt competent about their academic performance, and could relate to and had meaningful relationships with others in their college or university. These variables are believed to drive motivation to do well in college. Additionally, students reported the degree to which they were required to use math in courses. The dependent variable was student-reported GPA (overall grade average at the time of the study). The study aim was to determine whether and to what extent enjoyment, control, competence, relatedness, and level of math estimate academic performance as measured by GPA.

GPA is coded using a 4.00 scale. Age is reported in years. Gender is coded 1 = men and 2 = women. All of the other variables are formatted in a nine-point sliding scale from 1 to 9, where a higher score represents more of the variable attribute. The bar sliding scale allows for selections two places to the right of the decimal point. Please explain your responses and answer the study questions in the proper reporting format as covered in this textbook. Alpha is .05. The data file name is "Student Motivation Study Data."

(1) Provide descriptive statistics for all numeric variables as well as the percentage breakdown by gender.

The "Descriptive Statistics" table provides the means and standard deviations of the numeric variables. The same size was 1,000, composed of 51.8% (n = 518) women and 48.2% (n = 482) men.

Descriptive Statistics

	N	Mean	Std. Deviation
Control	1000	5.0000	1.00000
Competence	1000	5.0000	1.00000
Enjoy	1000	5.0000	1.00000
Relatedness	1000	5.0000	1.00000
Math_Level	1000	4.2106	.11052
GPA	1000	2.5500	.51000
Age	1000	21.01	.481
Valid N (listwise)	1000		

Gender

		Frequency	Percent	Valid Percent	Cumulative Percent
Valid	Men	482	48.2	48.2	48.2
	Women	518	51.8	51.8	100.0
	Total	1000	100.0	100.0	

(2) Screen the data (all variables) for univariate normal distribution. Report any violations of the normality assumption.

All of the numeric variables meet the normal distribution assumption because the Shapiro-Wilk statistics were $p > .05$, ranging from .268 to .783. The chances that the distributions do not vary from normality are well above .05 or the acceptable risk level.

Tests of Normality

	Kolmogorov-Smirnov[a]			Shapiro-Wilk		
	Statistic	df	Sig.	Statistic	df	Sig.
Control	.014	1000	.200*	.998	1000	.268
Competence	.020	1000	.200*	.999	1000	.668
Enjoy	.017	1000	.200*	.997	1000	.111
Relatedness	.017	1000	.200*	.998	1000	.297
Math_Level	.018	1000	.200*	.999	1000	.783
GPA	.015	1000	.200*	.999	1000	.600
Age	.014	1000	.200*	.999	1000	.743

*. This is a lower bound of the true significance.

a. Lilliefors Significance Correction

(3) Before analyzing the data in the aggregate, examine for gender effects.

Because all of the independent samples *t*-tests are not significant, there are no differences by gender. Therefore, the data can be analyzed together.

Group Statistics

	Gender	N	Mean	Std. Deviation	Std. Error Mean
Age	Men	482	21.01	.477	.022
	Women	518	21.01	.485	.021
GPA	Men	482	2.5587	.51096	.02327
	Women	518	2.5419	.50947	.02238
Control	Men	482	5.0048	.98911	.04505
	Women	518	4.9956	1.01097	.04442
Competence	Men	482	5.0152	1.00370	.04572
	Women	518	4.9858	.99731	.04382
Enjoy	Men	482	4.9746	1.01353	.04617
	Women	518	5.0236	.98763	.04339
Relatedness	Men	482	5.0022	1.01499	.04623
	Women	518	4.9980	.98682	.04336
Math_Level	Men	482	4.2069	.10298	.00469
	Women	518	4.2141	.11708	.00514

Independent Samples Test

		Levene's Test for Equality of Variances		t-test for Equality of Means					95% Confidence Interval of the Difference	
		F	Sig.	t	df	Sig. (2-tailed)	Mean Difference	Std. Error Difference	Lower	Upper
Age	Equal variances assumed	.792	.374	-.163	998	.870	-.005	.030	-.065	.055
	Equal variances not assumed			-.163	994.935	.870	-.005	.030	-.065	.055
GPA	Equal variances assumed	.011	.917	.523	998	.601	.01688	.03229	-.04648	.08024
	Equal variances not assumed			.523	992.412	.601	.01688	.03229	-.04649	.08025
Control	Equal variances assumed	.677	.411	.146	998	.884	.00921	.06332	-.11504	.13346
	Equal variances not assumed			.146	995.486	.884	.00921	.06327	-.11494	.13337
Competence	Equal variances assumed	.334	.563	.465	998	.642	.02942	.06331	-.09482	.15366
	Equal variances not assumed			.465	991.887	.642	.02942	.06333	-.09485	.15369
Enjoy	Equal variances assumed	.370	.543	-.775	998	.439	-.04903	.06330	-.17325	.07518
	Equal variances not assumed			-.774	988.515	.439	-.04903	.06336	-.17337	.07530
Relatedness	Equal variances assumed	1.440	.230	.066	998	.947	.00420	.06332	-.12005	.12845
	Equal variances not assumed			.066	988.077	.947	.00420	.06338	-.12018	.12858
Math_Level	Equal variances assumed	6.981	.008	-1.032	998	.302	-.00722	.00699	-.02094	.00651
	Equal variances not assumed			-1.037	994.880	.300	-.00722	.00696	-.02088	.00644

(4) Based on the results in Question 3, run bivariate data screening to examine for bivariate normality, linearity, and homoscedasticity.

Control and competence clearly meet the bivariate normality, linearity, and homoscedasticity assumptions. The other three bivariate distributions appear to have some degree of bivariate normality and weak linearity. They do not appear to be homoscedasticity (oval-shaped along the line). In reality, the three assumptions are not often met.

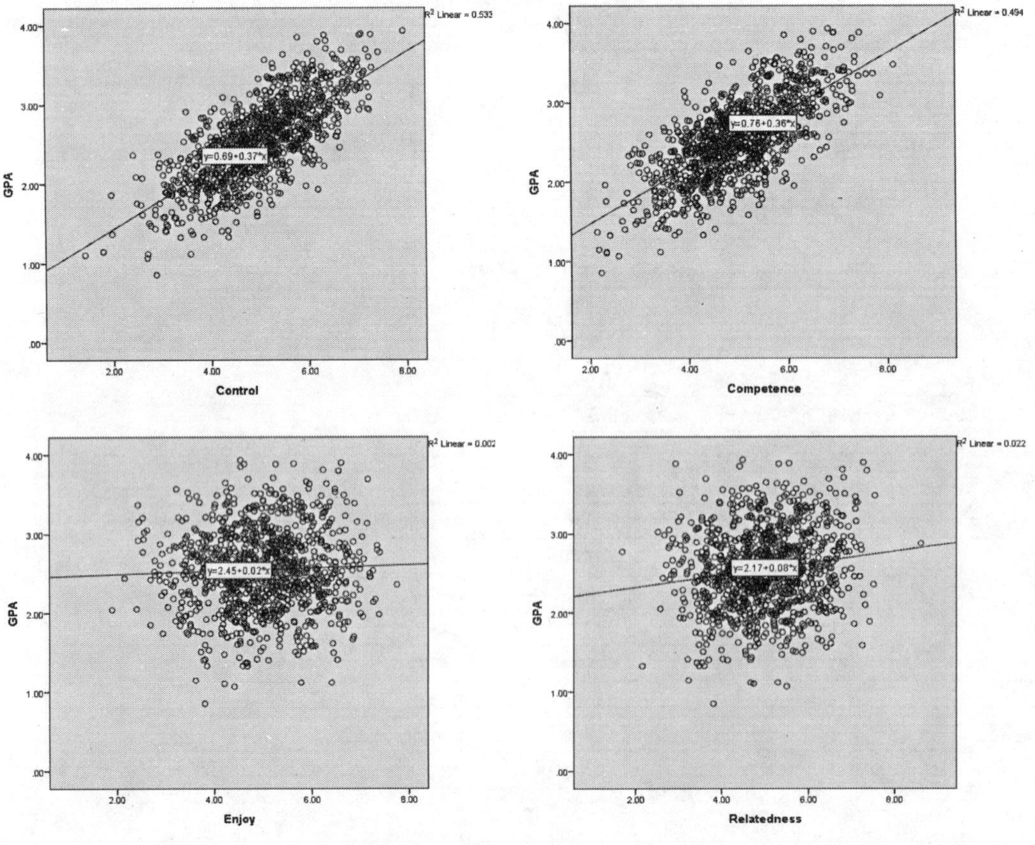

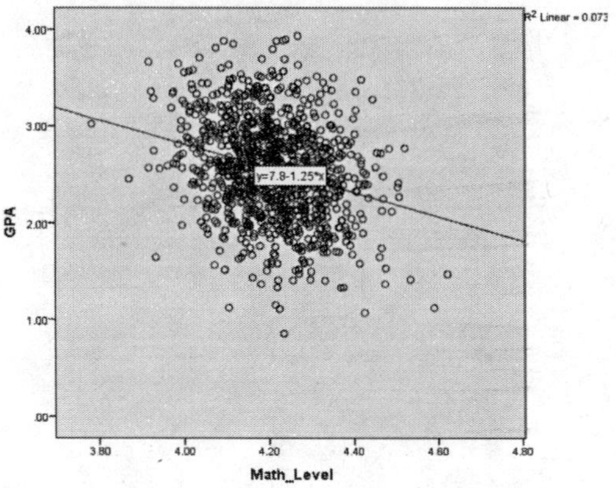

(5) Based on the results in Question 3, run a MLR.

For illustrative purposes, we ran the analysis with all of the predictors. The model is significant at $p < .001$. It explains 61.6% of the variance in GPA. However, relatedness is not significant ($p = .337$). The model will be rerun without relatedness.

ANOVA[a]

Model		Sum of Squares	df	Mean Square	F	Sig.
1	Regression	159.976	5	31.995	318.467	.000[b]
	Residual	99.864	994	.100		
	Total	259.840	999			

a. Dependent Variable: GPA

b. Predictors: (Constant), Math_Level, Enjoy, Control, Relatedness, Competence

Model Summary

Model	R	R Square	Adjusted R Square	Std. Error of the Estimate
1	.785[a]	.616	.614	.31696

a. Predictors: (Constant), Math_Level, Enjoy, Control, Relatedness, Competence

Coefficients[a]

Model		Unstandardized Coefficients B	Std. Error	Standardized Coefficients Beta	t	Sig.	95.0% Confidence Interval for B Lower Bound	Upper Bound
1	(Constant)	1.227	.429		2.860	.004	.385	2.068
	Control	.247	.014	.485	17.311	.000	.219	.275
	Competence	.175	.015	.344	12.052	.000	.147	.204
	Enjoy	.032	.013	.062	2.384	.017	.006	.058
	Relatedness	.013	.013	.025	.961	.337	-.013	.039
	Math_Level	-.240	.095	-.052	-2.524	.012	-.427	-.053

a. Dependent Variable: GPA

The revised model is significant at $p < .001$. It explains 61.5% of the variance in GPA. All of the regression coefficients are significant.

ANOVA[a]

Model		Sum of Squares	df	Mean Square	F	Sig.
1	Regression	159.883	4	39.971	397.883	.000[b]
	Residual	99.956	995	.100		
	Total	259.840	999			

a. Dependent Variable: GPA

b. Predictors: (Constant), Math_Level, Enjoy, Control, Competence

Model Summary

Model	R	R Square	Adjusted R Square	Std. Error of the Estimate
1	.784[a]	.615	.614	.31695

a. Predictors: (Constant), Math_Level, Enjoy, Control, Competence

The 95% confidence intervals are displayed. For example, we are 95% confident that a one-point increase in perceived control will result, on average, in an increase in GPA from .219 to .275 (based on a 4.00 scale).

Coefficients[a]

Model		Unstandardized Coefficients		Standardized Coefficients	t	Sig.	95.0% Confidence Interval for B	
		B	Std. Error	Beta			Lower Bound	Upper Bound
1	(Constant)	1.241	.429		2.894	.004	.399	2.082
	Control	.247	.014	.484	17.294	.000	.219	.275
	Competence	.178	.014	.348	12.385	.000	.150	.206
	Enjoy	.040	.010	.078	3.881	.000	.020	.060
	Math_Level	-.240	.095	-.052	-2.525	.012	-.427	-.054

a. Dependent Variable: GPA

(6) Interpret the MLR results.

The motivational variables sense of control, feeling of competence (or doing tasks well), and the enjoyment when doing tasks positively predict a higher GPA. As more math is involved in course work, GPA decreases. The reasons may be the challenges associated with math and/or perhaps its abstract nature, along with other factors.

More specifically, for every one-point increase in control, GPA increases, on average, by .247 out of 4.00. For every one-point increase in competence, GPA increases, on average, by .178. For every one point in reported task enjoyment, GPA increases, on average, by .040. For every one point of reported need to do math in courses, GPA decreases, on average, by .240. These are incremental changes that must consider the y-intercept (GPA when the predictors are zero) when calculating prediction values.

Providing that the sample represents the target population, these findings can be applied to the population.

Psychological Effects of the Workplace

This case study is meant to delve into real world situations, sometimes with imperfect information where alternative courses of action are viable. Interpretation of the results may vary based on different perspectives and topical expertise. The following are possible responses.

In an effort to understand and reduce employee stress, a major corporation surveyed a cross section of 500 employees. The study aim was to determine whether and to what extent employee age, salary, education, the informal company support network, and perceptions of job insecurity explain overall employee self-perceived depression, anxiety, and stress.

Age is reported in years. Salary is reported in dollars annually. Education is formatted in years completed, allowing for partial years. Workplace support network is formatted in a six-point scale, ranging from 0 = no support to 5 = great deal of support. Job insecurity is formatted in an eight-point scale, ranging from 0 = no job insecurity to 7 = complete job insecurity. Anxiety and stress are formatted in an 11-point scale, from 0 = no anxiety or stress to 10 = completely anxious or stressed. Overall depression is anchored in a six-point scale, from 0 = not depressed at all to 5 = deeply depressed. These measures are self-perceptions of the attributes and do not necessarily meet the clinical definitions of the conditions.

Please explain your responses and answer the study questions in the proper reporting format as covered in this textbook. Alpha is .05. The data file name is "Workplace Study Data."

(1) Screen all of the variables for normal distribution. Report each variable mean and standard deviation score. Interpret the results. All of the variables meet the normality assumption according to the Shapiro–Wilk statistic. They have *p*-values greater than .05. The means and standard deviations are also reported in the "Descriptive Statistics" table below.

Tests of Normality

	Kolmogorov-Smirnov[a]			Shapiro-Wilk		
	Statistic	df	Sig.	Statistic	df	Sig.
Age	.053	500	.002	.995	500	.138
Salary	.025	500	.200*	.998	500	.841
Education	.029	500	.200*	.997	500	.429
Support	.033	500	.200*	.996	500	.331
Job_Insecurity	.022	500	.200*	.997	500	.635
Stress	.031	500	.200*	.995	500	.093
Depression	.023	500	.200*	.996	500	.340
Anxiety	.019	500	.200*	.998	500	.789

*. This is a lower bound of the true significance.

a. Lilliefors Significance Correction

Descriptive Statistics

	N	Mean	Std. Deviation
Age	500	42.0390	2.92131
Salary	500	$66,930.67	$3,626.574
Education	500	4.71	.487
Job_Insecurity	500	4.2118	.40969
Stress	500	6.1963	.47177
Depression	500	2.2461	.20967
Anxiety	500	6.8391	.51201
Support	500	2.5165	.20511
Valid N (listwise)	500		

(2) Consider overall depression, anxiety, and stress as outcome variables. Run bivariate screening of each outcome variable with age, salary, education, the informal company support network, and perceptions of job insecurity. Interpret the results.

Only two predictor variables and each outcome variable met the assumptions of bivariate normal distributions, linearity, and homoscedasticity. They are work network support and depression, job insecurity and anxiety, and job insecurity and stress.

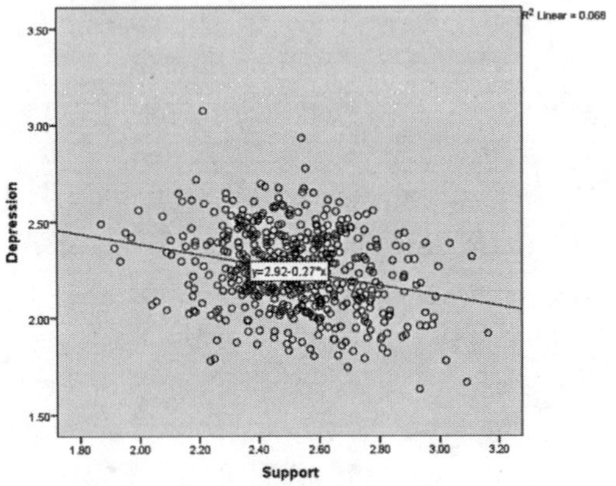

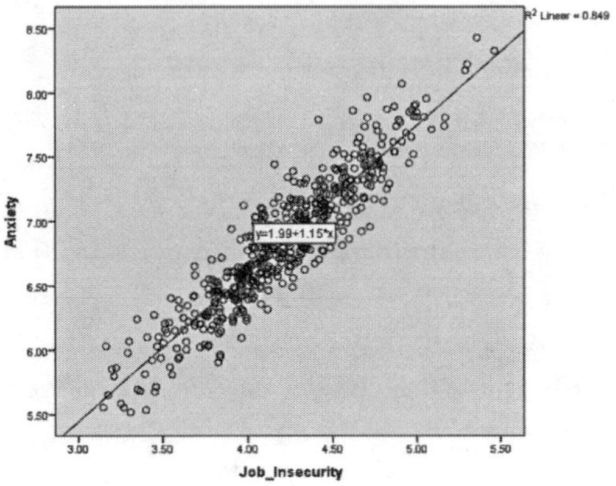

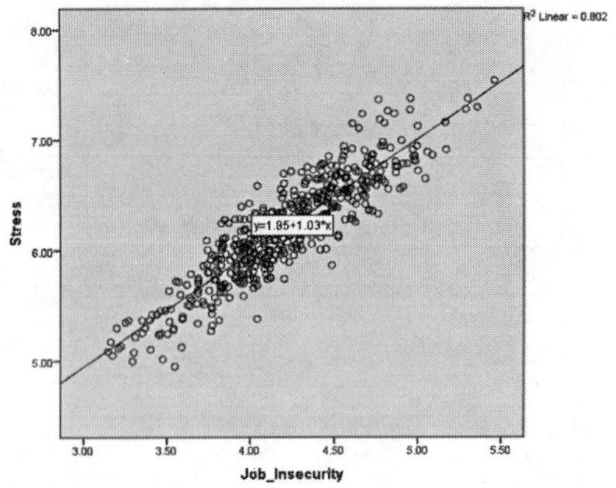

(3) Run three separate MLRs for each of the outcome variables. Interpret each model.

Since there is only one predictor for each outcome variable, we will run SLR.

Predictor: Work Support Network

Outcome: Depression

The SLR model is significant because the overall test is $p < .001$. The model only explains 6.8% of the variance in depression. For every one point in support, there is an incremental decrease in depression of .266. Both variables are based on a five-point scale. We are 95% confident that for every one point in reported support, depression will decrease from .18 to .353.

ANOVA[a]

Model		Sum of Squares	df	Mean Square	F	Sig.
1	Regression	1.490	1	1.490	36.284	.000[b]
	Residual	20.447	498	.041		
	Total	21.937	499			

a. Dependent Variable: Depression

b. Predictors: (Constant), Support

Model Summary

Model	R	R Square	Adjusted R Square	Std. Error of the Estimate
1	.261[a]	.068	.066	.20263

a. Predictors: (Constant), Support

Coefficients[a]

Model		Unstandardized Coefficients B	Std. Error	Standardized Coefficients Beta	t	Sig.	95.0% Confidence Interval for B Lower Bound	Upper Bound
1	(Constant)	2.917	.112		26.119	.000	2.697	3.136
	Support	-.266	.044	-.261	-6.024	.000	-.353	-.180

a. Dependent Variable: Depression

Predictor: Job Insecurity

Outcome: Anxiety

Again, we have a significant model because the overall test is $p < .001$. The model explains 84.9% of the variance in anxiety. For every one point in job insecurity, there is an incremental increase in anxiety of 1.152. Job insecurity is based on an eight-point scale and anxiety is based on 11 points. We are 95% confident that for every one point in reported job insecurity, anxiety will increase from 1.109 to 1.195.

ANOVA[a]

Model		Sum of Squares	df	Mean Square	F	Sig.
1	Regression	111.111	1	111.111	2808.044	.000[b]
	Residual	19.705	498	.040		
	Total	130.816	499			

a. Dependent Variable: Anxiety

b. Predictors: (Constant), Job_Insecurity

Model Summary

Model	R	R Square	Adjusted R Square	Std. Error of the Estimate
1	.922[a]	.849	.849	.19892

a. Predictors: (Constant), Job_Insecurity

Coefficients[a]

Model		Unstandardized Coefficients B	Std. Error	Standardized Coefficients Beta	t	Sig.	95.0% Confidence Interval for B Lower Bound	Upper Bound
1	(Constant)	1.988	.092		21.614	.000	1.807	2.169
	Job_Insecurity	1.152	.022	.922	52.991	.000	1.109	1.195

a. Dependent Variable: Anxiety

Predictor: Job Insecurity

Outcome: Stress

Again, we have a significant model because the overall test is $p < .001$. The model explains 80.2% of the variance in stress. For every one point in job insecurity, there is an incremental increase in stress of 1.031. Job insecurity is based on a seven-point scale and stress is based on 11 points. We are 95% confident that for every one point in reported job insecurity, stress will increase from .986 to 1.076.

ANOVA[a]

Model		Sum of Squares	df	Mean Square	F	Sig.
1	Regression	89.092	1	89.092	2019.781	.000[b]
	Residual	21.967	498	.044		
	Total	111.059	499			

a. Dependent Variable: Stress

b. Predictors: (Constant), Job_Insecurity

Model Summary

Model	R	R Square	Adjusted R Square	Std. Error of the Estimate
1	.922[a]	.849	.849	.19892

a. Predictors: (Constant), Job_Insecurity

Coefficients[a]

Model		Unstandardized Coefficients B	Std. Error	Standardized Coefficients Beta	t	Sig.	95.0% Confidence Interval for B Lower Bound	Upper Bound
1	(Constant)	1.852	.097		19.074	.000	1.662	2.043
	Job_Insecurity	1.031	.023	.896	44.942	.000	.986	1.076

a. Dependent Variable: Stress

(4) Which model is most appropriate and why?

Both models where job insecurity predicts anxiety and stress are strong models because of their explanatory power. The results indicate that it is situational job insecurity more than age, salary, education, or work support network that drives work related anxiety and stress. As one might expect, these findings suggest that job uncertainty can have a negative effect on an individual's psychological state.

Providing that the sample represents the target population, these findings can be applied to the population.

Appendix D

Research Goal and Objectives

D.1 Research Goal

Quality quantitative research is a systematic, logical, and well-organized process. A **research goal** is what we intend to achieve. It guides the research process. Goals are inspired by a problem, challenge, or opportunity that requires data-driven decision-making.

Some goals examine existing topics from different perspectives. Some types of research goals explore new topics or methodologies. For instance, researchers have applied family communication patterns to help understand how organizations communicate. Other researchers are applying network theory to analyze website word content.

The following are a few examples of research applications:

- An organization seeks to know why there is high employee turnover in some of its customer service districts.
- A marketing department wants to know the extent of consumer demand for a new product under development.
- A company considers whether to acquire a competitor and its customer list or take another approach in a move to increase market share. Feasibility research that explores these options would help identify the most attractive strategy to increase market share.
- Other research might explore the costs and benefits of capital equipment upgrading in light of long-term marketing opportunities.

D.2 Research Objectives

Attainment of a research goal is often measured through objectives. A **research objective** is the means by which we achieve a goal. It is often stated as a research statement to be tested for its truth or falsity or as a research question to be answered. Both guide the design of a study, selection of sampling strategy, and planned statistical analyses, all of which address objectives and ultimately achieve the research goal. Most of the time, a study has more than one objective, each addressing a specific aspect of the goal.

Developing and Testing Research Statements

If researchers have a clear picture of what they seek to address, they can frame objectives as statements (often called **hypotheses**). A **research statement** is a claim that is tested through the process of falsification. **Falsification** tests the probability of a statement being untrue. More specifically, through statistical significance testing, analysts determine if a research statement is false. The statement can be framed in the affirmative or non-affirmative, which is guided by the research goal and what is known about the topic.

For instance, statements exploring motivation and job performance might be framed as follows: "Individual motivation is positively linked to job performance" or "Individual motivation is not positively linked to job performance." In this kind of study, there usually are other research statements relating to types of motivation, types of job performance, or the individual attributes of the respondents. For example, additional research statements exploring the level of intrinsic and extrinsic motivation could be incorporated because they are likely to be associated with job performance in different ways.

Another example is: "Intervention Z is more effective than Intervention Y," "Intervention Z is not more effective than Intervention Y," or "There is no difference between Interventions Z and Y." An intervention is effective at various levels or in different ways depending on the treatment and attributes of the participants. In order to provide a more comprehensive picture of what is studied, additional research statements that address these issues would be included.

In both examples, these statements would be tested for their falseness.

Developing and Answering Research Questions

If researchers do not have a clear picture of what they seek to address and/or are exploring for answers to questions (some of which may be more general than specific research statements), they can ask questions that will shed light on the phenomenon. A **research question** is an objective framed as a question to be answered. Applying the examples above: "Is there a positive relationship between individual motivation and the individual's job performance?" "Is there a difference in effectiveness between Interventions Z and Y?" This approach is open-ended.

D.3 The Interconnected Parts of Research Goals and Objectives

Once the research problem is defined, a goal is developed in order to address the problem. The research goal is achieved through research objectives. Research objectives are achieved through the implementation of target population representative sampling techniques, as discussed in Chapter 5, followed by appropriate data collection methods. Once the data are collected, then they are analyzed and results are reported in a manner that reflects the research objectives.

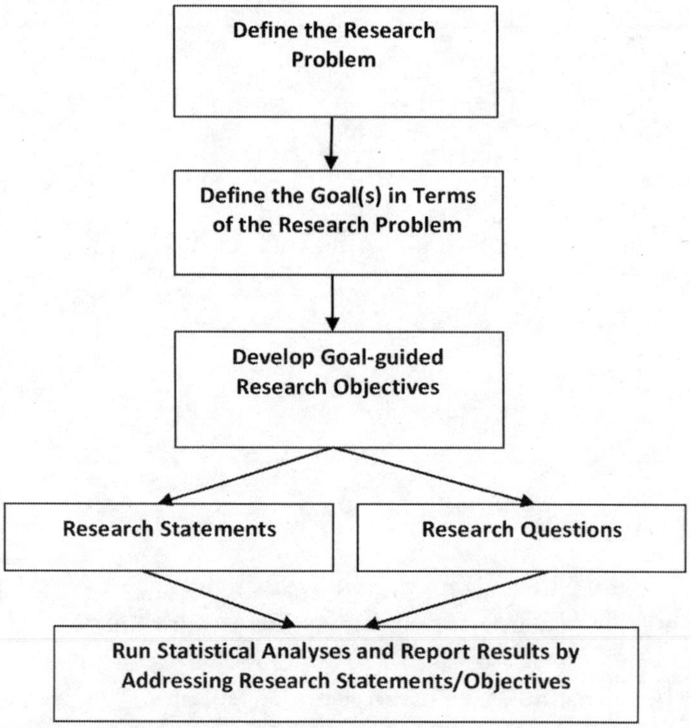

Figure D.1 The Flow of Goals and Objectives in Quantitative Research

Appendix E

Types of Research Design

E.1 Introduction to Research Designs

Studies come in various research designs. The designs covered in this appendix are by no means comprehensive. A **research design** is the strategy and plan that specifies the methods for collecting and analyzing data.

One way to classify designs is by the nature of the data to be collected. From this perspective, designs fall into three broad categories: survey, experimental, and observational. Survey data are directly provided from research participants, thus there is an element of participant subjectivity. Experimental studies generate data relevant to an experimental condition. Depending on how the data are collected, subjectivity and objectivity may be introduced. Observational studies offer a wider variety of sources. They can be researcher recorded behaviors, secondary economic or financial data, content analysis, Web surfing data, and so forth. Observational research is likely to be objective.

These design types often share similar attributes. For instance, an experimental study may involve surveys or include recorded observations. These studies can be exploratory, descriptive, evaluative, and causal. The type of research and design details are shaped by research goals, objectives, target population characteristics, accessibility to a representative sample, and available study resources. We will discuss survey, experimental, and observational designs, as well as a number of related research designs.

E.2 Survey or Self-Report Research Design

Surveys are questionnaires that are given to a sample to complete in order to measure something. For instance, if a social service agency suffers from high social worker turnover, surveying the staff on their work conditions might reveal the causes of the high turnover.

A **survey design** approach implies subjective responses. For instance, if you ask children if they think that their parents are too strict, generally they may respond that parents are stricter compared to the replies of the parents. An employee may claim to be a hard worker, which may vary from those perceptions of the employee's supervisor. Thus, survey studies likely measure participant perceptions.

Survey differentiation rests with the mode of data collection. There are two basic types of survey data collection. As depicted in Figure E.1, there are those surveys that are person-to-person administered and those that are self-administered.

Person-to-Person Administered Survey

A **person-to-person administered survey** can be directly administered in-person by a researcher in real time. The survey interview can be mediated by technology such as telephone or digital devices using applications such as Skype, Google Plus, and many more. A person-to-person method has a higher response rate compared to self-administered surveys. A major drawback is that persons may not provide candid answers to sensitive questions, especially when the researcher is face-to-face with the survey participant.

Self-Administered Survey

A **self-administered survey** is when invited respondents complete the surveys on their own time. They are provided with the survey or access to it. Participants answer questions using any of the following formats: hard copy (which is returned via mail), text message, email, email-linked, and Web-based such as Qualtrics and Zoomerang. Compared with person-to-person data collection methods, respondents tend to be more candid. However, the response rates are lower than person-to-person survey recruitment and data collection.

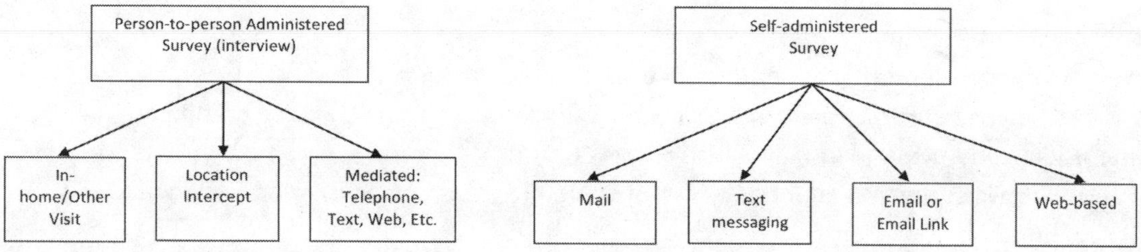

Figure E.1 Survey Design

Person-to-person interviews occur in real time. Examples are special U.S. Census studies and door-to-door polling. Some interviews are work-related. A typical location intercept is a mall intercept, where someone approaches a mall customer and invites the person to participate in a survey, which consists of a brief interview where responses are recorded on a tablet or clipboard. Other real-time methods are mediated by technology, such as a telephone call interview, a text message interview or instant chat, and other various types of Web-based communication platforms involving text, audio, and/or video.

Self-administered surveys are completed on the respondent's time frame. It might arrive in the mail, including a self-addressed, stamped, return envelope. Text messaging format usage is another method. The survey may be in the message, which is ideal for short surveys, or a link may be provided that redirects the participant to a Web-based survey. Email survey invitations follow a similar approach to that of text messaging.

E.3 Experimental Research Design

An **experimental design study** introduces a condition in a laboratory or field (natural) setting and tests to determine if the condition affects the study participants or results in some way. Thus, the study focuses on the presence and absence of a condition and establishes whether there is a cause and effect relationship. The condition is known by various names, such as **treatment**, **manipulation**, or **stimulus**. Generally, a baseline is established before exposure to the treatment, which is done through a measurement of what is studied. Then, the study participants are exposed to the treatment followed by one or more measurements, usually including the same measures. The pre-exposure and post-exposure measurements are then compared to determine if they are statistically different from each other. If they are different, then exposure to the treatment had an effect.

For example, we can determine whether high school students who enrolled in a special weekend college program designed to increase teen interest in science, technology, engineering, and mathematics (STEM) are more likely to major in a STEM major upon entering college.

Cause and Effect Relationship

Experimental studies aim to establish a cause and effect relationship where change in the independent variable causes change in the dependent variable. The experimental treatment is the independent variable and the pre- and post-tested measures are the dependent variable. For example, do different teaching styles influence motivation to learn? The teaching style is the treatment. Does the introduction of a support group reduce the rate of recidivism (returning to prison)? The support group is the treatment. The exposure to the treatment is the cause. The change in motivation and the reduction in recidivism are the effects.

Lab Experiment

A **lab experiment** occurs in an artificial setting such as a lab. It is highly structured, which makes it much easier to manage factors that can affect results. For example, a marketing company seeks to determine if its newly developed video ads increase Brand A's appeal. Customers visited a theater setting and were each given a tablet. By way of the tablet, they were asked about their attitude toward the brand before being exposed to the ads and after seeing the ads. The environment was controlled and free from distractions. The major drawback of a lab experiment is that findings are limited to conditions that are replicated in the lab setting.

Field Experiment

A **field experiment** occurs in a **natural setting** because it is where the experimental treatment exists in real life. There is less structure and there is less control of the experiment. Accounting for extraneous variables is challenging. Extending the above example, participants would be asked questions about Brand A. Then, at home, they would be asked to watch a certain network during a specific time range. After the time passed, they would be asked once more about the brand. Differences in responses would suggest that the commercials influenced their attitudes toward Brand A.

Manipulation Check

Another important component of an experimental design is the **manipulation check**, which is a test that determines whether the participants were aware of the treatment. In the marketing example, recall of the ads or details about the ads are indicators that participants were aware of the experimental treatment.

External Influences

There are potential external influences on the dependent variable that are not part of the study. Sometimes researchers are unaware of them. These are called **extraneous variables** and are external to the study. In our classroom motivation study, since the focus is teaching style, variables such as teacher gender or class subject matter are extraneous. In the recidivism study, the emphasis is on the program's effectiveness, and not such factors as the participant's history of substance abuse or family support structure.

If extraneous variables are identified, then they can be accounted for and statistical adjustments can be made accordingly. The ones that we can account for are called control variables. Control variables are usually measured during the pre-test or before the introduction of the treatment.

Managing the Effects of Unaccounted for Extraneous Variables

It is not always possible to know all extraneous variables in an experimental study. Although they may not be identified, usage of a control group can help discover the effects of unknown variables on the study. The control group is a sample that is measured two or more times like the treatment group, but it is not exposed to the experimental condition. If the treatment made a difference, then there should be a difference between the pre- and post-treatment groups, and there should not be a difference between the pre- and post-control groups. A difference between the two pre-treatment groups (experimental and control) and the post-treatment groups (experimental and control) suggests that the difference was accounted for by unknown extraneous variable(s) and not the experimental treatment. Figure E.2 summarizes the process.

The Experimental Design Process Model

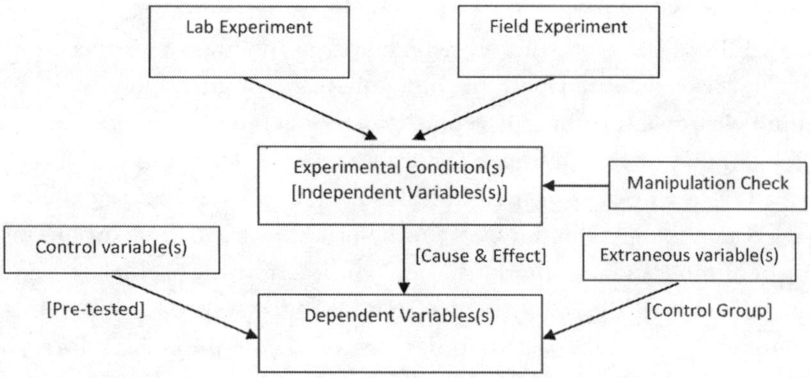

Figure E.2 Experimental Design

Let's examine an application of the experimental design. A manufacturer sought to discover if a new software upgrade for automated manufacturing equipment reduced the amount of routine maintenance per month. Over a period of time, measurements were taken from a representative sample of the pre-upgrade condition and later the same sample was measured again after the upgrade. Additionally, two measurements were taken from a sample that was not upgraded, which was the control group. The pre-upgrade and post-upgrade maintenance records revealed that maintenance decreased after the upgrade; however, the control group remained unchanged. As a result of this finding, the upgrade was scheduled for all equipment.

E.4 Observational Research Design

An **observational research design** involves the observing, collecting, and recording of data from people, objects, and events in a systematic manner by human and/or mechanical methods. The observer does not question any people and data may have been gathered from secondary sources. Personal observation, mechanical observation, audit, content or interaction analysis, and trace analysis are the major methods of observation. Let us cover these methods. Figure E.3 summarizes observational designs.

Personal Observation

Personal observation involves the researcher observing behavior without interacting with who or what is being observed. For example, an observer might record wait times in a hospital emergency room. A researcher might observe and record individuals negotiating terms of an agreement. The observer is vigilant to record as objectively as possible. Some observations are **structured**, where what is to be observed is specified, and others are **unstructured**, in which case what is observed is unspecified. Some observations may be **disguised**. For example, the researcher may observe through a one-way mirror. Other observations are **undisguised** because the participants are aware that they are being observed. Last, observations may occur in a natural setting or may take place in a **lab setting**.

Mechanical Observation

Mechanical observation requires a device rather than an individual to record observations. Observation may include video or audio recordings, Internet traffic and behavior, eyes-on-screen tracking, response latency devices, vehicle traffic counters, devices that record individual physiological responses, and so forth. For example, the functional MRI (fMRI) measures brain activity by recording the flow of blood to different areas of the brain. When persons are exposed to various visual stimuli, the fMRI can be used to locate which area of the brain becomes more active. The results can be statistically correlated with an individual's reported responses. Eyes-on-screen studies can determine what website content people watch on a monitor. The direction of the eyes is examined in the context of the website's features.

Data previously collected is a growing area of mechanical observation. Massive databases or **big data** can be explored using data mining techniques. Specific approaches are used incorporating statistics and computer programming. These methods deploy descriptive, predictive, and prescriptive analytics. Descriptive analytics is used to discover trends and the causes of such trends. Predictive analytics, as the name suggests, utilizes data to develop predictive models to forecast future behaviors and events. Prescriptive analytics combines the first two and adds data-driven decision-making to the mix. Many domains have adopted the analytics term in their disciplines, such as marketing analytics, medical analytics, insurance analytics, educational analytics, and so forth.

Content Analysis

Content analysis focuses on the analysis of communication content. Words, the relationships among words, themes, images, and the overall message are systematically studied. Organizations can content analyze messages posted on an internal discussion board or blog in order to develop a sense of how organizational members think and feel about the organization. Literature on new medical procedures can be content analyzed to determine whether they show promise and warrant further investigation. Companies can content analyze competitors' websites in order to learn about how competitors position or reposition their brands. Studying the content of social media communication and interaction can help us understand what is important to people, how these people spend their free time, identify social influencers, and so forth.

Some methods are qualitative while others are quantitative, and still others combine both approaches via a two-stage methodology where mutually agreed upon coding schemes are quantified for statistical analysis. nVivo is a popular content analysis application.

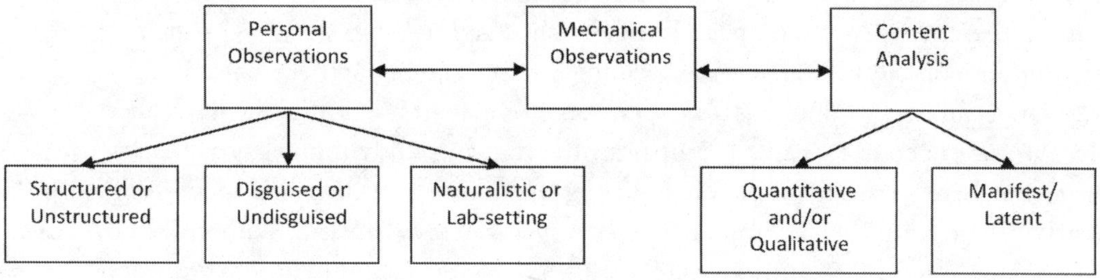

Figure E.3 Observational Design

Computational approaches rely on **manifest content analysis**, which counts actions, words, and co-occurrence of words. For instance, an analysis might seek to determine how many times do specific emotional words co-occur with the words "leadership" and "children." On the other hand, in addition to actions, words, and word co-occurrence counts, **latent content analysis** has an interpretative component. For example, research might look for patterns in the relationships among television stereotypical characters and their ethnicity as well as the gender of actors.

E.5 Other Research Designs

There are others ways to view research design. The following discussion briefly covers some design types.

Single Time vs. Repeated Measures Designs

Some research designs involve a single data collection point while others include collecting data more than once, which can extend over a number of years.

Cross-Sectional Design

A **cross-sectional design** involves collecting data from a sample at a single point in time. It is a snapshot. For example, a satisfaction survey sent to discharged hospital patients is a cross-sectional study. This type of research can describe and establish associations; however, it cannot be used to discover cause and effect relationships between variables.

Longitudinal Design

Generally, **longitudinal designs** usually involve collecting the same data from the same sample over a period of time (usually at least three times). The analysis involves examining for trends over time and can be applied to nearly any type of study. This approach looks for change over time. For example, pollsters may wish to monitor whether individuals who voted for presidential Candidate X continue to support her. Researchers may wish to learn whether children's media habits influence how they respond to stress as young adults. What follows is a brief discussion of the major types of longitudinal designs.

A **panel study** entails collecting data from the same sample over time whether they are persons, devices, records, or some other type of data source. This is called a **within-subjects design** because the purpose is to examine for consistency or change within each individual sampling unit. For instance, monitoring the same group of children's academic performance from elementary school through and including college is a panel study. The key drawback is response bias. People simply answer the same way over time regardless of change.

A **tracking study** involves collect data over time. Different samples are drawn from the same sampling frame (representative source or list from which sampling units are drawn such as an email list) so that response bias is minimized. For example, marketing researchers may monitor the change in new brand awareness by drawing from a customer email list and surveying a number of customer samples during the course of an ad campaign. If a tracking study focuses on a similar group of individuals who share a specific experience during the same time, then it is specifically called a **cohort study**. For example, a researcher may survey social issue awareness in children starting from ages 5 to 9 and then follow this group for 30 years asking the same questions every five years from samples drawn from the same sampling frame.

Longitudinal study designs can suggest cause and effect relationships over time. A drawback to such studies is cost and time requirements. Over time, other variables come into play, which can affect the study variables. For this reason, careful planning is required in order to anticipate and control for such situations.

Mixed Research Designs

Many times research designs are combined because of the nature of the study. This is called a **mixed research design**. For example, focus groups and surveys are often used together. First, focus groups are conducted in order to provide depth by drilling down into an issue. What is discovered informs subsequent survey development. Inversely, focus groups may follow survey data collection because some findings might require further exploration. Focus group data is an expeditious approach to addressing questions in survey results. Moreover, focus group participant quotations can be included in support of survey findings.

Some experimental designs are combined with a pre-test survey and personal observation. Participants may complete a pre-test survey that collects basic demographic and control data. Researchers may observe and record participant behaviors before and after the participants were exposed to an experimental treatment. The treatment could be background music or a program on a television in a room. There are many combinations of study designs suitable for various types of research.

Appendix F

Comparing Counts of the Same Sample Measured More Than Twice Using a Categorical Variable

F.1 A Categorical Variable Measured More than Twice Using the Same Sample

This appendix is a brief discussion about the tests applied to measure the same sample measured more than twice using a categorical variable with two categories. The nonparametric test for several related samples, **Cochran's Q**, is used when there are more than two measurement points. It is an extension of the McNemar chi-square test, which is discussed in Chapter 15. Since the same source provides the data at various times (e.g. same participants measured more than twice), this is a within-subjects analysis. Significance testing is used to determine whether there are any differences among the counted frequencies. The analyses includes all possible unique paired comparisons.

The Cochran's Q is an overall test that reveals whether at least one paired significant difference exists. The specific differences are discovered by running a series of McNemar chi-square paired comparisons. For example, in a pharma study aimed at measuring the effectiveness of a new antidepressant over a six-month period of time, patients were asked if they "feel better" compared to the previous month. The same patients would be asked at the end of each of the six months. The question must be framed as a binary response such as "yes" or "no." The test reveals if there is an overall difference in wellness over time and where those specific time differences lie.

F.2 Data Assumptions

Since we are analyzing sample data, we need to use probability statistics in order to discover whether any sort of relationship exists between or among the counts. For this type of analysis, there are a number of assumptions.

First, the sample is random and representative of the population under study. Second, the groups being compared are related in some way, which is usually indicated by the same data source for each count point. Third, the response choices are binary. For instance, there are only two choices or levels of data, such as "supportive" or "non-supportive" or "yes" or "no." Fourth, the two responses are assumed to be mutually exclusive and exhaustive. In other words, if a response is "yes," then it cannot be "no." Fifth, since this is a repeated measures procedure, each time point has an equal number of cases. Last, each combined time/category cell must contain at least five frequencies or counts.

Appendix G

More on Linear Regression

G.1 Introduction to Other Tools in Regression Analysis

Linear regression, and especially multiple linear regression (MLR), offers a vast array of diagnostics and statistics that provide insights about data. For those readers intrigued by MLR, this appendix briefly introduces the impact of outliers on results, major regression methods, dummy coding, interaction terms, residual analysis, and multicollinearity. Understanding and interpreting these concepts and their associated techniques will add valuable skills to an analyst's toolbox.

G.2 The Influence of Outliers on Linear Regression Results

Keep in mind that bivariate outliers can easily shift the prediction line of best fit so that results differ compared to results once the outliers are removed. The scatter plot in Figure G.1 depicts the prediction line and equation with five outliers and Figure G.2 represents the model without the outliers. Notice the difference in results. This is so because outliers fit the line to minimize error, thus the results are biased closer to outliers rather than where the majority of bivariate data points rest.

Table G.1

Years of College & Income Outliers

Years of College	Annual Income
2	\$175,000
3	\$160,000
7	\$10,000
7	\$15,000
8	\$20,000

Note: $N = 575$

Referring to the data in the prediction line, removing five outliers from a dataset of 575 is not problematic. In Table G.1, the outliers represent the following combinations of the predictor (years of college) and outcome (annual income in dollars) variables. The two cases with 2–3 years of college have unusually high annual incomes, whereas the three cases with 7–8 years of college education have unusually low annual incomes.

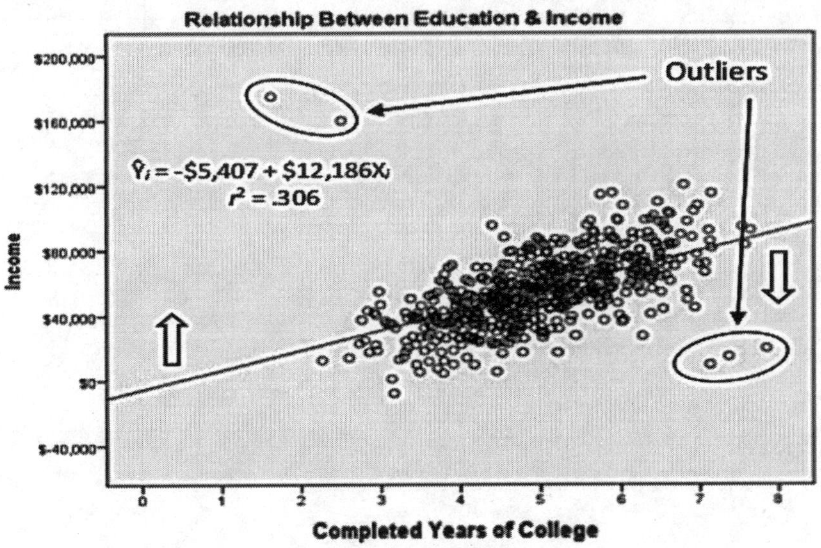

Figure G.1 Scatter Plot with Five Outliers (N = 575)

As we can see in Figure G.1, the outliers tend to draw the prediction line in the direction of the outliers.

On the other hand, Figure G.2 illustrates the prediction line without the five outliers. The line shifts to where most of the data points are located. The removal of the outliers provides a model that predicts more of the change in income as a result of education. The coefficient of determination (r^2) is .466 as opposed to .306 in the model with the outliers. In the model without the outliers, completed years of college predicts 46.6% of income, whereas with the outliers, education predicts 30.6%.

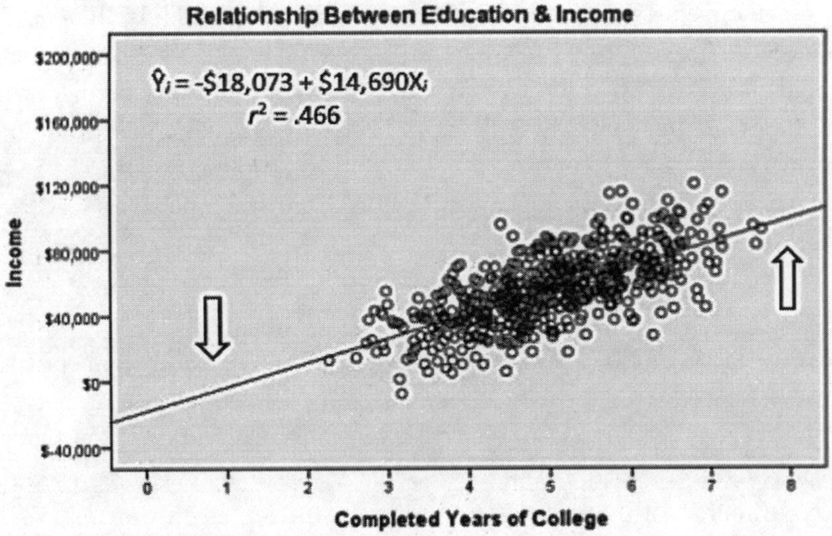

Figure G.2 Scatter Plot without Five Outliers (N = 570)

If we were to calculate income based on five years of college for both models, the predicted income would be as follows:

Model with Outliers

$$\hat{Y} = -\$5{,}407 + \$12{,}186X_i$$
$$\hat{Y} = -\$5{,}407 + \$12{,}186(5)$$
$$\hat{Y} = -\$5{,}407 + \$60{,}930$$
$$\hat{Y} = \$55{,}523$$

Income = $55,523

Model without Outliers

$$\hat{Y} = -\$18{,}073 + \$14{,}690X_i$$
$$\hat{Y} = -\$18{,}073 + \$14{,}690(5)$$
$$\hat{Y} = -\$18{,}073 + \$73{,}450$$
$$\hat{Y} = \$55{,}377$$

Income = $55,377

Incrementally, in the original model, for each year of college, income increases, on average, by $12,186. In the revised model, for each year of college, income increases, on average, by $14,690. The difference is $2,504.

G.3 Linear Regression Methods

Stepwise

Stepwise linear regression allows for the predictor that contributes most to R^2 to be entered first and alone in the regression equation, thus creating Model 1. The automatic process repeats by entering a second predictor that makes the second largest contribution to R^2. Thus, there are two predictors and it is Model 2. However, in Model 2, if the predictor in Model 1 is not one of the top two contributors, then it is dropped in favor of the top two contributing predictors. This automatic process continues adding a single predictor to each subsequent model until all the significant predictors are incorporated based on the entry and removal parameters set in SPSS, which also offers a significance test for the change in R^2 as models are stepwise built. This feature can also be used when predictors are entered in blocks.

Hierarchical

Hierarchical linear regression allows us to enter variables as forced groups based on conceptual clusters, for example. The researcher assigns the blocks or groups of predictors. For instance, psychological variables can be entered as a group, followed by a group of behavioral variables, and so forth. In addition to each predictor's relation to the outcome variable, hierarchical regression helps discover the unique contribution of the variable group to the model, as measured by its incremental contribution to the R^2. The incremental change is significance tested. This approach is often used with the Enter method, but can be used with the Stepwise method as well, thus generating all sorts of predictor variable combinations. The latter technique is appropriate when there are conceptual groups and uncertainty about the contributions of the predictors within the groups.

G.4 Dummy Coding

Dummy coded predictors are a special case of binary categorical variables that can be included in MLR. A **dummy coded** predictor measures the presence or absence of an attribute such as "yes" or "no;" "front-wheel drive" or "four-wheel drive;" "right" or "left" handed; and "aware" or "unaware." The presence of the attribute is usually coded "1" and its absence is coded "0." The presence of the attribute usually predicts variance in the outcome variable and its absence has no prediction potential because it is not considered. A significant regression coefficient will represent the change in the outcome as a result of the presence of the dummy coded predictor.

In the example below, let us assume that we wish to measure weekly grocery store sales per customer. The predictors are number of food items on sale at a discount and the presence or absence of a holiday in a given week.

$$Y_i = b_0 + b_1X_{1i} + b_2X_{2i}$$

where

Y_i = Y, the specific predicted amount of weekly sales per customer when the predictor variables takes on specific values, i

b_0 = y-intercept, which is the value of the outcome variable when the predictor variables are 0

b_1 = the slope of the line of best fit, which is the predicted unit amount of incremental change in weekly grocery store sales in dollars as a result of a one-unit change measured in single items available at a discount, not considering the presence or absence of a holiday

b_2 = the slope of the line of best fit, which is the predicted unit amount of incremental change in weekly grocery store sales in dollars as a result of the presence or absence of a holiday, not considering the number of items available at a discount

Assuming the following equation, each item available at a discount generates 5 cents in purchases per customer, and if there is a holiday during a given week, the customer spends an additional \$50.00.

$$Y_i = \$75.000 + \$.051X_{1i} + \$50.002X_{2i}$$

Thus, if there are 1,000 sales items and a holiday, it is likely that, on average, each customer will spend:

$$Y_i = \$75.00_0 + \$.05_1 1{,}000_{1i} + \$50.00_2 1_{2i}$$
$$Y_i = \$75.00 + \$50.00 + \$50.00$$
$$Y_i = \$175.00$$

The average predicted individual customer sales for the week = \$175.00.

The presence of the holiday is represented by multiplying \$50.00 by 1 so that it is accounted for in the calculation. If there is no holiday in a given week, the average individual customer sales will be:

$$Y_i = \$75.00_0 + \$.05_1 1{,}000_{1i} + \$50.00_2 0_{2i}$$
$$Y_i = \$75.00 + \$50.00 + \$0$$
$$Y_i = \$125.00$$

Average predicted individual customer sales for the week = \$125.00.

Notice that when there is no holiday, a zero is entered into the equation. This removes the \$50.00 in sales that would have been present had there been a holiday during the week.

G.5 Interaction Terms (Variables)

In regression analysis, only the relationship between a predictor variable and the outcome variable is analyzed. The influence of the relationship between predictors on the outcome variable is not considered. Yet there may be instances where we wish to know whether two variables uniquely predict change in the outcome variable not addressed by each of their individual influences. Each predictor's influence alone is called a **main effect**. Two predictors acting together provide an **interaction effect**. It is called so because the two independent variables interact together to co-predict the outcome.

For example, there may be synergy between the independent variables in how they predict the outcome variable. Think about income and how education and experience might have a stronger relationship on income when combined. Those individuals with a degree generally earn more than those individuals without a degree. Those individuals with experience may earn more than those persons without experience. Together, those individuals with both a degree and experience may earn more than the total for those persons with only education and with only experience. It is having both education and experience in combination that demands higher salaries than from each alone.

There are numerous methods for constructing an **interaction term (variable)**. At least two predictors are required. The simplest involves taking the cross-products of the two predictors for each paired case. This involves pairing each of the observations on the two variables and then multiplying the values by each other for all cases. For example, multiplying the years of college and years of experience for each case would provide an education/experience interaction term. Other approaches take this method a step further by removing the duplicated information in the interaction term from the individual predictors through a centering process. Since the interaction term is derived from the predictors, there is often a high correlation between and among the individual predictors of the interaction term and the term. Still other methods first standardize the variables before constructing an interaction term so that there is a common "measurement" between predictors. A basic centering approach is described below.

Basic **centering** involves subtracting the variable mean from each observation in the variable in order to create a new centered variable ($X_C = X - \bar{X}$). This is done for all predictors, including those not in the interaction term. The outcome variable remains in its original measurement. Centering removes the interaction term predictors' main effects and what remains is the interaction effect.

The formula for an interaction term using basic centering is:

$$X_I = (X_1 - \bar{X}_1) \times (X_2 - \bar{X}_2) \times \ldots \times (Xk - \bar{X}_k)$$

where

X_I = interaction term
X_1 = first predictor
$\bar{X}_1$ = first predictor's mean
X_2 = second predictor
$\bar{X}_2$ = second predictor's mean
X_k = additional predictors
$\bar{X}_k$ = additional predictor(s)' mean(s)

Providing that the basic data assumptions are met, then the mean of centered variables will be 0 or very close to 0. This centering approach is appropriate when the value of zero has no special meaning within the range of data values. For example, if age is examined, having a mean age of 0 would be difficult to interpret.

Below is the centered prediction equation for three predictor variables and one interaction term. The interaction term and all three predictor variables are centered. Equations can include more than one interaction term and any number of predictors, some of which may or may not be included in the interaction term(s). Decisions to include or exclude predictors in the interaction term are guided by prior knowledge, prior research, expertise, situational factors, and the results of the regression analysis.

$$Y_i = b_0 + b_1X_{1i} + b_2X_{2i} + b_3X_{3i} + b_4X_1X_2$$

where

Y_i = Y, the specific predicted value of the outcome variable when the predictor variables takes on a specific value, i

b_0 = y-intercept, which is the value of the outcome variable when the predictor variables are 0

b_1 = the slope of the line of best fit, which is the predicted unit amount of incremental change in the outcome variable as a result of a one-unit change (as measured) in the predictor variable, not considering variables X_2, X_3, and X_1X_2

b_2 = the slope of the line of best fit, which is the predicted unit amount of incremental change in the outcome variable as a result of a one-unit change (as measured) in the predictor variable, not considering X_1, X_3, and X_1X_2

b_3 = the slope of the line of best fit, which is the predicted unit amount of incremental change in the outcome variable as a result of a one-unit change (as measured) in the predictor variable, not considering X_1, X_2, and X_1X_2

b_4 = the slope of the line of best fit, which is the predicted unit amount of incremental change in the outcome variable as a result of a one-unit change (as measured) in the interaction term consisting of predictors X_1 and X_2, not considering X_1, X_2, and X_3

G.6 Residual Analysis

Residual analysis involves screening for error normality, linearity, and homoscedasticity after linear regression analysis is conducted. SPSS generates residual output as part of the regression analysis. A scatter plot with the residuals on the y-axis and the predicted outcome variable on the x-axis provides a visual representation for assessment.

Figure G.3 depicts a scatter plot that meets the assumptions of bivariate normality, linearity, and homoscedasticity. As we can see, and ideally, there is a concentration of data points near the line, and especially near the center, which becomes less and less dense as points move away from that area. The mean residual value should equal zero or be close to zero. This is so because the values are symmetrical. Half the values should be below the line and half should be above the line, thus they cancel each other out or come close to doing so. The scatter plot approximates constant variance in the relationship between the two variables.

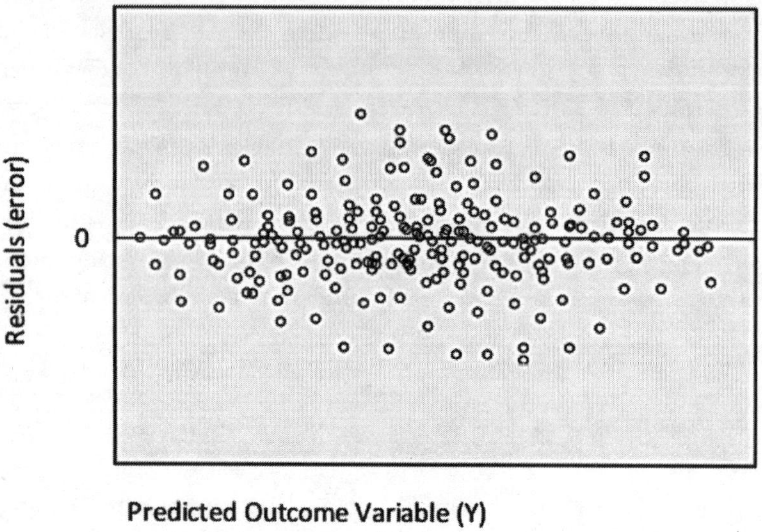

Figure G.3 Normality, Linearity, and Homoscedasticity Met in Residuals

Figure G.4 represents a failure to meet bivariate normality. There is a lack of symmetry; in fact, the distribution appears left-skewed. The data are densely packed above the line (positive residuals) and spread out below the line (negative residuals). The positive residuals are generally smaller than the negative ones. There is less variance in values higher than the means of the two variables. For example, above average SAT scores may not vary as much as below average scores because there may be other factors that are relevant when scores are lower.

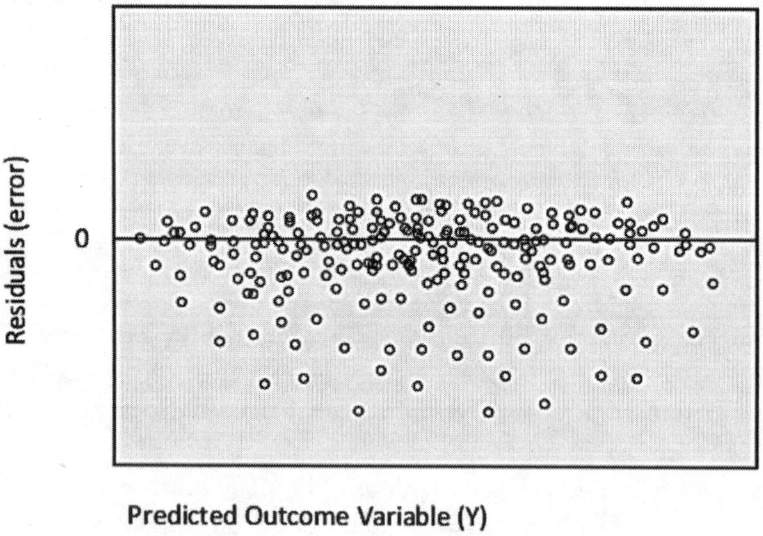

Figure G.4 Normality Not Met in Residuals

Figure G.5 violates the linearity assumption. It actually represents a curvilinear relationship. As we can see, initially, negative residuals dominate the distribution, followed by positive residuals, and then returning to negative residuals. Thus, the relationship between the two variables changes, as observed in the change of slope directionality. For instance, people's attention to viewing TV news about violence may increase until viewers become desensitized over time and pay less and less attention to such stories.

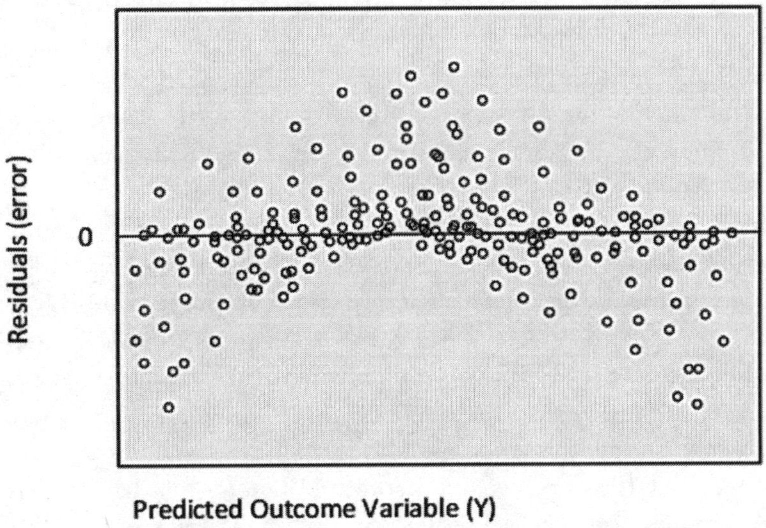

Figure G.5 Linearity Not Met in Residuals

Figure G.6 represents a relationship where the outcome variable's variance increases with increases in the predictor variable, whether the residuals are positive or negative. This condition violates homoscedasticity. For example, the effects of a training program may be fairly consistent shortly after completing the program. Yet, over time, the training's effectiveness may vary more and more. This pattern may also be the case in analyses that evaluate the efficaciousness of a new drug regimen. Early on, the drug's effectiveness is fairly constant, but changes over the longer term for various reasons, including the patient's condition.

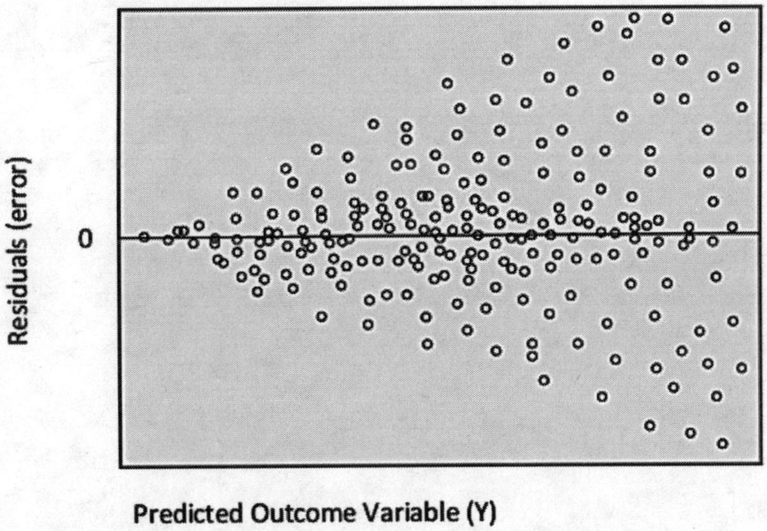

Figure G.6 Homoscedasticity Not Met in Residuals

G.7 Multicollinearity

In the interaction term section, we briefly mentioned that the predictors comprising the interaction variable and the variable are usually highly correlated. This can destabilize results. In such cases, the data do not generate a solution, the R^2 becomes unreasonably high, the coefficients do not make sense, one among a number of predictors accounts for most of the change in R^2, the standard errors are very high, and/or regression coefficient are the opposite of their correlations with the outcome variable.

High correlations between and among predictors are said to exhibit **multicollinearity** and can produce inaccurate results. They can be highly correlated because they are essentially the same thing. If three variables in a MLR are highly correlated, then they share a large amount of variance. There are two tools in SPSS that measure the degree of multicollinearity. They are tolerance and the **variance inflation factor (VIF)**. Since tolerance is more intuitive and VIF is the reciprocal of tolerance, we shall focus on tolerance as a measure of multicollinearity.

Tolerance is the proportion or percentage of change or variance in a predictor not accounted for by the other predictors in the model. It is $1 - R^2$, if you will, when R^2 pertains to a particular predictor and when the other variables (other than the outcome variable) serve as its predictors. Thus, tolerance is a predictor variable's unique variance not accounted for by the other predictors.

As a general rule, a tolerance of <.10 is problematic because it denotes that less than 10% of a predictor's variance is not unique. Note that some statisticians set the tolerance test point at <.20. Of the predictors in this model, the one that contributes most to predicting the outcome variable should be retained. The other multicollinearity predictors should be removed unless there is a sound reason to retain any of them.

Appendix H

Statistics Flow Chart

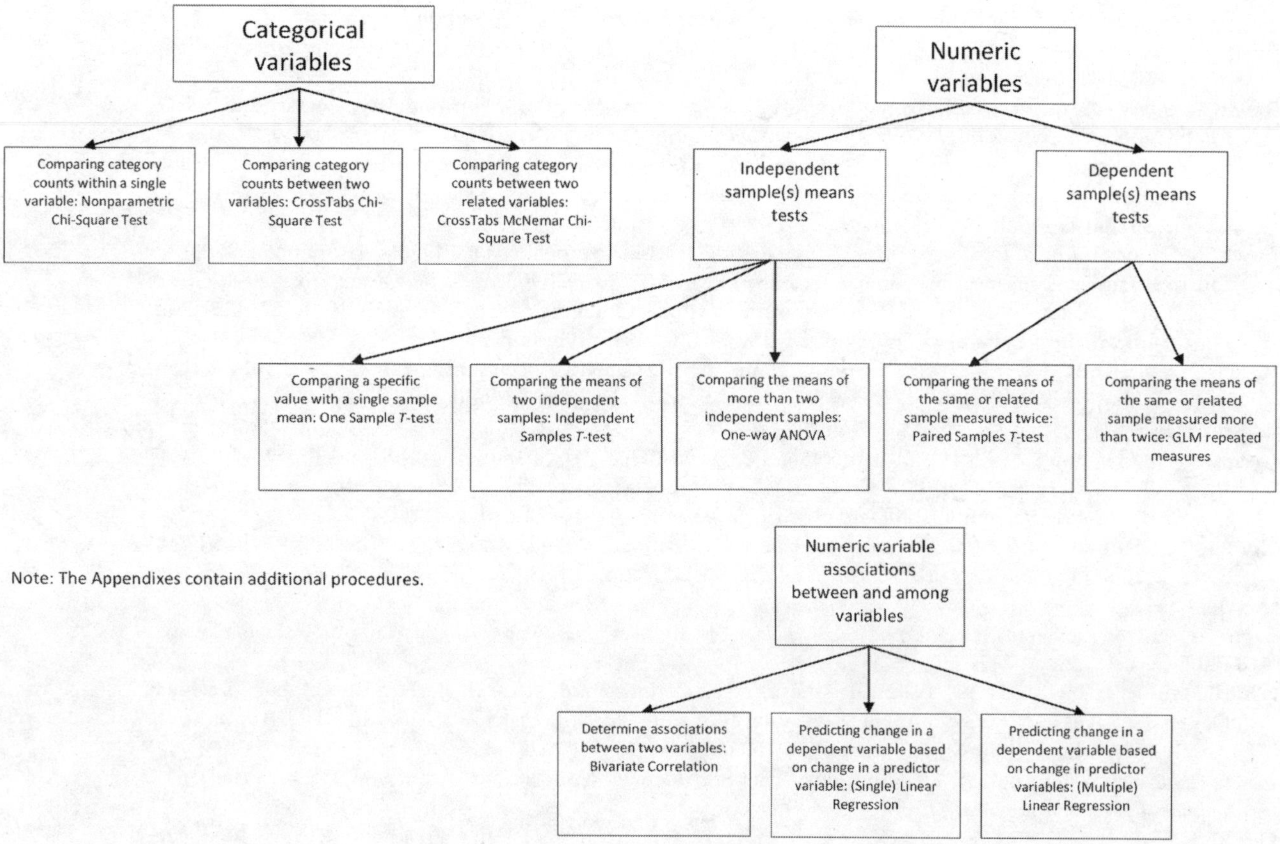

Note: The Appendixes contain additional procedures.

References

Barrows, C., & Vieira, Jr., E. T. (2012). Recommendations for the Development of a New Operational Classification System for the Foodservice Industry. *Journal of Hospitality & Tourism Research*, *37*(3), 349–376.

Borenstein, M., Rothstein, H., & Cohen, J. (2008). *IBM SPSS SamplePower Version 3.0*. Chicago, IL: SPSS, Inc. an IBM Company.

Bowman, S. (2013). Impact of Electronic Health Record Systems on Information Integrity: Quality and Safety Implications. *Perspectives in Health Information Management*, *10*(Fall), 1c.

Braum, C., Stangler, T., Narveson, J., & Pettingel, S. (2009). Animal-Assisted Therapy as a Pain Relief Intervention for Children. Nursing Faculty Publications, Paper 9. Available at: http://digitalcommons.csbsju.edu/nursing_pubs/9.

Brock, T. P., & Smith, S. R. (2007). Using Digital Videos Displayed on Personal Digital Assistance (PDAs) to Enhance Patient Education in Clinical Settings. *International Journal of Medical Informatics*, *76*, 829–835.

Caple, C. (2016). Complex Regional Pain Syndrome, Type 2. Quick Lesson, ICD-9 (355.71), ICD (G57.70). Cinahl Information Systems, a Division of EBSCO Information Systems.

Carifio, J., & Perla, R. J. (2007). Ten Common Misunderstandings, Misconceptions, Persistent Myths and Urban Legends about Likert Scales and Likert Response Formats and Their Antidotes. *Journal of Social Sciences*, *3*(3), 106–116.

Cohn, D., & Caumont, A. (2016). 10 Demographic Trends That Are Shaping the U.S. and the World. Pew Research Center: FACTANK News in the Numbers. Available at: www.pewresearch.org/fact-tank/2016/03/31/10-demographic-trends-that-are-shaping-the-u-s-and-the-world/.

Cortesi, F., Giannotti, F., Sebastiani, T., Bruni, O., & Ottaviano, S. (2004). Knowledge of Sleep in Italian High School Students: Pilot-Test of a School-Based Sleep Educational Program. *Journal of Adolescent Health*, *34*, 344–351.

Eagly, A. H., & Chaiken, S. (1993). *The Psychology of Attitudes*. New York, NY: Harcourt Brace College Publishers.

Edimansyah, B. A., Rusli, B. N., Naing, L., Rusli, B. A., Winn, T., & Ariff, B. R. H. (2008). Self-Perceived Depression, Anxiety, Stress and Their Relationships with Psychosocial Job Factors in Male Automotive Assembly Workers. *Industrial Health*, *46*, 90–100.

Faber, A., & Kuo, F. E. (2009). Children with Attention Deficits Concentrate Better after Walk in the Park. *Journal of Attention Disorders*, *12*(5), 402–409.

Gottfredson, D. C., Najaka, S. S., & Kearley, B. (2003). Effectiveness of Drug Treatment Courts: Evidence from a Randomized Trial. *Criminology & Public Policy*, *2*(2), 171–196. DOI: 10.1111/j.1745-9133.2003.tb00117.x.

Hasan, S., & Padman, R. (2006). Analyzing the Effect of Data Quality on the Accuracy of Clinical Decision Support Systems: A Computer Simulation Approach. *AMIA Annual Symposium Proceedings*, 2006, 324–328.

Howell, D. C. (2014) *Fundamental Statistics for the Behavioral Sciences*. Belmont, CA: Wadsworth Cengage Learning.

Horrigan, J. B. (2016). Lifelong Learning and Technology. *Pew Research Center Numbers, Facts, and Trends Shaping the World*, 1–69. Available at: www.pewresearch.org.

IBM SPSS Statistics 23. Statistical software from SPSS, an IBM Company. Chicago, IL.

IBM SPSS Statistics Base 23. Available at: ftp://public.dhe.ibm.com/software/analytics/spss/documentation/statistics/23.0/en/client/Manuals/IBM_SPSS_Statistics_Base.pdf.

IBM SPSS Statistics 23 Brief Guide. Available at: ftp://public.dhe.ibm.com/software/analytics/spss/documentation/statistics/23.0/en/client/Manuals/IBM_SPSS_Statistics_Brief_Guide.pdf.

IBM SPSS Statistics 23 Command Syntax Reference. Available at: ftp://public.dhe.ibm.com/software/analytics/spss/documentation/statistics/23.0/en/client/Manuals/IBM_SPSS_Statistics_Command_Syntax_Reference.pdf.

IMA Ltd. (2016) Website section on case studies. Available at: www.imaltd.com/#!case-studies/fzz5l.

Klion, R. (2013). Know Your N: The Importance of Sample Size. Available at: www.panpowered.com/know-your-n-the-importance-of-sample-size/.

Lilienfeld, S. O., Lynn, S. J., Ruscio, J., & Beyerstein, B. L. (2009). *50 Great Myths of Popular Psychology: Shattering Widespread Misconceptions about Human Behavior*. Hoboken, NJ: Wiley-Blackwell.

Marotzke, J., & Forster, P. M. (2015). Forcing, Feedback and Internal Variability in Global Temperature Trends. *Nature*, *517*, 565–570. DOI:10.1038/nature14117.

Martin, B. (2015). More Than Just Writing: Handedness and Substance Use. Master of Social Work Clinical Research Papers. Paper 490. Available at: http://sophia.stkate.edu/msw_papers/490.

Norman, G. (2010). Likert Scales, Levels of Measurement and the "Laws" of Statistics. *Advances in Health Science Education*, *15*, 625–632.

Parmesan, C., & Yohe, G. (2003). A Globally Coherent Fingerprint of Climate Change Impacts across Natural Systems. *Nature*, *421*(2), 37–42.

Quality Gurus. Avaialble at: www.qualitygurus.com/.

Rainie, L. (2016). Libraries and Learning. Pew Research Center. Available at: www.pewinternet.org/2016/04/07/libraries-and-learning/.

Ramirez, C., Schau, C., & Emmioglu, E. (2012). The Importance of Attitudes in Statistics Education. *Statistics Education Research Journal*, *11*(2), 57–71.

Rosenbaum, D. E. (1970, January 4). Statisticians Charge Draft Lottery Was Not Random. *New York Times*, 66.

Six Sigma. Available at: www.isixsigma.com/new-to-six-sigma/getting-started/what-six-sigma/.

Skaalvik, E. M., & Skaalvik, S. (2009). Does School Context Matter? Relations with Teacher Burnout and Job Satisfaction. *Teaching and Teacher Education*, *25*, 518–524.

SPSS, Inc. (2000). Missing Data: The Hidden Problem. SPSS White Paper. Chicago, IL: SPSS, Inc. Available at: www.whitepapercentral.com/browse/marketing/missing-data-the-hidden-problem/.

Tabachnick, B. G., & Fidell, L. S. (2013). *Using Multivariate Statistics*. New York, NY: Pearson.

Vieira, E. T., Jr. (2014). The Relationships among Girls' Prosocial Video Gaming, Perspective-Taking, Sympathy, and Thoughts about Violence. *Communication Research*, *41*(7), 892–912. DOI: 10.1177/0093650212463049.

Index